THE HISTORY of ERIE COUNTY PENNSYLVANIA

from Its First Settlement

New and Enlarged Edition

Laura G. Sanford

HERITAGE BOOKS
2010

HERITAGE BOOKS
AN IMPRINT OF HERITAGE BOOKS, INC.

Books, CDs, and more—Worldwide

For our listing of thousands of titles see our website
at
www.HeritageBooks.com

A Facsimile Reprint
Published 2010 by
HERITAGE BOOKS, INC.
Publishing Division
100 Railroad Ave. #104
Westminster, Maryland 21157

Copyright © 1991 Heritage Books, Inc.

Copyright © 1861 J. B. Lippincott & Co.
and 1894 Laura G. Sanford

— Publisher's Notice —
In reprints such as this, it is often not possible to remove blemishes from the original. We feel the contents of this book warrant its reissue despite these blemishes and hope you will agree and read it with pleasure.

International Standard Book Numbers
Paperbound: 978-1-55613-511-8
Clothbound: 978-0-7884-8568-8

PREFACE.

IF in every State we had those who were unprejudiced and truth-loving to examine and test the supposed history of their respective localities, and to record the testimony of the aged, "before they go hence and be no more," truth would be vindicated, much that is interesting rescued from oblivion, and a correct and minute history of our country secured.

For the encouragement of those attempting this duty, Sallust says: "Among the different ways of employing one's abilities, that of writing history is of eminent use; but I shall say nothing of its excellence, because many have already shown it, and lest I should be charged with vanity for extolling what I am myself engaged in."

Grateful acknowledgments are due to the many friends who have contributed to the History of Erie County by the use of their libraries, by the loan of valuable unedited manuscripts, and by their pertinent suggestions. Of these are Dr. U. Parsons, of Providence, Rhode Island; Madams William A. Brown, Chas. Pollock, J. C. Reid, J. H. Bliss, H. Russel, J. Dickson, and Miss I. Williams; Gen. C. M. Reed, Capt. W. W. Dobbins, William Nicholson, G. J. Ball, J. Sill, J. B. Johnson, B. B. Vincent, J. C. Spencer, T. G. Colt, A. H. Caughey, and G. W. Starr, Esqs.; Rev. Wm. M. Blackburn, and Rev. T. St. John, of Erie; Rev. S. M. Eaton, Franklin; Mr. I. Eaton, Fairview; Miss H. R. Cutler and Mr. R. Barnett, Girard; Miss Sarah Vincent and Mrs. McGill, Waterford; Rev. A. H. Carrier and Wm. E. Marvin, Esq., Northeast; and Mrs. M. Courtright, New York.

In this new edition we have given in the form of a supplement events of latter years only of main importance, the want of space being our plea for not giving much that is worthy of record.

The Editors of the county are entitled to many thanks for their files, and for favorable mention of the work.

CATALOGUE OF WORKS CONSULTED.

American State Papers; American Archives; Proud's History of Pennsylvania; Colonial History of New York; Documentary History of New York; Pennsylvania Colonial Records; Pennsylvania Archives; Western Annals; History of Western Pennsylvania; Thatcher's Lives of the Indians; Naval Monument; Hennepin's Discoveries in America; Historical Collections of Pennsylvania; Shea's Discovery of the Mississippi; Shea's Jesuit Missions; Annals of America, by Dr. Holmes; Schoolcraft's Indian Tribes; Conspiracy of Pontiac; Niles's Register; Burgess's Account of Perry's Victory; McKenzie's Life of Perry; Dawson's American Battles; Dr. Parson's Discourse; Calvert's Oration; Battle of Lake Erie Monumental Association; Bancroft's United States; Irving's Life of Washington; Stone's Life of Brandt; Elements of History, by J. E. Worcester; Historical Account of Erie County, by Dr. W. M. Wood; Dwight's Travels; Goodrich's History of the United States; Smith's Laws of Pennsylvania; Howe's Historical Collections of the West; State Geologist's Report; Poor's History of Railroads; Files of the Mirror, Erie; Erie Gazette; Erie Observer; Girard Republican; Encyclopedia Americana; Allegheny Magazine; Pennsylvania Gazetteer, by Thos. F. Gordon; Pennsylvania State Book, by Burrows; Old Fort Le Bœuf, by a Waterfordian; Inauguration of the Perry Statue, Cleveland; History of the Railroad War, by Wilson Laird, Esq.; Buffalo Express; Buffalo Commercial; History of Erie County, published in Chicago, 1884, Warner, Beers & Co.; Illustrated History of Pennsylvania, by W. H. Egle, M.D.; Old Portage Road, by H. C. Taylor, M.D.; Ship-yard of the Griffon, by C. K. Remington.

COMPLIMENTARY NOTICES.

The following note from the Hon. Geo. Bancroft explains itself, and is indirectly a flattering tribute to the worth of the book from the very highest source:

"NEW YORK, February 3d, 1862.

" . . . Your charming work on Erie County has so much merit, that I cannot bear to lie under your misapprehension of my judgment on a point, which has cost me a good deal of research. If you turn to page 163 of Vol. III., in the copy I sent to Erie, or any edition since 1853, you will find that I put the first ship yard at the 'Mouth of the Cayaga Creek.' It cost me a world of trouble to find the authorities to correct my mistake, and I am sorry you charged upon me the sins of my earlier years, instead of the revised opinion of mature study.

"Very truly yours,
"GEO. BANCROFT."

"The History of Erie County, Pennsylvania, by Laura G. Sanford is *in manibus*. It is an interesting book to any one, being full of Indian traditions, antiquarian gossip, and facts relating to cotemporary American heroes, all connected together in a very agreeable style. To a resident of Erie County, we think the work invaluable, comprising as it does the history of places and persons, forming subjects of his own daily conversation and observation. The tremendous 'War of the Gauges" has not received as much attention from the fair historian as we could wish. She passes it with a bare mention. Possibly a lady could not do justice to an event which above all others requires a manly pen to portray."

From Erie Gazette.

"'History of Erie County.' This is the title of a neatly printed and handsomely bound volume, just issued from the press of J. B. Lippincott & Co., Philadelphia, for a copy of which we are indebted to the authoress, Miss Laura G. Sanford, of our city. It consists of 347 pages, and embodies much interesting and valuable information relative to the County, from an early date to the present time. Biographical notices of well-known citizens form a prominent feature—citizens like Seth Reed, R. S. Reed, P. S. V. Hamot, Hon. Thos. H. Sill, Giles Sanford, Judah Colt, Rev. Robert Reid, Daniel Dobbins, and Hon. John Galbraith, accompanied in several cases by finely executed steel engraved likenesses. The work bears marks of careful preparation, and is doubtless strictly correct in its statements of material facts and events. We regard it as quite creditable to the authoress and the publishers, and cordially recommend it to all who would possess a reliable 'History of Erie County.' It is thus spoken of by a gentleman long and favorably known here:

"PROVIDENCE, R. I., October 8, 1860.

"It has been my privilege to be allowed the perusal of many of the sheets of Miss Sanford's History of Erie in manuscript, and I cordially bear testimony to its great value as embodying about all the material facts relating to that frontier city that such a work should contain, sought out with great industry, and carefully and candidly stated.

"USHER PARSONS."

From Providence (Rhode Island) Daily Journal.

"This is a valuable contribution to the history of our western frontier. It begins with the history of the Indians and their sway over the lake shores. It then gives us an account of the arrival of the first French settlers from Montreal, as missionaries, on Lake Erie and the upper lakes, and of the trappers and hunters who soon followed in their train, their first landing after leaving Lake Ontario being at this port. Here they established one of the first forts west of Niagara Falls, and opened a road eighteen miles south of Le Bœuf, now called Waterford, at the head waters of the Ohio. At that place, Washington, a century after, commenced his military career, at the age of twenty. Beyond this they established other forts at Venango and Pittsburg, and moved on further south; intending to secure the trade for Canada of the vast regions west of the Ohio and Mississippi rivers. An account is given of the first vessel that traversed the lakes and of the gradual increase of shipping until the War of 1812, when Perry's fleet was commenced and equipped. A faithful description is also furnished of the fleet's armament and crews, and of the celebrated battle of the 10th of September, with portraits of some of the officers (Commodore Perry and Dr. Parsons among them), and also of many of the prominent citizens who first settled in Erie.

"Erie is now a beautiful city, its inhabitants having increased from 300 or 400 at the time of the war to 12,000.

"The venerable Giles Sanford, Esq., who arrived there in 1810, is the father of the author, and being engaged since then as a prominent merchant and furnisher of supplies for the army and navy, is better acquainted with the history and concerns of Erie than any person living. He has been able to furnish his daughter with many of the materials of this valuable work, which we cordially recommend to the attention of all persons interested in the times, localities, and events of which it treats. It is written with great candor and truthfulness, and evinces a vast amount of industry and patient research."

From the Crawford Democrat, February 25, 1862.

"This is a work of great value as a depository in which are treasured up, so as to secure them in a permanent form, the facts and incidents of the early settlement of the portion of our State of which it is the history. The accomplished authoress has done the task she assigned herself in a way to deserve the thanks of the whole country, but particularly the inhabitants of this State, and most especially of the dwellers in Erie County. Her book will be read with satisfaction and pleasure because of the important information it contains—information collected by much industry and perseverance—and for the attractive manner in which it is imparted. Erie County is fortunate in having one to write its history who is so well qualified by possessing both the literary and scientific ability and taste, and the love of the work necessary to success.

"The plan adopted—and, indeed, required by the subject—is such as to give the 'History of Erie County' more than a merely local interest. Interesting sketches are given of various Indian tribes, whose braves formerly roamed over this then great western wilderness, following on the war path; whose hunters pursued their game through the vast forests that then, unbroken, covered all this region; whose young men and maidens whispered their tale of love by the sparkling brooks in the waters of which the speckled trout sported, while over them the green boughs meeting formed Nature's sweet bowers; and whose frail canoes were the only craft which then furrowed the lakes and rivers. The difficulties met and vanquished by the hardy early settlers are well narrated, and examples given. The naval operations on the lakes, and the victories gained on them by American heroes, receive attention. Besides these, other matters of general interest are noticed—such as relate to the occupancy of this region by the

French; the fortifications built by them, and final surrender of their claims to the English.

"A number of sketches of the lives of early settlers in Erie County are given, which add much to the attractiveness and interest of the volume.

"Miss Sanford did not perform her work a day too soon. The knowledge of the facts of the early history and settlement of this part of our country is fast passing away along with those—of whom so few yet remain—in whose memory that knowledge is stored. A very few more years, and those facts, now, happily, secured, would have perished from the living generations.

"I have said that Erie County is fortunate in having one so well qualified and, at the same time, disposed to write its history. The object of this notice of her book, besides being to call attention to a really meritorious work, is to ask, where is the historian of Crawford County? It is necessary he, or she, shall appear very soon, else it will be too late. Already, indeed, much that would have been among the most valuable history of this county has gone into the graves of the old settlers. Every year--every month —something of importance is perishing.

"Crawford County affords material—has an unwritten history— not less abundant, certainly, nor less attractive, than Erie; and as capable, in equally competent hands, of being made into a written history like that, in regard to interest, which is the subject of this notice. Have we no one with both the mind and heart to do it? Let the historian of Crawford County appear, and quickly, too, before those in whose memory it now lies pass away, and that person—man or woman—will deserve and have the gratitude of this and future generations.

"J. V. R."

"Mr. Fillmore, as President of the 'Buffalo Historical Society,' accepts with pleasure and thanks the interesting History of Erie County, Pennsylvania, from the author.

"*Buffalo, July 26, 1862.*"

CONTENTS.

CHAPTER I.

An Account of the Eries—Traditions concerning them—Their Destruction—Symbols found on Kelly's or Cunningham's Island—Indian Remains. 15

CHAPTER II.

La Salle—The Griffon—Relics—Gov. Shirley's Proposition—Braddock's Advice — Gov. Delancy's Plan — Estimating Presqu'ile—Hudson's Bay Company. 24

CHAPTER III.

The English and French Claims — Construction of Forts Presquile (Erie) and Le Bœuf (Waterford)—Washington's Visit—Condition of these Forts in 1756, '57, '58, and '59—Their Desertion after the taking of Fort Niagara—Tradition in Erie—Major Rogers takes Possession for the English in 1760. 29

CHAPTER IV.

Pontiac—Destruction of Forts Presqu'ile and Le Bœuf, as described by Bancroft, Parkman, and Harvey—Col. Bradstreet at Presquile, in 1764—Col. Bouquet's Treaty—A Detachment of British Soldiers and Indians embark at Chautauqua Lake—Hannastown burnt—Mr. Adams's Suggestion. 48

CHAPTER V.

Penn's Charter—Boundaries of Pennsylvania—Mason and Dixon's Line—Review of said Line by Col. Graham—Western Boundary of Pennsylvania fixed in 1786—Boundary between New York and Pennsylvania confirmed by Act of Assembly in 1789—Purchase of Triangle, 1791—Anecdote of Mr. William Miles. 56

CONTENTS.

CHAPTER VI.

Arrangements for the Settlement of the Triangle—Pennsylvania Population Company—Act to lay out a Town at Presqu'ile; afterward repealed—Block-house at Le Bœuf—Indian Murders—Gov. Mifflin to the President—Attorney-General Bradford's Opinion—Ransom's Deposition—Letters of Capt. Denny—Andrew Ellicot and Gen. Chapin—Joseph Brandt—Cornplanter—A Present of Land—Treaty of Peace at Canandaigua. 62

CHAPTER VII.

An Act to lay out the Towns of Erie, Waterford, Franklin, and Warren—To protract the Enlistment of Troops at Le Bœuf—Deposition of Tho. Rees, Esq.—Actual Settlers—Memorial to the Population Company—Deacon Chamberlain's Story—Capt. Martin Strong to William Nicholson, Esq.—Louis Philippe at Mr. Rees's—Murder of Rutledge and Son—Mr. Augustus Porter's Visit—Mr. Judah Colt's MS. Autobiography—Number of White Settlers on the Lakes west of Genesee River—General Wayne's Death at Presqu'ile, 1796. 76

CHAPTER VIII.

Erie County from 1785—Organization in 1803—Its Geography, etc.—Original Townships—Changes—Extent of Townships and Population—Population decennially from 1800—Census Items—Vote of 1808 and 1860—Receipts and Expenditures do.—Extract from Auditor-General's Report—Post-offices in 1830, 1856, 1860—List of Judges—Members of Congress—State Senate—Representatives—Prothonotaries—Registers and Recorders—Sheriffs—Coroners—First Section incorporated—Courthouses—Act for Public Landing—Borough Charter altered in 1833—Canal Basin—Peninsula—Poorhouse—Several Acts—Government of Erie changed to that of a City—Present Population and Business—List of Burgesses and Mayors—Collectors of Customs—Postmasters in Erie. 91

CHAPTER IX.

First Road—Population Company Roads—Erie and Waterford Turnpike—Salt Trade—Gen. O'Hara's Contract—Road to Buffalo—First Coaches—Erie Canal—Railroads—Erie or Wattsburg Railroad—Sunbury and Erie—Erie and North-

CONTENTS. xi

east—Franklin Canal Company—Pittsburg and Erie Railroad
—Plank-roads. 107

CHAPTER X.

Shipping—The Washington, the First Vessel built on the
South Shore of the Lake—Hudson's Bay Company—British
Government Vessels—American Government Vessels—The
Salina—Valuable Cargoes—Walk-in-the-Water—First Lighthouse—William Penn—First Steamer at Chicago—Cholera—
Tonnage and Number of Vessels in 1810-20-31-36-47-60—Lake
Disasters—Commerce of Port of Presqu'ile—Vessels and
Tonnage registered at Presqu'ile in 1860—United States
Steamer Michigan—Revenue Cutters. 123

CHAPTER XI.

Banks—Gas Company—Insurance—Fire Companies—Volunteer Military—Agriculture—Mutual Aid—Cemeteries—Moral,
Benevolent, and Literary Societies. 132

CHAPTER XII.

Newspapers—Common Schools—Academies—Normal School—
Sabbath School—First Protestant Missionaries West of Utica
—Moravians in Venango County, 1767—First Religious
Service in Erie County—First Church Edifice—A Religious
Experience—Presbytery of Erie—Revs. Patterson and Eaton
—Extract from Rev. A. H. Carrier's Historical Sermon—
Rev. R. Reid—Churches of different Denominations in Erie
—Revivals. 147

CHAPTER XIII.

Waterford—Edinboro—Northeast—Wattsburg—Girard—Union
Mills — Albion — Cherry Hill — Wellsburg — Cranesville —
Lockport—Pageville — Lexington — Fairview—Manchester—
McKean Corners—Wesleyville—West Springfield—Springfield—Beaverdam—Concord Station. 178

CHAPTER XIV.

Biographical Sketches of Col. Seth Reed—Rufus Seth Reed—
Judah Colt—Dr. U. Parsons—Dr. John C. Wallace—Rev.
Robert Reid—Thos. Wilson—P. S. V. Hamot—Capt. D. Dobbins—T. H. Sill—G. Sanford—Judge J. Galbraith. 195

xii   CONTENTS.

CHAPTER XV.

War declared—Commodore Perry—Capt. Dobbin's Correspondence—Commodore Chauncey, Mr. Henry Eckford, and Noah Brown—Difficulties in fitting out the Fleet—Gen. Mead—Capt. Perry at Fort George—Five Vessels brought from Buffalo—Provincial Marine Corps—Difficulties in procuring men—Letters to Commodore Chauncey and the Secretary of the Navy—A Providence recognized in the War—Getting the Vessels over the bar—Commodore Barclay at Port Dover—Seven of the Vessels make a Cruise—Officers and Men from Lake Ontario—August 12, Perry sails for Sandusky—Interview with Gen. Harrison—They proceed to Malden—Kentucky Militia—Sickness—Letters from the Secretary—Ohio dispatched to Erie—Strength of the British Force—The American Force—Americans look in at Malden—Corrected Instructions for the Battle. 214

CHAPTER XVI.

British Vessels appear—Commodore Perry remodels his Line, and other Preparations—A brief Description of the Battle of September 10, by Dr. Parsons—The Vessels return to Erie with the Wounded and Prisoners—Capt. Perry promoted—His Reception at Erie—A Remark of McKenzie—President Madison—Congress—Prizes. 238

CHAPTER XVII.

Block-houses built in 1813-14—State of Society—Buffalo burned—Alarms at Erie—Capt. Sinclair arrives—Bird, Rankin, and Davis executed—Disposition made of Government Vessels—List of Commanding Officers at Erie from 1813 to 1825—Topography of Presqu'ile Bay and the Peninsula—Misery Bay—Gen. Bernard and Maj. Totten's Survey—Appropriations made by the State and the United States—Changes since 1813—Rise and fall of Water in Lake Erie—A singular Phenomenon—Lake Survey. 246

CHAPTER XVIII.

Geology from Professor Rogers—Character of the Soil—Calcareous Marl—Bog Ore—Petroleum—Mineral Waters—Description of the Sink-hole by Mr. R. Andrews—The Devil's Backbone and Nose—Botanizing. 255

CONTENTS. xiii

CHAPTER XIX.

Miscellaneous Items, among which are: A Tradition—Gen. Wayne—An Anecdote—Price of Provisions—Wm. W. Reed, Esq.—First National Celebration—Churches—The Garrison —A Relic—Saturday Afternoon—Game—Mrs. P.'s Reminiscences—H. Russel's Journal—An Early Settler in Fairview— La Fayette's Visit in Erie—Cholera—Perry Monument—An Informal Meeting—Speculation—Fires—Sad Accidents—Ex-President Adams — Patriot War—Old Courthouse Bell—Pioneers—Perry—Lieut. Yarnall—Survivors of the Battle of Lake Erie—Perry Monument at Cleveland—Inventions—Moravian Lands—Omissions—Bankers and Exchange Brokers. . 270

SUPPLEMENT.

SECTION I.

The Shipyard of the Griffon — Northern State Boundary — Ownership of the Peninsula—The Pontiac Conspiracy—Le Bœuf—Letters of a Surveyor, etc.—Scenery. 303

SECTION II.

Magnitude of the Great Lakes—Lake Currents—Fish Exhibit —Hatcheries — Ancient Mariner—The Lighthouses — Flash Lighthouse—Life-saving Station—Waterworks—War for the Union—Soldiers and Sailors' Home. 319

SECTION III.

Johnson Island Plot—United States Steamer Michigan—Revenue Cutters — Railroads — Rapid Transit — Liberty Bells— Erie — Some Towns and Townships — Grapes — Postoffices— Census—City Hall—Government Building—Petroleum—Gas —The Weather—Parks—Massassauga—Height of Lakes. . . 341

SECTION IV.

Biographies of Dr. Usher Parsons—Capt. W. W. Dobbins (an extract)—Oliver H. Perry—Maj. Andrew Ellicott—Two Foreigners—Dr. F. N. Thorpe—Rev. C. Dickson, D.D.—William Wallace, Esq.—Wallace Family—Judge Converse—Rev. T. H. Robinson, D.D. — Judge A. Tourgee — Bishop J. F. Spaulding—Rev. Dr. Stuckenberg—Dr. Artemas Martin—Rev. Dr. Chamberlain—Miss E. Ditto—Dr. and Ernest Ingersoll — Rev. K. Fullerton — Messrs. Perkins — Judge James Thompson and family—Hon. William L. Scott—Visits of Nine Presidents—Citizens mentioned . . , ... 376

SECTION V.

Churches — Revivals — Missionary Annual Meeting — Public Schools—Academy—Villa Maria—Lake Shore Seminary—St. Benedict—Clark's Business College—W. C. T. U.—Y. M. C. A. —Hamot and St. Vincent Hospitals—Home of the Friendless —Three New Charities—Bequests of John Weis and R. Wilcox—Sisters of St. Joseph. 407

SECTION VI.

Water Commissioners—Hon. W. L. Scott—Palatial Residences —The Wadena—Ore Docks—Trestle—Metric Metal—Railroads —County Roads—Freight Report—Banks—Disasters—Storage —Homeopathic Hospital—A Synopsis—World's Fair Awards. 434

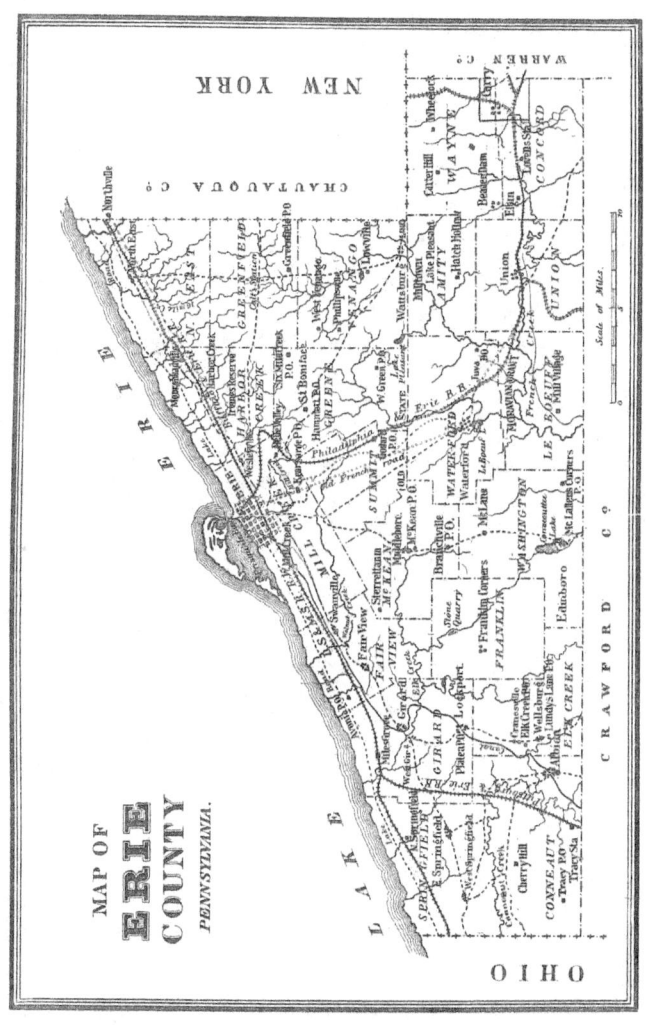

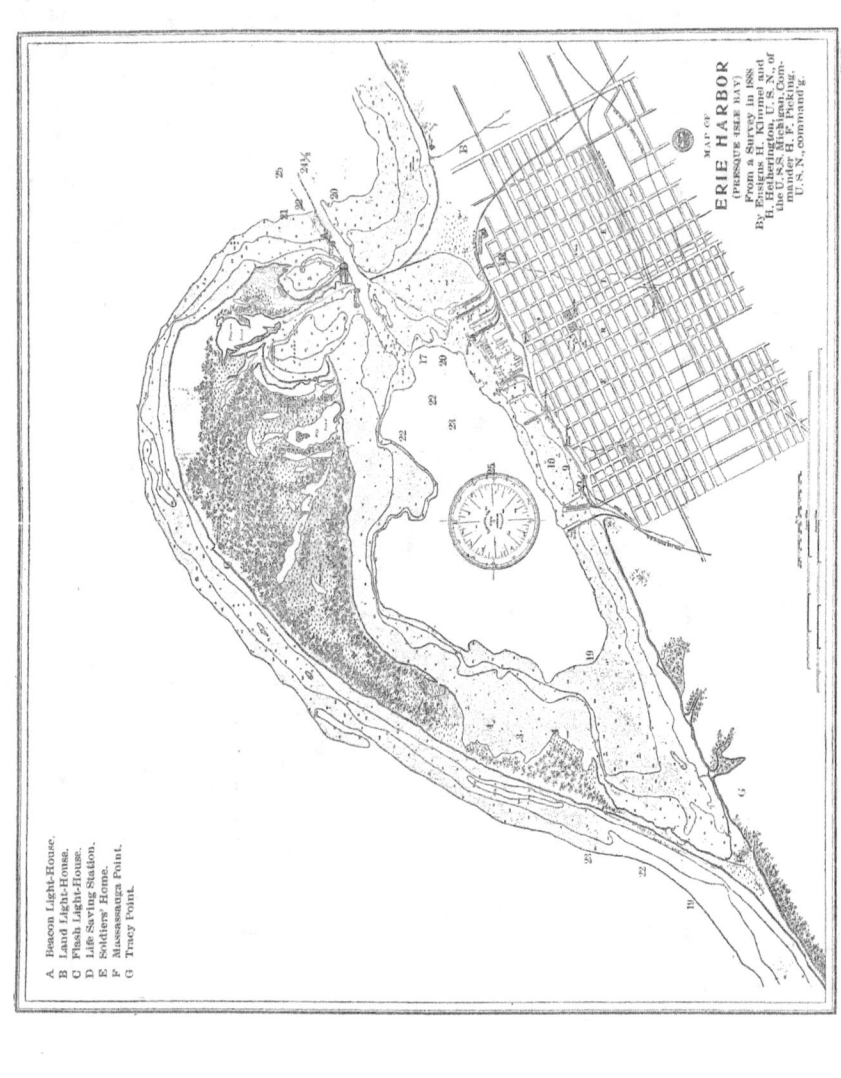

HISTORY OF ERIE COUNTY.

CHAPTER I.

An Account of the Eries—Traditions Concerning Them—Their Destruction—Symbols found on Kelly's or Cunningham's Island—Indian Remains.

> " A noble race! but they are gone,
> With their old forests wide and deep,
> And we have built our homes upon
> Fields where their generations sleep."—BRYANT.

AT the beginning of the seventeenth century the fierce and powerful Indian tribe called Erigas, Eries, Erie-honons, Mad Spirits or Cat tribe, occupied the southern borders of the lake now bearing their name. The same tribe was known to the French as the Neutral nation or Chats, and to the Dutch as Shaonons or Satanas. Champlain, in his first map, made no mention of them, locating other tribes in their territory; subsequently he heard of them when in the Huron country. The territory they occupied, according to Charleroix, was the celebrated valley of the Niagara River. On its northern margin they were found spreading both east and west on the shores of Lakes Erie and Ontario, but not to any great distance. Shea describes the localities of the tribes thus: "The Wyandots, traders of the West, lay in their densely-peopled villages, well fortified by ditch and palisade, on a small peninsula in Lake Huron; southwest lay their allies, the Tionontates, whose luxuriant fields of tobacco won for them and their fertile hills the name of Petuns; and south and east of these, stretching beyond the Niagara and its marvelous cataract, lay the many clans of the Atiwandaronk, friends to the Huron and Algonquin, friends, too, to the Iroquois, and called by the French the Neutral nation; east of these, in

New York, stretching from the Genesee to the mouth of the Mohawk, lay the five clans of the Hohnnonchiendi, whose name remains in the natural features of New York, and who are now known collectively by the French name Iroquois; west of these, on the southern shore of Lake Erie, lay the far-famed archers, the Eries or Cat tribe, who have melted away like a dream; on the Susquehanna were the Andastes or Conastagues, friends of the Huron and Swede, few but brave." The Eries at this time numbered twenty-eight villages, and twelve large towns or forts; these contained 12,000 souls, 4,000 of whom were fighting men.

In 1653, Le Moyne, an adopted Indian and priest, took his departure from Quebec, and landing at Oswego proceeded to the town of Onondaga. Here he was received with pomp, and after offering the authorities presents from the French governor, he commended to them peace and the faith of which he was the minister. Captive Hurons, of whom there were no less than a thousand in their midst, had prepared the way for the missionary by their instructions, causing the adults and children to desire baptism at his hands. Among others, a chief setting out against the Eries, on the eve of his departure begged for baptism. The prudent missionary counseled him to defer the rite to a future time, when he would visit them again. "Ah, brother!" exclaimed the chief, "if I have the faith can I not be a Christian to-day? Art thou master of death, to prevent its striking me without thy order? Will the shafts of the foe be blunted for me? Must I, at every step in battle, dread hell rather than death? Unless thou baptize me I shall not dare to meet the blows. Baptize me, for I will obey thee, and give thee my word to live and die a Christian." Such entreaties could not be resisted, and Le Moyne being persuaded of the chieftain's fitness, baptized him by the name of John Baptist, and the next day each set out on his different career. The baptized warrior was successful. Inspired by his zeal, the braves when surrounded by the Eries, invoked the God of the Christian, and vowed to embrace the faith if victory were granted. The tide of battle was changed, and the thousand braves of Onondaga drove an Erie force, which quadrupled theirs, from a strong post and won the day. Thus does even a corrupt Christianity inspire its possessors, and thus may paganism ever fall before the gospel.[1]

A semi-educated Tuscarora, David Cusic, published a pamphlet of Indian traditions, in Western New York, in 1825. This writing, though crude, ill digested, and generally obscure, throws much light on the history of the Eries. In 1626, among the first efforts made by New France to civilize the Indians, the Eries were visited; and the peculiarity for which they are most celebrated was first brought into notice, that of neutrality among fierce and powerful tribes. Hence they are called by the French the Neutral nation.

They were under the government of a queen, called Yagowanea, or as called by the French and Senecas, Gegosasa. According to Cusic, she was a second Zenobia. The settlement of Canada by the French produced a division in the great Iroquois family—the Wyandots adhering to the Gallic side, and the Five Nations to the Dutch and English. In this feud of the Iroquois, the Algonquins or Adirondacks, who were at war with them formerly, were glad to make allies of the French and Wyandots. Between these the Eries occupied a geographical position on the banks of the Niagara, and had already become closely allied to the Wyandots and Five Nations.* *Neutrality* was their only salvation—they were in a delicate position, and great wisdom was indispensable to its preservation. Gegosasa was called the mother of nations, and her wampum and peace-pipe were held sacred. Protected by the sanctity of Gegosasa's character and office as keeper of the symbolic house of peace, she received messengers and ambassadors from the Five Nations, Wyandots, Mississaqués, and others. Her authority extended much farther than her territory, but one inconsiderate act brought destruction to her nation after long and bloody wars. Two Canandaigua warriors (Senecas) were announced at her lodge, and began to smoke the pipe of peace, when a deputation from the Mississaqués was also announced. The object of

[1] The name of Le Moyne is again found as a leader when Schenectady, in 1690, was destroyed, and the most inhuman cruelties were perpetrated by a party of Canadian French Indians, being one of the three parties fitted out by Count Frontenac to distress the British Colonies.

their visit was soon made known, and their request, which was to demand vengeance for the murder of their chief's son, was immediately granted. Intelligence of this violation of neutrality on the part of Gegosasa spread in every direction. The queen dispatched messengers to explain her position to Ragnatha (Buffalo), where the principal commander of the Eries resided. She even undertook herself to execute the commission; but a meddling woman also stepped off quietly, taking a canoe along the shore of Lake Ontario, and communicated the death of the Canandaigua chief. Spies were sent by the Senecas to ascertain the truth of the rumors, who, without exciting suspicion, learned the facts from some boys found hunting squirrels, and an army was raised in hot haste. As a decoy, a man was dressed in bear-skin and directed to sit in the path, and when pursued, to lead the way into ambush. The plan succeeded, and the Eries were brought into the midst of crouching Senecas, who sounded the war-whoop most terrifically, but themselves, after a severe contest, were forced to flee. Afterward they rallied and fought with great desperation, and the Eries were compelled to yield, leaving 600 slain warriors on the battle-field.

In this first war of the Eries, which occurred in 1634, they proved themselves no despicable enemy. In 1653 they again engaged in war with the Iroquois. In this contest "Greek met Greek," and the event, otherwise doubtful, was decided by a pestilence which prevailed and swept off greater numbers even than the club and arrow. After their defeat, according to Seneca tradition, they fled down the Ohio, and the once sacred peace-lodge of Yagowanea was demolished. They were compelled to leave the land where Niagara pours its echoes and animates to heroic deeds. The Iroquois they found the worst of conquerors—inordinate pride, thirst of blood and dominion were the mainspring of their warfare, and their victories were stained with every excess of passion. When their vengeance was glutted by the sacrifice of a sufficient number of captives, they adopted the survivors as members of their confederate tribes, separating wives from husbands and children from parents, and distributing them among different villages, in order that old ties and associations might be more completely broken. This policy, as Schoolcraft informs us, was designated among them by a name which signified "flesh cut into pieces and scattered among the tribes." Jefferson says of them: "They fled to distant regions of the West and South, and wherever they fled they were followed by the undying hatred of the Iroquois. In accordance with the threat of the Onondagas, their council fire was put out, and their name and lineage as a tribe lost."

When the Jesuits visited the Onondagas, a Neuter was the first adult baptized. They were living then among them as helots, and bore their chains impatiently. They panted for freedom, their numbers giving them confidence. At one time they formed a plot to cut off their oppressors, but when aid was refused them by the French missionaries to whom they applied, they ceased to hope for deliverance. In 1674 the Eries are mentioned as constituting a part of the Christian village just then formed at La Prairie.

The various nations have long since fused into one, losing all distinctive trace of origin, and no clue of names can enable us to distinguish the Neutral element in the present Iroquois race. In the history of the Jesuit missions we find several of that order penetrated the country of the Eries or Neuters from the year 1626 to the year 1640. Among them are the names of Father Joseph De la Roche, D'Allyon, Brabœuf, Noue, Chaumount, and Sayard. They were received with coldness and distrust, in spite of which they remained some months preaching in ten of their villages and endeavoring to enter and obtain a knowledge of the country.

The efforts of De la Roche (who at first was quite a favorite) to find the mouth of the Niagara, excited their jealousy, and after they had robbed and beaten him severely, he was forced to depart.

The missionaries described the country as being finer than Canada, and producing an abundance of tobacco and grain. Brabœuf and Chaumount, by the aid of a charitable and intelligent native woman, compared the Huron and Neuter dialects. The result is lost, but Chaumount, in his manuscript, makes the Neuters, Hurons, and Iroquois use parts of the same language. They dressed in the most primitive style. In their manners they resembled the Hurons, but did not, like them, engage in commerce.

Brabœuf foresaw that the French must have a post among them in order to extend commerce and Christianity, but their jealousy prevented his taking out his astrolabe to find the latitude of the Niagara River, and he had to content himself with roughly estimating it at 42 degrees. The missionary, Sayard, suffered at the stake, and the cognizance of the Jesuits was from that time withdrawn from the Eries. When the valley was finally opened it was in possession of the Senecas, and a tradition was rife corresponding with that of Cusic, that the Eries had been expelled in a bloody war and exterminated.

And these traditions extend down almost to our own day. David Eddy, a resident of Hamburg, near Buffalo, and who settled there in 1804, relates that in early times there was an Indian living upon the reservation who probably was 115 years of age. He was a Christian, and had been a peacemaker through life, and related to Mr. Eddy the following: That a nation called the Eries once inhabited all that region—that they were a powerful, warlike people, dreaded and feared by all other tribes, but were finally warred upon and their country conquered by the Senecas.

Fortifications and mounds in Western New York indicate a race more skillful and persevering than the Senecas or the Indians known to the first white travelers. In many cases the mounds have trees growing upon them, the circles of which date them back a period of 300 years. Symbols of this extinct race have been found on Cunningham's or Kelly's Island, near Sandusky, Ohio. This island is about three miles long and two broad, and in consequence of the fine air, and its facilities for fishing and bathing, is a favorite summer resort. It is now, also, highly cultivated, and noted for producing an abundance of the finest grapes. The island is described as having a horizontal limestone basis like the main land, and rises fifteen feet above the water level. Where the rock is exposed, it appears to have been polished by diluvial or glacial action. The Indian remains discovered there consist of pictographic characters on the rocks, and earth-work embankments.

A drawing of these was made upon strong paper in 1851, and transmitted to Mr. George Johnson, of Sault St. Marie, a gentleman well versed in Indian languages, and by him was submitted to the examination of Shingowank, or Little Pine. The result of his inquiries was, that the island was the stronghold of the Eries during their fierce and unsuccessful contest with the Iroquois. On the south side of the island there is a crest-shaped and irregular earth-work, which has the general appearance of an embankment or circumvallation intended to inclose and defend a village. The embankment is 1246 feet around the crest-shaped part, and about 400 feet on the rock brink of the island. Another embankment on the western side is 614 feet front and 1243 feet around. Within these have been found stone axes, pipes, perforations, bone fish-hooks, fragments of pottery, arrow-heads, net-sinkers, and fragments of human bones. The arrow-heads were found in a fissure of the rock in large quantities, were evidently new, and had been concealed in this kind of rude armory; with them was found the largest species of axe figured, which had been apparently used. Five small mounds or burrows were also found on the southern and western parts of the island. On the north shore, on a bay, there is a brief pictographic inscription on a boulder, which has been reversed by the force of the waters in a tempest.

The interest of this, however, is inferior to that excited by a sculptured rock thirty feet by twenty-one, lying on the south shore of the island, about 200 feet from the west angle of the inclosure. The surface is smoothly polished, as well as the deeply-cut inscription, apparently by glacial attrition. According to Schoolcraft "it is the most extensive, and well-sculptured, and well-preserved inscription of the kind ever found in America." Its leading symbols are readily interpreted, and tell a thrilling story, in which the European acts a part. There are many subordinate figures which require study. In some, the atmosphere and lake action have destroyed the connection, and others are of an anomalous character. The whole inscription is manifestly connected with the occupation of the basin of the lake by the Eries, the coming of the Wyandots, and of the final flight of the people which have left their name upon the lake. There is an attempt to denote the position of Lake Erie; pictures of two brothers surveying a scene of carnage—a pipe reversed, which indicates that they are despairing and agonized. They are wild forest Indians, being drawn without hats. The date of these inscriptions is placed at 1625.

The Eries were known to be in "the plenitude of their power and barbaric boast of strength and influence" at the period of the first discoveries of the French in the beginning of the seventeenth century. From the French they learned the use of firearms, and the Iroquois from the Dutch about the same time.

About five miles south of Franklin, Venango County, or nine by the river, on the left bank of the Allegheny, is a large rock covered with symbols or hieroglyphics, known by the present inhabitants as the "Indian God." Among the figures may be distinguished a turtle, a snake, an eye, an arrow, a sun, etc., symbols which undoubtedly record the exploits and illustrious actions of departed and forgotten nations. They have never been examined, that we are aware of, by any one capable of deciphering them. Many Indian graves are in the vicinity.

The only traces of an Indian village in Erie County are near Waterford, where there is a burying ground, plum orchard, and other evidences of the Indians having chosen the hills around Lake Le Bœuf, and the beautiful creeks which flow into and from it, for their homes and hunting-grounds. The Six Nations were found in this region by the first white travelers (in fact, it was purchased from them), and yet comparatively few Indian remains are discovered. On the ridge a mile south and east of Erie, in making excavations, perhaps twenty years ago, a great number of human bones were found and graves opened, so that Mr. Colt, the owner of the land, considered it almost desecration to disturb them, and ordered the workmen to desist, feeling that it would be more appropriate to place a monument there.

An Indian mound was opened near the mouth of Walnut Creek (in which vicinity many relics are found), and some fragments of decomposed human skeletons were all that could be discovered. Two miles west of this mound is an embankment covered with the ordinary forest growth, which is known as the Old Indian Fort. A small stream near by is called *Fort Run*.

There are also remains of an Indian fort between Girard and Springfield. From a grave in this vicinity, some years ago, a thigh bone was exhumed which measured four inches longer than that of a man with which it was compared, who was six feet and two inches in height. About a mile south of Girard, arrow-heads, pipes, pestles for pounding corn, etc., have been found. Near Mr. Gould's, in Springfield, four or five years since, more than fifty arrows, axes, etc., were found in one collection, just below the surface in the public road.

An ancient double fortification, inclosing about two acres, upon the Pomeroy farm, a mile or two northwest of Cranesville, has been pretty much farmed over. On the top of the bank, in 1830, oak trees four or five feet in diameter were growing. Skinning-stones, arrow-heads, an enormous skeleton, and many other relics were found within the fort. A bed of coals a foot and a half below the surface appeared to be the remains of the fire of the occupants.

About one hundred yards above, on the opposite bank of the creek, was another fort, similar in appearance, and containing about the same quantity of ground. They are supposed to have been the encampments of two opposing armies.

In Scouler's woods, east of Erie, is an Indian buryingground. Mr. Fredrick Zimmerman described a very large skeleton which was found there; with it were two copper bowls perforated at the edges and laced together with a buckskin thong, which fell to dust soon after being exposed to the air. The bowls, which would contain about a pint each, were found filled with beads.

A year or two since, on the farm of Judge Sterrett, four or five miles east of Erie, several skeletons were found in a sitting posture, facing the east, with drinking vessels near them. The same posture has been observed in other Indian graves in this vicinity. We are not aware that any antiquarian has particularly examined these relics, or whether they resemble in their general features those of New York and

24 HISTORY OF ERIE COUNTY.

Ohio, which are said to give evidence of a race more skillful and persevering than the Iroquois. There is a tradition, as we have seen, that the Eries two hundred years ago possessed our soil ; and still another, that the Massassagués had their hunting-grounds and lighted their council fires near the head waters of the Allegheny. It is difficult to realize that our fair lands were so recently under the dominion of the hideous, painted savages, and that but little more than two generations have passed since heathenish rites and ceremonies prevailed, and the bow and arrow gave place to the peaceful arts of civilized life.

CHAPTER II.

La Salle—The Griffon—Relics—Governor Shirley's Proposition—Braddock's Advice—Governor Delancy's Plan—Estimating Presqu'ile—Hudson's Bay Company.

AMONG the adventurers who sought fame and fortune in the American wilderness, stood conspicuously Robert Cavalier, Sieur de la Salle, a young man of eminence and learning. He had received from Louis XIV. the rank of nobleman, a large domain, and an exclusive trading privilege with the Five Nations, but his ambition was far from being satisfied with these. To extend the bounds of New France and to open commerce with Europe seemed to be his great object, and to this end he proposed a plan which was carried out many years after—that of establishing military posts on the waters of the Mississippi.

August 7, 1679, he launched the first wooden vessel that ever floated upon Lake Erie and called it "The Griffon," in allusion to the arms of Count Frontenac, Governor-General of Canada, and who had honored La Salle with his friendship. [1]

[1] There has been a diversity of opinions as to the locality of the Griffon ship-yard. Schoolcraft says near Buffalo; General Cass, at Erie; Sparks, on the Canadian side of the Niagara; Bancroft, in his first edition, at the mouth of Tonawanta Creek (see his letter). Others, who have carefully examined the subject, and have had the best opportunity for judging, are firm in the belief that the keel was laid at the mouth of Cayuga Creek, on the American side of the Niagara, about six miles above the Great Falls. In the vicinity, it has long been known by the name of the "Old Ship-yard." La Salle is now a railroad station there. Bancroft's statement is in the *first edition only* of the History of the United States. See Bancroft's note on the subject.

The Griffon was of sixty tons burden, and built at Cayuga Creek, six miles above the falls, on the American side. The Iroquois had gone to war beyond the lake while the Griffon was building; the few that remained manifested their dissatisfaction, and one, affecting to be drunk, attempted to kill a blacksmith. They were advised that some Senecas intended setting fire to the vessel while on the stocks, but a very strict watch was kept constantly. The Senecas refused to sell them Indian corn, and they had many fears of a failure of provisions, but Sunday exhortations kept up the courage of the workmen. Two savages of the Wolf tribe were engaged to hunt the roebuck, and other species of deer, for their use. The workmen were stimulated by the impression that the enterprise had sole reference to the glory of God, and the welfare of the Christian colonies. When the vessel was launched, it was blessed according to the Church of Rome. It was a moving fort, causing the savages to tremble wherever it was known. The Griffon passed the violent rapids of Lake Erie almost by miracle, the pilot himself having fears. They spread all sail, the wind being stormy, and in the most difficult places the sailors threw out lines which were drawn by ten or twelve men on the shore. After having chanted Te Deum, they fired all their cannon or arbesques in the presence of the Iroquois warriors and the captives they had brought from Tin-ton-ha, or people of the prairie.

It was freighted with provisions, merchandise, and seven small cannon, and had on board thirty-two passengers, being mostly fur traders and priests. In twenty days this perilous voyage was accomplished, and the pioneer vessel cast anchor in Green Bay. On the passage they encountered a severe storm. Among other tarryings, they gathered fruits, and made wine of the wild grapes of Michigan, discussed the question of planting a colony at Detroit, and established a trading-house at Mackinaw. At Green Bay the vessel was loaded with the finest furs, and again set sail for Niagara, but was never afterward heard from with certainty. Hennepin says: "It came to anchor at the mouth of the Lake Illinois, where it was seen by some savages, who told us that they advised our men to sail along the coast, and not toward the middle of the lake, because of the sands that make the lake dangerous when there are high winds. Our pilot, as I said before, was dissatisfied, and would steer as he pleased, without hearing to the advice of the savages, who, generally speaking, have more sense than the Europeans think at first. But the ship was hardly a league from the coast when it was tossed up by a violent storm in such a manner that our men were never heard from since; and it is supposed that the ship struck upon a sand, and was there buried. This was a great loss, for the ship and cargo cost 60,000 livres. The rigging, anchors, and goods were brought by canoes from Quebec and Fort Frontinac, which is such a vast charge that the carriage of every hundredweight cost eleven livres." Another author says the Griffon was lost a few days after leaving the Bay of Fetid. This and other misfortunes completely disheartened the daring traveler, as evinced by the name "Crevecœur," which he gave his fort built the same winter. After seven years of wanderings and adverse fortune, La Salle was basely robbed and murdered by one of his own men, and left without sepulture on the prairie, to be devoured by the wild beasts.

Parkman says of La Salle: "Ten years of his early life had passed in connection with the Jesuits, and his strong mind had hardened to iron under the discipline of that relentless school. To a sound judgment and penetrating sagacity, he joined a boundless enterprise and an adamantine constancy of purpose. But his nature was stern and austere—he was prone to rule by fear rather than love—he took counsel of no man, and chilled all who approached him by his cold reserve."

There was a tradition among the Jesuits that the Griffon was driven ashore in a gale, the crew murdered, and the vessel plundered. Judging from relics found at different times, this may have occurred near Buffalo. In the Buffalo *Commercial Advertiser*, of January 26, 1848, a communication appears from James W. Peters, of East Evans, Erie County: "Some thirty-five or forty years ago, on the Ingersoll farm, in Hamburg, below the Eighteen-mile Creek, and on a high bank in the woods, was found by Mr. Ingersoll a large quantity of wrought-iron, supposed to be 700 or 800 weight. It was evidently taken off a vessel, was of superior quality, much eaten by rust, and sunken deep in the soil. A large tree had fallen across it which was rotted and mixed with the earth. There were trees growing over the iron from six to twelve inches in diameter, which had to be grubbed up before all the iron could be reached. About twenty-seven years since, a man by the name of Walker, after a heavy blow on the lake, found on the beach, near where the irons were found, a cannon, and immediately under it a second one. I was there not forty-eight hours after they were found; they were much defaced by age and rust, and filled up with sand. I cleared off enough from one to lay a number of the letters bare. The words were French, and so declared at the time. The horns or trunnions were knocked off."

The venerable D. Eddy, of Hamburg, says: "In 1805 there was found upon the lake shore, where a large body of sand and gravel had been removed during a violent gale, a beautiful anchor. It was taken to Buffalo and Black Rock, and excited a good deal of curiosity; but no one could determine to what vessel it belonged." A record of the loss of a vessel at a later period than that of La Salle would in all probability have been preserved, and we may reasonably conclude that the iron, cannon, and anchor were those of the Griffon.

In the *Maryland Gazette*, August 23, 1759, we find the following: "By a letter from Niagara, of the 21st ult., we learn that by the assistance and influence of Sir William Johnson there were upwards of eleven hundred Indians convened there, who by their good behavior have justly gained the esteem of the whole army; that Sir William being informed that the enemy had buried a quantity of goods on an island about twenty miles from the post, sent a number of Indians to search for them, who found to the value of eight thousand pounds, and were in hopes of finding more; and that a French vessel, entirely laden with beaver, had foundered on the lake, where her crew, consisting of forty-one men, were all lost." This vessel, lost eighty years after the Griffon, we have no account of elsewhere. The relics found at Hamburg were but forty-six years after this time—not a sufficient period to cause the appearance those relics presented, the anchor deeply imbedded in sand and gravel, the timber growth, etc.

About 1750, Governor Shirley, of Massachusetts, in writing to Secretary Robinson, proposed the plan of building one or two vessels on each of the lakes—Erie and Ontario—with which, and a few small fortified places of shelter upon the Ohio, he expected to curb the French, who were at this time the frequent occasion of difficulties and murders. Two years after, General Braddock named Presqu'ile as a suitable place to build vessels for securing the navigation of Lake Erie, which, he says, "together with those designed for Lake Ontario, would make the English masters of the great lakes and the Ohio country, until the French can get a force upon those lakes, which it seems very difficult, if not impossible for them to do when our vessels are cruising upon them." General Braddock also requested that a magazine of provisions in the back of Pennsylvania be established, from whence to supply himself by a road through the mountains to the waters of the Ohio—"the road to extend to Venango and Niagara, which would be of infinite use in subsisting the troops, as that region abounds more with provisions than any other colony in North America."

The estimation in which Presqu'ile was held one hundred years ago will be seen in a letter dated August 7, 1755, from Lieutenant-Governor De Lancy to Secretary Robinson : "The third method of distressing the French is by way of Oswego ; to go thither we pass, as I observed before, through the country of our Indian friends—by water it is a much less expensive carriage than by land—from Oswego we may go westward by water through Lake Ontario to Niagara. If we become masters of this pass, the French cannot go to reinforce or victual their garrisons at Presqu'ile, Beeve River, or on the Ohio but with great difficulty and expense, and by a tedious, long passage. From the fort at Niagara there is a land carriage of about three leagues to the waters above the falls ; thence we go to Lake Erie, and so to the Fort Presqu'ile ; and if we take that, the French can carry no supplies of provisions, nor send men to the head of Beeve River (Le Bœuf) or to the Fort Du Quesne on the Ohio, and of course those forts will be abandoned. The same batteaux which carry the train, provisions, etc., for the army to Oswego may carry them to

Niagara, and being transported above the falls, the same may carry them to Presqu'ile, the fort on the south side of Lake Erie, so that it will be practicable to bring the expense of such an expedition into a moderate compass—far less than the expense of wagons, horses, etc., which are necessary in an expedition by land from Virginia to Ohio; besides that, proceeding from Virginia to Fort Du Quesne, if it be taken, it is only cutting off a toe, but taking Presqu'ile you lop off a limb from the French and greatly disable them."

Relating to the commerce of Lake Erie, we find that as early as 1669 the Hudson's Bay Company was incorporated, and transported its goods, provisions, and peltries in batteaux for many years after.

In 1789 the British had vessels on Lake Erie for the transportation of his Majesty's troops and effects. The subject of commerce and shipping on Lake Erie is continued in Chapter XI.

CHAPTER III.

The English and French Claims—Construction of Forts Presqu'ile (Erie) and Le Bœuf (Waterford)—Washington's Visit—Condition of these Forts in 1756, '57, '58, and '59—Their Desertion after the Taking of Fort Niagara—Tradition in Erie—Major Rogers takes Possession for the English in 1760.

THE treaty of Aix-la-Chapelle, of 1748, which closed the war in Europe, left the boundaries of the French and English possessions in America undefined. In the opinion of the French, the discovery of the mouth of the St. Lawrence and of the Mississippi entitled their sovereign to the territory watered by those streams. The abstract of Sieur de Champlain, 1612, claims for them the possession of all the countries from Florida to Cape Breton prior to any other Christian nation. Afterward this was renewed by Sieur de la Salle, with thirty Frenchmen, among whom were Mons. Joliet, priest and superior of the seminary at Montreal, and Father Marquette, who made a tour of Lake Erie and took possession of the circumjacent lands. Celeron de Bienville, with a company of 300 men, was sent out by the Governor of Canada in 1749 to make peace among the tribes and to renew the French possession of the country. He dispensed presents to the Indians, reminded them of their former friendships, and warned them not to trade with the English. He also nailed leaden plates to the trees, and buried them in the earth at the confluence of the Ohio and its tributaries. One of these plates was found a few years since at the junction of the Great Kanawha and Ohio, dated January 18; another at Muskingum the 16th of August; and a third at Venango (Franklin). The following is a literal translation of the one last named : " In the year 1749, in the reign of Louis XV., King of France, we, Celeron, commandant of a detachment by Monsieur the Marquis of Galissoniere, commander-in-chief of New France, to establish tranquillity in certain villages of these cantons, have buried this plate at the confluence of Toradakoin, this 29th of July, near the River Ohio, otherwise beautiful river, as a monument of renewal of possession which we have taken of the said river, inasmuch as the preceding kings of France have enjoyed this possession and maintained it by their arms and by treaties, especially by those of Ryswick, Utrecht, and Aix-la-Chapelle."

The Indians regarded these plates with suspicion, and said, "They mean to steal our country from us"; and these suspicions were not groundless, for in a few years the French unceremoniously possessed themselves of their best tracts for trading-houses and fortifications.

June 30, 1749, a letter was received by express from General Clinton, purporting that two New England men, on their return from Canada, where they had been to solicit the release of some prisoners, reported that they saw an army of 1,000 French ready to go on some expedition, and they were informed it was to prevent any settlements being made by the English on Belle Riviere; whereupon it was determined to dispatch a messenger to Mr. George Croghan, with a request that he would go immediately to Allegheny, and on his arrival send away a trader, or some person he could confide in, to the lakes or to the eastward, to discover whether any French were coming in those parts, and if any, in what number, and what appearance they made, that the Indians might be apprised and put upon their guard.

January, 1750.—The Governor informed the council that three several letters, of an extraordinary nature, in French, signed "Celeron," were delivered to him by the French traders who came from Allegheny, informing him that this Captain Celeron was a French officer, and had the command of three hundred French and some Indians sent this summer to Ohio and the Wabash from Canada, to reprove the Indians for their friendship to the English, and for suffering the English to trade with them. The Governor sent one of the letters to the proprietaries in London, and another to the Governor of New York, that the same might be laid before the ministry.

A letter from George Croghan, dated Logstown, in Ohio, December 16, 1750, contains the intelligence that he arrived the 15th, and was told by Indians that they saw Jean Cœur 150 miles up the river, where he intended building a fort. The Indians he had seen were of opinion that the English should have a fort or forts on this river to secure the trade. They expected a war with the French the next spring.

February 6.—In a letter of Governor Clinton, dated Fort George, January 29, 1750, is the following: "I send you a copy of an inscription on a leaden plate stolen from Jean Cœur, in the Senecas' country, as he was going to the Ohio."

The claim of England to this region was founded on a grant of King James the First, dated 1606, and confirmed in 1620, to divers of his subjects, of all the countries between north latitude 48° and 34°, and westward from the Atlantic Ocean to the South Sea—not a right only to the seacoast, but to all the inland country from sea to sea. England had, also, through commissioners from Maryland, Virginia, and Pennsylvania, purchased western lands from the Six Nations. This treaty was held at Lancaster in 1744, between 252 Indians, with Conrad Weiser as friend and interpreter, and the Governor of Pennsylvania, with Col. Thomas Lee and Col. William Beverly, of Virginia. The commissioners of Maryland paid for their purchase £220 in goods; Virginia, £220 in gold and the same amount in goods, with promises that more should be paid as settlements increased. The chief subsequently disputed the sale of any lands west of the Warrior's Road, which was at the foot of the Allegheny ridge. In reality the Indians were intoxicated through the whole conference, and it was only through much ingenuity and persuasion that they were induced to sign a deed confirming the Lancaster treaty in its full extent, which was effected at Logstown, seventeen miles below Pittsburg, in 1752.

The year before, in 1751, it was rumored that the French were aware of the difficulties they would have to encounter in maintaining their position in New France, and were taking measures to meet them. Capt. Lindsay wrote Col. Johnson, to whom all such affairs were referred, "that Bunt and Black Prince's son with their fighters had come in, and that the French had built two forts, one at Niagara carrying place, and the other on the Ohio River by Joncaire; that they had heard a bird sing that a great many Indians from his castle, and others from the Five Nations, were gone to Swegage"; in fine, that the English would lose all the Indians if they did not bestir themselves.

Early in 1753 the French sent out a detachment from Montreal to erect other fortifications, to make good their claim by force of arms if they met with opposition, and to oblige all English subjects to evacuate. Oswego they were instructed not to molest in consideration of Cape Breton—any other post the English had settled near or claimed was to be reduced if not quitted immediately. A narrative of this expedition from Montreal, and the building of Forts Presqu'ile and Le Bœuf, is to be found in the following deposition of Stephen Coffin, which was made to Col. Johnson, of New York, January 10, 1754. Coffin was a New Englander who had been taken prisoner by the French and Indians of Canada, at Menis, in 1747. He had served them in different capacities until 1752, when, being detected in efforts to escape to his own country, he was confined in jail in Quebec; on his release he applied to Governor Du Quesne to be sent with the forces to Ohio. In his own words—"The deponent then applied to Mayor Ramsey for liberty to go with the army to Ohio, who told him he would ask the Lieut. de Ruoy, who agreed to it;

upon which he was equipped as a soldier and sent with a detachment of 300 men to Montreal under the command of Mons. Babeer, who set off immediately with said command by land and ice for Lake Erie. They in their way stopped to refresh themselves a couple of days at Cadaraqui Fort, also at Taranto on the north side of Lake Ontario, then at Niagara Fort fifteen days from thence.

"They set off by water, being April, and arrived at Chadakoin (Chautauqua) on Lake Erie, where they were ordered to fell timber and prepare it for building a fort there, according to the Governor's instructions; but Mr. Morang coming up with five hundred men and twenty Indians, put a stop to the erecting a fort at that place, by reason of his not liking the situation, and the River Chadakoin being too shallow to carry out any craft with provisions, etc. to Belle Riviere.[1] The deponent says there arose a warm debate between Messieurs Babeer and Morang thereon, the first insisting on building a fort there, agreeable to instructions, otherwise, on Morang giving him an instrument in writing to satisfy the Governor on that point, which Morang did, and then ordered Mons. Mercie, who was both commissary and engineer, to go along said lake and look for a situation, which he found, and returned in three days, it being fifteen leagues to the southwest of Chadakoin. They were then ordered to repair thither; when they arrived, there were about twenty Indians fishing in the lake, who immediately quit on seeing the French. They fell to work and built a square fort of chestnut logs, squared and lapped over each other to the height of fifteen feet. It is about one hundred and twenty feet square, a loghouse in each square, a gate to the southward, another to the northward, not one port-hole cut in any part of it. When finished, they called it Fort Presqu'ile. The Indians who came from Canada with them returned very much out of

[1] Lieutenant Holland of the English fort at Oswego observed Morain (or Morang) with his fleet pass that point on the fourteenth of May, and dispatched letters immediately to Colonel Johnson and Governor Clinton. He stated to the latter that there were "thirty odd French canoes," and that common report in Canada made the French army to consist of 6,000 men and 500 Indians of the Coyhnawagas, Scenondidies, Onogonguas, Oroondoks, and Chenundies tribes, who would not engage to go to war with the English, but would hunt at so much per month for the army.

temper, owing, it was said among the army, to Morang's dogged behavior and ill usage of them; but they (the Indians) said at Oswego it was owing to the French misleading them, by telling them falsehoods, which they said they now found out, and left them. As soon as the fort was finished, they marched southward, cutting a wagon road through a fine, level country twenty-one miles to the river—(leaving Captain Derpontency with one hundred men to garrison the Fort Presqu'ile). They fell to work cutting timber boards, etc., for another fort, while Mr. Morang ordered Mons. Bite with fifty men to a place called by the Indians Ganagarahare, on the banks of Belle Riviere, where the River Aux Bœufs empties into it. In the meantime, Morang had ninety large boats made to carry down the baggage, provisions, etc. to said place. Mons. Bite, on coming to said Indian place, was asked what he wanted or intended. He upon answering said, 'it was their father, the Governor of Canada's intention to build a trading house for them and all their brethren's convenience'; he was told by the Indians that the lands were theirs, and that they would not have them build upon it. The said Bite reported to Morang the situation was good, but the water in the River Aux Bœufs too low at that time to carry any craft with provisions, etc.

"A few days after, the deponent says, that about one hundred Indians, called by the French the Loos, came to the Fort La Riviere Aux Bœufs to see what the French were doing; that Morang treated them very kindly, and then asked them to carry down some stone, etc. to the Belle Riviere, on horseback, for payment, which he immediately advanced them on their undertaking to do it. They set off with full loads, but never delivered them to the French, which incensed them very much, being not only a loss, but a great disappointment. Morang, a man of very peevish, choleric disposition, meeting with those and other crosses, and finding the season of the year too far advanced to build the third fort, called all his officers together, and told them that, as he had engaged and firmly promised the Governor to finish these forts that season, and not being able to fulfill the same, he was both afraid and ashamed to return to Canada, being sensible he had now forfeited the Governor's favor forever. Wherefore, rather than live in disgrace, he begged they would take him (as he then sat in a carriage made for him, being very sick sometimes) and seat him in the middle of the fort, and then set fire to it and let him perish in the flames, which was rejected by the officers, who had not the least regard for him, as he had behaved very ill to them all in general. The deponent further saith, that about eight days before he left the Fort Presqu'ile, Chevalier Le Crake arrived express from Canada in a birch canoe worked by ten men, with orders (as the deponent afterward heard) from the Governor Le Cain (Duquesne) to Morang to make all the preparation possible against the spring of the year to build them two forts at Chadakoin, one of them by Lake Erie, the other at the end of the carrying place at Lake Chadakoin, which carrying place is fifteen miles from one lake to the other. The said Chevalier brought for M. Morang a cross of St. Louis, which the rest of the officers would not allow him to take until the Governor was acquainted with his conduct and behavior. The Chevalier returned immediately to Canada.

"After which, the deponent saith, when the Fort La Riviere Aux Bœufs was finished (which is built of wood stockaded triangularwise, and has two log-houses on the inside) M. Morang ordered all the party to return to Canada for the winter season, except three hundred men, which he kept to garrison both forts and prepare materials against the spring for the building of other forts. He also sent Jean Cœur, an officer and interpreter, to stay the winter among the Indians on the Ohio, in order to prevail with them not only to allow the building of forts over there, but also to persuade them, if possible, to join the French interests against the English. The deponent further says that on the 28th of October last, he set off for Canada under the command of Capt. Deman, who had the command of twenty-two batteaux with twenty men in each batteau, the remainder being seven hundred; and sixty men followed in a few days. The thirtieth arrived at Chadakoin, where they stayed four days, during which time M. Peon, with two hundred men, cut a wagon road over the carrying place from Lake Erie to Lake Chadakoin, being fifteen miles, viewed the situation, which proved to their liking, and so set off November the third for Niagara, where we arrived the sixth. It is a very poor, rotten, old wooden fort with twenty-five men in it. They talk of rebuilding it next summer. We left fifty men there to build batteaux for the army against the spring, also a storehouse for provisions, stores, etc. Stayed here two days, then set off for Canada. All hands, being fatigued with rowing all night, ordered to put ashore to breakfast within a mile of Oswego garrison; at which time the deponent saith that he, with a Frenchman, slipped off and got to the fort, where they were concealed until the enemy passed. From thence he came here. The deponent further saith, that beside the three hundred men with which he went up first under the command of M. Babeer, and the five hundred Morang brought up afterward, there came at different times, with stores, etc., one hundred men, which made in all fifteen hundred men, three hundred of which remained to garrison the two forts, fifty at Niagara; the rest all returned to Canada, and talked of going up again this winter, so as to be there the beginning of April. They had two six-pounders and seven four-pounders, which they intended to have planted in the fort at Ganagarahare (Franklin), which was to have been called the Governor's Fort; but as that was not built, they left the guns in the Fort La Riviere Aux Bœufs, where Morang commands. Further the deponent saith not."

The Indians of New York and the Allegheny country, as we have seen, were allied to Great Britian. A deputation of seven French Indians had been sent to Onondaga, the headquarters of the Six Nations, to conciliate them and to prepare the way for this expedition from Canada. Although many of the Indians favored the French, yet the deputation were informed promptly that they would not be allowed to settle upon their lands. Andrew Montour, an Indian interpreter who was present at the conference, having some commission from the Governer of Virginia, on his return conveyed the intelligence to him, and also to Governor Hamilton of Pennsylvania. The latter addressed the Colonial Assembly on the subject, urging the necessity of protection for the friendly

Indians, and suggesting the discomfort of having French forts within the limits of the province, together with the probability of the Indians deserting them for a power willing to afford them protection.

The same year (1749) Celeron, in the name of Louis, took possession of the Ohio valley. An association was formed by twelve Virginians, among whom were found the names of George and Augustus Washington, called the Ohio Company, which petitioned the king for a grant of land beyond the mountains. Their object was not so much to cultivate the soil or promote settlement, as to monopolize the Indian trade, to purchase and export furs, to sell goods, and erect trading houses and stores. The government readily assented to the project, as it promised quiet and prompt possession of the Ohio valley, in opposition to the advances of the French, and granted them 500,000 acres of land west of the Alleghenies. Of this land, two fifths was to be selected immediately, the whole was to be free from quit rent ten years, one hundred families were to settle upon it, and a garrison was to be maintained at the expense of the company as a defense against the Indians.

Christopher Gist was sent out to explore and report to the corporation, and in 1752 he, with eleven other families, made the first settlement west of the mountains. This was upon land presumed to belong to the company, and is now called Mount Braddock, being in Fayette County.

The news of the encroachments of the French having obtained, and the Ohio Company feeling aggrieved, applied for aid to Governor Dinwiddie, who claimed the country as a part of Virginia, and was also interested as a stockholder of the company. In Gen. Washington, then but a youth, Governor Dinwiddie saw one fitted to lead in this difficult expedition.

On the 30th of October, 1753, accompanied by Gist, the pioneer, Van Braem, a retired soldier, who had a knowledge of French, and John Davison, Indian interpreter, he set out for the wilderness.

The instructions given Washington were to communicate at Logstown with the friendly Indians, and to request of them an escort to the headquarters of the French, to deliver his letter and credentials to the commander, and demand of him an answer in the name of the British sovereign, and an escort to protect him on his return. He was to acquaint himself with the strength of the French forces, the number of their forts, and their object in advancing to those parts, and also to make such other observations as his opportunities would allow.

The Indians were not well satisfied as to the rights of either the French or English. An old Delaware sachem exclaimed, "The French claim all the lands on one side of the Ohio, and the English on the other; now where does the Indian's land lie?" "Poor savages! between their father the French, and their brothers the English, they were in a fair way of being lovingly shared out of the whole country." Three of the sachems, Tanacharison, or Half-King, from his being subject to another tribe, Jeskakake, and White Thunder, accompanied Major Washington from Logstown, as they had been directed by Governor Dinwidde, as well as for the purpose of returning to the French commander the war belts they had received from them. This implied that they wished to dissolve all friendly relations with their government. These Ohio tribes had been offended at the encroachments of the French, and had a short time previously sent deputations to the commander at Lake Erie, to remonstrate. Half-King, as chief of the Western tribes, had made his complaints in person, and been answered with contempt. "The Indians," said the commander, "are like flies and mosquitos, and the numbers of the French as the sands of the seashore. Here is your wampum, I fling it at you." As no reconciliation had been offered for this offense, aid was readily granted by them to the English in their mission.

From Washington's journal we get the following particulars: On their arrival at Venango [1] (Franklin) they found the

[1] "The original drawing of Fort Venango by the French engineers is still in existence, being in the possession of William Reynolds, Esq., Meadville. In the vicinity of the fort several choice species of grapes are still growing, a line of them extending from its center to the base of the hill. They have been bearing so long that the minds of men 'runneth not to the contrary.' No doubt the original shoots were brought from ' La Belle France.'"

The draft, it is said, was made in 1758 or 1759, and exhibited the stockade on the embankment, the bastions and gates of the fort, together with the very strong block-house in the center, which had no less than sixteen chimneys. Below the southeast corner of the fort stood a saw-mill, erected on the little stream that passes it. The draft has no notes or explanations annexed.

French colors hoisted at a house from which they had driven John Frasier, an English subject. There they inquired for the residence of the commander. Three officers were present, and one Capt. Jean Cœur informed them that *he* had the command of the Ohio, but advised them to apply for an answer at the near fort, where there was a general officer. He then invited them to sup with them, and treated the company with the greatest complaisance. At the same time they dosed themselves plentifully with wine, and soon forgot the restraint which at first appeared in their conversation. In this half-intoxicated state they confessed that their design was to take possession of the Ohio, although the English could command for that service two men to their one. Still their motions were slow and dilatory. They maintained that the right of the French was undoubted from La Salle's discovery sixty years before, and that their object now was to prevent the settlement of the English upon the river or its waters, notwithstanding several families they had heard were moving out for that purpose.

Fifteen hundred men had been engaged in the expedition west of Lake Ontario, but upon the death of the general, which had occurred but a short time before, all were recalled excepting six or seven hundred, who now garrisoned four forts, being one hundred and fifty men to a fort. The first of the forts was on French Creek (Waterford), near a small lake, about sixty miles from Venango, north-northwest; the next on Lake Erie (Presqu'ile), where the greater part of their stores were kept, about fifteen miles from the other; from this, one hundred and twenty miles to the carrying place, at the Falls of Niagara (probably Schlosser) is a small fort, where they lodge their goods in bringing them from Montreal, from whence all their stores are brought; the next fort lay about twenty miles farther, on Lake Ontario (Fort Niagara).

The second day at Franklin it rained excessively, and the party were prevented from prosecuting their journey. In the meantime, Capt. Jean Cœur sent for Half-King, and professed great joy at seeing him and his companions, and affected much concern that they had not made free to bring them in before. To this Washington replied that he had heard him say a great deal in dispraise of Indians generally. His real motive was to keep them from Jean Cœur, he being an interpreter and a person of great influence among the Indians, and having used all possible means to draw them over to the French interests. When the Indians came in, the intriguer expressed the greatest pleasure at seeing them, was surprised that they could be so near without coming to see him, and after making them trifling presents, urged upon them intoxicating drinks until they were unfitted for business. The third day Washington's party were equally unsuccessful in their efforts to keep the Indians apart from Jean Cœur, or to prosecute their journey. On the fourth day they set out, but not without an escort planned to annoy them, in Monsieur La Force and three Indians. Finally, after four days of travel through mire and swamps, with the most unpropitious weather, they succeeded in reaching Le Bœuf.

Washington immediately presented himself, and offered his commission and letters to the commanding officer, but was requested to retain both until Mons. Reparti should arrive, who was the commander at the next fort, and who was expected every hour. The commander at Le Bœuf, Legardeur de St. Pierre, was an elderly gentleman with the air of a soldier, and a knight of the military order of St Louis. He had been in command but a week at Le Bœuf, having been sent over on the death of the late general.

In a few hours Capt. Reparti arrived from Presqu'ile, the letter was again offered, and after a satisfactory translation a council of war was held, which gave Major Washington and his men an opportunity of taking the dimensions of the fort and making other observations. According to their estimate, the fort had one hundred men, exclusive of a large number of officers, fifty birch canoes and seventy pine ones, and many in an unfinished state.

The instructions he had received from Governor Dinwiddie allowed him to remain but seven days for an answer; and as the horses were daily becoming weaker, and the snow fast increasing, they were sent back to Venango, and still further to Shannopin's town, provided the river was open and in a navigable condition. In the meantime Commissary La Force was full of flatteries and fair promises to the sachems, still hoping to retain them as friends. From day to day the party were detained at Venango, sometimes by the power of liquor, the promise of presents, and various other pretexts, and the acceptance of the wampum had been thus far successfully evaded.

To the question of Major Washington, "by what authority several English subjects had been made prisoners?" Captain Reparti replied, "that they had orders to make prisoners of any who attempted to trade upon those waters." The two who had been taken, and of whom they inquired particularly, John Trotter and James McClochlan, they were informed had been sent to Canada, but were now returned home. They confessed, too, that a boy had been carried past by the Indians, who had besides two or three white men's scalps.

On the 15th, the commandant ordered a plentiful store of liquors and provisions to be put on board the canoes, and appeared extremely complaisant, while he was really studying to annoy them, and to keep the Indians until after their departure.

Washington, in his journal, remarks: "I cannot say that ever in my life I suffered so much anxiety as I did in this affair. I saw that every stratagem which the most fruitful brain could invent was practiced to win the Half-King to their interests, and that leaving him there was giving them the opportunity they aimed at. I went to the Half-King and pressed him in the strongest terms. He told me that the commandant would not discharge him until the morning. I then went to the commandant, and desired him to do their business, and complained of ill treatment; for keeping them, as they were part of my company, was detaining me. This he promised not to do, but to forward my journey as much as possible. He protested that he did not keep them, but was ignorant of the cause of their stay; though I soon found it out: he promised them a present of guns, etc., if they would wait until morning." Their journey to Franklin was tedious and very fatiguing. At one place the ice had lodged so their canoes could not pass, and they were obliged to carry them a quarter of a mile. One of the chiefs, White Thunder, became disabled, and they were compelled to leave him with Half-King, who promised that no fine speeches or scheming of Jean Cœur should win him back to the French. In this he was sincere, as his conduct afterward proved. As their horses were now weak and feeble, and there was no probability of the journey being accomplished in reasonable time, Washington gave them, with the baggage, in charge of Mr. Van Braem, his faithful companion, tied himself up in his watch-coat, with a pack on his back containing his papers, some provisions, and his gun, and, with Mr. Gist fitted out in the same manner, took the shortest route across the country for Shannopin's town.

On the day following they fell in with a party of French Indians, who laid in wait for them at a place called Murdering town, now in Butler County. One of the party fired upon them; but, by constant travel, they escaped their company, and arrived within two miles of Shannopin's town, where trials in another form awaited them. They were obliged to construct a raft, in order to cross the river; and when this was accomplished, by the use of but one poor hatchet, and they were launched, by some accident Washington was precipitated into the river, and narrowly escaped being drowned. Besides this, the cold was so intense that Mr. Gist had his fingers and toes frozen. At Mr. Frasier's, (Turtle Creek,) they met twenty warriors going southward to battle, and at the Monongahela, seventeen horses, loaded with materials and stores for a fort at the forks of the Ohio, and a few families going out to settle. On the 16th of February Washington arrived at Williamsburg, and waited upon Governor Dinwiddie with the letter he had brought from the French commandant, and offered him a narrative of the most remarkable occurrences of his journey.

The reply of Chevalier de St. Pierre was found to be courteous and well guarded. "He should transmit," he said, "the letter of Governor Dinwiddie to his general, the Marquis Du Quesne, to whom it better belongs than to me to set forth the evidence and reality of the rights of the king, my master, upon the lands situated along the Ohio, and to contest the pretensions of the king of Great Britain thereto. His answer shall be a law to me. . . . As to the summons to retire you send me, I do not think myself obliged to obey it. Whatever may be your instructions, I am here by virtue of the orders of my general, and I entreat you, sir, not to doubt one moment but that I am determined to conform myself to them with all the exactness and resolution which can be expected from the best officer. . . . I made it my particular care to receive Mr. Washington with a distinction suitable to your dignity, as well as his own quality and merit. I flatter myself that he will do me this justice before you, sir, and that he will signify to you, in the manner I do myself, the profound respect with which I am, sir, etc."

Governor Dinwiddie and his council understood this evasive answer as a ruse to gain time, in order that they might in the spring descend the Ohio and take military possession of the whole country.

This expedition may be considered the foundation of Washington's fortunes. "From that moment he was the rising hope of the country. His tact with the Indians and crafty whites, his endurance of cold and fatigue, his prudence, firmness, and self-devotion, all were indications of the future man."

Relating to the French forts, April, 1757, we have the following: "Colonel Johnson, British Indian agent, residing at Tribeshill, New York, received intelligence through savages, that a strong detachment was ascending the St. Lawrence and entering Lake Ontario, and supposing it concerned the Mohawk country, he assembled his militia and marched to Palatine, where another company of eleven or twelve hundred men joined him, sent out by the commandant at Oswego. He intrenched himself and remained in camp fifteen days, when he received intelligence that the French detachment had passed by to reinforce Belle Riviere."

A year before, in 1756, a prisoner among the Indians, who had made his escape, gave the following particulars: "Buffaloes Fort, or Le Bœuf, is garrisoned with one hundred and fifty men and a few straggling Indians. Presqu'ile is built of square logs filled up with earth; the barracks are within the fort, and garrisoned with one hundred and fifty men, supported chiefly from a French settlement begun near it. The settlement consists, as the prisoner was informed, of about one hundred families." [This French settlement is not spoken of by any other person. M. Chauvignerie, as will be seen, states that there were no settlements or improvements near the forts Presqu'ile or Le Bœuf.] "The Indian families about the settlement are pretty numerous; they have a priest and schoolmaster, and some grist-mills and stills in the settlement."

In 1757, M. Chauvignerie, Jr., aged seventeen, a French prisoner, testified before a justice of the peace to this effect: "His father was a lieutenant of marines and commandant of Fort Machault, built lately at Venango." [On the authority of an old map at Quebec, Fort Machault was the opposite side of the river from Fort Venango.] "At the fort they have fifty regulars and forty laborers, and soon expect a reinforcement from Montreal, and they drop almost daily some of the detachments, as they pass from Montreal to Fort du Quesne. Fort Le Bœuf is commanded by my uncle, Monsieur de Verge, an ensign of foot. There is no captain or other officer there, above an ensign; and the reason of this is, that the commandants of those forts purchase a commission for it, and have the benefit of transporting the provisions and other necessaries. The provisions are chiefly sent from Niagara to Presqu'ile, and so from thence down the Ohio to Fort du Quesne. Sometimes, however, they are brought in large quantities from southward of Fort du Quesne. There are from eight hundred to nine hundred, and sometimes one thousand men between Forts Presqu'ile and Le Bœuf. One hundred and fifty of these are regulars, and the rest Canadian laborers, who work at the forts and build boats. There are no settlements or improvements near the forts. The French plant corn about them for the Indians, whose wives and children come to the fort for it, and get furnished also with clothes at the king's expense. Traders reside in the forts, that purchase of them peltries. Several houses are outside of the forts, but people do not care to occupy them, for fear of being scalped. One of their batteaux usually carries sixty bags of flour and three or four men. When unloaded, it will carry twelve men."

Frederick Post's journal, dated Pittsburg, November, 1758, says: "Just as the council broke up, an Indian arrived from Fort Presqu'ile, and gave the following description of the three upper forts. Presqu'ile has been a strong stockaded fort, but is so much out of repair that a strong man might pull up any log out of the earth. There are two officers and thirty-five men in garrison there, and not above ten Indians, which they keep constantly hunting, for the support of the garrison. The fort in Le Bœuf River is much in the same condition, with an officer and thirty men, and a few hunting Indians, who said they would leave them in a few days. The fort at Venango is the smallest, and has but one officer and twenty-five men, and, like the two upper forts, they are much distressed for want of provisions."

On the 17th of March, 1759, Thomas Bull, an Indian employed as a spy at the Lakes, arrived at Pittsburg. At Presqu'ile, he stated that the garrison consisted of two officers, two merchants, a clerk, priest, and one hundred and three soldiers. The commandant's name was Burinol, with whom Thomas was formerly acquainted, and who did not suspect him. He treated him with great openness, and told him thirty towns had engaged to join the French and come to war. He saw fifteen hundred billets ready prepared for their equipment. He likewise understood that they were just ready to set out, and were stopped by belts and speeches sent among them by the English, but would decide when a body of over-lake Indians would arrive at Kaskaskie. Burinol described a conversation he had had with the Mingoes; that he had told them he was sorry one half of them had broken away to the English. They replied that they had buried the tomahawk with the French; that they would do the same with the English; and wished that both would fight as they had done over the great waters, without disturbing their country; that they wished to live in peace with both, and that the English should return home. Burinol replied, that he would go home as soon as the English would move off. Thomas Bull described Fort Presqu'ile "as square, with four bastions. They have no platforms raised yet; so they are useless, excepting in each bastion there is a place for a sentinel. There are no guns upon the walks, but four four-pounders in one of the bastions, not mounted on carriages. The wall is only of single logs, with no bank within, a ditch without. There are two gates, of equal size, being about ten feet wide : one fronts the lake, about three hundred yards distant, the other the road to Le Bœuf. The magazine is a stone house covered with shingles, and not sunk in the ground, standing in the right bastion, next the lake, going from Presqu'ile to Le Bœuf. The other houses are of square logs. They have in store a considerable quantity of Indian goods, and but little flour. Twelve batteaux they were daily expecting from Niagara with provisions. No French were expected from Niagara, but about five hundred from a fort on the north side of the lake, in the Waweailunes country, which is built of cedar stockades. The French were to come with the Indians before mentioned. There were four batteaux at Presqu'ile, and no works carrying on, but one small house in the fort. Some of the works are on the decay, and some appear to have been lately built." The officers made Thomas a present of a pair of stockings, and he went on to Le Bœuf, telling them that he was going to Wyoming to see his father.

Le Bœuf he describes "as of the same plan with Presqu'ile, but very small; the logs mostly rotten. Platforms are erected in the bastion, and loopholes properly cut; one gun is mounted on a bastion and looks down the river. It has only one gate, and that faces the side opposite the creek. The magazine is on the right of the gate, going in, partly sunk in the ground, and above are some casks of powder, to serve the Indians. Here are two officers, a storekeeper, clerk, priest, and one hundred and fifty soldiers, and, as at Presqu'ile, the men are not employed. They have twenty-four batteaux, and a larger stock of provisions than at Presqu'ile. One Le Sambrow is the commandant. The Ohio is clear of ice at Venango, and French Creek at Le Bœuf. The road from Venango to Le Bœuf is well trodden; and from thence to

Presqu'ile is one half-day's journey, being very low and swampy, and bridged most of the way."

A few months after this time, twelve hundred regular troops were collected from Presqu'ile, Detroit, and Venango, for the defense of Fort Niagara, which had been besieged by the English under Gen. Prideaux. Four days before the conquest, the general was killed by the bursting of a cannon, and the command devolved on Sir William Johnson, who carried out the plan with judgment and vigor, and the enemy were completely routed. The utmost confusion prevailed at Forts Venango, Presqu'ile, and Le Bœuf after the victory, particularly as Sir William sent letters by some of the Indians to the commander at Presqu'ile, notifying him that the other posts must be given up in a few days.

August 13, we find that the French at Presqu'ile had sent away all their stores, and were waiting for the French at Venango and Le Bœuf to join them, when they all would set out in batteaux for Detroit; that in an Indian path leading to Presqu'ile from a Delaware town, a Frenchman and some Indians had been met, with the word that the French had left Venango six days before.

About the same time, three Indians arrived at Fort du Quesne from Venango, who reported that the Indians over the lake were much displeased with the Six Nations, as they had been the means of a number of their people being killed at Niagara; that the French had burned their forts at Venango, Le Bœuf, and Presqu'ile, and gone over the lakes. At Venango, before leaving, they had made large presents to the Indians of laced coats, hats, etc., and had told them, with true French bravado, that they were obliged to run away at this time, but would certainly be in possession of the river before the next spring. They were obliged to burn everything and destroy their batteaux, as the water was so low they could not get up the creek with them. The report was probably unfounded, of the burning of the forts, unless they were very soon rebuilt, of which we have no account.

A tradition has prevailed in Erie, that at this time treasures were buried, either on the site of the fort or on the line of the old French road. From the above account, we learn that

48 HISTORY OF ERIE COUNTY.

their hasty departure was made by water, and the probability is that the company returned before winter. Spanish silver coins were found twenty years ago, to the value of sixty dollars, while plowing the old site for the purpose of making brick ; but, from appearances, they had been secreted there within the present century. The wells have been re-excavated time and again, but with no extraordinary results. Pottery of a singular kind has been found, and knives, bullets, and human bones confirm the statements of history.

In 1760, Major Rodgers was sent out by government to take formal possession for the English of the forts upon the lake, though it was not until 1763 that a definite treaty of peace was signed and ratified at Paris.

CHAPTER IV.

Pontiac—Destruction of Forts Presqu'ile and Le Bœuf, as described by Bancroft, Parkman, and Harvey—Col. Bradstreet at Presqu'ile, in 1764—Col. Bouquet's Treaty—A Detachment of British Soldiers and Indians embark at Chautauqua Lake—Hannastown burnt— Mr. Adams's Suggestion.

AT Detroit Major Rodgers first met with the Ottawa chief Pontiac, who had the largest empire and the greatest authority of any chief that had yet appeared in our continent. The chief treated him with distant ceremony, and intimated that, though the French had been conquered by the English, *he* had not ; but, at the close of the interview, they smoked the pipe of peace, and afterward he rendered the English good service in protecting their stores when passing through savage tribes. How he became inimical to the English is not certainly known. He may have feared their power, and also felt with sadness the absence of French courtesy. Prejudice arose, too, from the ill behavior and offensive conduct of Irish and other convicts, who had been transported for their crimes, and been bought and employed in carrying goods up among the Indians. " When the French first arrived," said a Chippewa chief, "they came and kissed us; they called us children, and we found them fathers. We lived like children with them in the same lodge." . . . "If the English did us no harm, they also manifested no interest in our affairs. They gave us no missionaries, made us no presents; they even would not consent to trade; and further, they were unjust to our friends, the French."

Mr. Henry, an English traveler, who passed through Canada and the Indian territories, about 1760, was compelled to disguise himself as a Canadian. At one time, when surrounded by Indians, he was coolly addressed by a chief in something like this strain: "The English are brave men, and not afraid of death, since they dare to come thus fearlessly among their enemies. You know that the French king is our father. You are his enemy; and how, then, can you have the boldness to venture among us his children? You know that his friends are our friends." They delighted to extol the power of the French, and to compare the king to an old man asleep, who would shortly arouse himself and execute vengeance upon his enemies. They also charged upon the English that, when fighting for them, their young men had been slain, and that the spirits of the slain had not been satisfied. This, according to their custom, could only be effected in one of two ways—by pouring out the blood of the nation by which they fell, or by covering the bodies of the dead, and allaying the resentment of the relations by presents. The English had never offered them presents or treaty, and they must therefore be considered still at war with them. But their hearts seemed to soften toward Mr. Henry, who came among them unarmed, and they even offered him a pipe, as a token of their friendship.

When Pontiac had formed his plan for restoring to his people their homes and hunting grounds, and "had mused until the fire burned," he determined to call around him his own tribe, the Ottawas, and disclose to them his determination to banish forever the proud, unconciliating Englishman. He appealed with eloquence and art to their fears, ambition, patriotism, and cupidity—the love and gratitude they owed to the French, and their hatred of the English. He next convened a grand council of the neighboring tribes at the River

Aux Ecores, and invited them to action, by assuming that the Great Spirit had recently made a revelation to a Delaware Indian as to the conduct he wished his red children to pursue. He had directed them to abstain from ardent spirits, and to cast from them the manufactures of the white man—to resume their bows and arrows, and skins of animals for clothing. "Why," said the Great Spirit indignantly to the Delaware, "do you suffer these dogs in red clothing to enter your country and take the land I gave you? Drive them from it, and when you are in distress I will help you." A plan of campaign was concerted on the spot, and belts and speeches sent to secure the co-operation of the Indians along the whole line of the frontier. The Ottawas, Chippewas, and Pottawatamies were the most active of the tribes; the Miamies, Sac and Foxes, Monononomies, Wyandots, Mississagués, Shawnees, Pennsylvania and Ohio Delawares, and the Six Nations, participated, and all the British posts, from Niagara to Green Bay and the Potomac, were comprehended in the attack. So well arranged and executed were their plans, that nine out of eleven of the forts were captured.

Bancroft, in his history of the United States, gives the following account of the destruction of Fort Presqu'ile: "The fort at Presqu'ile, now Erie, was the point of communication between Pittsburg and Niagara and Detroit. It was in itself one of the most tenable, and had a garrison of four and twenty men, and could most easily be relieved. On the 22d of June, after a two-days' defense, the commander, out of his senses with terror, capitulated, giving up the sole chance of saving his men from the scalping-knife. He himself, with a few others, were carried in triumph by the Indians to Detroit."

A more detailed account is found in the "Conspiracy of Pontiac," by Parkman. He says: "There had been hot fighting before Presqu'ile was taken. Could courage have saved it, it never would have fallen. The fort stood near the present site of Erie, on the southern shore of the lake which bears the same name. At one of its angles was a large blockhouse, a species of structure much used in the petty forest warfare of the day. It was two stories in height, and solidly built of massive timber; the diameter of the upper story exceeding that of the lower by several feet, so that, through the openings in the projecting floor of the former, the defenders could shoot down upon the heads of an enemy assailing the outer wall below. The roof being covered with shingles, might easily be set on fire ; but, to guard against this, there was an opening, through which the garrison, partially protected by a covering of plank, might pour down the water upon the flames. This block-house stood upon a projecting point of land, between the lake and a small brook which entered it nearly at right angles. And now the defenders could see the Indians throwing up earth and stones behind one of the breastworks ; their implacable foes were laboring to undermine the block-house, a sure and insidious expedient, against which there was no defense. There was little leisure to reflect on this new peril, for another, more imminent and horrible, soon threatened them. The barrels of water, always kept in the block-house, were nearly emptied in extinguishing the frequent fires ; and though there was a well in the parade-ground, yet to approach it would be certain death. The only resource was to dig one in the block-house itself. The floor was torn up, and while some of the men fired their heated muskets from the loopholes to keep the enemy in check, the rest labored with desperate energy at this toilsome and cheerless task. Before it was half completed, the cry of fire was again raised, and, at the imminent risk of life, they tore off the blazing shingles and averted the danger. By this time it was evening. The little garrison had fought from earliest daybreak without a moment's rest. Nor did darkness bring relief, for the Indian guns flashed all night long from the intrenchments. They seemed determined to wear out the obstinate defenders by fatigue. While some slept, others in their turn continued the assault, and morning brought fresh dangers. The block-house was fired several times through the day, but they kept up their forlorn and desperate defense. The house of the commanding officer sank into glowing embers. The fire on both sides did not cease till midnight, at which hour a voice was heard in French, calling out that further defense was useless, since preparations were made to burn above and below at once. Christie demanded if any one spoke English, upon which a man in Indian dress came forward. He had been made a prisoner in the French war, and was now fighting against his own countrymen. He said, if they yielded, they would be saved alive; if not, they would be burned. Christie resolved to hold out as long as a shadow of hope remained, and while some of the garrison slept, the rest watched. They told them to wait until morning. They assented, and suspended their fire. When morning came, they sent out two persons, on pretense of treating, but in reality to learn the truth of the preparations to burn the block-house, whose sides were pierced with bullets and scorched with fire. In spite of the capitulations, they were surrounded and seized, and, having been detained for some time in the neighborhood, were sent as prisoners to Detroit, where Ensign Christie soon after made his escape, and gained the fort in safety."

Mr. H. L. Harvey, formerly editor of the *Erie Observer*, a gentleman of research and integrity, in a lecture delivered in Erie, introduced the following account of the same event, differing, as will be seen, from both the above-named accredited historians. He says: "The troops retired to their quarters to procure their morning repast; some had already finished, and were sauntering about the fortress or upon the shore of the lake. All were joyous in holiday attire, and dreaming of naught but the pleasure of the occasion. A knock was heard at the gate, and three Indians were announced in hunting garb, desiring an interview with the commander. Their tale was soon told. They said they belonged to a hunting party, who had started for Niagara with a lot of furs; that their canoes were bad, and they would prefer disposing of them here, if they could do so to advantage, and return, rather than go farther; that their party were encamped by a small stream west of the fort about a mile, where they had landed the previous night, and where they wished the commander to go and examine their peltries, as it was difficult to bring them, and they wished to embark where they were, if they did not trade. The commander, accompanied by a clerk, left the fort with the Indians, charging his lieutenant that none should leave the fort, and none be admitted, until his return. Well would it probably have been had this order been obeyed. After the lapse of sufficient time for the captain to visit the encampment of the Indians and return, a party of the latter, variously estimated—probably one hundred and fifty—advanced toward the fort, bearing upon their backs what appeared to be large packs of furs, which they informed the lieutenant the captain had purchased and ordered deposited in the fort. The stratagem succeeded; when the party were all within the fort, it was the work of an instant to throw off their packs and the short cloaks which covered their weapons, the whole being fastened by one loop and button at the neck. Resistance at this time was useless, and the work of death was as rapid as savage strength and weapons could make it. The shortened rifles, which had been sawed off for the purpose of concealing them under their cloaks and in the packs of furs, were at once discharged, and the tomahawk and knife completed their work. The history of savage warfare presents not a scene of more heartless and bloodthirsty vengeance than was exhibited on this occasion. The few who were taken prisoners in the fort were doomed to the various tortures devised by savage ingenuity, and all but two who awoke to celebrate that day, had passed to the eternal world. Of these, one was a soldier who had gone into the woods near the fort, and on his return observing a party of Indians dragging away some prisoners, escaped, and immediately proceeded to Niagara; the other was a soldier's wife, who had taken shelter in a small stone house, at the mouth of the creek, used as a washhouse. Here she remained unobserved until near night of the fatal day, when she was made their prisoner, but was ultimately ransomed and restored to civilized life. She was afterward married, and settled in Canada, where she was living at the commencement of the present century. Capt. D. Dobbins, of the revenue service, has frequently talked with the woman, who was redeemed by a Mr. Douglass, living opposite Black Rock, in Canada. From what she witnessed, and heard from the Indians during her captivity, as well as from information derived from other sources, this statement is made."

About the same time the fort at Le Bœuf was furiously attacked by a large body of Indians, and the block-house fired at night. While the enemy believed them consumed, the ensign and his seven remaining men effected their escape, by means of a secret underground passage, having its outlet in the direction of the swamp adjoining Le Bœuf Lake. Tradition says that only one of these reached a civilized settlement. At Venango, a party of Senecas gained entrance by stratagem, and massacred the garrison, after having tortured Lieut. Gordon, the commander, for several nights over a slow fire. Afterward they fired and consumed the fort.

It was not the stockaded garrison alone, at this trying period, that suffered from the fury of the savages. Through the whole West the tomahawk and scalping-knife made fearful havoc. More than one hundred traders were struck down in the woods—the husbandman in the field and the child in the cradle shared the same unhappy fate. Emigrants were compelled to leave their homes and planted fields, and by toilsome journeys seek protection and shelter in distant settlements. Nearly five hundred families from the frontiers of Maryland and Virginia fled thus to Winchester, being destitute of every comfort. The regions of New York were happily exempted from similar outrages, through the influence of Sir William Johnson.

On the 12th of August, 1764, Col. Bradstreet and his army landed at Presqu'ile, and there met a band of Shawnees and Delawares, who feigned to have come to treat for peace. Col. Bradstreet was deceived by them (although his officers were not), and marched to Detroit to relieve that garrison. He found Pontiac gone, but made peace with the Northwestern Indians, in which they pledged themselves to give up their prisoners ; to relinquish their title to the English posts and the territory around for the distance of a cannon shot ; to give up all the murderers of white men, to be tried by English law ; and to acknowledge the sovereignty of the English government. Soon he discovered, as the war still raged, that he had been duped. He received orders to attack their towns; but, mortified and exasperated, his troops destitute of provisions and every way dissatisfied, he broke up his camp and returned to Niagara. Col. Boquet afterward met the same deceptive Shawnees, Delawares, and Senecas, and succeeded in bringing them to terms; so that in twelve days they brought in two hundred and six prisoners, and promised all that could be found—leaving six hostages as security. The next year one hundred more prisoners were brought in, between whom and the Indians, in many cases, a strong attachment had sprung up, they accompanying the captives, with presents, even to the villages.

The region west of the Ohio and Allegheny Rivers, prior to the year 1795, was only known as the Indian country. On the Canada side of Lake Erie there were a few white settlements. On the American side Cherry Valley, New York, was the most western settlement, and Pittsburg the nearest settlement on the south.

In the year 1782, a detachment, consisting of three hundred British soldiers and five hundred Indians, was sent from Canada to Fort Pitt. They had embarked in canoes at Chautauqua Lake, when information, through their spies, caused their project to be abandoned. Parties of Indians harassed the settlements on the borders, and under Guyasutha, a Seneca chief, attacked and burned the seat of justice for Westmoreland County, Hannastown, and murdered several of the inhabitants.

In 1785, Mr. Adams, Minister at London, writes to Lord Carmarthan, English Secretary of State : "Although a period of three years has elapsed since the signature of the preliminary treaty, and more than two years since the definitive treaty, the posts of Oswegatchy, Oswego, Niagara, Presqu'ile, Sandusky, Detroit, Mackinaw, with others not necessary particularly to enumerate, and a considerable territory around each of them, all within the incontestable limits of the United States, are still held by British garrisons to the loss and injury of the United States," etc. As we do not hear from any other source of the rebuilding of the fort at Presqu'ile or of a garrison there, the probability is that Mr. Adams only had reference to Presqu'ile as an important strategic point.

CHAPTER V.

Penn's Charter—Boundaries of Pennsylvania—Mason and Dixon's Line—Review of said Line by Col. Graham—Western Boundary of Pennsylvania fixed in 1786—Boundary between New York and Pennsylvania confirmed by Act of Assembly in 1789—Purchase of Triangle, 1791—Anecdote of Mr. William Miles.

IN the charter of Charles II. to William Penn, 1681, the first section describes the boundary of his grant as "east by Delaware River from twelve miles distance northward of Newcastle town, unto the three-and-fortieth degree of north latitude, if the said river doth extend so far northward ; but if the said river doth not extend so far northward, then by the said river so far as it doth extend ; and from the head of the said river the eastern bounds are to be determined by a meridian line, to be drawn from the head of said river unto the said 43d degree. The said land to extend westward 5 degrees in longitude, to be computed from the said eastern bounds ; and the said lands to be bounded on the north by the beginning of the three-and-fortieth degree of north latitude, and on the south by a circle drawn at 12 miles distance from New Castle northward and westward unto the beginning of the fortieth degree of north latitude, and then by a straight line westward to the limits of longitude above mentioned." Explicit as this description appears, Maryland and Virginia disputed for many years, each claiming to itself the whole space or extent of the land south of the fortieth degree of latitude. The controversy was at length settled in 1732, chiefly in favor of Maryland, which rendered the real extent of Pennsylvania one hundred and fifty-five miles instead of two hundred and eight, and the square miles forty-one thousand, exclusive of the Triangle.

Lord Baltimore had, in 1683, petitioned King Charles II. that no fresh grants of land in the territories of Pennsylvania might pass in favor of William Penn until the said lord was heard in his pretension of right thereto. This petition was referred to the committee of trade and plantation, which, after many attendances and divers hearings of both parties, made their report to King James II., who in 1685 determined the affair between them, by ordering a division of the tract of land between Delaware and Chesapeake Bays, from the latitude of Cape Henlopen to the south boundary of Pennsylvania, in two equal parts, of which the side of Delaware was assigned to the king and Pennsylvania, and the Chesapeake side to Baltimore. In 1732, commissioners were appointed both from Pennsylvania and Maryland for the actual running, marking, and laying out the boundary lines between both the province and territories of Pennsylvania and Maryland, according to articles of agreement concluded between Charles, Lord Baltimore, the proprietary of Maryland, and John, Thomas, and Richard Penn, proprietaries of Pennsylvania. The boundaries between Pennsylvania and Baltimore were as follows: That a due east and west line shall be drawn from the ocean, beginning at Cape Henlopen, which lies south of Cape Cornelius, upon the eastern side of the peninsula, and thence to the western side of the peninsula, which lies upon Chesapeake Bay, and as far westward as the exact middle of that part of the peninsula where the said line is run. That from the western end of the said east and west line in the middle of the peninsula, a straight line shall run northward up the said peninsula till it touch the western part of the periphery or arc of a circle, drawn twelve English statute miles distant from New Castle, westward toward Maryland, so to make a tangent thereto, and there the said straight line shall end. That from the western end of the last-mentioned straight line drawn northward, a line shall be continued due north, as far as to that parallel of latitude which is fifteen English statute miles due south of the most southern part of Philadelphia, and from the north end of the last-mentioned north and south line, a line shall be run due west, across the Susquehanna River to the western boundary of Pennsylvania. Notwithstanding this agreement, the performance was long delayed by disputes of the parties about the mode of doing it, said to have been occasioned mostly by the proprietary of Maryland, in consequence of which the inhabitants on the

Pennsylvania side, near where the boundary line ought long before to have been ascertained and marked out, were sometimes exposed to unreasonable demands from Maryland claims. It was not finally executed until the year 1762, when these families or proprietaries agreed to employ two ingenious English mathematicians, Charles Mason and Jeremiah Dixon, after their return from the Cape of Good Hope, where they had been to observe the transit of Venus, in the year 1761, finally to settle and mark out the same, which was accordingly performed by them.[1]

At the end of every fifth mile they placed a stone graven with the arms of the Penns on the one side, and of the Baltimore family on the other, marking the intermediate miles with smaller stones having "P" on one side and "M" on the other. The stones with the arms were all sent from England. This was done on the parallel of latitude as far as Sideling Hill; but here all wheel transportation ceasing, in 1766 the further marking of the lines was the vista of eight yards wide, with piles of stones on the crests of all the mountain ranges, built some eight feet high, as far as the summit of the Allegheny, beyond which the line was marked by posts, around which stones and earth were thrown the better to preserve them. Of these stones, the one which marked the northeast corner of Maryland became in the course of time undermined by a brook, and was removed and used in a farm-house chimney. After this occurrence the Legislatures of Pennsylvania, Maryland, and Virginia appointed a joint commission for a new survey, and appointed Col. Graham of the United States Topographical Engineers to superintend the work, and review the line of Mason and Dixon as far as might be judged necessary. Though their work was corroborated in the main, better instruments and a more accurate knowledge of the art enabled their successors to detect some errors. By their corrections Maryland gained about two acres, and a

[1] After they had surveyed the distance of 23 miles, 18 chains, and 21 links from the place of beginning, and were at the bottom of a valley on Dunkard's Creek, a branch of the Monongahela, an Indian path crossed their route, and their aboriginal escort informed them that it was "the will of the Sioux nation that the surveys cease;" and they terminated accordingly, leaving 36 miles, 6 chains, and 50 links as the exact distance remaining to be run west to the southwest angle of Pennsylvania.

gentleman who had served as a member of the Delaware Legislature found his residence located full half a mile within the State of Pennsylvania. Thus was established and perfected the line, "having no breadth or thickness, but length only," which threatens to make "enemies of nations which had else, like kindred drops, been mingled into one."

It is said the survey of Mason and Dixon cost the Penn family nearly $100,000; and that an arc of the meridian measured by them at that time is cited in works of astronomy, having been one of the measurements by which the figure of the earth was ascertained. Of these two mathematicians, to whom political disputes have given a notoriety as lasting as the history of our country, Dixon, it is said, was born in a coal mine, and returned to his own country, Durham, where he died in 1777. Ten years later Mason died in Pennsylvania.

It was not until 1786, after many difficulties between the States of Pennsylvania and Virginia, that the western boundary of the former was surveyed by extending Mason and Dixon's line five degrees west from the Delaware River, and a meridian drawn from the western extremity to the northern limit.

In 1785 commissioners were appointed, on the part of Pennsylvania and New York, to ascertain the northern boundary of the former from the River Delaware westward to the northwest corner. The commissioners first appointed were David Rittenhouse on the part of Pennsylvania, and Samuel Holland, on the part of New York. They proceeded to act in pursuance of that appointment, and in December, 1786, ascertained and fixed the beginning of the forty-third degree of north latitude, erected suitable monuments there at and near the River Delaware, but were prevented by the inclemency of the weather from proceeding further in the survey. The next year Andrew Ellicot was appointed a commissioner for the above purpose, on the part of Pennsylvania, and James Clinton and Simeon Dewit on the part of New York. In 1787 they completed the running and marking of this northern boundary 259 miles and 88 perches from its commencement at the Delaware River to its termination in Lake Erie, five or six miles east of the Ohio State line, and marked the whole distance throughout by milestones, each one indicating the number of miles from the Delaware River. In addition to these stones there are also mile-trees marked in the same manner. In 1789 an act of Assembly confirmed the acts of the commissioners, and established the line run by them as the boundary between New York and Pennsylvania.

The Indians being recognized as owners of the soil, the whole was purchased from them by different treaties : one at Fort Stanwix, now Rome, extinguished their title to the lands of Western Pennsylvania and New York, excepting the Triangle or Presqu'ile lands, which were accidentally left out of Pennsylvania, New York, Massachusetts, Connecticut, and Virginia, and were supposed at different times to belong to each. Gen. Irvine discovered, while surveying the donation lands, that Pennsylvania had but a few miles of lake coast, and not any harbor, and in consequence of his representations, the State of Pennsylvania made propositions for its purchase to Phelps and Gorham, the reputed owners in the year 1788. At their request the United States government sent out the Surveyor-General, Andrew Ellicot, for the purpose of running and establishing lines. Mr. Frederick Saxton, on behalf of Phelps and Gorham, accompanied Mr. Ellicot. As the line was to commence at the west end of Lake Ontario, there was some hesitation whether the western extremity of Burlington Bay or the peninsula separating the bay from the lake was intended. It was finally fixed at the peninsula, and by first running south, and then offsetting around the east end of Lake Erie, the line was found to pass twenty miles east of Presqu'ile. This line, as it was found to comply with the New York charter, being twenty miles west of the most westerly bend of the Niagara River, became the western boundary of the State of New York between Lake Erie and the old north line of Pennsylvania, and the east line of the track known as the Presqu'ile Triangle, which was afterward purchased by Pennsylvania of the United States. The Massachusetts charter, in 1785, comprehended the same release that New York had given, and that of Connecticut which retained a reservation of one hundred and twenty miles lying west of Pennsylvania's western boundary. On the 6th of June, 1788, the board of treasury was induced to make a contract for the sale of this tract described as bounded "on the east by New York, on the south by Pennsylvania, and on the north and west by Lake Erie." On the 4th of September, it was resolved by Congress "that the United States do relinquish and transfer to Pennsylvania all their right, title, and claim to the government and jurisdiction of said land forever, and it is declared and made known that the laws and public acts of Pennsylvania shall extend over every part of said tract, as if the said tract had originally been within the charter bounds of said State." By an act of the 2d of October, 1788, the sum of £1200 was appropriated to purchase the Indian title to the tract, in fulfillment of the contract to sell it to Pennsylvania. At the treaty of Fort Harmer, on the 9th of January, 1789, Cornplanter and other chiefs of the Six Nations signed a deed, in consideration of the sum of £1200, ceding the Presqu'ile lands of the United States to be vested in the State of Pennsylvania, and on the 13th of April, 1791, the Governor was authorized to complete the purchase from the United States, which, according to a communication from him to the Legislature, was accomplished in March, 1792; and the consideration—amounting to $151,640.25—paid in continental certificates of various descriptions. A draft annexed to the deed of the Triangle shows it to contain two hundred and two thousand one hundred and eighty-seven acres.

An amusing anecdote, relating to the period of these surveys, is mentioned in "Pennsylvania Historical Collections:" "When Mr. William Miles set off with a corps of surveyors for laying out the donation lands, the baggage, instruments, etc., were placed in two canoes. Fifteen miles above Pittsburg, at the last white man's cabin on the river, the party stopped to refresh themselves, leaving the canoes in the care of the Indians. On returning to the river, all was gone—canoes and Indians had all disappeared. Mr. Miles asked if any one had a map of the river. One was fortunately found, and by it they discovered the river had a great bend just where they were. Their compass was gone, but, by means of Indian signs, mosses on trees, etc., they found their way out above the bend, secreted themselves in the bushes, and waited for the canoes to come up, which happened very soon. When the old chief found he had been detected, he coolly feigned ignorance and innocence, and, stepping out of the canoe with a smile, greeted the surveyors with 'How do?' 'How do?'"

CHAPTER VI.

Arrangements for the Settlement of the Triangle—Pennsylvania Population Company—Act to lay out a town at Presqu'ile; afterward repealed—Block-house at Le Bœuf—Indian Murders—Gov. Mifflin to the President—Attorney-General Bradford's Opinion—Ransom's Deposition—Letters of Capt. Denny—Andrew Ellicot and Gen. Chapin—Joseph Brandt—Cornplanter—A Present of Land—Treaty of Peace at Canandaigua.

PENNSYLVANIA formed and adopted her Constitution September 2d, 1790. The State had adopted the Constitution of the United States and become a member of the Union December 12th, 1787. In 1790, a committee, composed of Timothy Matlack, Samuel McClay, and John Adlum, Esqs., was appointed by Gov. Mifflin to examine the western rivers of the State; to proceed up the western branch to Cinnamahoning, and thence to any creek that might discharge itself into the Allegheny nearest the mouth of French Creek, and thence examine French Creek up to Le Bœuf, and the portage to Presqu'ile. They were also to examine and explore any nearer and more convenient communication which might be effected, by land or water, with Lake Erie, and to return down the Allegheny and examine the same from the mouth of French Creek to the Kiskiminetas. . . . As a result of this examination, in 1791, even before the completion of the purchase of the huge cantle, or Triangle, an act passed the Legislature of Pennsylvania to open and improve navigable waters and roads, and included an expenditure of £100 for French Creek from its mouth on the Allegheny up to the road leading therefrom to Presqu'ile.

In 1793, on the 8th of March, the Pennsylvania Population

Company was formed for purposes set forth in their articles. The managers were John Nicholson, John Field, Theophilus Casenove, and Aaron Burr, Esqs. The following provisional plan of settlement was agreed upon :

"Whereas the said company have purchased considerable bodies of land in Pennsylvania, on the waters of Beaver Creek and Lake Erie; and whereas there is some prospect of a speedy termination of the Indian war, and the company are desirous of encouraging the settlement of these lands, as well for their own interests as for the following considerations, viz.:—

"1st. For promoting the interests of the State, by increasing the population thereof.

"2d. For establishing a barrier along the extremity, so that all the other unsettled parts of Pennsylvania, being within the same, may be settled with greater rapidity, etc.

"3d. To encourage the industrious inhabitants, who may encounter the difficulties always attending first settlements, by liberal grants of land.

"Under the influence of these motives, the society aforesaid, by their president and managers, offer as follows, viz.:

"1st. To the first ten families who may settle on their lands on the waters of Beaver Creek, one hundred and fifty acres each.

"2d. To the first twenty families on the waters of French Creek, one hundred and fifty acres each.

"3d. To the first twenty families on Lake Erie territory, one hundred and fifty acres each.

"4th. To the next twenty families (after the first ten) who shall so settle on the waters of Beaver Creek, one hundred acres each.

"5th. To the next forty families (after the first twenty) who shall so settle on the waters of French Creek, one hundred acres each.

"6th. To the next forty families (after the first twenty) who shall so settle on the lands of the company in the Lake Erie territory, one hundred acres each.

"7th. That such settlement be made on such parts of the lands of the company as settlers may choose. The parties respectively so settling shall have their several deeds for the land after two years' residence thereon, and having also cleared at least ten acres thereof, and erected a comfortable dwelling-house; in case they, or any of them, should be driven off by the Indians, no part of the aforesaid two years shall be deemed to run during the time they shall be so expelled; and in case of their leaving the lands before they receive their deeds, no title shall vest in them, their heirs and assignees, unless they procure the residence of their assigns in like manner as required of themselves, and in case of death, their successors to reside in like manner.

"8th. That the company will sell thirty thousand acres of land to actual settlers, not exceeding three hundred acres each, and those only at one dollar, paid at the choice of the purchasers, payable one third in two years without interest, and one third the next year, with one year's interest, and the residuary third in the succeeding year, with two years' interest.

"9th. That the surveys be made under the direction of the company, the expense of the surveys to be paid by the grantee or purchaser.

"By order of the Board.

"J. W. NICHOLSON."

A month after the formation of this company, an act passed the Legislature for laying out a town at Presqu'ile, "in order to facilitate and promote the progress of settlement within the commonwealth, and to afford additional security to the frontiers thereof."

Gov. Mifflin transmitted to the President of the United States a copy of this act, apprehending the difficulties which soon manifested themselves. Prior to this he had sent to Capt. Denny a commission, appointing him captain of the Allegheny company, and instructing him to engage four sergeants, four corporals, one drummer and fifer, two buglers, and sixty-five rank and file, or privates, and to stipulate with the men to remain longer than the appointed eight months, should the state of the war require it. Early in the month of May, Messrs. Irvine, Ellicot, and Gallatin were to engage in laying out the town, with Capt. Denny's company to protect and defend them. For the same object, a post had been established at Le Bœuf, two miles below the site of the old fort, and all persons employed by government were particularly cautioned against giving offense to the English or British garrisons in that quarter. A letter from Gen. Wilkins, at Fort Franklin, to Clement Biddle, quartermaster-general of Pennsylvania, informs us of his arrival, with forty of Capt. Denny's men and thirty volunteers from the county of Allegheny, and that the news was not favorable toward an establishment at Presqu'ile. Those most conversant with the Indians were of the opinion that they were irritated by the British, and meditated an opposition to the government, and that the question of peace or war depended upon a council then convened at Buffalo Creek. To this council Cornplanter, and other Indians on the Allegheny River, had been invited; and as the English had summoned it, the prospect was not favorable for peace. He also adds that it is his intention to proceed to Cassawago, and should a serious opposition seem to be meditated by the Indians, he would proceed no farther with the stores, until reinforced by more men and enabled to establish himself at Le Bœuf. He also mentions the very low water as a serious impediment. In a letter addressed to A. J. Dallas, he says: "The English are fixed in their opposition to the opening of the road to Presqu'ile, and are determined to send a number of English and Indians to cut them off. The chief Cornplanter communicated the same thing to the commanding officer at Franklin. To heighten the excitement, a friendly Indian was murdered by a dissolute man, named Robertson. The Indians were very much incensed that the murderer was not given up to them, and fears were entertained that some innocent person would be made to suffer in his place. 'The English,' said they, 'always promise to punish crimes, but have never done it.' The father of Robertson sent for John Nicholson to endeavor to appease the Indians, which he effected by calling a council, and offering one hundred dollars to replace, in an Indian way, the man that was dead."

May 24th, Gov. Mifflin applied to the President to order one thousand militia from the western brigades, for the purpose of supporting the commissioners, who were authorized to lay out the town. The brigade inspectors of Westmoreland, Washington, Allegheny, and Fayette accordingly made a draft for that number, to co-operate with Capt. Denny's detachment, under the command of Gen. Wilkins. The citizens of northwestern Pennsylvania urged on improvements, and the President, fearful of giving offense to the Indians, advised to a temporary cessation. Gov. Mifflin, in writing to the Secretary of War, says: "Some old grievances, alleged to have been suffered from the Union, the inflammatory speech of Lord Dorchester, the constant machinations of British agents, and the corruption of the British tribes, had, in truth, previously excited that hostile disposition, which you seem to consider the effect of the measures pursued by Pennsylvania for establishing a town at Presqu'ile. . . . . I desire to be clearly understood, that, on my part, no assent is given to any proposition that shall bring in doubt or controversy the rights of the States. . . . At the same time I am anxious to promote the views of the general government, and to avoid increasing the dissatisfaction of the Six Nations, or in any manner extending the sphere of Indian hostilities." The bounty offered to settlers by the Population Company was limited to those who should actually inhabit and reside in the town before the first of January, 1794; the time was consequently extended to May 1st, 1795, by an act of the Legislature. Capt. Denny also had orders to proceed no farther with his detachment than Le Bœuf, where, under the direction of Brigadier-General Wilkins, two small block-houses had been erected for the protection of the commissioners.

Attorney-General Bradford having been written to by the Secretary of War as to the constitutionality of raising four companies of troops "for the port of Philadelphia and the defense of the frontiers," replied as follows: "There is nothing in the Constitution, I apprehend, which prohibits the several States from keeping troops *in time of war*. If peace shall be made with the Indians, and the United States be engaged in no other war, these troops cannot be constitutionally kept up in Pennsylvania, although the war should continue to rage in Europe."

Some particulars of interest relating to the Indian difficulties in this region will be found in the following deposition and letters:

Deposition of D. Ransom.

ALLEGHENY COUNTY, ss.

"Personally appeared before me, John Gibson, one of the Associate Judges of the above county, Daniel Ransom, who, being duly sworn, deposeth and saith, that he, this deponent, hath for some time past traded at Fort Franklin with the Senecas and other Indians, and that a chief of the Senecas, named Tiawoncas, or Broken Twig, came there and informed him the time would soon be bad, and advised him to move off his family and effects. On this he, this deponent, asked him how he knew the time would soon be bad. The Indian then informed him that the British and Indians had sent a belt of wampum to him, inviting him to council at Buffalo Creek; that he had declined going, and that the messengers then informed him of the intended plans of the Indians; they said that the Cornplanter had been bought by the British, and had joined them; that he (the Cornplanter) intended soon to come to Fort Franklin, on pretense of holding a council respecting the Indian who was killed by Robertson; that then the British and Indians were to land at Presqu'ile, and there form a junction with Cornplanter on French Creek, and were then to clear it, by killing all the people and taking all the posts on it; that he was so much affected as to shed tears, and said, 'What shall I do? I have been at war against the Western Indians, in company with Cap. Jeffers, and killed and scalped one of them. If I now go back to the Indians, after having discovered this, they will kill me.'. He also informed this deponent that a number of cannon had been purchased by the British, and collected at Jurisadagoe, the town where Cornplanter lives, for the purpose of conveying the Indians down the river.

"He, this deponent, further saith, that the Standing Stone, a chief of the Onondagoes, also informed him, at Fort Franklin, that he thought the times would soon be bad, and pressed him very much to leave Fort Franklin, and assisted him in packing up his goods, etc.; that from what he had heard and seen from other Indians, he has every reason to believe the above account to be true; that seven white men came down the Allegheny, a few days ago, to Fort Franklin, who informed him, they saw the above-mentioned cannon at Jurisadagoe; and the Indians appeared very surly, and had not planted any corn on the river at their towns.

"Sworn and subscribed at Pittsburg, this 11th June, 1794."

A letter from Capt. Denny, dated Fort Franklin, June 14, 1794, says:

"SIR:—I have the honor of acknowledging your two letters, dated the 9th and 11th inst. After receiving the first, we concluded it would be best to proceed upon our march. We arrived here the day before yesterday, all well. The account of Ransom's people being killed was too true, but by what nation of Indians is doubtful. Mr. Ellicot and Mr. Wilkins have written and sent two runners from Cornplanter, and they have requested me to wait the return of the express. When they arrive you shall be informed of the success of the message. I am suspicious the old fellow will not show himself. The fact is, that the Indians about here, from twenty downward, have been exceedingly insolent, treated the officers, the fort, and every person about it, with the utmost contempt; but since our arrival they have altered their tune. So says Lieut. Polhemus and Dr. McCray. We have written to Le Bœuf and given the officers there a caution. The day after to-morrow the runner is to be back. Van Horn and Bales, the two men who brought your last letter, saw one Indian on the plain, about twenty miles this side of Pittsburg, and the trace of six or seven."

A second letter, dated June 16, says:

"Yours, inclosing a copy of Polhemus, came yesterday. The Cornplanter's nephew arrived from the town about the same time. He delivered a long speech from his uncle to Lieut. Polhemus. Upon summing up the whole, we have not a shadow of doubt but that a plan was formed to destroy all the posts and settlements in this quarter. It was all done upon the strength of the prospect of a war between the British and ——. That subsiding, the other, I am in hopes, has also done so. There is no doubt but the English will urge them to join the Western Indians, and have done everything possible, and perhaps a few may; but I rather think that, unless we have a war with them, we'll have none with the Six Nations generally. The Cornplanter has gone to another council at Buffalo; he set out at the same time the nephew started for this place, and will return in about ten days. He says he is very sorry for the mischief done lately, and is extremely concerned at the account given of their going to take up the hatchet. Says they were bad men that reported it; that it's a lie; and insists upon knowing whom the information came from, as it is evident that a stroke was meditated, but now perhaps dropped. Every apology which he can possibly make won't be sufficient to clear him of the imputation of a traitor. Some of the nation say the English have bought O'Beil. We shall spend two days to come in helping Mr. Polhemus to put his garrison in some state of defense; for should anything happen it, we should fare the worse above."

ANDREW ELLICOT TO GOV. MIFFLIN.

"June 29, FORT LE BŒUF.

"DEAR SIR:—In my last letter to you from Pittsburg I mentioned that you might expect to hear from me, both from Fort Franklin and Le Bœuf; but from a variety of circumstances no opportunity occurred of writing at first. On my arrival there, the place appeared to be in so defenseless a situation that, with the concurrence of Capt. Denny and the officer commanding at the fort, we remained there some time, and employed the troops in rendering it more tenable. It may now be considered as defensible, provided the number of men is increased. The garrison at present consists of twenty-five men, one half of whom are unfit for duty, and it is my opinion that double that number would not be more than sufficient, considering the importance of the safety of the settlement on French Creek. At Fort Franklin, Gen. Wilkins and myself wrote to Cornplanter to attend there, that we might have an opportunity of explaining to him the nature of our business, and of obviating any difficulties that might arise in our proceedings. However, he did not come as we expected, having gone some days before to a council of the Six Nations at Buffalo. With this letter you will receive a copy of their message, presented by Gen. Chapin and Mr. Johnson to Capt. Denny and myself, with our reply to the same. I leave to yourself to consider the propriety of a British agent attending a considerable number of Indians, with a superintendent of Indian affairs of the United States to order the people of Pennsylvania to remove from those lands which have been ceded to them by treaty, by the king of Great Britain, and since that time regularly purchased from the Six Nations, and punctually paid for. After repairing Fort Franklin, we proceeded to this place, and are now beginning to strengthen the works here, so as to render it a safe deposit for military and other stores; and in doing which, agreeable to instructions, economy shall be strictly attended to. The line described by the Indians on the map will take from the State of Pennsylvania the Cassawago settlement (Meadville), being part of the purchase of 1784, and the whole of the purchase of 1788. But with respect to this claim they can be serious only so far as encouraged by the British agents and the countenance shown them by the late interference of the United States. The objection made by Mr. Brandt to Gen. Chapin, that the establishment at Presqu'ile would cut off the communication between the Six Nations and the Western hostile Indians, and thereby diminish their joint strength, is the strongest argument that can be urged in favor of that establishment. Gen. Chapin and myself are of the opinion that all differences between the State of Pennsylvania and the Six Nations might be accommodated by treaty, which treaty ought not to be held in the neighborhood of any British post, the United States, and this State at present, and that Presqu'ile is the most eligible place for such a treaty. Gen. Chapin, I presume, has communicated his sentiments to Gen. Knox on this subject. Standing Stone, a chief resident at Conyat, has informed us, since we arrived at this place, that the late mischief on the Allegheny River and Venango path was done by a party of eight warriors from Huron River, which falls into Lake Erie about twenty-six miles above Cuyahoga. One of his brothers saw them on their way to commit these depredations. Those Indians are only to be chastised by way of the lakes, but it is neither the interest of the British, Brandt, nor the other agents to have them punished—it is the interest of the United States; and yet the United States, by directing a suspension of the business at Presqu'ile, have taken effectual measures for the security of this nest of murderers, whose cruelties have for some years past been severely felt by the citizens of this State. You must recollect that I always had my doubts respecting the fulfillment of the contract for opening the navigation of French Creek, and a road from Le Bœuf to Presqu'ile, and agreeable to my expectations, have hitherto not been able to discover anything done in that business. For the further security of the frontiers of this State, it would be necessary to erect two block-houses on the Venango path, between Fort Pitt and Venango, and a third between Venango and this place. At present, Mead's settlement appears to me the most proper situation.

"I am, with great respect, your real friend,
"ANDREW ELLICOT."

GEN. CHAPIN'S LETTER TO THE SECRETARY OF WAR.

"FORT LE BŒUF, June 26th, 1794.

"I left Canandaigua on the thirteenth of this month, in order to attend a council at Buffalo Creek. I waited more than a week after my first notification for my son to return, that I might have an answer from you; but the chief growing impatient, kept constantly sending runners, and I was obliged to set out at last, to my great disappointment, without having received any information from you. On my arrival I found the minds of the Indians much agitated with regard to the movements made by the State of Pennsylvania. On the eighteenth I met the Indians in general council, the proceedings of which you see here inclosed. At this council I was requested to go to Presqu'ile (as you will see by their speech), to desire those people to move off who had made encroachments on their lands. I found that no excuse could answer, and was finally obliged to comply with their request. On the nineteenth I left Buffalo Creek, accompanied by a delegation from the Six Nations, consisting of sixteen chiefs and warriors. I arrived at Presqu'ile on the twenty-fourth, but finding no person there, proceeded to Le Bœuf, where I found Mr. Ellicot and Capt. Denny. After informing those gentlemen of the business I came upon, I gave them a copy of the speech which had been delivered me at Buffalo Creek. The answer which they made I send you, inclosed with the other speeches. Although the minds of the Six Nations are much disturbed at the injuries which they say they have sustained, they are still opposed to war, and wish, if possible, to live in peace with the United States. They are much opposed to the establishing of garrisons in this quarter, as they think it will involve them in war with the hostile Indians. They are likewise displeased with having their lands surveyed, which they say were not legally purchased. In this critical situation, would it not be best to have commissioners appointed to treat with the Six Nations, that all difficulties may be settled which subsist between them and the United States, especially those that regard the State of Pennsylvania? And it is the wish of the Six Nations that this treaty should be held at their council fire at Buffalo Creek. I shall return by Buffalo Creek," etc., etc.

A rumor prevailed that a large body of Indians, assisted by the British, had been seen crossing the lake, the others descending the Allegheny; that their object was to take Fort Franklin, destroy the settlement at Cassawago, and make an establishment at Presqu'ile.

Capt. Denny removed to Venango with his men, and ordered the brigades to be ready to be called out should the reports appear well founded.

Three men on their way to Pittsburg, of the names of Wallace, Power, and Van Tickler, were overpowered by the Indians. A party sent out by Lieut. Polhemus found them shot, scalped, and tomahawked.[1]

Joseph Brandt, in a letter to the British authorities, dated July 19, 1794, says: "In regard to the Presqu'ile business, should we not get an answer at the time limited, it is our business to push those fellows, and therefore it is my intention

[1] This statement is made on the authority of a public record, but is not true. The name is Van Sickle. Mr. Jas. Van Sickle, a grandson, residing at Albion, Erie County, says his grandfather was taken up for dead, but recovered and lived for many years.

to form my camp at Point Appineau (a few miles above Fort Erie); and I would esteem it a favor if his Excellency the Lieutenant-Governor would lend me four or five batteaux. Should it so turn out, and should those fellows not go off, and O'Beil (Cornplanter) continue in the same opinion, an expedition against those Yankees must of consequence take place. His Excellency has been so good as to furnish us with a hundredweight of powder, and ball in proportion, which is now at Fort Erie; but in the event of an attack upon Le Bœuf people, I could wish, if consistent, that his Excellency would order a like quantity in addition to be at Fort Erie, in order to be in readiness; likewise I would hope for a little assistance in provisions."

At Buffalo Creek, June 18th, at a council of the Six Nations, Gen. Chapin was addressed by O'Beil, or Cornplanter, in substance as follows :—"That they depended upon the Americans to do all in their power to assist them; they wished Col. Johnson, British agent (who slyly prompted them), and Gen. Chapin to remove back over the line which they had laid out. This line began at O'Beil's town, and in a direct line crossed French Creek, just below Meade's, and on the head of the Cuyahoga; from thence to the Muskingum, and down the Ohio and to its mouth, and up the Mississippi; leaving a small square for a trading house at the mouth of the rivers, and one where Clarksville now stands. If this removal was attended to immediately, they should consider them friends; if not, they must be considered enemies." Mr. Ellicot and Capt. Denny desired an interval of an hour to prepare an answer; at the expiration of which they replied as follows : "By the peace of 1782 the king of Great Britain ceded all the lands of Pennsylvania which they claim, but from regard to justice they desired to fairly purchase it from the Six Nations—the real owners of the soil. The purchase north of the north boundary of Pennsylvania, west of the Conawango River, Lake Chautauqua, and the path leading from thence to Lake Erie, and south of said lake, was made of your chiefs at Fort Harmer (by Gens. Butler and Gibson,) and the money and goods punctually paid them. They had also sold those lands to such people as chose to settle and work them, and it was their duty to protect them from depredations. Their military preparations were intended as a defense from hostile Western Indians, not supposing they needed any from the Six Nations, whom they considered their friends and allies. They could not consistently with their duty remove from the lands they had purchased, unless directed to do so by the great council of the people, to whom they would immediately send their message. They had been ordered by the great council of Pennsylvania to their present post, and they could not move from thence until orders came for that purpose."

At another conference, held at the same place, the Indians maintained that "they had decided upon their boundaries, and wished for nothing but justice (forgetting their former contract); they wanted room for their children; it would be hard for them not to have a country to live in when they were gone. Congress and their commissioners had often deceived them, and if these difficulties were not removed, the consequences would be bad. A number of their warriors were missing, and they supposed they had been killed by the Americans. Big Tree was one of the number, and a nephew of theirs (a Delaware); and it had been customary to make satisfaction (to pay a sum of money), which had not been done. If a garrison were established at Presqu'ile, the Southern Indians might do injury, and the Six Nations be blamed for it." Gen. Chapin replied that he was bound to look to the interests of both the Indians and the United States, and would accede to their wish, which was to accompany ten of their warriors and two chiefs to Presqu'ile, and to send their message immediately to the President.

They made the journey to Presqu'ile by water, and finding no one there (from fear of the Indians), they proceeded on foot to Le Bœuf, where they made known their business, which was to see the surveyors and forbid their running lines. They were informed that they had shortly before left the country by way of the river, and assurances were given them that the whole matter should be laid before the President. On their return to Buffalo Creek another council was held, when Cornplanter again insisted that their former request should be granted; they were determined the line should remain. Capt. Brandt, a Seneca, the year before, at a council, claimed the same line, the Muskingum. Where lands were actually settled and improved they were to be circumscribed by a line drawn around them, and no claim admitted beyond such line. He added : "They must not suspect that any other nation corrupted their minds ; the only thing that corrupted their minds was not to grant their request. There was but one word said that they liked at Le Bœuf, that was the gift of some land to O'Beil ; and to complete his wishes, he desired they would give all the Six Nations land."

This refers to Mr. Ellicot, relating the particulars concerning the treaty at Fort Harmer, and informing the Indians that the State of Pennsylvania had made these grants of land to Capt. O'Beil. This present to Cornplanter was at the suggestion of Gen. Richard Butler, who had been witness to his usefulness in all the treaties since 1784. [He mentions that it would be good policy to secure the chief's attachment ; and that his ideas of civilization would make the present grateful—that it could be made in such a manner as not to excite the jealousy of his own people, and wishes for the quiet and interest of the State, as well as the merit of the man, had prompted him in the liberty he was assuming.]

Gen. Chapin replied to Brandt that he hoped the Indians would "sit easy on their seats until they heard Gen. Washington's voice," and that he would forward their speech to him immediately.

In reply to this, the President appointed a conference at Canandaigua in October, for the purpose of establishing a firm and permanent friendship with the Six Nations, and appointed Timothy Pickering sole agent for this purpose. Cornplanter was charged by his people at their council " with having been bribed in the sale of Presqu'ile, and that he and little Billy received $2,000 at Fort Harmer, and a like sum at Philadelphia " ; but these and all other difficulties were amicably settled. A large tract of land west of the Phelps and Gorham purchase in New York was reserved to them, with $14,500 in goods ; and fifty-nine sachems signed a treaty of perpetual peace and friendship with the United States.

CHAPTER VII.

An Act to lay out the Towns of Erie, Waterford, Franklin, and Warren—To Protract the Enlistment of Troops at Le Bœuf—Deposition of Tho. Rees, Esq.—Actual Settlers—Memorial to the Population Company—Deacon Chamberlain's Story—Capt. Martin Strong to Wm. Nicholson, Esq.—Louis Philippe at Mr. Rees's—Murder of Rutledge and his Son—Mr. Augustus Porter's Visit—Mr. Judah Colt's MS. Autobiography—Number of White Settlers on the Lakes west of Genesee River—Gen. Wayne's Death at Presqu'ile, 1796.

ALL difficulties being removed, April 18th, 1795, an act passed the Legislature to lay out a town at Presqu'ile, at the mouth of French Creek, at the mouth of Conewango Creek, and at Le Bœuf—being the towns of Erie, Franklin, Warren, and Waterford.

Two commissioners were appointed by the Governor to survey at Presqu'ile sixteen hundred acres for town lots, and thirty-four hundred adjoining for out lots (the three sections of about a mile each, only one half of which is now occupied), to be laid out into town lots and out lots; the streets not less than sixty feet in width, nor more than one hundred; no town lots to contain more than one third of an acre; no out lot more than five acres; and the reservation for public uses not to exceed in the whole twenty acres. After the commissioners had returned the surveys into the office of the secretary, the governor was to offer at auction one third of the town lots and one third of the out lots, upon the following conditions: that within two years one house be built at least sixteen feet square, with at least one stone or brick chimney. Patents were not to be issued till the same was performed, and all payments to be forfeited to the commonwealth in case of failure. (This condition was afterward repealed.) Exclusive of the survey of in lots and out lots, sixty acres were reserved on the southern side of the harbor of Presqu'ile for the accommodation of the United States, in the erection of necessary forts, magazines, dock-yards, etc.; thirty acres to be on the bank, and the remainder below, comprehending the point at the entrance of the harbor; and upon the peninsula thirty acres at the entrance of the harbor, and one other lot of one hundred acres. The situation and forms of these lots were to be fixed by the commissioners and an engineer employed by the United States. Andrew Ellicot had previously surveyed and laid out Waterford, and an act was now passed to survey these five hundred acres for out lots, to reserve for public uses not more than ten acres, and to give actual settlers the right of pre-emption.

At this time, also, provision was made to protract the enlistment of troops at Le Bœuf, not to exceed one hundred and thirty for the term of eight months. These were to protect and assist the commissioners, surveyors, etc.; and if occurrences should take place which, in the opinion of the Governor, should make a greater force requisite than the aforesaid, or Indian hostilities continue, and a defense be requisite for the western frontier, a complete company of expert riflemen might be raised.

Thomas Rees, Esq., for more than half a century a citizen of Erie County, made a deposition in 1806, which contains much information in a concise form. It is as follows: "Thomas Rees, of Harbor Creek Township, in Erie County, farmer, being sworn according to law, doth depose and say, as follows: I was appointed deputy surveyor of District No. 1, north and west of the Rivers Ohio, Allegheny, and Connewango Creek, now Erie County, in May, 1792, and opened an office in Northumberland County, which was the adjoining. The reason of this was, all accounts from the country north and west of the Rivers Ohio, Allegheny, and Connewango Creek, represented it as dangerous to go into that country. In the latter part of said year I received 390 warrants, the property of the Penn. Population Company, for land situated in the Triangle, and entered them the same year in my book of entries. In 1793 I made an attempt to go; went to the mouth of Buffalo Creek to inquire of the Indians there whether they would permit me to go into my district to make surveys.

They refused, and added that if I went into the country I would be killed. At the same time I received information from different quarters which prevented me from going that year. In 1794 I went into District No. 1, now Erie County, and made surveys on the 390 warrants mentioned above, in the Triangle, except one or two for which no lands could be found. Among the surveys made on the warrants above mentioned, was that on the warrant in the name of John McCullough. Before I had completed I was frequently alarmed by hearing of the Indians killing persons on the Allegheny River, in consequence of which, as soon as the surveys were completed, I removed from the country and went to Franklin, where I was informed that there were a number of Indians belonging to the Six Nations going to Le Bœuf, to order the troops off that ground. I immediately returned to Le Bœuf. The Indians had left that place one day before I arrived there. I was told by Major Denny, then commanding at that place, that the Indians had brought Gen. Chapin, the Indian agent, with them to Le Bœuf; that they were very much displeased, and told him not to build a garrison at Presqu'ile.

"There were no improvements made, nor any persons living on any tract of land within my district during the year 1794. In the year 1795, I went into the country and took a number of men with me. We kept in a body, as there appeared to be great danger, and continued so for that season. There was no work done of any consequence, nor was any person, to my knowledge, residing on any tract within my district. In the course of the summer the commissioners came on to lay out the town of Erie, with a company of men to guard them. There were two persons killed within one mile of Presqu'ile, and others in different parts of the country; such were the fears that though some did occasionally venture out to view the lands, many would not. We all laid under the protection of the troops.

"I sold, as agent of the Pennsylvania Population Company, during that season, 79,700 acres of land, of which 7,150 acres were a gratuity. The above quantity of land was applied for and sold to two hundred persons. That fall we left the country. In the spring of 1796 a considerable number of people came out into the country, and numbers went to the farms that they had purchased from the Population Company. The settlements during this year were very small.

"The latter part of this year, the opposition commenced against the Population Company on the waters of Elk and Conneaut Creeks, by an association under the title of ———, which impeded considerably the progress of the settlements under the Population Company. In the latter part of the month of May or the beginning of June, 1797, a second association made its appearance in opposition to the title of the Population Company on the waters of French Creek, near the New York State line, under the title of ———; and another on the northeast corner of the Triangle; and were active in their opposition to the claims of the Population Company, and to the exertions of its agents for the improvement and settlement of the country. . . . They took great pains to impress upon the minds of persons who came into the country with the intention of settling in it, that the Population Company had no title to the lands which they claimed, and induced all over whom they could gain any influence to settle and claim in opposition to the Population Company."

Compromises were afterward effected with many of the actual settlers, and their course was not unjustifiable until after the decisions of the courts. To show the ground taken by them I have inserted the following article: "Memorial of ——— to the Pennsylvania Population Company, March 4, 1799. Agreeable to the encouragement held out to settlers in the western part of the County of Allegheny, I moved in the year 1795 within sixteen miles of Presqu'ile, on Lake Erie. I entered into an article of agreement with a number of persons in Northumberland County, previous to my moving to Presqu'ile; the purport of the article was that I was to go and purchase or improve lands in that county, and that they were to share equal with me in all purchases or improvements that I should make.

"One very great encouragement to my going there was that the Pennsylvania Population Company published in different parts of Pennsylvania, offering, as an encouragement to the first settlers that would go, one hundred and fifty acres of land, valued at one dollar per acre, to each of the first settlers, with the remainder to make up a tract of four hundred acres; which remaining part was to be bought. And in order to give greater encouragement to settlers, the State of Pennsylvania offered, in a law passed in the year 1792, land at seven pounds ten shillings per one hundred acres, and ten years to pay it. Under these prospects I moved to that county, being one of the first settlers. The law then existing provided that an office would be opened in each district, which was not the case when I moved there; but I went and applied to Thomas Rees, who was agent for the Pennsylvania Population Company, and district surveyor, as I had the land improved. Before my applying to Rees, I mentioned if the land belonged to the company I would comply with their terms, and if the land belonged to the State of Pennsylvania I would comply with the terms the State held out to settlers. Finding no surveys made I believed the land belonged to the State, and improved upon it with these intentions, as being the proper person who should hold it by virtue of my improvements. I applied to Mr. Rees, district surveyor, and he entered my name in a book kept for that purpose as a claimant for so much land, and gave me a certificate for those lands, and had them surveyed, and I paid him five dollars for each tract, for surveying.

"After I had lived two years peaceably upon the land, without meeting with any opposition whatever, the agent for the company came out and requested of me to know how I wished or intended to hold the land. I answered, that I intended holding it upon the same principles that I made my applications in 1795. He then asked me for the privilege of building a vessel and storehouse upon my tract of land. I told him that there were more persons concerned in this land than myself, and if I granted any privilege of that kind, he must consider that I did not intend him to hold any right of any kind to the tract of land by making these improvements; and upon these conditions I granted him liberty to build the vessel and storehouse. Afterward in my absence he took possession of a mill-seat upon the same tract, and engaged the millwright I had verbally engaged to build a mill upon the same seat, and gave them possession. On my return, finding he had abused those privileges I had granted him, I went and discharged the millwrights and ship carpenters."

Deacon Hinds Chamberlain, of Le Roy, New York, in company with Jesse Beach and Reuben Heath, journeyed to Presqu'ile in 1795. Deacon Chamberlain describes the tour as follows: "We saw one white man, named Poudery, at Tonawanda village. At the mouth of Buffalo Creek there was but one white man, named Winne, an Indian trader. His building stood just as you descend from the high ground (near where the Mansion House now stands, corner of Main and Exchange Streets). He had rum, whisky, Indian knives, trinkets, etc. His house was full of Indians, and they looked at us with a good deal of curiosity. We had but a poor night's rest—the Indians were in and out all night getting liquor. The next day we went up the beach of the lake to the mouth of Cattaraugus Creek, where we encamped; a wolf came down near our camp, and deer were quite abundant. In the morning went up to the Indian village; found 'Black Joe's' house, but he was absent. He had, however, seen our tracks upon the beach of the lake, and hurried home to see what white people were traversing the wilderness. The Indians stared at us; Joe gave us a room where we should not be annoyed by Indian curiosity, and we stayed with him over night. All he had to spare us in the way of food was some dried venison; he had liquor, Indian goods, and bought furs. Joe treated us with so much civility that we remained until near noon. There were at least one hundred Indians and squaws gathered to see us. Among the rest there were sitting in Joe's house, an old squaw and a young, delicate-looking white girl dressed like a squaw. I endeavored to find out something about her history, but could not. She seemed inclined not to be noticed, and had apparently lost the use of our language. With an Indian guide provided by Joe we started upon the Indian trail for Presqu'ile.

"Wayne was then fighting the Indians, and our guide often pointed to the West, saying, 'bad Indians there.' Between Cattaraugus and Erie I shot a black snake, a racer, with a white ring around his neck. He was in a tree twelve feet from the ground, his body wound around it, and measured seven feet and three inches.

"At Presqu'ile (Erie) we found neither whites nor Indians—all was solitary. There were some old French brick buildings, (why did they make bricks, surrounded as they were by stone and timber?) wells, block-houses, etc., going to decay, and eight or ten acres of cleared land. On the peninsula there was an old brick house forty or fifty feet square. The peninsula was covered with cranberries.

"After staying there one night we went over to Le Bœuf, about sixteen miles distant, pursuing an old French road. Trees had grown up in it, but the track was distinct. Near Le Bœuf we came upon a company of men who were cutting out the road to Presqu'ile—a part of them were soldiers and a part Pennsylvanians. At Le Bœuf there was a garrison of soldiers—about one hundred. There were several white families there, and a store of goods. Myself and companions were in pursuit of land. By a law of Pennsylvania, such as built a log-house and cleared a few acres acquired a presumptive right—the right to purchase at five dollars per hundred acres. We each of us made a location near Presqu'ile. On our return to Presqu'ile from Le Bœuf, we found there Col. Seth Reed and his family. They had just arrived. We stopped and helped him build some huts; set up crotches, laid poles across, and covered them with the bark of the cucumber-tree. At first the Colonel had no floors; afterward he indulged in the luxury of floors made by laying down strips of bark. James Baggs and Giles Sisson came on with Col. Reed. I remained for a considerable time in his employ. It was not long before eight or ten other families came in.[1]

"On our return we again stayed at Buffalo over night with Winne. There was at the time a great gathering of hunting parties of Indians there. Winne took from them all their knives and tomahawks, and then selling them liquor, they had a great carousal."

Capt. Martin Strong, in a letter to William Nicholson, Esq., dated Waterford, January 8, 1855, says: "I came to Presqu'-

[1] This is double the number given in the article by Capt. Strong, whose testimony from the circumstances ought to have the preference.

ile the last of July, 1795. A few days previous to this, a company of United States troops had commenced felling the timber on Garrison Hill, for the purpose of erecting a stockade garrison ; also a corps of engineers had arrived, headed by Gen. Ellicot, escorted by a company of Pennsylvania militia commanded by Capt. John Grubb, to lay out the town of Erie.

"We all were in some degree under martial law, the two Rutledges having been shot a few days before (as was reported by the Indians) near the site of the present Lake Shore railroad depot. Thomas Rees, Esq., and Col. Seth Reed and family (the only family in the Triangle) were living in tents and booths of bark, with plenty of good refreshment for all itinerants that chose to call, many of whom were drawn here from motives of curiosity and speculation. Most of the land along the lake was sold this summer at one dollar per acre, subject to actual settlement. We were then in Allegheny County. . . . Le Bœuf had a small stockade garrison of forty men, located on the site of the old French fort ; a few remains of the old entrenchment were then visible. In 1795 there were but four families residing in what is now Erie County. These were of the names of Reed, Talmage, Miles, and Baird. The first mill built in the Triangle was at the mouth of Walnut Creek ; there were two others built about the same time in what is now Erie County : one by William Miles, on the north branch of French Creek, now Union ; the other by William Culbertson, at the inlet of Conneauttee Lake, near Edinboro.

"Half a century ago the winters were more regular, and snows deeper than in late years, and I think are become more favorable for vegetation."

When Mr. Rees was living in his tent on the bank of the lake, "with plenty of good refreshment for all itinerants that chose to call," he was honored with a royal visitor. Louis Philippe, his younger brother, and an attendant, spent a day or two with him, to refresh and rest themselves in their travels. After expressing themselves delighted with the lake scenery, they proceeded on their journey, Mr. Rees providing them with an Indian guide to Canandaigua. The brother, who was delicate and engrossed much of the care of the others, was suspected of being the Dauphin, but it proved otherwise.

The two persons spoken of by Esquire Rees and Capt. Strong, "as having been killed by the Indians, as was reported," were a father and son, who were rather prominent actual settlers. The site of the City Mills, near the "Lake Shore Depot," was for a long time known as "Rutledge's grave," and was the terror of the ignorant and superstitious. The elder Rutledge was dead when found, the son scalped and also shot, but still alive, and placed against a tree. He was attended by Dr. Kennedy, a skillful physician, of Meadville, but survived only a short time. A rumor was current at the time that these murders were committed by white men disguised as Indians; but no evidence admissible in a court of justice was adduced. Several suits brought by the Population Company against the actual settlers turned upon this point, namely, that the company had been prevented from settling their lands by the enemies of the United States, the purchasers considering it unsafe to bring their families out, or even themselves to be away from the protection of the fort. The murders were certainly fortunate, financially, for the Population Company, as under the most favorable circumstances they could not have brought out fifty thousand families in the two years alloted them. Had it not been for these depredations, the company must have forfeited their lands.

The respectability of the managers would not allow us for a moment to entertain such thoughts; and when we consider the strong inducements the actual settlers had for ferreting out the iniquity, their whole property in many cases being at stake, we must conclude that the murderers were what they appeared to be—Indians.

In the "Holland Purchase" we find an account of a visit of Augustus Porter, of Niagara Falls, made to Presqu'ile with Judah Colt, in 1795. He says: "At that time, all that part of the State lying west of Phelps and Gorham's purchase was occupied by Indians, their title not yet being extinguished. There was of course no road leading from Buffalo eastward except an Indian trail, and no settlement whatever on that trail. We

HISTORY OF ERIE COUNTY. 85

traveled on horseback from Canawagas (Avon) to Buffalo, and were two days in performing the journey. At Buffalo there lived a man of the name of Johnstone, the British Indian interpreter, also a Dutchman and his family by the name of Middaugh, and an Indian trader by the name of Winne.

" From Buffalo we proceeded to Chippewa, Upper Canada, where we found Capt. William Lee with a small rowboat about to start for Presqu'ile and waiting only for assistance to row the boat. Mr. Colt, Mr. Joshua Fairbanks, now of Lewiston, and myself joined him. Two days of hard rowing brought us to that place, where we found surveyors engaged in laying out the village now called Erie. Also a military company under the command of Gen. Irvine, ordered there by the Governor of the State to protect the surveyors against the Indians. Col. Seth Reed (father of Rufus S. Reed) was there with his family, living in a marquée, having just arrived. A Mr. Rees was also there, acting as agent for the Population Company. We returned in the same boat to Chippewa, and from thence on horseback by way of Queenstown, on the Indian trail through Tonawanda Indian village to Canandaigua.

"During this expedition from Buffalo to Erie, a very remarkable circumstance presented itself, the like of which I had never before seen, nor have I since witnessed. Before starting from Buffalo we had been detained there two days by a heavy fall of rain, accompanied by a strong northeast gale. When off Cattaraugus Creek on our upward passage, about one or two miles from land, we discovered, some distance ahead, a white strip on the surface of the lake, extending out from the shore as far as we could see. On approaching this white strip, we found it to be some five or six rods wide, its whole surface covered with fish of all the varieties common to the lake, lying on their sides as if dead. On touching them, however, they would dart below the surface, but immediately rise again to their former position. We commenced taking them by hand, making our selection of the best; and finding them perfectly sound, we took in a good number. On reaching Erie we had some of them cooked, and found them excellent. The position of these fishes on their sides in the water placed their mouths partly above and partly below the surface, so that they seemed to be inhaling both water and air; for at such effort at inhaling, bubbles would rise and float on the water. It was these bubbles that caused the white appearance on the lake's surface. I have supposed these fish had, from some cause growing out of the extraordinary agitation of the lake by the gale from the eastward, and the sudden reflux of water from west to east after it had subsided, been thrown together in this way, and from some unknown natural cause had lost the power of regulating their specific gravity, which it is said they do by means of an air bladder furnished them by nature. I leave others, however, to explain this phenomenon."

Mr. Judah Colt, in a manuscript autobiography, says : " In August, 1795, Augustus Porter and myself set out from Canandaigua for Presqu'ile, for the purpose of purchasing lands—went on horseback to Niagara, where we left our horses and took passage with Capt. Wm. Lee in a small shallop to Presqu'ile. On our arrival there we found a number of men encamped in that quarter. The United States troops were erecting a fort. Gen. William Irvine and Andrew Ellicot, State Commissioners, were laying out the town of Erie, and had in their service about one hundred militia troops. We purchased and took certificates of four hundred acres of land each—made but a short stay, and returned the way we came. The season was extremely dry and warm. We suffered much from heat, drought, and mosquitoes. Shortly after my return I was taken sick with bilious fever, which reduced me very low."

The next March, Mr. Colt being in Philadelphia, made an offer to the Population Company of one dollar per acre for thirty thousand acres of land off the east end of the Triangle ; they declined selling in so large a body, but contracted with him to be their agent at a salary of fifteen hundred dollars per year, and all expenses paid by them. Powers of attorney and letters were made out, maps of the country were furnished, and money advanced to purchase provisions, hire labor, etc. In the month of April he set out for the Geneseo country ; at New York laid in stores of provisions, sundry kinds of goods, farming and cooking utensils such as are generally wanted in a new country. They were shipped to Albany, thence across the portage in wagons, from thence in batteaux up the Mohawk River and through the lakes to Presqu'ile. On their arrival at Oswego, they were stopped by the British garrison there, and only an empty boat allowed to pass to Niagara and obtain of Gov. Simcoe permission to proceed with their loading. Shortly after this they were informed of the treaty being ratified by Congress, which was made by Mr. Jay with the British government, and which had been for some time under consideration.

Mr. Colt says: "I arrived myself at the town of Erie on the 22d of June, and my boats with the provisions the 1st of July following, and shortly after proceeded to business. I erected my tent or marquée near the old French garrison, and continued to reside there through the summer. There was a captain's command stationed at this village, in a garrison laid out and builded in the summer of 1795. In August I rode down to Pittsburg, and attended a vendue for the sale of parts of the Erie Reserve; visited the agent who had the superintendence of a portion of the company's lands on the waters of the Beaver; found the country new, with but few inhabitants; roads bad, and accommodations poor; encamped at night, and tied my horse head and foot. The journey was very fatiguing, owing to the dry and warm season. Returned to Erie in safety, and in September went on horseback, principally alone, through the wilderness to Canandaigua. After making a short visit to my family, returned to Erie, where I continued the business of my agency until the 1st of November. During the season met with considerable opposition from adverse settlers. After arranging the affairs of the company for the winter, and leaving the agency in the care of Elisha and Enoch Marvin, we set out again for Philadelphia (by way of Canandaigua) on the 4th of November, and after about two weeks of hard labor, and running much danger of losing ourselves, we arrived with our boat at the mouth of Genesee River," etc.

It is said all the white inhabitants west of this river, on the lakes, were those in the garrison of Niagara; two families at

Lewiston ; a British Indian interpreter, two Indian traders, and one family at Buffalo ; a few settlers and a garrison at Presqu'ile ; a party of New England surveyors with two families at Conneaut, Ohio ; one family at Cleveland ; a French trader at Sandusky, and the settlement at Detroit.

The first settlers in Erie County were mostly, as in the case of the Reeds, Colts, Strongs, Judsons, etc., from moral, thrifty, intelligent New England ; or, like the Mileses, Vincents, Kings, Hamiltons, etc., perhaps a more numerous class, of the illustrious, historic race of Scotch-Irish—"memorable for their devotion to liberty and religion, and ever ready to die upon the battle-field in the defense of the one, or to burn at the stake as a testimony for the other."

The following touching story, which we have condensed, is found in the *Chardon Gazette.* Those who emigrate from New England to Ohio in these days (about 1830) when thirty-five steamboats plow the waters of Lake Erie, and hundreds of white sails are spread to the breeze, and pride themselves on their enterprise and self-denial, would do well to consider a case of real endurance and privation which occurred on the Reserve in 1796.

Between Utica and the French settlement on the River Raisin, there were not half a dozen white families, when we except a few scattering infant settlements in Western New York, and the military post at Presqu'ile. Mr. K., the father of one of these families at Conneaut, had important business with the Connecticut Land Company, and was compelled to make the journey before winter. His family had subsisted on provisions brought from New York, with fish and game, and it was supposed a sufficiency was in store until his return. The oldest male member of the family, a boy of fifteen, having been placed in charge, he took his departure. On his return to Buffalo the winter had fully set in, the snow being two and a half feet deep. His absence had already been prolonged—the family might be in a starving condition, and there seemed to be no alternative but to venture into the wilderness. Having loaded his horse with such necessaries as could be procured for his family, he pursued his course on foot, following the beach of the lake. At an Indian settlement on the Cattaraugus he employed a guide, Seneca Billy, as the projecting bluffs prevented his following longer the shore. After camping out several nights on the snow, he reached Presqu'ile and dismissed his guide. Here he purchased a bag of corn, paying for it three dollars per bushel, and set out for home on the ice. At a fire spring near the mouth of Elk Creek, the horse broke through, and was so injured as to be of no further use, and taking his corn upon his back he reached home the same day. But it was only to consummate his grief, for the family were nearly in a famishing condition. An infant being deprived of its natural nourishment by the low diet of the mother, slowly expired of starvation. The Connecticut Company having a small store of provisions for the surveyors at Cleveland, Mr. K. made a journey there on foot, and returned with a barrel of salt beef. This, with the assistance of the man who related the story, he conveyed home on a handsled.

A circumstance worthy of note occurred in Erie, December 15, 1796, which was the death of Gen. Anthony Wayne at the garrison. For six years the Indians northwest of the Ohio, consisting of the Delaware, Shawnee, Miami, and other tribes had greatly annoyed the United States, being instigated by Great Britain. A peace was finally negotiated by our Minister, Mr. Jay, and Lord Greenville, and signed at Greenville in 1795. As the English were dispirited by the brilliant achievements of Gen. Wayne, and the Indians had lost confidence in them, and withdrawn their assistance, the terms of the treaty were advantageous to the United States, and the peace establishment proved permanent. Gen. Wayne, on his return home, was everywhere welcomed as the savior of his country; at Philadelphia all business was suspended, the streets festooned with evergreens and flowers, and all classes participated in the general joy.

The next year (1796) Gen. Wayne received an appointment from Government to conclude a treaty with the Northwestern Indians, and having accomplished this arduous task, embarked at Detroit, in the sloop Detroit, for the purpose of returning to his home in Chester County. Soon after leaving port he was violently attacked by his old malady, the gout, and the usual remedy, brandy, through an oversight of the steward, not being at hand, he became very much prostrated, and in this condition was landed at Erie. As there was no resident physician of any repute, Dr. J. C. Wallace, a skillful surgeon of the army, then at Pittsburg, was sent for with the greatest dispatch, but on arriving at Franklin, met a messenger with the news of his death.

When Gen. Wayne was brought into the garrison, he expressed a wish to be placed in the northwest block-house, the attics of the block-houses being comfortably fitted up and occupied by the families connected with the garrison. Capt. Russel Bissell probably had command at the time, and it is said the illustrious sufferer met with every possible kindness.

A fit death-bed and silent resting-place for a brave officer and patriot was the old military post of Presquile and its picturesque bay. He named the spot for his grave at the foot of the flagstaff. "A. W." on a single stone was placed at the head, and a neat railing inclosed it.

The remains were removed in 1809 by a son, Col. Isaac Wayne, of Chester County, and deposited in Radnor churchyard (St. David's Episcopal Church) which is fourteen miles west of Philadelphia. Dr. J. C. Wallace superintended the disinterment of the body, which was found in a remarkable state of preservation.

On a monument erected by the Pennsylvania Society of the Cincinnati is found the following: "Major-General Anthony Wayne was born at Waynesboro, in Chester County, Pennsylvania, in 1745. After a life of honor and usefulness, he died in December, 1796, at Erie, Pennsylvania, then a military post on Lake Erie, Commander-in-chief of the Army of the United States. His military achievements are consecrated in the history of his countrymen. His remains are here deposited."

CHAPTER VIII.

Erie County from 1785—Organization in 1803—Its Geography,etc.— Original Townships—Changes—Extent of Townships and Population—Population decennially from 1800—Census Items—Vote of 1808 and 1860—Receipts and Expenditures do.—Extract from Auditor-General's Report—Post-offices in 1830, 1856, 1860—List of Judges—Members of Congress—State Senate—Representatives— Prothonotaries—Register and Recorders—Sheriffs——Coroners First Section incorporated—Courthouses—Act for Public Landing —Borough Charter altered in 1833—Canal Basin—Peninsula— Poor-house—Several Acts—Government changed to that of a City— Present Population and Business—List of Burgesses and Mayors Collectors of Customs—Postmasters in Erie.

WE find Erie County, or rather that part south of the "Triangle," included in Westmoreland County by act of April 8, 1785. It reads as follows : " That all the land within the late purchase from the Indians, not heretofore assigned to any other particular county, shall be taken and deemed, and they are hereby declared, to be within the limits of the Counties of Northumberland and Westmoreland, and that from the Kittanning up the Allegheny, to the mouth of Conewango Creek, and from thence up said creek to the northern line of this State, shall be the line between Northumberland and Westmoreland Counties in the aforesaid late purchase."

September 24, 1788, we find the northwestern part of the State, being parts of Westmoreland and Washington Counties, constituting the new County of "Allegheny," with Pittsburg for the seat of justice.

March 12, 1800, the Triangle having been purchased and added in 1792, Erie County was erected into a separate county, and Erie designated as the place of holding courts of justice. At the same time, Crawford, Mercer, Venango, Warren, and Erie were constituted temporarily one county, with all county privileges, called Crawford, Meadville being the seat of justice.

April 2, 1803, Erie County was organized for all judicial purposes; this took place at the house of George Buehler, on the corner of Third and French Streets. [This house is still standing, though in ruins, and has been known for many years as the "McConkey House." In 1813 it was Duncan's and Perry's headquarters; next the house was kept by Thomas Rees, Jr., and lastly by James McConkey.]

McCONKEY HOUSE, 1861.

Judge Jesse Moore held the first court.

Erie County is 36 miles in length and 20 in breadth, with an area of 720 square miles, or 460,800 acres; its central latitude is 42° north, and longitude 3° west.

Its principal streams are Four Mile, Six Mile, Twelve Mile, Sixteen and Twenty Mile Creeks; west it has Walnut Creek, Trout Run, Elk, Raccoon, and Crooked Creeks. Mill Creek empties into the lake within the city limits. French and Le Bœuf Creeks empty into the Allegheny River. Conneaut Creek flows through the southwestern part, and also, for a short distance, Conneauttee.

These streams afford abundant water power for manufacturing purposes; and while the valleys and rivers are sometimes wild and picture-like, as at Elk, Walnut and Twenty Mile Creeks, the broken and unproductive acres in Erie County are few indeed.

It has three small beautiful lakes : Conneauttee, in Washington township; Le Bœuf, in Waterford; and Pleasant, in Venango township.

The dividing ridge which crosses from southwest to northeast (particularly described elsewhere) marks a striking distinction in the county on each side. The bank of the lake at Erie and in the vicinity is about sixty feet in height, and the surface rises gently from ten to twelve miles back, which is the summit of the level between the waters of the lake and the Allegheny River. The southern portion produces excellent grass, but is not fertile in grain; the northern, sloping to the lake is well adapted to wheat. One hundred bushels of corn, 30 bushels of wheat, 35 bushels of rye, 60 bushels of barley, 50 bushels of rape, and 500 bushels of potatoes have been raised to the acre.

The original townships were sixteen in number, namely : Mill Creek, Harbor Creek, Northeast, Greenfield, Venango, Brokenstraw, Union, Le Bœuf, Waterford, Conneauttee, McKean, Beaverdam, Elk Creek, Conneaut, Springfield, and Fairview. Brokenstraw, in 1820, was changed to Wayne and Concord. Amity was taken from Union in 1826. Girard was set off from Springfield and Fairview in 1832, and received its name from Stephen Girard, who had large tracts of land in the neighborhood. Washington was changed from Conneauttee in 1834; Greene from Beaverdam in 1840; Franklin was formed of parts of McKean, Washington, Fairview, and Elk Creek in 1844; and Summit, of Greene and McKean in 1854.

In 1800 the population of Erie County was 1468; in 1810, 1358; in 1820, 8553; in 1830, 17,041; in 1840, 31,344; in 1850, 38,742; and in 1860, 49,697. From 1840 to 1850 the increase in Erie was nearly 100 per cent.

In 1850 the cash value of farms was $4,782,858, and of farming implements and machinery, $294,726. The number of horses, 7014; of milch cows, 16,575; of sheep, 66,705; of swine,

AREA AND POPULATION OF THE TOWNSHIPS OF ERIE COUNTY.

Townships.	Greatest Length.	Greatest Breadth.	Area in Acres.	Population of Townships in						
				1820.	1830.	1840.	1850.	1860.	1870.	1880.	1880.
Amity	7	5	22,400	142	385	560	739	1016	924	1033	912
Beaverdam	7	5½	24,640	631	443						
Conneaut	8½	6	32,640	438	1324	1796	1942	1255	1538	1546	1386
Conneauttee	7	7	31,360	53	743						
Concord	7	5	22,400	288	225	652	882		1112	1171	991
Elk Creek	8	7	35,840	288	562	1645	1535		1462	1564	1325
Fairview village	8	7	23,040	536	1529	1481	1760		1674	1482	305
" township											1295
Greenfield	6	5½	19,200	281	664	862	731	880	1039	1020	1432
Harbor Creek	8	5½	23,860	555	1104	1843	2084	2033	1974	1781	1660
Le Boeuf	8	5	25,600	505	554	876	990	1483	1748	1420	1215
McKean	7½	7	32,280	440	984	1714	1921	1600	1427	1394	1330
Mill Creek	7½	7	24,960	1017	1783	2682	3064		2745	3279	3279
Northeast	7	5½	19,200	1068	1706	1793	2379	1900	2313	2152	2124
Springfield	8	6	24,320	896	1520	2344	1916	1054	1742	1792	1652
Union	7	5	22,400	200	235	583	1076	1224	1334	1377	1366
Wayne	7	5	22,400		197	738	1122	1950	1295	1306	1124
Waterford	7	5½	22,400	579	1006	1144	1545	1301	1884	1822	1537
Venango	6	5½	21,120	290	683	812	1019	2453	1370	1445	1351
Girard	6½	6	22,020			2660	2443	1450	2018	2338	2280
Greene	6½	5½	13,143			1081	1542	1038	1395	1531	1511
Summit	5	4½	27,473					1943	1047	1047	903
Washington	6½	8	16,096					979	1943	1880	1790
Franklin	5	5				1551	1706			1020	963
Erie				635	443	3412	5858	11,113	15,516	27,737	40,634
Waterford Borough	1	½	500			403	498	900	790	784	838
Northeast "					1329	339	386	560	900	1396	1534
Girard "							400	616	704	703	626
Wattsburg "	1	⅔	250			132	227	337	286	389	382
Edinboro "						232	363	474	801	876	1107
Albion "	1		500					443	452	433	366
Elgin "										154	169
Lockport "										345	240
Millvillage "											320
Union City "	1	1	1,700						500	2,171	2261
Corry (city)									6,809	5,277	5677

15,417; and the value of live stock, $1,070,519. The quantity of wheat raised in 1850 was 147,825 bushels; of rye, 10,203; of Indian corn, 433,692; of oats, 433,765; of tobacco, 8,000 pounds; of wool, 179,103; of peas and beans, 3,141 bushels; of potatoes, 171,855; of sweet potatoes, 170 bushels; of barley, 42,352; of hay, 69,422 tons; clover seed, 1,720 bushels; grass, 1,253; hops, 1,260; flax, 3,729; flax seed, 860; buckwheat, 27,272; orchard products, 17,327; 129 gallons of wine were made, 252,843 pounds of butter, 754,452 of cheese, 333,748 pounds of maple sugar, 1,875 gallons of molasses, 23,239 of beeswax and honey. The value of home manufactures was estimated at $28,581.

In 1860 the farms in the county numbered 4,474; manufacturing establishments, 383; dwellings, 9,759. The amount of property subject to tax, fixed by revenue commissioners in March, 1860, was $4,475,857.

In 1808 the full vote of the county for Governor was 589; 345 for Simon Snyder, and 244 for James Ross, Federalist. Erie and Mill Creek polled 156 votes.

In 1860 the vote for Governor was 8082—for Andrew G. Curtin, Republican, 5,613; for Henry D. Foster, Democrat, 2,469. One month later, the whole vote for President was 8,798—6,160 for Lincoln, 2,531 fusion, 90 for Bell, and 17 for Douglas.

In the report of the Auditor-General of Pennsylvania for the year 1860, are the following items relating to Erie County:

Tax on real and personal estate..........................$	11,006 91
Tavern licenses...	315 00
Retailers' licenses...	2,090 02
Brokers' licenses...	228 00
Theater, circus, etc., licenses...............................	76 00
Distillery and brewery licenses.............................	254 28
Billiard room, bowling saloon, etc., licenses.........	105 00
Eating-house, beer-house, and restaurant licenses...	671 00
Patent medicine license.......................................	67 00
Pamphlet laws...	19 00
Militia tax...	10 61
Millers' tax..	65 10
Tax on writs, wills, deeds, etc..............................	513 30
Tax on foreign insurance agencies.......................	200 00
Common schools...	3,514 44
Abatement of the State tax..................................	536 84
Value of real and personal estate.......................	4,475,857 00
Assessment of tax...	11,501 42
Population...	49,697 00
Taxables..	11,335 00

HISTORY OF ERIE COUNTY.

POST-OFFICES AND POSTMASTERS IN ERIE COUNTY IN 1830.

Beaverdam..Samuel Smith.
Elk Creek..Joseph Wells.
Erie..James Hughes.
Fairview..W. W. Warner.
Gray's Settlement..Amos Graves, Jr.
Greenfield...Elijah J. Woodruff.
Harbor Creek..Daniel Goodwin.
Lexington..David Sawdy.
Northeast..Jas. Smedley.
Northville..Orrin Wyllys.
Phillipsville...James Phillips.
Springfield X Roads..J. P. Woodworth.
Union Mills...William Miles.
Waterford..Joseph Derrickson.
Wattsburg..Levi Wilcox.
Wesleyville..Almond Fuller.

Post-offices in Erie County, July 1, 1856, and the revenue in 1855, showing the business importance of every town. The figures at the right hand show the net revenue of the office to the Department; left hand column the compensation of the postmaster.

Post-offices.	Postmasters.	Comp.	Rev'e.
Albion....................................	Josiah Sullivan......................	$ 164 57	$ 1 65
Belle Valley...........................	Joseph Vance (estab. in 1856)	....	....
Carter Hill..............................	David White..........................	8 38	4 51
Cherry Hill.............................	Ira Harrington......................	18 79	9 87
Cook.......................................	Harvey Davis.......................	26 10	12 64
East Greene...........................	Joseph Smith........................	4 00	2 50
Edenville................................	Robert H. Frisbee.................	....	....
Edinboro................................	Marcus Saley.......................	159 40	90 61
Elk Creek...............................	Daniel M. Wood...................	42 02	26 81
Erie (C. H.)............................	B. F. Sloan............................	2000 00	2 59
Fairview.................................	Daniel Weidler.....................	165 11	63 23
Franklin Corner....................	Ivory Hawkins.....................	10 32	5 26
Girard.....................................	Monroe Hutchinson............	345 04	267 00
Greenfield.............................	Wm. P. Barbie.......................	11 93	7 58
Harbor Creek.........................	Clarilla Stimson...................	78 01	36 19
Le Bœuf..................................	Pery G. Stranahan................	9 29	3 96
Lundy's Lane.........................	Wallace Sherman.................	73 58	41 86
McKean..................................	Titus D. Chillis.....................	86 38	32 06
Moorheadville......................	J. T. Moorhead.....................	33 27	8 47
Northeast...............................	Mrs. Rebecca Brawly...........	318 48	224 46
Northville..............................	John Taylor..........................	50 51	21 56
Platea.....................................	Samuel Cisson.....................	113 95	39 22
Springfield X Roads.............	Timothy S. Cowles...............	153 92	75 22
Sterrettania...........................	Elias Brecht..........................	13 04	7 16
Stewart...................................	Robert McCrea, 4th.............	11 06	3 21
Swan Station.........................	Samuel Selden.....................	51 89	27 05
Union Mills............................	Roswell H. Brown................	94 81	39 48
Waterford...............................	Henry Colt............................	372 14	234 21
Wattsburg..............................	W. B. Williams.....................	167 59	71 93
Wayne....................................	Roswell B. Adams................	55 80	23 65
Well's Corners.......................	Henry Hill.............................	22 21	9 66
Wesleyville............................	Samuel L. Potter..................	82 36	23 83
West Springfield...................	Gilbert Hurd.........................	82 63	59 08

In 1861 one other office was added, that of Oak Grove. The distributing office at Erie was discontinued after January 1, 1838; afterward restored, and again discontinued in 1858. In order to defray expenses in 1860, the boxes were rented at two dollars each per annum.

In 1808 the county treasurer reported $9,890.31½; of this, $4,055.84½ was in the treasury, December 31, 1807. The county expenses amounted to $2,763.15. The same year $1,178.47½ was expended in building and materials for the courthouse, and $20.20 appropriated to clear French Creek.

In 1860 the receipts of the county were $58,178.51, and the expenditures $50,592.91.

Courts and Judicial Districts.—Erie being a part of Crawford, for all county purposes, from 1800 to 1803, it belonged to the fifth judicial district.

By the judiciary act of February 24, 1806, Butler, Mercer, Venango, Crawford, and Erie composed the sixth judicial district.

In 1818 Erie, Crawford, Mercer, Venango, and Warren composed the sixth.

In 1830 Erie, Venango, Mercer, and Crawford were the sixth; and afterward Erie, Crawford, and Warren became the sixth.

Jasper Yates held a circuit court in Erie on the 15th of October, 1806; Judge Breckenridge one in October, 1807.

In 1839 Crawford, Erie, and Venango had a district court, which was in 1841 extended also to Mercer County. Judge James Thompson presided. The court expired by limitation in five years.

David Derrickson was elected an additional president judge, with the same associates, in 1856.

A session of the Pennsylvania Supreme Court was held in Erie in 1854. Judges present: Lewis (president), Woodward, Lowrie, and Knox.

President Judges of the Court of Common Pleas and Quarter Sessions.—Judge Addison, 1800; Jesse Moore, 1803; Henry Shippen, 1825; N. B. Eldred, 1839; Gaylord Church, 1849; John Galbraith, elected in 1851. Judge Galbraith died in 1860, and Rasselas Brown was appointed by Gov. Packer to fill the vacancy until the next election. S. P. Johnson was elected in 1860; L. D. Wetmore, 1870; J. P. Vincent, 1874; W. A. Galbraith, 1877; Frank Gunnison, 1887.

Associate Judges.—John Bell, John Kelso, John Cochran, Wilson Smith, John Vincent, John Grubb, Myron Hutchinson, John Brawley. In 1851 James Miles and J. M. Sterrett were elected, and in 1856 Samuel Hutchins and John Grier.

Erie is annexed to the western district of the Supreme Court.

In 1810 Erie, Beaver, Mercer, Crawford, Warren, and Venango constituted a congressional district. In 1820 Beaver was apportioned to another district.

In 1830 Erie County, with Crawford, Mercer, Warren, and Venango formed the Eighteenth Congressional District.

In 1843 Erie, Warren McKean, Potter, Jefferson, and Clarion were constituted the Twenty-third Congressional District. It was styled the "Gerrymander," from Elbridge Gerry, as it was supposed to have been thus divided for political purposes. The Whigs, notwithstanding, elected their candidate, C. M. Reed, by a majority of forty the same year.

In 1852 Erie, Crawford, and Warren became the Twenty-fifth Congressional District.

Members of Congress.—William Hoge; Samuel Smith; Robert Moore; Thomas Wilson; Abner Lacock; P. Farrelly, 1820; P. Farrelly died 1822, and T. H. Sill was elected to fill his unexpired term of one year; Stephen Barlow, 1824; T. H. Sill, 1828; John Banks, 1830; John Galbraith, 1832-4; A. Plumer, 1836; John Galbraith, 1838; A. Plumer, 1840; Chas. M. Reed, 1842; J. W. Farrelly, 1848; James Thompson, 1845; C. B. Curtis; John Dick, 1852-54-56; Elijah Babbitt, 1858-62.

In 1801 the State apportionment included twenty-five Senators, and Crawford, Venango, Mercer, Warren, and Erie (forming one county under the name of Crawford, for all county purposes) elected one member, the returns being made at the courthouse in Meadville.

March 8, 1815, the State had thirty-one Senators, and Mercer, Erie, Warren, Venango, and Crawford still were entitled to but one. In 1830 Erie, Crawford, and Mercer constituted the Twenty-third Senatorial District. In 1843 Erie and Crawford became the Twenty-seventh, and entitled to one member. An apportionment in 1856 gave the State thirty-three Senators, Erie and Crawford being still entitled to but

HISTORY OF ERIE COUNTY. 99

one. In 1836 Erie and Crawford became the Twenty-first District.

Members of State Senate.—William McArthur, 1801; Wm. Bell; Wilson Smith, 1809; Joseph Shannon, 1813; Henry Hurst, 1817; J. Herrington, 1821-22.

In 1820 the Twentieth Senatorial District was composed of Erie, Crawford, and Warren. Jacob Herrington, 1821-22-23; John Leach, 1825 to 1827; Thomas Cunningham, 1829 to 1836; J. M. Sterrett, 1837 to 1839; J. W. Farrelly, 1842; Elijah Babbitt, 1844; James D. Dunlap, 1845; J. B. Johnson, 1846; J. H. Walker, 1849-51; James Skinner, 1852-54; Darwin A. Finney, to 1860.

House of Representatives.—In 1800 Allegheny, Beaver, Butler, Mercer, Crawford, Erie, Warren, and Venango jointly elected two members.

The Assembly in 1801 consisted of eighty-six members, the Counties of Crawford, Venango, Erie, Warren, and Mercer being entitled to one member.

In 1815 it had ninety-seven members, and the representation from Erie, Crawford, Venango, Warren, and Mercer was increased to three.

In 1843 Erie and Crawford were entitled to two members in the House.

In 1856 Erie became entitled to two members.

Members of Assembly.—Samuel Ewatt, District of all the Northwest, 1800; Alexander Buchanan, 1801; John Lytle, Jr., 1802; Wilson Smith, 1805; John Phillips and James Herrington, 1808; John Phillips and Roger Alden, 1809; John Phillips and Patrick Farrelly, 1811; James Weston and James Burchfield, 1813; Jacob Herrington, James Weston, and Ralph Marlin, 1815; S. Hays, R. Marlin, and J. Herrington, 1816; S. Hays, Thomas Wilson, and R. Marlin, 1817; J. Herrington, James Cochran, and J. Hackney, 1818; W. Smith, James Cochran, and William Connelly, 1819.

From the district composed of Erie, Crawford, Mercer, Venango, and Warren—Wilson Smith, William McConnelly, Jacob Herrington, 1820; David Brown, James Cochran, George Moore, 1821; James Weston, 1822; T. H. Sill, from Erie and Warren, 1823; Gen. John Phillips, 1824; Stephen

Woolverton, 1825-27; George Moore, 1828-29; John Riddel, 1831; J. H. Walker, 1832-35; E. Babbitt, J. K. Miller, 1836; Charles M. Reed, David Sawdy, 1837; William M. Watts, Samuel Hutchins, 1838; S. Skinner, J. D. Dunlap, 1840; Stephen Skinner, L. Robinson, 1842; J. D. Dunlap, David A. Gould, 1843; J. D. Dunlap, Mark Baldwin, 1844; J. B. Johnson, L. Robinson, 1845; William Sanborn, D. A. Gould, 1846; G. J. Ball, William Sanborn, 1847; G. J. Ball, T. Ryman, 1848; J. C. Reid, L. Hart, 1849; J. C. Reid, A. W. Blaine, 1851; C. W. Kelso, A. W. Blaine, 1851; C. W. Kelso, H. A. Hill, 1852; W. Warner, G. J. Ball, 1853; G. J. Ball, James Thompson, 1854; G. J. Ball, M. Whallon, 1855; J. W. Campbell, W. Laird, 1858; J. Gunnison, H. Teller, 1859; H. Teller, G. J. Ball, 1860.

Previous to 1840, the offices of prothonotary and register and recorder were united, and the incumbent appointed by the Governor.

The first appointment was of Callender Irvine, 1803; James E. Herron, 1808 (Major Herron, U. S. A., died in Syracuse in 1818); John Kelso; Thomas Wilson, 1820, who died in 1824, and was succeeded by E. J. Kelso; William Kelley, 1836; James C. Marshall, 1839; Wilson King, 1842 and 1845; James Skinner, 1848; Samuel Perley, 1851; Alfred King, 1854; James Skinner, 1857 and 1860, and was re-elected and served to 1863; Samuel Rea, 1866.

In 1839 E. D. Gunnison was appointed first register and recorder, and held the office until after the fall election. William Kelly was elected 1839 and 1841; Thos. Moorhead, Jr. 1845; R. J. Sibley, 1849; D. McAllaster, 1851 and 1854; William P. Trimble, 1857; Samuel Rea, Jr., 1860-61.

Sheriffs.—Wilson Smith, 1804; Jacob Carmack, 1809; Jacob Spang, 1812; David Wallace, 1813; James Weston,[1] 1815; acting John C. Wallace, 1818; Thomas Laird, 1822; Stephen Woolverton, from 1816 and 1822-25; A. Thayer, 1826; A. W. Brewster, William Fleming, Thomas Mehaffy, 1835; A. Scott,[2]

[1] James E. Herron received the same number of votes; the Governor being a Democrat, it was decided in favor of James Weston.

[2] During Mr. Scott's term of office the sentence of the law was carried out in the execution of Henry Francisco, whose death warrant was issued December 12, 1837. This is the only instance of capital punishment in the history of Erie County, though others have doubtless been guilty of the crime of murder.

1838 ; E. M. W. Blaine, William E. McNair, M. W. Caughey, 1846 ; Peter E. Burton, 1849; Thomas Vincent, 1852 ; J. Killpatrick, 1855 ; John W. McLane, 1858, and served to 1861.

Coroners.—Abraham Smith, October 26, 1803 ; John Milroy, November 14, 1806 ; John Gray, November 17, 1807; John C. Wallace, November 8, 1809 ; John McCord, December 21, 1813 ; John Morris, April 23, 1816 ; Benjamin Russell, January 8, 1822 ; Rufus S. Reed, February 8, 1825 ; William Fleming, 1827 ; David Wallace, 1830 ; David McNair, 1833 ; Samuel Keefer, 1836 ; J. K. Caldwell, 1839 ; H. Bates, 1841 ; Thomas Dillon, 1845 ; S. L. Forster, 1848 ; S. Dunn, 1851 ; D. Burton, 1854 ; T. Dillon, 1857 ; R. Gaggin, 1860.

In July, 1805, the first section of the town of Erie was erected into a borough, and the May following the first borough officers were chosen.

In 1807 the sum of $2,000 was granted by the State to the

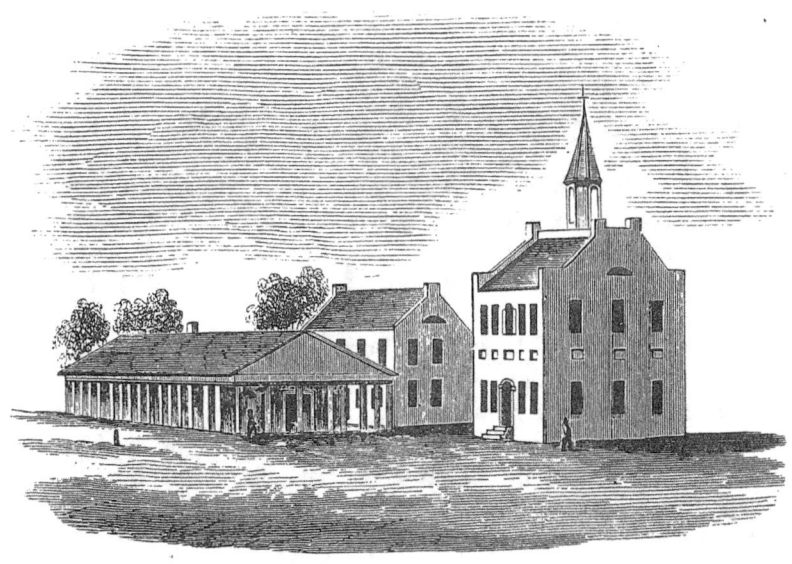

COURTHOUSE BUILT IN 1824.

commissioners, to expend in erecting buildings for county purposes. This courthouse was destroyed by fire March 23, 1823, with all the records. Another was immediately erected upon the same foundation, and after the same plan, which was not superseded until 1853. This second building served not only for courts and county purposes for thirty years, but for all lectures and public meetings of the citizens. Almost every church originated and held its meetings there, until otherwise provided. The famous railroad convocations were the last held there, and at that time it had become decidedly a gloomy and out-of-date edifice.

In 1852 the corner stone of the present commodious and imposing structure was laid. Judge John Vincent, who was present at the ceremony, and had filled the office of associate judge since 1805, remarked that he himself had selected and purchased the ground for the county commissioners forty-eight years before.

The ground plan of the building is sixty-one feet by one hundred and thirty-two, and the height from the ground to the top of the vane one hundred and twenty-eight feet. It is of the Roman-Corinthian order, and was designed by Thomas H. Walter. The whole cost of the building was between $64,000 and $65,000.

March 20, 1811, an act passed the Legislature "that the beach of the lake from the upper corner of the garrison tract, and for twenty perches back from the water's edge, down the lake to the out lots, and from thence down the same, including all the land between the out lots and the water's edge to the tract of land No. 38, shall be and remain a public landing for the use of the inhabitants and others."

In 1833 the inhabitants of the borough petitioned for an alteration in the law incorporating the borough, "stating that on a fair experiment they had found the existing laws insufficient to promote conveniency and good order and public utility." This resulted in the alteration of the whole charter, excepting a part of the tenth section.

In 1833 a fine was imposed, of five hundred dollars or imprisonment not exceeding six months, for cutting timber on the peninsula or setting fire to the shrubbery. R. S. Reed was appointed superintendent for five years.

In 1833 the third section, belonging to the commonwealth, of in and out lots was granted to the borough of Erie to con-

HISTORY OF ERIE COUNTY. 103

struct a canal basin in the Bay of Presqu'ile opposite the borough of Erie; provided that one hundred acres of the said land be reserved for the use of a county poorhouse, to be selected by three persons appointed by the county commissioners.

The question of having a poorhouse was put to vote soon after, and carried by a small majority. Suitable buildings were soon after erected. The number of inmates during the year 1860 was 107; the number of deaths, 4; 4 were bound out, and 44 discharged. The receipts and cash in the treasury, $10,375.94. Expenditures, which include some old debts and expenses for a new building, $7,629.14. A requisition of $8,000 annually has been made on the county for several years past, for the support of the institution.

In 1834 the bounds of the borough were extended northwardly 1300 feet into the Bay of Presqu'ile.

In 1835 a resolution passed to proceed against any who might erect any tenement on the peninsula or upon any part of the work erected to deepen the entrance to the harbor, or to place wood or other materials upon the public works or any sandbar.

Also, in 1835, Erie was authorized to borrow $50,000 to supply the borough with water. This contemplated improvement was never carried out.

In 1841 Erie was supplied with water by wooden pipes communicating with a spring a mile or two distant, the expenses being paid by the consumers.

In 1838 a sale of one row of water lots in the second section was authorized, to pay the expense of grading and improving the streets and grounds of the second section.

In 1841 an act passed the Legislature to prevent the picking or gathering of cranberries on the peninsula, between July and October, with a fine of not less than ten dollars or more than twenty-five against every person so offending.[1]

[1] The first day of October has been from that time denominated "cranberry day," and in the popular sense has become an "institution." Whole families cross, the night before, kindle a fire, and are in readiness by the earliest dawn to proceed to the marshes where the cranberry abounds. The uninitiated may search and wander the day long and scarcely find a handful, while many a thrifty family has been provided with comforts for the winter, or even their dwellings respectably furnished by this day's profits. The number of boats being limited, toward evening an undue eagerness sometimes results in the swamping of boats and other accidents, which are often aggravated by intemperance.

In 1843 an act passed the Legislature repealing the Nicholson Court of Pleas, which had been instituted in 1840. Without affording time for investigation, this court threatened to sell many of the farms in Erie County, as well as in other parts of the State, and dispossess those who had resided upon them for more than forty years. John Nicholson, President of the Population Company, was also State Treasurer and a defaulter; hence, a lien was supposed to rest on the lands once held by him. In the central part of the State the plea was more plausible; most of the lands in Erie County having been purchased after John Nicholson was divested of all interest in them.

In 1851 the government of the borough of Erie was changed to that of a city, and divided into the East and West Wards. It now has four, bounded as follows: First Ward—East of State, and north of Eighth Streets; Second Ward—East of State, and south of Eighth Streets; Third Ward—West of State, and south of Eighth Streets; Fourth Ward—West of State, and north of Eighth Streets.

Erie, in 1860, had 11,113 inhabitants within its city limits of about four square miles; thirteen churches (particularly described in Chapter XII.); two fine public schoolhouses; a flourishing academy, and several excellent select schools. There are no incorporated banks in the county at present, but six private banking houses. For manufactures in iron there are two foundries, and the Eagle Furnace of Atchison & Henry, just without the city limits. The "Erie City Iron Works" of Liddell & Marsh employs 90 men, and manufactures steam engines, freight and passenger cars, drilling tools and pipe for oil wells, agricultural implements, mill gearing, farm bells, etc. They have also a planing mill and moulding room in connection with the furnace. The "Old Furnace" of Barr & Johnson employs 60 men, and manufactures stoves, farming implements, and mill, building, and machinery castings.

There are four grist mills in the city: Fairmount Mills, Crouch & Brother, has three runs of stone; Erie City, C. McSparren, four runs of stone; Canal Mill, William Kelley, three runs of stone; and Reed's Mill, Mrs. R. S. Reed, two runs of stone. Near the city are Elliot's Mill, J. Elliot, three runs of stone; Hopedale Mill, H. Gingrich, two runs of stone; six flour and feed stores, one wholesale.

There are three planing mills, two machine shops, two sash, etc., two stone potteries, and several petroleum oil refineries in different stages of progress. A piano-forte manufactory of Wm. Willing sometimes employs twenty men; the instruments are of a fine tone, and in demand. The pump manufactory of L. W. Olds supplies the home market, and sends a large number West. Besides this there are five breweries, one brass foundry, one gun shop, five watch shops, five saddle and harness shops, three for hats and caps, three coffinmakers, five cabinet and furniture stores, two soap and candles, four tin shops, four drugstores, two book, five hardware, eight millinery, one shirt manufactory, four dentists, three confectionery, two carriage manufactories and several small wagon shops, four daguerrean artists, four commission merchants on the dock, eleven dry goods stores—wholesale and retail, eight shoe stores, five clothing stores, five wholesale groceries, twenty-one retail groceries, and ten dealers in bituminous coal.

The first borough election was held May 5, 1806, and resulted as follows: John C. Wallace, Burgess; Judah Colt, Rufus S. Reed, George Buehler, Robert Hays, George Schantz, Town Council; Robert Irwin, High Constable.

At the first meeting James E. Herron was appointed Town Clerk; Thomas Forster, Wm. Wallace, James Baird, Street Commissioners; Wm. Bell, Treasurer. Burgesses—Thomas Wilson, 1807; George Buehler, 1808 and 1809; John C. Wallace, 1810 and 1811; Samuel Hays, 1812; Judah Colt, 1813; George Moore, 1814 and 1815; Thomas H. Sill, 1816 and 1817; George Moore, 1818 and 1819; Judah Colt, 1820 and 1821; John Morris, 1822, 1823, and 1824; John C. Wallace, 1825, 1826, and 1827; Tabor Beebe, 1828; Thomas H. Sill, 1829; Wm. Johns, 1830; Geo. A. Elliot, 1831; Thomas Forster, chosen 1832, Tabor Beebe acted instead; Thos. H. Sill, 1833; J. M. Sterrett, 1835; J. B. Laughead, 1836 and 1837; James L. White, March, 1838; Wm. Kelley, 1839; Myron Goodwin, 1840; Rufus S. Reed, 1841; Thomas Stewart, 1842; Thomas H. Sill, 1843 and 1844;

Charles W. Kelso, 1845; Wm. Kelley, 1846 and 1847; Charles W. Kelso, 1848; A. W. Brewster, 1849; B. B. Vincent, 1850; Thomas G. Colt, first Mayor, 1851, from May acting Mayor; M. Whallon, April, 1852; A. King, March, 1853 and 1854; W. Laird, 1855 and 1856; James Hoskinson, 1857; W. Laird, 1858; S. Smith, 1859 and 1860; P. Metcalf, 1862 to 1865; F. F. Farrar; W. L. Scott, 1866; O. Noble, 1867 to 1871; W. L. Scott; C. M. Reed until H. Rawle, 1874 to 1875; J. W. Hammond, 1876; Selden Marvin, 1877; D. I. Jones, 1878; I. J. McCarter, 1881 to 1882; P. Becker, 1883 to 1884; F. F. Adams, 1885; F. A. Mizener, 1886; J. C. Brady, 1887 and 1888; Charles S. Clarke; Walter Scott, 1893.

The first city officers were elected May 15, 1851.

Mayor—T. G. Colt.

High Constable—A. C. Landon.

Select Council—East Ward: A. W. Brewster, F. Sevin, Clark McSparren. West Ward: S. M. Carpenter, John Zimmerly, Wm. M. Gallagher.

Common Council—East Ward: P. Metcalf, L. L. Momeyer, O. D. Spafford, J. D. Dunlap, A. A. Craig, Josiah Kellogg. West Ward: James Skinner, Wilson King, Thomas Dillon, S. W. Keefer, D. G. Landon, Adam Atchison.

Collectors of the Customs for the District of Presqu'ile—Thomas Forster, 1801; Edwin J. Kelso, 1836; Charles W. Kelso, 1845; William M. Gallagher, 1849; Murray Whallon; James Lytle, 1853; John Brawley, 1857; Murray Whallon; Charles M. Tibbals, 1859.

District of Presqu'ile embraces the whole coast line of the State of Pennsylvania on Lake Erie; it contains about forty miles of shore, and has three shipping points—Erie, the port of entry, Northeast, and Elk Creek, the business of the two latter being principally the shipment of staves and lumber.

Postmasters in Erie—John Hay; John Gray, 1809; Robert Knox, 1811, who resigned after having filled the office to general acceptance seventeen years; James Hughes, 1828; Robert Cochran, 1833; Smith Jackson, 1840; Andrew Scott, 1842; Robert Cochran, 1845; T. H. Sill, 1849; B. F. Sloan, 1853; Joseph M. Sterrett, 1861.

CHAPTER IX.

First Road—Population Company Roads—Erie and Waterford Turnpike—Salt Trade—Gen. O'Hara's Contract—Road to Buffalo—First Coaches—Erie Canal—Railroads—Erie and Wattsburg Railroad—Sunbury and Erie—Erie and Northeast—Franklin Canal Company—Pittsburg and Erie Railroad—Plank Roads.

THE opening of the first road in Erie County, as we have seen in Chapter III., was by the French, in 1753, from Erie to Waterford. This is still a good road, and in use for seven miles in a southerly direction from Erie; it is then scarcely traceable, but soon after is merged into the Erie and Waterford plank road, the site of the "new Shun-pike." In 1795, when the first settlers came to the Triangle, the traveled road was in pretty much the same location, as they allude to trees growing up in its path.[1]

The Pennsylvania Population Company made many of the roads. T. Rees, Esq., their agent, opened one in Harbor Creek in 1797, and Mr. Colt, who succeeded him, says: "June 3, 1797, set a number of men at opening roads leading to the intended station, nine and a half miles south of the mouth of Sixteen Mile Creek."

There was a road to Forster's mill (being the first erected in the county on Walnut Creek); to Conneauttee Lake, where Alexander Powers was located; to Conneaut Creek, Col. Dunning McNair's station; and to the headwaters of Beaver Creek, where Mr. Jabez Colt was assistant agent.

August, 1801.—Mr. Colt says: "Gen. Paine called to obtain a subscription in money for the purpose of opening a road from

[1] The first intention seemed to have been to make a military road, to level the hills and elevate the valleys; and cavities where the roots had been grubbed out, could be discerned for about half the distance from Erie. Hence it has been called the grubbed road, not as is usually supposed from the families of the name of Grubb on its line. Cannon balls, accoutrements, harness, and various implements were found along this route as late as 1825.

107

the east end of the Triangle to Buffalo Creek, and presented a letter from Mr. Kirtland, agent of the Connecticut Land Company, on the subject." Mr. Colt waived the matter until he should write to his principals, and after dinner Gen. Paine was furnished with provisions to carry him through the woods to Buffalo. The latter part of October a road was completed from Buffalo, westward, eighteen miles, at the expense of the Connecticut Company.

In 1805 the first election was held at Waterford for officers of the Erie and Waterford Turnpike Company. Col. Thomas Forster was chosen President, and Henry Baldwin, John Vincent, Ralph Marlin, James E. Herron, John C. Wallace, Wm. Miles, James Brotherton, and Joseph Hackney, Managers; Judah Colt, Treasurer.

This road was completed in 1809, and was a desirable improvement. Its location was less direct, and on higher ground than the French road, for the purpose of accommodating the farmers who were large shareholders.

The Waterford Turnpike was a particularly useful improvement, as all the salt for Pittsburg, and even down to the Falls of the Ohio (Louisville), passed from Erie to Waterford. Besides this, manufactures of iron and glass, whisky and flour from the Monongahela, and bacon from Kentucky, came up the Allegheny to Waterford, and from thence to Erie, which was then the depot for the lake country. The road was from two to five miles wide, diversified with stumps, logs, logheaps, and very deep mud holes. With such hindrances by the way, and from four to six oxen to guide, it was not unusual for a load of salt or provisions to be four days crossing the portage of fifteen miles. Often a part of the burden had to be abandoned. An instance is related of a barrel of whisky having been rolled at least half the distance by one of our most persevering and wealthy citizens.

At the risk of losing "the thread of the discourse," a few remarks will be introduced on the subject of the salt trade. Vessels leaving Buffalo for the West, from 1805 to 1810, were freighted principally with salt. In 1808, 6,000 barrels were registered at the custom house at Erie, and it is said 18,000 were at another season. It was the currency of the county.

In Mr. H. Russel's journal we find, "January, 1808, exchanged a pair of oxen for eight barrels of salt." In the *Erie Mirror*, dated January, 1809, is a well-written letter, signed "An Old Salt-hauler." It had been questioned whether the salt trade was beneficial to the county ; that perhaps it interfered with the cultivation of farms. In reply, he says the farmers were obliged to haul salt to procure the comforts, if not necessaries, of life, such as sugar, tea, coffee, wearing apparel, etc., as salt seemed to be the current medium of trade during the existence of the embargo. Indeed, it was the only commodity they had for market or exchange, and in proportion to the increase of the traffic the farmers of the county progressed in the improvement of the soil. Freightage from Buffalo to Erie was 87½ cents per barrel, and 12½ cents was the charge for storage; 12,000 barrels, in 1809, had been landed, according to the collector's books, which would amount to $12,000. The price of hauling from Erie to Waterford had been hitherto $1.50, amounting, on the same quantity, to $18,000. One dollar more was paid to convey it by water to Pittsburg. These several items made the aggregate receipts to the transporters of the county $42,000 in one year. The newly-finished turnpike diminished the cost of transportation to 50 cents per barrel : but it facilitated the carriage proportionably, as a team on the road could transport thirty-two barrels in the same time, and with greater ease than it formerly had done six. Salt was ordinarily from four to six months on the road from Salina to Pittsburg, and of one hundred barrels leaving the springs, seventy-five were required to pay the charges. Boats were built at Waterford expressly to float it down the river, and their construction was such as to prevent their return—this did not, however, add to the expense, as families removing still farther down were glad to purchase them.

The opening of the salt wells on the Kanawha and Kiskiminitas, about 1813, by affording a supply to that region, after a time, materially affected transportation here.

In *Pennsylvania Historical Collections* we find the following : "Gen. James O'Hara at an early day entered into a contract to supply Oswego with provisions, which he supposed could be furnished cheaper than from the settlements on the Mohawk. He had obtained correct information in relation to the manufacture of salt at Salina, and had in his contract an eye to supplying the Western country with salt.

"This was a project few would have undertaken, and fewer still carried out. The means of transportation had to be created: boats and teams must be constructed to get the salt from the works to Oswego, a vessel built to land it below the falls, wagons to carry it to Schlosser, and boats provided to carry it to Black Rock; there another vessel was required to convey it to Erie. The road to the head of French Creek had to be improved, and the salt carried across the portage in wagons; and, lastly, boats built to float it to Pittsburg.

"Mr. O'Hara packed his flour and provisions in barrels suitable for salt, and these were reserved in his contracts. Two vessels were built—one on Lake Erie, and another on Lake Ontario. The plan succeeded: salt of a fair quality could be sold at four dollars per bushel—half the price charged for that packed over the mountains. The vocation of packers was gone. Soon after, Onondaga salt was sold at twelve dollars per barrel of five bushels."

A duty of four cents per bushel was paid the State of New York, and it was forbidden by law to sell at the works for more than sixty cents per bushel.

The journey from Erie to Buffalo by land was much dreaded even to the completion of the railroad; previous to 1815 or 1820 it was absolutely dangerous. Travelers finding the land road through Cattaraugus woods almost impassable for wagons, would be induced, if the weather was not very boisterous, to pass around the point of rock projecting into the lake. Many fatal instances are recorded of persons unacquainted with the country being overwhelmed by the waves. The nature of the soil through the woods would scarcely admit of a good road, and a journey once made was scarcely forgotten, for passengers felt that then and there, they escaped narrowly with their lives. In "December, 1829, the road from Buffalo to Fredonia (in some places having been turnpiked late in the season) was so bad that two yoke of oxen were attached to the stage to draw it through, and all the male passengers worked their passage. The mail was three hours—more than a mile an hour—coming from Buffalo."

The following advertisement is found in the *Erie Gazette* for September 15, 1820 :

"Proposals will be received at the General Post-office for carrying the mail on the following route, until the fourteenth day of October next :

"From Buffalo, by Hamburg, Hanover, Fredonia, Portland, Westfield, Ripley, and Northeast, to Erie, Pennsylvania, once a week, ninety miles.

"Leave Buffalo every Saturday noon, and arrive at Erie the next Monday by six o'clock in the afternoon. Leave Erie every Tuesday at six a. m., and arrive at Buffalo the next Thursday by noon."

The mail to Pittsburg and by Philadelphia was more sure for the East. This, too, came in but once a week. The day this was due, people were seen standing in the street looking for "McGill," who, at first, with his mail came on horseback ; afterward, the increased weight required a horse for the mail alone, which he led by his side. On one occasion the eager expectants looked and looked in vain ; a bear had crossed the carrier's path, and the frightened mail horse fled to the woods, where, after a search of two or three days, he was found.

In the *Erie Gazette* for December, 1820, we find the following, being something new : that a stage for the conveyance of passengers as well as the mail would run regularly once a week from Erie to Buffalo and back, after the first of January. It would leave Erie every Tuesday, and arrive at Buffalo on Thursday ; leave Buffalo on Saturday, and arrive at Erie on Monday. The proprietors (Messrs. Bird & Deming) did not expect to make money in the business ; the convenience of the public seemed to require the experiment to be made, and if it met with support was to be continued and enlarged.

January 8, 1824, we find a stage had commenced running twice a week between Erie and Cleveland. Arrangements were also making for carrying the mail twice a week.

February 10, 1825, the mail coach commenced running

through in a day from this place to Buffalo. This may be said to terminate the ancient history of highways and conveyances in Erie County.

In the *Erie Gazette*, July, 1826, is an article intended to arouse Pennsylvanians to the importance of a canal, and it was well adapted to the purpose. It speaks of the wondrous improvement in this region in the previous thirty years. "Then the site of the village was a wilderness, and the path of the Indian the only guide for the daring traveler. Now it has upwards of a thousand inhabitants, and roads leading to Buffalo, Cleveland, and Pittsburg, three great points of intercourse equal to any in the western part of the Union. From these three places we have twenty-seven arrivals of stages every week, all of which remain here over night. From Buffalo there are fourteen arrivals, from Cleveland ten, and from Pittsburg three. Three years ago we had three arrivals: once a week from Cleveland, in a one-horse wagon; once a week from Buffalo, in a two-horse wagon; and once from Pittsburg, in a hack. Now there is not a vehicle enters our village for the conveyance of travelers but post-coaches, with teams equal if not superior to any in Pennsylvania.

"In addition to this, three steamboats for the conveyance of passengers enter and leave our harbor every week, and in a few days there will be five. There are also from two to ten schooners which enter and clear our harbor each week. What an important point this would be to Pennsylvania, if she would do her duty! This unexampled increase of travel and business owes its existence entirely to the New York Canal. . . . Pennsylvania is waiting for experience. She will soon have more of it than she wants in contrasting Philadelphia with New York."

There was much delay in prosecuting the Erie extension of the Pennsylvania Canal, for the want of decision as to the route; one of the first efforts at settling the question was the appointment in 1823, of Thomas Forster, of Erie, James Herrington, of Crawford, and William Marks, Jr., of Allegheny, commissioners to explore the different routes, and report to the Governor.

In 1825 a survey was made by Major Douglass, of the army.[1] In 1835 an appropriation of $200,000 was made, and a loan of $150,000 authorized should the appropriation be expended before another could be had. In 1837 the Governor borrowed $200,000, at an interest of four and a half per cent, authorized by the resolution of 1835. In 1838 two appropriations were made: January 9, one of $100,000, and April 14, one of $300,000. July 4, 1838, the breaking of ground for the canal was united with the celebration of American independence. A procession was formed under the direction of Capt. Dobbins, consisting of the orator of the day (J. H. Walker), the clergy, and committee of arrangements, forty or fifty of the earliest settlers with plows, wheelbarrows, spades, shovels, etc., and a large concourse of citizens. The breaking of ground was by one of the pioneers, Capt. M. Strong, who had resided in Erie County since 1795, and who related some very interesting facts and reminiscences.

In 1838 the route from Conneaut Lake was not determined, the commissioners insisting that the Legislature decide. Shortly after the western one was chosen.

The Erie Canal Company was incorporated in 1843, and accomplished the work which united the Ohio and the lakes, and which had been talked of a quarter of a century. The State had expended upon it upwards of $4,000,000, and but $211,000 was required to complete the one hundred and thirty-six miles, which was the shortest connection that could be made between the Ohio and the lake, and which opened to the market immense fields of coal of a superior quality.

The stockholders elected for managers of the company were R. S. Reed, President; T. G. Colt, Wm. M. Watts, B. B. Vincent, J. A. Tracy, Erie; M. B. Lowry, Crawford; James M. Power, Mercer; C. M. Reed, Treasurer; and Wm. Kelley, Secretary.

---

[1] The latter part of October, 1825, while the surveyors of the canal route were engaged in sounding the lake off the mouth of Elk Creek, a melancholy accident occurred. The boat, having in it four persons, was much dashed by a fresh breeze, and began to fill. Mr. Cranch, a son of Judge Cranch, of the District of Columbia, being an expert swimmer, for the purpose of lightening the boat deliberately plunged into the lake, having first with care placed an elegant gold watch, which he highly valued, between his teeth, to prevent its being injured by the water. He had gone a few perches from the shore when he suddenly sank. He was immediately taken out, but could not be resuscitated.

December 5, 1844, the first boats came through to Erie. First the *R. S. Reed*, Capt. Drum, laden with Mercer County coal; next, the packet boat *Queen of the West*, Capt. Armstrong, her deck and spacious apartments literally crowded with a dense mass of human beings, each desirous of being numbered among the first passengers by canal packet to the lake.

When the *Queen* entered the harbor, the deep-mouthed cannon gave out its thunder tones, and a shout, long, loud, and hearty, went up from the multitudes. To W. Milnor Roberts, chief engineer, special thanks were due for the early completion of the work after its abandonment by the State. The Wayne Greys paraded the streets during the day, and a ball at the Reed House concluded the celebration.

In December, 1840, two tons of bituminous coal were brought from Evansburg, Crawford County, a distance of forty miles, partly by canal, and sold at five and a half dollars per ton, at which it was thought cheaper fuel than wood at one dollar per cord. The amount of coal received at Erie by canal is as follows:

Year	Tons	Year	Tons
In 1845	15,000	In 1853	123,031
" 1846	27,000	" 1854	95,611
" 1847	51,000	" 1855	141,184
" 1848	70,000	" 1856	112,811
" 1849	79,613	" 1857	126,159
" 1850	57,741	" 1858	99,924
" 1851	72,943	" 1859	128,856
" 1852	76,650	" 1860	129,807

The first coal ever sent to this city, by way of the canal, was two boat loads, containing about one hundred tons, shipped some twelve or fifteen years ago by William Fruit, Esq., from a mine near Clarksville, Mercer County. It being a new article of traffic, says the *Meadville Republican*, Mr. Fruit found it difficult to dispose of his small cargo; but after running about, from one dealer to another, for two days, he finally disposed of it to Gen. C. M. Reed, at less than cost, taking a "slow note" for pay.

The officers of the Canal Company, 1860, were C. M. Reed, President; J. C. Marshall, A. Scott, P. Metcalf, D. McAllister, J. A. Tracy, J. Hearn, Directors; D. McAllister, Treasurer; A. H. Caughey, Secretary; William W. Reed, Superintendent.

HISTORY OF ERIE COUNTY.

Tolls for 1858	$ 52,968 38
" " 1859	68,574 65
" " 1860 ....$104,336 12	
Water rents 975 32	
Total receipts for 1860	$105,311 44
Expenditures for repairs and supervision	$ 45,783 70
Building a new aqueduct over Walnut Creek	17,039 60
Salaries of secretary, treasurer, superintendent, and collectors	6,370 50
Incidental expenses, including legal services, printing, rent, etc.	1,185 38
Expenditures for 1860	$70,379 18

By a resolution of the directors, $25,000 were appropriated to the payment of three per cent interest on the bonds and interest certificates of the company for the year ending January 1, 1861.

Railroads.—In 1831 a railroad convention met at Fredonia, for the purpose of making arrangements for the construction of a railroad from Buffalo to the State line of Pennsylvania. Erie sent C. M. Reed, P. S. V. Hamot, and T. H. Sill, a delegation having been invited. The president of the convention was Thomas B. Campbell; secretaries, Oliver Lee and James Mullet. It was understood that their road should be met on the part of Pennsylvania.

In 1835 a railroad from Philadelphia to Erie was first talked of; it was to be laid out by way of Harrisburg, West Branch, Clarion River, and Franklin, and it was thought to possess the great advantage of not requiring one inclined plane.

A macadamized road was petitioned for about this time, to connect Erie with the national road.

In 1836 books were opened, and the capital stock subscribed of the Erie Railroad Company. This was to connect with the Cassadaga Road, a branch of the New York and Erie, thirty-five miles in length, extending from the mouth of the creek, three miles from Jamestown, to the State line, three miles from Wattsburg. The Erie Railroad would have been twenty-three miles in length, but the New York and Erie was not completed for many years, and consequently by that route there could be no connection with New York. The Erie and Northeast seemed to better meet the views of all parties.

In 1837 the Sunbury and Erie Railroad bill passed, and this road was to form the last link in the chain of improvements between Lake Erie and Philadelphia. From Harrisburg to Philadelphia was completed; from Harrisburg to Sunbury was incorporated. At Erie and Warren the event was the cause of rejoicings, and a new era seemed to dawn on Pennsylvania. The stock necessary to secure the charter was taken by the United States Bank. During the years 1838 and 1839 a corps of engineers, under Edward Miller, explored the country between the points mentioned in the charter.

The whole distance from Sunbury to Erie is 270 miles; from Erie to Warren, 66 miles; Warren to Lock Haven, 136 miles; Lock Haven to Williamsport, 28 miles; Williamsport to Sunbury, 40 miles. At this latter place three distinct railroads from New York, Philadelphia, and Baltimore now converge.

This road is ninety miles less, in distance to the sea-board, than the New York and Erie, and the local trade of the road it is supposed will maintain it. An unsuccessful effort was made in 1852 to have the road terminate at Cleveland.

In 1854 the City of Philadelphia subscribed $1,000,000, and shortly after doubled the subscription. The City of Erie subscribed $300,000 and 150 acres in water lots, and Erie County $200,000. The State of Pennsylvania conveyed her canals to the company for $3,500,000 of Sunbury and Erie Railroad bonds.

December, 1854, the completion of the road to Williamsport was celebrated by about five hundred citizens of Philadelphia, including the president of the road, Hon. James Cooper, the directors, city councils, etc. The party arrived at Erie *via* Elmira and Niagara, and were hospitably entertained by the citizens. At a ball and supper given them at the Reed House, Hon. James Thompson presided.

The rails used upon this road are from the Montour and Rough and Ready Mills at Danville, Pennsylvania, and the Lackawanna Mill at Scranton. Lock Haven is the site of the company's workshops.

The company in 1859 had just one half of the road (135 miles) ironed: eighty-one miles being on the eastern, and fifty-four on the western division. More than half the work on the remaining one hundred and thirty-five miles was finished, and sixty-eight miles actually graded and ready for the superstructure. Liddell & Marsh, of the Erie City Iron Works, constructed twenty-five or thirty cars for the western division.

A celebration, numerously attended, was held at Warren, December, 1859, on the opening of the road from Erie to that place.

The earnings of the western division have equaled nearly $3,000 weekly, or six per cent on the cost of construction.

The discovery of petroleum in Northwestern Pennsylvania has added materially to the receipts of the Sunbury and Erie Road, which has been a very great convenience in getting the commodity to market.

Receipts of oil at the Erie station for

1859.					
November............	21	barrels.	July....................	1,432	barrels.
December.............	304	"	August...............	2,341	"
			September..........	2,227	"
1860.			October...............	2,775	"
January..............	63	"	November...........	3,069	"
February.............	115	"	December...........	6,431	"
March.................	414	"	1861		
April...................	980	"	January...........15,092		"
May...................1,159		"	February............	9,421	"
June....................	772	"	March.................	4,383	"
			April..................	5,521	"

A bill supplementary to the act incorporating the Sunbury and Erie Railroad Company was passed in the spring of 1861. The first section changes the name of the company to the Philadelphia and Erie Railroad Company.

The second section authorizes the company to issue five thousand bonds, not exceeding in amount the aggregate sum of one million pounds sterling or five millions United States currency. The bonds are to draw six per cent interest per annum, payable semi-annually, the principal to be paid in twenty years. The bonds are not subject to taxation, and as security for the payment of principal and interest the company is authorized to execute in trust a mortgage of the whole line of its railroad, finished and unfinished, from Sunbury to the harbor of Erie, and its appurtenances, including all locomotives and cars which may at any time be placed thereon, together with all its real estate, rights, and privileges. The mortgage to be delivered to trustees therein named, and recorded in the several counties in which the property may be situated, and shall remain the first mortgage on all the property therein described until fully satisfied, excepting the road extending from Sunbury to Williamsport, on which a mortgage of one million dollars now exists.

The third section authorizes the company to issue forty bonds for $100,000 each, payable in forty years from the date thereof, bearing six per cent interest from and after January 1, 1872. A second mortgage on the road to be executed to secure the payment of said bonds, which bonds and mortgage the company are to deliver to the commissioners of the sinking fund, to be retained as collateral security for payment of the five per cent bonds for $3,500,000 now in the sinking fund. The Treasurer of the Commonwealth shall cancel and surrender all the bonds belonging to the company and deposited in his office for safe keeping, under the provisions of the act for the sale of the State canals.

Section fourth extends the time for the payment of the $3,500,000, now in the sinking fund, till the maturity of the $4,000,000, which when paid will be in full satisfaction of the said $3,500,000 bonds : provided that the whole amount of principal and interest so to be paid by the company shall not be less than the debt now owing by the company to the State with the stipulated interest thereon till the time of payment.

When this and other railroads in progress are completed, it is expected that Erie will assume her true importance, so that the census of 1870 will find it a flourishing, noisy, and ambitious city, rivaling in size and trade the two large cities of Cleveland and Buffalo, which have hitherto overshadowed it.

"Pennsylvania is blest in having three border outlets through ports on the three great water ways—the Atlantic Ocean, the Ohio River, and the great lakes. Philadelphia, Pittsburg, and Erie City are the portals of the Commonwealth, all other ways of ingress and egress being only as windows in the stately edifice. The public men of an earlier generation purchased and annexed the Triangle which made Erie City a harbor in Pennsylvania, and yet, down to this day, there is no direct communications between that lake port which was acquired and the seaport where the State was cradled, although a route to the lakes was one of the objects of the acquisition." [The Sunbury and Erie was incorporated for this purpose, and in 1846, in the incorporation of the Pennsylvania Central, a branch was authorized deflecting to Erie.] "Here we have the proof that in the minds of men devoted to the consideration of commercial subjects, and to carrying lines, the thought was ever present, that the three custom house cities should have direct and unclogged railroad facilities, uniting each with the other, and opening from the interior of the State to its border cities a cheap and convenient transit." In its unfinished condition the Sunbury and Erie Railroad is a double failure, for it fails to pay interest on the bonds held by the State, and fails to meet public expectations inasmuch as it is not all open for traffic.

The Erie and Northeast Railroad Company was incorporated April 12, 1842, with a capital of $5,000,000. March 11, 1846, the capital stock was reduced to $600,000. Books for subscription were opened October 19, 1846, and sufficient stock subscribed to secure the charter. Letters-patent on the charter were granted December 16, 1846. The first election was held January 22, 1847, and resulted in the choice of C. M. Reed, President; William Kelley, Henry Cadwell, Smith Jackson, A. W. Brewster, M. Courtright, James Williams, Directors; and G. Sanford, Treasurer.

In the spring of 1849 the road was surveyed under the direction of M. Courtright; July 26, 1849, contracts were made for the construction of the road.

By an agreement entered into April 27, 1850, with the Dunkirk and State Line Railroad, the Erie and Northeast agreed to lay a six-foot track, that the cars of the New York and Erie might run directly to Erie, and this city be virtually the terminus of that road. Previously the Dunkirk and State Line Road had adopted the Erie and Northeast to do their business on the same, and by this arrangement expected to have an advantage over their great rival, the New York Central.

This led to a warm controversy between the two companies, and a parallel road was contemplated, which was the Sheridan Road, with a six-foot track, to connect with the Erie and Northeast *via* Westfield and Fredonia, and stock sufficient to secure the charter was taken. Finally, a compromise was effected by which it was intended that neither company should have the advantage, and a gauge foreign to both was adopted, viz., the four foot ten inches, being the gauge of the road constructing from Erie west to Cleveland.

The Erie and Northeast being laid according to agreement, a six-foot track compelled two changes of all freight and travel within nineteen miles, viz., at Erie and at the State Line.

The first cars came in on this road January 10, 1852. The Franklin Canal Company had constructed a railroad to the Ohio State line, and a connection through to Cleveland was effected in November of the same year. The formal opening of this road was November 23, 1852, when the cars left Erie at nine a. m. for Ashtabula, and returned at three o'clock, with their numbers greatly increased. A party of three hundred partook of a sumptuous dinner at Brown's Hotel. Speeches were made by Judge Galbraith, Alfred Kelly, Wm. S. Lane, and M. B. Lowry, and a change in the gauge law (which law compelled a break at Erie) was denounced.

The Franklin Canal Company was incorporated on the 27th of April, 1844, for the purpose of reconstructing and repairing the Franklin Division of the Pennsylvania Canal from the aqueduct on French Creek to the mouth of that creek, it having decayed and become dilapidated. On April 9, 1849, a supplement was passed, authorizing the company to construct a railroad instead of repairing the canal, the graded line or towing path of the canal to be the bed of the road, and giving the company the privilege of increasing its stock to $500,000, and extending northward to the lake and south to Pittsburg. In the building of this road, Judge John Galbraith was the influential manager.

A few months after the completion of the railroad from Erie to Cleveland, the Pennsylvania gauge law was repealed, and a contract was entered into November 17, 1853, between the Buffalo and State Line and Erie and Northeast Companies, by which the latter agreed to alter their track to one of four foot ten, thereby making a continuous gauge from Buffalo to Cleveland.

The first attempt of the Erie and Northeast Company to

change their gauge occasioned the contentions of 1853 and 1854, better known as the "railroad war."

The particulars of this severe but bloodless struggle can doubtless be more profitably discussed at a future period.[1] The citizens of Erie felt highly aggrieved, and not less so the railroad company and the traveling community. The loss financially to each of these parties was immense. In the fierce and prolonged excitement men grew prematurely old, and the tax on temper and nerves to all concerned was not of small account. In the course of time the courts settled the exciting question ; the two breaks between Buffalo and Cleveland have disappeared, and the city, once distracted by civil discord, is again peaceful and prosperous.

An act of the Legislature, passed in January, 1854, annulled the charter of the Franklin Canal Company, always considered doubtful, and invested the Governor with plenary power to make such a disposition of the road as in his judgment would best promote the interests of the State and the great objects to be attained.

The same winter Gov. Bigler visited Erie in person, and was received with the greatest enthusiasm, being met at the depot by the military and firemen with torchlights, and a large concourse of citizens.

In June, 1854, the Franklin Canal Company was merged into the Cleveland, Painesville, and Ashtabula Railroad Company.

In 1855 an act passed the Legislature repealing the charter of the Erie and Northeast Road, on the ground that it did not come to the borough, as stipulated in the act of incorporation. Hon. J. Cassey held it for the State, and afterward our late Governor, Wm. F. Packer.

April 22, 1856, it was reincorporated, the directors being required to subscribe $400,000 to the Pittsburg and Erie Road.

The earnings of the Cleveland and Erie Railroad for 1860 amounted to $1,063,405.23 ; operating expenses, $429,758.49. The road paid during the year, as dividends, five per cent in cash January 1, 1860 ; five per cent in scrip January 1, 1860 ; and five per cent in cash July 1, 1860.

[1] See supplement.

Number of through passengers on the road.................162,172
Number of way passengers...88,199
Total tonnage of freight carried over the road..........254,594 tons.
Merchandise carried over the road................................68,815 "
Lumber   "   "   "   ....5,096 "
Iron   "   "   "   ....2,004 "
Live stock   "   "   "   ....74,712 "
Flour   "   "   "   ....198,802 "

At a meeting of the stockholders of the Erie and Northeast Railroad, held at the office of the company January 17, 1854, the following named gentlemen were elected directors for the ensuing year: John A. Tracy, Milton Courtright, John H. Walker, Dean Richmond (of Buffalo), Prescott Metcalf, Andrew Scott, and John Brawly.

The Pittsburg and Erie Railroad Company was incorporated in 1850. C. M. Reed, President; M. Courtright, William Kelley, James Williams, A. W. Brewster, C. McSparren, James C. Marshall, John A. Tracy, P. Metcalf, J. McClure, B. B. Vincent, Smith Jackson, Directors; and David McAllister, Secretary.

The road was made to Jamestown, sixty miles, in 1859, and its final completion is soon expected.

Erie City Railroad was chartered in 1853, to extend from the harbor at Presqu'ile to a point on the New York and Pennsylvania State line in Northeast, Greenfield, or Venango townships. This, as a communication with New York, will have an advantage over the Dunkirk Road of twenty miles.

The first officers were M. Courtright, President; C. M. Reed, J. H. Walker, James Skinner, P. Arbuckle, M. W. Caughey, J. C. Spencer, J. W. Hart, J. McClure, William M. Arbuckle, J. A. Tracy, William C. Curry, and P. Metcalf, Directors; J. C. Spencer, Secretary and Treasurer. The road between Little Valley and Jamestown was put under contract in 1852.

The Erie and Waterford plank road was completed in 1851; Irvin Camp, President. The Erie and Wattsburg the same year; J. H. Williams, President. The Erie and Edinboro plank road was completed December, 1852; John Galbraith, President.

The plank roads have all been a benefit to the country and to the towns through which they pass. The one connecting with Wattsburg has wrought a great change in the aspect of the country. It was estimated in the summer of 1859 that one

hundred cords of hemlock wood were brought in daily, besides large quantities of hemlock bark, which was shipped for the West.

CHAPTER X.

Shipping—The Washington, the First Vessel built on the South Shore of the Lake—Hudson's Bay Company—British Government Vessels—American Government Vessels—The Salina—Valuable Cargoes—Walk-in-the-water—First Lighthouse—William Penn—First Steamer at Chicago—Cholera—Tonnage and Number of Vessels in 1810-20-31-36-47-60—Lake Disasters—Commerce of Port of Presqu'ile—Vessels and Tonnage registered at Presqu'ile in 1860—United States Steamer Michigan—Revenue Cutters.

CAPTAIN WILLIAM LEE'S vessel (name not known) propelled by sails and oars, was the only one on the south side of Lake Erie in 1795. Capt. Lee had no crew, and made trips only when he could have "passengers enough able and willing to man his boat." He resided at Chippewa, and it was in his boat Col. S. Reed, family, and goods came up in the spring of 1795.

Mr. Colt's journal says: "May 30, 1798, Mrs. Colt and myself took passage at Fort Erie in sloop Weasle, Dennaw, master. Set sail about two o'clock p. m. The wind continuing from the east, we were under way until about twelve at night, and lest we should run past the harbor of Presqu'ile, the vessel was hove to, and lay in that situation until six o'clock in the morning of Thursday.

"31.—We found ourselves off Chautauqua Creek, about twenty miles from our desired haven; at evening arrived in the harbor of Presqu'ile. We were much seasick during the passage."

In September, 1798, Eliphalet Beebe launched a sloop of thirty-six tons at the mouth of Four Mile Creek (east of Erie), called the sloop Washington. This was probably the first vessel built on the south side of the lake. It was built for the use of the Population Company, was sold in November, 1801, to Joshua Fairbanks of Queenston, for land and salt, was taken across the portage from Chippewa to Queenston, and lost on its first trip on Lake Ontario.

In 1799 Capt. William Lee built the Good Intent, thirty tons, R. S. Reed part owner, at the mouth of Mill Creek. Lost at Port Abino in 1806, with all on board.

In 1800 Eliphalet Beebe built the Harlequin, which was lost during her first season, with all on board.

In 1805 Thomas Wilson built a schooner of one hundred tons at Erie, called the Mary; in 1808 one half was sold to James Rough and George Buehler, and the remainder to Porter, Barton & Co. It was sailed by Capt. Rough until the war, when it was purchased by the United States.

The Erie Packet, a sloop of twenty tons, was built by Capt. William Lee, at Fort Erie, in 1796, for the Presqu'ile trade—Presqu'ile being the principal settlement at that time.

In 1803 the Niagara, of thirty tons, was built by the United States government, and bought by Porter, Barton & Co. Her name was changed to the Nancy; sailed by Capt. R. O'Neil.

In 1802-3 Porter, Barton & Co., contractors for the army, built at Black Rock the sloop Contractor, of sixty-four tons. Sill, Thompson & Co., at the same place, built the Catharine. These were both purchased by the government in 1812; the name of the former was changed to the Trippe, and the latter to the Somers.

In 1808 Major Carter built a schooner at Cleveland (which was the first built there) of forty-five tons, called the Zephyr. She was sailed by Capt. Cummings.

We have alluded, in Chapter II., to the Hudson's Bay Company and British vessels on Lake Erie in 1789. The Speedwell is heard of at Malden in 1792, and in 1796 they had in commission two armed vessels—the Ottawa, commanded by Capt. Cowan, and the Chippewa, by Capt. Grant, each of about ninety tons.

In 1804 they built the brig Camden, of one hundred tons and six guns; in 1806, the brig Hunter; and in 1807, the armed sloop Hope, which was lost near St. Joseph's, on Lake Huron. In 1809 the Queen Charlotte was built, and in 1810 the armed schooner Lady Prevost. These vessels did not belong to the royal navy, but to what was called the provincial marine service; or, as a London newspaper stated the matter (and which was true before 1812) after Commodore Perry's victory: "It may serve to diminish our vexation at the occurrence to learn that *the flotilla* in question *was not any branch of the British navy*, but was solely manned, equipped, and managed by the public exertions of certain Canadians, who had formed themselves into a kind of *Lake Fencibles*. It was not the royal navy, *but a local force*—a kind of mercantile military." A fictitious consolation, truly! Commodore Barclay, Captain Finnis, etc., were not distinguished from "mercantile military," in the editor's mind.

As to the American vessels, at the time Gen. Wayne took possession of Detroit, in 1796, the quartermaster purchased from a merchant the sloop Detroit, of fifty tons, for the use of the government. It was the same vessel that conveyed Gen. Wayne to Erie previous to his decease. She was wrecked the next fall, near Erie.

The Wilkinson, of sixty-seven tons, is heard of in 1801.

In 1802 the government built two vessels at Detroit—the brig Adams, of one hundred tons, sailed by Capt. Breevoort, and the schooner Tracy, of fifty-three tons—the latter was wrecked about 1809, on the reef off Fort Erie. The Adams continued in commission until the war of 1812, and was taken by the British at the surrender of Gen. Hull, and called the Detroit. She was one of the vessels cut out from Fort Erie, by Capt. Elliot, on the night of the 8th of October, 1812.

The British had in the merchant service, at an early day, the sloop Nancy, thirty-eight tons; the schooner Nancy, ninety-four tons; the Charlotte, eighty tons; the Caledonia, a brig of eighty-five tons; the sloop Hunter, of forty tons; and schooner Thames, of eighty tons.

In 1809 Mr. R. S. Reed and Capt. Dobbins purchased a schooner called the Charlotte, of ninety tons, from Alex. McIntosh, of Moy, Canada. Her name was changed to Salina, and Capt. Dobbins sailed her until 1812. Being at Mackinaw at its capture, this vessel was also taken by the British, and its captain, crew, and Messrs. R. S. and Wm. W. Reed made prisoners. She was converted into a cartel, and sent down, in company with the Mary, with provisions to

Detroit. At Detroit Gen. Hull received her from Capt. Dobbins, and she was included in the general surrender by him to the British. Here Capt. Dobbins left her and returned to Erie. While the Detroit and other vessels were building, the British made use of the Salina to transport provisions and stores from different parts of the lake. At last she was frozen up in the ice near Malden, in December, 1812, and being abandoned, drifted down the lake, inclosed in ice; was discovered opposite Erie, and, after having property taken from her by the citizens to the amount of about $2,000, was set on fire.

In 1811 the Salina had a remarkable cargo for value,[1] which consisted of $120,000 worth of furs, at the Mackinaw valuation—at Montreal their worth would be doubled. The agent of the Northwest Company, to whom the furs belonged, was on board, and the furs were stowed upon deck as well as below.

The schooner Mariner, Capt. Blake, August, 1825, landed a cargo at Buffalo still more valuable—that of furs belonging to the American Fur Company worth $267,000. Usually the finer furs were conveyed to Montreal by an inland route. From Mackinaw they were taken to the mouth of Canadian River, which communicated by portage with Grand River, and thence down to the St. Lawrence in bark canoes. The skins and coarser portions were taken in vessels to Fort Erie, and by boats to Chippewa; across the portage to Queenston, and by vessels to Kingston; thence down the St. Lawrence in boats.

May 28, 1818, the first steamboat on Lake Erie was launched at Black Rock. This was the Walk-in-the-water, of three hundred tons, and commanded by Capt. Job Fish. She was not able to ascend the rapids with her engine, but was drawn up by ten yoke of oxen. She was built by Noah Brown, of New York, for Gilbert and J. B. Stewart, of Albany, and was visited as a curiosity by the whole country.

[1] A modern costly cargo: "May 21, 1861. The steamer Illinois arrived at Detroit yesterday, from Lake Superior, with a cargo second in value only to that brought by the Mineral Rock, which arrived the day previous. The Illinois cargo was composed entirely of copper, and was valued at $101,452.80."

In the *Detroit Gazette* we find an account of her first passage to that city. "The Walk-in-the-water left Buffalo at one and a half p. m. and arrived at Dunkirk thirty-five minutes past six on the same day. On the following morning she arrived at Erie—Capt. Fish having reduced her steam in order not to pass that place, where he took in a supply of wood." [The boat was visited by all the inhabitants during the day, and had the misfortune to get aground for a short time in the bay, a little west of French Street.] "At half-past seven p. m. she left Erie, and arrived at Cleveland at eleven o'clock Tuesday; at twenty minutes past six p. m. sailed, and reached Sandusky Bay at one o'clock on Wednesday; lay at anchor during the night, and then proceeded to Venice for wood; left Venice at three p. m., and arrived at the mouth of Detroit River, where she anchored during the night.

"The whole time of this first voyage from Buffalo to Detroit occupied forty-four hours and ten minutes—the wind ahead during the whole passage. Not the slightest accident happened during the voyage, and her machinery worked admirably.

"Nothing could exceed the surprise of the 'sons of the forest' on seeing the Walk-in-the-water move majestically and rapidly against wind and current, without sails or oars. Above Malden they lined the shores and expressed their astonishment by repeated shouts of 'Taiyoh nichee!' [An exclamation of surprise.]

"A report had been circulated among them that a 'big canoe' would soon come from the 'noisy waters,' which, by order of the 'great father' of the 'Chemo Komods' (Long Knives or Yankees), would be drawn through the lakes and rivers by a *sturgeon*. Of the truth of the report they were perfectly satisfied."

The cabins of the Walk-in-the-water were fitted up in a neat, convenient, and elegant style; and a trip to Buffalo was considered not only tolerable, but truly pleasant. Friday she made an excursion to Lake St. Clair, with a party of ladies and gentlemen, and returned to Buffalo in time to be again at Detroit the following week.

Tradition has it that Capt. Fish was not particularly pleased with the lake, and returned in a short time to his former command on the Hudson—the Firefly, running between Poughkeepsie and New York; that the pilot Davis being a thorough and accomplished seaman (which Capt. Fish did not profess to be) amused himself by exciting his fears and magnifying the dangers of lake navigation. The pilot had the command previous to the appointment of Capt. Jedediah Rodgers.

The first of November, 1821, the Walk-in-the-water stranded on the beach at Buffalo, having a full and valuable cargo, at a loss to her owners of $10,000 or $12,000. Her engine was placed in the Superior, which was built by a chartered company, and had an exclusive privilege in the navigable waters of New York. This privilege was abandoned after a decision of the Supreme Court of the United States.

The first steamboat launched at Erie was the William Penn, of two hundred tons, May 18, 1826. She was ninety-five feet keel, twenty-five feet beam, and eighty feet hold; being the sixth steamboat on the lake, and was built by the Erie and Chautauqua Steamboat Company. The company was incorporated the 10th of April, 1826, with Walter Smith, E. L. Tinker, Charles Townsend, R. S. Reed, P. S. V. Hamot, Josiah Kellogg, John F. Wight, Daniel Dobbins, and Peter Christie, Managers. A supplement in 1831 provided that the principal offices should be held by citizens of Pennsylvania. In 1832 the company paid a dividend of ten dollars on each share of the stock.

In 1832 the first steamboat visited Chicago. There were few traces of civilization after passing the Straits of Mackinaw—not a single village, town, or city being in the whole distance. Four steamers—the Henry Clay, Superior, Sheldon Thompson, and William Penn—were chartered by the United States government for the purpose of transporting troops, provisions, etc. to Chicago during the Black Hawk war, but owing to the fearful ravages made by the breaking out of the Asiatic cholera among the troops and crews on board, two of these boats were compelled to abandon their voyage, proceeding no farther than Fort Gratiot. On the Henry Clay nothing like discipline could be maintained. As soon as the steamer came to the dock, each man sprang on shore, hoping to escape from a scene so terrifying and appalling. Some fled to the woods, some to the fields, while others lay down in the streets and under the covert of the river bank, where most of them died unwept and alone.

On the Sheldon Thompson, commanded by Capt. A. Walker, with Gen. Scott aboard, eighty-eight deaths occurred by the pestilence. Not one officer of the army nor any officer of the boat was attacked with such violence as to result in death, though nearly one fourth of the crew fell a prey to the disease while on the passage from Detroit to Buffalo.

In 1810, on Lake Erie, there were eight or nine vessels, averaging sixty tons. In 1820, thirty vessels of fifty tons each, and one small steamboat. In the summer of 1831 there were one hundred vessels averaging seventy tons each, and eleven steamboats, with an aggregate capacity of 2,260 tons. In 1836 there were on Lake Erie forty-five steamboats, with 9,119 tons, and 217 ships, brigs, and schooners, of 16,645 tons; that year many vessels from Lake Ontario found employment on Lake Erie, and still there was a demand for more. In 1847 there were sixty-seven steamers, twenty-six propellers, three barks, sixty-four brigs, and three hundred and forty schooners.

The marine register for 1860, including Lake Ontario, numbers:

Craft.	No.	Tonnage.	Value.
Steamers	138	69,150	$2,720,200
Propellers	197	61,550	2,478,300
Barks	58	28,417	544,200
Brigs	90	25,047	423,200
Schooners and sloops	974	198,661	4,489,300
Total	1457	377,825	$10,655,200

The loss of property on the lakes by disasters, in 1860, amounted to $1,020,100, being an increase of $135,915 over the year previous. The loss of life in 1860 was 578, being an increase of 473 over 1859.

At the port of Presqu'ile the importations for 1851, consisting principally of assorted merchandise, flour, fish, and manufactures of iron, amounted to

Imports coastwise $1,979,913
Imports foreign 3,455

Total importation $1,983,368

130   HISTORY OF ERIE COUNTY.

The *Chicago Republican* says the loss of life by disasters on the lakes, during the year 1865 was one hundred and seventy, being an increase over that of 1864 of thirty-six. The largest and most lamentable loss was that of the Pewabic, on Lake Huron, by which it is generally supposed that not less than one hundred persons found a watery grave.

The exports consist of wool, lumber, wood, bark, glass, stoves, bar iron, coal, and merchandise received by canal, with a small quantity of grain, the whole amounting to the following aggregate:

```
    Exports coastwise............................................$2,207,582
    Exports foreign.................................................    15,415
                                                                   ──────────
    Total exportation ........................................$2,222,997
```

The entire commerce of the port in the same year amounts to a total value of $4,206,483.

The licensed and enrolled tonnage amounts to 7,882 tons.

TONNAGE OF SHIPPING OWNED AT THE PORT OF PRESQU'ILE IN THE SPRING OF 1860.

Class of Vessels.	Tons.	95ths.	Class of Vessels.	Tons.	95ths.
STEAMBOATS.			Brought up......................	1850	91
John B. White (tug)............	39	79	Sch. Arrow...........................	281	28
Queen City	906	...	Bark American Republic....	459	31
S. C. Brooks...........................	62	62	Sch. Armada.........................	235	44
Keystone State......................	1354	09	Brig Paragon........................	212	26
			Sch. M. Courtright...............	389	41
Total steamboat tonnage...	2362	55	Sch. Illinois...........................	110	31
SAIL VESSELS.			Sch. St. James.......................	286	47
			Sch. St. Paul.........................	303	69
Sch. Post Boy........................	95	24	Sch. Pacific...........................	186	30
Sch. Silas Wright (scow)......	70	02	[1]Sch. W. A. Adair.................	81	56
Sch. North Carolina..............	141	71	Sch. C. E. Williams..............	156	60
Sch. Susquehanna	270	86	Sch. Columbia.......................	165	90
Sch. Huntress........................	350	88	Sch. St. Andrew....................	444	48
Sch. L. D. Coman	178	62	Sch. W. M. Arbuckle............	170	09
Sch. Mary M. Scott...............	361	02	[2]Sch. Washington Irving.....	111	44
Sch. Mary Morton.................	246	48	Sch. M. G. (scow).................	60	79
Sch. Hudson..........................	136	08	Sch. Citizen...........................	149	60
	1850	91	Total tonnage sail vessels..	5656	42
			Total tonnage	8018	97

[1] Schooner W. A. Adair sprang a leak on Lake Erie, ran ashore at Dunkirk, and was a total loss. Her cargo was coal.

[2] The Washington Irving, Capt. Vannatta, left Erie for Buffalo July 7, and it is supposed foundered, as she was never again heard from. She had seven persons on board, and was heavily laden with coal, iron, oil, etc.

November 7, 1843, the United States steamer Michigan, of five hundred and thirty-eight tons, was launched; her tonnage and force being regulated by treaty with England. She was finished and accepted by government August 15, 1844; built entirely of iron, excepting the spar deck, which was of three-and-a-half inch pine plank; drew eight feet when ready for a cruise. She was pierced for twelve guns (32-pounders), which, with two 68-pounder Paixham guns on pivots, upon the quarterdeck and forecastle, made her broadside equal to that of a vessel mounting sixteen guns. Her engines, two inclined low-pressure ones, of the collective power of one hundred and seventy horses, were designed by Charles M. Copeland, United States engineer, and were very similar to those of the Harriet Lane. The cost of her construction to the United States was about $165,000. The contractors were Messrs. Stackhouse and Tomlinson, of Pittsburg, and the naval constructor, Samuel T. Hart. Her first officers were: Commander, William Inman; First Lieutenant, James McKinstry; Second Lieutenant, James McDougal; Surgeon, Dr. P. Christie; Purser, William A. Bloodgood; Chief Engineer, Andrew Hibbard. T. H. Stevens, a son of Lieut. Stevens, in command of the Trippe in the battle of Lake Erie, was a past midshipman and acting master.

In 1860 the Michigan was supplied with two new boilers of the Martin vertical tubular description, and her machinery thoroughly repaired under the supervision of chief engineer Zeller.

A commission was appointed by the Secretary of the Navy to test, upon a large scale, the advantage or disadvantage of using steam expansively. This was in consequence of experiments having been made upon a single horse engine by Mr. Isherwood, and resulted in the decision that no economy followed the use of expanded steam. A petition was sent to Honorable Secretary Toucey, requesting the government to have the experiment tested upon a larger scale. With commendable alacrity a board was appointed composed of B. F. Isherwood, Theo. Zeller, Robert H. Long, and Alban C. Stimer, chief engineers in the naval corps, and Capt. Joseph Lanman, executive officer of the steamer Michigan. The steamer Michigan, being in winter quarters at Erie, was placed at their disposal.

Erie has always been the station for the revenue cutters. In March, 1833, one was launched of sixty-two tons; the collector gave it the name of Lewis McLane, but the Secretary changed it to Erie. The Benjamin Rush, of thirty-five tons, was launched September, 1828, being intended for the Upper Lakes.

Six revenue cutters were built in 1857, being one for each of the lakes; the Jeremiah Black, of Lake Erie, was commanded by Capt. Ottinger.

CHAPTER XI.

Banks — Gas Company — Insurance — Fire Companies — Volunteer Military — Agriculture — Mutual Aid — Cemeteries — Moral, Benevolent, and Literary Societies.

Banks.—The act incorporating the Erie Bank passed in 1829. The first officers were R. S. Reed, President; P. S. V. Hamot, Cashier; J. A. Tracy, C. M. Reed, Samuel Brown, William Fleming, Thomas Moorhead, Jr., E. D. Gunnison, and D. Gillespie, Directors. The capital stock was not to exceed $200,000, and it commenced business with $50,000. On the expiration of its charter, in 1850, its outstanding circulating notes were redeemed and its business closed.

The United States Bank of Pennsylvania established a branch at Erie in 1837, to be discontinued in 1850. The first officers were T. H. Sill, President; Josiah Kellogg, C. M. Reed, Wm. Kelly, G. A. Elliot, Samuel Hays, William Fleming, J. G. Williams, H. J. Huidekoper, Directors; Peter Benson, Cashier. When the parent institution at Philadelphia failed, in 1840, William C. Curry was appointed to settle the affairs of the branch in Erie.

The fine building erected for its use at an expense of $70,000, was purchased by the government in 1849 for a custom house and post office for $29,000. The banking-house is faced with white marble, and has steps and columns made of the same material.

The Erie City Bank was incorporated in 1753, with a capital of $200,000. The first officers were Smith Jackson, President; C. M. Tibbals, W. A. Brown, D. S. Clark, C. Seigel, John Brawley, James Webster, J. H. Fullerton, Ira Sherwin, M.D., J. D. Clark, Charles Brandes, J. C. Beebe, Directors; J. P. Sherwin, Cashier; Brua Cameron, Bookkeeper; S. E. Neiler, Teller. Suspended, 1857.

Bank of Commerce (Erie City Bank revived) commenced business in April, 1858. Directors—B. Grant, President; G. J. Ball, Cashier; C. B. Wright, Vice-President; W. F. Rindernicht, James Hoskinson, B. F. Sloan, Charles Metcalf, A. W. Blaine, G. F. King, J. W. Douglas; A. W. Guild, Teller. Suspended December, 1860.

The Erie Gas Company was chartered March 5, 1852, with a capital of $60,000. This was to be divided into twelve hundred shares of $50 each. The Board of Directors have the privilege of increasing the capital from time to time, as they may deem necessary, to $100,000.

The company purchased ten lots for $10,000, and expended $50,000 on buildings, machinery, etc.; the gas-holder is forty-five feet in diameter and eighteen feet deep, and capable of holding thirty thousand cubic feet. Pipe, the length of three and a half miles, was laid in the streets; it was first used August 22, 1853, by thirty-one consumers; at the end of the year, by one hundred and fifty; burners, six hundred.

Mr. Meredith superintended the construction of the works, and Mr. P. Metcalf, who was the heaviest stockholder, contributed materially to the success of the enterprise.

Insurance.—In 1834 the Erie County Mutual Insurance Company was incorporated (the business to be transacted at Erie), with the following names, and those of any other persons that might hereafter associate with them in the manner afterward prescribed: John A. Tracy, William Kelley, Peter Pierce, J. W. Hitchcock, James Williams, Smith Jackson, Samuel Low, Conrad Brown, Jr., B. B. Vincent, Bester Town, Jabez Wight, David G. Webber, and Stephen Skinner.

The Farmers' Mutual Insurance Company of Harbor Creek was incorporated 1857, with the following officers: John Dodge, President; Peter E. Burton, Vice-President; Henry

Gingrich, Treasurer; Robert Henry, Secretary; John Dodge, J. Y. Moorhead, John W. McLane, Calvin Leet, G. H. Wagoner, Jesse Saltsman, Robert Sewall, G. J. Ball, Thomas McKee, S. M. Brown, Henry Gingrich, Martin Warfel, and P. E. Burton, Directors.

Fire.—Active Fire Company, formed February 22, 1826. R. S. Reed, Chief Engineer; E. D. Gunnison, Secretary; John Riddel, Treasurer.

Red Jacket, No. 1, was formed in 1837.

Perry and Eagle Fire Companies formed in 1839.

Mechanics' Fire Company, No. 3, E. B. S. Landon, Secretary, formed in 1844.

Vulcan, 1848.

Phœnix Hook and Ladder Company, 1852.

The Parade Street Fire Company was organized in February, 1861, in Cloughsburg. The councils entrusted to them the engine Pennsylvania.

Officers of the fire department in 1859—William Murray, Chief Engineer; A. E. Yale, First Assistant; Robert T. Shank, Second Assistant; Richard Dudley, President; John Constable, Jr., Vice-President; E. D. Hulbert, Secretary; G. A. Bennet, Water Commissioner.

Military Companies.—The first military company formed in Erie was the "Erie Light Infantry," in 1806; the names of the officers and privates were as follows:

Officers—Captain, Thomas Forster; Lieutenant, Thomas Rees; Ensign, Thomas Stewart; Sergeant, Thomas Wilkins; Second Sergeant, John Hay; Fifer, Rufus Clough; Drummer, J. Glazier.

Privates—Archibald McSparren, Simeon Dunn,[1] Adam Arbuckle, George Kelley, John Sloan, William Murray, Jonas Duncan, John Woodside, William Duncan, George Slough, John Eakens, George Russel (died in 1813), John Lapsley, Peter Grawosz, Jacob Carmack, William Henderson, Robert Irwin, Ebenezer Dwinnel, John Bell, Robert McDonnel, Samuel Hays, Thomas Laird, Thomas Hughes, Robert

---

[1] Mr. Simeon Dunn was recommended to Commodore Perry in 1813 as capable and trustworthy, and was in his employ carrying important express to Buffalo.

Brown, John Morris, George Buehler, William Lattimore, James Herron, Stephen Woolverton, Francis Scott, Thomas Vance.

This company tendered its services to the President, in the war of 1812, and was accepted. The brigade rendezvoused at the Flats, near Waterford, and chose Adamson Tannehill, of Pittsburg, Brigadier-General. At Buffalo, where they were ordered, Capt. Forster was made Brigade Inspector, and James E. Herron chosen Captain.

This brigade of Pennsylvania volunteers was at Buffalo during the winter of 1812–13, being the year before Buffalo was burnt. Many of the volunteers deserted—sometimes by whole companies. This was not true of the Erie Light Infantry in a single instance.

In 1808 the Presqu'ile Rangers were in existence. William Moore, Orderly Sergeant.

Erie Greens were organized in 1821.

The Washington Artillery, in 1824.

Erie Guards, in 1825. Thomas Forster, Jr., Captain.

An Artillery company, in 1831. C. G. Howell, Captain.

Cavalry, 1836. F. Strong, Orderly Sergeant.

About 1841 two spirited German companies were formed: German Guards, Capt. Dutlinger, and the Washington Guards, Capt. Erhart.

In 1842 the Wayne Greys were organized. John W. McLane, Captain; William Curran, Orderly Sergeant.

In June, 1846, the Wayne Greys held a meeting, Lieut. John Graham in the chair, and in consideration of a proclamation of the Governor relative to the war with Mexico, requesting all citizens, especially those having in their possession public arms, to hold themselves in readiness to respond to the call of the Executive of the Union at a moment's warning, resolved to have themselves in readiness for any order from the Governor of the State for their services, and also to appoint a committee of four to procure an armorer to put all the arms and accoutrements of the company in complete order immediately.

Franklin Pierce Rifle Company was organized in 1858.

The Wayne Guards in 1859; John W. McLane, Captain.

The Fairview Guards in 1858; T. Beckman, Captain.
Girard Guards, 1860; commanded by D. W. Hutchinson.
Erie Perry Artillery Company, Gustavus Jarecki, Captain, organized in 1859.

An agreeable incident in the history of the Wayne Guards occurred in Cleveland at the dedication of the Perry Monument, September 10, 1860. After the historical address by the Hon. George Bancroft, the Wayne Guards were drawn up in front of the stand, and, in behalf of the company, Capt. McLane presented Mr. Bancroft with a beautiful cane. The presentation was made with a few remarks in very good taste. Capt. McLane said the cane was made of wood from Com. Perry's flag-ship, the Lawrence. The Wayne Guards, he said, were proud to honor the hero, and the historian whose graceful pen preserved untarnished the luster of the heroic deeds of 1813.

Mr. Bancroft accepted the gift in a few felicitous remarks. He was happy to receive the memento from the Guards, and particularly as they bore the name of one ever to be revered, brave in battle, correct and kind in private life. He should keep the cane while he lived, and bequeath it to his son with an injunction to cherish it, and remember that it came to him with the benediction of the Guards. It would comfort the few years of old age yet left to him.

The whole transaction passed off very pleasantly, and at the close of Mr. Bancroft's remarks he was greeted by cheers, which were repeated for the Wayne Guards.

The gold head of the cane was the work of Mr. T. M. Austin, of Erie, and cost one hundred dollars, and was beautifully wrought. On one side was engraved "September 10, 1813. We have met the enemy and they are ours." On the other, " Wayne Guards of Erie to Honorable George Bancroft, at the inauguration of the Perry Statue, September 10, 1860. ' Perry's fleet was built at, sailed from, and returned to Erie.' American patriotism embalms the memories of its heroes."

In November, the Guards had the pleasure of receiving from Mr. Bancroft eight volumes of his History of the United States, superbly bound in Turkey morocco and gilt, accompanied by the following note :

"NEW YORK, October, 1860.

"*Capt. John McLane, and the Wayne Guards of Erie:*

"DEAR SIRS:—The very great pleasure and enduring satisfaction which I derived from my friendly interview with you at Cleveland, excites in me a strong desire to secure a permanent place in your memory. For that purpose, I beg your acceptance of the volumes which accompany this note. Accept, also, I entreat you, very sincere assurances of grateful and affectionate regard from

"Your friend,
"GEORGE BANCROFT."

Agriculture, etc.—In 1820 a Mechanical Association was formed, S. Ball, Secretary, the object of which was to improve the condition of mechanics.

In 1822 an Agricultural and Mechanical Society was organized, which held one or two fairs or exhibitions. The first officers were: Judah Colt, President; Charles J. Reed, Treasurer; G. Sanford, Secretary; John Vincent, Waterford, R. S. Reed, Erie, Wm. Miles, Union, Martin Strong, McKean, Benjamin Russell, Mill Creek, Elisha Marvin, Greenfield, Moses Barnet, Fairview, John McCord, Northeast, Simeon Leet, Harbor Creek, and Mathias Brindle, Springfield, Directors.

The members contributed one dollar each, and the county fifty dollars; seventy-eight dollars were paid out in premiums, which were awarded for farming commodities and domestic manufactures. The highest premium was eight dollars, which was offered for the best two acres of wheat. In the words of the *Gazette*, "the exhibition of stock was large, and we can safely say was not surpassed in quality at any exhibition in the State. But few articles of domestic manufacture were offered, but these were worthy of notice."

The Mill Creek and Erie Agricultural and Manufacturing Association was formed in April, 1842, Robert Cochran, Secretary.

The Agricultural Society was formed in 1848, and the following offcers elected: John Brawley President; J. C. Spencer Treasurer, and J. D. Dunlap Secretary. The first fair was held at the market house, and $150 offered in premiums. These were increased every year. A flag was offered to the town entitled to the largest number of premiums, which was found to be

Harbor Creek. Next, an agricultural library was offered on the same conditions, and Harbor Creek again claimed the prize, but generously donated the books to the County Society.

In 1860 this society was merged into a joint stock association, chartered by the Court of Common Pleas, styled the Erie County Agricultural Society for the promotion of agriculture, manufactures, fine and useful arts, with $5,000 capital, to be afterward increased as the society should determine. The capital stock to be represented by shares of ten dollars each, the first stock to be invested in the purchase and improvement of thirty acres of ground. The land purchased was in East Mill Creek, being a part of the farm of Mr. Ebersole. A building designed to be a wing of the main building was completed in 1860. When the first fair was held, $355 were awarded in premiums.

Hon. James Miles in 1855 made an offer of 200 acres of land, situated in Girard township, to the State Agricultural Society, provided that organization locate an agricultural college on said land. To this was added an offer to sell land adjoining at a reasonable rate if required.

The Pennsylvania Farm School was located in Centre County, and in 1858 the Agricultural Society of this county voted $1,000 to its support.

The Union Agricultural Society of Girard adopted its constitution July 15, 1856, and at its first fair in September offered $170 in premiums. This society was intended as an auxiliary and not a rival of the Erie County Society, and was instituted in view of the distance of the western and southwestern townships from Erie. At the sixth annual meeting the following officers were chosen : P. Osborne, President ; Wm. Cross, J. W. Blair, J. Robertson, W. W. Eaton, Wm. Holliday, C. Bowman, A. Frances, S. Washburn, C. Leet, A. Nicholson, Vice-Presidents ; H. Ball, Treasurer ; J. McClure, Recording Secretary ; H. Hart, Corresponding Secretary.

The Wattsburg Agricultural Society was formed in 1856.

Masons.—Wayne Lodge, No. 112, was instituted in 1813. G. Sanford, Master ; T. Rees and Dr. J. C. Wallace, Wardens ; R. S. Reed, Treasurer.

Presqu'ile Lodge was organized in 1852. H. Pelton, W. M.,

HISTORY OF ERIE COUNTY. 139

Dr. William F. Owen, of Spring, in February, 1861, was appointed D. D. G. H. P. for the counties of Erie and Crawford.

Presqu'ile Lodge (Odd Fellows), No. 107. In 1859, the officers were William Mallory, N. G.; John Graham, V. G.; John Sweeney, Recording Secretary; G. A. Bennet, Financial Secretary; John Abell, Treasurer.

Philallelia Lodge, No. 299. Otis N. Gray, N. G.; A. T. Thomas, V. G.; A. M. Tarbell, Secretary; A. M. Guild, Treasurer.

Officers of the German Beneficial Society, in 1859, were A. T. Fiesler, President; F. Fiesler, Vice-President; Michael Koch, First Secretary; and F. M. Wagner, Treasurer.

Erie Temple of Honor, No. 5, a temperance association, was instituted in 1854, Wm. A. Galbraith, Esq., being the first W. C. T. It was reorganized in 1859 as No. 9. In 1861 the officers were A. H. Caughey, D. G. W. T.; James Lytle, W. C. T.; E. P. Bennett, W. V. T. and W. R.; John Fairburn, W. F. R. A lodge of the Good Templars, which had been in prosperous operation for two or three years, was merged into the Temple of Honor at its reorganization.

Exodus Lodge, No. 343, I. O. of G. T.; Edgar Olin, Degree Master; in existence at Girard in 1855.

Constellation Lodge, No. 210, I. O. of G. T., at Springfield.

In 1846 the society of Odd Fellows, still in existence, was organized in Waterford; there were also at one time organizations of the Temple of Honor, Sons of Temperance, and Good Templars.

Northeast Odd Fellows' Lodge, No. 412, established in 1850. Number of members, 92; of P. G., 17.

Albion Lodge, No. 376, I. O. O. F., was probably established about the same time.

The St. George's Benevolent Society of Erie has for its object charity to its sick members. Officers in 1861—Jacob Boty, President; J. Singer, Vice-President; M. Knoll, First Secretary; P. Rochenwald, Second Secretary; P. Schotten, Treasurer.

Cemeteries.—On the 6th of July, 1801, a number of persons collected at Greenfield to cut and clear off about an acre of ground for a burying-place. These were Enoch Marvin, Joseph Shadack and family, Henry and Dyer Loomis, Samuel, Hezekiah, and Philo Barker, Wm. Scott, Israel Wanever, James Heaton, Stephen Hazelton, Joseph Webster, Thomas Prentice, —— Dagget, and one or two others.

In 1805 lots on the corner of Eighth and French streets were set apart for a burying-ground. The trustees of the United Presbyterian congregation paid the purchase money due the State for them, and after removing the bodies to the city cemetery, disposed of the ground to purchasers. At an early day we observe an Obituary Association in existence, P. S. V. Hamot, Secretary, which probably managed its affairs. Previous to 1805, all interments were made on the bank of the lake, east of the town, where also were buried many of the soldiers of 1812.

About 1826 the Presbyterian Society purchased four lots on Seventh and Myrtle streets for burial purposes. After the Erie Cemetery was opened in 1851, the graves were removed from this, and, by an act, the trustees of the First Presbyterian Church disposed of the property.

The Episcopalians, Roman Catholics, and Lutherans also had separate grounds.

The Erie Cemetery was incorporated in 1850, and is handsomely situated south of the city. It embraces seventy acres beautifully planned and ornamented with trees, shrubs, and flowers, and also contains at this time many fine monuments. The first managers were C. M. Reed, William Himrod, G. A. Elliot, William Kelley, A. W. Brewster, J. Galbraith, and E. Babbitt. G. A. Elliot was chosen President; J. C. Spencer, Treasurer; and Wm. A. Brown, Secretary. Mr. Brewster, who was in perfect health at the time he was made an officer, was the first person interred there, having died of smallpox.

In the immediate vicinity the German Roman Catholics consecrated a cemetery in 1853, and likewise St. Paul's German Evangelical Congregation in 1859.

The Northeast Cemetery was incorporated April 15, 1852. The following corporators were elected May 8: John Brawley, John Schouller, James Smedley, Calvin Spafford, John Greer, William Griffith, A. W. Blaine. Twelve and a half acres of ground were purchased of the heirs of P. S. V. Hamot, to which five acres were added that had been used as a burying-ground for nearly fifty years. It is handsomely designed.

In Girard application was made by several citizens for an act of incorporation to establish a cemetery at or near that borough. The application was granted March 14, 1861.

Moral and Benevolent.—A Moral Society was organized at Waterford, December, 1815. The object, as expressed in the preamble, being to aid each other, and strengthen the hands of the magistrates in the suppression of vice and immorality, by every prudent, and, if necessary, by every legal method, hoping to meet the approbation of God, and the assistance of good men of every political sentiment and religious denomination. Officers—Rev. John Mathews, Chairman; Dr. Wm. Bacon, Secretary; Amos Judson, Treasurer; George W. Reed and Henry Woodworth, Corresponding Committee; John Boyd, Esq., John Way, Esq., Archibald Watson (elder), and Capt. Martin Strong, Standing Committee.

The County Bible Society was organized in 1824, and has, without intermission, fulfilled its duties to the present time. The first officers were Rev. Johnston Eaton, President; Rev. R. Reid, Vice-President; E. D. Gunnison, Treasurer; G. Selden, Secretary; Managers, William Gould, Robert Porter, John McCord, Col. Joseph Selden, Judah Colt, Robert McClelland, Gen. John Phillips, Rev. Oliver Alfred, Rev. R. C. Hatton, James Flowers, Philip Bristol, and G. Sanford. At the thirty-seventh annual meeting, in 1861, Rev. G. A. Lyon, D.D., was chosen President; S. S. Spencer, Secretary; and J. C. Seldon, Treasurer. The amount of receipts for the year, $750.18; disbursements for the same period, $514.13; balance in treasury, $522.28; value of Bibles and Testaments purchased during the year, $134.60; amount sold and donated, $120.43; amount in value at depository, $289.48.

In 1828 a Colonization Society was organized in Erie, but was sustained only a few years. Rev. Robert Reid, President; G. A. Elliot, Secretary; Rev. D. McKinney, Josiah Kellogg, R. O. Hulbert, and G. Selden were a committee to solicit signatures. In the spring of 1860, Alex. Simms, wife, and eight children, with eight other colored persons from Erie County, left for Africa under the auspices of the Pennsylvania society. In 1836 a Colonization Society was formed at Northeast. Henry Frey, President; John Brawley, Vice President; J. D. Dunlap, Secretary, and Clark Putnam, Treasurer. The same year a County Anti-Slavery Society was formed, Col. James Moorhead, President, and William Gray, Secretary; and also one at Northeast, Truman Tuttle, President; James Duncan, Vice-President; Dr. E. Smedley, Secretary, and R. L. Loomis, Treasurer.

About the same time an anti-abolition meeting was called at Springfield, H. G. Davis in the chair, and Daniel G. Webber, Secretary. The meeting in its resolutions highly approved of the Colonization Society, but not of a crusade against the South.

About 1824 a Female Tract Society was formed in Erie, which was useful for many years. Mrs. J. Colt, Directress; Mrs. G. Sanford, Treasurer; Miss E. Wight, Secretary.

At Wattsburg a Tract Society was formed in 1828, Rev. A. McCreary, President; James Nelson, Secretary, and Wm. K. Black, Treasurer.

A society was formed in Erie in 1844 for abolishing capital punishment. In 1845 a committee, composed of Irvin Camp, W. H. Knowlton, Smith Jackson, Oliver Spafford, and Wm. A. Galbraith, gave notice that they would meet a committee who might be appointed to discuss the question, "Ought capital punishment to be abolished in Pennsylvania?" The question was discussed at the courthouse, and excited general interest; John Galbraith and Irvin Camp in the affirmative, Elijah Babbitt and J. H. Walker, negative, and James C. Marshall, Moderator.

A Lady's Benevolent Society was formed in 1843, which for many years possessed the confidence of the public, and relieved much suffering.

In 1845 a Sabbath Convention was called that resulted in the organization of a Sabbath Association, which for several years held meetings, and attempted to promote the better observance of the Sabbath by travelers, on the canal, lakes, etc.

The Erie City Tract Society, which represented five evangelical denominations, and had for its object tract distribution and aid to the poor, was active for seven years. It was formed in 1854, with the following officers: D. S. Clark, President; W. F. Liddell and J. D. Dunlap, Vice-Presidents; Rev. Joseph Pressley, M. R. Barr, James Metcalf, C. Doll, and M. B. Cook, Managers.

Among so many efforts to repress vice, we are sorry to record one attempt to promote immorality. In 1840 a petition was sent to the Legislature from the county, signed by forty persons, asking that the Sabbath might be abolished, to legalize blasphemy, and extend the privilege of giving testimony in court to all persons, whether believers or not.

Temperance societies were formed in Erie and Wattsburg in 1829, and in Wayne Township in 1832, which year the county society had seven hundred and forty-two members. Judah Colt, President; R. McClelland, Vice-President; R. O. Hulbert, Secretary; G. Selden, Treasurer; G. Sanford, Hugh Wilson, William Gray, John Cook, Chauncey Graves, Benjamin Whitley, Ira Phelps, James Smedley, Samuel Beedy, James Nelson, and Rev. Edson Hart, Managers.

In 1840 they had a temperance society in most of the townships. In 1842 the jailer *complained* (as his apartments were vacant) that the temperance people had combined to injure the business of the house.

In 1851 a Division of Sons of Temperance was formed, which continued in operation for several years.

In 1852 a Harp and Shamrock Temperance Society was formed. J. W. Duggen, President.

One hundred ladies of the first standing in Erie and in Wattsburg petitioned for a prohibitory liquor law in 1853.

The same year, Cadets of Temperance appeared in Erie, being a society of youths between twelve and eighteen years of age, with rules similar to those of the Sons of Temperance; they were also to abstain from tobacco, profane language, etc.

The Carson League, formed in 1854, was an efficient aid to temperance.

The "Young Men's Christian Association" was formed in September, 1860. A. McD. Lyon, President; S. E. Blackall, Secretary; A. H. Caughey, Corresponding Secretary; C. E. Gunnison, Treasurer; James Metcalf, Librarian. It numbered about fifty members. Besides the usual religious work of such a society, a course of first-class literary and scientific lectures was sustained during the winter of 1860-61. A general reading room was opened in May, 1861, for the free use of the young men of the city, a subscription of $175 having been raised for the purpose of establishing the enterprise on a substantial basis. The library of the Irving Literary Institute, consisted of about seven hundred volumes, and was placed in their hands.

In 1828 quite a respectable contribution was made to the Greeks from Erie and vicinity, and several public meetings held. We regret that the particulars were not published.

In 1847, for the relief of Ireland, $150 from officers and seamen of United States steamer Michigan, $50 from the revenue cutter, and $79 from the other ship hands at the port were acknowledged. Gen. C. M. Reed gave notice that he would store and transport to Buffalo, free of charge, all grain intended for this object. A meeting was also called in Waterford, and about $2,000 in provisions were shipped from the port of Erie.

In February, 1861, $1,000 were collected in Erie for the Kansas sufferers. For this benevolent object, Waterford subscribed $155; Girard, $100; Springfield township, $500; Belle Valley, $15; probably in all $2,500 from Erie County.

Among the German Roman Catholics was a school society, the object of which was to give educational advantages to poor children. John Gensheimer, President; C. Englehard, Vice-President; F. Schlaudecker, Secretary; F. Peiffer, Treasurer.

Literary.—In 1806 thirty of the citizens of Erie formed themselves into a library company, Judah Colt being President; Thomas Forster, James Baird, John C. Wallace, and William Wallace, Directors; and Thomas Forster, Librarian. The company at first expended $200 for standard works, and the institution was well sustained for several years. In 1821 an effort was made to revive it, but without success. The books were loaned to the Irving Literary Institute.

In 1826 there was a Franklin Literary Association; T. Moorhead, Jr., Librarian.

In 1833 the Conneauttee Library Company (Edinboro) was incorporated.

In the winter of 1835, a lyceum held its meetings first at the Erie Academy and afterward at the courthouse, interesting the inhabitants by the debates and literary exercises of the members. The Apprentices' Literary Society originated about 1839, with fifty members and a library of one hundred and ten volumes, and soon after had a course of lectures. In 1841 an Adelphic Literary Society existed; A. King, Corresponding Secretary. The Irving Literary Institute had a nucleus for an excellent library. It was organized in 1843 by the union of the Apprentices' and Adelphic Societies.

In 1859 a Young Men's Literary Association was formed at Girard, and about the same time a literary union at Waterford, which sustained courses of lectures.

At West Mill Creek an association called Custos Morum (Guardian of Morality) was formed in April, 1860, with twenty-five members; Jackson McCreary, President. The object of the society was to procure a library, and for intellectual culture.

A Youths' Literary Society at Northeast has existed since 1858.

A County Medical Society was formed in 1829. Dr. William Johns, President; Dr. A. Thayer, Vice-President; Dr. F. M. Miller, Recording and Corresponding Secretary; Dr. A. Beebe, Treasurer; Dr. J. Smedley, Dr. J. Vosburg, and Dr. A. N. Molton, Censors.

In 1836 the Presqu'ile hospital was incorporated, the act to continue in force for the term of twenty years. It was expected a medical college and a medical society would form a part of the establishment, with a lunatic asylum and an asylum for the deaf and dumb. In consequence of the depression in business affairs soon after, the project was abandoned.

A County Geological Society was formed in 1843. G. Sanford, President; J. D. Dunlap, Vice-President; L. G. Olmstead, Corresponding Secretary; William C. Kelso, Recording Secretary; and J. C. Spencer, Treasurer; William Fuller, Keeper of the Cabinet and Library; Jacob Vosburg, Peter

Pierce, Galen Foster, J. B. Johnson, and Richard Sill, Members of the Executive Committee.

The objects of the society were commendable, and it is to be regretted that it had an existence of but a year or two. As stated in the constitution, the society were to thoroughly survey the county in order to develop its mineral wealth and resources; for the advancement of geology and the collateral branches of natural science, and the promotion of intercourse between those who cultivated them.

In 1846 the citizens assembled in town meeting at the courthouse, B. B. Vincent in the chair, and Carson Graham, Secretary, and resolved that the public square be planted with trees. E. Babbitt, W. C. Lester, C. McSparren, and S. Jackson were appointed a committee to coöperate with the town authorities in carrying out the resolution.

A reading room association was formed in 1850, B. B. Vincent, President, but, for want of adequate support, was discontinued in a few months.

In 1852 a city hall association was incorporated for the purpose of erecting a building for the accommodation of the city authorities, as well as for lectures, benevolent societies, a reading room, etc.

A sacred music society was formed in 1858. John Galbraith, President; Thomas Stewart, Sr., Vice-President; H. Catlin, Secretary; and J. L. Lints, Treasurer.

In 1852 the Erie County Education Society, for the advancement of education, was in existence; C. W. Kelso, President, and J. W. Wetmore, Secretary.

In 1855 the Girard Lyceum was formed; Harmon D. Hunt, Secretary.

The Arion Musical Society was organized in Erie in 1860.

CHAPTER XII.

Newspapers—Common Schools—Academies—Normal School—Sabbath School—First Protestant Missionaries West of Utica—Moravians in Venango County, 1767—First Religious Service in Erie County—First Church Edifice—A Religious Experience—Presbytery of Erie—Revs. Patterson and Eaton—Extract from Rev. A. H. Carrier's Historical Sermon—Rev. R. Reid—Churches of different Denominations in Erie—Revivals.

Newspapers.—The first newspaper, *The Mirror*, is dated May 21, 1808, George Wyeth, printer. In size it was ten inches by sixteen; terms, two dollars semi-annually, in advance. It advocated the Federal Constitutional Republican party, whose candidates at that time were James Ross, for Governor; Alexander W. Foster, Congress; and John W. Hunter and William Wallace for Assembly. *The Mirror* was discontinued after a two years' existence.

In 1813 R. J. Curtis established the *Northern Sentinel* (the size of a sheet of foolscap), and in 1815 made arrangements for removing his establishment to Detroit. For want of encouragement he failed to accomplish his purpose, and in 1816 recommenced business in Erie, having changed the name of his paper to the *Genius of the Lakes*. The name of John Morris was added as publisher. The "terms, two dollars and fifty cents by post rider—if neglected to the end of the year, three dollars."

The *Erie Patriot* was issued in 1818 by Zeba Willis, and continued one year. It was then removed to Cleveland, and made the basis of the *Cleveland Herald*, Mr. Howe being associated in its publication.

In 1819 Mr. Curtis enlarged his paper and called it the *Phœnix and Erie Reflector*. This was soon removed to Mayville, New York, and discontinued in April, 1820.

Mr. Curtis, in speaking of his editorial experience in Erie, says: "For two or three years during the war I had a very good support, but afterward it was poor indeed. The most of my subscribers paid in produce. For six months I taught school and printed my paper at the same time, with the assistance only of an apprentice and my sister." We might suppose a newspaper published in Erie during the war would contain interesting information; but it was not the case, as the government prohibited the publication of facts which might have been suggestive to the enemy.

In January, 1820, the *Erie Gazette* was published by Joseph M. Sterrett. In 1822 James Buchanan was editor for six months. In 1825 J. Hoge Waugh, for a short time; and in 1836 John Shaner was associated in its publication. In 1842 J. P. Cochran and G. W. Riblet took charge. I. B. Gara became associated with Joseph M. Sterrett in 1846. In politics it has been Anti-Masonic, Whig, and Republican.

The *Erie Observer*, a Democratic paper, was issued in 1830, T. B. Barnum, editor. H. L. Harvey being editor in 1836, issued a specimen daily paper, to be continued provided there was sufficient encouragement. In 1848 a paper was issued tri-weekly for several months. Thomas Laird, H. Beebe, J. M. Keuster, and S. W. Randall were successively editors. In 1840 it passed into the hands of Durlin & Sloan. Mr. Durlin withdrew from the firm in 1855 and removed to Wisconsin. The paper passed into the hands of Mr. Andrew Hopkins, January 1, 1861.

The *Erie Chronicle*, a conservative Whig paper, was issued by S. Perley in 1840. In 1855 the editor removed to Girard and revived the *Girard Republican*.

The *Girard Free Press* was first issued in 1845, being neutral in politics. S. D. Carpenter, editor. November 7, 1854, T. C. Wheeler and William S. Finch purchased the interest of L. F. Andrews in the *Girard Express*, and commenced the publication of the *Girard Republican*. The conservative character of the paper was indicated by the motto, "Independent on all subjects, rabid on none." As we have mentioned, Mr. Perley took charge of the paper in 1855.

In 1846 J. P. Cochran commenced the publication of the *Commercial Advertiser*, which was Whig in politics. After his death it passed in 1852 into the hands of A. H. Caughey, who continued its publication for a year and a half and then sold it to J. B. Johnson, who gave it the name of the *Constitution*. In 1855 the press was destroyed by a mob—an outgrowth of the railroad excitement. The *Constitution* was continued by R. L. White, and for a few months was issued daily—being the first experiment of the kind. The *Daily Bulletin*, as it was called, suspended issue in 1858. The large number of weeklies issued in Erie probably accounted for the want of success in daily or tri-weekly papers.

The *Herald*, a monthly temperance paper in quarto form, was published at the office of the *Commercial Advertiser* during the year 1852.

In 1853 the *True American* appeared, Compton & Moore, editors. From the first this paper gave temperance and anti-slavery a large share of attention. In 1855 this and the *Erie Chronicle* merged into one; James Perley and Henry Catlin, publishers.

The *Unsere Welt* (Our World), a German paper, was first published by Carl Benson, in 1851. Its name was changed to *Frei Presse* about 1856. It advocated Fremont and Lincoln for Presidents.

In 1852 the *Zushauer* (Spectator) appeared; Mr. Scheufflen, editor. In 1855 C. Moeser took charge, and in 1861, Ernst Sturzneckle. This paper was at first Whig in politics, but became independent. Both the German papers were under Protestant influence.

In 1859 the *Express* appeared, with E. C. Goodrich editor; this was soon merged into the *True American*, afterwards edited by H. Catlin.

The *Waterford Museum*, Mr. Lewis, editor, changed its name to the *Enquirer* in 1857, Amos Judson, publisher and editor; in 1858 it suspended issue for a few months on account of the ruinous rates at which it was afforded; recommenced with Judson and Lynn, editors; afterward alone by C. R. H. Lynn.

The *Northeast Guard* was published for a few months in 1855.

Two newspapers were issued in Edinboro in 1855: the *Gem*

expired in 1856, and the *Museum* was removed to Waterford the same year. The *Edinboro Express* appeared in 1859, at fifty cents per year; Henry Lick, editor; "independent on all occasions, neutral in nothing." Issued the last number December 29, 1860, the materials having been sold to Mr. Clute, who was expecting to publish a paper at Three Rivers, Michigan.

In 1851 the *Waterford Dispatch* was issued at Waterford; Joseph S. M. Young, editor. In 1856 the paper was removed to Erie and called the *Erie City Dispatch*. It was independent on all subjects, and was said to have a larger circulation than any other paper in Northwestern Pennsylvania.

In 1855 we hear of the *Native American*, a monthly at Edinboro.

Schools.—April 2, 1831, a law passed the Legislature of Pennsylvania introducing our present system of education for all. At that time it was shown that out of 400,000 children in the State, more than 250,000 capable of instruction were not within a school the previous year. This was not for want of effort in that direction.

In 1809 an act was passed to provide for the education of the poor, and in 1824 an act that it was hoped would prove effectual, but which was repealed in 1826.

In 1834 an act was passed designating the Secretary of the Commonwealth as Superintendent, and, including other valuable provisions, stating that $546,563 had accumulated under the act of 1831.

Next came the act of 1836, "to consolidate and amend the several acts," to settle the mode of taxation, and the application of the whole for school purposes. The fund accumulated since 1831 was set apart, and a fund from the State treasury pledged for school purposes, and the system became a settled fact as a part of the policy of the State.

In 1854 the election for county superintendents was provided for in each county.

In 1848–49 the provisions of the law were extended over non-accepting districts, as it had been previously optional.

In 1849 an act to provide for the training of teachers for the common schools of the State was passed, and the State was divided into twelve normal school districts—Lawrence, Mercer, Venango, Crawford, and Erie were made the twelfth district. William H. Armstrong, of Wattsburg, was elected to the office of Superintendent of Common Schools in Erie County, with a salary of $800, and was re-elected in 1857. In 1860 L. Savage, of Springfield, was elected his successor.

According to the seventh census report, Erie County had, in 1850, 7 academies, with 13 teachers, 375 pupils, and an annual income of $3,357. Public schools, 293, with 308 teachers, 9,928 pupils, and an income from taxes, etc., of $22,120. In 1857 the number of schoolhouses in the county was 276 ; 34 were well adapted to the purpose, 120 capable of being improved, and 102 to be rejected. Erie had three graded schools, and Northeast one.

According to the eighth census report (which we have only in part), Waterford borough had 2 schools; Northeast borough, 1; Girard borough, 1, and 1 academy; Wattsburg borough, 1; Union, 2; Wesleyville, 1; Girard township, 16 ; Springfield township, 15, and 1 academy ; Franklin township, 10 ; Fairview township, 11, and about 500 pupils ; Summit township, 8, and 160 pupils ; McKean township, 11, and 511 pupils; Le Bœuf, 11, and 258 pupils; Washington township, 14, and 642 pupils ; Greenfield township, 8, and 342 pupils ; Amity township, 8, and 424 pupils ; Venango township, 10, and 488 pupils ; Wayne township, 12, and 504 pupils ; Union township, 12, and 752 pupils ; Concord township, 9, and 417 pupils ; Harbor Creek township, 17 ; Greene township, 8, and 450 pupils ; Northeast township, 16, and 1,083 pupils ; Waterford township, 15, and 450 pupils.

The State Superintendent of Schools reports, for the year ending June 4, 1860, as follows : Erie County—

Whole number of schools	288
Number yet required	6
Average number of months taught	6–8
Number of male teachers	157
Number of female teachers	232
Scholars learning German	167
Average attendance of scholars	8195
Cost of teaching each scholar per month	$0 51
Tax levied for school and building purposes	$42,053 25
State appropriation	3,922 70
Received from collectors	35,747 95
Cost of instruction	35,696 44
Fuel and contingencies	4,040 25
Cost of schoolhouses	14,824 76

In Erie a fine schoolhouse for the East Ward was completed in 1859, at a cost of $20,000. In this building there are ten teachers and about five hundred scholars. German, algebra, geometry, chemistry, and philosophy are attended to among the higher branches.

The West Ward has, besides the principal school, a branch in the upper part of the city which is considered and numbered as such. In this ward there are eight teachers and about five hundred and thirty pupils; a library of three hundred and fifty volumes belongs to the school.

There is a school for boys attached to the German Roman Catholic church, which is divided into two departments, English and German, and has at present over one hundred scholars.

A school for girls was conducted by the Sisters of St. Benedict, who in 1861 completed their new convent in connection with the church. It has three school rooms, well arranged and provided with maps, globes, etc., and four teachers, two being English and two German. The name of the Prioress is Sister Scholastica Burkhard. The ordinary English branches are taught, with Christian doctrine, sacred history, drawing, instrumental music, embroidery, etc.

In August, 1804, the lot in Erie, No. 1378, corner of Holland and Seventh streets, where the East Ward schoolhouse now stands, was purchased from the State for the use of Presqu'ile Academy, in the name of James Baird. The only stockholders known were Daniel Dobbins, Thomas Stewart, and Samuel Hays. A school committee was in existence in 1805.

In 1806 the first schoolhouse was built of hewn logs by John Greenwood. Thirty dollars had been collected from citizens for this purpose. Erie had about one hundred inhabitants who resided mostly in that vicinity. The names of the teachers were Mr. Anderson, Mr. Blossom, Dr. Nathaniel Eastman, and, in 1812, Mr. Ebenezer Gunnison.

In 1811 Waterford Academy was incorporated. The trustees appointed by the Legislature were John Vincent, John Boyd, John Lytle, Aaron Himrod, Charles Martin, Henry Colt, and

Amos Judson.[1] It was endowed with five hundred acres of land near the village, and fifteen in-lots; in 1816 eight other in-lots were added.

By an act of February 24, 1820, the trustees were authorized to sell five hundred acres at a price not less than ten dollars per acre, and required to vest the proceeds in some productive fund, the interest to be applied for the compensation of the teachers.

The trustees erected their building in 1822, and in 1826 it was occupied as a school.

LIST OF PRINCIPALS.

John Wood	1826	R. R. Nichols	1843
Irvin Camp	1832	Peter Wright	1844
William Boyden	1832	A. O. Rockwell	1844
R. W. Starr	1833	James C. Reed	1845
R. W. Orr	1833	A. Davidson	1846
John Livingston	1834	A. Davidson	1847
E. R. Geary	1835	W. R. Marsh	1848
James Park	1836	J. H. Reed	1849
J. W. Miller	1837	C. J. Hutchins	1850
Irvin Camp	1838	A. H. Caughey	1851
William Benson, Jr	1838	J. R. McCaskey	1852
F. A. Hall	1839	S. S. Sears	1853
L. S. Morgan	1840	J. R. Merriman	1854–1857
Charles Woodruff	1841	J. P. Gould	1857
R. T. Stewart	1842	J. A. Austin	1857–1861

The present officers are John Wood, President; William Benson, Secretary; William Judson, Treasurer; C. C. Boyd, David Boyd, Miles Barnet, J. L. Cook, and J. M. White, Trustees. The permanent fund is $5,170.18; the common fund is $1,874.66.

The legislative acts incorporating the Erie Academy were approved March 25, 1817. At the same time the State donated to the trustees of said Academy 500 acres of land in Millcreek township, adjoining the borough, and later fifteen in-lots in the borough of Erie and $2,000.

At the meeting of the Board of Trustees, June 10, 1817, it was decided to divide the farm lands donated to the Academy into pieces of not less than five nor more than fifty acres.

April 12, 1818, it was decided by a majority vote to lease these lands for a term of 999 years to tenants.

---

[1] Mr. Judson held the office of treasurer from the beginning to December 31, 1858. He died in Waterford, November, 1860, aged eighty-seven, having resided there since 1795. Of him it was said with truth "that he lived a blameless life, and was honest, industrious, liberal, and devoted to objects of public utility."

On Saturday, April 25, 1818, the following notice appeared in *The Genius of the Lake*, a newspaper then printed in Erie:

"PUBLIC NOTICE.

"That the Academy land situate on the Turnpike road, in the township of Millcreek, Erie County, will be offered on lease in convenient lots (with the exception of the one on which the schoolhouse is erected) for the term of 999 years, at public auction, at the house of Robert Brown, in the borough of Erie, on the first Wednesday of June next, when the terms will be made known. In the meantime, any person wishing to lease may see a plot of the lots by applying to Thomas Forster, Esquire, at Erie.

"By order of the Trustees.
"THOMAS FORSTER, Sec'y."

There is an episode at this point in the affairs of the Erie Academy that does not show the most friendly spirit in the world to a rival school. The "Walnut Creek and Millcreek School Association" had erected a school building on the public land before it was donated by the State to the Erie Academy. This association, as poor and struggling, no doubt, as any in that early day of public schools, petitioned the Erie trustees to set apart the fraction of a lot on which the school building stood and confirm them in possession of it, that the schoolhouse and land might remain. But the Erie trustees passed a resolution leasing that particular tract of land for $20 per acre for 999 years; and that the lessees bind themselves to reimburse the association for the money actually laid out in erecting the building.

On June 3, 1818, the auction sales of the lands took place upon the following conditions: No bid to be considered that fell under the valuations previously fixed by the trustees. The bids to be for the lease of each acre or fraction for the term of 999 years; the legal rate of interest to be paid semiannually on the amount of the bid, during the term of the lease.

Owing to an indisposition of some of the purchasers to take their leases, or from a suspicion that they had bid too low, a new sale was held May 4, 1819, and the lots were resold at lower prices than the first bids.

The yearly interest on the pieces sold amounted to $451.44,

which was later increased by the sale of some pieces previously unsold. This interest, which was to be paid semi-annually, was the permanent educational fund of the Erie Academy. Subsequent acts of the Legislature empowered the trustees to give title to the lands of lessees, on payment of the price bid by them.

At the next meeting of the Academy Board of Trustees, composed as follows: Rev. Robert Reid, President; Thomas Forster, Secretary; Rufus S. Reed, Robert Brown, Judah Colt, John C. Wallace, Thomas Wilson, Giles Sanford, and Thomas H. Sill, it was decided to begin the Academy work. Judah Colt, Thomas Wilson, and Thomas H. Sill were appointed a committee to take the matter under consideration.

It was decided that on October 1, 1819, the Erie Academy be opened in Col. Forster's new house, with Rev. Robert Reid as principal, and Mr. Brewster as assistant, the latter teaching under the "Lancasterian system of school-keeping," the fad of that day, embodying rewards and punishments, and so-called "monitors," to report bad conduct of pupils. Before the day set for beginning school, Mr. John Kelley, of Waterford, versed in the "Lancasterian system," was engaged as a teacher.

On June 7, 1820, the trustees were notified that the State had appropriated $2,000 for a school building.

It was found on examination that the fifteen lots donated by the State were not conveniently located for the Academy building, and the committee were instructed to examine other available localities, including the "public square for the purpose aforesaid." Plans for a building were also ordered prepared of these dimensions: "60 feet in length and 30 feet in width; the lower story to be 12 feet in height; the second story to be 11 feet in height, the structure to be either stone, brick, or frame."

October 21, 1820, the proposal to sell to the trustees the four lots numbered 733-5, inclusive, owned by Enoch Marvin, at $75 each, payable in two years without interest, for an Academy site, was accepted. The Legislature was asked for and granted the trustees permission to sell the fifteen in-lots donated for an Academy site, the money from the sale to be used in paying for the new site.

Early in the spring a contract was made with Rufus S. Reed for the building of a stone Academy, as per dimensions previously stated, for the sum of $2,500, $2,000 of amount to be collected from money due the State on lands sold, and the other $500 to be paid after the building was fully completed and accepted by the trustees.

In 1799, at the sale of reserved tracts adjoining Erie, Franklin, Waterford, and Warren, five hundred acres were set apart for the use of schools and academies. To this fund fifteen town lots and two thousand dollars were afterward added—the latter to be collected by the trustees from debts due the State for lands in this vicinity. In 1821 other lots in town were added.

From 1819 to 1827 Erie Academy was conducted as an English high school by the following principals: Rev. Robert Reid, John Kelley, A. W. Brewster, George Stone, E. D. Gunnison, A. S. Patterson, and John Wood. In November, 1827, it became a classical school, conducted by the following as principals:

A. E. Foster, A.M.	November, 1827.
Richard Gailey, A.B.	April, 1836.
James Park, A.M.	July, 1836.
G. R. Huntington, A.M	April, 1838.
James Park, A.M.	August, 1830.
Lewis Bradley, A.M.	March, 1841.
John Limber, A.M.	February, 1842.
Reid T. Stewart, A.B.	September, 1843.
James C. Reid, A.B.	October, 1845.
R. S. Lockwood	December, 1847.
J. H. Black, A.B.	September, 1848.
J. A. Hastings, A.B.	October, 1851.
Fayette Durlin, A.B.	December, 1851.
C. L. Porter, A.B.	October, 1853.
W. B. Carpenter	December, 1854.
W. C. Bissel.	August, 1855.
G. W. Gunnison, A.M.	April, 1856.
L. G. Olmstead, A.M.	September, 1858.
E. W. Gale, A.M.	September, 1860.

This academy purchased a fine library, and chemical and philosophical apparatus, and a telescope seven feet in length, magnifying six hundred times.

The number of pupils in attendance during the sessions of 1859–60 was two hundred and thirty-nine, of whom one hundred and fifteen were males and one hundred and twenty-four females. A teachers' department has been connected with it, in which preparation for the profession can be obtained.

HISTORY OF ERIE COUNTY. 157

In 1838 the Erie Female Seminary was incorporated; Robert Reid, G. A. Lyon, T. H. Sill, G. Selden, C. M. Reed, George Kellogg, A. W. Brewster, Wm. Kelley, and James Williams, Trustees. For a few years the State appropriated three hundred dollars annually to the support of the institution. Miss E. D. Field, Rev. William Fuller and lady, and Madame Sosnowski successively were teachers.

Springfield Academy, at Springfield Cross Roads or East Springfield, is reputed to be one of the best institutions in Northwestern Pennsylvania. B. J. Hawkins was the first principal. The officers in 1858 were L. W. Savage, Principal; William Holliday, Thomas Webster, Dr. G. Ellis, J. Day, J. Teller, William Warner.

West Springfield Academy was founded in 1853. The Trustees were Z. Thomas, S. Devereux, N. Gould, D. Mershom, S. Rea, Sr., G. Ferguson, J. Eagley, P. Brindle, G. Hurd. W. H. Heller was principal in 1857. In 1855 eighty-four males and eighty-one females were in attendance. The second year of the institution John A. Austin, with three assistants, had charge. James H. Colt, of Waterford, held the office in 1858, and C. C. Sheffield in 1859. In this institution pupils had the privileges of a full college course at a moderate expense. In December, 1859, the building was destroyed by fire, with the furniture, books, etc.

Girard Academy was erected by a few enterprising citizens acquainted with the wants of the community. The building is of brick, finely arranged, and surrounded by spacious grounds. A students' boarding-house, with rooms partially furnished, has been provided. The school opened with 150 scholars. Mr. Pillsbury was the first principal, and N. J. McConnel succeeded, and in 1857 John A. Austin. In 1858 A. C. Walshe had charge, who was succeeded by Mr. Couse in 1859. There were in 1862 three teachers and about one hundred scholars. The same year the Trustees were James Miles, Homer Hart, Henry McConnel, L. S. Jones, George Porter, L. Hart, G. H. Cutler, P. Osborn, and James Webster.

The Northeast High School, under the management of P. H. Stewart as principal, two female assistants, and Professor Heimburger, teacher of languages and music, at present offers rare inducements for those desirous of securing a thorough and finished education.

Edinboro has the most expensive school buildings in the county. Ten acres of land eligibly situated were purchased, and commodious buildings erected at the cost of $25,000, contributed by citizens of the county. There are four buildings, assembly hall, academy hall, and two boarding-houses. The assembly hall is sixty-six feet by forty-four, and two stories in height, and is occupied by the model or public school, now numbering one hundred and twenty pupils. The upper story is devoted to the purposes of a lecture hall, and will accommodate a large audience. Academy hall is forty by fifty feet, and two stories in height. The upper story of academy hall has seven recitation rooms, and a library valued at one hundred dollars. The two boarding halls are three stories in height, and have accommodations for three hundred students, the dormitories being partially furnished.

The trustees of the academy, in 1857, when the first frame was erected, were P. Burlinghame, E. W. Gerrish, F. C. Vunk, Lewis Vorse, C. Reeder, J. W. Campbell, and N. Clute.

The Board of Trustees of the Edinboro Normal School applied, on December 3, 1860, to the Superintendent of Common Schools, for inspection and recognition, under the "act to provide for the training of teachers for the common schools of the State." Hon. Joseph Ritner, of Cumberland County; J. R. McClintock, Allegheny; H. L. Diffenbach, Clinton; J. Turney, Westmoreland, were appointed Inspectors, and the several county superintendents composing the Twelfth Normal School District were duly notified to attend for the inspection and examination of the school, on January 23, 1861. After a careful inspection of its arrangements and facilities for instruction, the school was found to have fully complied with the provisions of the act, and was officially recognized as the State Normal School of the Twelfth District, composed of the counties of Erie, Venango, Mercer, and Lawrence, by the name of the Northwestern Normal School; is to enjoy all the privileges and immunities, and be subject to all the liabilities and restrictions contained in the act and its supplements. The institution is under the guidance and control of Prof. Thompson. The trustees had reasons to expect an appropriation of $10,000 from the State—the Legislature, however, appropriated to the institution but $5,000.

The first Sabbath school in the county was established in 1817, at Moorheadville, in a log schoolhouse, which was removed in 1857. Rev. Mr. Morton, now of Corning, New York, and Col. James Moorhead were the founders.

As Erie has now a dozen Sunday schools and more than one thousand scholars, it is interesting to note the small beginnings of this excellent institution. Mrs. J. Colt, who had returned from a visit in New England where these schools were being introduced, suggested the subject in Erie. Mrs. R. S. Reed and Mrs. Carr were the first teachers, and the few girls constituting the school met alternately at the houses of Mrs. Colt and Mrs. Reed. The brothers of the girls soon asked to be admitted. Fears were entertained that boys would be difficult to manage, but these vanished and the school rapidly increased in numbers. Col. Forster tendered for its use a vacant room on his premises, which was accepted. In order to systematize the matter and place it on a more permanent basis, a call was made on the citizens to assemble at the courthouse, March 25, 1821, for the purpose of forming a Sunday school and moral society. The following gentlemen were appointed a committee to draft a constitution, to be submitted at an adjourned meeting, viz.: R. S. Reed, T. H. Sill, and G. A. Elliot. The committee reported as follows :

"Whereas, the united testimony of all Christians confirms the importance of instructing the rising generation in the principles of religion, as they are contained in the Holy Scriptures ; and as the most happy consequences have resulted from the Sunday schools established in Great Britain and America, and wishing to see one of these excellent establishments brought into operation among ourselves, therefore, we whose names are annexed to this paper do cheerfully unite and promise to adopt, as the basis of our union, the following articles," etc. The substance of the articles was as follows :

That a committee of three persons be appointed to provide proper teachers and suitable books ; that the school be opened and closed with prayer or reading a portion of Scriptures, and singing, if convenient. Though the teachers and managers are expected to render their services gratuitously, yet a small fund for the purchase of books to be awarded by the committee to meritorious scholars, will be required. Children and adults are to be freely admitted without regard to denomination, sect, or party, and parents and guardians requested to visit the school, and to exert themselves for its prosperity. Then follow the names of thirty citizens, with their contributions for the purchase of books, amounting to twenty-eight dollars and fifty cents.

From the first report it appears that the school commenced in May, with sixty-four scholars; that during the term of six months the average attendance was eighty-one, and the number of teachers eighteen.

The scholars had committed to memory and recited 16,525 verses of Scripture, 9,453 answers in the catechism, 1,625 verses of hymns, and the Lord's Prayer and Ten Commandments. They reported also that among the scholars were twenty-one persons of color, whose attendance and recitations had been good.

The utmost harmony and good will had prevailed, and the efforts of all had been to promote the welfare of the school. The next six months (for the school for many years had an intermission through the winter) the number of scholars diminished, and the managers urged its importance with renewed vigor—and it would seem successfully, for the institution has continued and prospered to this time. One of the most interested and useful citizens in the cause, for thirty years, was Mr. George Selden. Horace Greeley, who was in the printing office of the *Erie Gazette*, attended this school near its commencement, and was in the class of Mr. Joseph Chase.

Asa E. Foster, long principal of Erie Academy, and afterward of a high school, each Sabbath, for twenty-five years, engaged in the Christian and self-denying work of giving instruction and distributing tracts to the criminals in the county jail.

To show what a wilderness was New York, and not less

Pennsylvania, as well as to speak of the first Protestant missionaries in this region, we make the following extract:

"The Rev. Gideon Hawley, with Deacon Woodbridge, in 1753 (the year Fort Presqu'ile was built by the French) made a journey to Oquago, upon the Susquehanna, fourteen miles from the village of Binghampton; it is a beautiful valley, from three to four miles in length, and was the ancient dwelling-place of a tribe of Indians for a long series of years.

"Mr. Hawley had been solemnly set apart as an evangelist among the Western Indians; at Stockbridge he had a school attended by many Indians who wintered there. May 22, he set out with Mr. and Mrs. Ashley (the latter being an Indian interpreter), and Deacon Woodbridge, upon the errand of planting Christianity one hundred miles beyond any settlement of Christian people. Col. Johnson, Indian agent, who resided near Utica, favored their mission, and kindly met them in person. But they were not always so favored. A drunken Indian, named Pallas, who was acting as guide, fired at Mr. Hawley when the party were in a boat, on pretense of aiming at a duck. Mr. Hawley providentially moved his head just at the moment and was saved. The missionaries showed the Indians their credentials, and, among other things, preached temperance to them, at which they appeared to be religiously moved, and even converted, and disclaimed the ill-behaved Pallas as a foreigner."

In 1767 we hear of the Moravian missionary Rev. David Zeisberger, an unarmed man, of short stature, remarkably plain in his dress, and humble and peaceful in his demeanor, preaching to the Senecas at the mouth of the Tionesta, in Venango County. He built a block-house, planted corn, and gathered around him several huts of believing Indians. The surrounding tribes were said not to be equaled for wickedness and thirst for blood. Soon he retired from this hamlet called Goshgoshunk, fifteen miles farther up the river, to the present site of Hickorytown. Here he built a dwelling and chapel, and suspended the first church-going bell in Northwestern Pennsylvania. In consequence of broils with the Cherokees, the station was removed to Butler County. In 1770 the Christian colony again removed, setting out in sixteen canoes for the mouth of Beaver Creek, and establishing a station in the center of Beaver County, called Friedenstadt, or Town of Peace.

Sunday, July 2, 1797, we have an account of probably the first religious service held in what is now Erie County. Mr. Judah Colt, in his manuscript "Life," says, "About thirty persons assembled at Colt's station, who gave decent and becoming attendance while a sermon was read from Dr. Blair's collection, 'on the importance of order in conduct': 1st Corinthians, chapter xiv, verse iv. 'Let all things be done decently and in order.'" The selection of the subject, "Order," was suggested by circumstances. Immediately preceding, we find: "This season was one of much business, and, owing to the opposition of adverse settlers, one of much trouble and perplexity. We were compelled to keep from forty to eighty or one hundred men in the service of the company to defend the settlers and property. More than once, mobs of men, from twenty to thirty, would assemble for the purpose of destroying houses, and other mischief, some of whom I had indicted, and bills were found against them by the grand jury of the then Allegheny County, the courts being held in the borough of Pittsburg."

Some of the earliest settlers in the county, who were located at Northeast, were Presbyterians from Ireland, and brought their Bibles with them. Among these was a ruling elder, named William Dundass, and others of the names of Lowry and Campbell. They held their meetings in private dwellings, and in fine weather in the open air. An occasional missionary was sent out by the Ohio and Redstone Presbyteries, but this was of rare occurrence until after 1800. The first church edifice erected in Erie County was at Middlebrook, near Lowville, two miles from Wattsburg, in 1801. It was built of logs and is still standing, though not occupied as a church.[1]

To show the customs of the times with regard to religious services, as well as to give an interesting event in the life of one of the most enterprising as well as excellent citizens of Erie County, we make the following extract:

[1] Mr Colt's journal, 1801: "Rev. Mr. Wood, from Washington County, intended preaching at the Middlebrook church, but getting lost by taking the wrong path, could not find the meetinghouse, and returned to Colt's station after a fatiguing day's ride."

"In 1801, in the course of the summer and fall, we were visited by a number of clergymen who were sent out by the Ohio and Redstone Presbyteries, who preached in a number of places, and took much pains to collect and establish churches, and to convene the scattering inhabitants for religious service. Among those who came among us was the Rev. McCurdy, who appeared a very zealous man and well calculated to be useful as a traveling minister. On the Sabbath of the 27th of September (the first time the Sacrament was administered in the county) it was appointed and agreed upon to have the Sacrament of the Lord's Supper administered in the township of Greenfield, on a plantation then occupied by William

MIDDLEBROOK CHURCH, ERECTED IN 1801.
Sketched by Miss F. L. Spencer, in 1860.

Dundass, and a congregation of three hundred assembled. The day was pleasant, I accompanied Mrs. Colt to the place of meeting; on our way the conversation turned upon religious subjects, and my consort had come to the determination to offer herself as a communicant, and to become a member of the church—her mind appeared much occupied meditating upon the subject. While conversing with her I became more thoughtful than usual, and shortly after arriving at the place of meeting, I became more and more impressed with the evil nature of sin, and of the importance of leading a sober, orderly, and religious life, and it was not long after service that I found myself much distressed in mind, and my body considerably agitated. Although I felt a load of guilt upon me, I resolved to come forward and make a request to become a member of the church, provided I could be admitted at that late period. Accordingly, at the interval between those who sat down at the first table and those who were preparing to come to the second, I came forward and kneeled at the feet of the minister and elders, and explained to them as well as I could the situation I was in, and what I had a desire to do. After asking me a few questions, and after having a short conference among themselves, I was invited to rise, being overwhelmed with grief. A token of admittance was given to me by one of the elders—I arose and took my seat at the table. So it was that I and my beloved consort were both permitted to partake of the Sacrament of the Lord's Supper on the same day, and I hope and trust it will be a day of grateful remembrance while we live, and of unceasing praise beyond the grave.

"The ministers present were Revs. McCurdy, Satterfield, Wick, and Boyd, from the Ohio and Redstone Presbyteries. After service we were invited to go home with Mr. McCord, and on Monday, being the last day of the feast, people were again assembled and a sermon preached—it appeared a good day to me. Toward evening, service being ended, they returned to their respective homes, this being a new epoch to my life as it was a beginning of years."

From another source we find that this service was held at Northeast, and that about forty persons sat down at the tables.

The Presbytery of Erie was organized April 13, 1802. The enabling act was passed by the Synod of Virginia (under whose jurisdiction the territory then was) at their meeting at Winchester, Virginia, October 2, 1801. The first meeting was held at Mount Pleasant, Westmoreland County, Pennsylvania, on the day above mentioned. Erie Presbytery then embraced that portion of Pennsylvania west and northwest of

HISTORY OF ERIE COUNTY.   165

the Allegheny and Ohio Rivers, with a portion of the Western Reserve. It now embraces Erie, Crawford, and parts of Mercer, Venango, and Warren Counties. From it, have been constituted Beaver, Allegheny, Allegheny City, and part of New Lisbon Presbyteries. The New School Presbytery of Erie held its first meeting at Meadville, Pennsylvania, in June, 1838. It is proper to state, that at the time of the division of the General Assembly in 1838, the New School had the majority in the Erie Presbytery. At the meeting in June following, the Old School members withdrew, taking all the old records, as directed by the General Assembly. The New School Presbytery now embraces Erie County, with a part of Crawford.

September 1, 1803, Rev. Robert Patterson, of Ohio Presbytery, was ordained pastor of the church of Upper and Lower Greenfield for two thirds of his time, and immediately after arrangements were made by which he was to preach occasionally in Erie. The names of those who signed the call from Upper Greenfield were Thomas Robertson, Judah Colt, Timothy Tuttle, and Seth Loomis; the salary for two thirds of his time was two hundred dollars. The ordination took place at Mr. John McCord's bark house, Rev. Mr. Badger preaching the sermon, and Rev. Mr. Tate giving the right hand of fellowship. The Rev. Mr. Stockton was also present, and the people, as was the custom, were favored with preaching for several days.

In 1806 Mr. Patterson petitioned the Presbytery of Erie and desired leave to resign his charge. The reasons offered were that his salary was insufficient, and "impediments in the way of realizing any land as his own by purchase, embarrassed and disturbed his mind so that he had neither leisure nor due composure to engage in that reading, meditation, and study which were necessary to a faithful and profitable discharge of ministerial duties." With regard to the citizens, he says, "In their intercourse I have found them respectful, obliging, and friendly; and though the dispensation of the Gospel and its ordinances have not been attended by any remarkable success, yet we are not without some encouragement and dawnings of hope." Writing from Pittsburg, where he established himself in 1807, in reference to his successor in the county, Rev. J. Eaton, he says: "I would be rejoiced to be informed that the prospect of their religious horizon is becoming brighter than it has ever yet been, for to me it appears very nearly a land 'sitting in the region and shadow of death.'" Rev. Mr. Patterson died in 1832, near Pittsburg, where he had resided many years.

The Rev. Johnston Eaton preached a few Sabbaths at the mouth of Walnut Creek (Manchester) in 1805. In 1807 he returned, and was ordained in 1808 as pastor of the churches of Fairview and Springfield. The services were held in the barn of William Sturgeon, in what is now the village of Fairview.

The first preaching by Mr. Eaton was at Swan's tavern, on the east side of the mouth of Walnut Creek. This building was removed but a few years ago, when it was said to be the first house erected in the county.

In a year or two the congregation erected a log meeting-house opposite the dwelling of R. L. Perkins, where still are the remains of the burying-ground by which it was surrounded. Directly in front of the church was an Indian mound about six feet in height and fifteen in diameter, covered with grass, on which the hardy pioneers reclined at the noon recess. The house of worship soon became too strait, and it was enlarged,—even then, on fine days the services were conducted in the open air.

The first elders were Andrew Caughey, George Reed, and Wm. Arbuckle. Of the twenty-five original members at Fairview, but five survive (1861); their names are Jane Caughey, Agnes McCreary, Elizabeth Eaton, Jane Sturgeon, and Wm. Arbuckle.[1]

The Rev. Mr. Eaton was appointed chaplain of the army at Erie during the war of 1812-13, the most of his people being called to the defense of their country. After this he preached a part of his time in the Dunn settlement and in Northeast. From the organization of the Presbyterian church in Erie, in 1815, he labored there a portion of the time until 1822. Mr.

---

[1] Mr. Arbuckle died in Mill Creek, February 25, 1862, aged 91 years, being one of the earliest and most respected citizens of the county.

Eaton sustained the pastoral relation at Fairview until his death in 1847, a period of nearly forty years. He was a student of Rev. John McMillan, and a faithful servant, enduring hardships and encountering difficulties with indomitable resolution, and with ardent devotion to the Master.

At Erie there was no preaching for several years excepting by an itinerant or missionary occasionally. The inhabitants attended church at Northeast or Fairview, particularly on sacramental occasions. In 1807 the Rev. John Lindsay was employed by the General Assembly of the Presbyterian church for two or (if he preferred it) three months to preach in the new settlements in the Holland purchase, and to go as far as the town of Erie.

We need offer no apology for quoting largely from a historical sermon of Rev. A. H. Carrier, preached at Northeast, February, 1861, on the occasion of the occupancy of their old meetinghouse for the last time.

"The church at Northeast was organized, under the name of the church of Lower Greenfield, in the year 1801. The spot upon which those who formed it assembled was a place in the woods nearly in the rear of Amos Gould's residence. The services of the occasion were held in the open air, and they continued to be thus held until the log church was built. The minister who organized the church was the Rev. Elisha McCurdy. In Dr. Sprague's 'Annals of the American Pulpit,' an interesting and detailed account is given of the labors of this servant of Christ in Western Pennsylvania. He was a native of Carlisle, Pennsylvania. At twenty-nine he began preparation for the ministry, and pursued his studies seven years, mostly at Cannonsburgh. He was licensed to preach by the Presbytery of Ohio, in Washington County, Pennsylvania, in 1799. For some time after his licensure he was engaged in missionary labor in the region bordering on Lake Erie. He had an important agency in connection with the great revival in Western Pennsylvania, which commenced about 1801-2. It must have been while laboring in connection with that revival that he organized the church of Lower Greenfield, as it was called. Mr. McCurdy's last days were spent at Allegheny. He died in the triumphs of the Gospel on July 22, 1845, in the eighty-third year of his age. Though the founder of the church at Northeast, it does not appear that he labored either as its pastor or stated supply. The church at its organization consisted of twenty-five members, of whom none, so far as I am aware, are surviving, with the single exception of the aged Mrs. Moorhead,[1] in Harbor Creek. The church did not enjoy the services of religion each Sabbath, but through many years of its existence divided with other churches the labors of such ministers as could be obtained.

"In 1802 Rev. Robert Patterson accepted a call to take the pastoral charge of the Presbyterian churches of Erie and Upper and Lower Greenfield. In 1803, he was ordained and installed pastor of Upper and Lower Greenfield. He continued their stated pastor four years and a half, when he applied to the Presbytery for a dismission, and was accordingly dismissed. The church here consisted then of about forty members. After this there was a long interval during which the church did not enjoy the stated ministrations of any minister. In 1812 a Rev. Mr. McPherrin was employed for six months, and then, after another long interval, bringing us down to 1815-16, we find that the Rev. Mr. Eaton was engaged to preach either one third or one fourth part of his time at Northeast.

"Rev. Mr. Tate often labored at Northeast about these years, during seasons of religious interest, and at four days' meetings, held, as usual in those times, in connection with communion seasons. Rev. Mr. Eaton's residence was at Fairview, and his parish was somewhat extensive, consisting as it did of the place of his residence, together with Erie and the township of Northeast. There are several of the church and congregation who distinctly remember Mr. Eaton as their minister. In his day, worship was held in a log church on Cemetery Hill. When this house (the log one) was built, I have not been able to ascertain, but probably not long after the organization of the church. Thither from all the country round the people resorted, coming, not as now, over the best of roads and in comfortable carriages, but through the mire of swamps, and over stumps, treading their way upon horseback

[1] Died in December, 1861, aged 94.

or slowly moving in a cart drawn by oxen. The elder female members of the church have told me of frequently taking a child in their arms, and, upon horseback, riding eight, ten, or a dozen miles over not the best of roads to attend preaching. Sometimes the log church would be too contracted to hold all who came; then they would adjourn to the open air, and under the shelter of the trees would worship God. Thus the grove which adorns our attractive cemetery has often been made to resound with praise, to hear the voice of prayer, and to ring with the message of peace—the glad tidings of a Saviour.

"In 1818 it appears that Rev. Mr. Camp, a missionary, was employed statedly, one month, in which time a revival commenced which resulted in an addition to the church of about twenty members.

"The old log church now began to be too strait for its occupants, and perhaps it was argued by some of the younger members of the society that it was not 'up with the times.' This would seem, however, to have hardly been a valid argument, judging from the picture which one of our older members gives me of the appearance of the present village and surrounding country in those days. The few scattered houses along the main street were built substantially of logs; and interposed between them were wide tracts of girdled trees, which gave to the place the aspect of a harbor filled with masts. The worthy people, however, with commendable zeal for the cause of religion, determined that they would have for the house of God something better than their own. We are not in possession of any records stating precisely what steps were first taken, what debates were had upon the subject, what arguments were used in favor of the project, and what objections were urged against it; but I have heard it intimated that, with that tenacity of habit which generally characterizes elderly people, much was said by the more aged members against changing the location of the house. They had become accustomed to climb the hill where the sanctuary stood, the graveyard was there, their religious associations clustered around that spot, and they were unwilling that those associations should be disturbed. But the log village prevailed. Its inhabitants considered themselves centrally located, and succeeded in securing the new structure as an ornament for their street. The work undertaken was no slight enterprise. The record of the mode by which it was built proves under what difficulties it was prosecuted. Money was an article which played but a small part in the erection of the house which we desert to-day. The members of the congregation seemed to say in effect, by their contributions, what Peter said to the lame man at the Beautiful Gate of the temple: 'Silver and gold have I none, but such as I have give I thee.' The list of items constituting payments is a perfect curiosity, very significant of the condition of the times, and indicative likewise of much zeal that an excellent house of worship should be built. As scarcely any could furnish money, there was given what was equally serviceable—lumber of all kinds, and such labor as was needed. But besides this, unlimited amounts of grain and flour, and every merchantable article, were furnished as equivalents for the amount of subscription or for the price of the pews and slips. Some items credited are calculated to excite a smile, such, for instance, as 'bread and apple pies,' which were appropriated to the object in a way not precisely explained. Our notions of propriety, too, are somewhat startled, unless we understand how the temperance question stood in those days, by finding a more peculiar item credited. In one instance a barrel of whisky, price eleven dollars, is set down as a part payment for the price of a pew! Where it went to, and what was done with it does not appear. Our fathers unquestionably apprehended no difficulty in the way of such a barter. We may be thankful that the interval of years since then has created a more enlightened conscience in regard to the use of spirituous drinks.

"Through much labor and sacrifice the walls were at last inclosed and the house covered, and then, while the seats were yet not built, the people turned into the new house for worship. Doubtless it seemed, notwithstanding its then unplastered walls, a luxurious place to those who had occupied the old log house. All who had a hand in building it, or who were interested in worshiping in it, considered themselves exceedingly fortunate in possessing so imposing a structure. We who sit and shiver here these winter Sabbaths may do well to let our imaginations run back to those days when stoves for churches were not thought of, and when the congregation, within unplastered walls, managed as they could to keep comfortable. Not that it would be desirable to bring back those times, when any method of warming a church was considered a desecration of it, but it may be wholesome to remember what experiences have preceded ours. Some, even of the middle-aged members, have told me that they remember to have seen the minister preaching, winter Sabbaths, with hands well fortified against the cold in thick, woolen mittens.

"The work continued on the church, to a greater or less extent, for several years. The galleries were finally erected and the interior completed. At that day the building was considered by the surrounding people an architectural wonder. People, I am told, came long distances in order to see it. Doubtless it excited more remark, and was regarded with higher interest than is the case with our beautifiul new edifice. And indeed it was, for that time, a most creditable structure—in greater contrast with the dwellings of the people, and indicative, therefore, it is possible, of more zeal for the outward prosperity of Zion than the building which now so eminently graces our village. Owing to the gradual manner in which it was constructed, this house was never formally dedicated. The congregation were anxious to occupy it while, as yet, they were unable to finish it; and when finished, it had been already dedicated by their long-continued acts of worship, and, as we may hope, by the conversion therein of many a soul.

"After the erection of the church, the first minister who appears upon the records is a Mr. Ely, a licensed minister of the Buffalo Presbytery, who was employed one half his time for six months. This was in 1823. The church was commenced about 1818, and finished in 1822. In 1824 Rev. Giles Doolittle was invited, by regular calls, to take the pastoral charge of the congregation in Northeast and Ripley, New York. On April 15, 1825, he was ordained by the Presbytery of Erie, and installed by them pastor of the united congregations above named.

"The number of church members, when he took charge, amounted to sixty-eight. The only elders, two in number, at the time were John McCord and Thomas Robinson. The oldest surviving members of the church are Edmund Orton, Dr. James Smedley, and Harmon Ensign, who united at about the same time, having come from the same town in Connecticut; and among the females, Mrs. Robinson, who united about 1803, Mrs. Hall, and Mrs. Baldwin. Their connection with the church dates back to the times of the old log meetinghouse. Of those who joined during the same periods, some, however, are still surviving, but are connected now with the church at Harbor Creek.

"Mr. Doolittle continued his labors with this church from 1825 to September 14, 1832. He died at Hudson, Ohio, at which place he was laboring as pastor. In 1832 the church was divided. Fifty-eight members, living in Harbor Creek and vicinity, were constituted a church, leaving a membership here of one hundred and five.

"November 15, 1833, Rev. W. A. Adair was ordained and installed over the congregations of Northeast and Harbor Creek. It was during the years of prevailing religious interest—a period of revivals—that Mr. Adair was connected with this church, and during his ministry, in connection particularly with the labors of Rev. Samuel G. Orton, large accessions were made to the church. In 1836 the membership amounted to one hundred and eighty-three, and in April, 1838, to two hundred and fifteen—a larger number than are now in communion with us. In June, 1838, Rev. Nathaniel West commenced labors with this church. His pastoral relation with it ceased July 17, 1841. January, 1842, Rev. Miles Doolittle began to preach to the Presbyterian congregation of Northeast, and continued their pastor until some time in 1844. November of that year, Rev. Samuel Montgomery became their stated minister, followed by Rev. Mr. Paine in 1848, who was succeeded by Rev. Mr. Cochrane in 1850. August, 1852, Mr. Cochrane gave place to Rev. D. D. Gregory. During the continuance of Mr. Gregory with this people, a lot was purchased and a parsonage built thereon. March, 1859, the present minister took charge of the congregation. February, 1859, a meeting was called, and a committee appointed to take into consideration the purchase of a lot for a new church.

"The committee reported the twenty-eighth, were empowered to purchase March seventh, and March twelfth resolved to build. The result of that resolution is the beautiful structure which adorns our village."

In 1811 the Rev. Robert Reid, a minister of the Associate Reformed denomination, organized a church in Erie, which was incorporated as the "First Church of Erie." The congregation met in the schoolhouse until 1816, when they erected a comfortable building near their present site—Eighth Street, east of French. The frame, re-covered, is now occupied as a store, it having been removed to State Street.

The first elders of the church were Archibald McSparren, Thomas Hughes, Alexander Robinson, and James Barr.

The Associate Reformed denomination in 1841 erected a large and substantial church, and in 1845 called as pastor Rev. Joseph Pressly.

In 1816 the Rev. Charles Colson, a Lutheran minister from Germany who had settled in Meadville, organized four churches in this vicinity, expecting to have the oversight of them. One was at Meadville, another ten miles above, on French Creek, a third at Conneaut, and a fourth at Erie. He took a severe cold returning to Meadville, from the effects of which he died the same year.

In 1824 the First Presbyterian church of Erie erected a large and substantial building on the site at present occupied by their new edifice. The trustees were Judah Colt, P. S. V. Hamot, G. Sanford, R. McClelland, B. Russell, J. Evans, R. Brown, S. Hays, T. Laird, G. Selden, J. Kellogg. At the ceremony of laying the cornerstone, Rev. Timothy Alden offered prayer, and Rev. Johnston Eaton made a few pertinent remarks. Rev. David McKinney was ordained and installed April 13, 1825. Rev. George A. Lyon was installed September 9, 1829.

In June, 1859, the cornerstone of their rich and elaborate

structure was laid on the site of the former building. Rev. Dr. Chester, of Buffalo, Rev. C. J. Hutchins, and Rev. D. C. Wright took part in the exercises. Its cost, exclusive of the ground, is estimated at $25,000, and it is capable of seating nine hundred persons. The organ of this church cost $2,000.

March 17, 1827, a meeting was held at Mr. Hamot's for the purpose of organizing an Episcopal church. Col. Thomas Forster was called to the chair, and P. S. V. Hamot appointed Secretary. George Miles, G. A. Elliot, Taber Beebe, C. M. Reed, Thos. Forster, Jr., D. C. Barrett, Wm. Kelley, G. Knapp, and J. A. Tracy were elected vestrymen. Rev. Charles Smith accepted the office of rector, but resigned December 8. He was succeeded by Rev. B. Hutchins, and afterward by Rev. John W. James. Rev. Bennet Glover was next appointed, July 17, 1828, and held the office until his death in 1838. St. Paul's church was erected in 1831, on West Sixth Street.

The First Baptist church was organized in 1831. July 31, 1832, at a meeting held at the courthouse, Rev. Wm. H. Newman was called to the chair and O. N. Sage appointed secretary. The following gentlemen were nominated trustees: E. D. Gunnison, Abijah Frost, O. N. Sage, Wm. Kelly, James Lytle, Warren Foot (did not serve), Adonijah Fuller, George Moore, and D. J. Lloyd. The first pastor was Rev. Wm. Newman, and they erected their building in 1833, on the corner of Peach and Fifth streets.

In 1838 the Methodist Episcopal denomination erected a frame building on Seventh Street. In 1860 they dedicated their new house of worship on the corner of Sassafras and Seventh. This is one of the finest churches in the city. The house and ground cost $17,000. Trustees: J. Hanson, J. S. Sterrett, T. Willis, John Burton, Wm. Sanborn, A. A. Craig, J. W. Ayers, A. Yale, N. Murphy. In 1858 the same denomination completed a house of worship a short distance south of the town, at a cost of $4,000, called the Simpson Church. Messrs. E. Goodrich, Heman Jaynes, and Capt. Thomas Wilkins were liberal contributors.

In 1841 the Lutherans built a church. Rev. Mr. Hartman, pastor.

In 1844 the Universalists organized a church, and in 1845

erected their building on Ninth Street. First pastor, Rev. Henry Gifford. Trustees, Henry Caldwell, R. Huston, and Porter Warren. S. H. Kelsey, collector.

The first Roman Catholic church erected in Erie was a small frame building on German Street, in 1839. The cornerstone of St. Patrick's, on Fourth Street, was laid in 1850, and about 1858 a dwelling for the bishop and a schoolhouse were erected on the premises. In 1854 the diocese of Erie was created, and the Rev. Joshua Young made bishop.

In 1854 St. Mary's, a German Catholic church, was commenced, and completed in 1858. This is probably the largest, as it is the most expensive church in the city, its cost having amounted to $28,000. It has two spires 135 feet in height, and is furnished with three bells, one weighing 1991 pounds, another 1085 pounds, and the third 708 pounds. The bells cost $1,400, and are remarkable for their clearness of tone; they were consecrated by the Rt. Rev. J. Young, April 15, 1860. The church has an organ which cost $1,200, the Society of St. Cecilia engaging themselves in the choir. The Benedictine Fathers have had charge of the congregation since July, 1859, Rev. F. Celestine Engelbrecht, pastor.

Two societies for the propagation of the faith are connected with St. Mary's—St. Aloysia's for young men, and the Society of the Blessed Virgin for young ladies—each of which has a library.

The German Methodists about 1845 erected a comfortable house of worship near Fifteenth Street.

About 1850 the German Presbyterians erected a brick church on South Peach Street.

In 1855 an Old School Presbyterian church was organized by Rev. Wm. Willson, and immediately after the congregation erected Park Church at a cost of $17,000. First Trustees: G. Sanford, Joseph Arbuckle, J. C. Spencer, Wm. C. Curry, I. W. Hart, J. Moore, D. W. Fitch. Treasurer and Secretary, D. B. McCreary. In 1856 Rev. W. M. Blackburn was installed pastor. The first attempt of the General Assembly (O. S.) to establish a church in Erie was in 1842, when Rev. J. H. Townley was sent as a missionary. In 1853 the Presbytery of Erie made appointments for preaching for several months, having previously named a committee to establish a church when Providence should direct.

In 1847 the Wesleyan Methodist Society (colored) erected their building on Third Street, in Jerusalem, the western part of the town. The founders were H. E. Waters, John Clifford, Amos Burgess, Luman Harris, and Wm. Messick. The African Methodist Episcopals (also colored) formed a society and erected a building soon after.

The Protestant Episcopal church, Rev. Mr. Abercrombie, held services for a few months in 1858 in the Wesleyan church, when it was not otherwise occupied, and organized a Sunday school there. At the same time the Rev. Mr. Bowman, of the same church, held services at the depot.

The first instance of Christian worship after the manner of the Protestant Episcopal church, at Girard, was in June, 1858, in the Methodist Episcopal church, a large audience being in attendance. Rev. John Bowman officiated.

Girard township has five churches : one Protestant Methodist, three Methodist Episcopal, and one Roman Catholic.

Springfield township has six churches : two Methodist Episcopal, one New School Presbyterian, one Universalist, one Christian, and one Calvinistic Baptist.

Franklin township has no church edifice.

Fairview township has seven church organizations : one Methodist Episcopal, one German Methodist, one Old School Presbyterian, two New School Presbyterian (though but one house of worship), and two German churches, the denominations not known. In this statement are included the churches of Manchester and Fairview or Sturgeonville.

Summit township has two churches : one Methodist Episcopal that will accommodate three hundred persons, valued at $850, and one United Presbyterian, seating four hundred, and valued at $800.

McKean township has one Methodist Episcopal church, seating five hundred, and valued at $1,500 ; and a Roman Catholic, seating five hundred, which cost $1,300.

LeBœuf township has one Methodist Episcopal church, seating three hundred, and valued at $1,000 ; and a second one, seating five hundred, and valued at $1,500.

Washington township has one Christian Communion church, accommodating three hundred, valued at $1,200.

Concord township has one Methodist Episcopal church with two hundred sittings, valued at $1,000.

Harbor Creek township has four churches.

Greene township has two Methodist Episcopal, and one Presbyterian church.

Northeast township has three churches: one Presbyterian, valued at $1,000, seating three hundred; one Methodist Episcopal, valued at $3,000, seating three hundred and fifty; and one Baptist, valued at $3,400, that will accommodate four hundred.

Greenfield township has one Methodist Episcopal church.

Waterford township has six churches: one Roman Catholic, seating three hundred persons, valued at $3,000; one Lutheran, seating one hundred and fifty, valued at $300; one Presbyterian, seating two hundred, valued at $450; one Methodist Episcopal, seating two hundred and twenty, valued at $400; another of the same denomination, seating three hundred, valued at $500; one Baptist, seating three hundred, valued at $450.

Amity township has one Methodist Episcopal church, valued at $800, which will accommodate two hundred persons.

Venango township has one Methodist Episcopal church, besides the churches in Wattsburg.

Wayne township has two churches: a Methodist Episcopal, valued at $1,000, which will accommodate three hundred, and a Presbyterian one valued at $800, seating two hundred and fifty persons.

Union township has three churches: one Methodist Episcopal, valued at $1,000, with three hundred sittings; one Presbyterian, valued at $1,500, with three hundred sittings; and a Roman Catholic, valued at $800, with two hundred sittings.

The census statistics (which include those of the churches) of Mill Creek, Elk Creek, Conneaut, and the West Ward of Erie have not yet been published or filed in the Prothonotary's office, nor have they been aggregated, excepting in population.

Erie has been favored with revivals of religion at several

periods. In 1831 Rev. Mr. Stone held a series of meetings, and more than thirty persons united with the Presbyterian church.

In 1834 Rev. Mr. Orton, a zealous evangelist, held a protracted meeting, and about one hundred persons connected themselves with the different churches.

In 1842 the Rev. Mr. Clark preached for several days in the Presbyterian church—sixty-five persons united with the church at that time. Again, in 1858, more than two hundred persons united with the different evangelical churches in Erie.

Rev. O. Parker, an evangelist, labored successfully in the Presbyterian churches of Girard and Edinboro in 1860. At the latter place there were many converts in the Normal School.

CHAPTER XIII.

Waterford — Edinboro — Northeast — Wattsburg — Girard — Union Mills—Albion—Cherry Hill—Wellsburg—Cranesville—Lockport—Pageville—Lexington—Fairview—Manchester—McKean Corners—Wesleyville—West Springfield—Springfield—Beaverdam—Concord Station.

WATERFORD, beautifully situated at old Fort Le Bœuf,[1] the history of which has been given in a former chapter, is distant fourteen miles southeast of Erie.

In the act for laying out the towns of Erie, Franklin, Warren, and Waterford, is to be found the following : " Whereas, Andrew Ellicot lately surveyed and laid out a town, within

---

[1] Old Fort Le Bœuf being inland, was not ranked or fortified as a first-class station; yet, being situated on the "headwaters" of the Allegheny River, and at the nearest point of water communication between Lake Erie and the river, it was considered of much importance as a trading fort. It afforded protection to traders, hunters, and to many adventurers who passed between Canada and Fort Duquesne and the French possession farther south. The portage between Presqu'ile and Le Bœuf being only a little more than four leagues, the necessary goods, munitions of war, implements of agriculture, etc., were conveyed overland from the lake, and at Fort Le Bœuf embarked upon radeaux or rafts, to be transported to forts to the south and west along the river.

the tract heretofore reserved for the public use at Le Bœuf, near the head of the navigation of French Creek, and the draft and plan of the said town being communicated by the Governor to the General Assembly, was by them approved : therefore, be it enacted by the authority aforesaid, that the said draft and plan of the town so surveyed and laid out by the said Andrew Ellicot, . . . being first recorded in the office of the Secretary of the Commonwealth, and the original thereof deposited in the office of the Surveyor General, shall be, and the same is hereby, in all respects accepted, ratified, confirmed, and established, as fully and effectually as if it had been made by virtue of a law previously authorizing a town to be surveyed and laid out at Le Bœuf ; . . . and the commissioners hereinbefore directed to be appointed shall also survey five hundred acres of land, adjoining the said last mentioned town, for out-lots : and the same shall be divided in such manner, and with such streets, lanes, and alleys as the said commissioners shall direct, but no out-lot shall contain more than five acres, nor shall the reservation for public uses exceed in the whole ten acres ; and the said last mentioned town shall be called 'Waterford,' and all the streets, lanes, and alleys thereof, and of the out-lots thereto adjoining, shall be and forever remain common highways."

And in section thirteenth, "that it shall be lawful for the Governor, with the consent of the individuals, respectively, to protract the enlistments of such part of the detachment of State troops, or such part as may be in garrison at Fort Le Bœuf, or to enlist as many men as he shall deem necessary, not exceeding one hundred and thirty, to protect and assist the commissioners, surveyors, and other attendants intrusted with the execution of the several objects of this act : provided always, nevertheless, that as soon as a fort shall be established at Presqu'ile, and the United States shall have furnished adequate garrisons for the same, and for Fort Le Bœuf, the Governor shall discharge the said detachment of State troops, except the party thereof employed in protecting and assisting the commissioners, surveyors, and other attendants as aforesaid, which shall be continued until the objects of this act are accomplished, and no longer."

And section fifteenth, "that in order to defray the expenses of making the survey at Fort Le Bœuf, and the various surveys and sales herein directed, and to maintain the garrison at Fort Le Bœuf, there shall be, and hereby is, appropriated the sum of $17,000, to be paid by the Treasurer on the warrants of the Governor."

When Judge Vincent[1] settled in Waterford in 1797, he says: "There were no remains of the old French fort excepting the traces on the ground, and these traces were very distinct and visible." Fifteen years after, a cellar and a deep well were the only visible remains. Cannon, bullets, etc., have been found occasionally below the surface, and fragments of human skeletons pervade the soil. From the first settlement to the present time men have, at intervals, been searching for treasures on the sites of Le Bœuf and Presqu'ile, with all the helps afforded by the magnet and mineral rod. At Le Bœuf, in 1860, a man, digging under the direction of the "spirits," discovered below the surface a stone wall laid up with mortar, which would probably have a radius of one hundred feet. Within this was the foundation of a blacksmith's forge, or indications of one—as burnt stone, cinders, pieces of iron of all shapes, and of no conceivable use, guns, gun-locks, bayonets, and parts of many implements of war.

Judge Vincent says further, on the same ground, in 1797, stood a stockade fort built by Maj. Denny in 1794; it was commanded by an officer of the army, Lieut. Marten, with twelve or fifteen soldiers. The same year (1797) a new fort was built, which is still occupied by a family, though very much dilapidated, and some parts apparently ready to fall. This blockhouse was at one time a storehouse; in 1813 (after the

---

[1] Judge John Vincent was born in Newark township, Essex county, New Jersey, February 4, 1772. The family were originally from France, where his great-grandfather was born, in 1676. Several of the brothers were residing at West Branch, Pennsylvania, and in Fort Freeland when captured by the Indians.

Judge Vincent was appointed Associate Judge in 1805. He discharged the duties of the office for more than thirty-four years, being absent but twice from the sittings of the court. When he removed to Waterford in 1797, he found in the vicinity William Miles, Capt. Pollock, Capt. Martin Strong, and Amos Judson; and a strong friendship was engendered by common dangers and privations, and which was interrupted only by death. Judge Vincent was industrious, energetic, and persevering, and lived to enjoy the benefits his industry had accumulated. He died in February, 1860.

battle of Lake Erie) a body of prisoners and wounded men were there quartered; it was next connected with other buildings, the whole being weatherboarded, and a respectable hotel constituted. The main street of the borough running from north to south passes in front of the "Blockhouse Hotel," and over the same ground which was occupied by the French and first American forts. The whole is now the property of A. M. Judson, Esq.

In the neighborhood of the depot, two miles northeast of the blockhouse, spikes, bullets, cannon balls, etc. have been found. In another part of the town, a quarter of a mile from the fort, a hillock is called "Washington's Mound," from the fact (as tradition has it) that Washington, when on his mission in 1753, spent a night there.

One of the first appropriations for the northwestern part of the State, in 1791, was £400 for the improvement of French Creek (besides £400 for the road from Le Bœuf to Presqu'ile), and in 1807 we find five hundred dollars were to be set apart from the sale of town and out-lots of the Commonwealth, adjoining Erie, for clearing and improving the navigation of Le Bœuf and French Creeks from Waterford to the south line of the county.

Here it may not be out of place to give a short description of French Creek. It was formerly called Venango Creek, or rather, In-nan-ga-eh, and is a beautiful, transparent, and rapid stream. For many miles from its confluence with the Allegheny it is less than one hundred feet in width. At some seasons its waters are navigable to Waterford for boats carrying twenty tons, yet for a few weeks of summer it cannot usually be navigated by any craft larger than a canoe.

Washington, in his journal, calls Le Bœuf Creek the Western Fork, which is correct; but besides this there are three others, and these are now particularly so designated. In addition to many small streams, in all directions, proceeding northerly from the mouth of French Creek, its most noted contributary waters, all of which have mill privileges and are furnished with sawmills and gristmills, are Big Sugar Creek, Deer Creek, Little Sugar Creek, the outlet of Conneaut, Cassewago, Woodcock, the outlet of Conneauttee, Muddy Creek, and Le Bœuf Creek, on which Waterford stands, three or four miles above its union with French Creek.

In the articles on roads and the salt trade Waterford is conspicuous. Salt on its arrival from Erie was deposited in storehouses at the landing to await a freshet. There were four of these large storehouses, being the property of Judge Smith, Judge Vincent, Capt. Tracy, and Thomas King. Messrs. Tracy and King did not build until 1815 or 1816. The last load of salt carried down the river to Pittsburg was by Judge Smith, in 1819, the boat containing four hundred barrels.

In the days of the salt trade Waterford contained no churches, and the people assembled in the storehouses to hear the word of God. On one occasion when Mr. Matthews was preaching, the freshet reached the point that made it necessary, or at least desirable, to start the boats. The barrels were rolled out and the boats filled in the midst of the service, and the divine prayed for "the success of the boats that were obliged to start on the Lord's day."

The keelboats gave employment to many, who seemed to form a peculiar and vigorous class by themselves. An "up-the-river boatman" was quite a different specimen of the *genus homo* from all others. "He could drink, swear, smoke, and fight in a manner that would quite astonish his *degenerate* great-grandchildren of these days. The race is nearly extinct."

It was the custom to give the men who went with the boats every tenth barrel of salt for their pay. There was a Dutchman by the name of Jacob Kitelinger (as it was pronounced), who said to Judge Smith on one of his trips, "Judge, you are an old friend of mine, and, I believe, a good one. Prove it by giving me every *twelfth* barrel. I think I deserve it." The Judge thought about it, and finally, for *friendship's* sake, agreed to do it. Kitelinger was delighted, and when they reached Pittsburg worked industriously, setting aside for himself every twelfth barrel. But when he found that the others received ten barrels for every hundred and he only eight, the poor fellow was in despair. The Judge, however, was a man of honor, and gave him his due, but Jacob could never understand it.

Keelboat fare has been pronounced, even by some epicures, the very sweetest, owing, undoubtedly, to the fresh air and a good appetite. A mass composed of flour and water was well kneaded on the top of a barrel, the large loaf then placed on a board before the fire, and when well browned the lower side placed in the same position. Some slices of bacon were then roasted on the points of sticks, to complete the variety. Their drink was usually chocolate, with the bacon held over while roasting, some drops of the fat imparting a richness and flavor to the beverage.

To impel by poles against the current (as they were obliged to do on their return) was a most laborious employment; keelmen not unfrequently at that day had the side flayed and raw as a poor draught-horse long galled by the harness. "*No more going ahead, backward,*" was the expressive toast of an old boatman at the Meadville canal celebration; and well did his class appreciate the improvement.

On April 8, 1833, the town of Waterford was erected into a borough, being bounded and limited as follows: beginning at a white ash at the northwest corner of the Waterford reserve, adjoining lands of J. Vincent, Esq., on the north and west; thence east 276 perches along the north side of Circuit Street, adjoining lands of J. Vincent, Esq., and the heirs of A. Himrod, to a post at the northwest corner of G. W. Reed's land; thence south along the reserve line 159 perches to a post at the southeast corner of said Reed's land; thence east 69 perches along the southern boundaries of the same and the reserve line to a post; thence south 26 degrees, east 125 perches, along the eastern boundaries of out-lots numbers 30, 23, 22, 94, and 1, to a post adjoining land of Amos Judson on the south; thence south 64 degrees, west along the line dividing the out-lots and reserve tracts, 261 perches to a post at the southwest corner of out-lot number 12; thence north 26 degrees, west 40 perches, along the western boundary of said out-lot to a post on the south side of Water Street; thence south 64 degrees, west 126 perches along the south side of Water Street, to a post on the west side of Circuit Street; and thence north 422 perches along the west side of Circuit Street to the place of beginning.

The first borough officers were elected in 1834. Amos

Judson, Burgess; John Boyd, Henry Colt, William Benson, John Tracy, Isaac M. White, Wilson King, Town Council; Charles C. Boyd, High Constable; B. B. Vincent, Town Clerk and Treasurer; Samuel Hutchins and Daniel Vincent, Overseers of the Poor.

Waterford has a plank road connecting it with Erie and with Meadville, and the Philadelphia & Erie Railroad, which as yet has appeared to be of no advantage to the town.

It has four churches, of the United Presbyterian, New School Presbyterian, Protestant Episcopal, and Methodist Episcopal denominations. The Presbyterian church was organized in 1810, Rev. John Mathews being the first pastor, and William Bracken, John Lytle, and Archibald Watson, the first trustees.

In 1832 the Presbyterians united with the Protestant Episcopal denomination in erecting a church, which now belongs to the latter exclusively. In 1835 they erected their present house of worship.

The Associate Reformed church (United Presbyterian) was organized in 1816, Rev. Robert Reid being the first pastor. This is much the largest congregation in Waterford, and, like the same denomination in Erie, composed almost entirely of Irish Protestants. The founders were William Smith, Robert Kincaid, and William Carson. A year or two since they enlarged and improved their building.

The Methodist Society was organized as early as 1814, but did not erect a house of worship until 1854. Rev. Mr. Paddock, first pastor.

A Protestant Episcopal church was organized in 1827, and they erected their building, as mentioned above, in 1832. Rev. Bennet Glover was their first clergyman. Dr. M. B. Bradley, Timothy Judson, Amos Judson, Martin Strong, John Vincent, James Pollock, and John Tracy were the first officers.

Waterford Academy is the oldest institution of the kind in the county, as we have mentioned.

Waterford has eight factories and one banking establishment.

The borough officers are William Judson, Burgess; David

HISTORY OF ERIE COUNTY.

Boyd, William C. Smith, Samuel C. Stamford, J. L. Cook, J. L. McKay, Owen McGill, Town Council; J. M. White, Town Clerk and Treasurer.

EDINBORO, in Washington township, is twenty miles south of Erie, and but two miles from Crawford County. It was incorporated April 3, 1840, and is the most enterprising interior town in the county. Mr. Culbertson built a mill here about 1800, being one of the first mills erected in the county. Families of the name of Hamilton and Reeder were also among the first settlers. It was formerly called Conneauttee or Little Conneaut, an Anglicized aboriginal word.

Eight miles in a southwesterly direction from Meadville, is a beautiful lake three or four miles in length and one in breadth, called Conneaut, or as the Senecas pronounce it, Kon-ne-yaut, "the snow place." The Indians of the neighborhood had observed the snow to remain some time on the frozen lake after its disappearance elsewhere.

Here are church organizations of the Baptist, Methodist Episcopal, and Old and New School Presbyterian denominations.

The Old School Presbyterians, under the pastoral charge of the Rev. James Dickey, erected their building in 1855, at a cost of $2,000. It has sittings for five hundred and fifty persons. The Methodist Episcopal church will accommodate two hundred and fifty persons, and cost $500. The New School Presbyterian church cost $3,000, and will accommodate five hundred. The Baptists are yet without a house of worship.

In 1833 the Conneauttee Library Company was incorporated. Edinboro has the most expensive school buildings in the county, and the citizens have exhibited a commendable spirit of liberality and enterprise in their efforts connected with the establishment of the Normal School of the twelfth district in their midst. About $25,000 have been raised by them in subscriptions and expended in buildings and improvements, and the success of the school promises to compensate for the investment, and add to the population and prosperity of the town. The Normal School has at present four teachers and about eighty pupils. There is also one common school with two teachers and one hundred and thirty-six pupils.

M. Saley was elected burgess in 1861. A plank road connects Edinboro with Erie and Meadville.

For manufactures there are two cooper shops, two for the manufacture of sashes and blinds, one of shovel handles, three of cabinetware, a tannery, gristmill, sawmill, and tin shop.

The water power of Conneauttee Lake, obtained by the damming of the outlet, is one of unsurpassed excellence, and many factories working wood and lumber are found along the stream below. This lake is noted for its double, white pond lilies, which are exquisitely beautiful, and peculiar, we believe, to the American continent; springing from the bottom of the lake, they expand their flowers when they reach the surface and sunshine.

NORTHEAST was formerly called Gibsonville, and later Burgettstown, and is seventeen miles east of Erie, on the Buffalo and State Line Railroad. This vicinity has been long settled, and is highly cultivated and populous. The inhabitants are mostly Eastern people, while in other parts of the county the Scotch-Irish element predominates.[1]

Northeast has three churches, one public school, and a flourishing high school, at present under the management of P. H. Stewart, with three assistants. Rev. Mr. Carrier's very interesting history of the Presbyterian church in this place is found under the general head. The Methodist Episcopal church was formed at an early day. The Baptists dedicated a neat and commodious house of worship February 1, 1860. For many years this people had maintained public worship two miles east of the borough; in July, 1858, a church was organized denominated "The First Baptist Church of Northeast." Officers: E. C. Heath, A. Partridge, Deacons; E. C. Heath, A. Partridge, S. Malick, Trustees; and H. Partridge, Clerk.

An account of Northeast cemetery is found elsewhere.

For manufactures it has four shoe shops, two tin and two wagon establishments, one plow manufactory, a cabinet shop,

---

[1] The first brick building erected in the county was the residence of Mr. Silliman in 1809 or 1810, which is still firm and good. It is said the contractor was to have so much a thousand for all the brick he put in, and in accordance with a law of human nature, he used an enormous quantity, which in the end has proved good economy.

ashery, etc. It has also one banking office. At Freeport, two miles distant, the Franklin Paper Mill, owned by J. S. Johnson, is in excellent order, with every modern improvement. In 1860 they manufactured 4,000 reams of wrapping paper, 2,000 of writing paper, and 2,000 of printing. In 1838 a paper mill on the same site, the property of Mr. W. S. Hall, was consumed by fire, at a loss of $15,000.

In 1860 the borough officers were Philetus Glass, Burgess; J. M. Conrad, Richard Bran, John Greer, Rufus Loomis, Levi Jones, and Harley Selkregg, Town Council.

WATTSBURG, Venango township, is seventeen miles east of southeast from Erie, at the forks of French Creek. Provisions and stores from Pittsburg were landed here for Colt's Station and Northeast from their first settlement. There was also a landing at Bissel's mill, seven miles above Wattsburg, on French Creek, where at first provisions were landed for Colt's Station, being but two miles distant. In 1797 Mr. William Miles built "the upper storehouse," in which was deposited a few dry goods for the convenience of the settlers, and to exchange for furs, besides being a depot for provisions. Mr. David Watts (of the company known at an early day as Watts, Scott & Co.), from whom the town was named, owned a tract of 1,400 acres in the vicinity.

In 1796 Adam Reed and a Mr. Tracy, with their families, settled up the stream, a little above Wattsburg. Messrs. Reed and Tracy built a small gristmill on the east branch of French Creek at an early day.

In April, 1833, Wattsburg was erected into a borough, with the following boundaries: beginning at French Creek where the old State line crosses the same, being the south boundary of Venango township; thence east along said line 180 perches; thence north 180 perches; thence west 180 perches (more or less) to French Creek; thence southwardly by the windings of said creek to the place of beginning.

Wattsburg had, in 1840, one hundred and thirty-one inhabitants, and in 1860, three hundred and thirty-seven. It has three churches, a select school, and a common school with two teachers and one hundred and two scholars, which has a new building in progress. The Presbyterian church was organized at an early day—the church being of the New School branch dedicated a house of worship in 1854. It is valued at $1,500, and will seat three hundred persons. The Baptist and Methodist Episcopal denominations have also churches ; the Methodists completed a new one the past year at an expense of $4,000, which will seat four hundred. The Baptist will accommodate two hundred, and cost $1,200.

For manufactures it has two sash, door, and blind factories, two boot and shoe shops, one tannery, one harness, one of cabinetware, one ashery, etc.

This borough and the vicinity has been greatly benefited by the building of the Erie and Wattsburg plank road. In 1836 a bill for a railroad called the "Erie and Wattsburg Railroad" (a connection being intended with the New York and Erie) became a law, but for want of means the road was never built.

Wattsburg has a fine water power, an extensive flat and bottom lands up both branches of the Creek, and on the main stream. The forests are of pine, cherry, and other valuable timber. The soil is productive, the water clear and wholesome, and the climate salubrious.

L. S. Chapin was elected Burgess of the borough, in 1861, and Lyman Robinson, Justice of the Peace.

GIRARD was named from Stephen Girard, who, at the time the village was laid out, had a large tract of land in Conneaut township adjoining.

In 1814 the site of this pleasant borough was a part of the farm of John Taylor, and his residence was the only building.[1] It is fifteen miles south of west from Erie, and ten miles from the Ohio State line, and overlooks some of the finest scenery in the country. The valley of Elk Creek, winding toward the east, has precipitous banks—the stream having worn its bed in some places to the depth of two hundred feet. The rocky formation here is a soft, friable slate, in which are many fossil shells, and which appears solid, but on exposure soon crumbles to clay. On the creek there are several mills, and the water power is sufficient for an indefinite number.

[1] The names of some of the earliest inhabitants in this vicinity were Miles Taggart, Joseph Wells, James Laughlin, James Silverthorn, and Willard Badger.

Around is a rich agricultural country, dotted with pleasant farm houses and well-cultivated fields, and owned by a people who are excelled by none in all the qualities of good citizenship.

The borough was incorporated in 1846. The first officers were Mason Kellogg, Burgess; John McClure, Jr., Lefferet Hart, H. McConnell, and George H. Cutler, Town Council; L. S. Jones, Clerk. It contains four churches and a fine academy capable of accommodating two hundred pupils—this is particularly described elsewhere. Of the churches, the Methodist was organized at a very early day; the Presbyterians were organized in 1830, and after the division of the General Assembly in 1837, the New School branch retained the building. Three of the elders, Messrs. Bristol, Porter, and Blair, remained with the Old School, and for some years the possession of the church property was disputed by the two parties. The Old School, for some time, had preaching in the Methodist Episcopal church, and in 1852 erected a building. The Universalist church was organized in 1853, and their house of worship was erected soon after. A Roman Catholic church (Irish) was consecrated in 1856. This is outside of the borough limits.

The Erie Canal crosses the principal street on its west end, thus increasing its business without marring its appearance. The depot of the Lake Shore Railroad and the Pittsburg and Erie Railroad is about two miles north of Girard; from this place to Erie both roads use the same track.

For manufactures Girard has two carriage shops, a steam planing mill, and the requisite stores and shops for the population of the town and vicinity.

The buildings and grounds of the citizens are quite tasteful; the streets and walks are delightfully shaded by elms, maples, and locusts; the society is cultivated, and altogether Girard is quite a desirable place of residence.

West Girard has about twenty dwellings, Methodist, Episcopal, and Baptist churches, three machine shops, a mill, etc.

UNION CITY, or MILES'S MILLS, the third town in population, having 807 inhabitants, is situated twenty miles southeast of Erie, on the Philadelphia and Erie Railroad. Mr.

William Miles, from whom the place derived its name, was a soldier in the revolutionary army, and at the capture of Fort Freeland, on the West Branch, was taken prisoner and carried to Canada, where he remained until the peace. He then returned to Northumberland County, and in 1785, with Mr. David Watts, was appointed (by Gov. Mifflin, we believe) to survey the tenth Donation Tract.[1] In June, 1795, he returned and settled on the flats of French Creek, in what is now Concord township, Erie County. Accompanying him were his wife and children, and Mr. William Cook with his family. The manner in which Mr. Miles's children were conveyed from Franklin, Venango County, is worthy of especial notice. A sack was provided, partly open at the side, but closed at the end. The sack was thrown across the horse and a child placed in each side. Mrs. Miles carried her youngest child before her on the horse. Mrs. Miles and Mrs. Cook, her sister, were, next to Mrs. Reed, the first white women in the county.

Mr. Miles resided in Concord about five years, removing in 1800 to Union, where he erected the same year a sawmill and gristmill, and a frame dwelling house, which, from its being an unusual improvement, Mr. Judah Colt recorded in his diary at the time its dimensions, being twenty by seventy feet, and a story and a half in height. The nearest station was in distance eight miles. All provisions, in 1795, were transported by means of pack-horses, from Pittsburg to Concord; shortly after, they were brought up the Allegheny, and thence by its tributaries to Union City.

In 1796 Mr. Miles commenced clearing land where Wattsburg now stands, and built, in addition to his dwelling house, a store for provisions, where also a few dry goods were kept to exchange for furs. Wattsburg was laid out by him some

[1] The provisions of the party being procured in Harrisburg, were packed on horses and conveyed to a point near Wattsburg. An incident is related of the Indian steward: "The duties of Messrs. Miles and Watts being very severe, they hired an Indian, who was to act in the capacity of general cook, furnish meat, etc. 'Mr. Indian,' as is natural to the race, in time became remarkably lazy in his endeavors to procure meat, giving, as his excuse, the *scarcity of it in the wilderness;* but the trick was carried too far, and Messrs. Miles and Watts becoming cognizant that he was deceiving them, cut short *his* allowance of food, which brought 'the native of the forest' to a strict sense of his duty, which he never neglected afterward."

thirty years after. Mr. Miles died in Girard township in March, 1846, aged eighty-seven years. "As a pioneer he was hardy, intelligent, and sagacious. Endowed by nature with a mind of uncommon vigor, his talents were early called into action by the settlers, who, for a series of years, gathered around him as the guardian of their interests."

In the year 1796 families named Hurd, McCrea, Wilson, and Findley settled in the neighborhood of Union Mills. Three years ago Union Mills had but 293 inhabitants; its real and personal property was then valued at $98,217; it is now estimated at $267,380, which is a greater proportional increase than any other town in the county, and may be attributed to the facilities afforded by the railroad, and the transhipment of oil.

For religious privileges it has a Presbyterian church (New School), one Methodist Episcopal church, and one Roman Catholic church. It has two schools.

The Penn Rock Oil Refining Company, Mr. Parsons, manager, procured ground and erected a building, in which it is estimated fifty barrels will be refined daily. Clark, Andrews & Co. have established recently a factory for the manufacture of oil and flour barrels, firkins, etc. In this establishment they expect to manufacture eighty to one hundred oil barrels per day, and twice that number of flour barrels. The whole cost of machinery and buildings will be $4,000. The town has three oil refineries, one steam shingle factory, one for fork and shovel handles, one for wagons and sleighs, one sash, door, and planing mill, one of tin and sheet iron ware, one boot and shoe shop, and one cabinet shop.

Union township abounds in oak, white wood, cherry, second growth of ash, pine, and hemlock timber.

ALBION, Conneaut township, became a borough in 1860, and elected officers in March. In 1861 Perry Kidder was elected burgess. It is an active, thriving town, and in 1860 numbered 443 inhabitants; has a Methodist Episcopal church, and an academy with two teachers, and about seventy-five pupils in attendance.

Messrs. North and Denis manufacture at this place shovels, forks, hoes, hammers, etc., on quite an extensive scale. The power is steam; the articles are made of steel, manufactured at a branch of the firm in Central New York, whence they are forwarded to this point, where handles are affixed to them for the Western trade, while for the Eastern trade, handles are forwarded to that branch of the concern. The articles are all finished in the best style and defy competition. The number annually manufactured is counted by the hundred thousand.

This enterprise has been long enough prosecuted to acquire stability and permanence, and the management evinces a skill and discretion that augurs well both for the proprietors and the communities in which they are operating. A horserake factory in the same vicinity is on quite an extensive scale. It has also a machine shop and oar factory. The Erie Canal and Pittsburg & Erie Railroad pass through the place.

CHERRY HILL, in the same township, has about one hundred inhabitants, a church, one store, and several shops. It has but lately come into existence, but has good prospects, and ambition in abundance.

WELLSBURG is a pleasant little place on the east branch of Conneaut Creek, in Elk Creek township. It has 310 inhabitants, one Free Baptist church, one Methodist Episcopal church, and a Universalist church, erected in 1855. It has the largest tannery in the county, twelve shops of different kinds, and perhaps a dozen sawmills in the village and vicinity. The inhabitants are peaceful, temperate, and industrious.

Quite an unusual excitement prevailed within a few months, on the cleaning of a salt well which had been opened forty years since. An artesian well 300 feet deep three times violently ejected gas, etc., giving indications of oil. The occurrence brought to the locality many strangers and speculators.

CRANESVILLE is a village very pleasantly located in Elk Creek township. The first settlement was made here in 1796 or '97, by Elihu Crane, Sr., a veteran of the revolution. It has about thirty dwellings, a tavern, and a few stores and shops, one school, and a Methodist Episcopal church, midway between the village and Wellsburg. It is twenty-four miles from Erie and on the canal.

LOCKPORT, in Girard township, is twenty-one miles from Erie on the canal, and so named from having twelve locks in the vicinity. It was laid out and settled at the time the Extension Canal was being built. It has a Methodist Episcopal church, a Baptist church, and two public schools, averaging sixty scholars each. An extensive oar factory was built here by Messrs. Page, being 180 feet in length, 60 feet wide, and four stories high, but it is closed at present. It has several stores and shops, a printing office, windmill, small furnace, warehouse, etc., with a population of about 200.

PAGEVILLE is seven miles from Lockport, and has about 100 inhabitants, mostly employed manufacturing oars. Its post office is Platea. This village was built up principally by the enterprise of Mr. E. Page, near the edge of a large, dense forest of heavy ash and oak timber, which he has manufactured largely into oars and sent to all parts of Europe as well as the United States.

At LEXINGTON (a few miles south of Girard) the Pennsylvania Population Company had a station about 1797, Col. Dunning McNair being the acting agent.

FAIRVIEW, or STURGEONVILLE, is about twelve miles from Erie, being near the Lake Shore Railroad and Pennsylvania Canal. It has three churches, five stores, one carriage factory, one brewery, and several other shops. The inhabitants are mostly German, and are honest, diligent, and happy. It has 423 inhabitants. In 1814 there was but one dwelling where this village stands, which was owned and occupied by Mr. Wm. Sturgeon.

A contest between the Old and New School Presbyterian churches arose in Fairview shortly after the division of the General Assembly. Mr. Wm. Sturgeon died previous to 1837, and bequeathed to the Presbyterian church of Fairview, after the decease of his widow, about fifty acres of land and twenty town lots for church purposes. A burying-ground and schoolhouse upon the premises were to remain undisturbed. Six months after the decease of the widow, the church was to be organized, and a house of worship erected within one year. If these conditions were not complied with, the property was to be a donation to the Presbyterian Board of Publication.

Both branches of the church erected buildings within the stated time. The Court of Common Pleas decided in favor of the Old School, and the Supreme Court confirmed the decision. In 1860 the New School removed their building.

MANCHESTER, at the mouth of Walnut Creek, has some fine scenery and a few pleasant residences. There are two paper mills here. The Keystone Mills, R. L. Perkins, proprietor, manufactures printing, colored, and manilla paper, and employs six men and four girls. Adelphic Mills, J. C. Perkins, proprietor, manufactures manilla and wrapping paper, and employs four men and one girl.

MCKEAN CORNERS is on the old State line. It has a Methodist church and parsonage, twenty or thirty dwellings, etc.

WESLEYVILLE has 164 inhabitants, a Methodist church, several shops and stores, and one gristmill.

WEST SPRINGFIELD has a Methodist Episcopal church and a Universalist church, an academy and boarding hall, described elsewhere. The Lake Shore Railroad passes near.

SPRINGFIELD also has an academy and a Presbyterian church.

BEAVERDAM, in Wayne township, has a Methodist Episcopal church, a Presbyterian church, and several shops and stores.

At CONCORD STATION, on the Philadelphia and Erie Railroad, the gristmill known as Hall's lately passed into the hands of Norton & Miller, and has been repaired and remodeled to equal any in the county. Mr. Bedient erected a large turning and planing mill, and the carding machine of Mr. Reynolds has given place to a large woolen factory. Mr. Barry, late of Chautauqua County, recently erected a large hotel; and an oil refinery, with a capital of $2,500, is in progress, being directed by Mr. Ensign Baker, an experienced chemist from Fredonia, New York.

CHAPTER XIV.

Biographies of Col. Seth Reed—Rufus S. Reed—Judah Colt—Dr. U. Parsons—Dr. J. C. Wallace—Rev. Robert Reid—Thomas Wilson —P. S. V. Hamot—Capt. D. Dobbins—T. H. Sill—G. Sanford— Judge J. Galbraith.

COLONEL SETH REED was a native of Rhode Island, but at an early day removed to Uxbridge, Massachusetts. By profession he was a physician, and served in the revolutionary army at Bunker Hill with the rank of colonel. About 1790 he removed to Ontario County, New York, where he came in possession, probably by purchase from the Indians, of a very valuable tract of land eighteen miles in extent, known as the "Reed and Ryckman location." This he disposed of, and in 1795 removed with his family to Erie.

In Historical Collections of Pennsylvania we find: "Mr. William Connelly, now of Franklin, came out to Erie in the spring of 1795 with his cousin, Thomas Rees. They saw Col. Reed land—the first white settler[1]—who came in a bark boat with a quantity of groceries, liquors, and Indian goods. He erected a log cabin, soon after made it a double one, and called it *Presqu'ile Hotel*, where he entertained traders and travelers on the lake shore." In the "Holland Purchase" we find an extract from Deacon Hinds Chamberlain's journal, being an account of a journey to Waterford in 1795. "On our return from Le Bœuf to Presqu'ile we found there Col. Seth Reed and his family. They had just arrived. James Baggs and Giles Sisson came on with Col. Reed. I remained for a considerable time in his employ."

Col. Reed's wife and sons, Manning and John Charles, came with him; Rufus Seth a few months after, and George with

[1] Mr. William Miles settled on the flats of French Creek, at a point where two or more roads cross, a little northwest of the place where the Stranahans now live, in Concord township, in the month of June, 1795.

the daughters, Mrs. T. Rees and Mrs. J. Fairbanks, the following year.

Col. Reed died March 19, 1797, aged fifty-three years. Mrs. Reed (who was Hannah Manning, of Dedham, Mass.) died December 8, 1821, at the age of seventy-three, having lived to see great changes, and to tell those who came after of the trials and hardships of life in the wilderness.

RUFUS SETH REED was the third son of Col. Seth Reed, and was born at Uxbridge, Mass., Oct. 11, 1775. In 1798 he was married to Dolly Oaks, daughter of Jonathan Oaks, Esq., of Palmyra, who died the same year. In 1801 he was married to Agnes Irwin.

Rufus S. Reed was long regarded as the father of the town, his residence here being coeval with its settlement. From the first efforts to dispel the gloom of the surrounding forest to the hour of his death he was a master spirit, conspicuous for his enterprise, perseverance, excellent judgment and penetration, remarkable business talent and success.

As a man, Mr. Reed was kind hearted, entirely free from ostentation, easy of approach, and took delight in a generous action. "Early seeing the advantageous position of the lake country as a theater of enterprise, he was one of the first to lead off and plant the germs of a commerce that under his eye attained a growth which equaled that of one third of the Union. Possessed of a vigorous constitution, with an active mind and body, he earnestly engaged in extensive business undertakings which spread over a wide district of country, and amply repaid him for his enterprise and labor, as evinced by the immense estate he was in possession of at his death." To his various commercial, banking, and mercantile employments he added that of farmer, and applied himself with a zest and with his usual success to agriculture.

After a protracted illness, his mind retaining its accustomed clearness to the last, he expired on the first of June, 1846, aged seventy years. Mrs. Reed and his only son and child, Gen. C. M. Reed, still survive.

JUDAH COLT was born at Lyme, Conn., July first, 1761. As his history is identified with that of the western country, a brief sketch and some extracts from his journal will be given.

HISTORY OF ERIE COUNTY. 197

Until the age of twenty-three he assisted his father on the farm, and the last three winters taught school in the neighboring towns. He then resolved to see something of the world, and took passage in the sloop Betsy for North Carolina. As they were driven off the shore by adverse winds, they landed at the island of Bermuda, disposed of their perishing cargo, and repaired the vessel. They then made the harbor of Ocracock, N. C., and Mr. Colt visited the larger towns and taught school in the vicinity until spring, when he returned home after an absence of over six months. As was the custom, the prayers of the church at home had been offered for his safe return. In the autumn he made a tour to Vermont, taught school in Williamstown, Mass., in the winter, and next engaged himself as a clerk in the dry goods store of Mr. Thomas Shelden, of Lansingburg, N. Y.

When he returned to the parental roof, after an absence of eighteen months, his father made him proposals "such as a kind parent would do," but having seen a better country for obtaining an estate by labor, he excused himself from accepting his offer, and returned to Lansingburg to enter the employ of Mr. Nathaniel Gorham, a respectable merchant. Mr. Colt's father dying, he returned and settled his estate, spending the winter there. Finally, after several other tours, in 1789 he, with thirteen persons, with their goods, farming utensils, etc., set out for the Genesee country. At German Flats their wagon broke, and they proceeded from thence on horseback, each traveler carrying his own baggage. Through the scattering Dutch settlements the accommodations were poor. At Fort Schuyler (Utica) they crossed the Mohawk where there were but one or two small log houses; ten miles west they put up at Mr. Blackman's; from thence proceeded through the Oneida castle, following a bridle path, and at night encamped on the Canasaraga Flats. Here Mr. Colt's horse failed to keep up with the company, and Mr. E. Curtis agreed to move with him, as his horse could travel. Two days after leaving Utica they reached Onondaga river, and put up at Maj. Danforth's, near the salt spring, which was the only white family they found after leaving Blackman's. (One man resided in Oneida castle named Alburt or Talbut.) At

Cayuga Lake a family by the name of Richardson resided, who ferried them and their horses over in two canoes lashed together; ten days from Utica they arrived at Geneva, and put up at Gilbert R. Boney's, Mr. Colt's horse having failed after crossing the outlet of Seneca Lake. After remaining a day or two in Geneva he walked to Canandaigua and took shelter in a cabin occupied by Gen. Israel Chapin, being much fatigued. Provisions were brought in boats from Albany and Schenectady, and there was a great scarcity of the necessaries of life.

Mr. Colt contracted with O. Phelps, Esq., to survey a township situated on the Genesee River, known as No. 11, Honeoye township. On July 1, 1789, he purchased a town lot (forty acres) of O. Phelps, cleared the timber, and afterward erected a dwelling in which he resided for many years. He sowed wheat upon three acres of his lot the same fall, which was the first sown in that part of the country. N. Gorham and others sowed large fields the same season. [Mr. Colt's yielded twenty bushels to the acre.] In August a treaty was held for the purchase of the Indian lands, attended by the chief, Red Jacket, and 1,700 Indians, including women and children. The payment was made them in cash and merchandise. Rations of bread, meat, and occasionally rum were served out, and they came and went hungry. One hundred head of cattle were killed for them, but of flour there was a scarcity—one barrel made into bread sold for one hundred dollars in silver plate, of which various kinds of Indian ornaments were made. Many horses died distempered during the treaty, and the Indians fed on them freely, and also on the blood and entrails of all the beef slaughtered. While the treaty continued but little else was attended to, and although no serious accident happened between the whites and Indians, there were several narrow escapes in consequence of the Indians making too free use of spirits, and the misconduct of the white people, who were often the aggressors.

The winter following, Mr. Colt spent in Connecticut, his health having become impaired by frequent attacks of fever and ague. In September, 1790, he received the appointment from Gov. Clinton of sheriff of Ontario County; and on the third of the same month a court of quarter and general sessions of the peace was held at the dwelling-house of O. Phelps; Oliver Phelps, Esq., presided as judge, and James Parker and Israel Chapin as assistant justices.

In January, 1792, Mr. Colt was married to Elizabeth Marvin, of Lyme, Connecticut. During the winter of 1794, he continued in Canandaigua for the first time. The inhabitants were under serious apprehensions of an invasion by the Indians in the spring, if measures were not taken by the general government to quiet them. Early in the spring, news was brought to I. Chapin, Esq. (Geneva), superintendent of Indian affairs, that Capt. Brant had assembled with his warriors at Buffalo Creek, and was proceeding to Presqu'ile, Pennsylvania, to prevent the survey of the Triangle. To prevent serious consequences, Mr. Chapin repaired to Buffalo Creek, Mr. S. Colt accompanying him as secretary, and Horatio Jones as interpreter. The Indians were assembled, and after consultation, a part of the young men were dismissed, and a few of the chiefs took passage by water, with the superintendent, secretary, and interpreter, to Presqu'ile. From this they went on foot to Le Bœuf, where was stationed a small command of State troops, under Capt. Ebenezer Denny. On the Indians making their errand known, viz., to see the surveyors and to forbid them running lines, etc., they were informed that they shortly before left the country and had gone down the river. The Indians agreed to return home on assurances being given that the matter should be laid before the President of the United States.

It was agreed to hold a treaty with them the ensuing fall. Timothy Pickering, Esq., was appointed for that purpose, and met them at Canandaigua, in the month of October, when all matters of difference were amicably settled.

In August, 1795, Mr. Colt, accompanied by Mr. Augustus Porter, visited Presqu'ile for the purpose of purchasing land; and February, 1796, Mr. Colt made a journey to Philadelphia to confirm the purchase of his lands, as well as to make an offer to the Population Company of one dollar per acre for a tract of 30,000 acres in the eastern part of the Triangle. The company declined to sell in so large a body, but appointed Mr.

Colt their agent, at a salary of $1,500 per year, besides expenses for traveling, board, etc. In 1798 the salary was increased to $2,500, a clerk furnished, and all reasonable traveling expenses paid. May, 1798, Mr. Colt brought his family to Greenfield, where they resided until their removal to Erie in 1802. The history of Erie County, during its first thirty years in business and society affairs, is closely interwoven with that of its two most prominent citizens, Judah Colt and R. S. Reed. In October, 1825, Mr. Colt was elected first elder of the First Presbyterian church, and was distinguished for his piety and benevolence, as well as esteemed and respected in all the various relations of life.

The evening of October 11, 1832, without the least premonition, Mr. Colt suddenly expired, when seated with his family by the cheerful fireside. Mrs. Colt died March 13, 1834, aged sixty-six years; they left no children, two sons and a daughter having died in infancy.

USHER PARSONS, M.D., formerly of the United States Navy —the last surviving commissioned officer of Perry's squadron— was a native of York County, Maine. When war was declared with Great Britain in 1812, he was a surgeon's mate on board of the *John Adams.* The officers and crew volunteered for the lake service and joined Perry at Erie in June, 1813. Dr. Parsons was attached to the flagship *Lawrence,* and, owing to the illness of the two other medical officers of the squadron, was the only acting surgeon on the bloody and eventful tenth. Respecting his valuable services on that trying occasion, the commodore made most honorable mention in a letter addressed to the Secretary of the Navy.[1] Soon after (1814), he was commissioned full surgeon and sailed with the squadron to Mackinaw, and was present at the disastrous attack on that fort by Col. Croghan. Com. Perry was soon after ordered to the command of the frigate *Java,* and allowed the privilege of selecting his officers, when Dr. Parsons was appointed surgeon.

[1] "Of Dr. Usher Parsons, surgeon's mate, I cannot say too much. In consequence of the sickness of Drs. Barton and Horsely, the duty of operating, dressing, and attending nearly a hundred wounded and as many sick, fell on him; and it must be gratifying to you, sir, to know that of the whole number only three have died. I can only say that in the event of my having another command, I should consider myself particularly fortunate in having him with me as a surgeon."

In 1818 he again sailed to the Mediterranean in the *Guerriere*, commanded by Com. McDonough, and after one year obtained leave of absence and visited the hospitals and medical schools in France and England. On his return he had charge of the hospital in Charlestown, Mass., for a year or two; afterward he was appointed to a professorship in Dartmouth College, which he resigned the following year. Since then Dr. Parsons has resided in Providence, Rhode Island, excepting the winter of 1831, when he was Professor in Jefferson Medical College, Philadelphia.

In 1822 he married Mary Jackson Holmes, a sister of Dr. Oliver Wendell Holmes, the celebrated author and *littérateur*, and daughter of Abiel Holmes, D.D., LL. D., of Cambridge (author of *Annals of America*). Mrs. Parsons deceased in 1825, leaving one son, Dr. C. W. Parsons, of Providence.

Dr. Usher Parsons resigned his commission in the United States Navy in 1823. He was for some years connected with Brown University as professor of anatomy and surgery. In 1852 he was chosen first vice-president of the National Medical Association. He wrote the Life of Sir William Pepperell, several medical works, Reforms in the Navy, and probably he had a more complete knowledge of Indian traditions and history than any other person.

Dr. Parsons combined not only eminence as a professional man and scholar, but all the virtues and graces of a Christian gentleman. The period he was stationed in Erie, and the arduous duties which then devolved upon him, made a lasting impression, and in its growth and prosperity, and in the friends of those early and exciting times he ever manifested a warm interest.

DR. JOHN CULBERTSON WALLACE, the first resident physician in Erie, was born in Dauphin County, Pennsylvania, February 14, 1771. He was a good classical scholar, and graduated as Doctor of Medicine, at Philadelphia, under Rush and other celebrated medical men. In 1796 he accompanied Gen. Wayne as surgeon in the Indian war; was stationed at Fort Fayette, Pittsburg, and in 1801 went to Kentucky with Gen. Wilkinson's command. The same year he was married to Miss Margaret Heron, daughter of Capt. James Heron, of the army, being a couple remarkable for personal grace and beauty. Dr. W. resigned his commission as surgeon in the army, and after a residence of three years in Franklin, removed to Erie.

Dr. Wallace commanded an Erie County regiment at the commencement af the War of 1812, and was called into service with his regiment in the alarm that arose on the burning of Buffalo. Dr. Parsons, of the navy, was acting-surgeon of Col. Wallace's regiment for a short time. In attending upon the wounded after the batttle of Lake Erie, Dr. Wallace assisted Dr. Parsons at the hospital (courthouse) during the months of November, December, and January.

Dr. Wallace was elected the first Burgess of Erie, in 1806, and also held the offices of Justice of the Peace, County Commissioner and coroner. He was possessed of very considerable talents, being endowed by nature with unusual discernment, which he exercised as well on ordinary occasions as in his profession. He died December 8, 1827, being but little past the meridian of life. The direct descendants in Erie are Maj. R. A. Pollock and Miss Elizabeth Pollock (1893).

REV. ROBERT REID [1] was the son of James and Elizabeth Craig Reid. He was born at Reid's Hill, Hillsborough, near Belfast, Ireland, on November 5, A.D. 1781. Owing to the troublous state of the times in their native country, his father, James Reid, and the three sons, Robert, Isaac, and James, then their sole family, the mother having died young, emigrated to this country in the fall of 1798, during the political troubles then raging; in which, as most Protestants had done, he and his connections had taken sides with the government and Orangemen. This was not remarkable, as their ancestor, Capt. John Reid, had emigrated to that country from England under William of Orange, and was under him at the famous battle of the Boyne over a hundred years before, and after the final success of that struggle, remained in the country where most of his descendants are still.

James Reid settled in Philadelphia, and died there in 1821, and was buried in the then Spring Garden Cemetery. James Reid, the son, removed to Boston, but died young in Philadelphia, leaving an only daughter, Elizabeth, wife of Dr. Koch,

[1] Biography of Rev. Robert Reid, written by his son, James C. Reid, Esq.

the paleontologist, of St. Louis. Isaac Reid became a shipowner and trader to the Guianas and South America. He died in Philadelphia in 1854, leaving an only son now living, Dr. Neville Craig Reid, of Philadelphia; while Robert, the oldest and subject of this sketch, deeply imbued with the idea of religious duty, determined to devote himself to the service of the Gospel of Christ. He entered, as a student, the University of Pennsylvania, in Philadelphia, in 1801, and graduated with honor in 1805, being appointed immediately thereafter tutor in the chair of mathematics, which post he continued to fill during the following year.

Then entering the Theological Seminary of the Associate Reformed Presbyterian church, at that time located in the City of New York, he continued his clerical and professional studies under the presidency of the celebrated Dr. John Mason. Having engaged in the necessary preparations for the sacred calling with a zeal and perseverance characteristic of him through life, his studies were deep and thorough. Religion was in him not only practical piety, but a science as profound as the great Author of the universe, into the workings of whose mind we might by means of it obtain some faint glimpses; while his study of the original languages of the sacred writings continued and prosecuted they became one of the main pursuits of his life—one hour of every secular day when in his study being ever after devoted to the critical study and examination of the Scriptures in the original, as "containing the only rule of faith and practice," and as being the emanations and teachings of the Divine Spirit. Having completed the usual course and trials, he was licensed in 1809 under the authority of the Presbytery of Philadelphia, and for the next two years the field of his labors was in Virginia, Maryland, and Pennsylvania; principally in and west of the mountains, fulfilling Presbyterial appointments.

During his licentiate, he traveled over much wild and then thinly settled country, and preached in many neighborhoods, sometimes a sermon for each day in the week.

In the fall of 1811, in company with the Rev. Samuel Wier (afterward his brother-in-law), also a licentiate of the same Presbytery, under the authority of the Presbytery of Monongahela, he arrived at Erie, and in 1812 he was regularly ordained and installed as pastor of the Associate Reformed Presbyterian church, then the only organized religious association in Erie.[1]

Some years after, another congregation of the same church was organized in Waterford, and for many years thereafter he continued to preach. During the war of 1812-13, he often officiated as chaplain to Perry's fleet here and to the army on shore, and in alarms, like most of our older citizens, was sometimes on duty in the ranks.

He was married on April 11, 1816, to Elizabeth, daughter of David Calhoun, Esq., of Allegheny County, Pennsylvania, an elder of the Associate Reformed church, who died young. In 1828, he was again united in marriage with Elizabeth, daughter of Rev. Matthew Lind, an eminent clergyman of the Associate Reformed church, and long pastor of the famous Paxton church, near Harrisburg.

In 1819 the Erie Academy was incorporated, and he was elected President of the Board of Trustees, the duties of which office he continued to perform for twenty-five years, to the close of his life. In him the cause of popular education from the earliest times here, and during all that period, had a constant, efficient, and devoted friend; and after the organization of the Erie Academy, until a competent principal could be procured, he occupied the position of the first principal of the institution.[2] After a service of more than a third of a century in the ministry, he died on the 16th of May, 1844, in the sixty-third year of his age.

---

[1] "On Wednesday, October 21, 1812, Rev. Robert Reid was ordained pastor, the Rev. Messrs. David Kerr, Mungo Dick, and James McConnell were the members of the Presbytery who were present. On Wednesday, April 21, 1813, the Rev. Mr. Galloway, of Mercer, and Mr. Junkin, ruling elder, assisting, Archibald McSparren, Thomas Hughes, and David Robinson were ordained, and Alexander Robinson was installed, ruling elders, and James Dumars ordained deacon of the congregation."—*Copied from the original records, pp. 83, 84, of the Associate Reformed Church of Erie, Pennsylvania.*

[2] One of Rev. R. Reid's parishioners informed me that his custom was to visit every family of his congregation once in six weeks. This, with memorizing all sermons, in accordance with the practice of the denomination, must have called for untiring industry. Two hundred and fifty dollars, and at the utmost never more than three hundred dollars, was the salary allowed for the support of the pastor and his family. Mr. Frank G. Carpenter, the traveler and lecturer, of Washington City, is a grandson.

L. G. S.

His published works are:
1. A Funeral Sermon on the Death of Lieut. Brooks, United States Navy, published in 1813.
2. A Sermon, "The Reign of Truth and Righteousness about to commence," in 1824.
3. A Tract, "Observations on Dr. Watt's Preface to the Psalms of David," etc., in 1825.
4. "The Seven Last Plagues, being Dissertations on the Prophecies of the Book of Daniel, and on the Book of Revelations." 1 Vol., in 1828.
5. "Helps to Christian Devotion"; consisting of critical translations of, and dissertations on, the first twenty-three Psalms. 1 Vol., in 1833.
6. Two "Tracts on Church Government," published in 1839 and 1841.

As a scholar, he was distinguished for a profound and critical knowledge of the original languages of the sacred writings and their cognates, and as a mathematician. To the study of the exact sciences much of his leisure was appropriated, and his occasional contributions to the scientific periodicals of the day are still evidences of his extra-clerical lucubrations.

THOMAS WILSON was born near Sunbury, Northumberland County, Pennsylvania, in 1772. His father, John Wilson, who, was one of the earliest settlers of Northumberland County, died in 1774, and his sister Agnes soon after was married to Gen. David Mead, the pioneer to the waters of French Creek, and the first settler of the pleasant town which bears his name. In 1782 a band of Indians entered the residence of Mrs. Wilson, being led by a chief who had frequently been fed there, and after emptying the ticks and filling them with the most valuable household goods, departed with the mother and Margaret, a little daughter, prisoners. Seeing one of Thomas' garments on the grass, the chief angrily demanded him also, but fortunately he could not be found. Before evening they sent the mother back, but she feared to enter the house lest the Indians should return, and remained through the night in the stable. The child was redeemed three years after at Detroit, and afterward married a Mr. Barry, of Toronto. In 1802 Mr. Wilson was married at Waterford to

Miss Mary Naylor, who resided with her brother, James Naylor, Esq., being stationed there as Issuing Commissary for many years. Mr. Wilson removed to Erie in 1805. He had, for many years, been in partnership with Mr. Oliver Ormsby, of Pittsburg, in contracts for supplying all the Western military posts from Niagara to New Orleans; his last contract, which was at the time when Louisiana was ceded to United States, proved unfortunate, and involved him financially beyond recovery. The year of his removal to Erie he built two vessels, one on Lake Erie, called the *Mary*, and the *Fair American* on Lake Ontario, being the best on those lakes; afterward he built the *Lark* at Erie.

Mr. Wilson was a man of remarkable business talent and enterprise. His popularity in the county and among his acquaintances was only equaled by his large hearted beneficence. He held various offices of trust in Erie with credit, being successively Justice of the Peace, County Treasurer, County Commissioner, member of the Legislature, and member of Congress, and at the time of his death, in 1824, he held the office of Prothonotary.

His eldest daughter, Jane L., who deceased in 1860, was an agreeable and interesting writer, and the author of several works published by religious societies. The titles of the principal ones are "Broken Cisterns," "Arthur Singleton," and "Ruth Elmer."

P. S. V. Hamot was born in Paris, France, on November 28, 1784. His father was a captain in the French army, and a royalist, and left France for Russia, where he resided during the "reign of terror." Returning to France after the establishment of the "Republic," he offered to procure for his son a lieutenancy in the army; but such a position not being in accordance with his tastes, and his attention having been turned to the new republic of the West, he preferred to come to America and to try his fortune in a new and strange land. His father consenting, he came to Philadelphia, with the French consul, in 1802, as "*l'homme de confiance*," as expressed in his passport. The consul died soon after his arrival, leaving Mr. Hamot a friendless youth, and among a people in whose language he was little versed. His self-reliance, peculiarly a trait of his character, did not allow him to despond. A mercantile situation offering, he started for the West, as the clerk of a French house, in charge of a stock of merchandise. The vessel on the route was wrecked on Lake Ontario, but, with the goods recovered, he opened a store at Niagara, Canada, and from thence removed to Lewiston, and in 1805 to Erie. In 1810 he formed a partnership with Messrs. E. & D. Alvord, of Salina, who dealt largely in salt. This business connection continued many years. He was also engaged in general mercantile business on his own account, and was one of the first and most successful merchants of the place.

Mr. Hamot held responsible and honorable offices under the government; being at one time Canal Commissioner, and at another Superintendent of Public Works at Erie. He was the first cashier of the Erie Bank and one of the principal stockholders. As a business man, he was fortunate, and noted for his activity and energy in the prosecution of his plans, and for sound judgment. He engaged warmly in politics, his sympathies and feelings being with the Democratic party; and his politeness and hearty hospitality won for him many attached friends. Mr. Hamot was twice married : to Adeline Woodruff, of Lewiston, New York, in 1818, who died in 1821 ; and to Elizabeth Coltrin, widow of Dr. Asa Coltrin, and daughter of George Keefer, of Thorold, Canada, in 1825. He died October 17, 1846.

CAPT. DANIEL DOBBINS was born near Lewistown, in Mifflin County, Pennsylvania, January 5, 1776. He came to Erie with Esquire Rees' party of surveyors in 1795, when all was a wilderness. In July, 1812, while lying with his vessel, the *Salina*, at Mackinaw, he was taken prisoner by the British, it being his first intimation that war had been declared. Having landed the night before on the north side of the island, they took possession of the fort and the vessels in the harbor. R. S. Reed and William Reed, of Erie, were on the *Salina* as passengers, but were dismissed on parole. Capt. Dobbins was also allowed to return home.

In Chapter XV. is found an account of Capt. Dobbins' services in forwarding the construction of the squadron in

1813; and that through his discernment and perseverance Erie became the naval station.

While in the navy as sailing-master, he was also engaged in the merchant service. He had command of the *Washington* in 1816, which the same year conveyed troops to Green Bay, and was the first vessel which had entered that harbor, it being a difficult task to navigate it. On this first visit, Washington Harbor was called for the vessel; Boyer's Bluff, for Col. Boyer, who was aboard; Chambers' Island, for Col. Chambers, aboard; Green Island, for an officer of the name, aboard; and the Captain's own name, Dobbins, was given to a small group of islands.

In 1826 Capt. Dobbins was ordered to sea in the vessel fitted out to bring home the remains of Com. Perry, and resigned his commission. In 1827 he was engaged in constructing piers at Ashtabula. In 1829 Gen. Jackson appointed him to the command of the revenue cutter *Rush*, to which he was re-appointed by President Polk in 1845, and he left active service in the revenue department in 1849.

Capt. Dobbins was possessed of sterling qualities, and being a close observer, recorded many interesting incidents connected with the navigation of the lakes and life on the frontier. He died at the age of eighty, February 29, 1856.

THOMAS HALE SILL.[1]—Among the early residents of Erie, and belonging to that set of men who found it a frontier settlement in what was then the distant West, and of those who devoted their energies and talents to the building up of the place, the development of its resources, and the welfare of its inhabitants, the name of Thomas H. Sill may well be mentioned.

A daily familiarity with the city and harbor, their natural advantages and all the improvements which skill has devised and industry added, may indeed cause the present generation to forget the unremitting and varied exertions, extending through the past half century, by which those advantages, now regarded as a matter of course, were first developed and secured.

Of the men who during this period thus actively exerted

[1] From the pen of his son, Hon. James Sill.

themselves, hardly a survivor remains; and a history of Erie County would be incomplete were no mention made of them. Mr. Sill having in early life selected Erie as his home, and become identified with its people and interests, and having for nearly half a century participated in the vicissitudes, hopes, struggles, and triumphs always incident to a settlement through the various steps of its progress and development into a city, the very incidents or events of the life of such a citizen are inseparable from and part of its history.

We give, therefore, from the *Erie Gazette* next succeeding Mr. Sill's decease, the following biographical notice:

"This gentleman, who closed his earthly career at his residence on Sixth Street last Thursday evening, was the senior member of the Erie County bar as well as one of the best known and most esteemed citizens of Northwestern Pennsylvania. He had so long and conspicuously figured in the affairs of this section of the State, and particularly of our city and county, that his name had become a household word— and seldom was that name mentioned without deep-seated respect. Aside from his qualifications as a lawyer, which were of the first order, he possessed traits of character calculated to inspire universal regard and admiration. His deportment was unassuming yet dignified, his disposition kind and accommodating, his general course of conduct based upon principles of acknowledged integrity. As a husband he was attentive and affectionate; as a father, kind and indulgent; as a neighbor, generous and sympathizing; as a citizen, active, honest, and true. In short, in all the relations of life, whether as a lawyer, legislator, friend, or neighbor, he exhibited a commendable spirit of interest in the welfare alike of the county, State, and country, ever sustaining his endeavors to promote and secure the same by a strong and well-cultivated intellect and ready and effective eloquence.

"Mr. Sill was born at Windsor, Connecticut, on October 11, 1783. His father, Capt. Richard L. Sill, served in the Revolutionary War, and occupied an honorable position in his day. Graduating at Brown University, in September, 1804, and his health failing him, he traveled in the Southern States and made a voyage to the West Indies—at intervals, as health permitted, studying law. Completing his law studies with the Hon. Jacob Burnett, of Cincinnati, in 1809, he commenced practice in Lebanon, Warren County, Ohio. His health again failed, and after going back to Connecticut and returning to the West as far as Pittsburg, he was induced to locate at Erie, then a naval station, where he arrived in July, 1813, and remained until his death. From 1816 to 1818 he held the office of Deputy United States Marshal. In 1816 he married Joanna B. Chase, daughter of Rev. Amos Chase, of Litchfield County, Connecticut. In 1819 he was appointed Deputy Attorney-General for Warren County, and was present at the opening of the first court—practicing from that time until a recent period in the several courts of Erie, Warren, and Crawford Counties. The confusion occasioned by the burning of the courthouse, with the records, in 1823, induced a general movement in favor of sending him to Harrisburg in the capacity of a representative. In compliance therewith he relinquished his practice, and represented the district during the session of 1823-24. By dint of earnest effort he procured the passage of an act remedying the losses and inconveniences resulting from the destruction of the county records, connected with an appropriation from the State to assist in rebuilding the courthouse. He succeeded Hon. Patrick Farrelly in Congress in 1826, and was re-elected in 1828—being at that period the only anti-Jackson member from Pennsylvania. He declined a re-election at that time. He was appointed President of the United States Branch Bank in 1837, and held the office to the close of the existence of that institution. At various times he was elected burgess of the then borough of Erie, and for nearly thirty years filled the office of trustee of the Erie Academy; ever exhibiting a deep interest in the educational affairs of the city and county. He was elected in 1836 to the Convention to amend the Constitution of Pennsylvania—a body composed of the ablest and best men in the State—men like Forward, Sergeant, Meredith, Chauncey, Chandler, and Reigert—and it is due to his memory to say that in this body he acquired and maintained a position of commanding influence. He was chosen Presidential Elector in 1848, and, in accordance with the expressed voice of the State, as well as his own preference, voted for Taylor and Fillmore. Feeble health having, in a great measure, incapacitated him for the laborious practice of his profession, he was appointed postmaster of Erie by President Taylor, on April 16, 1849. President Fillmore reappointed him, and he continued to serve until June, 1853. He died February 7, 1856, 'full of years and full of honors.'

"Mr. Sill was confessedly one of the *first* members of his profession. He excelled particularly as an advocate, never failing, by his clear logic, smooth diction, strong sympathies, and unvarying candor and courtesy, to produce a deep impression, and frequently carrying the jury with him against the instructions of the court and the *apparent law* of the case. In this respect he had few, if any, superiors, and was always considered a dangerous competitor in the prosecution of important suits. Taking him all in all, he was a great and good man, enjoying the confidence and respect of all classes of society, and dying without a known enemy."

GILES SANFORD was born in Norwich Farms, now Franklin, New London County, Connecticut, September 18, 1783, and with his father's family removed to Herkimer County, New York, in 1801. Mr. Sanford came to Erie to reside in 1810.

The family can be traced back directly to John Sanford, President of Rhode Island in 1655. In 1637, having been disarmed for sympathizing with Wheelright in his famous opinions, in connection with Coddington, Hutchinson, and other well-known colonial men of wealth and eminence, Rhode Island was purchased. On the maternal side Giles Sanford was descended from Richard Edgerton, who, in 1655, was one of the thirty-eight original proprietors of Norwich, Connecticut.

In 1814 Mr. Sanford formed a mercantile partnership with Mr. R. S. Reed, which continued until 1824. In 1823 the firm in his name was contractor for supplying the military posts of Fort Dearborn (Chicago), Mackinaw, St. Mary's, and Fort Howard (Green Bay).

Mr. Sill and Mr. Sanford were delegates to the Canal Convention, which met at Harrisburg (in 1824, we believe), and which convention gave the first impetus to internal improvements in the State. The Board of Trade and the Natural History Society he was the first to suggest.

Mr. Sanford was ever a zealous and disinterested friend of public improvements, did much for the promotion of agriculture and horticulture in the county, and contributed liberally to benevolent and Christian enterprises. In consequence of his business connections, habits of observation and general information, he has rendered valuable assistance in this work.

JOHN GALBRAITH was born in Huntingdon County, Pennsylvania, August 2, 1794. His father was a soldier of the American Revolution, and took part in the battle of Long Island, where he was taken by the enemy, and being, with many others, imprisoned in New York, he there suffered hardships and privations, from the effects of which he never fully recovered. He resided in Huntingdon County after the war, when he removed with his family to Butler County, Pennsylvania, where he passed the remainder of his life. He gave to his children such opportunities for learning as were attainable in a new and thinly settled country. The subject of this sketch early exhibited a fondness for study, and although the facilities afforded to him were but meager and limited, he yet managed to acquire a liberal education.

Like many others who have attained a prominent position, he at one time, and when yet quite a youth, taught a country school. He served an apprenticeship to the printing business in the same office in Butler where James Thompson, afterward Chief Justice, was employed. He married Miss Amy Ayres, daughter of Rev. Robert Ayres, an Episcopal clergyman, of Brownsville, Pennsylvania. He studied law in the office of Gen. William Ayres, of Butler, at that day one of the leading lawyers of Western Pennsylvania, and was admitted to the bar in the year 1819. He began the practice of his profession soon afterward at Franklin, Venango County. He soon took a prominent place as a lawyer and acquired a large practice. In 1828 he was elected to the Pennsylvania Legislature, and was twice re-elected. In 1832 he was elected to Congress, from the district at that time composed of the Counties of Venango, Crawford, Warren, and Erie. He was re-elected to Congress in 1834, and again in 1838. On the expiration of his third con-

Engraved by J.C. Buttre, N.Y.

G. Sanford

ERIE, PA. April 6th 1861

gressional term in 1840, he resumed the practice of the law at Erie, to which place he had removed in the year 1837.

In 1851, the Constitution of the State having been so amended as to require the election of judges by the people, Mr. Galbraith was placed in nomination by the Democratic party as their candidate for President Judge of the Sixth Judicial District; and, although his party was in a very decided minority in the district, he was elected by a large majority—a marked evidence of the great personal popularity he always enjoyed. He continued to discharge the duties of his new position until his death, which occurred from a stroke of paralysis, on June 15, 1860.

Few men in the State had a wider circle of acquaintance than Judge Galbraith. Of remarkably gentle disposition and winning manners, he had a strong hold upon the popular heart. He was always the friend of the poor.

As a lawyer, he was studious and learned, rather than brilliant. He was never a fluent speaker, although very successful as an advocate. As a judge, he was distinguished for his thorough knowledge of the law; but it was more particularly in the administration of criminal justice that he was noted for a humane and discriminating appreciation of his duties. Avoiding the heartless and indiscriminate severity, which appears by many to be regarded as indispensable in the treatment of offenders, he always sought to temper justice with mercy, and, if possible, to reform as well as to punish.

It was as a judge of the criminal courts that his attention was drawn to the defects in our present penal system, and some of which he sought to remedy by his project of an Industrial Reform School. The charter for this institution was obtained by his efforts, and its list of managers numbered some of the most respected and honored names in the country.

CHAPTER XV.

War declared—Com. Perry—Capt. Dobbins' Correspondence—Com. Chauncey and Mr. Henry Eckford—Mr. Brown—Difficulties in fitting out the fleet—Gen. Mead—Capt. Perry at Fort George—Five Vessels brought from Buffalo—Provincial Marine Corps—Difficulties in procuring Men—Letters to Com. Chauncey and the Secretary of the Navy—A Providence recognized in the War—Getting the Vessels over the Bar—Com. Barclay at Port Dover—Seven of the Vessels make a Cruise to Long Point—Officers and Men from Lake Ontario—August 12, Com. Perry sails for Sandusky—Interview with Gen. Harrison—Squadron proceeds to Malden—Kentucky Militia—Sickness—Letters from the Secretary—Ohio dispatched to Erie—Strength of the British Force—The American Force—Americans again look in at Malden—Corrected Instructions for the Battle.

IN June, 1812, during the administration of James Madison, war was declared by the United States against Great Britain. The grounds given in the Message were "the impressment of American seamen by the British; the blockading of the ports of their enemies; the orders in council; and a suspicion that the Indians had been instigated to acts of hostility by British agents."

The bill for a declaration of war passed the House of Representatives by a vote of seventy-nine to forty-nine, and in the Senate by one of nineteen to thirteen. The day after the bill passed the Senate it was signed by the President, and in five days, as it afterward proved, the British orders in council were repealed.

The minority opposed the war on the ground of its being unnecessary and impolitic; that the aggressions of the French had been greater than those of the English; and they entered a solemn protest against the measure. These views had the sympathy of a considerable proportion of the people of the United States, and the war was consequently prosecuted with much less energy and success than it otherwise would have been.

Although hostilities had been meditated a long time, the country was in an imperfect state of preparation, and by land, the first year, the American arms were entirely unsuccessful. In the attempt of government to conquer Upper Canada, Gen. Hull and his army surrendered at Detroit, and Gen. Van Renssalaer met with defeat at Niagara, thus leaving the British in full possession of Lake Erie. Having five armed vessels, they captured the *Adams*, a brig of 150 tons, and the only armed vessel of the Americans,[1] and at any time could strike a fatal blow upon the South Shore settlements.

These disastrous expeditions urged the necessity of a naval force upon the lake to coöperate with Gen. Harrison, who had command of the Northwestern army.

The construction of this force was commenced in the autumn of 1812, at Erie, and gained the following year a most brilliant victory. Com. Oliver Hazard Perry, to whose judgment and bravery it was mainly to be attributed, with the blessings involved, was a native of Rhode Island, and entered the navy as a midshipman at the age of fourteen—this was on board the *General Greene*, a frigate of twenty-eight guns, in 1799, his father being in command. His ancestors were of the first respectability, and the following anecdotes of his childhood indicate that his mother was a woman of rare sense and excellence. On the removal of the family to Newport, "Oliver was placed at the school of Mr. Frazier, under whose skillful and judicious tuition he made rapid proficiency in all his studies. The relaxed discipline of the country schools, where, the numbers being small, everything was conducted somewhat upon the principle of brotherly love, furnished but an imperfect preparation for the sterner rule which the Highland gentleman found it necessary to exercise among his more numerous and heterogeneous disciples at Newport. The early days of Oliver's admission into Mr. Frazier's school were signalized by a very untoward occurrence—no less a one than his

[1] Some years ago, in a letter to a gentleman in Erie, J. Fenimore Cooper claimed the honor of wearing the first navy button on Lake Erie, being a midshipman on the brig *Adams*, which was not generally commanded by navy officers.

receiving a broken head, one day, for some trifling, and perhaps unconscious, misdemeanor, from a heavy ferule hurled by Mr. Frazier, in an ungovernable fit of passion, such as he was often subject to. Seizing his hat, without leave asked or granted, Oliver went immediately home, and told his mother he could never enter that school again. Mrs. Perry was a woman of strong feelings, eminently courageous temperament, and commanding character. She was necessarily indignant at the treatment of her child; but she was not much edified by Oliver's determinations as to what he would or would not do, nor disposed to yield to them. She did not reply to his decision not to return to Mr. Frazier's school, but quietly bound up his wounded head, and soothed him with expressions of maternal solicitude. Had she consulted only her resentment, it would have led her, at every hazard, to withdraw her child from the authority of one who had abused it. She wisely reflected, however, that Oliver being an unusually high-spirited boy, and his father generally absent, as he happened to be at that time, if she yielded to his wishes in this instance, he might expect the same indulgence whenever he felt discontented with a school from motives less well founded. This would not only be a disadvantage to him with regard to his studies, but might tend to weaken her control over him. She then wrote a note to Mr. Frazier, stating in subdued terms her indignant feelings at the outrage upon her child, coupled with the motives which restrained her from withdrawing him from the school, and concluding by the expression of a hope that she would not have cause to regret the mark of renewed confidence which she thus gave to Mr. Frazier by again intrusting her son to him. On the following morning, as the usual hour came around, she called to Oliver as if she had heard nothing of his declaration of the previous day, and told him it was school-time; at the same time she placed the note for Mr. Frazier in his hand, and told him she did not think he would receive similar treatment again. The proud boy's lip quivered, and a tear stood in his eye, but the thought of disobeying his mother had never entered his head, nor did it probably ever do so until the day of his death. She lived to rear five sons, all of whom entered the naval service of their country, and whom she fitted to command others by teaching them thus early to obey. Mr. Frazier was conscious of his own culpable violence, and alive to the good sense and magnanimity of Mrs. Perry's conduct. He devoted himself unremittingly to Oliver's improvement, and became warmly attached to him, and won his attachment in return—for Oliver, though high tempered, was a stranger to vindictiveness and cherished resentment. Newport was then an eminently commercial port. As many of the young men were intended for sea, Mr. Frazier had an evening class for the purpose of teaching mathematics, and their application to navigation and nautical astronomy. He took a peculiar pleasure in initiating Oliver into these sciences, and in the intervals between school hours, and on holidays, would frequently walk to the beach with him, where a horizon could be obtained, to take astronomical observations, and otherwise render his lessons more practical. Before Oliver left Mr. Frazier's school, the latter was wont to boast that he was the best navigator in Rhode Island."

Another interesting circumstance of Perry's youth is related by McKenzie. "When Oliver was but eleven years old, Bishop Seabury came to Newport, in the course of an episcopal visitation of the Eastern States, for the purpose of ordaining clergymen and confirming the young. Oliver's parents scarcely considered him old enough to receive and appreciate that solemn rite; but the Bishop having been greatly pleased by his appearance and manners, and by the maturity and seriousness which his conversation indicated, requested that he might come forward for confirmation. Afterward, when the Bishop came to take leave of Oliver's parents, he laid his hand upon the boy's head and blessed him in a manner so solemn and emphatic as to make an indelible impression upon all who were present. His mother was greatly touched by the incident, and received the impression that the blessing had been heard and answered, and would follow him through life. Toward the close of the year 1797, Capt. Perry, having secured a small competency, retired from his profession and settled in the village of Westerly, in a remote part of the State. Oliver was now entering his thirteenth year, his education unusually advanced for his age—for he had been a diligent student at Mr. Frazier's during the last five years—and an unbounded fondness for books, kept up from the early period when his mother had first taught him to read, had imparted to him an unusual share of general information. Fortunately for the youth of those times, novels were not so abundant nor so universally diffused as now, and the reading of Oliver was confined to Plutarch, Shakspeare, the Spectator, and works of a similar character, suited to instruct and furnish the mind and give force to his character." In after-life he was an earnest student, particularly of mathematics and astronomy. During his leisure hours his modesty and amiability, with his fine personal appearance and conversational talents, made him a favorite in intelligent and refined society. Though of a quick and excitable temperament, he was not disposed to be unreasonable or implacable. He was an elegant and fearless rider, possessed a fine musical talent, and added to these the more questionable accomplishment of playing an admirable game of billiards, but without the taste for gambling too often accompanying it.

At the age of twenty-two he was married to Miss Elizabeth Champlin Mason, of Newport, a lady of extraordinary gifts and loveliness; and it was said by one who knew Capt. Perry intimately, "that he was through life a model of every domestic virtue and grace."

Com. Rodgers had been his able instructor in seamanship; and previous to his command on Lake Erie, although then but twenty-seven years of age, he had been in charge of a flotilla of gunboats at Newport. Having the rank of commander, in November, 1812, he tendered his services for the lakes, as he had before applied for a post where he might serve his country and distinguish himself. On February 1, 1813, he received a letter from Com. Chauncey, who had the command of Lakes Erie and Ontario, stating that he had applied to the Secretary of the Navy to have him ordered to the lakes; and added, "you are the very person that I want for a particular service, in which you may gain reputation for yourself and honor for your country." A few days after, he also had the pleasure of hearing from his friend, Com. Rodgers, in Washington, that the new Secretary, Mr. Jones, had decided to order him to Lake Erie; and "you will, doubtless," he adds, "command in chief; the situation, I think, will suit you exactly; you may expect some warm fighting, and, of course, a portion of honor."

On February 17, he received orders to proceed to Sackett's Harbor with all the best men in the flotilla under his command, where he would be further instructed by Com. Chauncey with regard to his duties on Lake Erie. The same day Capt. Perry sent off a detachment of one hundred and fifty men and officers under the command of Sailing-master Almy; on the 19th, fifty men under Sailing-master Champlin; and fifty men on the 21st, under Sailing-master Taylor. His object in thus dividing the men was that they might the better procure conveyances and accommodations on the road. On the morning of February 22, he set forward on his mission, visiting his parents by the way, and taking with him his brother Alexander, a midshipman, then but twelve years of age. He arrived at Sackett's Harbor the evening of March 3, having waited three days at Albany for Com. Chauncey. As an attack was expected at Sackett's Harbor on the squadron and vessels on the stocks, the Commodore detained him there until March 16. On his journey to Erie (where he arrived on the 24th), he remained one day in Buffalo, examining the navy yard at Black Rock, then under command of Lieut. Pettigru. He then made some arrangements to have stores forwarded to Erie, and on the 26th set out himself in a sleigh upon the ice. At Cattaraugus, where he spent the night, the innkeeper informed him that he had recently been on the Canada side, and there had been questioned as to the vessels building at Erie, and the force stationed there, and his opinion was that the British intended to make an attack when the ice should break up. On the evening of the 27th, Capt. Perry arrived at Erie, and immediately acquainted himself with the state of affairs and the progress of the work. Here six months before, Gen. David Mead, who commanded the militia, had appointed Mr. Daniel Dobbins bearer of dispatches to Washington. Mr. Dobbins, with his vessel, had been taken by the British at Hull's surrender, and his experience on the lakes gave him an acquaintance with its harbors, commerce, and inhabitants. He received from the Navy Department the appointment of sailing-master, and was ordered to repair immediately to Erie and commence building the fleet, with instructions to draw upon the Department for funds to meet the expense, and to report to Com. Chauncey at Black Rock or Sackett's Harbor for further instructions. Accordingly, on his return he addressed the commanding officer, and in reply received the following :

"SIR :— "BUFFALO, OCT. 2, 1812.

"Your letter of the thirteenth ultimo, directed to Com. Chauncey or the commanding officer on Lake Erie, I have received, together with its inclosed, a copy of your instructions from the Honorable the Secretary of the Navy, each of which, together with a copy of this letter, I have inclosed to him for his consideration. It appears to me utterly impossible to build gunboats at Presqu'ile ; there is not a sufficient depth of water on the bar to get them into the lake. Should there be water, the place is at all times open to the attacks of the enemy, and in all probability when ready for action will ultimately fall into the hands of the enemy, which would be a great annoyance to our force building and repairing at that place. From a slight acquaintance I have with our side of the lake, and with what information I have obtained from persons who have long navigated the lake, I am under an impression that Lake Erie has not a single harbor calculated to fit out a naval expedition, and the only one convenient I am at present at, which is between Squaw Island and the main, immediately in the mouth of Niagara River. I have no further communication to make on the subject. Probably in a few days I shall be in possession of Commodore Chauncey's impressions, when you shall again hear from me.

"With esteem, yours respectfully,
"J. D. ELLIOT.
"*Mr. Daniel Dobbins.*"

Capt. Dobbins replied as follows :

"DEAR SIR :— "ERIE, Oct. 11, 1812.

"Yours of the second instant is received. In regard to the

idea entertained by you that this place is not a suitable one to build gunboats at, allow me to differ with you. There is a sufficiency of water on the bar to let them into the lake, but not a sufficiency to let any heavy armed vessel of the enemy into the bay to destroy them. The bay is large and spacious, and completely land-locked, except at the entrance. I have made my arrangements in accordance with my own convictions, for the purpose of procuring the timber and other materials for their construction. I believe I have as perfect a knowledge of this lake as any other man on it, and I believe you would agree with me, were you here, that this is the place for a naval station.

"I remain, very respectfully, etc.,
"DANIEL DOBBINS,
"Sailing-master U. S. N.
"*To Lieut. J. D. Elliot, U. S. N., Black Rock.*"

The letter of Lieut. Elliot was the only information Mr. Dobbins could get from that quarter; not being satisfied with this, he hastened to Black Rock, where he found Lieut. Angus in command, and as he had not heard from Com. Chauncey, or from any other quarter, of the building of gunboats at Erie, he expressed himself at a loss what course to pursue. Capt. Dobbins, however, employed Ebenezer Crosby as master carpenter, which Lieut. Angus sanctioned, and returned to Erie determined to urge forward the work with such house-carpenters as he could procure.[1]

[1] Extract of a letter from Capt. Dobbins to the Secretary of the Navy:

"ERIE, PA., Dec. 12, 1812.
"SIR:—
"I have expected workmen, or orders to employ them, but have received none, owing, in all probability, to the Commodore [Chauncey] not coming on [to Black Rock] as was expected. I have, however, gone on with the work, and at this time have two of the boats on the stocks, and will engage to have them *all* ready by the time the ice is out of the lake if required.

"Their dimensions are 50 feet keel, 17 feet beam, and 5 feet hold, and I think will be fast sailers. If it is desired that I should proceed with the work, please authorize me to draw upon the Department, as I have already expended a considerable sum over the $2,000 already drawn, the vouchers of which expenditure I will forward by the next mail. I have found a merchant [R. S. Reed] in this place who will advance money on drafts. I have negotiated those already received with him, and have continued to draw, as I feel satisfied the Department do not wish the work to stop. It appears the Commodore [Chauncey] has been so engaged on the lower lake as to have taken all his attention; but the ice will soon lock him, as it has the harbor at this place, which forms a complete barrier against the enemy this winter. I have not been able to make contracts for the construction, in ac-

Early in January Com. Chauncey and Mr. Henry Eckford, his principal carpenter, came on and inspected and approved the work, and gave instructions to get out timber for two sloops of war. Mr. Noah Brown, a master shipwright from New York, came on early in March with twenty-five carpenters.

In a letter from Mr. Dobbins to the Secretary of the Navy, dated March 14, we find the following: "The keels of the two brigs are ready to lay; the gunboats are ready for caulking. Although everything looks encouraging, yet I have my fears of the secret incendiary as well as the prowling spy of the enemy, and that in a moment our labor may be destroyed. I find I cannot raise any volunteers to guard the vessels, but have made arrangements with the carpenters in the yard to stand guard until I hear from you. Mr. Brown joins me in my opinion in regard to the danger, and the course I intend to pursue to secure a guard for the vessels." This guard, with a well-armed volunteer company of sixty citizens, commanded by Col. Thomas Forster, constituted for some time the only protection of the town and vessels.

Capt. Perry immediately on his arrival dispatched Mr. Dobbins to Buffalo for seamen and muskets, and, if possible, two 12-pounders. After a most perilous and fatiguing expedition, Mr. Dobbins returned with one 12-pounder (having left Buffalo with three), four chests of arms, ammunition, etc. The difficulty of creating a squadron where most of the supplies must come from the seashore—the cordage, cannon, powder and balls—at an inclement season, through a half-settled country, with miserable roads, can scarcely be conceived.

cordance with the wish of the Department, as the people in this country are poor and would fail to comply. I have made individual contracts with each workman. The iron I procure at Pittsburg, which comes high, as the roads are bad and transportation expensive.

"Please send me instructions at your earliest convenience.

"I have the honor to be, very respectfully, etc.,
"DANIEL DOBBINS,
"Hon. Paul Hamilton, Secretary of the Navy." "Sailing-master U. S. N.

It still being urged at the Department that Black Rock was a more suitable place for a naval station than Erie, Capt. Dobbins addressed a letter to the Secretary on the subject, dated December 19, 1812, from which the following is an extract: "In regard to the vessels cut down and lying in an unfinished state at Black Rock, there can be but little confidence placed in their safety. The yard is within reach of the batteries of the enemy, and if finished the vessels would be cut to pieces with their shot in passing up the rapids into the lake."

On the evening of the 30th of March, Sailing-master W. V. Taylor arrived from Sackett's Harbor with twenty officers and men, and the next day Capt. Perry left for Pittsburg to procure necessary stores, and to hasten, if possible, the coming of the expected carpenters. He arrived there on the 4th of April, and made arrangements to procure from Philadelphia canvas for the sails of the squadron, and also passed two days in visiting the different shops of the mechanics employed in working for his vessels. Many of the articles they had never before manufactured, and in such cases minute directions were required. Capt. A. K. Woolley rendered him great assistance in supplying necessary stores by loaning him four small guns and some muskets, and in superintending the casting of the shot. The carpenters, he found, had passed on to Erie, but their tools were yet to come, and the blockmakers were equally unfortunate. Having impressed upon the manufacturers the necessity of all being completed by the first of May, he departed on the 7th of April, and reached Erie on the 10th. In his absence he found the work had progressed rapidly.

At Capt. Perry's earnest request, Gen. Mead had stationed five hundred militia at Erie, so that a defense could be set up in case the British attempted the destruction of the vessels. Two of the gunboats, the *Porcupine* and *Tigress*, were launched the 15th of April, and were soon equipped for service. The *Scorpion* had been lengthened twelve feet by Mr. Eckford's order, and was not launched until the first of May. All were built at the mouth of Lee's Run, near the foot of Sassafras Street—afterward known as the "Navy Yard"— the government having rented the ground for a term of years and erected there a storehouse, hospital, and other buildings. The two brigs that were laid down shortly before Com. Perry's arrival were launched about the 24th of May. The *Lawrence* and *Niagara* were built and rigged precisely alike.[1] Their frames were of white and black oak, and the decks of pine. They were each 110 feet in length, and 260 tons burden; were pierced for 20 guns, and carried 132 officers and men. These, with the pilot boat schooner *Ariel*, were

[1] The *Lawrence* was the better sailer. Com. Sinclair, a year or two after the battle, suggested alterations in the *Niagara* which much improved it.

built at the Cascade, about one mile west of the town, where there was a good depth of water.

On the 23d of May, Capt. Perry suddenly took his departure for Lake Ontario, and was absent until the 17th of June. Capt. Perry was promised the command of the seamen and marines that might land when an attack was made on Fort George, and accordingly when he heard that Com. Chauncey expected to be at Niagara in a day or two, and the attack be made, joined him immediately. Capt. Perry left Erie in a four-oared boat at evening, and after a journey full of discomforts and perils, rendered valuable service by superintending the embarkation of the troops. Com. Chauncey, in his official report, mentioned that "Capt. Perry was present at every point where he could be useful, under showers of musketry, but fortunately escaped unhurt." The capture of Fort George led to the evacuation by the British of the whole Niagara frontier, and Capt. Perry was enabled to return with five small vessels of the government which had been detained in Seajaguady Creek, back of Squaw Island, by the enemy's batteries on the Canada shore. One of the vessels, the *Caledonia*, 3 guns, 85 tons, Lieut. Elliot had surprised and taken from the enemy; the *Somers*, 2 guns, 65 tons, formerly the *Catharine;* the *Trippe*, 1 gun, 63 tons, formerly the *Contractor;* the *Ohio*, 1 gun, 62 tons; and the *Amelia*, formerly the *Gen. Wilkinson*, built at Detroit, 1802, 1 gun, 72 tons, had been purchased and fitted for service by Mr. Eckford.[1] On the 28th of May commenced the laborious work of towing the five vessels against the current of the Niagara, which varied in strength from five to seven knots. To aid Capt. Perry in the work, two hundred soldiers, under command of Capts. Brevoort and Young, were detailed by Gen. Dearborn; he had also a party of officers and fifty seamen, that remained with him until after the battle. At Black Rock navy stores were taken aboard; and after two weeks of incredible fatigue the vessels passed the rapids. On the evening of the 14th they set sail from Buffalo, and reached Erie on the evening of the 18th without having been molested, though the enemy had a force in the vicinity six times that of

---

[1] The *Amelia* was condemned, on examination, immediately after the vessels reached Erie, and sunk in the harbor.

the Americans. The British ship *Queen Charlotte* and schooner *Lady Prevost* lay at Long Point when the vessels passed up. When hovering afterward around Sturgeon Point, they discovered a boat passing up the lake, which had left Buffalo Creek the preceding evening loaded with valuable property. The vessels immediately gave chase and fired several guns, but the Yankee skipper was too wide awake for them, and ran into Cattaraugus Creek and escaped. It is certain Capt. Perry manifested as much his skill and address *here*, as his indefatigable perseverance in stemming the rapids.

Previous to the war the English had upon the lakes what was termed a Provincial Marine ; the vessels had a slight armament, and were used to transport troops, Indian goods, and sometimes the property of individuals. This squadron was now commanded by Capt. Finnis, of the Royal Navy, and consisted of the ship *Queen Charlotte*, 17 guns, between 200 and 300 tons ; the schooner *Lady Prevost*, 13 guns, 96 tons ; the brig *Hunter*, 10 guns, 73 tons ; schooner *Little Belt*, 3 guns ; and *Chippeway*, 1 gun. Several of these vessels, and those of the Americans, were in sight from the same point on the bank of the lake, and just as the last vessel entered the harbor the enemy appeared in the distance. They must have greatly underrated the spirit as well as the strength of their adversary, and supposed they could be crushed without difficulty at any moment.

A letter awaited Capt. Perry on his arrival at Erie, from the Secretary of the Navy, highly complimenting his conduct at Fort George, as well as his exertions at Erie. In reply to this, Capt. Perry expressed diffidence as to his own capabilities, and says, " that no exertion should be wanting on his part to promote the honor of the service." He informed the Secretary " that one of the brigs was completely rigged and had her battery mounted, the other would be equally far advanced in a week ; the sails of both vessels were nearly completed, and on the arrival of the shot and anchors from Pittsburg, which were confidently expected soon, all the vessels would be ready for service in one day after the reception of the crews." Lieut. Brooks, of the marines, was engaged in recruiting, and had succeeded in enlisting thirty men at Erie and Pittsburg.

In place of an increase of forces which Capt. Perry so much needed, Gen. Dearborn, in consequence of an order from the Secretary of War, recalled the two hundred soldiers which had been loaned from Fort George to assist in bringing up the vessels. Capt. Brevoort, if it were agreeable to himself and Capt. Perry, he consented might be retained, and, as he had navigated the lakes, he would be particularly useful.

But five days after this reduction of Perry's forces, instructions came from the Secretary of the Navy to coöperate with Gen. Harrison in the Northwest for the recovery of Michigan. This presupposed that the squadron was provided with officers and men, and ready for action, when, in reality, Com. Chauncey had retained the crews at Sackett's Harbor. The plan of the Commodore appeared to be to overpower the enemy on Lake Ontario, and then repeat the action in person on Lake Erie. He seemed to forget the disadvantage of keeping officers and men strangers to one another and their vessel, until they were to encounter the enemy, and that but a handful of men, and these reduced by sickness, were expected to equip the vessels. Capt. Perry immediately wrote to Com. Chauncey, expressing a very great desire to have the officers and men that were to join him, especially a commander for the second brig. He had but seldom the satisfaction of a direct reply from the Commodore, but it was rumored that three hundred and fifty men would soon be on the way, and accordingly two boats were dispatched to Buffalo on July 18, in addition to the two that had conveyed the Fort George men to their destination. The sailing-master that had charge of the boats was directed to proceed with the greatest caution on account of the enemy's squadron, which was daily in sight of Erie, and nearly blockaded the port. On their return they were advised to keep close in shore, and call at Chautauqua and Twenty Mile Creek for instructions.

On July 19, Capt. Perry informed Gen. Harrison that he had but one hundred and fifty men fit for service, with fifty others on the sick list. On the same day he received a second order from the Secretary of the Navy, to coöperate with Harrison, under the belief that the squadron was manned, and also a letter from Gen. Harrison, stating that the enemy would soon launch their new ship, the *Detroit*, and that they had just received a reinforcement of experienced officers and prime seamen. Perry could only reply to the Secretary "that the enemy were then off the harbor, and the moment he had a sufficient number of men he would be able to sail, and trusted that the issue of the contest would be favorable." He then wrote to Com. Chauncey as follows :

" DEAR SIR :—

"The enemy's fleet of six sail are now off the bar of the harbor. What a golden opportunity if we had men ! Their object is no doubt either to blockade or attack us, or to carry provisions and reinforcements to Malden. Should it be to attack us, we are ready to meet them. I am constantly looking to the eastward ; every mail and every traveler from that quarter is looked to as the harbinger of the glad tidings of our men being on their way. I am fully aware how much your time must be occupied with the important concerns of the lake. Give me men, sir, and I will acquire both for *you* and myself honor and glory on this lake, or perish in the attempt. Conceive my feelings ; an enemy within striking distance, my vessels ready, and not men enough to man them. Going out with those I now have is out of the question. You would not suffer it were you here. I again ask you to think of my situation ; the enemy in sight, the vessels under my command more than sufficient, and ready to make sail, and yet obliged to bite my fingers with vexation for want of men. I know, my dear sir, full well you will send me the crews for the vessels as soon as possible ; yet a day appears an age. I hope that the wind or some other cause will delay the enemy's return to Malden until my men arrive, and *I will have them.*"

A day or two after this, the enemy were becalmed off Erie, and Capt. Perry pulled out to the bar with three gunboats to annoy them. A few shots were exchanged, and one of them struck the mizzen-mast of the *Queen Charlotte*, when a breeze springing up, they stood off.

On the 23d, Capt. Perry received another communication from the Secretary, urging the importance of immediately destroying the enemy's squadron. Again he replied, "that he was fully aware of the importance of the object—that his ships were ready but without crews." Had the men been sent directly from Philadelphia, in place of having to undergo what was familiarly called the "Sackett's Harbor examination," the object would have been better and more speedily effected. However, the same day that he replied to the Secretary, seventy men and officers arrived from Lake Ontario, and Perry wrote Com. Chauncey acknowledging the receipt of his letter and the seventy men, and earnestly requesting a full supply of officers and men for his vessels.

About this time a concentration of the enemy's troops took place at Long Point, directly opposite Erie, at the distance of forty miles, and fears were entertained lest an attack should be made upon Erie and the squadron destroyed before the arrival of the crews. Great consternation prevailed among the inhabitants of the village, many of them removing their families and goods back from the lake. Maj.-Gen. Mead was called upon for a reinforcement of the militia, who made a show of defense by parading on the high bank when the enemy were in sight. The officers were all kept aboard, and boats rowed guard throughout the night. Capt. Perry apprised the Secretary of the Navy and Com. Chauncey of the fact, and also that he had no apprehension for the fleet even though the enemy should get possession of the town, which he did not expect. It proved afterward that an attack had been planned, but failed for the want of troops at the proper time.

On July 27, Capt. Perry received a letter by express from Gen. Holmes, by order of Gen. Harrison, stating that the enemy had invested Fort Meigs a second time with a heavy force, and that the presence of the enemy's squadron off Erie was unfortunate, unless Capt. Perry could either elude or fight them. He urged in strong terms, for Gen. Harrison, that Capt. Perry's great object should be to coöperate with the army by sailing up Lake Erie, and concluded his letter with "assurances of the perfect conviction of the General, that on his part no exertion would be omitted to give the crisis an issue of profit and glory to the arms of our country." Capt. Perry immediately inclosed the letter of Gen. Holmes to Com.

Chauncey with the following, indicating his distress of mind in being so unnecessarily hampered:

"SIR :—

"I have this moment received by express the inclosed letter from Gen. Harrison. If I had officers and men, and I have no doubt you will send them, I could fight the enemy and proceed up the lake. But having no one to command the Niagara, and only one commissioned lieutenant and two acting lieutenants, whatever my wishes may be, going out is out of the question. The men that came by Mr. Champlin are a motley set, blacks—soldiers, and boys. I cannot think you saw them after they were selected. I am, however, pleased to see anything in the shape of a man."

On July 30 he received from Lake Ontario an additional reinforcement of sixty officers and men, and soon after opened a rendezvous for landsmen, to serve four months or until after a decisive battle, at ten dollars a month. He had now three hundred officers and men to man two twenty-gun brigs (each brig carried one hundred and thirty-two men) and eight smaller vessels, and an aggregate of fifty-five guns. The men were in general of an inferior description, and more than one fifth incapacitated for duty by disease incident to a change of climate. The able-bodied had been incessantly engaged in duties not relevant to their essential ones in a naval engagement, as gunners, boarders, pikemen, sail trimmers, etc.

The disposition throughout the country to recognize a Providence in the war deserves attention. Dr. Parsons says: "On Sunday, July 18, two respectable missionaries, who were passing through Erie, were invited by the Commodore on board one of the large ships, where as many officers and men as could be spared from all the vessels were assembled to hear prayers that were offered up for the success of the expedition. I shall never forget their fervent pleadings in our behalf, that we might subdue the hostile fleet, and thereby wrest from savage hands the tomahawk and scalping knife, that had been so cruelly wielded against the defenseless settlers on the frontiers, and that in the event of a victory, mercy and kindness might be shown to the vanquished."

Several of the States appointed days of "thanksgiving, fasting, and prayers, that He in whose hands are the mighty, would in the hour of battle be their strength and deliverance." A resolution is recorded in the Pamphlet Laws of 1812, requesting the President of the United States to recommend a day of public humiliation. It reads as follows:

"It being a duty peculiarly incumbent in a time of public calamity and war, humbly and devoutly to acknowledge our dependence in Almighty God, and to implore his aid and protection; therefore,

"*Resolved*, By the Senate and House of Representatives of the United States of America in Congress assembled, that a joint committee of both houses wait on the President of the United States, and request that he recommend a day of public humiliation and prayer, to be observed by the people of the United States with religious solemnity, and the offering of fervent supplication to Almighty God for the safety and welfare of these States, his blessings upon their arms, and the speedy restoration of peace.

"H. CLAY, *Speaker of the H. R.*
"WM. H. CRAWFORD, *President of the Senate, pro. tem.*"

The bay of Presqu'ile, as before mentioned, had a bar of light sand at its entrance, where the water (on an average eighteen feet in depth) varied from six to ten feet, and sometimes in a gale of wind was as low as five feet. Maj. James G. Totten, who surveyed the harbor in 1824, says: "In continuation of Presqu'ile, there is a sandbank under water, nearly a mile wide, which runs in a southeast direction to the shore of the main, a little eastward of the town of Erie, reducing the depth of the water in this part (the mouth of the basin) to about six feet on the average. A narrow and winding channel runs through this bank, in which there is from five to nine feet water." On Sunday, August 1, the large vessels arrived at the bar, and were visited by Gen. Mead and staff in full dress, about noon, and received a national salute, fired by Lieut. Holdup, in an excellent style. The firing drew people in from the country in great numbers, who lined the shore of the lake, filled with astonishment, as they had never before seen a square-rigged vessel. In the evening all hands engaged in the work of lightening the vessels preparatory to crossing the bar. The draught of the brigs required that they should be lifted at least four feet, and Mr. Brown had planned to effect this by scows or camels. Capt. Dobbins, who was present and actively engaged, says : " There was less water in the channel by three feet than the vessels required, and after the guns and stores of the *Lawrence* had been taken ashore (the guns being laid upon timbers on the sandbeach), the two lighters or scows were placed one on each side of her and large timbers put across the vessel and secured to the lighters. There were four holes in the bottom of the lighters, eight inches square, and plugs fitted to them, which reached above the tops of the lighters ; these plugs were taken out and the lighters sunk. The timbers were then blocked upon the lighters, the plugs placed in the holes, and the lighters pumped and bailed out, which raised the vessel to the height required to float her over. Before daylight on Tuesday, the vessel was afloat ; by two o'clock, her armament was all on board, mounted, a salute fired, and ready for action. The same plan was the next day pursued with the *Niagara*, and by incessant labor, day and night, she was in twenty-four hours also ready for action. When the *Niagara* was on the bar with the lighters under her, the British squadron hove in sight, standing in for Erie. It fortunately happened that the wind caused the *Lawrence* to head in the same direction with the *Niagara* on the bar, and the weather being quite hazy, the enemy must have supposed them both afloat. The headmost of the British vessels hove her main-top-sail to the mast, and lay by until the rest came up, and, after having exchanged signals, they hauled their wind and stood for Long Point. Here they put a courier ashore to proceed to Malden, with orders to get the *Detroit* out as soon as possible."

"The entire management pertaining to getting the vessels over the bar was of the most judicious kind, both in facilitating the work and protecting the *Lawrence* and *Niagara* when aground. While the *Lawrence* was on the bar, the *Niagara* and smaller vessels were moored inside, with their broadsides toward the roadstead and within point-blank range of the enemy, should they attempt to approach near enough to destroy her. Besides this, three long twelve-pounders were placed upon the bank about one hundred feet above the water (where the lighthouse now stands), protected by an earthen entrenchment; this was not more than three hundred yards from a line ranging directly over, and could have kept up a destructive fire upon the enemy before they could have reached the vessel."

It has been said that Com. Barclay lost the ascendency on Lake Erie by attending a dinner given him and his officers at Port Dover, which is situated on Ryerson's Creek, below Long Point. It appears there was a dinner given the officers there, about that time, and that Com. Barclay replied to a complimentary toast in rather boastful and contemptuous terms when alluding to the "Yankee brigs hard and fast upon the bar." The compliment of a dinner was undoubtedly accepted by the British officers, but that the day of battle was deferred on that account is scarcely worthy of belief. Capt. Perry had looked forward with great anxiety to the passage of the bar. In a letter dated July 27, to the Secretary, he says: "We are ready to sail the instant officers and men arrive; and as the enemy appear determined to dispute the passage of the bar with us, the question as to the command of Lake Erie will soon be decided."

On the 28th of July another urgent appeal came from Gen. Harrison. Capt. Perry replied: "I am of opinion that in two days the naval superiority will be decided on Lake Erie. Should we be successful, I shall sail for the head of the lake immediately, to coöperate with you, and I hope that our joint efforts will be productive of honor and advantage to our country. The squadron is not much more than half manned; but as I see no prospect of reinforcement, I have determined to commence my operations. . . . My anxiety to join you is very great, and had seamen been sent me in time, I should now in all probability have been at the head of the lake acting in conjunction with you." A call was made for volunteers, and a sufficient number offered to man the vessels for a cruise to Long Point, where the enemy were supposed to be. At three o'clock on the morning of the 6th of August the signal was made for the squadron to weigh anchor, and at four the vessels were all under sail. From daylight on the 2d to the 4th of August Capt. Perry, though in feeble health, had not closed his eyes, and not an officer or man of the squadron had enjoyed a moment's rest, excepting such as could be snatched upon the deck. As they were in search of the enemy, the vessels were cleared for action, and consequently there could be little opportunity for repose. In twenty-four hours the squadron returned to Erie without having seen the enemy, and they afterward heard that they had sailed up the lake to Malden. The list of vessels and commanders on this cruise were: the *Lawrence*, Capt. Perry; *Niagara*, Lieut. D. Turner; *Caledonia*, Purser Magrath; schooner *Ariel*, Lieut. J. Packett; *Scorpion*, Sailing-master S. Champlin; *Tigress*, Master's Mate A. McDonald; *Porcupine*, Midshipman G. Senat. The *Ohio* and *Trippe* were left behind for want of crews.

The evening of the 8th it was Capt. Perry's intention to set sail for the head of the lake, but he was happily detained by the arrival of officers and men from Lake Ontario. Mr. Hambleton, who was purser of the *Lawrence*, and Capt. Perry's confidential friend, has in his journal the following: "Went on shore and transacted a variety of business; paid off the volunteers, so that we have none but the four months' men who signed articles. Capt. Perry has just received a letter from Gen. Harrison, informing him of the raising of the siege of Camp Meigs, and of the unsuccessful attack on the fort at Sandusky, commanded by Lieut. Croghan. The prisoners taken there state that the new ship *Detroit* was launched at Malden on the 17th day of last month. Capt. Perry and I dined on shore. After dinner, being alone, we had a long conversation on the state of our affairs. He confessed that he was now much at a loss what to do. While he feels the danger of delay, he is not insensible to the danger of encountering an enemy without due preparation. His officers are few and inexperienced, and we are short of seamen. His repeated and urgent requests for men have been treated with the most mortifying neglect; he declines making another. While thus engaged, a midshipman, Mr. J. B. Montgomery, entered and handed him a letter. It was from Lieut. Elliot on his way to join him, with several officers and eighty-nine seamen. He was electrified by this news, and as soon as we were alone he declared he had not been so happy since his arrival." On the 10th the party from Lake Ontario arrived at Erie, numbering one hundred and two souls, including two acting lieutenants, eight midshipmen, a master's mate, and a clerk.

On August 12, Com. Perry's squadron again set sail from Erie, with a few short of four hundred officers and men, for the headquarters of the Northwestern army, which were then at Seneca, on the banks of the Sandusky. The order of sailing established by Perry's squadron was in a double column— the *Lawrence*, *Porcupine*, *Caledonia*, *Ohio*, and *Ariel* being on the right, and the *Niagara*, *Trippe*, *Tigress*, *Somers*, and *Scorpion* on the left. At first the *Ariel* and *Scorpion*, the best sailers of the small vessels, were placed opposite the enemy and near the Commodore; in a situation to render support in any part of the line. Afterward the *Scorpion* was brought into the line, and the distance between the vessels was fixed at a half-cable's length (three hundred and sixty feet). Finally, there was an order of attack, in which each vessel had an antagonist assigned to it in the British squadron. Perry reserved to himself the privilege of fighting the largest of the enemy's ships, and, accordingly in his diagram, placed the *Lawrence* opposite the *Detroit*, and the *Niagara* opposite the *Queen Charlotte*. Provision was made in case the vessels should be separated in the night, to recognize each other by the following signal: Hoist one light and hail the vessel to windward; first answer "Jones," to which the leewardmost would reply "Madison." These, with others, were well conceived to promote concerted action and prevent surprise, and indicated judgment and forethought. On the 16th the squadron arrived off Cunningham's or Kelly's Island, and on the 17th the *Scorpion*, which was in advance of the squadron, reconnoitering the islands, in looking into Put-in-Bay discovered a small vessel of the enemy. This was the *Ottawa*, of twenty-five tons, that had previously been captured at Maumee. She at once attempted to escape, but was closely pursued by the *Scorpion*, and would have been taken, but the *Scorpion* grounded in rounding a point off Middle Bass

Island, and the little craft made good her escape to the Canada shore. The squadron being under way at the time, working up to the islands, had a full view of the chase.

"The fleet on the 17th sailed to the mouth of Sandusky Bay, and on anchoring fired three guns, waited ten minutes, and fired three more, which was the signal previously agreed upon by letter between Capt. Perry and Gen. Harrison. Col. Gaines the same evening came aboard the *Lawrence* with a number of officers and Indians, and reported Gen. Harrison twenty-seven miles distant with an army of eight thousand militia, regulars, and Indians. Boats were sent to bring the General and his suite; the party arrived late in the evening, and consisted of Generals Cass and McArthur, Col. Gaines, Maj. Croghan, with his numerous staff, and twenty-six chiefs of the Shawnee, Wyandot, and Delaware Indians. Among these were three highly influential ones, Crane, Blackhoof, and Capt. Tommy; the Indians were brought that they might inform their friends among the British of the great force of the Americans. On the morning of the 20th a salute was fired in honor of the General's visit. Gen. Harrison not being ready to advance at this time, Capt. Perry resolved immediately to pursue the enemy and offer battle. Gen. Harrison and the Commodore spent the day in reconnoitering, and concerted a plan for removing the army to this point when it should assemble, previous to invading Canada. On the 21st the General returned to his camp, and Capt. Perry proceeded to Put-in-Bay and stood out for Malden, where he discovered the British squadron within Bar Point. At Put-in-Bay Gen. Harrison had furnished Capt. Perry with a reinforcement of thirty-six volunteers, which, after deducting a few deaths, carried the total of his muster roll to four hundred and ninety souls. Of the reinforcement a small number were river boatmen, and were mostly to serve as marines. Many of them were militia from Kentucky, and men who had volunteered from a love of adventure, having never seen a vessel until their arrival at Sandusky, and their astonishment and curiosity knew no bounds. They unceremoniously visited every part of the ship, from the masthead to the bottom of the hold, and expressed themselves in rapturous and enthusiastic terms.

Dressed in the favorite Kentucky hunting-shirt of blue linsey-woolsey fringed, they themselves were a curiosity to most of the officers and men, some of whom had never before seen a backwoodsman. After being allowed to indulge their curiosity, Com. Perry stated to them their duties, which they cheerfully undertook to perform. On their return from Malden, a few days were profitably employed in teaching the ill-assorted crews their duty, and in training them in their various evolutions preparatory to battle. They had returned to Put-in-Bay, as the wind was not favorable to their entering Malden; and they could here watch the enemy's movements. They had also much sickness aboard. Capt. Perry had been attacked with bilious-remittent fever; but owing to his strength of constitution it had not assumed a malignant form. His surgeon, clerk, and brother were also seriously ill. Dr. Usher Parsons, the assistant surgeon, though himself out of health, was obliged to prescribe for the sick of the *Lawrence*, as well as the small vessels. In the Commodore's case strong remedial measures were successfully applied. "On August 28, Dr. Parsons himself became affected with the prevailing fever and though unable to walk, with a humane self-devotion he continued at the bedside of the sick, to which he was carried; this was not only in the *Lawrence*, but the small vessels—being lifted on board of them in a chair, and the sick brought on deck for his prescription." By September 1, Capt. Perry was able again to be on deck; in the meantime the British had rigged and equipped their new vessel, the *Detroit*, and he was compelled to abandon all hopes of meeting the enemy on an equal footing.

Capt. Perry received two letters at this time from the Secretary of the Navy, one begging him to retain the command on Lake Erie (which he had resigned in consequence of some misunderstanding), with many soothing and complimentary expressions; the other full of fault-finding and bitterness, which was wholly unmerited. In Capt. Perry's reply, he vindicated himself in a mild and respectful manner from all charges.

On the 6th of September the *Ohio*, under command of Sailing-master Dobbins, was dispatched to Erie for stores and ammunition (where she had been the 22d of August on the same errand), and was enjoined to make every exertion to return with all practicable speed. Some citizens of Malden, as well as the family of Capt. Brevoort, who resided in Detroit, informed Capt. Perry as to the force of the enemy, and also that they were short of provisions and must engage our squadron to open the way to Long Point. Their force consisted of the new, strongly-built ship *Detroit*, 19 guns, 298 tons; the *Queen Charlotte*, 17 guns, 260 tons; the *Lady Prevost*, 13 guns, 96 tons; the brig *Hunter*, 10 guns, 71 tons; sloop *Little Belt*, 3 guns, 60 tons; schooner *Chippewa*, 1 gun, 35 tons—making an aggregate of sixty-three guns, thirty-five of which were long. The squadron was commanded by Capt. Robert Herriot Barclay, a skillful and experienced seaman, who had served with Nelson at Trafalgar; the second in command was Capt. Finnis, also a brave officer. The whole British force numbered thirty-two officers and four hundred and seventy seamen—in all five hundred and two. Of the American vessels, the *Lawrence* and *Niagara* were each 260 tons, with 20 guns; Capt. Perry commanded the *Lawrence* and Capt. Elliot the *Niagara;* the *Caledonia*, 3 guns, 85 tons, Lieut. Turner; the *Ariel*, 4 guns, ·Lieut. Packet; the *Scorpion*, 2 guns, Sailing-master Champlin; the *Somers*, 2 guns, 65 tons, Sailing-master Almy; the *Trippe*, 1 gun, Lieut. Holdup (Stevens); the *Tigress*, 1 gun, Lieut. Conklin; the *Porcupine*, 1 gun, Midshipman Smith—in all nine vessels, with fifty-four guns. The whole force of officers and men, four hundred and ninety; of these, one hundred and sixteen were on the sick list, seventy-eight being cases of bilious fever. The *Somers*, *Trippe*, *Tigress*, and *Porcupine* were dull sailers. The officers of the squadron were mostly young men from Rhode Island, and the sailing-masters were fellow-townsmen of Capt. Perry, taken from the merchant service. The superiority of the enemy in physical force must have brought to mind an admonition of Com. Chauncey to Com. Perry, "never despise your enemy"; yet he thoroughly understood himself, and felt armed in having a just cause.

On the 6th Perry sailed for Malden, and finding the British still at their moorings, returned to Put-in-Bay. He then signalled all the commanders to the *Lawrence*, and furnished them with corrected instructions for their government during the battle. The battle-flag, which had been privately prepared by Mr. Hambleton before leaving Erie, with the last words of the lamented Lawrence, "Don't give up the ship," in white letters on a blue ground, was produced, and its hoisting at the main-royal mast of the *Lawrence* was to be the signal for action. Capt. Perry stated to them his intention to bring the enemy from the first to close quarters, in order to get the benefit of his carronades. His last injunction to them was, in case of difficulty to follow the advice of Lord Nelson: "If you lay your enemy close alongside, you cannot be out of your place." The men had now become familiar with their weapons, and every preparation seemed complete. The sickness continued, and on the 8th the other medical officers ceased to perform duty, leaving Dr. Parsons, though but half recovered, in sole charge of the sick of the whole squadron.

CHAPTER XVI.

British Vessels appear—Com. Perry Remodels his Line, and other Preparations—A brief Description by Dr. Parsons of the Battle of September 10—The Vessels return to Erie with the wounded Prisoners—Capt. Perry promoted—His Reception at Erie—A Remark of McKenzie—President Madison—Congress—Prizes.

At sunrise of September 10, from the masthead of the *Lawrence*, the British fleet was discovered on the northwestern board, standing for Put-in-Bay. The fact was immediately reported by the officer of the deck, who ordered the signal made, "Enemy in sight," "Under way to get." Soon the whole squadron was moving out of the bay with a light southwest breeze. The wind was very unsteady, and at ten o'clock, having made little progress, Capt. Perry addressed his sailing-master, Mr. Taylor, as to the time in his opinion it would require to weather the islands. Mr. Taylor's reply caused Capt. Perry to order the master to run to leeward of the islands. Mr. Taylor replied, "they would then have to engage the enemy from the leeward." Capt. Perry said. "to windward or leeward they shall fight to-day." The signal was made accordingly; but before it could be executed they were relieved by the wind shifting to the southeast, which enabled them to engage the enemy to windward, as they much preferred. The newly-painted British vessels, with their unfolding banners in the morning sun, were an imposing and gallant sight.

Com. Perry remodeled his line, as he found Com. Barclay had placed the *Chippeway* in the van; second in the line, the *Detroit;* the *Hunter* third; *Queen Charlotte* fourth; *Lady Prevost* fifth; and *Little Belt* sixth. Capt. Perry placed the *Lawrence* so as to encounter the *Detroit*, with the *Scorpion* ahead, and the *Ariel* on his weather bow. The *Caledonia* came next, to encounter the *Hunter;* the *Niagara* next, to be opposite the *Queen;* the *Somers, Porcupine, Tigress*, and *Trippe* in the rear, to encounter the *Lady Prevost* and *Little Belt*. It was now ten o'clock, and they were distant five or six miles from the enemy, with a light wind from the southeast, so that the advance was at the rate of three knots; and Capt. Perry having called the crew about him elevated the burgée, exclaiming, "My brave lads, this flag contains the last words of Capt. Lawrence! Shall I hoist it?" "Ay, ay, ay, sir!" resounded from all quarters of the ship, and the flag was swayed to the main-royal masthead. As the flag unfurled and became visible to the other crews, hearty and enthusiastic cheers responded throughout the line. A luncheon was now served, and Perry carefully examined his battery, gun by gun, to see that all was in order, exchanging a pleasant or encouraging word with all. Seeing some of the *Constitution's*, he said to them, "Well, boys, are you ready?" "All ready, your honor!" was the brief reply, with a general touch of the hat or handkerchief, which some had substituted. To another group, "But I need not say anything to you; *you* know how to beat those fellows." Again, with a smile of recognition, "Ah! here are the *Newport* boys! They will do their duty, I warrant!"

A silence of an hour and a half succeeded, during which the

squadron was slowly nearing the enemy; this was spent in various ways, as the cares and consciences of the men about to engage in deadly combat might dictate. In the event of his death, Capt. Perry gave Mr. Hambleton directions how to act with regard to his private affairs, and a leaded package to Dr. Parsons, with instructions from government and letters from Mrs. Perry, to be thrown overboard.

At length a bugle was heard to sound from the *Detroit*, a mile and a half distant, and loud cheers followed throughout the British squadron. Soon after, at a quarter before twelve, a single shot was fired from the enemy's flag-ship at the *Lawrence*, which did not take effect. Signal was now made for each vessel to engage her opponent as previously designated. The dull sailers among the small vessels were a little out of their stations astern, so that our line overspread that of the enemy one thousand feet; besides this, the inferior size of our vessels gave the enemy a greater superiority than even his nominal one. A brief description of the battle, by Dr. Parsons, an eye-witness of high character and intelligence, is as follows: "Perry made more sail, and coming within canister distance, opened a rapid and destructive fire upon the *Detroit*. The *Caledonia*, Lieut. Turner, followed the *Lawrence* in gallant style, and the *Ariel*, Lieut. Packet, and the *Scorpion*, Mr. Champlin, fought nobly and effectively.

"The *Niagara* failing to grapple with the *Queen*, the latter vessel shot ahead to fire upon the *Lawrence*, and with the *Detroit*, aimed their broadsides exclusively upon her, hoping and intending to sink her. At last they made her a complete wreck, but, fortunately, the Commodore escaped without injury, and stepping into a boat with his fighting flag thrown over his shoulder,[1] he pushed off for the *Niagara*, amid a shower of cannon and musket balls, and reached that vessel

---

[1] In a letter dated Providence, June 28, 1861, Dr. Parsons says: "I yesterday visited the naval school, in Newport, on board the *Constitution*, and was delighted to see once more the identical flag, '*Don't give up the ship*,' which Perry hoisted on board the *Lawrence* on going into action, and took with him to the *Niagara* when he had fought his own ship to the last. The flag was immediately sent to Washington by Lieut. Forest, and has ever since been preserved—of late years in the naval school—and is exhibited only on particular occasions. The sight of it created such emotions and reminiscences of the past that I could not refrain from shedding tears over it."

unscathed. He found her a fresh vessel, with only two, or, at most, three persons injured, and immediately sent her commander to hasten up the small vessels. Perry boarded the *Niagara* when she was abreast of the *Lawrence*, and further from her than the *Detroit* was on her right. The *Lawrence* now dropped astern and hauled down her flag. Perry turned the *Niagara's* course toward the enemy, and crossing the bows of the *Lawrence*, bore down, head foremost, to the enemy's line, determined to break through it and take a raking position. The *Detroit* attempted to turn so as to keep her broadside to the *Niagara* and avoid being raked, but in doing this she fell against the *Queen*, and got entangled in her rigging, which left the enemy no alternative but to strike both ships. Perry now shot farther ahead, near the *Lady Prevost*, which, from being crippled in her rudder, had drifted out of her place to the leeward, and was pressing forward toward the head of the British line to support the two ships. One broadside from the *Niagara* silenced her battery. The *Hunter* next struck, and the two smaller vessels, in attempting to escape, were overhauled by the *Scorpion*, Mr. Champlin, and *Trippe*, Lieut. Holdup, and thus ended the action after three o'clock.

"Let us now advert for a moment to the scenes exhibited in the flag-ship *Lawrence*, of which I can speak as an eye-witness. The wounded began to come down before she opened her battery, and for one, I felt impatient at the delay. In proper time, however, as it proved, the dogs of war were let loose from their leash, and it seemed as though heaven and earth were at loggerheads. For more than two hours little could be heard but the deafening thunder of our broadsides, the crash of balls dashing through our timbers, and shrieks of the wounded. These were brought down faster than I could attend to them, further than to stay the bleeding or support a shattered limb with splints and pass them forward upon the berth deck. When the battle had raged an hour and a half, I heard a call for me at the small skylight, and stepping toward it I saw the Commodore, whose countenance was as calm and placid as if in ordinary duty. 'Doctor,' said he, 'send me one of your men'—meaning one of the six stationed with me to assist in moving the wounded. In five minutes the call was repeated and obeyed, and at the seventh call I told him he had all of my men. He asked if there were any sick or wounded who could pull a rope, when two or three crawled upon deck to lend a feeble hand in pulling at the last gun.

"The hard fighting terminated about three o'clock. As the smoke cleared away the two fleets were found mingled together, the small vessels having come up to the others. The shattered *Lawrence* lying to the windward was once more able to hoist her flag, which was cheered by a few feeble voices on board, making a melancholy sound compared with the boisterous cheers that preceded the battle.

"The proud, the painful duty of taking possession of the conquered ships was now performed. The *Detroit* was nearly dismantled, and the destruction and carnage had been dreadful. The *Queen* was in a condition little better—every commander and second in command, says Barclay in his official report, was either killed or wounded. The whole number killed in the British fleet was forty-one, and of wounded ninety-four. In the American fleet, twenty-seven killed and ninety-six wounded. Of the twenty-seven killed, twenty-two were on board the *Lawrence;* of the ninety-six wounded, sixty-one were on board the same ship, making eighty-three killed and wounded out of one hundred and one reported fit for duty in the *Lawrence* on the morning of the battle. On board the *Niagara* were two killed and twenty-three wounded, making twenty-five; and of these twenty-two were killed or wounded after Perry took command of her.

"About four o'clock a boat was discovered approaching the *Lawrence*. Soon the Commodore was recognized in her, who was returning to resume the command of his tattered ship, determined that the remnant of her crew should have the privilege of witnessing the formal surrender of the British officers. It was a time of conflicting emotions when he stepped upon the deck. The battle was won and he was safe, but the deck was slippery with blood, and strewed with the bodies of twenty officers and men, some of whom sat at table with us at our last meal, and the ship resounded with the groans of the wounded. Those of us who were spared and able to walk met him at the gangway to welcome him on board, but the salutation was a silent one on both sides—not a word could find utterance.[1]

"And now the British officers arrived, one from each vessel, to tender their submission, and with it their swords. When they approached, picking their way among the wreck and carnage of the deck, with their hilts toward Perry, they tendered them to his acceptance. With a dignified and solemn air, and with a low tone of voice, he requested them to retain their side arms; inquired with deep concern for Com. Barclay and the wounded officers, tendering to them every comfort his ship afforded, and expressing his regret that he had not a spare medical officer to send them, that he only had one on duty for the fleet, and that one had his hands full.

"Among the ninety-six wounded there occurred three deaths: a result so favorable was attributable to the plentiful supply of fresh provision sent off to us from the Ohio shore; to fresh air—the wounded being ranged under an awning on the deck until we arrived at Erie, ten days after the action, and also to the devoted attention of Com. Perry to every want.

"Those who were killed in the battle were that evening committed to the deep, and over them was read the impressive Episcopal service.

"On the following morning the two fleets sailed into Put-in-Bay, where the slain officers of both were buried in an appropriate and affecting manner. They consisted of three Americans: Lieut. Brooks and Midshipmen Laub and Clark; and three British officers: Capt. Finnis and Lieut. Stokes, of the *Queen*, and Lieut. Garland, of the *Detroit*. Equal respect was paid to the slain of both nations, and the crews of both fleets united in the ceremony. The procession of boats, with two bands of music; the slow and regular motion of the oars, striking in exact time with the notes of the solemn dirge; the

---

[1] In Dr. Parsons' address at Cleveland, on the 10th of September, 1860, is the following interesting item: "Perry walked aft, when his first remark was addressed to his intimate friend Hambleton, then lying wounded on the deck. 'The prayers of my wife,' said he, 'have prevailed in saving me.' Then, casting his eyes about, he inquired, 'Where is my brother?' This brother was a young midshipman of thirteen years. He had during the battle acted as aid in running with orders to different parts of the ship—for you must know that in the din and uproar of battle orders can hardly be heard at three feet distance. We made a general stir to look him up, not without fears that he had been knocked overboard, but he was soon found in his berth asleep, exhausted by the exercise and excitement of the day."

mournful waving of flags and sound of minute-guns from the ships, presented a striking contrast to the scene exhibited two days before, when both the living and the dead now forming in this solemn and fraternal train were engaged in fierce and bloody strife, hurling at each other the thunderbolts of war."

On the eighth day after the action, the *Lawrence*, with the wounded on board, was dispatched to Erie, where they were cordially welcomed and most kindly cared for. Soon after the British prisoners arrived in the *Detroit* and *Queen Charlotte*, and after the wounded of their number had been carefully attended, they were removed to Pittsburg for greater security from desertion. Immediately after the battle, Capt. Perry joined Gen. Harrison as a volunteer. The remainder of the vessels conveyed the army to Malden; here the enemy, under Gen. Proctor, had made a hasty retreat, but were pursued and captured.

Capt. Perry was promoted to the rank of post-captain, and leave granted him, according to his request, to return to his family; he was to resume also the command of the Newport station until a suitable ship should be provided for him. As the British were checked in the Northwest, Gen. Harrison received orders to repair with a part of his army to Fort George, and embarked with Capt. Perry on the *Ariel;* Com. Barclay, who was on parole, and on his return homeward as far as Buffalo, was also of the party.

On the morning of October 22, the *Ariel* was descried by the citizens of Erie, and preparations were immediately set on foot for an appropriate and enthusiastic reception of the hero, the magnitude of whose services they could better appreciate than others. Though Com. Perry expected to land unobserved, a large concourse of citizens with joyful acclamations met him at the beach at the foot of French Street, and two field pieces fired a national salute. The party, consisting of Com. Perry, Com. Barclay, with his surgeon, and Gen. Harrison, with Col. Gaines, came on foot up the steep hill to Duncan's tavern (which is still standing, though in ruins), on the corner of Third and French streets. In the evening the town was illuminated and a torch-light procession marched through the streets, bearing transparencies with the following devices:

"Com. Perry, 10th September, 1813"; on another, "Gen. Harrison, 5th of October, 1813"; on a third, "Free trade and sailor's rights"; on a fourth, "Erie"; cannon in the meantime being discharged at intervals of three minutes. During the afternoon, the *Niagara* arrived; and the next day the *Ariel*, with its distinguished party, left for Buffalo, the command at Erie devolving on Capt. Elliot. Capt. Perry's journey to the East was one succession of enthusiastic demonstrations, and the cities vied with one another in expressions of joy and gratitude for one who had restored tranquillity to the frontier and whose modesty or bravery they knew not which most to admire.[1] It has been said, "Nelson triumphed over Frenchmen and Spaniards; Perry was called on to meet the conquerors of these, led, moreover, by a veteran formed in the school of Nelson, and bearing upon his person the marks of Nelson's greatest victory. The battle of Trafalgar was won by the whole British fleet over a part of that of the allies; the battle of Lake Erie was over the whole British squadron by only a part of ours."

President Madison, in his message, calls it a victory never surpassed in luster, however much it may have been in magnitude.

Congress passed a vote of thanks to be presented to Capt. Perry, and all the officers and men of the squadron, for the decisive and glorious victory over a British squadron of superior force. The President of the United States also presented gold medals to Capt. Perry and Capt. Elliot, bearing an emblematical device of the action between the two squad-

[1] An hour after the battle, Com. Perry forwarded by express two letters, one to Gen. Harrison, the other to the Secretary of the Navy, as follows:

"DEAR GENERAL:—We have met the enemy and they are ours; two ships, two brigs, one schooner, and one sloop.
"Yours with great respect and esteem,
"O. H. PERRY."

"UNITED STATES BRIG NIAGARA, off the Western Sister,
"Head of Lake Erie, September 10, 1813, 4 p. m.

"SIR:—It has pleased the Almighty to give to the arms of the United States a signal victory over their enemies on this lake. The British squadron, consisting of two ships, two brigs, one schooner, and one sloop, have this moment surrendered to the force under my command, after a sharp conflict.

"I have the honor to be, sir,
"Very respectfully, your obedient servant,
"O. H. PERRY."
"The Hon. WILLIAM JONES, Secretary of the Navy."

rons; and a silver medal to each commissioned officer either of the army or navy service on board; a sword to each of the sailing-masters and midshipmen; and also a medal to the nearest male relative of Lieut. John Brooks; and a sword to the nearest male relative of Midshipmen Henry Laub, John Clark, and Thomas Claxton, Jr., with the expression of the deep regret of Congress for the loss of these gallant men. Three months' pay, exclusive of the common allowance, was voted to all the petty officers, seamen, marines, and infantry, who supported the honor of the American flag under the orders of their gallant commander on that signal occasion.

The British vessels were prized by a board of officers from Lake Ontario, assisted by naval constructor, Henry Eckford, and purchased for $255,000. Of this, Com. Chauncey was entitled to one twentieth of the whole, being $12,750; Captains Perry and Elliot each drew $7,140. As no portion of prize money could be awarded to Capt. Perry for his general command, Congress made a special grant to him of $5,000; $2,295 was the portion of each commander of a gunboat, lieutenant, sailing-master, and captain of marines; $811 for a midshipman; $447 a petty officer; and $209 for each marine and sailor.

CHAPTER XVII.

Blockhouses built in 1813-14—State of Society—Buffalo burned—Alarms at Erie—Capt. Sinclair arrives—Bird and Rankin shot, and Davis hung—Peace—Disposition made of Government Vessels—List of Commanding Officers at Erie from 1813 to 1825—Topography of Presqu'ile Bay and the Peninsula—Misery Bay—Gen. Bernard and Maj. Totten's Survey—Appropriations made by the State and United States—Changes made by Time and Art since 1813—Rise and Fall of Water in Lake Erie—A Singular Phenomenon.

For the better defense of Erie, in the winter of 1813 and 1814, a blockhouse was built on Garrison Hill, and another on the point of the peninsula. (The one on the shore was burned in 1853, an occurrence much regretted by the inhabitants).

Ten vessels, with their complements of men, were stationed in the harbor, and a large body of militia quartered upon the town. The winter is remembered by the old inhabitants as one of unusual excitement and dissipation. Like the idolatrous Israelites, the people sat down to eat and drink, and rose up to play. Victory and prize money, leisure and lax discipline were found to promote anything but peace and good morals. Deaths by dueling, suicide, and *mania a potu* were not unfrequent. As an instance of the folly of the times, an officer by the name of B——s provided himself with blank challenges in order to be in readiness, if insulted, to demand "the satisfaction of a gentleman." Near the corner of Third and Sassafras streets, a duel took place between Midshipman Senat, who commanded the *Porcupine* during the action, and Acting-master McDonald, which resulted in the death of the former. The cause of the difficulty, it is said, resolved itself into the number of buttons worn by McDonald. A singular fact is related of McDonald. A few minutes after committing the fatal deed, but before it was known, he addressed an acquaintance with some ordinary inquiry, but was not recognized by him excepting by his voice; and scarcely by that, so unnatural and ghost-like was his countenance. It is almost superfluous to add, that the legal authorities took no notice of such infractions of the law.

December 30, 1813, Capt. Isaac Barnes, of the militia near Buffalo, communicated to the commander at Erie the alarming intelligence that the British had that morning landed three thousand regulars, militia, and Indians, at Black Rock, and forced Maj.-Gen. Hall's company of militia to retreat to Buffalo, and afterward to surrender as prisoners of war. The village and large vessels at Black Rock had been consumed—the enemy had advanced eight or ten miles up Lake Erie destroying everything as they passed, and purposed burning the vessels at Erie. Full liberty was given the Indians to plunder in order to encourage them in the nefarious business. Capt. Barnes requested of Capt. Elliot men, arms, and ammunition, the communication being interrupted eastward by the Indians. Upon this Capt. Elliot, January 10, informed Gen. Mead that the Indians were collecting a great number of sleighs and sleds, and as soon as the ice would admit, expected to make an attack upon Erie—that the force of the British amounted to three thousand, and the one at Erie to but two thousand. Immediately the whole of the first brigade of Gen. Mead's division was ordered into service, and proceeded to Erie, which increased the force to four thousand. The boldness of the British at this time was owing to the removal of troops from Fort George, which left the frontier partially unprotected. False alarms were frequent in Erie during the winter as to the progress of the enemy, and more than once the whole village was astir at midnight packing goods and furniture for a hasty departure—assurances of safety and protection from the commanding officer having no effect. The parades of the militia at such times, in their begged, borrowed, or inherited uniforms, were occasions of special gratification to the young, and those fond of the ludicrous, the first brigade being mostly in the hands of substitutes. These were often of the lowest class, untaught and unteachable in manners and discipline. North and west of where the First Presbyterian church now stands, the ground was covered with log huts erected for a regiment of regular troops, and was familiarly known as Stumptown; most of the huts were afterward destroyed by fire—one of the largest, however, for many years served as a meeting-house. Among officers and men the all-absorbing topic was the share of honor or otherwise Capt. Elliot was entitled to in the battle of September 10. The sailors of the *Lawrence* and *Niagara* were never expected to meet peaceably. The following scene was often enacted: an "Elliot" champion would maintain that the wind was light and they could not get up; the "*Lawrence* man" would allude to "the main-top sail to the mast, and the jib brailed up," and immediately a trial of muscle would ensue, and blood flow unless prevented by the by-standers. In the spring Capt. Elliot left for Lake Ontario, and Com. Sinclair came on to Erie in April. In the fall three men were executed for desertion—Bird and Rankin, marines, were shot, and Davis, a seaman, hung to the yard-arm of the *Niagara*. Bird belonged to a volunteer company from Bellefonte. The company occupied a small blockhouse at the Cascade—being unaccustomed to military discipline they were impatient and restive under orders, and mutinied by shutting themselves up and refusing admission to others. Lieut. Brooks, of the marines, being much in need of men before the battle, these men were told that their offense would be overlooked provided they would enlist with him. Bird being a man of some standing was made sergeant, and placed in charge of a storehouse at the mouth of Mill Creek, and deserted from thence. He was found guilty by a court-martial, the President approved the sentence, and as it was thought on the frontier such an offense could not be overlooked, it was carried out with all its horrors.[1]

When the war in Europe ceased, that of the United States with Great Britain, as a branch, naturally fell to the ground, and a treaty of peace was concluded and signed at Ghent, December 24, 1814. The following disposition was made of the government vessels on Lake Erie: The *Lawrence* was repaired, and after making a cruise to Lake Huron was sunk in Misery Bay for her better preservation. Two years ago her stern was elevated and a portion secured for memorials. The *Niagara* lies under water near the *Lawrence.* The *Caledonia* was sold in 1815, called the *General Wayne,* and finally broken up at Erie. In 1814 the *Ohio* and *Somers* were cut out by the British at Fort Erie; the *Scorpion* and *Tigress* were taken the same year on Lake Huron; the *Little Belt* and *Trippe* were destroyed when Buffalo was burned; the *Ariel* went ashore and was wrecked in Buffalo Bay, and the *Porcupine* was transferred to the revenue department. The *Detroit* was sunk in Misery Bay, near the *Lawrence* (sailors say she would float off, and in spite of their efforts would keep at a respectable distance); she was, in 1835, raised, and rigged a bark, by Capt. George Miles, and navigated the lake some years; lastly, she was sent over Niagara Falls for a spectacle, and probably a speculation, too, on the part of the hotel keepers. The *Queen Charlotte* was sunk in Misery Bay, and afterward fitted out for

[1] The execution of Bird and the other deserters at Erie in 1814, constituted the romance of the war among children and the lower classes. A ballad on the theme, of not less than twenty verses, in the "gory" style, rehearsed or rather screeched by a servant girl with a doleful countenance, made a decided impression on a group of children.

the lake trade; the *Lady Prevost* was sold to a Canada merchant in 1815.

In 1820 an order was received to reduce the naval station at this place to a master commandant, one lieutenant, one purser, one surgeon, one surgeon's mate, one captain's clerk, one boatswain, one gunner, one carpenter, one armorer, one purser's steward, five able seamen, five ordinary seamen. The naval station at Erie was not completely broken up until 1825, when the public property was disposed of by auction. The following is a list of the commanding officers from 1813: Captains O. H. Perry, Jesse D. Elliot, Arthur Sinclair, Daniel S. Dexter (who died in 1818, leaving Lieut. George Pearce the senior officer), David Deacon, and George Budd.

Here it may not be out of place to give something of the topography of Presqu'ile Bay, and the changes made by time and art since 1812. The extreme length of the bay is about five miles, and nearly two in breadth, with an area of from six to eight miles, and is formed by a peninsula which extends in a northeasterly direction, being much in the form of a crab's claw. In some places the peninsula is three-fourths of a mile in width, and susceptible of cultivation, but a larger part is sand, and covered with a low growth of timber, the wild grape, and cranberry. The neck or west side in 1812 was two or three hundred feet in width; afterward the action of the waves and increased height of the water submerged it for the distance of half a mile. By an appropriation of government a passage eight feet in depth was made through this neck, so that vessels detained in the harbor by head winds might depart, and a saving of distance to steamboats be made of from four to six miles. This channel is again filled with sand, which is wearing way on the northwest side. At the east end of the peninsula sand has been and is accumulating, and just within is Misery Bay, a convenient shelter for vessels in a storm. This name was given it by Lieut. Holdup in 1814, from the comfortless condition of the vessels at the time—the weather being gloomy and the stock of falsely so-called good cheer exhausted. The depth of water in Presqu'ile Bay averages eighteen feet; at the entrance, the bar or sandbank under water has been removed, and the channel there is now about fourteen feet deep. Immediately after the war the opinion of Com. Perry was asked by the Navy Department on the subject of removing the bar, and his reply was favorable to the project.[1] In 1824 Gen. Bernard and Maj. Totten surveyed the harbor, and in their report we find the following interesting item : "The basin of Presqu'ile is situated so far above the commencement of the falls into Lake Ontario, and in so wide a part of Lake Erie that the current produced by the escape of water at the falls is here insensible—the only current here observable being entirely owing to the easterly or westerly winds. These latter currents have, however, sometimes considerable rapidity, and a curious fact appears in relation to the effect of these lake currents upon the waters of the basin, viz., that a strong current sets into the basin in direct opposition to the westerly winds when they blow hard, and conversely, a strong current sets out of the basin in direct opposition to violent easterly winds : or, in other words, the current out of or into the basin runs in a direct opposition both to the set of the lake's current and the direction of the winds, whether easterly or westerly.

"It is important to account for this before proceeding further, and in doing so we refer to the sketch herewith to make the matter more intelligible. We must first suppose the surface of the lake and of the basin to be of the same level, as will always be the case after a few days of calm weather, and represent the level by $0° 0' 00''$ and $0'''$. An easterly wind then setting in drives a part of the water of the easterly half of the lake into the western, raising the surface at $0''$ and $0'''$, and lowering it at $0'$; as the surface descends at $0'$ the water in the basin must also descend by running out against the wind, there being no issue at the west end of the basin.

"In like manner when a westerly wind heaps the water at $0'$ above the surface in the basin, it must rise in the basin by running in against the wind, there being no entrance at the west end. As the winds abate, the waters gradually take a level common to both lake and basin, but not the same as

[1] In 1822 the State appointed a committee composed of Thomas Forster, G. Sanford, and George Moore, to survey the Bay of Presqu'ile; to ascertain the depth of water in the bay, on the bar, and the anchoring ground outside of the bar.

before; for, the supply being nearly equable at all times, with westerly winds more is forced out of the lake over the falls, and with easterly winds less passes that way than when the surface is at a mean elevation. The basin has, therefore, higher to rise immediately after an easterly wind than it was depressed by it, and lower to fall after a westerly wind than it was elevated by that wind. But the return of the lake to its level is slow and gradual, the elevation and depression of the waters at its ends is sudden and violent, and amounts often to several feet. It is to this latter operation that we are to look for producing any considerable effect." They then proceed to recommend a plan carried out soon after, that of increasing the current by closing the whole mouth of the basin with the exception of a passage two hundred feet in width. By means of sinking piles and removing the sand between them with a dredging machine, as well as by the frequent passage of vessels, the object has been effected.

The different appropriations for the improvement of the harbor have been as follows: By the State, in 1822, $10,000; by the United States, in 1824, $30,000; in 1828, $6,223; in 1831, $1,700; in 1832, $4,500; in 1833, $6,000; in 1834, $20,000; in 1835, $5,000; in 1836, $15,000; in 1844, $40,000; in 1852, $30,000; for a steam dredge, $20,000.

About 1813 there was a fine drive on the beach from State Street to the Cascade, where there is not now even a footpath. Toward the middle of the day this was often overflowed, giving rise to the opinion entertained by Com. Perry and others that the lake was affected by tides. The year of the battle the water was unusually high, not only in the lake, but in the Allegheny and French Creek, and it was remarked by those well qualified to judge, that without this fortunate circumstance, this extraordinary rise, the squadron could not have been built, as it would have been impossible to transport the ordnance and necessary equipments over land, such was the state of the roads leading from Pittsburg.

In 1808 the water in Lake Erie was lower than it had ever before been known; in 1838 it was four and a half feet above the water-mark of 1808. Some pine trees, killed by the inundation, were found by their rings to be over one hundred years old, and from this it was inferred that the water had not been at so great a height for a century. In 1858 it was observed at the Buffalo lighthouse that for some years a gradual progressive rise of water had taken place, and the same year at Lake Ontario the water was higher than it had been for forty years. At Toledo the water gauged from two to six feet higher than in 1834. During the years 1815, 1816, and 1817, which were cold and wet seasons, the water was high; in 1818 it was higher still, but not equal to 1837-38. The summer of 1818 was very hot, and the evaporation reduced the height of the lake two feet, when the fall was gradual for several seasons. From 1822 to 1828 it remained without change.

Some have supposed that there exists a regular and periodical rise and fall of the waters of the lake once in seven years; but facts do not seem to favor this supposition. Previous to 1838 there had been six or seven uncommonly wet seasons, with heavy falls of snow, and this fact, together with the subsidence of the waters after extremely warm and dry seasons, *would seem* plainly to indicate the cause.

A singular phenomenon has sometimes been observed near the shore, which is the sudden rise and fall of water in particular localities without any apparent cause. May 30, 1823, a little after sunset, while the weather was fine and the lake calm, at the mouth of Otter and of Kettle Creek, being twenty miles apart in Canada, the water rose with astonishing rapidity and without the least warning—at the former place nine feet, and the latter seven. In both cases, after three swells, the lake seemed to have spent its force, and gradually subsided. The same effect was observed at different places along the shore; but the high steep banks did not admit of the same observation.

Two other cases of this kind were witnessed and described by a revenue officer; one at Cunningham Creek, Ohio, in 1826, which, in the space of five minutes, overflowed a bank fifteen feet in height, doing much damage. The other observed by him, was in 1830, at Grand River, Ohio, at three o'clock, p. m. There was an unusual waving of the water and a tremendous sea. The revenue cutter *Rush*, lying at the wharf, let go her anchor, and the current was so strong she drifted with both anchors ahead, and would have been ashore but for the man placed at the helm. The top of the pier when built was about five feet above the water, but so deeply was it submerged at this time, from appearance, a vessel drawing eight feet of water would have gone over it.

At the mouth of Sixteen Mile Creek, Erie County, Mr. Thomas Crawford witnessed a similar phenomenon about 1820.

Others have mentioned the same periodical flux and reflux on Lake Ontario, recurring at intervals of a few minutes, and ascribed it "to springs at the bottom of the lake, and the shock of rivers discharging into it."

A waterspout was witnessed at Cleveland, October, 1841. It was apparently the size of a large haystack, hollow and inverted. The wind had been blowing a strong current from the northeast, and suddenly changed to the west.

A few years before, three waterspouts occurred at the same moment, twenty-five miles west of Cleveland; ordinarily they may be said to be of rare occurrence on inland seas.

A whirlwind visited Conneaut, September, 1839, and the effects were felt both on sea and land. The waters were lifted forty or fifty feet, a barn unroofed near the shore, and much other damage sustained.

The *Conneaut Reporter*, 1859, has an article to this effect: "That the water of Lake Erie was never higher. Many acres of land that had borne crops were totally submerged, and Mr. J. Gilbert had had more than thirty acres of land destroyed by the encroachments of the water the last thirty years. The complaint was general along the lake shore, and many causes assigned: some believed it to be the back-water caused by the Black Rock dam, on the Niagara River, and petitions were circulated, asking of the Legislatures of Ohio and Pennsylvania the passage of memorial to Congress for an appropriation to pay the expense of a survey of Niagara River to determine the matter."

A survey of the lakes is now (1861) progressing slowly but steadily. An appropriation of $125,000 has been granted for carrying on the work.

The report drawn up by Capt. George G. Meade exhibits the

following summary of the year's work : " A recapitulation of the operations in the office and the field exhibits the projection of twenty-nine manuscript sheets of hydrography, topography, and water levels ; the reduction of four charts for engravings ; the drawing of one chart for the lighthouse board ; the publication of two charts ; the reduction and tabulation of 140 monthly sheets of meteorological observations, together with numerous other computations, astronomical, and geotic ; the survey of 303 miles of lake shore, covering 313 square miles of minute topography and hydrography ; the execution of two triangulations, extending over 2,200 square miles ; the sounding in deep water of 4,300 miles of lines ; the determination of the latitudes of three, and the longitudes of four points ; the observation of the magnetic elements at nine points ; and finally, the continuation of the meteorological water-level observations over the whole lake region."

The water-level and meteorological observations on Lakes Erie and Ontario, though in an imperfect state, sum up as follows : That the lakes are sensibly and rapidly affected by winds and storms, depressing the water from the side whence it blows, and raising it on the opposite side ; that, independent of wind fluctuations, a change of level arises from rains and draining of watersheds and from discharges arising from evaporation and the flow through their outlets ; that, as a general rule, these last fluctuations occur annually, the high stage being in summer, and the low in winter ; that these annual fluctuations vary in degree from year to year, being the effect of various causes, and the extreme range as yet reported between the highest and lowest waters has amounted to five feet five inches.

CHAPTER XVIII.

Geology, from Prof. Rogers—Character of Soil—Calcareous Marl—Bog Ore—Petroleum—Mineral Waters—R. Andrew's Account of Sink-hole—The Devil's Backbone and Nose—Botanizing.

A SURVEY of the State was commenced by H. D. Rogers, State Geologist, in the year 1836, in consequence of an act of the Legislature passed the same year. The law directed that an annual report be made by him to the Legislature of the progress of the work, with the various areas occupied by the different geological formations represented on the State map, and on the completion of the work a full account to be prepared of the Geology and Mineralogy of the State. On the organization of the survey, it was estimated that it would occupy at least ten years; appropriations being withheld after the sixth year, Mr. Rogers for three years pursued his explorations, and prepared his final report at his own expense; this was, however, afterward repaid.

In 1851 the Legislature adopted and provided measures and means to revise the field-work, in consequence of the rapid development of the mining districts, and for the publication of the reports, with the accompanying maps, etc. In 1858 the final report was published at an expense of $16,000, Mr. Rogers retaining the copyright and presenting 1,000 copies of the work to the State.

In 1836 the sum of $6,400 was appropriated to the work: $2,000 for the salary of the principal; $1,200 for each of the assistants; $1,000 for the chemist; and $1,000 for incidental expenses, should they occur.

In 1837 two other assistants were appointed, and $3,600 added to the future annual appropriation. In 1838 $6,000 was appropriated, and in 1841 $10,200, for the purpose of completing the mineralogical and geological survey of the State. Of this, $4,000 was lost by the want of proper management in its publication.

It was required of the State Geologist, from the first, to furnish specimens of all mineral products to the Secretary of the Commonwealth, and also of the minerals of each county to its respective commissioners (those for the counties seemed to be waved). In 1842 the Legislature required the preparation of three cabinets of all geological and mineral specimens for the use of the State, to be severally deposited at Harrisburg, Philadelphia, and Pittsburg. We have been informed that Mr. Rogers also made a promise of a similar one for Erie, to Mr. J. D. Dunlap; but that it was not added to the list, lest some might consider it favoritism. Such a cabinet might awaken in our county an interest in geology, which would manifest itself in the more general pursuit of that engaging science, as well as in the more profitable management of farms, and the opening up of its resources and mineral wealth.

According to Prof. Rogers, the northwest corner of the State, embracing Erie County, a large part of Crawford, and the north half of Warren, which he makes his seventh district, a mean breadth of forty miles, is much the simplest of all the natural divisions of the geological surface of Pennsylvania, as to its variety of strata and their structural features. It includes but two paleozoic formations, namely, the vergent flags[1] and vergent shales.[2] These strata (the most ancient or lowest great division of the fossiliferous strata) retain very nearly the horizontal position in which they were originally deposited, sustaining but a trivial inclination toward the southeast, which extends to the coal strata and gives them their trough-like configuration. The surface descends rather rapidly from the watershed to the lake by a succession of obscure, alternately gentle and steepish slopes. The declivation of the ground may be inferred from the difference in the elevation of its two margins : that of the watershed, in which it begins, being nearly twelve hundred feet, and that of the lake, in which it ends, being only five hundred and sixty-five feet above the level of the sea. This tract is cut transversely by numerous sharp ravines and long tortuous valleys (evidently carved by a tremendous rush of waters), carrying its streams to the lake ; and the borders of some of these afford many small, pleasing bits of scenery. But the characteristic, and altogether the most impressive pictures, are those of the lake itself. The first view which the traveler gets of this broad inland sea, as he passes the watershed, especially when the surface of the lake, crisped into gentle waves by a light western breeze, reflects the deep blue of the upper sky, never fails to charm and surprise him.

[1] *Vergent flags.*—A rather fine-grained gray sandstone in thin layers, parted by their alternating bands of shale. It abounds in marine vegetation.
[2] *Vergent shales.*—A thick mass of gray, blue, and olive-colored shales and gray-brown sandstone. The sandstone predominates in the upper part, where the shales contain many fossils.

This inclined plane extends from Cattaraugus County, New York, to Sandusky Bay, being a slope consisting rather of a succession of low terraces, themselves a little inclined. These terraces are made by the outcropping of the strata, and are parallel with the lake shore. The average inclination of the surface is about thirty-three feet to a mile; from eight or ten miles from the lake the downward sweep of the surface is much more rapid.

This Lake Erie slope is bounded on the southeast border by an abrupt, low, broken wall or escarpment, which constitutes the verge of the bituminous coal region. Between the Clarion and Tionesta, and also extending across the river southwest toward Mercer and Beaver, it rises gradually toward the northwest.

The rise of the Allegheny River, from Pittsburg to Franklin, does not exceed 755 feet, and the rise of French Creek, from its mouth to Meadville, is about 130 feet. The high dividing ridge which separates the waters of the Allegheny tributaries from Lake Erie crosses the New York State line near Colt's Station, where it is about 1,000 feet above the surface of the lake. It then passes in a straight line to Strong's on the turnpike, ten miles from Erie, where it is from 850 to 875 feet above the lake level. From Strong's southwestward it becomes less distinctly marked and much depressed, and is altogether lost previous to reaching Conneaut Creek. The summit of the Erie Extension Canal is at Conneaut Lake, and is little more than 500 feet above Lake Erie.

From this dividing ridge there are four tolerably well-marked terraces to, and parallel with, the lake. These terraces are higher and better defined near the New York State line, and become much depressed on reaching Elk Creek and Fairview townships, with the exception of the lower one, which extends into the State of Ohio. The streams which empty into the lake frequently run within one of these terraces for a considerable distance before they find an opening through which they can pass to a lower level—thus, Walnut, Elk, and Conneaut Creeks head very far to the east of their respective final outlets.

Between Cattaraugus Creek and Sandusky Bay the whole

lake coast displays only the upper or sandstone member of the flag formation, called in the New York Geological Survey the portage sandstones. This group of strata crossing Erie County in a southwest direction, almost precisely parallel with the bend of the lake coast, constitutes a belt ten or twelve miles in width, its upper limit pursuing the general watershed of the district. All the rocks between this line and the margin of the coal field are referable to the vergent shales.

The vergent flag or sandstone formation, in the type which the group wears upon Lake Erie, would not be recognized in its lithological composition by those who are only familiar with it in the Appalachian valleys. In the eastern and central tracts of New York the whole formation is far more arenaceous, and the proportion of the sandstone layers to the shales, or more purely argillaceous beds, is much greater, the upper or terminal subdivision of the mass especially containing, with a large amount of thin bedded or flagy sandstone, a considerable body of more massive strata. But advancing west the clayey element predominates, and in the belt of country bordering on Lake Erie but comparatively little true sandstone remains in the mass. The most arenaceous portion of the formation is even here near the top, and where well exposed, as it is in several places about eight miles south of the lake, where it is occasionally quarried, it may be recognized by its marine vegetation, and especially by a vertical stem-like form or species of scolithus.

The vergent shales also on Lake Erie are more argillaceous, and the two formations approximate so nearly in composition, and even in their organic remains, that a separation is not practicable.

The whole vergent mass between the lake and the coal rock is 1,900 feet thick, about 800 or 900 feet representing the thickness of the lower formation, and 1,000 or 1,100 the overlying vergent shales. The quarries near the road between Waterford and Erie, at an elevation of 800 feet above the lake, indicate nearly the highest portion of the inferior group. It would appear from the researches of Prof. James Hall, that the total thickness of the vergent flag formation or portage group of New York, amounts, in the longitude of Chautauqua

Creek, to nearly 1,400 feet; we are therefore to infer that in the region of Lake Erie some 500 or 600 feet of the formation are covered by its waters.

Ripple marks, so abundant in the vergent flags, are numerous in Erie and Crawford Counties. Concretions of various shapes abound in the more calcareous varieties of the finer-grained clay shales, particularly those of the lower or flag group. The commonest forms are spheroids, generally much flattened, and often curiously lobed by the addition of fresh materials on one or more sides. When very calcareous, these are seamed with little veins of carbonate of lime, filling cracks in more central portions—they are, in other words, true *septaria*.

Among the concretionary structures is one [1] which, from its singularity, and the doubts entertained by many in relation to its mode of origin, deserves a more special mention. It is the so-called " Cone-in-Cone " structure of the English geologist. In England it is met with occasionally in the finer shales and clay ironstones of the coal measures; but in one vast series of formations it is nowhere seen but in this particular horizon, near the vergent flag formation. It usually occurs in flat cakes of hardened calcareous shale imbedded in soft, mealy shale, the conical structure occupying a thickness of one or two inches on one surface of the cake. Its position in the strata is near the lake shore, and perhaps the best localities for it in Erie County are at the mouth of Sixteen Mile Creek, and at the Cascade near Erie; but it is to be seen in a corresponding situation bordering on the lake at a great number of spots throughout the entire length of the formation, from Chautauqua Creek in New York, to Cleveland in Ohio, and Prof. Hall speaks of it as abundant on the Genesee River.

A minute inspection of the strata, as disclosed on the lake shore and in the ravines, shows the first two hundred feet to consist of blue and olive-colored soft, calcareous clay-shales, brown bituminous shale and slate, and their alternating layers of fine-grained gray calcareo-argillaceous sandstone. All

---

[1] This structure was first observed by Dr. Samuel L. Mitchell, a distinguished geologist of New York, in 1827, and regarded by him with very great interest. His specimens were labeled " Argillaceous Schist of a peculiar conchoidal fracture."

these materials are in their beds, and in constant alternation, their dimensions being from one fourth of an inch to twelve inches. The carbonaceous shales and slates are the thinnest. Some of the finer-grained shales extend with little change of thickness over very considerable areas, while other beds change their dimensions rapidly. The shales, but more especially the sandstones, are slightly calcareous.

The level line of the shore enables us to detect, in the dip of the strata, a slight lateral or northeast and southwest undulation—but this feature is only local and inconspicuous. At the mouth of Elk Creek, and elsewhere, the strata exhibit even a very gentle dip toward the northwest; and when examined, this feature is connected with a low anticlinal arching of the rocks, the axis of elevation being near the bridge, half a mile above the outlet of the stream, not far from Girard. If it were practicable thus to refer all the inclinations of the strata to a succession of horizons absolutely level, we should discover a vast succession of very low but broad and obscure anticlinals, conforming in their northeast and southwest trend to the flexures of the Appalachian chain, and indicating the last expiring swells in the crust transmitted with abating intensity across the broad bituminous coal region, from the enormous billows which lifted the Appalachian chain.

Organic remains are rare in the strata near the side of the lake, but one slender layer, about three inches in thickness, occurring on the shore near the borough of Northeast, contains the little *Avicula speciosa* and *Ungulina suborbicularia*, the most abundant fossils of the formation. In other places the faces of the slabs of slate, especially when in contact with bituminous shale, are sometimes covered with fragments of plants, chiefly a delicate species of fucoid.

Eight or ten miles back from the lake the terrace outcrops consist of thinly-laminated olive and brownish shales, alternating with flagy layers of sandstone. These latter become gradually more abundant as we ascend in the series. The thickest arenaceous beds measure in some places twelve or fifteen inches, and where a number of them occur together, with only thin partings of shale, the mass is quarried as a building material.

A stratum of this kind appears about midway between Erie and Waterford, and has been quarried in an excavation known as Vincent's, about one mile west of the turnpike, the materials from it being used in the locks of the Erie extension of the Pennsylvania Canal. Near Elk Creek, at Elisha Smith's, east of Girard, and at Cranes' near Cranes' Mills, are the most extensive quarries of similar masses. It is seldom possible to trace a particular stratum of the sandstone for any considerable distance, for the beds soon thin off or deteriorate for economical uses, becoming too argillaceous. At an elevation of about 810 feet above the level of the lake there appear, in the vicinity of Waterford, two or three thin layers of calcareous sandstone, abounding in marine organic remains, chiefly bivalve shells. These strata, easily recognized by the profusion of their imbedded fossils, are to be seen at Whiteman's, and also at Wilcox's, near the village, as likewise along the streams at the head waters of Le Bœuf and Elk Creeks—one locality being near the house of Martin Strong. The species are characteristic of the vergent newer shales, the Chemung group of New York.

Upon these fossiliferous beds rest several bands of sandstone, the layers being from six to twelve inches thick. These have been quarried for building-stone, but approaching Waterford they deteriorate. East of the village occurs a stratum of yellow sandstone, coarser than the beds of the formation generally, and differing from them in aspect. It has been quarried on the borders of French Creek, where a good building material was obtained. At Smith's quarry the bed was about four feet thick. Upon it rest, first, thin bands of pebbly rock, the pebbles having the size of large shot; secondly, shale; thirdly, two layers of hard silicious sandstone, sixteen inches thick, and above them slate and flaggy sandstone. A similar section may be seen on the opposite side of the stream at A. Middleton's.

In the Moravian quarry (near Waterford) the sandstone bed is not so thick. At Carrol's quarry it is from four to six feet in thickness, some thin layers of pebbly rock or coarse grit, and other sandstone resting over it, separated by only a few inches of shale. All these beds are embraced within a thickness of ten or twelve feet. A little petroleum is found in all of these quarries. We have already seen that many of the clay shales are highly bituminous. The greater part of the surface of the northwest district is thinly strewed with Northern drift, and the valleys of all the principal streams are deeply filled with it, presenting some very instructive features in the forms of many bold terraces into which the waters have brought it.

Character of the Soil.—The cadent and vergent rocks, of which this northwest district consists, furnish by disintegration a soil in which clay is the predominating ingredient. It may be denominated a cold, clayey loam, better suited for grazing than for growing wheat. That derived from the inferior, more argillaceous strata nearer the lake, is in many belts a stiff clay, while that into which the sandy matter of the upper parts of the formation enters as an element is looser, and approximates to the character of a loam. A greater or less mixture of the materials of the Northern drift or transported gravel, with the proper soil of the region, modifies the quality of the latter, and gives to many localities agricultural peculiarities which the subsequent rocks themselves could never impart. In nearly all the larger valleys the depth of the drift is such as to confer on them a soil abounding in gravel. Though this very heterogeneous covering contains pebbles and sand derived from the limestones which outcrop to the north and east of Lake Erie, mingled with the less fertile materials of the crystalline and silicious rocks yet farther north, and with the fragments of the underlying shales, a soil exists usually well adapted to the culture of wheat and the finer kinds of grain.

The soil derived from the cadent and vergent rocks alone is too generally deficient in calcareous matter to possess a high degree of fertility, and, unfortunately for the domestic agricultural resources of the district, not a single bed or formation of good limestone either within it or cheaply contiguous to it, contributes to the land the element which it chiefly needs. As, however, much good agricultural lime is procurable from the immediate coast of the lake toward its west end, there cannot be a doubt that ultimately commerce, in her inexhaustible power to benefit, will be enlisted to convey the requisite quantity of this almost indispensable fertilizer not only to the coast of Erie County, but by the canals, to all the contiguous regions toward the southeast.

Calcareous Marl.—In the Pymatuning and Conneaut swamps there are shallow but rather extensive deposits of a soft calcareous tufa and shell-marl, the possible value of which to the agriculture of the surrounding districts is not enough appreciated. This is in Crawford County. Thus far we have cited the State geologist.

In Erie County, at Beaverdam, west of Union, thirty years ago, marl was burned for lime; and at Walnut Creek, quite recently, lime of the best quality was manufactured. At the Sink-hole, in Waterford, we have reason to suppose the quantity of shell-marl inexhaustible.[1] Many cords of hard blue limestone were quarried in excavating the canal in Erie. The very superior quality of the wheat produced in the vicinity of the lake confirms Prof. Roger's statement, that lime exists in the sand and pebbles. It is sometimes too, observed in bricks, in their disruption when the lime slackens.

For several years the blast furnace of Vincent, Himrod & Co. was stocked principally with Erie County bog ore.[2] It was brought from Laird's farm, Nicholson's, Elk Creek, etc., in the western part of the county. Near Cranesville there is a bed which is burned and used as a mineral paint. The ore yielded from fifteen to twenty, and sometimes even sixty per cent of iron—some was found to be one-fifth limestone. At the time the furnace discontinued operations, the supply of ore was supposed to be exhausted.

Coal in small quantities has been found, and also sulphate of alumina compounded with the sulphate of iron, from which

[1] Prof. Austin, of the Waterford Academy, put the marl to the test, and found it to be composed principally of lime; and adds, "the time will come when it will be extensively used as a fertilizer, and it can be burned so as to form lime—but the lime will not be as good as if obtained from some other source."

[2] As a proof of the quality of the metal, we find in the *Erie Gazette*, 1843: "An inspection of 1200 32-pound shot was made by the navy agent, at the Presqu'ile Foundery, from Erie County ore, and a contract was finished with government for 300 8-inch shot and 7,000 32-pounders, part of which were shipped for Buffalo and Sackett's Harbor."

Many years ago considerable quantities were shipped at Massassaqué for a small furnace in Conneaut, Ohio.

the alum of commerce is derived. Salt springs have been discovered in various places, but probably not of sufficient strength to justify the erection of works for the manufacture of salt.

Petroleum.—Boring for oil has been prosecuted in different parts, as yet not with any marked success. The well of C. McSparren, in the southeastern part of the town, reached the depth of 200 feet, mostly through rock. An abundance of gas was found, but the work has ceased for the present. In Summit township, Mr. C. Fronce bored a well on a branch of Le Bœuf Creek to the depth of 200 feet without finding oil in paying quantities. Afterward, near Strong's Mill, at a depth of 157 feet, a vein which it was thought would yield ten barrels per day was found. P. G. Stranahan drilled 200 feet in Union; and on Sturgeon's farm, at Fairplains, 100 feet through a stratum of coal four feet in thickness. Near the Springfield Depot, on the Cleveland and Erie Road, boring has been commenced. Nearly a dozen companies are now prosecuting the business in Conneaut township, on the banks of Marsh Run. Oil was found in that region twenty years ago, and collected for medicinal purposes, and in quarrying stone the workmen found it in small pools among the rocks. An old salt well which had been opened forty years ago, in Wellsburg, having become filled with rubbish, was cleaned, and jets of oil were thrown at three different times. This is on the east branch of Conneaut Creek. A company with a cash capital of $1,000 was formed in February, 1861, at Waterford, to drill in that neighborhood, and in Erie one hundred Germans formed an association with a capital of $10,000, and immediately commenced operations on Ninth Street.

The Germans carried on this work and drilled four hundred feet. On February 26, 1862, they struck a vein of gas which threw the water twenty feet into the air. About 9:30 the proprietor, Mr. Athof, and eight others visited the well to examine, carrying a lighted lantern. When they were within a few feet of the derrick, the gas took fire, and the whole party were more or less injured and one survived but a few hours.

Several mineral springs have been discovered—a burning

sulphur spring on the farm of Mr. Knox, south of the town, at one time claimed attention and excited much curiosity. Another burning spring is found on the Ohlwiler farm, on Six Mile Creek. A mineral spring on the ground formerly owned by P. P. Glazier, on Eighth Street, was, in 1840, improved and fitted up with baths for the benefit of invalids. A specimen of the water was sent for analysis to Prof. Booth, of Philadelphia. His experiments on one gallon of 60,000 grains resulted as follows :—

Chloride of potassium	20.56		Carbonate of lime	19.12
" sodium	110.16		" magnesia	0.96
" magnesium	45.36		" iron	1.44
" calcium	8.88		Silica	0.48
" iron	2.88			
Sulphate of lime	11.68		Total insoluble	22.00
Total soluble matter	199.52			

Prof. Booth explains insoluble matter to mean " the residue, which will not redissolve in pure water after evaporation to dryness. The carbonates in the insoluble portion are held in solution in the spring water by a small quantity of carbonic acid which escapes during the evaporation."

He adds: "It appears from the analysis that the spring water is of excellent quality and bears comparison with many European springs which have attained some celebrity." The waters have been successfully tried by invalids ; but the premises are now out of repair, and the water not to be obtained in its purity and strength.

The unforseen and repeated sinking of the Philadelphia and Erie track, at Le Bœuf swamp, near Waterford, attracted much attention during the construction of that road, and elicited the following statement in substance from Mr. R. Andrews, one of the engineers. When the location was made, the surface, excepting in a few places, appeared firm and hard. Le Bœuf swamp, in which the sinking occurred, is between two large mounds designated as the north and south mounds, as they lie in that course with the railroad. The level is about four feet higher than Le Bœuf Creek. The surface soil is mostly made up of vegetable mould, varying from three to seven feet in thickness, for the distance of 38,000 feet. The line of the railroad is perfectly straight through this swamp, and the height of the bank above it averages five feet. The grading of the railroad was begun in 1856, at both ends, and after making 100 feet of the bank near the south mound it first showed symptoms of settling, and went from bad to worse as the bank receded from the mound. At the north end better progress was made, and there were no indications that any settling would take place. When the work on the road was stopped, in 1857, 1,000 feet were made on the north end, and 175 on the south.

In 1858 the work was resumed, but little progress was made until January, 1859, when the efficient and energetic contractors, Russel, Barnet & Co., took charge. Soundings were made under the direction of the engineer through the swamp, the length of which, by previous advancement, was reduced to 2,600 feet. At the south mound no bottom could be found for a distance of 300 feet—an iron rod having been made thirty-five feet in length for the purpose. The soundings for the remaining 1,300 feet averaged from 1 to 25 feet, striking a good gravel bottom. The penetration of the rod in most places through the crust was somewhat hard ; but when through, it passed readily to the gravel.

There is every indication that at one time this was a large lake, and that it has become filled up by drift, logs, etc., which, by decay and vegetable matter decomposing, has formed the "crust" alluded to. For some time the two sides settled very materially, but particularly the one on the south, consuming an immense quantity of earth.

The height of the bank (as ascertained from a formula, the amount of yards put in and the distance made being known) is 55 feet, thus making a fill of this height when the original section called for only 6 feet. Some idea may be formed of the amount of work required to complete the south end, from the following calculation based on actual measurement : "In the month of February 7,500 yards were put in and only gained 30 feet. Had the swamp not settled, and with the original section, this amount of earth would have made something over three fourths of a mile. The settling is very gradual, and when the bank once ceases to settle, it never varies afterward.[1] A portion made up to grade in 1857 has not settled an inch, thus guaranteeing a good and safe bank, though a costly one.

"Large night forces were put on this work—200 men, 20 cars, and 18 horses worked day and night as faithfully as possible. It presented a lively appearance at night to see the fires and lanterns strung along the banks, and to hear the voices of the men, and the rumbling noise of the cars breaking the peaceful quietude."

To those in the vicinity who had never before witnessed *earth swallow earth*, or suspected an old lake under cover, with its gravel bottom forty feet below, it must have been a matter of very great surprise.

Near Union a similar but smaller sinkhole was found; and also at Hartstown, Crawford County, on the canal, one of twice the extent of the one at Waterford.

Meadows in the West have broken through and sunk, while others have been so like a spring floor that the weight of a cart was never hazarded upon them, but the harvest secured by long pitchforks. "All belong to a class of which there are myriads in the drift region of North America. The largest *Superior*, and others that scarcely hold a gallon, as to supply and position, are to be accounted for in exactly the same manner."

The Devil's Backbone.—About three and a half miles southeast from the borough of Girard is a most remarkable place, which deserves a better name than "The Devil's Backbone." The country is very romantic and extremely hilly, rising apparently to a very great height. Reaching the farm of Mr. Blair, one of the first settlers, the drive is along the edge of a fearful ravine, the road lying frightfully near, and but for the thick growth of trees on its border would be absolutely dangerous. Leaving the horses and carriage, a walk of a few moments opens to view a magnificent prospect. Beneath, appears a large hollow, the precipitous sides of which, as well as the bank beyond, are covered with magnificent forest trees. In the middle of this rises the "Backbone," a ridge of sand

[1] This treacherous swamp occasioned difficulty after the cars commenced running.

and slate one hundred feet in height, with a base of but sixty feet. This is two hundred feet in length, one side being partly covered with trees, while the other is entirely bare. The top of the back, which is from one to twelve inches in width, is a narrow but rather dangerous walk, but affords a view truly grand, Elk Creek being around the point and on both sides having worn its bed through the soil to a very great depth. The abrupt height of the ridge, its narrow base, the deep bed of the stream, with the beauty of the surrounding scenery, compose the extraordinary landscape.

Half a mile distant is another pyramidal ridge covered with grass, not so high or peculiar, called the "Nose." Here there are forks in the creek, and the whole is wild and picturesque.

The description is miserably unjust, but *none* could be fully adequate—in the worn out words, "it must be seen to be truly appreciated."

As to the flora of this region, we cannot do better than to quote a few words of Prof. L. G. Olmstead: "We consider the county and immediate vicinity of Erie by far the best botanizing district with which we are acquainted throughout a large district of country. We have upon the peninsula a very great variety of plants, many of which are not found on the main land, but are common only to Western prairies. The marshes, ponds, bogs, etc., afford a great variety of marsh and aquatic plants.

"Among the plants that some of our best florists would travel many miles to see, are the Saracenia purpurea or pitcher plant; several varieties of Potamogeton, which are aquatic; Batschia canescens, Enchococinea, found on the Western prairies; Hydopeltis purpurea, and several species of Utricularia."

The sweetbrier, which has been much admired and particularly adorns the green banks of the lake in the western part of the town, is not, like the wild rose, indigenous, the first plant having been brought from Carlisle, by Gen. Kelso. Some specimens of the double sweetbrier have been found on the Peninsula.

CHAPTER XIX.

Miscellaneous Items, among which are: A Tradition—General Wayne—An Anecdote—Price of Provisions—William W. Reed, Esq.—First National Celebration—Churches—The Garrison—A Relic—Saturday Afternoon—Game—Mrs. P.'s Reminiscences—H. Russel's Journal—An early Settler in Fairview—La Fayette's Visit in Erie—Cholera—Perry Monument—An Informal Meeting —Speculation—Fires—Sad Accidents—Ex-President Adams— Patriot War—Old Courthouse Bell—Pioneers—Perry—Lieutenant Yarnall—Survivors of the Battle of Lake Erie—Perry Monument at Cleveland—Inventions—Moravian Lands--Omissions.

A Tradition.—The Eries were alarmed when they heard of the confederation of the Mohawks, Oneidas, Onondagas, Cayugas, and Senecas residing in Central New York, and regarded them as natural enemies. To satisfy themselves, they sent a message to the Senecas, who resided nearest to them, inviting them to select one hundred of their most active, athletic men to play a game of ball against the same number selected from the Eries, for a wager worthy of the occasion and nation.

The message was received in the most respectful manner, but the challenge declined. The next year the offer was renewed and again declined. At the third offer, the young Iroquois could be no longer restrained, the wise councils which had hitherto prevailed were set aside, and the challenge accepted. After the selection, the party being the flower of the tribe, a most solemn charge was given them to acquit themselves as the worthy representatives of a great and powerful people, anxious to cultivate peace and friendship with neighboring tribes. The party then took up the line of march for Tu-shu-way (Buffalo), sent a messenger to notify the Eries of their approach, and the next day made a grand entrée. They brought no weapon. The bat was a hickory stick, about five feet long, bent over at the end, and thong netting woven into a bow. Their wager, which was matched by the Eries, consisted of piles of elegant wampum, costly jewels, silver bands, and beautifully ornamented moccasins. The game began, and though contested with desperation and great skill by the Eries, the Iroquois bore off the prize in triumph. The Iroquois having accomplished the object of their visit were about to return, when the Eries proposed a foot race between ten of their number, at "Kanswans" or Eighteen Mile Creek. The victor in the race was to dispatch his adversary with a tomahawk and bear off his scalp as a trophy. This the Iroquois accepted, secretly intending to waive the bloody part of the proposition should their tribe be victors. The Eries were again vanquished, but the Iroquois declined to execute their victim. At this the chief of the Eries came forward, and, quick as thought, himself dispatched the vanquished warrior, who was dragged out of the way and another champion placed in his stead. This was three times repeated, and the Iroquois seeing the great excitement that prevailed, made a signal to depart, and, gathering up their trophies, proceeded homeward.

The Eries knew no mode of securing peace but by the extermination of their enemies; it being no part of their character to cultivate and strengthen friendship. They knew to contend with them collectively would be useless. Immediately they organized a powerful party of warriors—hoping to be an equal match to their powerful neighbors by surprising the Senecas, who resided on Seneca Lake. But a woman residing among them who had a stronger interest in the Iroquois, secretly gave them warning, and five thousand warriors were organized and marched out to meet them. The two parties met at Honeoye, where a bloody and desperate battle was fought. The Eries were driven seven times across the stream and as often regained their ground. But a few of the vanquished Eries escaped to convey the news of their terrible overthrow, and these were pursued, and all that fell into the enemies' hands put to death. For weeks the pursuit was continued, and it was five months before the victorious party of the five nations returned with their trophies, having subdued their last and most powerful enemies. Tradition adds that the descendants of the Eries returned from beyond the Mississippi and attacked the Senecas, then settled in the seat of their fathers, Tu-shu-way; and that a great battle was fought, and the Eries slain to a man, near the site of the (Cattaraugus) Indian Missionhouse.

General Wayne.—The following newspaper article, by Rev. L. G. Olmstead, is copied partly for the purpose of adding a word of explanation in reference to the disinterment of Gen. Wayne, at Erie, in 1809:

"On arriving at Erie, he (Colonel Isaac Wayne) employed 'Old Dr. Wallace,' so called to distinguish him from the present Dr. Wallace, to take up his father's remains, pack the boxes in as small a space as possible and lash them on to the hinder part of his sulky. Dr. Wallace took up the remains and found them in a perfect state of preservation, except one foot. The body had been buried in full uniform, and the boot on the decayed foot was also decayed, while the other boot remained sound, and a man by the name of Duncan had a mate to it and wore them out. Duncan's foot, like the general's, was very large. Dr. Wallace cut and boiled the flesh off the bones, packed them in a box, lashed them to the carriage, and they were brought and deposited beside the rest of his family in the above named churchyard.

"I visited Gen. Wayne's old residence in the summer of 1857, and found everything much as he had left it. The house is an elegant, old two-story mansion, now occupied by his grandson. The parlors and sitting-rooms are as they were. There are portraits and engravings of men of the Revolution, hanging on the walls, as on the 3d of April, 1792, when he was appointed to the command of the Western army. Around the house and over the farm, while the fences and buildings are in a good condition, yet they assured me it is about as he left it. Everything appeared as though it had belonged to a gentleman of the old school, a race now said to be extinct. The premises looked, and I felt, as though the old hero, whose very name was once a terror to the murderous red man, might be expected back in an hour or so, and a dreamy impression seemed to steal over me that if I waited a little I should see him. I should have liked much to have questioned him about Three Rivers, and Brandywine, and Germantown, and Monmouth, and Stony Point, and Yorktown, and the Indians, and how the city appeared when she was only a year old. And I seemed to hold my breath and listen as many an old Indian had done, for his footsteps and his fearful oaths ; yet he did not come, and I passed on some three miles to his final resting place."

G. Sanford, who came to Erie in 1810, and was well acquainted with Dr. J. C. Wallace, heard him more than once allude to this circumstance. Mr. Sanford's impression is that Col. Wayne put up at Buehler's hotel, and did not visit the grave of his father, but sent for Dr. Wallace and made known the object of his visit, requesting him to superintend the removal and place the remains in a suitable condition for the journey. Dr. Wallace was a skillful surgeon of the army and a man of the first standing, and Col. Wayne could not have selected a more suitable person to carry out his design. Both must have supposed the body, thirteen years after death, to have returned to corruption. That Dr. Wallace pursued the wisest course the nature of the case would admit of, none who knew him would for a moment doubt. As a military man he was accustomed to obey orders, but it was with his operations as with other surgeons, not always an agreeable subject to discuss minutely.

An Anecdote.—The details of the first year's residence of a wealthy citizen of the county who settled near Waterford, present a model of patience and industry worthy of study and imitation. On landing, one of the few settlers offered him employment in going to the woods to split puncheons, for which he was to have fifty cents a day. This occupation consists in splitting fair chestnut logs two or three times and smoothing them with an axe, to be used as a substitute for boards in making a floor. After a week of hard work at the puncheons (with hoeing potatoes before breakfast added), reckoning day came, and he found he was charged seventy-five cents per day for board ! Legal redress was not to be thought of, as there was no law this side of Pittsburg, which was then almost as difficult of access as Pike's Peak. He tied up his effects in his yellow cotton handkerchief, and was about starting, when his employer called out, "Where did you split the puncheons?" (He had been called "the green Yankee.") "You call me green, and I am; but not green enough to tell you that!" was the spirited reply.

(Many years after he saw the decayed puncheons on the spot where he left them, near the site of the courthouse).

The settler then walked six or eight miles to the location of a farmer, and, finding no warrant upon the tract adjoining him, he secured it, and immediately put in a crop of potatoes. These, when the size of birds' eggs, he used for food, for he had no other. In November the potatoes were gone, and after having scooped out a log for a canoe, he floated down the river, seeking employment. At Pittsburg no engagement offering, he put himself up at auction, at the market, proclaiming from a horseblock, that he "could do any work that any other man could do," and a Dutchman gave him a bid of three dollars a month and board. (This time he was careful to mention the board). Here he remained three months, and was offered for the future three dollars and fifty cents per month, but he paid out his nine dollars for a barrel of flour and poled himself up to Waterford; from this he carried his flour, thirty pounds at a time, to his farm three miles distant.

Price of Provisions, etc.—Among Esquire Rees's papers we find a bill dated 1792, "For services in viewing the county, $193.43." Another, "To Indians for hunting, $50."

Other accounts, dated 1797, show provisions at the following prices: Potatoes, 12 shillings per bushel; corn 16 shillings; oats, 12 shillings; wheat, 20 shillings per bushel; pork, $30 per barrel; sugar, 33 cents; loaf sugar, 87 cents per pound, etc.

In 1813-14 provisions commanded a still higher price; corn $4, and oats $3 per bushel.

The first white man born in the "Triangle" was William W. Reed, son of John C. Reed, and grandson of Col. S. Reed, in Erie, February 20, 1797. He became a merchant in Ashtabula, Ohio, but had resided in Erie a few years previous to his decease, September 9, 1851.

The First Celebration of our National Independence recorded was the Fourth of July, 1797, near Colt's Station. Mr. Colt says: "Tuesday being the twenty-second anniversary of the Independence of America, at the expense of the Pennsylvania Population Company we gave an entertainment to about seventy-five people, settlers of the said company. A bower was erected under two large maple trees, and when the hearts of the people were cheered with good fare, sundry toasts were drunk suitable to the occasion. After I had withdrawn, one James Crawford offered the following: 'May Judah Colt, agent of the Population Company, drive the intruders before him as Samson did the Philistines! Three cheers!' and the woods rang with a roar of laughter for some time."[1]

First Court.—When the circuit court met for the first time in the county, several of the citizens rode out to escort Judge Yates into town, but were disappointed in not meeting him. The court met in a room rented by the commissioners, on French Street, between Second and Third Streets. As the first day was election day, business was postponed, and in the afternoon, in honor of the judge and strangers, a large sailing party of ladies and gentlemen went over to the peninsula.

Churches.—Previous to 1811 there was seldom church to attend, but the few who could do so conveniently would ride to Fairview or Northeast, where were church organizations and settled pastors at an early day. Among the itinerants at a later day was Rev. Mr. Judd, who periodically, for several years, held meetings in Col. Forster's vacant room, on the corner of French and Fifth streets. He was esteemed a man of zeal and strong faith, but somewhat eccentric; having been connected with the Presbyterian, Baptist, and Methodist churches, he was now free from all ecclesiastical rule. In the selection of elders, with him piety was of no account—influence was the indispensable qualification. Hence, his men in Erie were Captain Deacon, the commanding officer, Purser Carr, and Mr. Reed the wealthiest citizen. On one occasion, after reading the hymn, no one appeared "to raise the tune," and he remarked that he wished "Captain Deb. was there, and she could do it," meaning his wife. He then asked if there was not some lady who would undertake it, when one

[1] This refers to "actual settlers," and not Indians, as the agent often had perils in dispossessing them.

kindly volunteered, and in due time all went on in a becoming and reverential manner.

An anecdote is related which shows the class of people our ministers had to deal with, even long after this. On one occasion the parson thought proper to exclude from the communion one of his members who had been guilty of intemperance, by the name of Folwell. In consequence of this a near connection came *to thrash the parson.* After the matter had been discussed, and the irritated avenger (who, for the preacher's eye, had not been able to execute his threat) being somewhat restored to reason, he exclaimed, "Faith, sir, and when ye come till heaven ye'll find the Folwells *theer!*" With this ultimatum of his rage he departed.

At an early day *the garrison* seemed to be the general resort for citizens and strangers, an officer of the army having command until about 1806. At the time Gen. Wayne's remains were removed, in 1809, and previously, Captain D. Dobbins was residing in the large building, in the center of the ground, erected for the commanding officer; one of the gates was down and the works were going to decay. Gen. Wayne, when he was landed in an almost dying state, chose to be tenanted in the upper part of the east block house. It seems the attics of the three were fitted up as dwellings. We have mentioned elsewhere that these block houses were on the east side of the creek, and built in 1795 for the protection of the State Commissioners, General William Irvine and Andrew Ellicot, who were laying out the town. Captain John Grubb brought on a militia force at the time.[1] The names of the officers who commanded at different times were Captain Russel Bissel, in 1797; Captain Cornelius Lyman, until 1801; Captain McCall, and Gen. Callender Irvine. Captain Lyman is described as a perfect gentleman, notwithstanding which he was court-martialed in Erie, in 1798, for a want of hospitality (in what particular instance is not recorded), but was honorably acquitted. In 1801 (Mr. Colt notes), "Col. Hamtramck arrived from Pittsburg, on his way to Detroit. On entering the garrison a salute from the fort, of sixteen guns, was fired, and also one from the

[1] Captain Grubb was a worthy citizen. He received the appointment of Associate Judge about 1813, and resided on his farm in Mill Creek until his death in June, 1845.

United States armed vessel Wilkeson, in the harbor; at the same time a large brig from Fort Erie, of two hundred tons, came in." In April, 1802, a ball was given at the garrison, which, Mr. Colt remarks, " was a very agreeable affair."

A Relic.—In 1804 or 1805 an iron cannon, a three pounder, was found by Gen. Kelso, near the Cascade, partly imbedded in sand. The probability is that it belonged to the French. At the time of their occupation, and previously, there was a road on the sand beach, and in transporting stores this might have been for some reason abandoned. Gen. K. or his heirs disposed of it many years ago to a citizen of Black River, Ohio.

In a number of the newspaper *Mirror*, of 1808, we find that the sum of forty-two dollars was paid William Davidson for clearing the public square.

It has been remarked of Mill Creek, that in 1810 it contained four times the quantity of water that it does at present and was quite a large turbulent stream, and about Third Street there was quite a pretty cascade. The gradual diminution of streams has been remarked in all new countries. It is supposed to be the result of increased evaporation occasioned by the removal of trees, and also by the plowed ground, which absorbs large quantities of water.

Saturday Afternoon.—An early custom prevailed in Erie that must have been highly unpopular with some—that of calling out every man on Saturday afternoon to dig out stumps in the streets. This was before 1810.

There was an ordinance also compelling citizens *to dig three stumps from the highways of the town* as a punishment for every *bacchanal revel they engaged in.* This ordinance was repealed at an informal meeting held in front of the Reed House, in June, 1846, the principal object being in congratulation of the puplic benefit received by the adornment of the public square with trees, and when it received the name of Perry Square.

As to game, the early settlers found an abundance of deer, rabbits, foxes, squirrels, opossums, etc. As late as 1804, Mr. Hamlin Russel enters in his journal: " January 1—Cloudy morning; clears off; hunt bears, wolves, panthers, wild cats, etc." Panthers are not often spoken of in Erie County. In Buffalo we hear of one being shot, in 1827, one mile and a half from the present courthouse.

In 1808 are to be found, among county expenditures, $80 paid for wolf scalps. The bounty was probably $10 per head—afterward, for many years, it was $12. The few scalps presented for bounty at that early day indicate the sparseness of the population and their want of leisure for such pursuits. In 1813 Mr. Russel lost four sheep by wolves. In 1828 sheep could not be kept at Colt's Station on account of their frequent visits: $72.74 was paid by the county for scalps in 1834, $85.90 in 1836.

Probably the last of the wild cat species in the county was shot by Mr. Abram Knapp, at Lake Pleasant, in 1857.

A copy of the *Erie Gazette*, dated August, 1820, has the following advertisement:

"*A Hunting we will go!*—A party of gentlemen intend going to the head of the peninsula, on Wednesday morning next, if fair—if not, the next fair morning—for the purpose of forming a line across it at the head and marching abreast down to the point, where boats will be stationed to follow game that may take to the water. A meeting will be held on Monday evening next at the courthouse, for the purpose of making the necessary arrangements."

Foxes are still abundant. J. W. Silverthorn shot twenty in the neighborhood of Girard, in the winter of 1861, and many other sportsmen were quite successful in the same way.

In 1862 several minks were found and sold as high as 14 shillings a piece.

Mrs. P.'s Reminiscences.—Mrs. P., who remembers Erie in 1803, says: The pickets were standing around parts of old Fort Presqu'ile at that time. A ruined, peculiar looking house of stone and timber was also standing, and near by was a very deep well. Indian beads and other relics were found on the ground.

When the fleet was building, a small party returned from the peninsula very greatly excited, maintaining that they had seen three British spies, in red coats, and made oath to the fact before a magistrate. As fears were entertained of the destruction of the vessels while building, the militia were called out until the square was filled. The Burgess thought advisable, before proceeding further, to send over and make a strict search, which was accordingly done, and nothing found to justify the story unless it might be that three red oxen were there quietly feeding.

Soon after Buffalo was burned, an express came with the news that the British were eighteen miles west of Buffalo, on their way to destroy Erie and the fleet. Merchants removed their wares, and the greatest consternation prevailed. Families were called up at midnight, and, hastily packing their furniture and goods, fled from the lake, and many of them remained absent until spring. The most anxious fears were from the Indians, who had perpetrated such cruelties at Buffalo. Commodore Elliot was, through the whole, firm in the the opinion that the town and fleet were sufficiently protected. The young people were very much amused, during such excitements, by the conduct of the militia, as well as by their uniforms, which were made up of every variety of borrowed and inherited garments and nonfits. Some went so far as to maintain that they protected the town after the manner of scarecrows, and that they were nuisances second only to the British themselves.

In the *Journal of Mr. Hamlin Russel*, of Mill Creek, is the following:

"June, 1812.—Gen. Kelso ordered Captain Foot to call out his company of infantry for the defense of Erie. (Hamlin Russel volunteered).

"6th.—On duty. This day the general dismissed our company; so, for the present, myself and a number of my neighbors have volunteered to keep sentry at the head of the peninsula, three by rotation to stand a tour of twenty-four hours; my tour will commence on the eighth instant.

"August 25.—Expresses were sent through the county to call out the militia—a number of vessels being seen, apprehensions were entertained that a descent would be made at this place. I went to town, as did all the country; there heard the disagreeable information that General Hull had surrendered himself and army prisoners to the British, together with the post of Detroit. The general voice pronounces Hull a traitor.

"May 15, 1813.—Go to town; a great alarm; 600 or 700 British and Indians land on the peninsula under cover of a thick fog, and go off again without being seen by any one.

"July 26, P. M.— . . . Our harbor closely blockaded by the British vessels; the militia of this county are ordered out en masse.

"December 31.—Thus ends the year 1813, in which the war has been carried on in a manner becoming Democracy; Wilkinson's army is defeated and driven out of Canada, and likely to starve this winter; Fort George is evacuated; the enemy have burned Lewistown and Schlosser, surprised and taken Fort Niagara without the loss of a man, and still retain possession of it. Hurrah for Democracy!

"January 1, 1814.—Go to town; there learn that Thursday last the British crossed at Black Rock, drove the militia before them to the village of Buffalo, and then drove them out of the village, which they reduced to ashes. Report says that the enemy, 3,000 strong, are eight miles in advance of Buffalo, on the march for this place; the citizens of Erie are sending off their families and effects as fast as possible. Come home; make preparations to send off my wife and babes, should worst come to worst.

"Sunday, 2.— . . . Find that it is not true that the enemy are advancing to this, but in all probability they will be here, or attempt to come, before spring (on the ice); expresses sent off in every direction to call in the militia.

"3d.—Receive orders from Lieutenant-Colonel J. C. Wallace to appear immediately at Erie to perform the duties of my office in the regiment.

"February 7.—Receive my discharge from my tour and come home, having been engaged thirty-four days, during which I have been at home but seldom, and never but a few hours at a time, and expect now to be ordered out again shortly.

"May 18, 1815.—Went to Martin Strong's [1] to the battalion

[1] Captain Martin Strong was one of the earliest inhabitants. In a letter we find that he came to this county the last of July, 1795, when there was but one family in the Triangle. Captain Strong was not only one of our most prominent citizens, but a man of excellent sense.

review ; 200 or 300 bludgeoniers met ; hawed and geed about under as brave officers as ever raised potatoes. Hurrah for the militia of Pennsylvania!" [At this early day militiamen practiced with broomsticks, handspikes, etc., the proper weapons often not being obtainable.]

Reminiscences of an Early Settler in Fairview Township are as follows : "In 1810 my father bought a four-hundred acre tract of land in Fairview, ten miles west of Erie and one mile and a half south of the ridge road, of Jacob Ebersole, for five dollars per acre, on which were two cabins of round logs so near to each other that it was considered but one dwelling, the space between the two being the hall. There was also what was considered a large barn in those days. About fifty acres were partially cleared, much deadened timber yet standing in the fields, and some peach and apple trees. The nearest neighbors were of the names of Vance, James Moorhead, John Long, John Stewart, and Jacob Wise, all within the bounds of three miles, which was then considered near neighbors. Many of their descendants reside on the same lands, which have become quite valuable.

"It was seldom in those days that two improved lots joined each other ; generally, they were divided or separated by at least a strip of woodland. The dwellings were rude log cabins which in many instances were taken from the forest and erected into a dwelling in the space of two days, by the assistance of the neighbors. Some would be engaged cutting down trees, while others would be hauling together, building, splitting clapboards for the roof or puncheons for the floor, and thus a tenement would be completed speedily, and with but few nails or boards.

"Our crops were often injured by the depredations of bears, raccoons, deer, and wild turkeys, which were numerous.

"Our house of worship was near the mouth of Walnut Creek—the Rev. Johnson Eaton, pastor."

Memoranda of Mr. Richard Barnett.—"August 26, 1845.— Oppressively hot and dry ; the Beaverdam Run dry in many places, which was never known before by the oldest inhabitants. [Beaverdam Run empties into Walnut Creek.]

"January 5, 1847.—A terrific storm of wind passed over

Fairview, and leveled fences, roofs, sheds, etc., and a great many trees.

"December 16, 1850.—Steamboat May Flower beached above the mouth of Elk Creek,

"December 31, 1852.—A steamboat passed up the lake. January 10, 1853, another passes up. March 21, steamboat commenced running; navigation open most of the winter."

Gen. La Fayette's Visit to Erie.—On the 3d of June, 1825, Gen. La Fayette, on his way from New Orleans to New York, honored Erie with a stay of a few hours. A committee proceeded to Waterford and there received the committee from Pittsburg, with the illustrious guest, Gen. La Fayette, G. W. La Fayette, and M. La Vasseur. Judah Colt, Esq., of the Erie committee, in behalf of the citizens, gave him a cordial welcome to the county, to which the General made a suitable reply. After an early breakfast, the company, with a number of citizens from Waterford, proceeded to Erie. When within a mile of the borough they were received by a battalion of volunteers in full uniform, and a procession formed under the direction of Gen. B. Wallace, Chief Marshal. The procession passed down State Street to the public square; then down French to Third; across Third to the foot of State Street, where the General and suite alighted, and were received by Captain Budd, U. S. N., commanding officer of the naval station, Captain Maurice, of the engineers, and a number of other naval and military officers, and proceeded to the bank. The party being in full view of our beautiful harbor, a national salute was fired from the navy yard, after which the procession passed to the house of Mr. Dobbins, where accommodations had been provided and where he was welcomed in the name of the citizens by Dr. J. C. Wallace, Chief Burgess. Gen. La Fayette made a very appropriate reply, and was introduced to a great number of persons of every age, and then proceeded to the house of Judah Colt, where a large number of ladies were assembled, to whom he was severally presented. Having returned to his quarters he was escorted at half-past one to the bridge on Second Street, between French and State, where a dinner had been prepared by Mr. Dickson. The table extended the length of the bridge, one hundred and seventy feet, in full view of the lake, and was covered by an awning of the sails of the British vessels taken by Commodore Perry, and handsomely ornamented with flowers and evergreens. Among the toasts drank standing, with three cheers, were the "President of the United States," "Gen. George Washington," "Ex-Presidents," "The Greeks," "Bolivar, the Liberator," "the surviving heroes of the Revolution," severally, and lastly, "Gen. La Fayette—In youth a hero, in maturity a sage, in advanced life an example to the present and future generations." After which, Gen. La Fayette arose and gave the following: "Erie—A name which has a great share in American glory: may this town ever enjoy a proportionate share in American prosperity and happiness." The General and his suite were then escorted from the table to their quarters, and, after an affectionate farewell of the citizens, at three o'clock stepped into the carriage and were accompanied by a number of citizens to Portland, where the steamboat Superior was in readiness to receive and convey the party to Buffalo.

In 1827 the young men of Erie celebrated the tenth of September on board of the Queen Charlotte, in Misery Bay. The revenue cutter Dallas carried the company out with one of the flags that was in the action floating from her mast. Between the hours of three and four o'clock a national salute was fired, being the hour the British surrendered. One of Commodore Perry's officers took dinner with them, and one of his seamen fired the cannon.

Cholera.—During the prevalence of the Asiatic cholera throughout our country in 1832, a Mrs. Hunter was landed on the peninsula, in the last stages of the disease, and died thirteen hours after the attack. Her daughter who accompanied her died in twenty-four hours. Great anxiety existed among all classes lest the contagion should prevail. A board of health was appointed, which made frequent reports to the public, and through their exhortations to rigid cleanliness, cheerfulness, and temperance in eating and drinking, no cases originated in the town. This case of Mrs. Hunter, who was an emigrant, was one of the first that originated in the country. It will be remembered as the season when the disease prevailed so fearfully and fatally in many of the lake towns, and on several of the steamboats.

Perry Monument.—In November, 1835, a public meeting convened at the courthouse, to take into consideration the propriety of erecting a monument to the memory of Commodore Perry. Rufus S. Reed was chosen President; George Moore and Giles Sanford, Vice-Presidents; and William Kelley, Secretary. The meeting adopted several appropriate resolutions, and appointed eleven persons to collect funds, procure a site, etc., to fill vacancies in their own body, and to increase the number if necessary, and to attend to all business relating to the accomplishment of the object.

The names of the executive committee were Col. Thomas Forster, George Moore, R. S. Reed, P. S. V. Hamot, Giles Sanford, Thomas H. Sill, William Kelley, Daniel Dobbins, Robert Brown, John H. Walker, and Samuel Hays.

Buffalo made a move about the same time for the erection of a Perry monument in that city, but the depression in the money market, probably with both, prevented further action.

At an *informal meeting* of citizens, in front of the Reed House (probably an imaginary one, as the chairman was the "oldest citizen," and the secretary the man with the "Shaker hat"), held June 2, 1846, in congratulation of the public benefit received by the "recent adornment of the Diamond, the chairman christened the Park 'Perry Square,' and expressed the hope that he might see a cenotaph reared on this spot worthy of the fame of Perry. Let us formally consecrate this ground to the memory of the gallant dead; let it bear the name of Perry, and, by-and-by, a patriotic people shall rear in the midst of the rich foliage that surrounds us, an obelisk to perpetuate his fame, and on which shall be inscribed the enduring record of his achievements. The remarks of the venerable chairman were greeted with enthusiastic applause, amid frequent cries of 'We'll build the monument ourselves.'"

Order having been restored, the following resolutions were introduced and unanimously adopted:

"*Resolved*, That the public ground in Erie, heretofore known as the Diamond, be and the same is hereby named *Perry*

HISTORY OF ERIE COUNTY. 285

Square, by which appellation it shall be known and designated for all time to come.

"*Resolved*, That a monument to commemorate the brilliant naval victory achieved September 10, 1813, by Commodore Perry and his associates, on Lake Erie, be erected in this square; and for that purpose P. S. V. Hamot, Esq., Commodore S. Champlin, U. S. N., and Captain William W. Dobbins are appointed a committee, and are charged with the execution of the work, with power to appoint sub-committees everywhere to collect funds for this patriotic project."

In 1857 a petition was circulated asking Congress to appropriate $20,000 for a monument to Commodore Perry, to be placed in Erie Cemetery. Provided this was successful, a further appropriation was to be solicited from the State. We trust the cause is not abandoned in the minds of our people, and that the example of a neighboring city may be an additional incentive.

Speculation.—In the general stagnation of business, and the speculating mania which prevailed throughout our country about 1836, the inhabitants of Erie unfortunately participated. The immediate completion of the canal; the improvement of the harbor, which would make it second to none; a great diagonal railroad from the West Branch Canal to Erie, the route being perfectly practicable, and one hundred miles nearer the seaboard than any other, and without an inclined plane, being the Northumberland or Sunbury and Erie Road; all contributed to the briliant prospects of Erie, and increased the nominal value of real estate marvelously.

In February 1836, the sales exceeded $1,000,000, the purchasers being mostly Eastern capitalists and speculators.

Extracts from Erie newspapers, in 1830 and 1836, exhibit the position of matters in a business point of view.

"January 12, 1830.—The spirit of speculation which has wrought such wonders upon the line of the Erie Canal has never visited this borough. No extensive business is done on fictitious capital. The soil is owned by its occupants, and no part of it is covered by foreign mortgages. No branch of business is overdone, if we except, perhaps, one or two of the professions. The growth of Erie has at no time exceeded that of the surrounding country. Its increase has been commensurate only with the increase of business. It has, consequently, never felt those reverses which always attend villages of mushroom growth. Many men with small capital have become independent, and some opulent. Erie possesses advantages which must forever secure to it important and lucrative business. Its harbor is decidedly the safest and best on the lake. Our water privileges are equal to our present wants, and an increase may be expected from the construction of the Pennsylvania Canal.

"That Erie will be a successful rival of her sister villages on the borders of the lake, we have not a shadow of doubt; but let not her growth be forced; every doubtful or chimerical speculation should be discountenanced, and, above all, let not our village lots fall into the hands of those who calculate great speculations on their rise. This is the bane which is most to be dreaded in all our growing villages. We must construct a wharf out to Mr. C. M. Reed's pier, where there is deep water.

"February 27, 1836.—Erie bank. We are informed that the entire stock of $200,000 has been subscribed, and, we believe, paid in. [News at the same time of probable passage of appropriation in Congress for improvement of harbor.]

"February 27, 1836.—The receipt of positive news of the final passage of the canal and (U. S.) bank bill at this place, on Monday evening, gave a new impetus to the rise of real estate. It advanced immediately about one hundred per cent, and has since continued rising at the rate of from ten to twenty per cent a day. Sales have been made this week amounting to near half a million of dollars. The sales, too, are none of your sham sales got up for effect—they are bona fide, and liberal, almost invariably made by the purchasers, who are mostly men of heavy capital from the East—Buffalo, Rochester, and New York—and persons able to sustain prices, so far as they buy for speculation, and to improve what they buy for use. There is no danger of retrograde. The tide of prosperity has set in favor of Erie, and it must go ahead. The Fates cannot make it otherwise. Real estate will continue to rise, and we would sincerely recommend any friend of ours who wishes to purchase, to do so as soon as possible.

" March 1.—Real estate. Sales increase in briskness, and prices still rising. The amount of sales on Saturday and yesterday (Monday) amounted to over $300,000. Good bargains are yet offered to any who have cash to invest for first payments, and at prices which cannot fail of advancing in as great a ratio as they have done for several weeks back.

" It is estimated that the sales in our borough, last week, amounted to a million and a half of dollars. They are still going on and daily advancing in prices.

" A company has bought land at the mouth of Twenty Mile Creek, to construct a harbor there.

" A lot of ground sold in Erie, in February, for $10,000—was sold in March, in Buffalo, to a company, for $50,000.

" April 2, 1836.—For the sake of our numerous correspondents, who look with distrust on all excitement in the grave business of laying out bona fide capital, we will briefly and generally reply that there is no sham nor get-up to the land transactions hereaway ; and that neither collapse nor the ordinary fever and ague need be apprehended for this place ; it has grown steadily and slowly into public favor, and its present towering prospects have a foundation in the nature of things not only permanent and enduring, but natural and everlasting. Look at the position of Erie on the map ; read the reports of the United States Engineers as to the harbor ; above all, at this crisis, observe the enlightened legislation of the Commonwealth in anticipating the demand for commercial facilities at this favored spot.

" June 11.—Twelve water lots of thirty-two feet front sold, notwithstanding the severe pressure in the money market, at an aggregate price of over $40,000."

In consequence of the failure of the United States Bank, and delay in prosecuting projected improvements, prices gradually declined, and the depression was so great in a few years that property could scarcely be disposed of at the lowest rates. These fluctuations have been succeeded by times of more reliable and permanent valuation.

Fires.— January 22, 1839, Erie suffered from a destructive fire, in which the " Mansion House" and several frame buildings were consumed. Also the barn of Messrs. Hart and

Bird, stage proprietors, containing eleven horses and seven coaches. Loss estimated at $50,000.

April 1, 1851, the Eagle Hotel and several other buildings and stores were consumed by fire.

In 1857 a whole block was consumed on the west side of State Street and the public square. The buildings were principally wood, and much of the loss was covered by insurance. The printing offices of the *Dispatch* and *True American*, and about twelve shops and stores, were destroyed.

Sad Accidents.—The summer of 1841 was overshadowed by gloom in consequence of two very melancholy accidents. The first was the loss by drowning, under aggravated circumstances, of two children of Mr. Josiah King, of Pittsburg, with their nurse. Mr. K. and his family, which consisted of his wife, three children, and mother-in-law, were anticipating a visit to Mr. K.'s parents in Erie. On Saturday night they arrived at the public works in the steamboat *New England*, Captain Oliver, from Cleveland. The captain insisted that he could not enter the harbor in safety. Mr. K. requested then to be taken on to Buffalo; but being assured that the yawl was as safe as the steamboat, Mr. K., after consulting his family, acceded to the captain's wishes. Three other passengers and three deck hands, with Mr. K. and family, were then committed to the small boat, which through unaccountable negligence, had the plug removed. With the utmost exertions the boat succeeded in reaching the pier, but not without imminent peril to the whole, and the loss of two lovely children and their nurse. The dead bodies were not recovered until the third or fourth day.

The 9th of August, 1841, is noted for a most appalling calamity on Lake Erie, scarcely equaled in the number of sufferers by any similar event. This was the burning of the steamboat *Erie*, Captain Titus, being thirty-three miles from Buffalo, on her way up the lake. It was estimated that two hundred and forty-nine persons were, by this accident, launched into eternity in a few brief moments; twenty-six of these were from Erie County, among whom were Lloyd Gilson, clerk, Leander Jolls, steward, six members of the brass band, wheelsman, deck hands, etc.

The conduct of the wheelsman, Augustus Fuller, of Harbor Creek, is far famed for its heroism. He was at the wheel when the alarm of fire was given ; immediately headed the boat for the shore, and continued at his post until the wheelhouse, wheel, and his own person were completely enveloped in flames. In the vicinity of the wreck, in the course of a week, between one hundred and twenty and one hundred and thirty of the dead bodies arose to the surface, and mourning, burials, and funeral sermons sadly prevailed throughout the land.

The *Erie* had a cargo worth $20,000 ; the immigrants had with them $180,000 ; the boat was valued at $75,000 ; making a loss of little less than $300,000. The *Erie* was built by a number of citizens of Erie, and launched in October, 1837. At the time she was lost General C. M. Reed was the largest shareholder. Her tonnage was between six and seven hundred.

The coroner's jury certified that the destruction was accidental—that the fire was occasioned by the bursting of one or more demijohns of spirits of turpentine standing on the boiler deck—the boat having been newly painted, and the wind being high, the flames were driven through the entire boat with astonishing velocity.

Ex-President Adams.—In 1843 the town was honored by a call from Ex-President J. Q. Adams. The steamboat *Gen. Wayne*, on which he was a passenger, remained from seven to nine P. M. at the dock. The Wayne Greys and the three fire companies escorted him to the Reed House. Hon. T. H. Sill made him welcome in a short speech. The citizens in large numbers took him by the hand, and he was introduced severally to a number of the ladies, whom he addressed in a brief and appropriate manner. As Mr. Adams held no office, it was an expression of genuine, disinterested respect to a great and good man.

During the *Patriot War* (as the rebellion in Canada has been called) the arm-house in Erie was entered, and a quantity of muskets taken therefrom. They were discovered in Buffalo, and identified by Capt. Homans, U. S. N., then residing in Erie, by a peculiar kind of side-arm used by the company. The steamer *Gov. Marcy* was chartered by the United States government, and Lieut. Homans placed in command.

The *Old Courthouse Bell*, which could be heard at a greater distance than some of the larger bells that our city is favored with at present, belonged to the ship *Detroit* when taken, September 10, 1813. Commodore Sinclair had it afterward on the *Niagara* for a ship bell. In 1821 this brig was dismantled, and the bell, with other goods, placed in the navy storehouse at Erie. In 1825, when the station was broken up and the property disposed of by auction, the bell was bought by the county commissioners and placed upon the courthouse. After the new courthouse bell arrived in 1854, by a singular coincidence this old bell slipped from its hangings, and some mischievous persons purloined it. It was recovered after a few months, and bought for $105 by the city authorities.

Among the *Pioneers* of Erie County we find the name of James Tallmadge, who came in 1795, and died in McKean township in 1855, aged eighty-two years.

Mr. James Blair, of Girard, also came to the county in 1795, and died in 1855, at the age of eighty-one. He was an elder in the Presbyterian church, and a man of rare worth, respected and beloved.

Captain James Pollock died at Waterford, in May, 1857, having lived in Erie County sixty years. He was one of the members of the Convention to amend the Constitution of Pennsylvania in 1836.

Mr. Giles Badger died at Lexington, a few miles south of Girard, in 1857, aged eighty-nine years, having lived in Erie County sixty years. Upon the surrender of Hull he entered the army, and served under Gen. Harrison. "He enjoyed the confidence and respect of his fellows, both as a member of the Methodist Episcopal church and a citizen; and in peace and Christian hope passed away."

Mr. Stephen Oliver, a revolutionary soldier, died in McKean, in February, 1857, aged ninety-seven years. He was one of the survivors of the massacre of Wyoming, his name being inscribed upon the monument. He voted for Gen. Washington and Col. Fremont, and at every intervening Presidential election. He lived and died a Christian.

Mr. Thomas Dunn died in McKean, in 1854, aged eighty-two years. He came to Erie in 1797, and settled upon the farm where he died.

Mr. Burrell Tracy died in 1853, having removed to Erie County in 1797.

Perry's Squadron was but seventy days in building. The timber was mostly taken from the third section. Captain Daniel Dobbins claims to have cut the first stick of timber with his own hands.

At a dinner given to Commodore Perry, before leaving Erie on his momentous mission, he expressed his determination to return a conqueror or in his shroud.

Commodore Perry had a propensity for fine horses. The one he rode in Erie was a superior but not showy animal, which he had purchased at Cattaraugus. Mr. Judah Colt bought him when Commodore Perry left, and he always went by the name of the "Commodore." He died in 1829 and was buried with due respect, with his shoes on, near the garrison ground.

Peter H., a young gentleman of Meadville, came to Erie to volunteer with Commodore Perry, but when the decisive moment arrived and the squadron was to sail, altered his purpose and returned home. Wade, a law student of the same place, made this conduct the occasion for a practical joke, and in a week's time Peter H. received a communication through the postoffice, which he opened with due formality. Inclosed was a letter, a bank bill, and a tract or little book about three inches by four, such as the pious missionary, Mr. Osgood, distributed among the people. The letter purported to be from Com. Perry, stating that they had met the enemy and conquered—had killed Tecumseh and taken his private library, and the little book was his apportionment, and the note (a counterfeit of the broken Gloucester bank) his share of the prize money.

Extract from a letter dated—

"MARION, O., November 13, 1860.

. . "The last few years of his life (Lieutenant Yarnall's, of Commodore Perry's flagship *Lawrence*), were spent in Norton, a small town of Delaware County, where he earned a a small pittance by prescribing a few botanical medicines to the people of that vicinity, and telling fortunes or predicting the future of those who would reward him for the same, and pretending to be gifted with second sight, by which he could tell the persons calling upon him where to find property that had strayed away or been stolen from them. By these means he procured a livelihood for a number of years, and won for himself the name of old Pluto.

"He died about twenty years ago, and was buried with the honors of war. Many of the old veterans of the war gathered around the grave of the poor old man, when he was lowered to his last home, where 'he sleeps his last sleep,' and where 'no sound can awake him to glory again.' They shed tears over his grave as they remembered the time when they fought with him on the battle fields of their country.

"No monument, not even a slab, marks the last resting place of the old veteran. But his name is remembered by a people that know how to appreciate the liberty for which he fought. J. N. S."

The survivors of the battle of Lake Erie as far as known (1861):

Stephen Champlin, sailing-master and commander of the *Scorpion;* now a post-captain, and residing in Buffalo.

J. B. Montgomery, midshipman in the *Niagara;* now a post-captain, and in command of the Pacific squadron.

Hugh N. Page, midshipman in the *Tigress;* now a post-captain, and resides in Virginia.

Thomas Brownell, sailing-master on board the *Ariel*, resides in Newport, and is lieutenant.

Usher Parsons, acting surgeon of the flagship, and of the squadron, resides in Providence, and is the last surviving commissioned officer of the squadron.

Hosea Sargeant, a volunteer from Gen. Harrison's army, was a gunner on the *Lawrence;* lives in Boston.

W. T. Taliaferro, a volunteer from Harrison's army, now resides, as a physician, in Cincinnati.

Benjamin Talmon, gunner on the *Caledonia.*

John Tucker, powder boy of the *Caledonia.*

Benjamin Fleming, a sailor on the *Niagara*, lives in Erie.

Jonas Stone, carpenter on the *Lawrence*, resides near Milwaukee.

Alexander McClaskey, a volunteer from Erie, resides in Illinois.

Daniel Metzenburg resides in Erie; volunteered on board the *Niagara;* is now about seventy years of age, and has his medal.

J. Murray, a marine, resides in Girard.

The following, who were mostly volunteers from Harrison's army, are believed to be still living, to wit:

Thomas H. Bradford, Nathan Holburt, John Norris, William Blair, James Artus, Rowland S. Parker, and James Lanman.

Extract from the account of "The Inauguration of the Perry Statue, at Cleveland":

"The cost of the Perry Monument was $8,000, as agreed in the contract made with T. Jones & Sons. Nearly $5,000 of this sum was obtained by voluntary subscriptions, and the City Council, on the receipt of a communication from the Chairman of the Perry Monument Committee, stating the balance due to the contractors, September 25, 1860, passed the resolution offered by Mr. Ballard:

"*Resolved*, That the sum of three thousand and eight dollars be appropriated from the city treasury to T. Jones & Sons, in full of the balance due them on their contract for the erection of the Perry Monument, the same to be paid one third in six months and one third in twelve months. Adopted. Ayes, 18; nays, 1."

"October 30, 1860, the following action was had in the City Council, on the receipt of a communication from Harvey Rice, Chairman of the Perry Monument Committee, stating that he has received from O. H. Perry, only surviving son of Commodore Perry, a portrait in oil of the Commodore, copied by Mr. Lawson, of Lowell, from the original painting by Stuart. In compliance with the request of Mr. Perry, he presented the portrait to the City of Cleveland. In the note by Mr. Perry accompanying the portrait, he expresses his belief that 'so patriotic a people as the citizens of Cleveland will value the portrait of one they have been pleased to honor.'

"Received and filed.

"Resolutions of Mr. Clark:

"That the portrait of Commodore Perry, presented this evening to the City of Cleveland, in the name, and at the request of O. H. Perry, Esq., his only surviving son, be accepted ; and that the City Clerk be directed to cause the same to be handsomely framed and suspended in Council Hall.

"That the thanks of the City Council be, and the same are hereby tendered to O. H. Perry, Esq., for so valuable and acceptable a gift, and that the Mayor of the City be requested to communicate to him a certified copy of the foregoing resolutions.

"Adopted."

Inventions.—October 4, 1853, Ozias J. Davie and Thomas W. Stephens, of the City of Erie, obtained a patent for a punching and shearing machine. Improvements were afterward made by them, and the machine exhibited at the Crystal Palace, where its operations attracted much attention. Munn & Co., editors of the *Scientific American*, make mention of it as one of the best inventions of the kind with which they are acquainted. Liddell, Kepler & Co., of Erie, are proprietors. A car spring was afterward patented by Walter F. J. Liddell, which is considered a very great improvement.

Captain Douglass Ottinger invented a lifeboat which was exhibited at the Crystal Palace in 1853, and which is now in general use. From humane motives he refused to have it patented, but received, in 1858, a remuneration from Congress of $10,000.

J. W. Wetmore, Esq., invented a band railroad chair ; first patent, April 19, 1859 ; second patent, December 27, 1859. Sub-wedge railroad chair, which was first patented August 23, 1859, and a second time, May 15, 1860.

A legislative voting register, the object of which is to prevent the delay in taking the ayes and nays, was patented by him April 3, 1860. The gravimotometer was patented February 16, 1858, the object of the apparatus being to test or measure the effect of motion on attraction or gravitation. It is constructed by having horseshoe magnets attached vertically flatwise unto a wooden globe.

Also letters patent were granted June 16, 1861, for improved means of propelling vessels in shoal water. The model was submitted by Mr. Wetmore to a committee in 1858, which concluded their article as follows:

"On the whole, this method of propulsion seems to us to be practicable. In our opinion it is a valuable invention for the use proposed. The advantages consist principally of a great saving of power in the propulsion of boats and the extension of the use of steamboats to rivers where navigation by paddle wheel boats is now hardly practicable. The large appropriations expended or proposed for the improvement of the navigation of the various rivers of the country, and the difficulty and expense of such improvements, show the utility and necessity of successful efforts to overcome the impediment in these channels of commerce. This plan seems to us to meet the necessity, and to be the best improvement yet devised for shoal water navigation.

"DOUGLASS OTTINGER,   CHARLES M. REED,
"M. COURTRIGHT,   JOSHUA FOLLENSBEE,
"JOHN A. TRACY,   WILLIAM A. GALBRAITH,
"P. METCALF,   A. H. CAUGHEY,
"A. SCOTT."

In the Buffalo *Daily Republic* of March 20, 1861, we find an article on the "Suspended Purchase," an invention of Mr. William H. Brown, of Erie. The editor remarks: "To us it seemed to be rather more than a purchase, it was really a combination of purchases. Every part sustains such a delicate and positive relation to every other part, that it seems as if human ingenuity could go no further in the development of the idea which has lived in the brain of the inventor for over eight years. To perfect machinery by which massive bodies, or large quantities, should be lifted and transported to any given distance, or deposited at points difficult to reach, has been the great object of the inventor. That he has accomplished his undertaking, no one who has seen the performance of his model will undertake to question. . . . For quarrying purposes, bridge building, and unloading of vessels, the 'Suspended Purchase' is invaluable; in fact, it would require too much space to specify the purposes for which it may be successfully and economically used. In the work of construction, especially, it will be found by engineers to meet a necessity which nothing but rude muscle and great mental labor have heretofore met. In the unloading of vessels Mr. Brown guarantees to discharge 150 tons of iron ore or coal per hour, with the number of hands necessary to keep up with the operations of his machinery."

Also, in the New York *Times*, July 29, 1861, under the head "Improvised Army Bridges," after a statement by the editor of the difficulties of making passable, at short notice, the ordinary bridges of which the rebels have destroyed the superstructure, of rapidly transporting guns, stores, and horses over chasms which cannot speedily be bridged, the time required to construct rafts, etc., he adds: "A recent apparatus (Brown's Suspended Purchase), which has been employed to some extent in carrying and depositing the material of bridges, and in raising ore and coal from vessels and dumping it some hundreds of feet off—an apparatus indorsed by competent engineering authorities, seems to possess the features required in military purposes. . . . There is evidently the principle in this simple device for greatly aiding military operations by speedily repairing damaged bridges, improvising bridges, etc., and it is obvious that something of this sort will be specially useful in this campaign."

"The Society of the United Brethren for Propagating the Gospel among the Heathen," was incorporated by the act of Assembly, February 27, 1788. It is formed of members of the Episcopal church of the United Brethren or Unitas Fratrum —more generally known as the Moravian church.

April 17, 1791, an act was passed to grant this society 5,000 acres of land and allowance; 2,500 acres to be located "on the River Conneought near the northwestern corner of the State," and 2,500 acres "on the heads of French Creek."

The inducement thereto is stated in the act to be the fact that the United Brethren had sent and supported missionaries and teachers among the Indians since 1740, and in furtherance of which the aforesaid society was incorporated in 1788. The society asked for public aid because the missions had become both numerous and expensive, and hitherto had been maintained solely by the charitable contributions of the members of the Moravian church. The request was granted on the ground that the Commonwealth was " disposed to encourage all pious and charitable institutions, and the propagation of the Gospel, and the erecting and supporting schools among the Indian nations of America being of the first importance to this and other of the United States, and by the blessing of God conducive to the peace and security of the inhabitants and settlers of our frontiers by turning the minds of the savages to the Christian religion, industry, and social life with the citizens of the United States."

The patents are dated April 14, 1795.

The French Creek tract, called "Good Luck," contained 2,875 acres and allowance. Thirty-four pounds, eleven shillings and nine pence were paid for the excess above 2,500 acres.

The Conneaut tract, called "Hospitality," contained 2,797 92-100 acres and allowance, the payment being nineteen pounds, twenty-three shillings and ten pence for the excess.

Both tracts were subdivided and leased on "Improvement Leases," by the late William Miles, Esq., who for many years was the society's efficient agent in the improvement of these lands. Mr. Miles's health failing, his son, Judge James Miles, succeeded him in the agency of the "Hospitality" tract, and John Wood, Esq., in the "Good Luck" tract.

The lands were finally sold by the society in 1849, to N. Blickensdefer, Esq.

To the efficient care and superintendence of these gentlemen, particularly the Messrs. Miles, who were pioneers in the improvements, the society and the county are indebted for reclaiming from a wilderness a large portion of the best lands in Erie County—some 700 acres of "Good Luck" and 1,200 of "Hospitality" having been brought into a good state of cultivation up to the year 1850.

The terms of the leases were, in general, the use of the land by the tenant for a series of years, usually seven, in consideration of clearing and fencing a small portion annually. Subsequently leases included agreements to build houses and barns.

The society were induced to sell principally from the consideration that the annual interest of the proceeds of sale would be a more effectual and available aid to their work than any system of farming by tenants. After its purchase by Mr. Blickensdefer it was again subdivided and resold to actual settlers, a few of the best tenants becoming purchasers. Both tracts are now well improved in suitable-sized farms, and will compare favorably with any lands in Erie County.

In Chapter IX. mention of an act to open a road from near the Bald Eagle's Nest, in Mifflin County, to Le Bœuf, in the County of Allegheny, was omitted. This act passed April 10, 1799, and appropriated $5,000 for the purpose.

The following on the subject of railroads, from Poor's History, should be added: "In addition to the subscriptions made to the Philadelphia & Erie Road was $500,000 to the share capital by the Cleveland & Erie Railroad, at the time the Legislature of Pennsylvania confirmed the rights of this and the Erie & Northeast to the chartered privileges claimed by them.

"The Erie & Pittsburg Railroad was chartered as the successor of the Pittsburg & Erie Railroad, on April 15, 1858. In addition to the $400,000 subscribed to this by the Erie & Northeast Road as one of the conditions by which it enjoys quiet right of way through the State, it has a floating debt of $250,000 (advances by the Buffalo & State Line Company), and $30,000 from individual stockholders.

"In 1857 an act was obtained from the Legislature of New York, authorizing the Buffalo & State Line Road to lease or purchase, by exchange of stock or lands, the Erie & Northeast Railroad. Under this act nearly all the share capital of the Erie & Northeast has been exchanged for that of the Buffalo & State Line Road. Bonds have also been exchanged to the amount of $149,000. The funded debt of the Erie & Northeast Road is $400,000, in details as follows: First mortgage, seven per cent, coupon bonds $400,000, dated June 1, 1857, and payable, principal June 1, 1870, and interest semi-annually, June 1 and December 1, at New York. Of these bonds $149,000 have been exchanged for bonds of the Buffalo & State Line Railroad as a part of its own line; its earnings and expenses are embraced in those for that road. The same dividends have been paid by the two companies."

At Junction (afterwards Corry), in Concord township, where

the Atlantic & Great Western Railroad intersects the Philadelphia & Erie, quite a cluster of buildings has arisen in the woods within the last three months. The Atlantic & Great Western connects with the New York & Erie at Little Valley, in Cattaraugus County, having the same gauge. A large quantity of petroleum passed over this road on September 9, 1861; twenty-three car-loads were shipped at Junction for New York City on that day.

March 1, 1781, the State of New York made a deed of cession to the United States of lands lying between the northern boundary of Pennsylvania and Lake Erie, or rather judged it expedient to limit and restrict the boundaries of this State. April 19, 1785, the Commonwealth of Massachusetts made a similar deed of cession.

At the Assembly of Internal Commerce, in Philadelphia, September 15, 1783, a resolution was carried to "examine the navigation of the Susquehanna to the source of the same, and ascertain, as near as conveniently may be, where the northern boundary of this State will fall, particularly whether any part of Lake Erie is within the State of Pennsylvania, taking particular notes of the nature and geography of the country as to the practicability of roads, water carriage, air, soil, natural productions, etc."

September 20th William Maclay, James Wilkinson, and William Montgomery, Esqs., were duly elected to perform the duties prescribed in the resolution. These commissioners arrived at Erie, October 8, 1787, and determined by scientific observations that there was no lake harbor inside the State, and also that the land was of a fair quality. On motion of Gen. Irvine, in Congress, February 25, 1788, the Geographer of the United States was directed to proceed to run a line and ascertain the western limits of the States of New York and Massachusetts, comformable to their acts of cession.

June 16, 1788, Tho. Hutchins, Geographer of the United States of America, addressed Lord Dorchester, Governor-General of Canada, for permission to survey the most westerly bent or inclination of Lake Ontario, and to extend a meridian line from thence south to Lake Erie, etc.

September 4, 1788, by act of Congress the United States

relinquished and transferred to the State of Pennsylvania "the land contained in the interval betwixt a meridian line run between Lake Erie and the State of Pennsylvania, and the boundaries of the States of New York and Massachusetts, at the rate of three quarters of a dollar per acre," bearing interest, when the quantity should be ascertained by actual survey. An estimate of other expenditures that might be incurred in the purchase from the Six Nations, amounting to £950, is in details as follows : Various suitables articles, £375 ; provisions, £100 ; wagonage, boat hire, etc., £150 ; pay of commissioners, hire of interpreters, runners, etc., £250 ; presents to great men, £75.

September 8, 1788, P. Muhlenberg, Vice-President of the Board of Treasury, transmitted to Hon. Thos. Mifflin, Speaker of the General Assembly, an act of Congress passed the 4th of the same month, by which the United States relinquished and transferred to the State of Pennsylvania all their right and title to the tract of land on Lake Erie. September 13, 1788, the State of Pennsylvania in General Assembly heard the report of the committee and resolved to accept, on the part of the Commonwealth, the contract made with the Board of Treasury of the United States, and recommended to the succeeding House of Assembly fully to pay and discharge the consideration moneys due, at three fourths of a dollar per acre, as soon as it should be surveyed. Some estimated the number of acres (which proved to be 202,187) at 800,000, and others at 1,000,000. Provision was made immediately for the payment of £950 for contingent expenses.

October 1, 1788, Gen. Richard Butler and Gen. John Gibson were appointed by the Council of Philadelphia commissioners to negotiate and complete the purchase of the Lake Erie tract, and William Maclay and John Smilie to prepare and report to the board a draft of instructions to said commissioners. These instructions were in effect to make the purchase when they should find the Indians in a proper temper—at that time they were attending a convention at Muskingum.

The 9th of January, 1789, in open and public council, twenty-four chiefs and warriors representing the Senacas, Cayugas, Tuscaroras, Onondagas, and Oneidas, of the tribes of

HISTORY OF ERIE COUNTY. 301

the Six Nations, for themselves, tribes, heirs, and sucessors, and Richard Butler and John Gibson, Esqs., commissioners for and in behalf of the State of Pennsylvania (Onas) on the other part, made and concluded seven articles by which the Indians renounced their claims, and the title of the Presqu'ile lands vested in the State of Pennsylvania.

March 24, 1789, it was resolved by the General Assembly of Pennsylvania, that not exceeding 3,000 acres be surveyed for the use of the Commonwealth at each of the following points: Presqu'ile, Le Bœuf, at the mouth of Conewango, and at the fort of Venango. And also in the country of Lake Erie, 1,500 acres for Capt. O'Biel or Cornplanter, whose Indian name was Gyantwachia.

Bankers and Exchange Brokers in the City and County of Erie, with amount of capital invested by each firm and individual respectively, as reported to the Auditor-General of Pennsylvania, agreeably to act of Assembly passed A. D. 1861:

	Capital.
M. Sanford & Co., bankers, Erie City	$ 50,000
W. C. Curry, broker and private banker, Erie City	100,000
Vincent, Bailey & Co., Erie City	25,000
Neiler & Warren, " "	5,000
Clark & Metcalf, " "	12,000
Benson & West, Waterford	500

SUPPLEMENT.

SECTION I.

The Shipyard of the Griffon—Northern State Boundary—Ownership of the Peninsula—The Pontiac Conspiracy—Le Bœuf—Letters of a Surveyor, etc.—Scenery.

LA SALLE, born at Rouen in 1643, was of a good family, and at an early age evinced a taste for mathematics; was for a period a teacher, and expected to become a priest. Self-will and ambition predominated, and he followed his longings for adventure, discovery, and conquest. The influence of his elder brother, a priest in New France, settled his purpose for explorations, reciting his own adventures in the new discovered countries, and studying the habits and dialects of the Indians.

Mr. Orsamus H. Marshall, a lifelong resident of Buffalo, and a painstaking historian, in a lecture February 3, 1863, says: "Two leagues above the falls (on the American side) we find the Cayuga Creek, a stream which answers perfectly Hennepin's description. Opposite its mouth an island of the same name lies parallel with the shore, about a mile long and two or three hundred yards wide. It is separated from the mainland by a narrow branch of the river called by the early inhabitants 'Little Niagara'—wide and deep enough to float a vessel of the tonnage of the *Griffon*. Into this channel and opposite the middle of the island, the Cayuga Creek empties. On the main shore, just above the mouth of the creek and under shelter of the island, is a favorable site for a shipyard. So eligible is the position that it was selected by the United States government, in the early part of the present century, as a suitable point for building one or more vessels for the transportation of troops and supplies to the western ports. For that reason it was known in early times as the 'Old Shipyard'; and local traditions have been preserved in the memory of the early pioneers of the anterior occupancy, for the same purpose by the French. . . . The same site was selected by the United States government about the year 1804 for the construction of a small sloop of fifty tons burden, called the *Niagara*, which was used for conveying supplies to the western ports. The owner of this estate is Mr. Jackson Angevine, who has generously stated to me that it will be a pleasure for him to donate land sufficient for the erection of a testimonial commemorating the event."

The *Erie Morning Dispatch* of August 18, 1893, said: "A conference will be held in New York City early next week, when the agreement entered into yesterday at the Department of Internal Affairs between Col. Thomas J. Stewart, chief of that department, and Martin Schenck, of New York, who are charged with the duty of examining the boundary line monuments between Pennsylvania and New York and resetting and relocating them where it is found necessary, and to commence work at once. Allen W. Carson, of Norristown, the engineer who represented Pennsylvania in relocating and resetting the monuments three years ago, has again been chosen by Col. Stewart to act on the part of the Secretary of Internal Affairs. It would not appear too soon to examine, with a view to repairs, the work of one hundred and six years ago. The report from the 'mile trees marked' will also be of much interest. The commissioners will travel on foot along the entire line between the two States from the Delaware River to Lake Erie, and are required to examine every monument." [See page 59, chapter v.]

OWNERSHIP OF THE PENINSULA.
From The Erie Evening Herald, July 6, 1893.

Major John W. Walker a few days since received the following interesting public document from Henry W. Babbitt, Esq., son of the late Elijah Babbitt, who represented the Erie district in Congress a number of years ago. Mr. Henry Babbitt has been connected with the general land office for the last thirty years, and the letter here given is an authentic history of the purchase and sale of the land known as the peninsula:

"DEPARTMENT OF THE INTERIOR,
"GENERAL LAND OFFICE,
"WASHINGTON, D. C., Dec., 16, 1889.

"*Hon. W. C. Culbertson, House of Representatives, Washington, D. C.:*

"SIR—In reply to your verbal inquiry of December 7, 1889, as to whether the title to the peninsula or island in Lake Erie, near the City of Erie, Pennsylvania, known as 'Presque Isle,' is vested in the State of Pennsylvania or the United States, I have the honor to advise you that I find as follows:

In 1781 the State of New York ceded to the United States its claim for that portion of the State of Pennsylvania known as the 'Erie Purchase' ('Public Domain,' page 65). April 19, 1785, the State of Massachusetts ceded to the United States . . . . Also, 'a small portion on Lake Erie, just west of New York, being a triangular piece of land, also claimed by the State of New York, containing 315.91 square miles, which was sold by the United States to the State of Pennsylvania, March 3, 1792, for $151,640.25, or 75 cents per acre. The lands are now in the County of Erie, State of Pennsylvania, and patent was issued therefor by the President. It is known as the 'Erie Purchase,' and contained 202,187 acres.' (Public Domain, page 71).

"By act of Legislature of February 4, 1869, the State of Pennsylvania conveyed the said 'Presque Isle' to Marine Hospital at Erie, Pa. (*Congressional Record*, 49th Cong., first Sess., page 3,790). By act of the Legislature of Pennsylvania of May 11, 1871, title to said Peninsula or Presque Isle was tendered to the United States Marine Hospital at Erie, Pa. (*Ibid.*).

"By act of Congress approved August 5, 1886, (U. S. Statutes, v. 24, page 312), the Secretary of War is authorized and directed to receive and accept title from said Marine Hospital as tendered by said legislative enactment of May 11, 1871; $37,500 being the sum appropriated to pay for the same.

"From the letter of December 7, 1889, on this subject from

Thomas Lincoln Casey, brigadier general, chief of engineers U. S. A., to Hon. B. F. Gilkerson, second comptroler U. S. Treasury Department, I am advised that the deed of said Marine Hospital, coveying title to said Peninsula, or Presque Isle, to the United States, is dated May 25, 1871 ; that the acting judge advocate of the U. S. Army, on the 18th of November, 1886, rendered an opinion that the acceptance of said deed, under the provision of said act of Congress of August 5, 1886, might be signified by entering upon and taking possession of the land in behalf of the United States ; that the honorable Secretary of War approved this opinion and directed, December 14, 1886, that the necessary action be taken. Accordingly, in pursuance of this order, the land was entered upon, and taken possession of, in behalf of the United States, by the War Department.

" Very respectfully your obedient servant,

"GEORGE REDWAY, Chief Clerk.
" Per H. W. Babbitt.

" [The act of August 5, 1886, was introduced and pressed to passage by the late Hon. W. L. Scott.]"

Dr. Thomas H. Robinson, D.D., in his "Family Memorial," published in Pittsburg in 1867, says : " Our ancestry settled at their first arrival, it would appear, a few miles east of the Susquehanna, in Hanover township. Their farms were on the banks of the Swatara and its tributary creek, the Mavada. Here dwelt and intermarried at an early day the Robinsons, McCords, Blacks, Martins, Logans, Crawfords, with many others, nearly if not quite all of them of Scotch-Irish origin. The fort at Mavada gap, sixteen miles northeast of Harrisburg, sometimes is called Philip Robinson's, sometimes Samuel Robinson's—Samuel, as the eldest son of the household, taking charge of the paternal estate. There were many other forts in that neighborhood and throughout the country. We learn elsewhere that this was in April, 1756, and that twenty-seven persons were killed or captured by the Indians. Among the captured was Ann McCord, wife of John McCord, who was retaken from the Indians about five months later at the celebrated battle of Kittanning, in September.

"The French and English war over, our fathers hoped now

for a long and undisturbed peace. The French were driven from the continent. It was thought that the Indian tribes were conciliated. The valley of the Susquehanna and of the Juniata began again to wear the aspect of civilized life. Cabins were rebuilt, settlers pushed their way deeper into the forests and opened new farms. The militia of the middle and southern colonies were disbanded. The frontiers seemed to need protection no longer. The security of our fathers was doomed to be speedily and terribly broken up.

"The Indians beheld their old allies, the French, driven out of the whole country, yet scarcely had they received the rich presents that accompanied the treaty of peace before murmurs of discontent began to be audible among the tribes. A vast conspiracy was formed, greater in extent, deeper and more comprehensive in its design than any that before or since has been conceived by a North American Indian. The bloody belt of war was sent secretly from tribe to tribe, until everywhere, from the falls of Niagara and the pine-crowned crest of the Alleghenies to the forests of the Mississippi and the borders of Lakes Michigan and Superior, all the Indian nations had agreed to rise and attack the various English forts, which extended then nearly to the Mississippi, on the same day, and having massacred their garrisons, turn upon the defenseless frontier and with all their warriors ravage and lay waste the settlements, until, as the Indians fondly believed, the English would be driven into the sea, and the whole country restored to its original owners. Pontiac, the colossal chief of the Northwest, was the mighty spirit of this formidable conspiracy. The preparations for war were kept profoundly secret. Hatred of the English was excited to the highest pitch by stories of their rapacity and cruelty. Suddenly the terrible storm burst. An English party sounding the entrance to Lake Huron was seized and murdered. Seven Indians admitted into the port at Sandusky as friends, in an unsuspecting moment, murdered the entire garrison, save its commander, whom they carried away a prisoner. The fort at the mouth of the St. Joseph was entered by Indians under the guise of friendship, and in about two minutes all the garrison except three men were massacred. At Mackinaw, with similar deception, the fort was seized and all were murdered or borne away prisoners. The forts and garrisons at Lafayette, Indiana, and at Presqu'ile met the same horrible fate. Fort Le Bœuf, on the headwaters of the Allegheny, was attacked, but in the night the commander and garrison escaped secretly into the woods, while the Indians believed them all buried in the flames of the burning fort. As the fugitives passed Venango on their way to Fort Pitt, they saw nothing but ruins. The fort at that place was consumed, and not one of its garrison was left alive to tell the story of its destruction. Eight haggard and half-famished soldiers dying from fright and exhaustion, the remnant of the men who escaped from Fort Le Bœuf, staggered to the walls of Fort Pitt, bringing news of the coming tide of savages. They roamed the wilderness massacring all whom they met. More than one hundred traders were met in the woods, struck down, scalped, their bodies horribly mutilated, and their life-blood quaffed in savage glee. They laid siege to Fort Pitt, . . . but were beaten off after a hard day's fighting. . . . Rumors of these disasters and of the coming foe reached the country east of the mountains. . . . On Sunday, July 3, 1763, a soldier riding express from Fort Pitt galloped into Carlisle and alighted to water his horse at a well in the centre of the place. A crowd of country men were instantly about him to hear the news. 'Presqu'ile, Le Bœuf, and Venango are taken, and the Indians will be here soon,' he cried. Remounting his horse in haste, he rode on to make his report at the camp of Col. Boquet, who was raising a force for defense. All was consternation and excitement. . . . Every pathway and road leading into Carlisle was filled with the flying settlers flocking thither for refuge. . . . The Indian war parties at length broke out of the woods like gangs of hungry wolves, murdering, burning, and laying waste on every hand, while hundreds of terror-stricken families abandoning their homes fled for refuge toward the older settlements. Outrages were perpetrated and sufferings endured which defy all attempts at description. Cumberland County, which at that time formed the western frontier of Pennsylvania, was almost exclusively occupied by the descendants of the thrifty colony of Scotch, who for many

years had occupied the north of Ireland, and were Presbyterians. These acquitted themselves admirably in their own defense. The march of Col. Boquet in 1764 and the victory of Bushy Run, some twenty-five miles from Fort Pitt, dispirited the Indian warriors and caused a temporary lull. Afterwards, when they saw they were in the power of Boquet, they reluctantly sued for peace. Twelve days were given them to deliver up all prisoners in their hands—Englishmen, Frenchmen, women and children, and to furnish them with clothing, provisions, and horses to carry them to Fort Pitt. They hastened to fulfill the conditions, and upwards of two hundred were collected at the camp of Boquet. Many affecting incidents are on record of those who had become enamored of the wild forest life, and some even had to be borne back by force. When the army reached Carlisle, people met them there in great numbers to inquire for the friends they had lost. . . .
As the Indian tribes retreated, this hardy, freedom-loving race moved forward and took possession of the country. In the latter part of the eighteenth century we find them going south into Virginia, west to Kentucky, and a few families to the shores of Lake Erie. Dr. Thomas H. Robinson refers to several of our prominent divines, as Rev. Dr. Matthew Brown, at one time President of Jefferson College, Rev. D. H. Riddle, D.D., Rev. Francis Herron, D.D., the Hon. J. G. Blaine, and Col. Ephraim Blaine, of the Revolution, being of the same family or having intermarried, as in Northeast the families of Moorhead and Mills."

We have given this lengthy account to show what sufferings the ancestors of some of the best Erie County people endured, how a kind Providence preserved a remnant, and to contrast those trying times with the peaceful present.

LE BŒUF.

A very interesting visit was paid to Col. P. E. Judson, still landlord of the Eagle Hotel, Waterford, in the summer of 1892. A vestige of Fort Le Bœuf still remains, being the cellar with remnants of its stone wall as originally laid (Maj. Martin Strong selected a specimen with a shell impress for a cabinet). A chapter of the "Daughters of the Revolution" should have charge of it, though the quiet inhabitants have been very kind—the charm is to see it in its unremodeled condition and full of tall weeds. When it was in good condition in 1796 there were four block houses with no light from outside, but an underground passageway crossed the road diagonally to a spring. A picture of the fortifications hangs in the hall of the hotel. Col. Judson has lived in Waterford since he was fourteen years of age and for many years has occupied the fort as a public house. A cannonball that had served at his front door for seventy years was at last stolen a few months ago, and now a sword, very rusty but beautifully chased, is kept under lock and key; a tailor's goose also was found upon the premises and was gilded and deposited with other relics of the olden time in Washington. There is not a more beautiful drive than from Waterford south to Cambridgeboro.

An Erie merchant writes:

"ERIE, Sept. 10, 1813.

"DEAR BROTHER:

"I have been waiting all summer to get some news worth relating, but have been disappointed in this. It has been busy times here this summer. The Navy Department have built two brigs of 400 tons, carrying 18-32 carronades each, and four large gunboats carrying one and two long heavy cannon. There has been stationed here one regiment of Pennsylvania militia, about 800 men, and the militia have been called out frequently from the country in cases of alarm. The British squadron has been hovering round the mouth of the harbor frequently through the summer, sometimes near enough to exchange shots with the gunboats and batteries, but no damage has been done. Our squadron, consisting of ten sail, left this on the 12th ult., and are now off Sandusky, probably, waiting for Gen. Harrison to make a descent on Malden, which I think will be in a few days. I think it doubtful which will carry the day, as the English are rather superior on the lake and strongly fortified at Malden, where the fleet now lies."

"ERIE, March 4, 1814.

"SIRS:—Since my last, nothing of importance has transpired

in this vicinity until by the arrival of a gentleman on Monday evening last from the westward, who brings us the news that a considerable British force was on the march for Detroit. My informant saw a man who left Detroit on the 16th ult., who states that on the night of the 15th, a corps of British soldiers had crossed the St. Clair River about fifty miles from Detroit, and were marching down. That about four hundred Indians were coming down on the Canada side and that the inhabitants were in great confusion, endeavoring to save their lives and property. The commanding officer, Col. Croghan, would not permit any of the inhabitants to take shelter in the fort, it being too small to protect the inhabitants and make defense. An order had been issued to burn Malden and Sandwich, the first at ten and the other at eight o'clock on the 15th. From other sources we are informed that a heavy cannonading was heard at the river Raisin and at Vermillion on the 18th in the direction of Detroit. We were informed a few days since by express from Sackett's Harbor that a British regular force of 1,500 men and 500 seamen had passed that place from the westward. These circumstances and others, particularly that the most loyal inhabitants near Detroit have moved into the interior, leave but little room to doubt that an attack has been made. Through an interposition of Providence we have been permitted to remain unmolested thus far (except by the patriotic militia from the neighboring counties), the ice on the lake not having been strong enough for an army to come here, and the winter is so far spent that we apprehend no danger until the spring opens."

"In answer to your note," writes a pioneer March 30, 1861, "I would say that I know of no person nor can I learn of any person who attempted to reside in this county previous to the year 1795. Mr. Wm. Miles, I believe, was the first—at least he was the *first* settler *so far as I can learn.* Mr. Miles settled on the flats of French Creek at a point where two or more roads cross, a little northwest of the place where the Stranahans now live in Concord township, in the month of June, 1795. Accompanying him were his wife and children and Mr. Wm. Cook's family. The irregular manner in which Mr. Miles' children were carried is worthy of especial notice. A sack was made, open in the side instead of the end ; the sack was thrown across the horse, a child placed in each end of it, and in this manner they were conveyed to Concord from Franklin, Venango County. Mrs. Miles carried her youngest child before her on the horse. Mr. Miles resided in Concord township about five years, removing in 1800 to a place which he called Union Mills, from the fact of a saw and gristmill being built there. The nearest station was eight miles distant. All provisions in 1795 were carried by means of pack horses from Pittsburg to Concord township. After the year 1795 provisions were brought up the Allegheny River, thence by its tributaries to Union Mills. In the year 1796 families named Hull, McCrea, Wilson, and Findley settled in the neighborhood of Union Mills. A Mr. Stephen Oliver settled near there in the latter part of 1795 ; but before I forget I would remark that Mrs. Miles and her sister Mrs. Cook were the two first white women in the County of Erie. Families by name of Hamilton and Reeder settled in and about Edinboro between the years 1795 and 1800. They were the first settlers at that particular point. Lexington was first laid out by McNair and others, the time I do not remember. In 1796 Mr. Wm. Miles commenced clearing land, and built himself in addition to his dwelling house, a store for the storing of provisions on the tract of land where Wattsburg now stands. In the same year families by the name of Tracy and Reed (Adam Reed) built a small gristmill on the east branch of French Creek, and surveyed the tract of land known as ' Tenth Donation Tract.' Mr. Wm. Miles and Mr. David Watts were appointed by the Governor of Pennsylvania (Mifflin, I think) in the year 1785 to the survey. Their provisions being procured in Harrisburg were packed on horses and conveyed to a point near Wattsburg. An incident happened which might be worthy of note. The duties of the surveyors being severe they employed an Indian in the capacity of general cook and to furnish meat, etc. Mr. Indian, as is natural to the race, in time became remarkably lazy in his endeavors to procure meat, giving as his excuse *the scarcity of it in the wilderness*, but the trick was carried too far, and Messrs. Miles and Watts becoming cognizant that he was deceiving them cut short his allowance of food, which brought the 'native of the forest' to a strict sense of his duty, which he never afterwards neglected."

An original surveyor writes:

"FRANKLIN, February 6, 1862.

". . To your first query, 'How long were you making survey?' etc., I answer, we were engaged all summer; in the fall I went home to my father's. To the second, I answer, Rutledge and his son were out looking for land to settle, and in going from Le Bœuf to Erie were by the Indians shot and murdered within one mile or thereabouts from Presqu'ile and on the path leading from Le Bœuf to Presqu'ile. The elder Rutledge was killed on the spot; the young man was taken to Le Bœuf and taken care of by the surgeon of the fort, Dr. Thomas R. Kennedy, and lived but a few days. You ask, Why did they venture so far from the fort? It was common for travelers to travel the path in small companies, but very often dangerous on account of hostile Indians from the upper lakes, prowling through the woods to plunder and murder. I often saw signs of them when running lines in various parts of the district. I will give you an anecdote. One night about eight or ten miles from our main camp at P., *we*, our compass and hands, had encamped as usual for the night; after taking our supper we lay down by a good fire. In about half an hour we were alarmed by our dog running from the fire and barking very fiercely. We were very apprehensive that Indians were about, and concluded to move from the fire and lie down where we pleased. Each one of us took his own course; I went about one hundred yards from the fire, and with my blanket around me laid me down by the side of a large log. In about half of an hour the dog who had been near the fire, ran with great speed from the fire after something, and directly we found it to be deer, as they scented so as to satisfy me it was so. I arose and called the boys to come to the fire; all came and we fell fast asleep and rested quietly until morning. But I often conversed with Seneca Indians who told me that there were hostile Indians in the district. . . . . I will mention one thing further: Shortly after we got to Erie, perhaps in June or July, the State Commissioners came out to lay out the town, and about the same time the United States troops arrived to build the fort. However, I think it must have been about the first of June that Rutledge was killed. I am sorry I cannot furnish you with more items. Your object is a laudable one, and if you could give the circumstances of the country, it would be interesting. The young people now enjoying the blessings of civilization and refinement know but little of the privations the early pioneers suffered.

"WILLIAM CONNELY."

We cannot do better than copy from the *Erie Dispatch*, 1891, a description of the annual outing of the Natural History Society for some of our boldest scenery: "On leaving the morning Lake Shore train at Fairview station, Mr. G. I. Howard's fourhorse vehicle was in waiting to take the party to his residence and stone quarry at Fall's Run, about six miles south of Fairview. The route lay through a pleasant farming country and over a succession of hills, rising higher and higher until an elevation was reached of several hundred feet above the surface of Lake Erie. The creek is the largest stream in Erie County, and to members of the State Geological Survey it has been the most interesting. It rises on the highlands south of Erie City and runs in a westerly direction fifteen or twenty miles to a point south of Girard, where it forms a great oxbow curve around a long narrow ridge of rocks one hundred feet in height, known as the 'Devil's Backbone,' and then runs north through Girard to Lake Erie. The reason Elk Creek took a western direction while other streams that rose near that line ran directly north into the lake is because a high ridge lies between them, running parallel with the lake shore and named by the Geological Survey, 'First Divide.' From this watershed the rainfall on the north side runs into the lake through Mill Creek and other small streams, while the rainfall on the opposite side goes south into Elk Creek. In this stream is the second and most important subject of interest to the geologist, in having cut a deep channel in the rocks with perpendicular walls more than one hundred feet in height, and a personal inspection of the vertical walls has been made and the result published by members of the State Geological Survey. This is also an interesting stream to sight-seers. Not only are the great oxbow bend, the 'Devil's Backbone,' and further down the creek the 'Devil's Nose,' a high promontory of ashen gray rocks exhibiting that little-known mineral, cone-in-cone, jutting out from the vertical walls, but also the deep valley sloping gracefully away to the uplands which are, apparently, above the universal horizon. Here numerous landscapes along the entire water courses are as diversified with sheep, horses, and grazing cattle, clumps of bushes and shade trees, grain fields and farm buildings as any, perhaps, that may be seen in Northern Pennsylvania. There are many places where the air is fragrant with wild flowers, mint leaves and wintergreen, spice bushes, coniferous trees, and sweet birches. After crossing Elk Creek the party soon arrived at Fall's Run, and were driven into the maple grove in front of Mr. Howard's residence, where we were made welcome for the day. Mr. Howard showed us his creamery, ice house, and stone quarry, where we obtained many beautiful fossil shells and fossil marine plants.

"This quarry," Mr. Howard said, "is the northern outcrop of the Pennsylvania third oil sand about five hundred feet above the surface of Lake Erie. A lady asked ' Why is there no oil here?' His reply was, ' These rocks are the highest part of the strata, so hard and so fine that they can contain no oil. As the stratum dips down under the surface toward the oil-fields it becomes softer and coarser and so porous that it can hold an ocean of oil.' This corresponds with the Geological Survey. Some time was spent in looking at the waterfall. It is forty feet in height and sixty feet in breadth. The water cascades beautifully over the brink and down through a dark, narrow gulch about ninety feet in depth and pours itself into Elk Creek, singing its own glad song as it goes. Near the cascade is a mineral spring, clear, cool, and tasting fairly. It is said to be very healthy. Mr. Howard is not only an intelligent farmer and dairyman and quarryman, but is also an intelligent geologist. He did all he could to make our visit as pleasant as possible, and he and his family have the thanks of the entire company.

"There are hundreds of ravines in Erie County. The site

of Erie City was formerly gashed with them, but some are now entirely obliterated by refuse earth and other materials which have been deposited there from time to time, making them level with the surrounding earth. Upon such a new formed surface the City Hall and the Reed House square have been built. One of the ravines outside the city is now being used for another purpose. The Eighth Street motor car track has been extended from the Catholic Cemetery, accross the fields to a deep ravine situated about two hundred yards southwest of the head of Presque Isle Bay. The track continues on down through the ravine, where it curves around toward the east to the Massassauga Hotel. The descent is gradual, the rails are permanently laid, the gulch is cleared of fallen trees and bowlders, and its sides are dense with forest trees, twining vines, and flowers. A small crystal stream chatters its rights of passage from a small spring at the head down to the bay, where is a cool and refreshing lake breeze and an enchanting view of the lake.

"At a depth of three or four feet below the upper surface of the dark sand a fluid oozes out very slowly from a seam, having a metallic scum on the surface, tinged with a mixture of iron, copper and zinc. This stratum descends also with the track, showing how much the deposit was inclined toward the lake when this part of the earth was two or three hundred feet lower than it is now—so low that the high land along Twenty-sixth Street became the shore of a broad ocean many times wider than the waters of Lake Erie.

"T. D. I."

"Five miles from the Erie Union Depot the railway makes a true curve on the very brink of a 100-foot gulf, through which the Four Mile Creek descends to Lake Erie at the rate of about 100 feet per mile. The gulch is about 100 feet in depth and wide enough to be called a valley. This location is unrivalled for a picnic; the horizontal branches, forty feet in length, afford shade for the tables, the open, smooth grass plots are broad enough for baseball, football, and tennis, while the even, rocky bed of the meandering stream makes wading delightful for many children. There is ample room for strolling in all directions to enjoy the beautiful scenery. Passing a mile further up the stream we find groves and open spaces and reach the famous Wintergreen Gulch. In some places the banks are sufficiently sloping for the growth of shrubbery and forest trees, while the bank opposite is so precipitous and rocky that no kind of vegetation can take root. The face of the wall above shows the strata to be composed of alternate layers of sandstone and shale each several inches in thickness, but near the bottom the shale is several feet in thickness, and caused by the elements to break into thin scales no larger than the finger nail, which are washed away by every rainfall. Here and there are great bowlders in the valley and bed of the stream. They are of different kinds of rock, and entirely unlike any of the foundation rocks in this part of the country. They were formed in some past age of the world, and transported to this locality from some foreign country. There are, however, other loose rocks which were broken from the foundation rocks of this country, and crop out one or two miles south of these picnic grounds. They were brought down the gulch by ice and powerful floods. Some of the blocks are eighteen or more inches in thickness, and are filled through and through with beautiful fossil shells.

"T. D. I."

Lake Pleasant, in Amity township (and via Wattsburg 18¾ miles from Erie), is several hundred feet above Lake Erie, which is a still greater height above the ocean, ridges and valleys succeeding one another. As seen from high hills, the landscape is exceedingly beautiful, and a great distance appears between the observer and the horizon.

Lake Pleasant, near the corners of Venango, Green, Amity, and Waterford, is a beautiful body of water about three fourths of a mile long and a third of a mile wide, with a depth of twenty-five to fifty feet. Its outlet is a stream about the size of Le Bœuf Creek at Waterford, that never diminishes except in the dryest season. After furnishing power to several mills it falls into French Creek about three miles south, in Amity township. The wooden bridge over the West Branch at Wattsburg was the first bridge of the county and was originally built by the County Commissioners in 1822, through the influence of William Miles.

Dr. Ingersoll speaks poetically of the green woods and silent waters of the peninsula—Erie's wild natural park and pleasure ground. Since permanent habitation upon Presqu'ile has been forbidden by the United States government it has become wilder by the growth of plants in the trails made by pedestrians. If it would now transform this water-bound tongue of land into a public park with modern improvements, it would become a charming resort for health seekers and lovers of nature who live at a distance, as well as for those who dwell in its immediate vicinity. In this secluded and wild locality there is much that is interesting to the zoölogist, the botanist, and the sportsman. Wild birds of various species visit the peninsula semi-annually for food and rest as they migrate to and from distant parts of the country, both north and south, and many are the victims of sportsmen. As a variety of crafts and steamers in the warm season pass on both sides, the views through the trees and open spaces present pictures at various points of observation worthy of transfer to canvas and with exquisite color.

"Sixteen Mile Creek takes its rise in Greenfield township, within a mile of French Creek, passes the borough on its west side, and enters the lake at Freeport. Its length is about ten miles, and its general course due north. About two and a half miles south of the borough, Sixteen Mile Creek is joined by Graham Creek, which rises in New York, and is perhaps four miles long. At the point of junction there is a "hogsback" which is nearly perpendicular on the east side. The gully at the "hogsback" is not far from two hundred feet deep. The heads of Twenty Mile Creek are in Chautauqua County, N. Y., and its mouth is near the northeast corner of Northeast township, Pennsylvania. It enters the State about a mile above the crossing of the Lake Shore Railroad, and must have a length of ten or twelve miles. The deep gulf of this stream, which attracts so much attention from travelers begins three or four miles south of the Lake Shore Railroad culvert, and continues nearly to the lake, some three miles further by the windings of the creek. Its depth where the railroad crosses is about one hundred feet. The culvert at this point is a mammoth work and one of the finest pieces of masonry in the country. The Nickel Plate road has a fine iron bridge some distance above. The gully on the headwaters of Sixteen Mile Creek is nowhere as abrupt as that of Twenty Mile Creek, except at the junction above referred to. From Moorheadville to its mouth the Twelve Mile Creek has steep banks.

" A wonderful curiosity is to be found on Elk Creek where it makes a great oxbow bend around a very high point of rocks, hundreds of feet above the surface of Lake Erie. It is seventeen miles southwest from Erie, and a delightful drive. Arriving at the creek is a winding wagon path up to a plateau owned by Mr. Blair, and through cultivated fields to the middle of the bend where the promontory-like formation terminates in a long knife-blade ridge of bare rocks on which one may balance himself with a foot over a precipice on each side. Some are brave enough to attempt to walk the ridge single-file, and succeed without accident, though life depends on proper balance of the body—a single misstep would send one headlong to the bed of the creek more than a hundred feet below. This has been named the 'Devil's Backbone' and on the other side of the creek is another high rocky point called the 'Devil's Nose.'"—*From History of Erie County, 1884. Published by Warner & Co., Chicago.*

CHAPTER II.

Magnitude of the Great Lakes—Lake Currents—Fish Exhibit— Hatcheries—Ancient Mariner—The Lighthouses—Flash Lighthouse—Lifesaving Station—Waterworks—War for the Union— Soldiers and Sailors' Home.

From the Marine Review.

The story of a captain who took a schooner across the Atlantic with a cargo of wheat from the lakes, and being unable to get insured for the return trip, because no information of the great lake ports was to be found, is well known, as is also the one about English underwriters being surprised that lake vessels were navigated at night instead of tying up along the "bank," but a recent instance more interesting is given by a New York engineer. He accompanied Mr. Johnson, the English capitalist interested in the building of whalebacks in England, on his first trip up the lakes. While in the rivers Mr. Johnson asked if they would not reach Duluth by nightfall. When told he would have to pass through two large lakes on which he would be out of sight of land for several hours and cover some 600 miles, he shook his head and wondered. Nearing the end of his journey he ventured to suggest that it couldn't be far from the Pacific Ocean, but subsided when told that the halfway point in crossing the continent was still several hundred miles west of him. Some foreigners, as well as eastern business men, have had their doubts dispelled as to the immense traffic of the lakes, but many are still woefully ignorant of that as well as of their great area. The following will give an idea of the magnitude of the great lakes :

"The water surface of Lakes Ontario, Erie, Huron, Michigan and Superior, and connecting waterways, is 95,275 square miles, while the area of Great Britain, England, Scotland and Wales combined is only 88,781 square miles. The coast lines of the great lakes contain more than half the fresh water on the globe, and have a combined length of 3,075 miles. It is 1,279 miles from Ogdensburg to Duluth, and from the northern shore of Lake Superior to the southern end of Lake Michigan is 520 miles. The distance from Chicago to Liverpool is 4,500 miles, one half of which is covered by the great lakes and St. Lawrence River. From the Straits of Belle Isle to Duluth, at the head of Lake Superior, is 2,259¾ miles. From the Straits of Belle Isle to Kingston, Lake Ontario, is 1,164 miles. From Kingston to Duluth it is 1,186 miles, over one half of the distance from the Straits of Belle Isle across the Atlantic to Liverpool."

Observer W. B. Stockman, of the Cleveland Weather Bureau, has received for distribution among vessel masters and others interested in the welfare of the lake marine, a large number of copies of the newly issued current chart of the great lakes. This chart is the result of the effort put forth by the department last season to ascertain the trend of currents believed to exist on the vast sheets of inland water. At the

HISTORY OF ERIE COUNTY.   321

suggestion of Dr. H. J. Penrod, then marine agent of the Weather Bureau, with headquarters in Cleveland, a number of bottles were purchased from a Pittsburg firm that manufactured them to order. They much resembled what is known as a pop or ginger beer bottle, save that they were fitted with an ordinary cork. They were so blown that the weight was such as to immerse the bottle except about half an inch of the neck, leaving the smallest proportion possible to be affected by surplus influences. The bottles were packed in boxes, each box containing twenty-five bottles, and issued to masters of lake boats. The masters were instructed to drop bottles over board in certain localities, first filling out a blank containing the date, hour, and location of the casting away of the bottle, the paper being placed inside. Inside each bottle was another blank, with a franked envelope, which the finder was requested to fill out, naming the day and hour, and the spot where the bottle had been found.

The plan was carried out thoroughly in all its details, and the envelopes placed in three fourths of the bottles issued eventually found their way to Washington. In fact, so many more were returned than had been expected that the artist found considerable difficulty in making clear use of the information contained, and this delayed the issue of the charts. The charts just issued show excellent lithographic work. They are of the same size as the wreck chart issued last year, and give the outline of the lakes in blue upon an orange background, the degrees of latitude and longitude being very plainly marked.

In the upper right-hand corner, on a salmon-colored background, is a smaller map of the lakes, showing the general set of the currents as indicated by the drifting of the bottles, and giving a fair idea of the directions in which the water circulates. The light blue which indicates the water in the large chart is adorned with what at first glance appears to be a meteoric shower, in a darker blue. Small circles show the localities where some of the bottles, selected for the purpose of illustration, were thrown overboard, and lines follow their course to the spot where the bottles were picked up, this being indicated by an arrowhead. While the courses of the bottles were in many cases determined by the flow of the water through the rivers, a surprisingly large number took such apparently independent courses as to clearly argue the existence of very definite and permanent currents. The bottles cast overboard at Duluth started down Lake Superior, but in several instances showed a decided inclination, after passing Apostle Islands, to turn back toward Ashland. After passing Keweenaw some drifted in toward Marquette ; others took a more or less direct course for Whitefish Bay and the headwaters of the Sault ; while by far the greatest proportion were cast upon the inhospitable coast extending from Grand Marais to Whitefish Point. Remarkable exceptions to all these were noted, however, in bottles dropped overboard between Keweenaw Point and Point au Sable, these taking a northeasterly direction, and crossing the courses followed by other bottles, drifting upon the Canadian shore north and east of the Caribon Islands.

On Lake Michigan, bottles cast away between Beaver Islands and the entrance to Green Bay drifted toward the latter and found the shore for the most part at the north end of Green Bay. At the south end of the bay the water had little motion, and no bottles ever got out of it. The general drift of the bottles showed a current up the west shore, but steadily turning to the east shore and flowing back toward the straits, passing out through the south passage almost exclusively. On Lake Huron the courses were the most varied, the principal drifts being southeastward or southwestward. The bottles passed into Saginaw Bay at the lower side, then turned and came out at the north side, explaining the constant rough seas found at the mouth of this bay. Many bottles thrown overboard on the west side of Lake Huron found their way through the narrow island passages into 'Georgian Bay and were then washed ashore.

Bottles dropped in Detroit River showed currents setting against the north shore to Point au Pelee, and against the west shore far into Maumee Bay. Bottles coming through the north passage found the shore between Lorain and Buffalo. Those dropped overboard in midlake west of Lorain took a southwesterly course. Bottles starting from the locality where the *Wocoken* foundered, even when dropped close to the Canadian shore, drifted down past Long Point and ultimately reached the south shore. The drifting wreckage and bodies from this steamer have constantly followed the same course.

On Lake Ontario the bottles have uniformly taken a southeasterly course, most of them drifting upon the New York shore.

Chief Mark W. Harrington, of the Weather Bureau, in issuing his chart, expresses the hope that it may prove of material value to those interested in lake navigation, and extends the thanks of the bureau to the many persons, masters of vessels and others, who have aided in the work. The study of currents is to be continued, and the bureau hopes for the same coöperation and assistance in the future as in 1892.

FROM PENNSYLVANIA'S FISH EXHIBIT AT THE WORLD'S COLUMBIAN EXPOSITION.

By Col. John Fleeharty, of Erie.

Although Pennsylvania has but forty-five miles of frontage on Lake Erie, its interests in the fisheries of these waters are considerable, the City of Erie, a flourishing town on this great waterway, doing the bulk of the trade.

Upper Mill Creek, Walnut Creek and Trout Run were noted for their fine fishing in the memory of many now living. All the streams in Erie County were prolific in fish, and all of them contained many brook trout. . . . Log canoes for fishing purposes were as much a necessity to the early settlers along the lake as log cabins to shelter their families, and each went fishing as his wants required.

In 1796, some twenty or thirty Indian families belonging to the Seneca tribe resided at the head of the bay, now known as "the Head," or Massassauga Point, and were the first fishermen on the lake in Northwestern Pennsylvania. This was the last Indian village in Erie County. After their departure the site was occupied by a halfbreed negro named McKinney who lived by fishing. He subsequently removed to the upper Laird farm, and one of his daughters married Ben Fleming, who was the last survivor of Perry's fleet residing in

Pennsylvania. Following him came Moses Muzzy, and then Ben Fleming, both of whom made their living by fishing in the bay from log canoes. Black bass abounded, and with all varieties were taken with the hook prior to 1830. David Fowzier at that time became the first seine fisherman. The ponds in the peninsula and Pike Pond on the south side of the bay near the harbor entrance were the spawning grounds for a large variety of fish, particularly grass pike and some fine turtles. They lay upon the bottom, in about two and a half feet of water and were taken by shooting or spearing ; some were of extraordinary size.

Hon. James Hoskinson contributed some interesting items for Col. Fleeharty's article. About 1824-26 small vessels went from Erie to Mackinaw in the fall to fish for white fish and trout. Having cured and packed them in barrels they returned to Erie and a good market was found for them, and many were shipped to Pittsburg. There were eight or ten vessels engaged in this trade for several years. Messrs. Seth Reed, P. S. V. Hamot and Capt. John Dixon had vessels so engaged. Capt. John Dixon built the first dock and warehouse, and from there all of the limited fish business was transacted. For many years the names of Horton, Huntsburger and Buckingham also were connected with seine fishing. Little or no fishing was done in the lake, as the bay abounded. Misery Bay and the mouth of Mill Creek have always been fine places for rock bass fishing as well as sunfish and perch. The first white fishing at this point was in 1853 ; the first shippers were George Witter and John Sutter & Co.

In 1867 there were only nine fish boats out of Erie, and the first steam fish boat came to Erie from Ashtabula, Ohio, in 1874 or '75.

Capt. Clark Jones says : "Commenced gill net fishing in 1854 or '55. White fish was shipped east and west about 1856. At that time sturgeons were considered of no use and were taken to the peninsula and buried. Thousands have been buried there and to-day they are worth two dollars and fifty cents each. Smoked sturgeon is considered fully equal to smoked halibut, and the roe makes an excellent 'caviare.' Each fish yields from twelve to fourteen pounds. The meat is mostly sent to Sandusky, Ohio, for curing and smoking and is worth from five to eight cents a pound for that purpose. Though formerly thrown away this fish is now scarce and valuable. The Dash family is a family of fishermen of four generations. Capt. John Dash gave interesting items, as also William Terry, Capts. Jones and Wick. They speak of black bass, the gamiest fish in the lakes, becoming more and more scarce; herrings though plentiful are not as much so as formerly, but a great many are salted along the lakes. The muscalonge used to be quite plentiful in this vicinity—the largest one taken was sixty-two pounds—the average weight is twenty-five to thirty pounds.

"Mr. E. D. Carter embarked in the business of fishing and shipping fish in 1874, and to him is given the credit of opening up a permanent market abroad. Shipments of fish previous to this were at times when there was an overplus on the market. Mr. Louis Strueber went into the business in 1877, and the two were for years the only shippers from Erie. Frank W. Bacon & Co. have also been large shippers for some years.

"On the 24th of September, 1892, the Erie Fish Association was formed by consolidation of the following houses: E. D. Carter, Louis Strueber, Frank W. Bacon & Co., and E. Knoblock & Co. The first day after the consolidation the catch of fish was forty-eight tons. The statistical account on the lake, in Pennsylvania for 1892 shows that 28 steam fish boats, 14 sail boats, 40 pound nets, boats, etc., employ $250,000 total capital, and 500 men. An accurate account of the fish taken for commercial purposes during 1892 has been kept, the total number of pounds being 12,786,579. The herring was highest in number, being 8,300,633, and blue pike the next, 2,968,659, while black bass was only 4,286 and sturgeon 90,702, white fish 524,428, and trout 131,337."

STATE FISH HATCHERY.

In Erie is a beautiful cottage on the corner of Second and Sassafras streets under the supervision of the Fish Commission, and was opened in December, 1885, to propagate white fish in Erie waters. As hundreds of thousands of dollars are invested and a small army of men employed in the fishing business here, and there is also a wholesale destruction of spawn by sturgeons, as well as in the natural way, this is essential to keep up the supply. It is supposed one large sturgeon will consume millions of fish eggs in a day, which if undisturbed would be comparatively safe after hatching.

After entering a pleasant reception room the remainder of the floor is devoted to propagating purposes. On several long counters or tables are placed glass jars, each containing one gallon. One quart of spawn is put in each jar, which is filled with water and sealed airtight, excepting as two rubber tubes with glass nozzles run in a supply of fresh water, which keeps the whole in motion. By an ingenious plan all the "dead" spawn is removed also by the discharge tube. On the second floor a tank containing 1,000 gallons of water affords pressure. After hatching the small fry are kept in the jars about a week, when they are liberated in the lake, perhaps ten miles out. The Erie hatchery has the capacity for bringing out 30,000,000 small fry in a season. Rock bass, catfish, and when the season closes for white fish, blue pike are sometimes placed in the hatching jars.

The hatchery is under the supervision of the State Fish Commission, one or more members visiting it monthly, and the entire board makes an annual inspection. The Erie hatchery is in charge of Mr. John Maher, an enthusiast in fish culture.

"*Ancient Mariner,*" *1893.*

In 1837 the steamboat *Erie* was built by the Erie Steamboat Company at the foot of French Street, in the borough of Erie. Thomas G. Colt and Smith Jackson, being the chief men of the company, sold out in 1838 and 1839 to Gen. C. M. Reed. August 9, 1841, she was destroyed by fire off Silver Creek, N. Y., two hundred and forty-nine persons being lost, twenty-six being residents of Erie. . . .

Previous to the completion of the railroads on both sides of the lake, the New York Central and New York and Erie railroads built a class of steamers which for speed, elegance, and safety were marvels indeed. At the decline afterwards of passenger traffic, by the completion of railroads on the north and south shore, the propellers appeared which to-day are fine, large, seaworthy vessels, built and equipped regardless of expense, and in every respect fully equal to the best of ocean steamers. Iron ship building was commenced in 1862. The propeller and consort system was first established in 1870, and has become a great factor in solving the question of cheap transportation.

The navy has but one ship on the chain of lakes, the *Michigan*. The supply steamers of the lighthouse service are under the control of the Navy Department. Capt. John Richards built the first revenue cutter, *Benjamin Rush*, which was commanded by Capt. Gilbert Knapp, who was succeeded by Capt. Daniel Dobbins. The second was the *Erie*, which was succeeded by the iron steamer *Dallas*. This vessel was removed to the Atlantic coast by way of the Welland Canal and the St. Lawrence River in 1848. The six small revenue cutters, being one for each lake, at the outbreak of the war of 1861 were moved to the Atlantic coast under the direction of Capt. Douglass Ottinger by way of the Welland Canal. In 1864 the *Perry* was built on Niagara River and equipped with Capt. Whittaker's sidewheel propellers. She was remarkably fast, making nineteen miles an hour on her trial trip, but was sold, the present cutter *Perry* succeeding her.

THE LIGHTHOUSE.

On the mainland just within the eastern limits of the city is the land lighthouse site, which has been occupied since 1818. The first structure cost $3,000. In 1858 a new tower was built of Milwaukee brick. The foundation proved defective and in 1866 it was replaced by one built of Berea stone at a cost of $33,000. To secure a solid foundation an excavation twenty feet deep was made and filled with Portland cement, oak timber, and finely broken limestone. On this bed courses of stone were placed aggregating eight feet in thickness. It is sixty-seven feet in height from the water table to the focal plane of the lens, and one hundred and twenty-seven feet above the lake's level. The lens was manufactured in Paris and cost $7,000 when delivered in New York. It is a fixed white light and can be seen seventeen nautical miles. Mineral oil is used in the lamps. In 1880, on the recommendation of Commander G. W. Howard, U. S. N., Inspector of the Tenth Lighthouse District, notwithstanding many protests, the light was discontinued, and the same year the property was sold for $1,800. The next session of Congress ordered its repurchase and re-establishment as a light.

In 1828 an octagonal wooden tower was erected on the east end of the pier at the harbor entrance, and fish oil used for the lamps. This was carried away by a schooner being thrown against it in a gale in 1857. In 1858 a cast iron skeleton tower weighing nineteen tons was erected. Lard oil was then used and the lamps were the best. In 1880 this tower was taken down and transferred to the extreme end of the pier, which had been lengthened 2,000 feet. The light had been fixed white and was changed to fixed red, and was visible eleven miles—mineral oil being used. In 1830 a keeper's dwelling was erected but was destroyed by fire in 1841 and a larger one erected. In 1858 a neat residence was erected on the beach. In 1878 a fog bell weighing 1,200 pounds was placed on the pier near the lighthouse, but has been of no practical value to the merchant service.

The Flash lighthouse is a modern square tower of brick, with a convenient keeper's dwelling attached. It was erected in 1872 on the north shore of the peninsula at a cost of $15,000. The light, varied with red and white flashes, is inside of a fourth order lens, and is said to be the finest in the lighthouse service. Being isolated and on the sand with a background of evergreens, it presents a picturesque appearance as seen from passing vessels. The keepers of lighthouses must not be over fifty years of age, and they are not subject to removal when a change of administration occurs.

In February, 1878, Commander W. R. Bridgman, U. S. N., Lighthouse Inspector of the Tenth District, and Capt. D. P. Dobbins, Superintendent of Life-saving Stations, came to Erie and selected a site for the station on the lighthouse premises. In 1876, as the marine disasters usually occurred on the outer shore of the peninsula, a building which had been placed three miles from the beacon lighthouse, proved a mistake and was moved on trucks and the crew located in the present quarters.

Surfman William Clark was placed in charge and fulfilled its duties until 1891, when he was drowned, after many years of service.

WATERWORKS.

Up to 1840 the ordinary cisterns and wells supplied the inhabitants of Erie with water. The thickly settled parts were then provided with water from a large spring on the Reed farm south of Eighteenth Street. The Erie Water and Gas Company was incorporated in 1857, and in 1869 the works were completed at a cost of $675,000. The first engines were the Cornish Bull engines, invented by James Watt. In 1887 a new engine house was completed, with the Gaskill engine, pumping 5,000,000 gallons per day. This was purchased of the Holly Company, of Lockport, N. Y., the contract price for engine and foundation being $24,850.

The engine house is a solid brick structure, with stone foundation 30x35 feet, and 65 feet in height surmounted by an octagonal turret 14 feet high. The boiler house is 50x60 feet, and 12 feet high; smokestack 14 feet square at the bottom and 100 feet in height, with a draft of 25 feet. The standpipe tower, built to enclose the standpipe, is octagonal in shape. Forty-five feet above its foundation, throughout which distance the tower is brick, a belt of stones 5 feet high is placed; thence upward it is a circular tower. Its total height is 217 feet, and its total elevation 237 feet above the surface of the bay, while an additional 16 feet has been added to the standpipe since its erection, making it 253 feet above the water level, the highest standpipe in the world. In the interior a spiral stairway ascends to the top of the tower, which is suitably decked and enclosed by an iron railing. The visitor may here obtain the finest view possible of the city and lake.

The reservoir on Twenty-sixth Street, between Chestnut and Cherry, has a capacity of 35,000,000 gallons. In 1872 the Water Commissioners purchased seven acres of land and constructed a reservoir, the bottom of which is 210 feet above the surface of the bay, while the water is kept at an average depth of 25 feet. The construction account of the works up to 1888 amounted to about $1,000,000. The private street connections number from 5,000 to 6,000, with 60 miles of pipe, 300 fire hydrants, and 550 stop valves. Some of the citizens who have been most identified with the works are W. W. Reed, W. L. Scott, H. Rawle, B. Whitman, George W. Starr, Messrs. Selden, Sherwin, Sloan and others. In 1892 the new 12,000,000 gallon Worthington pump at the waterworks was started, and the workings are smooth and perfect.

The first volume of the annual report of the Chief of Engineers on the river and harbor improvements has been made public. This volume contains the reports of the officers in charge, which were suppressed by the chief last July. The report relating to Erie Harbor is as follows:

"Erie Harbor—The original survey of the harbor was made in 1819, at which time the channel was narrow and tortuous, with a depth of only six feet. In 1823 a plan for the improvement was adopted and constitutes the present work at the entrance to the harbor, excepting some changes which have been required either on account of the age of the structures already built or other causes. The piers have been extended from time to time, and are now in pretty good order and condition. The north pier needs considerable repairs. The present project contemplates the extension of the piers to the 16-foot curve in the lake, and the maintenance of a channel of navigable width, 16 feet in depth from the harbor, inside to the lake outside. Operations have been prosecuted with more or less interruption and suspension (no work was done from 1838 to 1842, from 1846 to 1853, and from 1855 to 1864) and have resulted in much benefit to the harbor and its channel entrance. The work during the year consisted in the extension of the north pier for 300 feet, of which five cribs were sunk at the end of the year and the last since that date. The total amount expended up to June 30, 1892, was $798,892.33. The amount expended during the fiscal year ending June 30, 1893, was $4,609.47.

"Presque Isle Peninsula, Erie Harbor—In a report upon the examination of Erie Harbor, made in 1885, it was recommended that the neck of the peninsula be protected by a breakwater, and the movement of sand around the eastern end of the peninsula be prevented at an estimated cost of $173,044.50. Work under this project was in progress until October, 1889, when it was abandoned, it having been found that the structures would not stand against the violence of the storms. No further work is at present contemplated, but the sum of $20,000 has been reserved from the appropriation for the improvement of Erie Harbor to be used in case of necessity in closing any breach which might occur. The total amount expended up to June 30, 1890, was $60,000. Nothing was expended during the fiscal year ending June 30, 1893.

THE WAR FOR THE UNION.

When the thrilling tidings were received that our people must resort to arms for the preservation of the country, patriotism was universally manifested by all parties. Men of all classes were united, and ministers of the gospel were equally outspoken. The national flag was displayed from hundreds of buildings in Erie and throughout the county, and a solemn faith in the ultimate triumph of this righteous cause prevailed. A meeting was held in Wayne Hall, on French Street, April 26, 1861, which was largely attended. William A. Galbraith, a leading Democrat, presided, and speeches were also made by John H. Walker, a leading Republican, George H. Cutler, and George W. De Camp.

A movement had already been inaugurated by Capt. John W. McLane to form a three months' regiment, which was speedily filled, and a fund for the support of the families was provided. Seven thousand dollars was subscribed at this meeting, and $10,000 soon after was added. Three dollars and fifty cents was allowed for the wife, weekly, and fifty cents added for each child. Throughout the county similar meetings were held and funds provided.

This first regiment encamped at the southeast corner of Parade and Sixth streets, being the grounds occupied by the Agricultural Fair, and volunteers were more in number than could be accepted, so that many returned home sadly disappointed. One hundred came from Waterford alone, and five companies were recruited in Erie. The regiment left Erie May 1 for Pittsburg, Mehl's brass band accompanying it, and many friends were at the depot to give them a parting blessing. The next morning they took up quarters in Camp Wilkins. In many cases the companies exceeded their quota, and members were discharged. A flag was presented them by the ladies of Pittsburg May 5, in the presence of 10,000 spectators. May 29 they received their arms and uniforms and were carefully drilled each day, but returned to Erie July 20, not being called into active service, much to the chagrin of both officers and men. They met with an enthusiastic reception on their return, and supper was prepared by the ladies at the West Park. One member had died in their absence.

The Eighty-Third Regiment.—The 24th of July, Col. McLane received an order to recruit a regiment, the President having issued a call for 300,000 men. Many of the three months' men had volunteered and they were dismissed August 1st to await an answer. Recruiting was active in the northwestern counties, and a camp was established about two miles east of the city by Capt. J. B. Bell of the regular army. Capt. Gregg, a recruiting officer for cavalry, enlisted a number of young men. The Perry Artillery of Erie offered its services and was accepted, with C. F. Mueller as Captain and W. F. Leutje as Lieutenant. An immense meeting at Farrar Hall was called on the 24th of August to aid in raising men for Col. McLane's regiment. The speakers were W. A. Galbraith, J. C. Marshall, G. W. DeCamp, Col. McLane, M. W. Caughey, Capt. J. Graham. In different parts of the county similar meetings were held and addressed by A. King, Strong Vincent, W. S. Lane, M. B. Lowry and Dan Rice. At Greenfield the Democrats and Republicans were united in a union pole raising. At the same time recruiting for the navy was being prosecuted by Lieut. T. H. Stevens, sixty persons from Erie recruiting, and by September, seven hundred seamen were forwarded to the seaboard at different times by Capt. J. C. Carter, of the U. S. Steamer *Michigan.* A Ladies' Aid Society had been organized in Erie and other towns to provide hospital stores and comforts for wounded soldiers, and many boxes were forwarded during the war.

Col. McLane's regiment being full was ordered to Harrisburg on the 16th of September. Those who were witnesses of its departure will never forget the scene. A flag was presented it by the State December 21st, and it was officially known as the Eighty-Third Regiment.

The One Hundred and Eleventh Regiment.—Maj. M. Schlaudecker of Erie, just before the departure, raised another regiment and occupied the same ground for his camp. This left the 25th of February, 1862, with every company full. It was presented with a stand of colors by Gov. Curtin, and took rank as the One Hundred and Eleventh Regiment. Its departure was fully as affecting as the former ones. Zimmerman's brass band accompanied the regiment.

A rumor of war with Great Britain prevailed in the early part of 1862, and in anticipation a naval depot on the lake was projected. The City Council urged the claim of Erie as the site, and citizens visited Washington for that purpose. March 8th newspapers were notified by the Secretary of War that the publication of army movements was prohibited. Money was raised in Erie for the wounded who might need attendance, and war was the chief topic. Rebel prisoners were taken through on the Lake Shore Railroad.

The Eighty-third suffered terribly in the battles around Richmond. Col. McLane was killed, and grief was general and mourning pervaded the community. Hospital stores for the wounded were hastily forwarded. This was in June, and in July the President made a call for 300,000 more troops, and it was announced that five companies of 100 men each was Erie County's proportion. A meeting in Wayne Hall to urge enlistments asked of the County Commissioners the appropriation of $100,000 to equip a new regiment. Discouragement prevailed in consequence of the Virginia disasters, and greater inducements must be offered. A bounty of $50 was offered each recruit by the City of Erie, and some townships followed their example. Another call for 300,000 men caused the County Commissioners to offer an additional bounty of $25,000. In August another regiment, the One Hundred and Fifty-fifth, was in camp at the same fairground. Recruits came forward, and the regiment left for the seat of war September 11th. At the same time the navy received many accessions, and the cavalry companies of Capts. Lennon, Miles, and Roberts were formed. From official reports Erie City alone had furnished for the navy up to the 16th of August two hundred men. The above cavalry companies were in camp at Pittsburg the 4th of

October. Notwithstanding great inducements to volunteers the quota of Erie County was still short, and a draft seemed inevitable. Insurance companies were formed, members paying from $20 to $50 to procure substitutes provided their names were drawn. Recruiting for both the army and navy went on vigorously. At the call for minutemen to defend Harrisburg, six companies, composed of many leading business men responded to the call of the Governor. Happily their services were not needed, and they returned the first of October. An enrollment of militia had been made, I. B. Gara having been appointed a commissioner. These proceedings were under the State militia law. W. P. Gibson was appointed a Deputy Marshal to prevent the escape to Canada of those liable to conscription. The officers to manage the draft were B. B. Vincent and Charles Brandes, surgeon. Gov. Curtin gave notice that volunteers for nine months would be accepted up to the day of drafting.

The draft was held in the grand jury room of the courthouse on the 16th of October, 1,055 being drawn for the whole County, who were to serve for nine months. A blindfolded man drew the slips from the wheel and read the name to the anxious bystanders. In filling the wheel persons above forty-five years were exempt: also ministers, teachers, and school directors. Substitutes were to be found at prices varying from $50 to $250. About 300 were exempted from physical disability, and probably not more than 500 of the drafted went into the army. In October and November about 350 men were forwarded. Andrew Scott was appointed Provost Marshal to find delinquents. The Councils of Erie voted $45,000 for the relief of their families, and the Ladies' Aid Society supplied each family with a Thanksgiving dinner. Those who reached the front soon returned without seeing much service. Prices advanced, money became scarce from levies for bounties, and silver and gold almost disappeared. The city issued scrip to meet the demands for small change of 50, 25, 20, 10 and even 5 cents. Greenbacks, "shinplasters" and various checks and duebills served as a medium of exchange. Political feeling became intense about 1863, and though a patriotic spirit influenced the large majority, still a fear of the results made great jealousy of "copperheads" and those who gave aid and comfort to the enemy, and fears of another class prevailed with Democrats—it was happy that the "war Democrat" party was numerous.

The Second Draft.—Early in 1863 Congress passed an act taking conscription out of the hands of the States, all persons being liable between twenty and forty-five and those exempt from physical causes furnishing a substitute or paying $300. Lieut.-Col. H. S. Campbell, late of the Eighty-third Regiment, was Marshal; Jerome Powell, of Elk County, Commissioner; Dr. John Macklin, of Jefferson County, Surgeon, to act for this Congressional district. Headquarters were established at Waterford, and a new enrollment made during May and June. The government was now enlisting negroes, and bodies of troops passed through Erie frequently. The news of the rebel invasion of Pennsylvania and of the battles at Gettysburg produced a deep and fearful excitement. The Governor appealed for militia to defend the State, and it met with immediate response. June 15 a vast meeting was held, addressed by Messrs. Walker, Lowry, Marvin, Sill, McCreary and others, earnestly calling for the enemy to be driven from the State. About 400 citizens enlisted for the State's defense, but on reaching Pittsburg, the news of Meade's victory, rendered their services unnecessary, and they returned home. The Ladies' Aid Society forwarded stores to the wounded at Gettysburg. The fall of Vicksburg was celebrated with great rejoicings.

In June Capt. Mueller was in Erie recruiting for another battery, and large numbers of young men entered the navy. The county was announced 1,400 short, and substitutes ran up to $300. September 26, it is stated that 83 of the conscripts had furnished substitutes, 245 paid commutations, 706 had been exempted and 127 were forwarded to Pittsburg. Impatience for the return of peace was general. In October President Lincoln made a call for 300,000 more men, and Gov. Curtin announced Pennsylvania's quota to be 32,268, and he asked for volunteers. A bounty of $402 was offered veterans. To this sum the county added $300 more, and most of the districts $50 to $100 more. During a part of the season the United States Steamer *Michigan*, which had been fully manned, guarded

Johnson's Island, where 2,000 rebel prisoners were confined, and fears were entertained that they might escape. In November a report was circulated that the rebels purposed an invasion from Canada, landing in Erie. Six hundred troops arrived from Pittsburg under the command of Maj.-Gen. Brooks. The citizens were called upon to aid in an intrenchment to be thrown up on Block House Bluff, and about 1,000 responded with picks and shovels. The rumor proved to be false, and the troops left for the South, the battery remaining. On the 14th of January, 1864, the One Hundred and Eleventh Regiment returned to recruit its ranks, and after a grand reception, were given by the ladies a sumptuous repast at Wayne Hall. They went into camp until February 25, when they returned with ranks nearly full. Many members of the Eighty-third, whose term had expired, came home in January and were received with deserved cordiality, and 75 more arrived in March.

Several negroes were accepted to supply the quota of Erie County and five or six were released from prison at May session on condition they would join the army. To the general joy no draft was needed, though a few names were drawn for the other counties of the Congressional district.

Another call from the President in July, 1864, was for 500,000 more men. Erie subscribed $20,000 to induce volunteers, besides the United States, county, and district bounties. The quota of the county was 1,289, and the city's share 150. Negroes were taken as substitutes, and Asa Battles, John W. Halderman, and Richard M. Broas were deputed to go to the southwest for this purpose. Ensign Bone shipped men by the hundred for the navy. About 1,000 entered the service through this channel, receiving a bounty of $400. The price of substitutes ranged from $550 to $700. President Lincoln was re-elected in November after a severe contest.

A last call for 300,000 men was made in January, 1865. The Councils of Erie offered to increase their bounty $150, and ultimately it was increased to $400. A draft took place at Ridgway March 6, where the Provost Marshal's office had been removed and 2,010 names were drawn from Erie County. Girard borough was the only district that escaped. The price of substitutes arose to $1,500 at times, and the Legislature had passed an act authorizing any district to pay a bounty of $400. Of the drafted men, some had guard duty assigned them at forts near or at Washington.

April 9 came the glad news of the surrender of Gen. Lee, which was hailed as the termination of the war. Rejoicings in Erie were more demonstrative than before in its history and manifested by illuminations, firing of cannon, the ringing of bells, and display of bunting, with shouts for the Union and the gallant soldiers. On the 12th, joy was turned to mourning and the deepest sorrow, by the assassination of President Lincoln. On Saturday all places of business were closed, and emblems of mourning were everywhere for the martyred President. A special train conveying the remains to Springfield passed through on April 27 and thousands gathered at the depot out of respect to the honored dead.

Remarks.—The Eighty-third Regiment was assigned to the Third Brigade of Porter's division, under Gen. Butterfield. It was highly complimented by Gen. McClellan, and awarded one of the French uniforms and equipments imported to present to the most proficient in drill. It was engaged in twenty-five battles, "more by two than any other Pennsylvania, infantry regiment." Col. McLane fell at Gaines' Mills the 27th of June, 1862, lamented not by his own men alone, but by the whole corps. Col. Strong Vincent, who succeeded him, and was in command of the whole brigade, fell mortally wounded at Gettysburg July 2, 1863. His appointment of Brigadier-General did not reach the regiment until after his death. After Gettysburg the members of the regiment were reduced by sickness and battle to 200, but later received accessions by draft and substitutes to the number 2,600, and disbanded July 4, 1865.

The One Hundred and Eleventh Regiment.—This third regiment was commanded by Col. Mathias Schlaudecker for three years' service. It reached the State capital January 27, 1862. In its first serious engagement at Cedar Mountain, August 9, it lost nineteen killed, sixty-one wounded, and thirteen missing. Until the regiment was transferred to Tennessee, September 24, 1863, it participated in the battles of

Virginia and Maryland, including Antietam, Chancellorsville, and Gettysburg. While stationed at Acquia Creek it was one of fifteen regiments specially commanded by Gen. Hooker in his general order of March 3. Col. Schlaudecker was honorably discharged in November, 1862, and the other field officers were promoted. The regiment joined Rosecrans' army and took part in the movement upon Lookout Mountain. After most of its members enlisting for a second term, they were given a furlough to come home, reaching Erie January 14, 1864. On returning to the southwest they took part in the march upon Atlanta, being one of the first to enter the city. Before reaching Atlanta Col. Cobham was shot, and died on the field of battle. Afterwards it joined the main body of the army in Sherman's famous "march to the sea." At Goldsboro, N. C., the One Hundred and Ninth and One Hundred and Eleventh were consolidated, with 885 members, retaining the name of One Hundred and Eleventh. It was mustered out July 19, 1865, and the northwestern portion reached Erie the 27th, the gallant veterans meeting a grand reception.

The One Hundred and Forty-fifth Regiment.—Its rendezvous was the same as that of the Eighty-third and the One Hundred and Eleventh, having been organized September 5, 1862. There was time for little training in military duty. After being furnished with arms they were in two days within sound of the enemy's guns at Antietam. About noon on the 17th they joined the extreme right of the Union line, and aided in preventing a flank movement of the enemy. After the battle the duty of aiding to bury the dead, some having lain four days on the field of battle, told seriously on the health of the regiment, two or three hundred being laid aside from duty, and many died. The One Hundred and Forty-fifth was assigned to the First Brigade, First Division, of the Second Corps. On December 13 it took part in the charge at Fredericksburg, under Gen. Hancock. Of the 5,000 of that division, 2,000 fell in that single charge. Of the 556 in the One Hundred and Forty-fifth, 226 were either killed or wounded. At Chancellorsville, a detail of 150 men failing to receive an order to retire were mostly captured. At Gettysburg the regiment entering 200 strong, lost in killed and wounded upwards of 80. Returning to Virginia it participated in most of the engagements until the close of the campaign in 1863. May, 1864, found the regiment recruited almost to its original strength. From this date the history of the army of Virginia, with its constant marches, was also the history of this. There were no braver men or better officers. In the charge in front of Petersburg about fifty were killed and wounded and ninety were captured. The remainder of the regiment was almost constantly under fire the rest of the season. In the spring campaign of 1865 it did good service with Sheridan, and was mustered out May 31, and returned to Erie on June 5, where they received a well merited and enthusiastic welcome. The colonel of the One Hundred and Forty-fifth was H. L. Brown. Of other officers we may say a few are at the present time in honorable and useful positions, as D. P. McCreary, J. W. Reynolds, and the Chaplain, Rev. J. H. W. Stuckenberg.

THE SOLDIERS AND SAILORS' HOME.

June 3, 1885, a bill was introduced into the Legislature by Hon. Isaac B. Brown, member from Erie County, and was approved by the Governor. The location of the Home was left to a commission composed of the Governor, State Treasurer, the Auditor-General, one Senator, and two members of the House of Representatives, and five honorably discharged soldiers appointed by the Grand Army of the Republic. After considering various sites the building known as the Marine Hospital at Erie was selected. Being nearly ready for occupancy and owned by the State, it was a matter of economy to use it. No more appropriate place could be chosen, for "it has echoed to the tramp of armed men for more than two centuries. Its location on the bluffs above the lake commanded the entrance to the harbor, and the fighting men, both among the original red men and more recent occupants, looked upon it as the point of advantage, and no other portion of the State has been the scene of so many battles and sieges as the garrison grounds on which the Home is built."

On February 26, 1886, the institution, having been repaired

and furnished, was open for inmates. Eight veterans presented themselves and were admitted. The commission appointed under the act were: Gov. Robert E. Pattison, Hon. William Livsey, Hon. J. B. Niles, Hon. W. F. Aull, Col. T. I. Stewart, Hon. C. R. Geutner, Gen. J. A. Beaver, Col. R. B. Beath, Hon. I. B. Brown, Col. J. M. Vanderslice, and Gen. L. Wagner.

The citizens of Erie being anxious to secure the Home, purchased a piece of land and promised in the matter of streets and sidewalks to render aid. The building originally was three stories high, with basements, the main building 56 x 153 feet, with a wing westward 40 x 130, and a shorter building two stories high to be used as a chapel. Extensions have been made in different directions and the capacity will be for 650 inmates when completed. There are 141 rooms now under the roof and a dining-room 44 x 100 feet, seating 500 people at table.

The infirmary is a two-story building, with all the latest appliances for the care of twenty-eight patients at one time. A corridor 180 feet long connects this with the main building, and serves for a conservatory in winter, being filled with rare plants, and is an agreeable resort for invalids at all times. Maj. William Webster Tyson is the commander of the Soldiers and Sailors' Home. He was born at Baltimore, Md., August 1, 1834, and by his judicious management it is an honor to the city and the State. It is not in any way connected with politics, but its tone is "clean, morally, bodily, and financially." Religious services are held in the chapel on Sundays; Thursday evening a prayer meeting and lecture is conducted by the chaplain. "Contemplating all these comforts of our brave defenders, one cannot help but say: God bless the Commonwealth."

Soldiers' Home Trustees 1893. Gov. Pattison, President; Gen. Robert B. Heath, Vice-President; Gen. Louis Wagner, Treasurer; Thomas J. Stewart, Secretary; Building Committee, Wagner, Brown, Morrison, and Nesbitt; Pension Committee, Gobin, Wagner and Lull; Legislation, Gobin, Nesbitt and Lull.

The amount now paid by the State has been reduced to $40,000 per annum, owing to the fact that a very liberal contribution is made each year by the national government. There are at the present time 330 inmates at the Home, 116 of whom are hospital cases. The population of the institution has been reduced 150 on account of the receipt of pensions from the national government.

SECTION III.

The Johnson Island Plot—U. S. Steamer Michigan—Revenue Cutters—Railroads—Rapid Transit—Liberty Bells—Erie, some Towns and Townships—Grapes—Postoffices—Census—City Hall—Government Building—Petroleum—Gas—The Weather—Parks—Massassauga—Height of Lakes.

THE JOHNSON ISLAND PLOT.

DURING the war for the Union an attempt was made at Sandusky to capture the United States Steamer *Michigan* by the Confederates, and release the prisoners at Johnson's Island. The *Philadelphia Press* of February, 1882, published a breezy story continued in three numbers, entitled "Pirate Cole's Conspiracy," which was founded on facts. A Confederate officer in the guise of a wealthy oil man from Philadelphia, with his lady, made a six weeks' stay at the hotel in Sandusky; he was apparently loyal to the government, and there was nothing tangible to justify suspicion. He dined and wined the junior officers, probably when off duty, for Capt. Carter never had met him personally until he made him his prisoner. Cole gave a supper as a decoy at the hotel and the same day at 12 o'clock Capt. Carter received a telegram from Detroit saying, "Thirty suspicious looking men have embarked on the steamer *Philo Parsons* to engage on a certain railroad in Ohio; look out for them." At the same time a dispatch was received from the Secretary of the Navy, repeating the same received from Detroit and saying: "We have reason to think your crew have been tampered with." Capt. Carter's prompt answer was, "Let them come; I am ready." Those dispatches and certain suspicious circumstances connected with a champagne supper to be given by Cole that night at the hotel, caused Capt. Carter to order Ensign Hunter to fully man and equip his boat, go to Sandusky, arrest Mr. Cole and bring him on board ship. On meeting Mr. Cole at the hotel the first salutation was, "You have come to the supper" (for it was then 4 o'clock p. m.). Mr. Hunter answered: "No, I cannot come, unless you go off to the ship and ask the captain, for I am an officer of the day, and we shall just have time before dark." Mr. Cole instantly caught at the bait, going with the officer to his room to get some money, where some of the drugged wine was politely refused by him under the protest of having a headache. An affectionate leave was taken of his wife, they embarked on the return trip, and a three mile row was probably never more vigorously accomplished. When Mr. Cole was landed on the quarter deck he turned to the officer and said: "You must introduce me; I do not know the captain." When the orderly opened the cabin door and Capt. Carter met the Confederate Cole with, "I arrest you in the name of the government," he dropped into a chair and then divulged the plot. At 9 o'clock he was to fire a photograph building as a signal for the *Philo Parsons* and her Confederate crew to take the *Michigan*, release the prisoners on Johnson's Island and make good their escape with all on board the *Michigan*.

In a letter written by Cole after his capture he says: "But for the vigilance and timely arrival of Capt. Carter, who had been ordered to Washington on official business, our plot would doubtless have succeeded."

In this connection I would add that letters were received by Com. Carter from ex-Governor Cox, of Ohio, and Gen. Dix commending the late Commodore for his loyalty on all occasions, his remark being, "In early manhood my allegiance was given to my country, not my State, and to it I earnestly adhere." Mr. Whitman's history of Erie (1884) in substance says: During a portion of the season the United States Steamer *Michigan*, which had been fully manned again, was guarding Johnson's Island, in the upper part of the lake, where about 2,000 rebel prisoners were confined, when rumor accused of a design to escape. In November there were reports of a proposed rebel invasion from Canada, Erie being named as the landing place. This was the most startling news, in a local sense, that had arisen out of the war, and citizens were greatly agitated. While the excitement was at its height, 600 troops arrived from Pittsburg with a battery, under the command of Maj.-Gen. Brooks. The latter directed intrenchments to be thrown up on the Block House Bluff, and called upon the citizens to lend him their assistance. Something like one thousand obeyed his summons, with picks and shovels, on the first day, but the workers dwindled woefully in number on the second day. The rumor, which was absurd from the start, unless explained by the above story, soon proved to be false, the work was abandoned, and the troops left for the South in a few days, with the exception of the battery.

The successive commanders of the United States Steamer *Michigan* were William Inman, Stephen Champlin, Oscar Bullus, — Biglow, — McBlair, — Nicholas, Joseph Lanman, John C. Carter, Francis A. Roe, A. Breyson, James E. Jouett, George Brown, James Gillis, — Wright, Charles Cushman, G. W. Hayward, Albert Kautz. The officers in 1892 are: Captain, Geo. E. Wingate; Lieutenant Commander, F. M. Symonds; Lieutenants, G. R. Clark, G. H. Stafford; Ensign, V. O. Chase; Past Assistant Engineer, C. F. Nagle; Surgeon, L. B. Baldwin; Past Assistant Paymaster, J. H. Chapman.

THE UNITED STATES STEAMER MICHIGAN.

Some newspaper extracts will describe the experiences of the *Michigan* the last two years.

Boilers Condemned—(March 21, 1892.) That the United States Steamer *Michigan* may never be allowed to take another cruise from this port is somewhat surprising, even as a possibility. It is learned that an inspection by line officers some time ago resulted in a report that the vessel was O. K. but that a recent commission has condemned the boilers in a report to the department and that as a result of their inspection, action by the authorities at Washington will utimately be an order to put the vessel permanently out of commission.

There is added color of probability given to unofficial statements by reason of a public desire that the great lakes should have a more modern vessel of war to display in the naval demonstration at the dedicatory exercises inaugurating the World's Fair. Under existing treaty arrangements the *Michigan* is the only war vessel allowed in these waters. If she were out of the way it is thought that a substitute or substitutes might be available in time for exhibition, as well as usefulness thereafter. Of course a report from the department alone will determine the reliability of rumors.

On the other hand it may be stated that the last outside scraping of the *Michigan* in dry dock revealed no weakness, and the Swedish wrought iron of which the hull is made appeared to be good for years to come in fresh water, and her last cruise down the lakes, although a rough one, did not bring out any visible rottenness of material.

The Michigan in Port.—(April, 1893.) The United States Steamer *Michigan*, which had wintered in Buffalo for the purpose of undergoing necessary repairs, and which has been expected here for several days, steamed into the harbor yesterday afternoon, resplendent in a covering of dazzling white with gold trimmings, to be in conformity with the rest of the "white squadron." The news of the old "man-of-war's" arrival soon spread about the city, and quite a number of people visited the docks despite the disagreeable weather, to gaze upon the "iron steamship," as she was formerly called here.

The *Michigan* is under orders from the Secretary of the Navy to proceed to Chicago, where she will remain during the World's Fair, and will probably stay but a day or two in Erie harbor. The vessel is at present officered as follows:

Lieutenant Commander R. M. Berry, commanding; Lieutenant C. P. Rees, Executive Officer and Navigator; Lieutenant J. M. Helm; Ensign, V. O. Chase; Chief Engineer, J. L. D. Borthwick; Surgeon, L. D. Baldwin; Past Assistant Paymaster, James H. Chapman.

The press and people of Erie extend a hearty welcome to the *Michigan* and her gallant officers and crew, and look forward with pleasure to the time when the steamer will return here "for good."

Return of the Michigan.—Wednesday morning, November 22, 1893, dawned dark, drizzly, and dreary. Storm signals were fluttering in a northwest breeze from the top of the government building and pedestrians hurried along the streets with their great coats buttoned to the chin and collars upturned to their ears. Up to 11 o'clock the rain continued to come down, not in the stereotyped buckets full, but in a sort of fine Italian hand manner that had a tendency every once in a while to become congealed and take the form of snow. It was a hard outlook for enthusiasm and no mistake. To make matters worse a rumor was in circulation that Mayor Scott was confined to his residence on account of illness and would not be able to participate in the proposed reception to the Steamer *Michigan*.

It had been authoritatively announced that the celebrated boat would arrive outside the harbor and be ready to receive its escort at precisely 2 o'clock at the harbor entrance. The escort was to consist of all the available flotilla in the harbor, preceded by the tugs *Scott* and *Erie*, which boats were to contain all the city officials and committee on reception. Then the batteries, one located at the Soldiers' Home and the other at Lake View Park, were to boom out a 21-gun salute each, and a whole lot of other pleasing episodes were to take place.

Old man Neptune, however, disarranged all this, for at 11:30 the good ship steamed into the harbor and cast anchor a little way out from the public dock. Her arrival was announced to the astonished citizens by the wild tooting of whistles. As soon as it was known that the *Michigan* had surely arrived and cast anchor, a large crowd rushed for the docks to see her.

It was the intention of the commander of the man-of-war to remain outside the peninsula until 2 o'clock to await the reception committee, but the wind was so high that it was necessary to enter the harbor and cast anchor.

From the time the vessel arrived until 2 o'clock a steady stream of people had been marching down State Street, so that when the band and reception committee reached the dock they found several thousand there to assist in extending greeting to the *Michigan's* crew.

Arriving at the dock the committee, accompanied by Kohler's Band, boarded the tug *W. L. Scott* and were conveyed to the *Michigan*. The water was very rough and the passengers were nicely sprinkled by large waves that dashed over the craft. The committee was taken aboard the *Michigan* from the tug by one of the small launches belonging to the old war vessel. They were cordially received by Capt. Berry and other officers of the ship. The band played a couple of selections and was returned to the dock by the *Scott*. It was altogether too rough for all on board the tug to reach the *Michigan*.

After the committee, consisting of Mr. Benjamin Whitman, Capt. John Fleeharty, City Treasurer Hanley, Mr. N. Leuschen and J. J. O'Brien, had been received, Mr. Whitman addressed Capt. Berry and his men as follows:

Mr. Whitman's Address.—"Capt. Berry: In the absence of the Mayor, whom illness has prevented from being here, I extend to you, and through you to your officers and crew, on behalf of our citizens and public authorities, a heartfelt welcome to our home. I use the word "home" because, although this may not be the actual place of residence of some of you, it is the home of your ship—the place of its birth, its station for more than half a century, and, we sincerely hope, its home port during the remaining years of its life. None of you may know or can fully appreciate the interest with which our people have followed the *Michigan* during the many months in which she has been gone from Erie Harbor. To the people of Erie she is more than a ship—more than a mere structure of wood and iron. She is very much like a member of our family, whose return we hail as we would that of a long-lost son or daughter. Welcome, then, sir—a thrice hearty welcome. Welcome to your gallant officers and crew, and a special welcome to the staunch old craft that has weathered the wind and waves of fifty years of difficult lake navigation. We trust that your return will be as agreeable to all of you as it is to our citizens, and that every one of you may be with us as long as the rules of the Navy Department will permit. May your stay with us be one round of pleasure, and may the Erie girls continue to find as warm a place in the hearts of your bachelor officers as they have done in the past."[1]

To this address of welcome Capt. Berry responded very

[1] It is said of the officers of the *Michigan* nearly twenty have married in Erie.

happily, expressing the appreciation of the commander and officers and men of the vessel of the kind feeling shown by the citizens of Erie upon their arrival. His response was brief and to the point.

Remarks were also made by City Treasurer Hanley and Mr. O'Brien. These gentlemen coincided with all that Mr. Whitman had said. They joined in the welcome to the officers and crew and said that it afforded the people of Erie great pleasure to have the boat return to Erie.

Lieut. Reese, of the *Michigan*, made a few remarks. He said that Capt. Berry voiced the sentiments of the naval officers in his kind reference to Erie and its people.

Had the weather been favorable the demonstration would have been a grand success. Much credit is due Capt. Fleeharty for his ceaseless effort in arranging the details for the reception.

The first revenue cutter was the *Benjamin Rush*, of thirty tons, built at Erie by Capt. John Richards about 1827, and first commanded by Capt. Gilbert Knapp, who was succeeded by Capt. Daniel Dobbins. The second was the *Erie*, of sixty-two tons, built at Erie in 1832-33. The *Erie* was succeeded in 1846 by the iron steamer *Dallas*. This vessel was removed to the Atlantic coast by way of the Welland Canal and the St. Lawrence River in 1848. In 1857 the Treasury Department built six small revenue cutters, being one for each lake. At the outbreak of the Civil War these vessels were removed to the Atlantic coast under the direction of Capt. Douglass Ottinger of the revenue service, by way of Welland Canal and River St. Lawrence. In 1864 the *Perry* was built on Niagara River and was equipped with Capt. Whittaker's sidewheel propellers, which with the steamer *Baltic* are the only propellers of the class ever used. She was remarkably fast, having developed on her trial trip a speed of over nineteen knots an hour for more than two hours. This vessel was sold, the present cutter *Perry* succeeding her.

In the spring of 1893 the revenue cutters *Grant* and *Perry* were ordered to Puget Sound to suppress opium smuggling. The *Perry* is esteemed one of the handsomest and staunchest of the vessels in the revenue marine service. Capt. A. A. Fenger is in command.

The *Perry* is a topsail-schooner-rigged steamer of 282 gross tons. Her principal dimensions are: Length, 165 feet; beam, 25 feet; depth, 11 feet 2 inches; draught 9 feet 10 inches. She is a single-screw steamer mounting two three-inch breechloading rifles. The complement of the *Perry* is seven officers and thirty-one men. Her speed is about twelve knots an hour.

Speaking of the removal Revenue Collector Glazier said that in his opinion a mistake was being made. Instead of moving the *Perry* from the great lakes, said Mr. Glazier, there is greater need of an additional boat here. The *Perry* has been cruising Lake Erie and Ontario as well and her services have been constantly in demand. The object of the boat on the lake is not merely that of revenue service, but it is supposed to render assistance to vessels in distress, and as is well known there has been much need of this.

RAILROADS.

The announcement of the contemplated change of gauge of the Erie & Northeast Railroad created the utmost indignation with a large majority of the citizens, as they had hoped that Erie might become the terminus of the New York & Erie Railway, and not a mere railway station. The facts stated in Warner's edition of "History of Erie," 1884 (Chicago), are in substance as follows: December 7, 1853, a large number gathered at the depot and tore down the bridges over State and French streets and removed the track across each street east of Sassafras. At Harbor Creek the same day the track was torn up in three places, and on December 28, while the railroad men were relaying the track, a fracus took place in which a pistol was fired by a train conductor and two citizens were slightly wounded. The excitement that ensued was the most intense ever known in the county. (The railroad question obliterated party lines to a great extent, and in each of the years 1854, 1855, and 1858, for the first time in a long period, one of the two legislative representatives elected from the county was a Democrat.) An appeal was made to the courts and the State and United States officials interposed. This state of affairs continued for two years, and the two months in which passengers were transferred by stages and wagons between Harbor Creek and Erie, at an inclement season, and unprepared, were trying indeed. April 16, 1856, the anti-railroad party, being embittered by the court legalizing the new gauge, and the newspaper *Constitution* expressing sympathy, or perhaps it was through some private grievance, a tumultuous crowd burned the office. The court afterwards awarded $3,000 damage for the loss, and the closing scene of the railroad war ended. An officer who had been through the war for the Union pronounced the railroad war, which he had also experienced, the more exciting of the two. A paragraph in the *Erie Gazette* of January 12; 1854, indicates the state of feeling at that date: "Never in the history of our city have we witnessed popular excitement equal to that which now prevails. God grant that it may speedily subside."

Extracts from Railroad Official Documents. — During the time that the track was up, from December 7, 1853 to February 1, 1854, the passengers, baggage, mail, and express were conveyed between Erie and Harbor Creek in wagons and sleighs, at a cost of $17,000 to the railroad company. . . . It was a war in which both parties expended large sums of money, employed the best legal talent of the country, and exhausted the courts and Legislature. At first local in its character, it grew in importance until on one side was arrayed practically the whole people of Pennsylvania, its courts and Legislature, and on the other the citizens of adjoining States, east and west, backed by the urgent demands of the trade and commerce of the country. And yet it was all for the purpose of maintaining what has since proved to be a mere shadow, as the broad treadwheel has quietly solved the problem; and since that a universal uniform gauge prevails.

First Report of the Directors to the Stockholders of the Erie and Northeast Railroad Company.—The Erie & Northeast Railroad is about twenty miles in length, commencing at Erie, Pa., and running to the State line of New York, and is a link in the South Shore Railroad between Buffalo and Cleveland, connecting the Central New York and the New York and Erie roads with the roads running to Cincinnati, St. Louis, Chicago, and other portions of the West. The road was opened for business about one year since, and was the first road completed in Western Pennsylvania. It is straight nearly its entire length, being but forty-seven feet longer than an air line, with no grades exceeding fifteen feet to the mile—runs mostly through material composed of gravel and sand, is well ballasted and now in perfect order.

There have been taken over this road since its opening in January last, 73,476 passengers without any accident or injury.

The receipts from the 10th of January to the 1st of July last were $31,260; the expenditures for repairs and supervision during the same time were $10,007.24; leaving for net earnings the first six months $21,253.65, sufficient to pay the interest on the indebtedness of the company and a dividend of three per cent on the stock which was made and paid in July last.

On the receipts for the first six months, all but about $5,000 was collected before the opening of lake navigation in the spring, at which time the road west of Erie was not completed, and there being no communication between Erie and the West except by stages, all through business was driven on the lake.

The receipts from July 1 to the 1st of January, inst., were $31,119, of which about $16,000 was collected since the 20th of November last, and after the completion of the road west to Cleveland. . . . The stock of the company, all of which has been taken and paid up, is $600,000. The present indebtedness of the company is $131,950, to which it is estimated it will be necessary to add for additional rolling stock, extension of depot buildings, etc., $18,050. Making the whole cost of the road and fixtures complete $750,000.

. . . The net earnings of this road are somewhat lessened, and all the trade and travel passing between us and the seaboard are subjected to a greatly increased expense and most serious inconvenience and delay in consequence of the track of the Buffalo & State Line Railroad Company—which connects this road with the New York & Erie and Central New York line of roads, being different in width from either of the roads mentioned, and different from *all* other roads in the State in which it has been introduced. The Erie & Northeast was the first commenced and the first road completed on the lake shore. It was made a six-foot track in accordance with a contract between this company and the Dunkirk & State Line Company, the latter having been got up by the New York & Erie, interest to be used for the purpose of making a six-foot connection with this road at the State Line, which connection the New York & Erie Company by a written agreement with this company guaranteed should be made. The Buffalo & State Line Company being identified with the Central line of New York roads, the gauges of which are four feet eight and one half inches, complained that our laying the six-foot track only, would be doing injustice to them. This company, therefore, with the consent of the New York & Erie Company agreed to furnish a track for each of the roads mentioned, corresponding to their respective tracks, six feet and four feet eight and one half inches. Thus matters remained for some weeks, when, for reasons best known to themselves, without notice or any consultation with this company, the New York & Erie argued with the Buffalo & State Line companies, the former in violation of their contract with this company, and both regardless of the wrong they were inflicting on the public, to introduce between this road and theirs a four-foot ten inch track—a track different from all the roads with which it connected, and between which it only formed an intermediate link, thus compelling all freight and passengers passing between the East and the West to change cars both at the State Line and at Dunkirk or Buffalo, as the case might be. Whatever inconvenience or expense, therefore, is incurred in consequence of these two changes, is solely attributable to the Buffalo & State Line Company, sanctioned by the New York & Erie Company. Much complaint is justly made on account of the unnecessary obstructions, and none regret their existence more than this company. It was out of the power of this company to prevent them, and is therefore out of its power to remove them—they can only be removed by those who placed them there. It is thought by some of our friends in Buffalo and Cleveland, that Congress, in the exercise of its power to establish post roads, may remove such nuisances. If so, it is but reasonable to suppose that the Buffalo & State Line Company will be compelled to change their *imported* gauge to one of their own State, and thereby remove the obstructions they have made on this important thoroughfare.

This being the first report of the directors to the stockholders, and a desire to place this company in its true position on the question of gauge alluded to, we trust will be considered a sufficient justification for this somewhat lengthy statement. By order of the Board of Directors,

Erie, January 18, 1853. J. C. SPENCER, Sec'y.

As to the Philadelphia & Erie Railroad, fears having been entertained by the stockholders that the enterprise could not be completed in consequence of the war alarm, the road was leased in 1862 to the Pennsylvania Railroad Company for a term of 999 years. Work was vigorously prosecuted by the lessees, and in October, 1864, the first passenger train came through with a large party of excursionists. A magnificent entertainment was given them by the City of Erie at a cost of $3,000, one half being the bill for wines alone.

The first General Superintendent of the road was Joseph D. Potts, 1864; A. L. Tyler, 1865; W. A. Baldwin, 1870; R. Neilson, 1881. The Superintendents of the Western Division have been S. A. Black, 1859; W. A. Baldwin, 1862; J. W. Reynolds, May 1, 1868. The general offices were at Erie until 1874, when they were removed to Williamsport.

Evening Herald, July 7, 1893.

Fastest time on record.—The Fast Mail on the Lake Shore Railroad gave that line an opportunity yesterday to show that in the matter of speed it is able to make as good a record as the best. The train consisted of seven mail cars and a baggage car, drawn by engine No. 568, with Engineer Charles Allen in charge. It left Buffalo 2 hours and 15 minutes late and was brought into Erie, 88 miles, in 1 hour and 48 minutes.

This time is two minutes faster than that of the Exposition Flyer, and the run with such a heavy train makes it remarkable. A stop was made at Dunkirk for water.

November 26, 1893.—The crowd that was at the Union Depot Saturday to get a look at the exhibition American and English railway trains on their way through Erie numbered fully 2,000 people, and they patiently endured the chilly blasts in their long wait for the arrival of the trains. The

Wagner vestibule train, drawn by the fleetest piece of wheeled machinery in the world, the famous "999," steamed into the station at 1:30 P. M., and was at once surrounded by the eager throng, who gazed with admiration upon the magnificent piece of mechanism. The engine was uncoupled and run over to the roundhouse to be oiled up and the tank filled with water for the run to Buffalo. After the engine was detached the crowd availed itself of the courtesy extended by the officials and passed through the vestibuled cars, admiring their magnificent appointments and the comfort they afforded the traveler. Attached to the rear of the train was a flat car upon which was arranged the De Witt Clinton train of an engine and three carriages, not unlike the oldtime stage coach. This train was the same that made the trip from Schenectady to Albany in 1831, and afforded the spectators an illustration of the revolution in railway travel that sixty years has wrought.

At 2 o'clock the English train, drawn by the "Empress-Queen," steamed in on the south side of the depot. It consisted of two English coaches, which the crowd at once declared were not to be compared with the Wagner or Pullman cars for elegance or comfort. The engine was an odd looking affair to the American eye, lacking the familiar "cowcatcher," and having a headlight no larger than those Erieites are accustomed to see displayed upon bicycles. The bell instead of being forward of the cab, is perched midway upon the tank, and the whistle of the "Empress-Queen," sounds more like the toot of the small boy's Christmas horn than the ear-splitting shriek that denotes the approach of the American locomotive. The train was in charge of Mr. C. A. Baratoni, general passenger and freight agent for America of the London & Northwestern Railway, and he afforded the crowd all the opportunity the short stay allowed to inspect the train.

The "999" drew away from the depot first, the English train following a "block" behind. The three vestibule cars attached to the latter train were occupied by a party of Erie gentlemen who availed themselves of the invitation extended by the railway official to ride as far as Ripley, where they were picked up and brought back to Erie by train No. 9.

The *old courthouse bell* was lost for a time after 1854, then was used at the fire engine house, at which place according to one version it became cracked. For many years it was in possession of the antiquarian P. Osborn, Esq., eventually coming into the hands of the Young Men's Christian Association, where it remained until a few days previous to the visit of the Liberty Bell of Independence Hall on its way to the World's Fair at Chicago. April 26, 1893, the city had a half holiday and on that occasion was visited by multitudes at the depot—and the Erie Liberty Bell was hung in the corridor of the City Hall to remain permanently.

For several years previous to the War of 1812 this bell was used in Fort Erie, Canada, where it was rung three times daily —7 A. M., 12 M. and 9 P. M.—as it was after being placed on the old courthouse in this city, where it remained until the building was torn down. It also has another war record which can be verified by many of our citizens. It was used to call the people together during the railroad war, and it only required three taps of this silver-toned relic to bring out hundreds of ablebodied men armed with guns to intimidate the railroad laborers. The bell was rung with more violence than it could stand in that exciting campaign, and became cracked in consequence.

September, 1893. It may be of interest to speak of the new Liberty Bell cast to the order of the Daughters of the American Revolution at the foundry at Troy, N.Y. It attracted general attention at the World's Fair, though not the reverence paid the old Liberty Bell in the Pennsylvania State building.

There are three inscriptions on the bell, one at the top ridge, another in the center, and one at the lower edge.

The upper one reads: "Glory to God in the highest; on earth good will toward men."

The central inscription is: "A new command I give unto you, that ye love one another."

The lower is: "Proclaim liberty throughout the land and unto the inhabitants thereof."

The bell is one of the finest castings ever made. Not a flaw is in the metal. It is composed of a curious compound of precious and base metals. More than $10,000 worth of old gold and silver ornaments, coins and jewelry was contributed by the patriotic members of the order.

An old cent which was worth $100 from its historical association was contributed. The tone is very sweet because of the quality of the casting and the metal. It weighs six and a half tons—13,000 pounds. Although it is one of the large bells of the world, it does not approach in size that of the enormous bell at Moscow, which weighs 25,000 pounds.

The bell is six feet high and eighteen feet in circumference at the mouth. It has a bright lustre of a brassy nature.

The City of Erie has 105 64-100 miles of streets opened and in use. Area of city, 6,916 square miles, and contains 4,426.69 acres. Population per acre, 11.

The electric motor cars run each way on the streets below named, according to the following schedule—subject to the fluctuations of business: On State Street every four minutes; on Peach Street every ten minutes; on Fourth Street every eleven minutes; on Sixth Street every eleven minutes; on Eighth Street, to city limits, every twelve minutes; on Eleventh Street every eleven minutes; on East Eighteenth Street every ten minutes; on West Eighteenth Street every ten minutes; French and East Twenty-sixth cars leave corner of State and Eighteenth streets every ten minutes; the East and West Eighteenth Street cars, as well as the main line cars, run on State Street.

Street Lighting.—The streets and public grounds of the city of Erie are lighted by 496 gas lamps at $21.50 each per annum, $10,664; and 220 electric arc lamps at $120.45 each (1,200 candle power) per annum, $26,499, making a total of $37,103.

Length of all sewers in the city.—Brick, 10.056 miles; cost $244,721.79. Tile, 21.131 miles; cost, $236,799.03. Total, 31.-187 miles; cost, $481,520.82.

Total paved streets in city.—Stone, 6.865 miles; asphalt, 7.981 miles; total, 14.846 miles.

Mayors since 1860—Hon. Sherburn Smith, 1859-1861; Hon. Prescott Metcalf, 1862-64; Hon. F. F. Farrar, 1865; Hon. W. L. Scott, 1866; Hon. Orange Noble, 1867-70; Hon. W. L. Scott, 1871; Hon. Charles M. Reed, 1872-73; Hon. Henry

Rawle, 1874-75; Hon. J. W. Hammond, 1876; Hon. Selden Marvin, 1877; Hon. D. I. Jones, 1878-80; Hon. Joseph McCarter, 1881-82; Hon. P. A. Becker, 1883-84; Hon. F. F. Adams, 1885; Hon. F. A. Mizener, 1886; Hon. J. C. Brady, 1887-88; Hon. C. S. Clarke, 1889-93; Hon. Walter Scott, 1893-96.

Prior to and including the year 1878, the term of office of the Mayor of Erie was one year; from 1879 to 1888 inclusive, two years; 1889, one year; 1890 to date, three years. The salary of the Mayor is $2,000 per year.

President Judges of Court of Common Pleas and Quarter Sessions since 1860. William A. Galbraith, 1876; Frank Gunnison, 1886.

SOME TOWNS AND TOWNSHIPS.

Summit Township is the smallest of the county and the last organized. Its name was given from its containing "the divide" between the waters of Le Bœuf and Walnut creeks, the first flowing into the Gulf of Mexico, via the Ohio and Mississippi; the latter into the Gulf of St. Lawrence, by way of Lake Erie.

Many years ago Col. Norris gathered oil from his quarry and sold it for medicine. This is known as Reynolds's quarry, being the nearest to Erie. A well was drilled for oil, but only yielded an abundance of gas. William Liddel has a smaller quarry.

The First National Bank is erecting a brownstone structure at Northeast. Northeast has now three banks, three newspapers and large manufacturing interests. A new national bank was organized August 1, 1893, with G. W. Blaine as president. The old bank of thirty years ago had the same, with A. W. Blaine, the father of G. W. Blaine, president.

St. Paul's German Evangelical church was organized in 1864, and erected its church building in 1867.

The German church of the Evangelical Association of North America completed their house of worship in 1871.

The Protestant Episcopal mission of the Holy Cross was organized in 1872, and erected a handsome church in 1879.

St. Gregory's Roman Catholic church was erected in 1870. A parsonage adjoins the church, and Father Riordy entered upon the duties at first in connection with the church at Girard.

Edinboro was incorporated in 1840, and included 500 acres of high, gravelly land at the foot of Lake Conneauttee. The third gristmill (the others being at Walnut Creek and Union) in Erie County was erected by William Culbertson in 1801, and he added a sawmill in 1802. The cemetery, which includes three acres, was the gift of William Culbertson, and has been in use seventy years. A Presbyterian church was organized there prior to 1819.

Waterford was the site of an Indian village, traces of which were visible thirty-five years ago.

A Mammoth Dairy Farm is at Belle Valley. It has 75 cows in very comfortable quarters. Twenty-five years ago Mr. H. H. Russell commenced selling milk in Erie with 17 cows. Then there were but two milk wagons in the city, A. Sullivan & Son's, and now Mr. Russell runs two wagons daily, or rather his three sons, N. W., Warner, and W. H. Russell.

A bridge of iron has just been finished to supply the place of one carried away by the flood. It is expected ere long that a new Presbyterian church will supersede the present one built about forty years ago.

Union City.—At a special meeting of councils of Union City, Nov. 17, 1893, a board of health was appointed by the Mayor, and his nominations confirmed by the councils are as follows: Frank P. Hatch, to serve one year; S. M. Hayes, two years; Prof. N. R. Luce, three years; G. Gary Smith, four years, and Dr. L. D. Rockwell, five years. The board at once held a meeting and elected the following officers: Dr. L. D. Rockwell, president; Dr. W. J. Humphrey, secretary and treasurer, and ex-Mayor Jonathan Canfield, health officer. The sanitary laws of the State are to be strictly enforced, and the board is made up of the right kind of material to do it.

Corry is near the east line of the county, and in both Concord and Wayne townships. It was named from Hiram Cory or Corry, in consideration of his liberal dealing at the time of the purchase of his farm of fifty acres by Mr. Hill, superintendent of the railroad. It had been selected as a site by W. H. L. Smith, and was laid out in town lots by Eugene Wright, and is at the junction of the Philadelphia & Erie, the New York, Pennsylvania & Ohio, and the Oil Creek and the Crosscut railroads, from Titusville to Brocton, now called the Buffalo, Pittsburg & Western. Corry was organized as a borough in 1863, became a city in 1866, and in 1870 the population was 6,809; in 1880 it was but 5,277. Until the panic of 1873 it was considered by some as bidding fair to rival Erie in the northwest. Samuel Downer, a wealthy oil refiner of Boston, selected Corry for refineries, as obviating the necessity of transporting crude oil to a distance. Thousands flocked to this as to the whole oil region, real estate increased rapidly in value, and at this time a part of Wayne township was included, tripling its size. It has few equals and no superior as an inland city. Having three important railroads passing through, and being in direct communication with bituminous and anthracite coal regions, as well as oil, it has rare facilities for manufacturing. Freight trains are almost constantly passing, and at times more than twenty passenger trains arrive daily. The Downer Oil Works originated the city in one sense, and Clark & Warren are thus spoken of in the *Oil, Paint and Drug Reporter:* " One of the best appointed oil refineries in the United States and of their painstaking and improved methods of manufacturing superior oils. The firm holds many patents on the construction of stills, etc." Other prominent manufactories are of woodenware, iron works, novelty, radiator, and many others.

Corry has three fine brick school structures and two smaller ones; three newspapes, two public halls, and three banks. Its churches are twelve in number, and it has an unusual number of secret societies. The State fish hatchery is about one mile west, in Wayne township, having nine acres, and fine cool springs which supply all the water requisite. Streams in all parts of the State to which they are adapted are supplied with fish. Mr. Seth Weeks, who is particularly qualified, has had charge from the commencement. In the words of an official, "It is the finest in the State. It has more ponds, better water, covers more ground, and does more business than any other in Pennsylvania. They hatch trout, brook trout, and other kinds of fish."

The board of directors of Young Men's Christian Association of Corry present the following statement for three months ending September 30, 1893 : Total attendance at the rooms 1,089 ; total attendance at meetings only 453 ; average daily attendance 12 ; total attendance at gospel meetings 375 ; the membership now numbers 225.

Benevolent Societies.—June 3, 1893, a Children's Aid Society was formed in Corry, the object being to provide homes for children who may have no friends able to take care of them. The annual meeting of the State society is held in Pittsburg, where methods of work are discussed. The aim is to have but one society in each county. Mrs R. G. Lindsey was elected president and Miss B. King secretary. A Children's Temperance Society was also organized in the Congregational church, Rev. Mr. and Mrs. Barnett, officers.

GRAPES.

When the French were at Franklin, Venango County, one hundred and fifty years ago, they introduced delicious grapes, and the vines were flourishing and bearing fruit not very long ago.[1] Wild grapes abounded in the wilds and after frost they were quite palatable. Sweet water and Malagas were found in a few gardens sixty years ago. About 1830 the Isabella and Catawba were cultivated to some extent, but the season was usually found too short for them to ripen well. From Kelly's Island, near Sandusky, the choicest Catawbas reached the market, and were disposed of at large prices. About twenty-five years ago grapes were introduced suited to our region— the Concord, Delaware, Salem, and Niagara. We have found that the Pennsylvania grape belt in some places is forty miles wide ; the length is said to extend from Harbor Creek, six miles east of Erie, to Silver Creek, New York. We may quote from Phillip D. Armour, of Chicago, who could not be said to have local prejudice. A present of a basket of mixed grapes from Mr. J. H. Phillips, of Maple Grove Vineyard, was sent him, which resulted in his ordering fifty baskets more, "and that

---

[1] Eight hundred bunches of grapes, off the famous vine at Hampton Court Palace, England, have been sent to Windsor, Osborne, and Balmoral. There were in all 1,200 bunches as the growth of the present year. The fruit is, however, what would be called meagre in size, this being due to the depleted strength of the parent stem, which is no less than 125 years old.

they were the finest he had ever eaten." We cannot do better than give some reliable newspaper items which have appeared.

The Chautauqua and Northeast Grape Union sent a car of grapes to Seattle, Washington. The freight amounted to $754.40. During the grape season one car is to be sent weekly.

"No one now doubts that the Chautauqua and Northeast Grape Union is a success in the largest sense of the word, because it has proved the claims made for it by its projectors early in the history of the movement. The union has shipped over 2,000 cars of grapes and has 600 or 700 yet to ship as the fruit is demanded. Not a basket has been sold for less than eighteen cents, and the fruit has been sold on the cars and not consigned.

"It is not generally known that the fruit commission men in the large cities attempted to combine to force down prices, and were aided by a few enemies among the grape growers, but the movement was abortive and failed of effect. At the present time all the growers along the grape belt recognize the benefits that have come to them through organization.

"The total amount of cash that has come into the Chautauqua and Northeast grape belt from the sale of grapes this season will not fall short of one and a half millions of dollars. In consequence of the great profit this year on vineyards the value of grape lands has gone up appreciably, and there is a strong demand for them as an investment. Probably no other form of producing property in Chautauqua County has yielded anything like the rich returns that have been received by the owners of vineyards on the lake shore.

"A private letter from a London (England) commission house to its representative in Ripley states that its customers say the grapes are bitter at the core. Growers here think that all that is indicated by this complaint is that the English buyers chew the pulp and seeds.

"Northeast, Nov. 10, 1893.—The secretary of the Chautauqua and Northeast Grape Union has received a telegram from Great Britian of great interest to all along the Chautauqua grape belt. The *Dispatch* has already noticed the fact that two car loads of grapes were sent to England as an experiment or trial trip across the Atlantic. The Liverpool car sold for 39 cents per basket and the London car from 45 to 57 cents. The freight from here there was about 15 cents a basket, nearly 10 cents less than it cost to Seattle, Washington. It goes without saying that the success of the Liverpool and London experiment is of much importance to the grape growers along the lake shore. The broad new field for marketing grapes must certainly have a tendency to enhance the future price in the Chautauqua belt.

"The sale in Europe will net some 6 or 7 cents more per basket than the fruit marketed this season in America.

"More than a quarter of a century has gone by without a single failure of the grape crop in Northeast, and now there is a good showing for a fine yield of fruit this coming fall.

"Never were real estate transfers so lively here as during the past winter and spring. Never was there so much building and rebuilding and beautifying of private residences as at present."

Another correspondent advises caution as follows: "All along the lake shore and especially in this locality thousands of acres of good bearing apple orchards are being torn out to make room for vineyards. Peach, pear, and plum orchards are going the same way, and it is an undeniable fact that all fruit excepting grapes will be at a premium the coming fall. A prominent Fredonia shipper of small fruits said yesterday:

"Everything is giving away to grapes, and unless we can get into the English markets and get there to stay, the grape growers of this section will be sadly disappointed. Last year the grape union had to hustle to secure a market for the product at eighteen cents per basket. This season we will have nearly 2,000 acres more of bearing vines, and next year over 2,000 acres; this spring nearly 2,000 acres of new vines will be set out, and fully as much a year hence. The grape industry is being overdone, and those who are tearing out good bearing orchards to make room for vineyards will see their mistake in a year. The grower will receive about fifteen cents per basket for his product the coming fall, and should the price drop one cent below this figure it will certainly mean disaster and ruin to this entire section of country.

"The business men in different towns in the grape belt are becoming alarmed, and are awake to the necessity of pushing the grape crop into the English market. To this end they now propose to establish a fund, taking the money from their own pockets, to be used exclusively for the purpose of securing the English market. They are aware that should the grape industry go down it would not only ruin the growers and the business men, but the property of this entire section, now considered so valuable, would be a drug upon the market. All classes of people are watching just now with deep interest the movement of the grape union in this important matter."

"Northeast, January 4, 1893.—A conference was held here yesterday afternoon between the grape growers of this section and Mr. J. C. Walker, chairman of the Pennsylvania World's Fair Horticulture, Viticulture and Floriculture Committee, and Mr. Benj. Whitman, member of the Pennsylvania World's Fair Executive Board.

"Mr. Walker said the object of the meeting was to give an opportunity to make a display of grapes and wines at the World's Fair, and that there is no reason why Pennsylvania should not be at the top at the great Chicago Exposition. Erie County is doubtless the banner county of the State, and although New York is older in her grape industry and has a larger area, it is believed by good judges that the territory here is equal if not superior to any in the grape belt.

"He said the State is willing to meet the grape men half way in whatever is necessary to make a creditable display, and the result of the conference showed that the grape men are ready to do their part. Mr. Whitman made a number of practical suggestions and was very patriotic to Erie County and Pennsylvania. Both gentleman, in fact, Walker and Whitman, took a very lively interest in planning for a fine display of the products of the vine of Pennsylvania.

"By a unanimous vote the following was adopted: *Resolved*, That the grape growers of Erie County will join with the board of World's Fair Commission of Pennsylvania in making an exhibit of grape culture and grape products such as will be creditable to the State and an object of interest to the World's Fair.

"*Resolved*, That the president of the meeting be authorized to appoint a committee of five to act in co-operation with the committee of viticulture of the board of World's Fair Commission of Pennsylvania for the purpose of carrying out the objects of the above resolution."

"The president, Mr. James H. Phillips, appointed from Northeast, Robert Dill, Charles H. Mottier, John B. Scouller, John A. Stetson; Harbor Creek, Charles Leet. It was decided to ask for one thousand (1,000) square feet of space at the Chicago Exposition.

"Mr. Foll stated that the South Shore Winery would have a display of wines at Chicago."

Northeast, October 5, 1893.—The Grape City Packing Company is putting up 10,000 baskets a day. There are two forces, each working ten hours. The proprietor, Mr. Morse, has 12,000 tons yet to pick, pack, and ship. There was no time last season when the grapes came into the different depots as fast as they have for the past few days, but the quality is fine, and there is a ready market.

The idea has been conveyed that the yield for this season is the greatest in the history of the grape industry, but this is a mistake. The crop in almost every vineyard will be found less than the estimate of three months ago. Old vineyards are not yielding on an average much more than three fourths what they did last year, owing to hail and wind in the different parts of the belt. The season will probably close two or three weeks earlier. The fruit is exceptionally fine, the clusters large and compact, with a beautiful bloom. At Dunkirk the grape crop this year is unusually large, the fruit large and sweet, and the weather favorable. Grapes are being put out at the rate of fifty or sixty car loads a day. The Ohio crop has just gone out of the market, and for that reason good prices are expected in this section.

At the close of the season of 1893 we find that more than a million of baskets of grapes were shipped at Northeast— which does not include those marketed in wagons. Some of.

the vineyards have yielded so bountifully that the fruit has brought over a hundred dollars an acre.

Messrs. Ryckman, Fuller & Fay, of Brocton, N. Y., gave the following interesting statistics regarding the shipments by the Grape Union last season, and including transient shipments as far as it has been possible to obtain the figures:

	UNION.	OTHER SHIPMENTS.	TOTAL.
Northeast	225	167	392
Ripley	209	204	413
Westfield	308	137½	445½
Portland	512	479	991
Pomfret	326	172¼	498¼
Dunkirk		70¼	70¼
Sheridan	74	16	90
Hanover	183	11	194
Totals	1837	1257	3094

The Northeast report includes Harborcreek, Ripley, Northville, State Line, and Forsyth; Westfield, West Portland, Portland, Pomfret, Brocton, Concord, Prospect; Pomfret, Fredonia, Laona, Van Buren, and a part of Dunkirk; Hanover, Silver Creek, Forestville, and Perrysburg.

In filling small orders, 3,000 baskets were taken for a carload.

The Grape City Packing Company will erect a house two hundred feet long, also a new depot will be built by the Nickel Plate Railroad Company on the McNeil property, which was recently purchased for $5,000, Mr. C. H. Morse negotiating the sale.

In Washington, according to the *Northeast Sun*, they talk of putting a strong internal revenue tax on wine made from domestic grapes. This will interest this section. California is reported to be arranging to oppose it. The grape unions here and in the neighboring States should confer regarding it.

POSTOFFICES.

Erie is a postoffice of the first-class, having the salary $3,200. Corry is of the second class, with salary $2,300. Union City is of the third class, with the salary $1,700. Edinboro is also third class, with salary of $1,200, and Northeast has a salary of $1,700.

Erie, Corry, Northeast, and Union City are known as "Presidential offices," the incumbents being appointed by the President, and confirmed by the Senate, the others are appointed by the Postmaster General.

HISTORY OF ERIE COUNTY. 365

The money order offices are: Albion, Corry, East Springfield, Edinboro, Erie, Fairview, Girard, Lundy's Lane, Mill Village, Northeast, Union City, Waterford, Wattsburg, West Springfield. Erie is the only letter carrier office.

POSTOFFICES IN ERIE COUNTY.

Albion.	Hammett.	Northeast.
Arbuckle.	Harbor Creek.	North Springfield.
Avonia.	Hatch Hollow.	Northville.
Bascobel.	Hornby.	Ovid.
Belle Valley.	Itley.	Pennside.
Cherry Hill.	Juva.	Philipsville.
Clipper.	Katan.	Platea.
Corea.	Kearsarge.	Pont.
Corry.	Keepville.	Sampsonville.
Delhil.	Lake Pleasant.	Sterrettania.
East Greene.	Lavery.	Swanville.
East Springfield.	Le Bœuf.	Tracy.
Edinboro.	Little Elk.	Union City.
Elgin.	Lovells Station.	Waterford.
Elk Creek.	Lowville.	Wattsburg.
Erie.	Lundy's Lane.	Wesleyville.
Fairview.	McKean.	West Greene.
Ferdinand.	McLane.	West Mill Creek.
Frances.	McLallen Corners.	West Springfield.
Franklin Corners.	Miles Grove.	Wheelock.
Girard.	Mill Village.	Washby.
Godard.	Moorheadville.	
Greenfield.	Mystic.	

CENSUS OF ERIE COUNTY, 1890, BY MINOR CIVIL DIVISIONS.

The cities, wards, boroughs, townships and villages, as shown by the census, compared with that of 1880: (From Census Buletin No. 105.)

	1890.	1880.		1890.	1880.
Albion borough	366	433	cluding Miles Grove Village	2,280	2,338
Amity township	912	1,033	Miles Grove village	570	
Concord township	991	1,171	Greene township	1,511	1,531
Conneaut township	1,386	1,546	Greenfield township	1,432	1,020
Corry City	5,677	5,277	Harborcreek township	1,660	1,781
Ward 1st 957			Le Bœuf township	1,215	1,420
Ward 2d, 1,357			Lockport borough	240	345
Ward 3d, 1,737.			McKean township	1,330	1,394
Ward 4th, 1,626.			Middleboro borough	195	210
Edinboro borough	1,107	876	Millcreek township	3,279	3,279
Elgin borough	169	154	Millvillage borough	320	388
Elkcreek township	1,325	1,564	Northeast borough	1,538	1,396
Erie City	40,634	27,737	Northeast township	2,124	2,152
Ward 1st, 6,492.			Springfield township	1,642	1,792
Ward 2d, 9,985.			Summit township	903	1,047
Ward 3d, 7,318.			Union City borough	2,261	2,171
Ward 4th, 7,292.			Union township	1,366	1,377
Ward 5th, 4,360.			Venango township	1,351	1,445
Ward 6th, 5,187.			Washington township	1,790	1,880
Fairview borough	305	425	Waterford borough	838	784
Fairview township	1,295	1,482	Waterford township	1,537	1,822
Franklin township	963	1,020	Wattsburg borough	382	389
Girard borough	626	703	Wayne township	1,124	1,306
Girard township, in-					
Totals				86,074	74,688

It will be seen that outside of Erie City the only minor civil divisions that have gained population are Corry, Northeast borough, Edinboro, Elgin, Union City, and Waterford. Millcreek township shows no change; all of the remaining divisions outside of the city show a loss.

The City Hall is located on the southwest corner of Peach Street and the West Park. It is a substantial and elegant edifice, and not surpassed by any other municipal building in Western Pennsylvania. The hall is 124 feet on Peach Street, 64 on the Park, 88 from the basement to the ridge of the roof, and 156 from the foundation to the top of the main tower. The basement is occupied by the police department, City Engineer, Street Supervisor, and Health Officer. There are sixteen cells strongly constructed for temporary confinement of prisoners.

The first floor has the offices of the Mayor, City Treasurer, Solicitor, Comptroller, and Water Commissioners. The second floor has council chambers and city clerk's office. The third floor has two halls, one 56 x 56, and the other 32 x 38; also committee rooms and the office of the fire department.

The cornerstone was laid with Masonic ceremony in July, 1884. Mr. D. K. Dean was the architect, and Erie contractors did most of the work. The iron cells were constructed by Cleveland parties, and the massive vault by Diebold & Co., Canton, Ohio. The brown stone trimmings (for it is built of brick) are of superior quality, from Twinsburg, Ohio. The foundation and entrance are of Medina stone. The heavy plate glass was from a Pittsburg manufactory. The joiner's work is of hard wood, the floors of marble, and the cells have boiler iron sides, and the floors are of solid stone. The best of ventilation is secured. Bath rooms, drinking fountains, and gas jets abound.

The entire cost of the building will be about $200,000. In the cornerstone were deposited the city ordinances, newspapers, a photograph of the edifice, this History of Erie County—but a copy of the Bible was not mentioned, though we trust its principles were included. Hon. William A. Galbraith, being introduced by Maj. P. A. Becker, made a fine oration.

The Government Building. — This the most elegant public building in the city, is on the southeast corner of State Street and the Park, which was purchased at a cost of $36,000. In 1882 an act was passed appropriating $150,000 for a new government building in Erie, which was afterwards increased to a limit of $250,000. Ground was broken for the foundation in April, 1885. The basement is of Maine granite, and the superstructure is of Amherst, Ohio, sandstone. The basement stone work was done by an Erie contractor, Mr. Henry Shenk ; and the superstructure by Messrs. Straub & Schmidt, of Buffalo. The roof is of tinned copper, and the plumbing was done and steam heating apparatus put in by Mr. J. W. Butler. Mr. Jacob Bootz served as superintendent. The basement is used for heating and storage—the entire first floor for postoffice purposes, with main entrances on State Street and the Park.

The offices of Collector of Customs, Internal Revenue Collector, United States District Attorney, United States Commissioners, etc., are on the second floor. The third floor has two court rooms with judge and jury rooms, and the fourth is occupied by the United States Signal Service. A large clock in the tower on the corner was purchased by the citizens.

The entire structure is absolutely fireproof, and the vaults provided for the postal service are burglar proof. Broad, easy iron stairways lead to the different stories, with the walls wainscoted with highly polished American marble. The whole building is beautifully finished and furnished, without exceeding the appropriation. Its dimensions are 114 feet on the Park, and 72 on State Street. The postoffice has 723 lock boxes.

In 1887 a sad accident occurred, resulting in the untimely death of two of the workmen, Andrew Guenther and Mark Shannon, who fell from a lofty height and were instantly killed.

"It will not be long before an elevator will be in full operation at the government building, and people having business with the signal officers will no longer have to climb up four flights of stairs for that purpose. The elevator, of the hydraulic passenger variety, is now being built by Eaton & Prince, of

Chicago. A representative of the firm took the necessary measurements yesterday. The elevator will cost $6,800, and will be run by steam, which will keep the building uncomfortably hot during the summer season. Those best able to judge are of the opinion that a dynamo should have been put in and electricity used as a motive power."

GAS COMPANIES.

The officers of the Pennsylvania Gas Company are C. N. Payne, President; J. P. Jefferson, Vice-President. General office at Warren, Pa. Offices at Jamestown, N. Y., Erie, Pa., Corry, Pa., and Clarendon, Pa.

Main line from the wells to Erie 82 miles; low pressure lines in the city 38 miles; service lines in the city 26 miles; gas turned into low pressure lines Thanksgiving 1886. First application for natural gas in Erie made by Mr. Frank E. Woods; first consumer Dr. H. A. Spencer. Regulation meters were introduced in 1889. Number of consumers, about 4,000.

The Pennsylvania Gas Company furnishes fuel in Erie for 9,000 fires. The gas is piped from the Ludlow field, near Kane, and on the main line there is a pressure of 125 pounds. New wells are constantly being bored to keep up the supply.

A letter, "Erie's big card," in the *Gazette* of 1870, alludes to our advantages over Pittsburg as a location for manufactories. Some newspaper clippings on the subject are as follows:

"At that city, coal is convenient and cheap, but at the best it is a never-ceasing item of expense, and every year the supply will become more scarce and costly. Here our fuel lies right underneath our feet, is brought to surface at a cost that bears no comparison to that of opening a coal mine, and when once reached the expense ceases. In respect to shipping facilities Pittsburg has no better railroad conveniences than Erie, while we have the great lake in addition, where the 'Smoky City' has nothing but an uncertain river."

A company of Pittsburg capitalists have leased several hundred acres near the location of the old Bootes well on French Creek, and will put down a well immediately. Mr. John M. Arters, of Pittsburg, was in Waterford looking after the company's interest. This is an old field, and the Bootes well that was drilled years ago was a paying gas well, but that was before natural gas was used to any extent, so the territory was not developed.

"A few days ago Janitor Avery, of the courthouse, noticed that all the grass within a radius of four feet in the rear of the yard had been killed. A little investigation proved that natural gas was escaping through the ground in small quantities. Some of the older men at the courthouse then remembered that in 1869, while Gen. Thomas Walker was acting Sheriff of Erie County, a well had been drilled in the jail yard to the depth of 700 feet.

"A small vein of gas was struck, but it was not obtained in paying quantities. A little investigation with a shovel brought to light the end of the pipe which was placed in position nearly twenty-five years ago. A plug through which a half-inch pipe was inserted was placed in the end of the old casing and as a result there is a small flame which is allowed to burn night and day at the end of the pipe."

"Mr. Colt's gas well at the corner of Ash Lane and Sixth Street, is now down 800 feet. The drillers say Mr. Colt has now all the gas he can use in his house, but the drilling will be continued."

"UNION CITY, April 20.—Mr. Rice, of Waterford, who has been drilling a well for oil or gas on Oak Hill, three and a half miles west of this city, has found the latter at a depth of about 800 feet in sufficient quantities to feed the boiler, and to-morrow will make the necessary attachments. The indications for a big well are said to be first-class, the sand resembling that found in the best gas territory. As soon as the boiler connections are made the drill will be again started and will be run night and day until the well is completed."

June, 1893, Mr. Casper Doll, who is building a house at the corner of Cherry and Eighth streets, has struck a very heavy flow of gas for this territory. The drill at 100 feet got a good flow and every ten or fifteen feet found a new vein. At 500 feet, the drill struck a vein of gas, the pressure of which was so heavy that it threw a shower of stones out of the hole. It is the intention to go down to 800 feet as soon as the pressure eases up.

Dr. Francis N. Thorpe says: "One matter has interested me in the History of Erie County: it is the effect of the discovery of oil. It is known that the climate and soil of the lake shore region are both the same as in the oil region. As soon as oil was made profitable, many of the best families in the oil country, selling their farms for much money, moved into the lake shore country, purchasing farms at advanced prices, locating in Erie, Northeast, etc., and there building costly and superior dwellings. The effect was to raise all values in Erie County along the lake; improvements were at once begun, the grape interest received an impetus and schools and churches were improved. Manufactures followed and social changes, incident to an influx of wealth and energy, at once were observable. It is an interesting phase of the country's history."

In 1850-56, while the railroad difficulties were pending in Erie, not far distant in Northwestern Pennsylvania another important matter was developing in the oil region of Venango County. In 1854 "Brewer, Watson & Co.," for the sum of $5,000, sold to Messrs. Eveleth & Bissel, for ninety-nine years, the territory where the principal oil springs were located. Prof. Silliman, of Yale College, had reported favorably on the value of the oil, and Col. E. L. Drake became superintendent of the "Pennsylvania Rock Oil Company."

Col. E. L. Drake was furnished with all necessary funds, but it required strong courage to bore the earth or solid rock—for he had no precedent, and was looked upon as Noah was by the antediluvians. It was supposed by some that the manufacture of salt was the main object. Rock oil was the principal one, and faith was rewarded by success when at a depth of seventy feet, on August 28, 1859, a cavity in the rock was reached with evidence of the pressure of oil in large quantities. At first ten barrels a day was the yield, soon after, forty. This was near the upper springs, in the northern portion of Venango County. Thousands rushed to the scene and speculators abounded in Franklin, Tidioute, up French Creek, the Two-Mile Run, and Oil Creek region. Companies were organized, lands leased or bought, machinery invented, and now the influence on general trade could hardly be overestimated. Its importance to the manufacturing interests of the country was great. New branches of mechanical business have been called into existence and all branches stimulated to new life and energy. For instance, the steam engines that were required, the cable and rope, the establishments in Pittsburg for the manufacture of lamps and chimneys—of the latter 4,000 dozen being made weekly. The influence upon the ocean trade has been felt in two ways: lessening the whale fisheries and building up the carrying of petroleum to foreign parts.

Dr. Mills Eaton describes a flood that visited that region on March 16, 1865, which was unexampled in modern times. Not only had snow fallen in quantities at the headwaters of the Allegheny and French Creek, but on the 16th rain descended in torrents and as though the clouds were rent asunder. The Allegheny was absolutely frightful—fifty houses, derricks, oil tanks, lumber, staves, and oil barrels floated down. A bridge in Franklin was lifted up in two pieces; Oil Creek bridge and Sugar Creek also. Oil City was completely inundated and the railroad swept away. The flood of 1806 was of much smaller dimensions. The loss in money was many millions, and yet only a temporary suspension of business ensued.

"Millions in Petroleum" is the title of the following article from the *Erie Morning Dispatch*, of October 10, 1893—eighty-two years after the discovery: "Fifty-nine freight steamers are now employed in transporting petroleum to foreign countries. The capital in Pennsylvania wells and lands is estimated at $87,000,000, and $65,000,000 is invested in plants for producing the crude petroleum. This is exclusive of such accessories as pipe lines, tank cars, refineries, docks, fleets of vessels, etc., and an estimate of $300,000,000 as the total valuation of all branches of the industry is not excessive."

The Navigator of 1811 gives as follows:

"Among the natural advantages of the waters of the Allegheny, is Oil Creek, which empties into that river about 100 miles from Pittsburg. This creek issues from a spring on the top of which floats an oil similar to that called Barbadoes tar, and is found in such quanties that a person may gather several gallons a day. The oil is said to be very efficacious in rheumatic pains, rubbed on the parts affected. The troops sent to guard the western posts halted at this spring, collected some of the oil and bathed their joints with it ; this gave them great relief from the rheumatic complaints with which they were afflicted. They also drank freely of the water, which operated on them as a gentle cathartic. This oil is called Seneca oil in Pittsburg, probably from its first having been discovered and used by a nation of Indians of that name. It is a wise plan in Nature to generally place an antidote where she has planted a poison. No climate perhaps is more subject to pains of the rheumatic kind than ours, arising from the sudden transitions from heat to cold, and *vice versa;* and if it be true that the qualities of this oil are so effectual in the cure of diseases to which we are more or less subject, from the nature of our climate, it is equally true that Nature in her wisdom has not been unmindful of her general plan of providing a good for an evil in this particular instance.''

The following statement from *The Navigator* also will show the increase in the article of salt at the port of Erie from 1800 till 1809, as registered by Mr. Foster, collector of the of the port, December 25, 1809 :

"In the year 1800, 723; 1801, 396 ; 1802, 834 barrels of salt were entered at this port and distributed along the lake in the States of New York, Pennsylvania, and Ohio, and a few barrels sent to Pittsburg.

"In the year 1803, 2,736; 1804, 3,778; 1805, 7,589; 1806, 7,261 ; 1807, 6,774 ; 1808, 9,349; 1809, 14,346 barrels of salt were entered at this port for the consumption of this neighborhood and Pittsburg market, not including the supplies to the States of New York and Ohio, making 52,776 barrels, or 263,880 bushels of salt, besides other articles of merchandise, though of less importance, yet to a considerable extent."

An extract from Rev. Dr. McKinney's "Family Treasure," 1866, gives the following list of provisions furnished by the contractors, Messrs. Reed & Sanford, for the inhabitants of Chicago in 1823. There were one hundred men garrisoned in Fort Dearborn, under Capt. I. Green. According to the contract they were required to deliver in June, 1823, and October,

1824, "120 barrels of pork, 250 barrels of fine flour, 1,400 gallons of whisky, 110 bushels of beans, 1,760 pounds of soap, 860 pounds of tallow candles (with cotton wicks), 28 bushels of salt, and 450 gallons of vinegar." The same year three times as much of each of these commodities was consumed at Green Bay, and more than twice as much at Sault de Ste Marie, and the same merchants had contracts for these places also. But Chicago has now left them both far in the background. The arrival of six barrels of salt would be no great event for Chicago now. The 430 pounds of tallow candles to their present gas and electricity could not "hold a candle" for one night only, and as for Chicago importing 250 barrels of fine flour from Erie, and living upon it sixteen months, so small a matter has not been heard of from them the last seventy years. "Where we are we know, whither we are going no man knoweth."

A Retrospective Glance of February Weather of the last Nineteen Years. Compiled by Weather Observer Wood.—The mean or normal temperature during nineteen years (which is the length of time this station has been established) has been 28 degrees, the warmest in February, 1882, with an average of 37 degrees, and the coldest in 1875, when the average was only 10 above zero. On February 16, 1883, the temperature was 70 degrees above, and on February 9, 1875, 16 below zero—the two extremes noted. In precipitation (rain or melted snow) the average has been 3.43 inches, with an average of seventeen days in February of each year on which the precipitation was .01 of an inch or more. The greatest monthly precipitation was 8.50 inches in 1887, the least, 0.33 inches in 1877.

The month has averaged four cloudless, ten partly cloudy, and fourteen cloudy days during this term of years, and prevailing winds have been from the south. Their greatest velocity was sixty-four miles per hour, in 1875.

For nineteen years the mean or normal temperature in Erie has been 33 degrees. The warmest December was in 1889, averaging 41 degrees, and the coldest was in 1876, with an average of 22 degrees. The highest temperature during any December was 70 degrees, on December 29, 1889. The coldest was 11 degrees below zero, December 30, 1890. The average monthly precipitation has been 3.36 inches; the greatest monthly precipitation, 6.44 inches, occurring in 1881, and the least, .75 inches, in 1876. The average number of cloudless days per month was three; partly cloudy, seven; cloudy days, twenty-one. The prevailing winds have been from the southwest, and the highest velocity of the wind was southeast fifty-two miles on December 24, 1875.

Parks.—Glenwood Park, just outside of the city limits between two much-traveled roads leading towards Waterford, is appropriately named. The *Central* Parks in the center of the old first section at the intersection of Sixth and State streets are the glory of the city. *Lake Side*, between State Street and French, has expended its appropriation by the city of $1,500, and is assuming an aspect of beauty; and *Cascade* will doubtless in a completed state creditably add to the number. These are mere breathing spots, but Glenwood has 93 acres from the Robert Evans farm, and enough from the John Elliott and Henry Shannon farms to aggregate 115 acres, with a fine mansion, a commodious barn, excellent spring-house and drinking water. Thirty acres are covered with forest trees, some being very fine and imposing. A gas well for many years past has enlightened the whole vicinity. Enjoyments of an unobjectionable nature are promoted, but nothing of a demoralizing tendency is allowed. The full board for the first year is composed of J. F. Downing, A. H. McMullen, William Spencer, William A. Galbraith, M. H. Taylor, George Selden, F. F. Adams, Richard O'Brien, Frank V. Schultz, William N. Nicholson, F. Brevellier, W. J. Sands, H. F. Watson, I. Sobel, Joseph Metcalf. Through their efforts $25,000 has been subscribed. Mr. J. F. Downing subscribed $5,000, Judge Galbraith, $2,000, and several others of the board $1,000. Much money is required for improving the grounds. Dedicatory exercises were held October 19, 1892.

Massassauga Point is at the head of Presqu'ile Bay, and is now a delightful summer resort, having been purchased in 1833 by Hon. William L. Scott. In 1796, twenty or thirty Indian families resided there, of the Seneca tribe, being the last Indian village in this vicinity. In 1800, Eliphlet Beebe, a ship carpenter, took up the land under the laws of the State, for a shipyard. It was next the farm of Thomas Laird. James C. Marshall and E. J. Kelso owned farms adjoining that had been Indian cornfields. The name Massassauga is supposed to have been that of a tribe having relations with the Eries. A short, thick rattlesnake also bore that name, which species disappeared before civilization. The Massassauga Hotel was burned in 1882. It is still a charming resort, and the electric cars as they pass through a wild ravine and descend to the lake level present a bit of scenery of unusual grandeur. An iron ore bed was discovered many years ago in the vicinity, and was quarried by a furnace at Conneaut, Ohio, and was used at the blast furnace of Vincent, Himrod & Co., but was exhausted after a few years. The road from the schoolhouse to the shore of the bay was laid out for hauling the ore to the vessels. At present sand has accumulated and would render an approach to a vessel impossible.

Some of Erie's wealthy citizens are erecting summer residences on the lakeside. Judge William A. Galbraith, about 1880, built a pretty villa at the mouth of Six Mile Creek, where is a park, bathing, and boating. Mr. Charles H. Strong has a costly log cabin on the bluff at the mouth of Cascade Creek. Ex-Congressman Griswold and Mr. H. F. Watson have beautiful sites at the mouth of Miles Run, seven miles west of Erie. On the Ball farm is a clubhouse, fishpond, etc. At "Harts' Farm" many Pittsburgers, as well as our own citizens, have picturesque, romantic summer retreats.

Chautauqua Lake is generally supposed to be the highest navigable body of water on the globe. It is well then to get at the facts and figures. Lake Canadohta, located 17 miles south of Union City, is 84 feet higher than Chautauqua and is navigable. The relative height of all the lakes in this vicinity is as follows: Erie, 573 feet above the sea; Conneaut Lake is 1,070; Lake Le Bœuf, at Waterford, is 1,180; Conneauttee, 1,196; Chautauqua, 1,305; Lake Pleasant, 1,325; Lake Canadohta, 1,389. These levels were taken by Prof. J. C. White, under the employ of the State, and are endorsed by Peter Lesley, State geologist.

SECTION IV.

Biographies of Dr. Usher Parsons—Capt. W. W. Dobbins (an extract)—Oliver H. Perry—Major Andrew Ellicott—Two Foreigners —Dr. F. N. Thorpe—Rev. C. Dickson, D.D.—William Wallace, Esq.—Wallace Family—Judge Converse—Rev. T. H. Robinson, D.D.—Judge A. Tourgee—Bishop J. F. Spaulding—Rev. Dr. Stuckenberg—Dr. Artemas Martin—Rev. Dr. Chamberlain—Miss E. Ditto—Dr. and Ernest Ingersoll—Rev. K. Fullerton—Messrs. Perkins—Judge James Thompson and family--Hon. William L. Scott—Visits of Nine Presidents—Citizens mentioned.

MEMOIR OF USHER PARSONS, M.D., OF PROVIDENCE, R. I.

By his son, Dr. Charles W. Parsons.

IT IS well known that a controversy arose between Com. Oliver H. Perry and Jesse D. Elliott in relation to the conduct of the latter in the naval battle of September 10, 1813; and that long after Perry's early death, the credit of victory was claimed for Elliott by himself and his friends. Dr. Parsons took a warm and active interest in this dispute. He was strongly attached to Perry and convinced that Elliott's conduct was disgraceful. In conversation, by newspaper articles, by contributions to writings published by others, and, lastly, in a public historical address, he vindicated the claims of Perry and the truth of history, as he understood it, often in terms reflecting severely on Elliott and his defenders.

In January, 1836, Tristam Burges read a discourse before the Rhode Island Historical Society, in which he gave a vigorous account of the battle. In 1839 this was published with copious notes and diagrams of the battle in different positions. Some of these notes were furnished by Dr. Parsons. The "extract from the logbook of the *Lawrence*" was taken from his diary. He contributed many notes to the "Life of Commodore Perry," published in 1840 by Alexander Slidell Mackenzie.

In 1852, having been invited to deliver the stated annual discourse before the Rhode Island Historical Society, he chose for his subject, the history of the battle of Lake Erie. "I have made this choice," he says, "first, because this battle is a part of Rhode Island history and, therefore, appropriate to the occasion; secondly, because I could speak of it from personal knowledge; and, thirdly, because a very inaccurate and perverted account of it has been written and imposed upon the public by the late J. Fenimore Cooper, Esquire." He narrates the circumstances which led to the formation of a fleet on Lake Erie, the difficulties under which it was created and got afloat, and the reasons why it is regarded as belonging to Rhode Island history. He relates the incidents of the battle quite fully, and then attacks Elliott and Cooper in a style of indignant sarcasm. In the words of Mr. Arnold: "He has done this in a style that leaves nothing to be said upon the points in dispute. His own testimony is direct and incontrovertible. His reply to the assaults of Cooper is comprehensive and complete. A certain irony pervades this portion of the address, which is the appropriate weapon wherewith to treat mendacity of statement when brought to the support of cowardice of conduct and infamy of character." Dr. Parsons always had a fondness for written controversy, and could handle the caustic pen as well as the scalpel or saw.

In his more advanced life, he became well known in the growing cities along the southern shore of Lake Erie, and often visited this region. The importance of Perry's victory was more appreciated and there were various plans for the erection of monuments. Dr. Parsons was the only surviving officer of the battle who had cultivated historical tastes and the powers of writing and oratory.

In 1858 the anniversary was celebrated at Put-in-Bay Island, near Sandusky, where Perry's fleet had anchored the night before the battle. There was a very large assemblage, and a brilliant display of yachts and steamers. Hon. Salmon P. Chase presided at the ceremonies on the island. Three surviving officers appeared on the platform; Capts. Champlin and Brownell speaking briefly, while Dr. Parsons read an elaborate narrative discourse. This was received with a great deal of interest by the large audience and published in the principal newspapers of the region. He afterward wrote in his notebook, "This anniversary was among the most delightful of my life, as well as the most interesting."

Two years later the forty-seventh anniversary was celebrated at Cleveland. That city alone successfully carried out the plan of erecting a monument to Perry, which on that day was dedicated. It stands in the park at Cleveland, and consists of a statue of Perry, and of other appropriate sculptures. The dedication, September 10, 1860, was very largely attended. The Governor of Rhode Island, with many of her civil and military officers, were present by special invitation. The two most important features of the literary exercises of that day were the oration by Hon. George Bancroft and a historical address by Dr. Parsons.

These three discourses relating to the battle of Lake Erie all give the story in essentially the same way, and show some unavoidable repetition. The two delivered at Put-in-Bay and Cleveland are not, however, controversial.

In his later journeys along Lake Erie, Dr. Parsons was regarded as a guest of the public, and was passed and entertained as such on the steamboats and railroads. These various acknowledgments of his early services, and the kind reception of his historical discourses, after he had passed the age of seventy, gave him the keenest pleasure.

In 1838, he revisited Erie, after an absence of nearly twenty-four years. In his diary he writes: "I called on Capt. Dobbins, who was a sailingmaster in the war, now commander of the revenue cutter. I went with him to the Peninsula, [Erie was formerly called Presqu'isle] and trod once more the deck of the *Lawrence*, now a hulk resting about east a quarter of a mile from the old blockhouse. Her deck is in a sound state; but the water comes nearly up to it, so that I could not see her hold. In this vessel I sailed in 1813, and was in battle. She was repaired the following year, and I went in her to Mackinac with troops under Col. Croghan. She was sunk and remained so till within the last two or three years, when she was raised and proved to be perfectly sound. Took some pieces from her to make canes of. This visit to Erie gave me indescribable pleasure. The thousand associations . . . the pleasure afforded in taking old friends by the hand after a separation of twenty-four years; . . . the grave yard, where lie the bodies of great numbers of early friends; the changes and vast improvements about the city—elegant houses and churches where there were then but a few humble dwellings—all, all tended to render my stay there one of the most intense interest, on many occasions so powerful as to take from me the power of speech. But what shall I say of the protecting mercy of Him who, through dangers seen and unseen, perils by land and perils in the deep, has surrounded my path, and preserved me to the present moment? May the remainder of my days be more devoted to His service."

After a decline of some months, Dr. Usher Parsons died on Dec. 19, 1868, aged 80 years. "Loved in life and honored in death, his memory will be revered by all who value these high qualities of manhood which were united in his character."

When Capt. George Miles purchased the *Lawrence, Detroit, Queen Charlotte,* and *Niagara* of Mr. B. H. Brown, he raised the vessels, intending to fit them up for the merchant service. The two prizes were found in tolerable condition, but the *Lawrence* required thorough repair, and was too shallow in the hold for a merchant vessel—being but nine feet. She was allowed to sink again and was brought to the surface, only to be viewed as a curiosity and cut into fragments to serve as relics. A part of the ship was transported by railroad to Philadelphia and placed on exhibition on the Centennial grounds in 1876. Capt. William W. Dobbins wrote in pamphlet form a "History of the Battle of Lake Erie," which accompanied it. The title of the owners is as follows:

Bill of sale from Benjamin H. Brown, of Rochester, New York, to A. Q. D. Leech (who transferred to George Miles), of *Lawrence, Niagara, Detroit,* and *Queen Charlotte;* said bill of sale being made to George Miles separately, bearing date as per acknowledgment, June 20, 1835.

        (Signed) B. H. BROWN.

Acknowledgment by George Mumford, Commissioner of Deeds.

Letters of Col. Thomas Forster, Collector of Customs for the District of Presqu'ile (Erie), to the Secretary of the Navy, in regard to any claim the government might have to said vessels. The inquiry being made for information enabling the collector to grant papers to the brig *Queen Charlotte*, then to be fitted out for the merchant service, bearing date April 7, 1835.

Also, answer of Mahlon Dickinson, Secretary of the Navy, disclaiming any interest of the government in said vessels, bearing date April 23, 1835.

Also, transfer of all right, title, and interest of George Miles in said vessel to Leander Dobbins, bearing date December 9, 1857.

       (Signed) GEORGE MILES.

Also, transfer of hulk of *Lawrence* to Thomas J. Viers and John Dunlap, bearing date September 10, 1875.

       (Signed) LEANDER DOBBINS.

Oliver Hazard Perry was born at South Kingston, Rhode Island, Aug. 23, 1785. His father, Christopher Raymond Perry, was born in the same place in 1761, and was a post-captain in the navy until the reduction in 1801, when he received the appointment of collector at Newport. He married Sarah Alexander in 1784, and of a large family descended from them almost every male member served with distinction in the navy. Mathew Calbraith joined in the Japan expedition in 1852; he was a brother ten years younger than the "Hero of Lake Erie." Oliver Hazard Perry entered the navy as a midshipman in 1799; served in the Tripolitan war; had charge of a flotilla of gunboats in New York Harbor in 1812, and in 1813 he served under Chauncey on Lake Ontario. Then, being only master-commander, he superintended building the fleet at Presqu'ile (Erie), and September 10, 1813, gained the complete and brilliant victory over the British squadron at Put-in-Bay, Sandusky. He received a vote of thanks from Congress for his bravery, and a gold medal, and was promoted to a post-captain. Late in 1813 he assisted Gen. Harrison in retaking Detroit. In 1815 Perry commanded the *Java*, of Decatur's squadron in the Mediterranean, and in 1819 was appointed to the command of a squadron for the coast of Columbia. In July, he ascended the Orinoco to Angostura, and on leaving the river was seized with yellow fever, which terminated fatally the day his vessel arrived at Port Spain, Trinidad, West Indies, being the 23d of August, 1819. His remains were buried there, and in 1826 a sloop-of-war removed them to Newport, R. I., where they were re-interred with great ceremony. The State of Rhode Island erected a fine granite monument to his memory. In 1860 a handsome marble statue of him by Walcutt was erected in a public square in Cleveland, O., with imposing ceremonies. At the unveiling Hon. George Bancroft, the historian, delivered an address; Dr. Usher Parsons, who was the surgeon at the battle, read a historical discourse, and at a dinner afterwards, about three hundred surviving soldiers of the war of 1812-15 sat down. The average of their ages was about seventy years, and the aggregate of the venerable company was about 20,000 years!—*Collated from Lossing.*

Maj. Andrew Ellicott.—The subject of this sketch devoted a long life to the service of his country, and illustrated in an eminent degree the valuable aid intelligence and learning can render in the settlement of a new country. He was born in Bucks County, Pennsylvania, January 24, 1754. His attainments in science soon drew public attention to him, and from the Revolution to the day of his death he was employed in the fulfilment of trusts conferred by the general of the State governments. Though belonging to the society of Friends, he commanded a battalion of Maryland militia in the Revolution. In 1784 he was employed on behalf of Virginia in fixing the boundary line between that State and Pennsylvania. In 1786 he was commissioned by the Supreme Executive Council of the State to run the northern boundary line of Pennsylvania, and in 1788 he was directed to make a survey of the islands in the Allegheny and Ohio Rivers within the bounds of the State. In 1789 he was commissioned by the United States government to locate the western boundary of New York State and ascertain the validity of the claim of that State to the site upon which Erie now stands. He located the line, after much hardship and trouble, some twenty miles east of Presqu'ile; his valuable service in this important and responsible survey seems to have been duly appreciated by Washington, for he writes in the year of its completion: "Gen. Washington has treated me with attention. The Speaker of Congress and Governor of the State have constantly extended to me most flattering courtesies." In 1790 he was employed by the United States government to survey and lay out the District of Columbia and Washington City; in 1796 he was appointed by Washington commissioners to fix the boundary line between the United States and the Spanish Possessions. One important trust succeeded another, for more than forty years, and up to the time of his death he was constantly employed in some public capacity. His high character and superior intelligence elevated him without special effort; he had an exalted sense of duty, and a well-sustained conception of personal responsibilities. In March, 1801, he was appointed by Jefferson surveyor-general of the United States, which office he accepted upon conditions imposed by himself. In 1813 he was appointed professor of mathematics in the military academy of West Point, and removed there with his family, and there he died August 28, 1820. He left a widow and nine children; Col. John H. Bliss, of Erie, is his grandson. President Hale, in his memoir of Maj. David Bates Douglass, the son-in-law of Andrew Ellicott, says: "The memoir of the late Andrew Ellicott, when written, will form a valuable addition to the history of our country, taking us away from the beaten ground of battle-fields and Senate chambers and cabinets to the services which science can render in the settlement of a new country in a civilized age.—*Extract from Stuart's "Civil and Military Engineers of America."*

Two distinguished foreigners are connected by marriage with Erie families: Richard Claverhouse Jebb, LL.D., regius professor of Greek at the University of Cambridge, England; the other, George H. Darwin, F.R.S., LL.D., of the Plumian chair of astronomy at Cambridge University, England. He has also the honor of being the third son of the eminent naturalist, Charles Darwin, whose investigations and writings have made a new epoch in the scientific world, and is himself a scientist of world-wide reputation, and an authority in his special department. Prof. Darwin was married in Erie, July 22, 1884, to Miss Maud De Puy, by Rev. G. A. Carstensen, of St. Paul's P. E. Church, at the house of her sister, Mrs. William

Spencer, No. 143 West Eighth Street, having an elegant entertainment and costly presents from friends on both sides of the ocean. "The fair representative of America who has drawn across the ocean this bearer of a distinguished name is the daughter of Charles M. Du Puy, of Philadelphia, whose Huguenot ancestors have been prominent in the past, and entitle him to the position he holds at the head of the Pennsylvania branch of the American Huguenot Society."

Prof. Jebb, above mentioned, in 1874, married the widow of Lieut.-Col. Slemmer, U. S. A.,[1] who is a sister of Maj. J. W. Reynolds, Superintendent P. & E. R. R., and aunt of Mrs. Darwin. Prof. Jebb has frequently visited our country. In 1892 he delivered the second annual course upon the foundation named the "Percy Trumbull Memorial Lectureship in Poetry," by special invitation of Johns Hopkins University. After completing the course on the Greek language and literature there, a similar course was delivered in Chicago. Maj. Reynolds and Mr. Spencer met him in Baltimore, and the party occupied the private car of Vice-President Thompson over the P. & E. road.

Of the published works of Prof. Jebb, "The Complete Works of Sophocles" has received very many favorable notices from reviewers. Other publications are "Theophrastus Characters," "Modern Greece," "Life of Bentley," "Erasmus," and many lectures.

Francis Newton Thorpe was born in Swampscott, Essex County, Massachusetts, April 15, 1857, and is descended from Miles and Rose Standish, who were of the Mayflower company. In 1865 Mr. Thorpe's parents moved into Erie County and settled at Northeast. He passed through the public schools of this place and in 1875 completed the four years' course of study in the Lake Shore Seminary, an institution of learning that flourished in Northeast from 1869 to 1883. Among his class-mates in the county are Mr. A. E. Sission and Mr. Walling, district attorneys; and Mr. J. M. Force.

After graduation he began teaching in the High School at

[1] Gen. Slemmer was famed for saving Fort Pickens after the Federal forces found it impossible to hold the Pensacola navy-yard. Pickens was the one stronghold on the mainland from the Chesapeake to the Rio Grande, over which the flag of the Union never ceased to float.

Pleasantville, Pennsylvania, and continued his studies. A year later he was elected teacher of the schools at Northeast and soon after put in charge of them. By his efforts a course of study was adopted which fits for college, and the schools soon took high rank in the county. In 1880 he traveled in Europe. Three years later he completed the post-graduate course in history at Syracuse University and received the degree of Doctor of Philosophy from that institution. The subject of his doctor's thesis was "The Federal Principle in American Government." Having registered for the study of law in 1879, with Judge John P. Vincent, of Erie, Mr. Thorpe entered Judge Vincent's law office in 1884, and in June, 1885, was admitted to the bar. On the day of his admission he was elected to the Fellowship in History and Political Science, in the Wharton School, in the University of Pennsylvania, and in September of that year he entered the law school of that university and began special studies in American history with John Bach McMaster, the historian. 1886 he was reelected fellow, and elected professor of History and Social Science in the Central Manual Training School of Philadelphia. In 1889 appeared his work entitled "The Government of the People of the United States," designed as a text-book on American institutions and which immediately was favorably received, passing through eight editions in the next four years. In 1891 appeared his "Story of the Constitution," written for the Chautauqua Literary and Scientific Circle, and in 1893 appeared his next work involving vast labor, entitled "Benjamin Franklin and the University of Pennsylvania," printed by the government of the United States. This is a critical account of Franklin as an educator, and of Franklin's influence in the United States, together with the history of the University of Pennsylvania (of which Franklin was the founder) from 1740 to 1893.

While at Oxford University in 1880, Mr. Thorpe conceived the idea of a school wholly devoted to the study and investigation of American history and institutions, and in 1886 he entered upon the foundation of such a school at the University of Pennsylvania. For five years he collected moneys, books, rare MSS., and material for the equipment of such a school. It was a noble conception and it was successfully carried out. In describing the schools in the history of the University, Mr. Thorpe writes: "The school was established in 1891 by the trustees of the university, as a result of the coöperative labors of William Pepper, M.D., LL.D., Provost of the University; Joseph D. Potts, John B. Gest, and Hon. S. W. Pennypacker, of the board of trustees; Charles Elmer Bushnell, Ferdinand J. Dreer, Hon. Thomas Cochran, Joseph G. Rosengarten, Richard L. Austin, John Bach McMaster, and Francis Newton Thorpe." The library of the school is specially rich in United States public documents, second in completeness to the collection in the British Museum.

In 1891 he resigned the chair of history in the training school and was elected professor of American Constitutional History in the University of Pennsylvania. In 1889 he was admitted to practice in the Supreme Court of Pennsylvania. Since 1885 he has rapidly won distinction and recognition in his chosen specialty, American constitutional history and law. He is widely known as a lecturer on these subjects and he has written on them for *The Century Magazine*, *The Atlantic*, *The Chautauquan*, and for numerous educational magazines. He has been closely identified with the growth of University Extension in this country. He is a member of several learned societies and is one of the council of the American Academy of Social and Political Science.

His library of rare originals and works on State constitutional history is not surpassed by any of the kind in this country.

He spends a portion of his summers at Northeast, and takes great interest in all pertaining to the history of Erie County. He is fond of music, art and literature; is a constant contributor to the press on questions of the day; is fond of assisting young men in their educational efforts, and is identified with many useful undertakings.

Rev. Cyrus Dickson, D.D., for eleven years one of the secretaries of the Presbyterian Home Missionary Society, and one of the most eloquent pulpit orators and successful pastors of our country, was a native of Erie County. His father, Elder Wm. Dickson, commenced life for himself in the southern part, and in 1801 removed to the head of French Creek—afterwards to the northeast township, one mile and a half from the lake. Dr. Dickson was born Dec. 20, 1816. His mother was Christina Moorhead, daughter of James and Catherine Moorhead. Though quiet and unassuming, "she was a woman of principle and of conscience, and in some things much in advance of her neighbors." Her heroic conduct at a barn-raising in her husband's absence has been much and deservedly published, and resulted in generally banishing spirits on such occasions. Dr. Dickson graduated at Jefferson College, and was licensed to preach by Erie Presbytery in 1839. His first pastorate was at Franklin, Venango County. In 1848 he had a call to Wheeling, West Virginia, where he remained until 1856, when he was installed in the Westminster Church of Baltimore. After his appointment as secretary in 1870 he with his family resided in New York. He was married in 1840 to Miss Delia McConnell, of Girard, Pa. In 1858 he received the honorary degree of Doctor of Divinity from Washington College. His continuous labors made relaxation desirable, and he planned a journey abroad, but the disorded state of that country prevented traveling in Palestine. In 1877 he attended as a delegate the Pan-Presbyterial Council, in Edinburgh, Scotland. Dr. Dickson was permanent clerk of the General Assembly from the reunion of the Old and New School branches until his decease, September 11, 1881.

William Wallace, Esq., a brother of Dr. J. C. Wallace, the first burgess of Erie, was a lawyer of prominence who came to Erie from Harrisburg in 1800, as the attorney for the Pennsylvania Population Company. He married in 1803 Rachel, daughter of Dr. A. Forrest, who died in Erie in 1804. In 1806, he married Eleanor Maclay, of Harrisburg, and returned there to reside in 1810. He resumed his profession, was elected the first president of the old Harrisburg Bank, and was burgess of Harrisburg at the time of his death. He was a polite, urbane man, of slight frame and concise address. His only daughter, Mary Eleanor, married Rev. W. R. De Witt, D. D., long the pastor of the Presbyterian church of Harrisburg. Dr. William M. Wallace, the prominent physician of Erie, and Irwin M. Wallace, Esq., his sons, were among our most valued citizens for over half a century. Miss Julia A. W. De Witt, a grandchild, is the author of "How he made his Fortune," and "Life's Battle Won," and is a frequent and able contributor to church papers, Rev. John De Witt, D.D., a professor of Princeton Theological Seminary, and the gifted preacher is also a grandson.

The Wallace and Heron families in the Army and Navy.
By Elizabeth Pollock, a descendant. (By request.)

Mr. Benjamin Wallace was in the War of the Revolution; was born in 1727, and died in 1803.

Dr. John C. Wallace was a Surgeon in the U. S. Army, came to Erie with Gen. Wayne, and resigned to settle here.

Benjamin Wallace (brother of Dr. J. C. Wallace), was a Major in the U. S. Army, commissioned in 1813.

James Gordon Heron was in the War of the Revolution, and afterward was a Major in the U. S. Army.

Margaret Heron married Dr. John C. Wallace, of the army.

Hannah Heron married Capt. Daniel S. Dexter, of the U. S. Navy. After his death she married Maj. Nelson, of the U. S. Army.

Nancy Heron married Lieut. Hopson, of the U. S. Army.

Jane Wallace (daughter of Margaret Heron) married Capt. Otis Wheeler, of the U. S. Army.

Hannah Foster, (daughter of Jane Heron) married Gen. Crosman, of the U. S. Army.

Hannah Irvine (daughter of Mary Ann Heron) married Lieut. Cutts, of the U. S. Army.

Otis W. Pollock (grandson of Margaret Heron Wallace), is a captain in the Twenty-third Infantry, U. S. Army.

Alexander Crosman (grandson of Jane Heron Foster) was lieutenant in the U. S. Navy.

Frederick Crosman (grandson of Jane Heron Foster) was lieutenant in the U. S. Army.

Mary E. Cutts (granddaughter of Mary Ann Heron Irvine) married Col. William Craig, of the U. S. Army.

Calvin De Witt (grandson of William Wallace, who was a brother of Dr. J. C. Wallace and Benjamin Wallace) is a Surgeon in the U. S. Army.

Lieut. S. K. Allen, U. S. N., and grandson of Col. Ethan

Allen married Miss Eleanor Wallace, daughter of J. M. Wallace, Esq.

All these I have mentioned were in the regular service of the United States, but when it comes to volunteer and militia service, a much larger list could be named.

Benjamin Wallace, son of Dr. J. C. Wallace, was a volunteer in the army of Texas, with the rank of major, in 1835 and 1836, when Texas fought for her independence from Mexico. He was taken prisoner by the Mexicans, and by the order of Santa Anna was, with other prisoners, shot in cold blood, at the massacre of Goliad.

Charles Crozat Converse, the son of Manning Converse, and grandson of Jacob, [whose distinction it was to unite, by his marriage, the lines of the Winthrop and Robinson settlements in America, as, after graduation from Brown University in 1790 he married Miss Ellen Robinson, of Plymouth, Mass., of the family of the Puritan leader, and whose ancestress, of the same name, was an heir of Capt. Miles Standish] is well known by his contributions to general literature and his success in his profession of the law. He also ranks as one of America's leading orchestral composers. "While pursuing his literary and legal studies in Germany, he took a course of instruction in musical composition under the great harmonist Richter, and his professional *confrères*, at Leipsic. Spohr, Mr. Converse's orchestral mentor, Liszt, and other composers highly praised his orchestral works, which embrace overtures, symphonies, cantatas, etc. His "American Concert Overture," for full orchestra, was played at the Boston Peace Jubilee, it being chosen from thirty works there offered. His "Im Frueling" has been played several times in New York under the direction of Theodore Thomas, and his "Psalm Cantata," on the 126th Psalm was performed at the concert of the Music Teachers' National Convention in Chicago, July 1888, under the same direction. The American overture on "Hail Columbia," which was played at the World's Fair on the Fourth of July, was enthusiastically received. The overture numbers fifty-eight printed pages. Its singular historic value concerning the formation of a school of American music is recognized by the purchase of its score, and the first proof copy of it in print for preservation with the collection of Columbia mementos now being formed in Chicago.

It was after examining this work that Spohr, Mr. Converse's musical mentor, made the notable prophecy that "If its composer devotes himself to musical composition, America need not look to Europe for works of the higher class."

"The words and music of Charles Crozat Converse's American national hymn, 'God for Us,' was one of the many special features of the *Mail and Express* souvenir Washington centennial edition to-day. This noble hymn is growing steadily in popularity and frequently makes its appearance at national and patriotic celebrations. It possesses every essential for a national song and has become a favorite in Grand Army circles. The *Mail and Express* printed 250,000 copies of 'God for Us' for its centennial souvenir."—*American Art Journal.*

The popular hymn "What a Friend we have in Jesus" has been translated into many languages and may be heard in strange lands.

Mr. Converse married Miss Lida Lewis, of Alabama, on January 14, 1858. Their only child and son, Clarence, is known as an author, his articles being published in *Youth's Companion, Little Men and Women of Boston, Argosy, Godey's Magazine, The World,* etc., and occasionally in Philadelphia and Chicago papers. He has been urged by New York critics to devote himself entirely to parlor comedies, and has been highly praised as a dramatic writer. He would seem "to inherit literary gifts which have marked his illustrious line, in which the names of Rev. Dr. Thomas Carter and Count Rumford are conspicuous."

Because of Mr. Converse's devotion to philology he has been engaged to assist Rev. Mr. Gregory, editor-in-chief of the "*Standard Dictionary*" now preparing, in that line of musical definition with which he is especially familiar.

A synopsis of a paper adopted and put upon record by the Presbytery of Erie. Taken from the Memoir by Rev. A. H. Caughey, Ph. D. :

Samuel John Mills Eaton was born at Fairview, Erie County, Pa., April 15, 1820. His father, Rev. Johnston Eaton, was one of the pioneers, and his mother, Eliza Cannon, was of the family that founded Cannonsburg, Pa., the seat of Jefferson College. He was educated partly at home and at Erie Academy, and entered the sophomore class at Jefferson College in 1842, graduating in 1845, being esteemed the finest essayist of his class. He spent three years at the Western Theological Seminary, and was licensed by the Presbytery of Erie in 1848. The same year he was ordained and called to succeed Rev. Cyrus Dickson at the churches of Franklin and Mt. Pleasant. November 5, 1850, he was married to Miss Clara J. Howe, who still survives, and in 1855 he devoted his whole time to the church of Franklin, which was his only pastorate, continuing there thirty-four years, until February, 1882. When he commenced his work there the church had 74 members; when he resigned the last name on the roll was numbered 772. During the revival of 1867, 111 persons were added to the church on examination. In 1869 Washington and Jefferson College gave him the title of Doctor of Divinity. In 1871 he visited Europe and the East, devoting himself particularly to the study of the Holy Land, and afterwards published the result of his observations under the titles of "Jerusalem" and "Palestine." He became stated clerk of the Presbytery of Erie in 1853, and held the position through life, and for many years held the same position in the old Synod of Erie. He was a member of the Board of Trustees of Washington and Jefferson College, and of the Western Theological Seminary. Was appointed chairman of a committee to investigate the workings of the Presbyterian Board of Publication, and made a valuable report to the Assembly in 1886. Dr. Eaton was identified with Chautauqua from its commencement, and at his death held the largest number of seals for courses of study mastered of any Chautauquan. He lectured there on "Palestine and Jerusalem," and was also a popular and valuable author. His works were "History of Petroleum," "History of the Presbytery of Erie," "Lakeside," "Ecclesiastical History of Centennial Missionary Work," "Memorial of Dr. Cyrus Dickson," "Chapters in the History of Venango County, Pennsylvania," "Biographical Catalogues," etc.

Dr. Eaton died suddenly at his home in Franklin July 16, 1889. It would be difficult to overestimate the character and work of Dr. Eaton. He was preëminently a manly man and a noble Christian.

Dr. Thomas Hastings Robinson, professor of Sacred Rhetoric, Church Government, and Pastoral Theology, in the Western Theological Seminary, at Allegheny, was born January 30, 1828, in Northeast township, Erie County. He graduated at Oberlin College, Ohio, in 1850 ; taught in public and select schools—was principal of the Academy at Ashtabula, Ohio, and was for six months principal of the Normal School at Farmington. He entered the Western Theological Seminary in 1851 and graduated in 1854, receiving a call soon after as colleague pastor of the Market Square Presbyterian church at Harrisburg, Pa., Dr. William R. De Witt, pastor, and was ordained and installed January 21, 1855, by the Presbytery of Harrisburg. After Rev. Dr. De Witt's withdrawal in 1864, and his decease in 1867, Dr. Robinson continued in sole charge of the church, a pastorate of thirty years, until his resignation to accept of the professorship at Allegheny.

Rev. Dr. Robinson in 1856 married Mary Wolf Buehler, daughter of Henry Buehler and Anna Margaretta, only daughter of Governor Wolf of Pennsylvania. We find also in "Pennsylvania Genealogies" Scotch-Irish and German, that Thomas Robinson, the father of Rev. Dr. Robinson, married Mary McCord, whose father, William McCord, removed to Erie County in the early days, and died there in 1806. The Blaines and Mooreheads were from central Pennsylvania, settling east of Erie, and their descendants formed a large community of thrifty and intelligent farmers, organizing two Presbyterian churches. Annie-Robinson Tuttle married, in Northeast in 1885, William H. Jeffers, D.D., LL.D., professor of Old Testament Literature, Ecclesiastical History, etc., in the Western Theological Seminary, Allegheny, Pa. John F., David, William, several of the brothers went to Pittsburg about 1850 and formed the banking firm of Robinson Brothers, now for many years well known, honored, and successful.

Albion Winegar Tourgee, Ph.D., LL.D., American author

and jurist, was born at Williamsfield, Ohio, May 2, 1838. He studied at Rochester University, 1859-61, then entered the Union Army as private in the Twenty-seventh N. Y. V. I.; was severely wounded at battle of Bull Run, in consequence of which he was discharged from the service; in 1862 was commissoned Lieutenant of Co. G., One Hundred and Fifth O. V. I.; resigned in 1864 on account of wounds; on editorial staff of the *Erie Dispatch*, and principal of Erie Academy, 1864-5. Removed to Greensboro, North Carolina, in 1865; was a member of the North Carolina Constitutional Conventions of 1868 and 1875; was one of the commission to codify and revise the State laws. Was elected Judge of the Superior Court of the State in 1868, and held that position until 1874. Was editor of *The Continent* Magazine, New York, 1882-4. Has been a professor of the Buffalo Law School since 1889. Is the author of several professional works,—"The Code with Notes" (North Carolina) 1878; "A Digest of Cited Cases" (North Carolina) 1879; "Statutory Decisions of the North Carolina Reports," 1879. Is the author of the following novels: "Toinette" (now entitled "A Royal Gentleman") 1874; "A Fool's Errand," 1879; "Figs and Thistles," 1879; "Bricks without Straw," 1880; "John Eax," 1882; "Hot Plowshares," 1883; "Black Ice," 1885; "Button's Inn," 1887; "With Gauge and Swallow," 1889; "Pactolus Prime," 1890; "Murvale Eastman," 1891; "A Son of Old Harry," 1892; "Out of the Sunset Sea," 1893. Author also of the following miscellaneous books: "An Appeal to Cæsar," 1884; "The Veteran and His Pipe," 1885; "Letters to a King," 1887. Since 1880, his residence has been at Mayville, on Lake Chautauqua, Chautauqua County, N. Y.

The Rt. Rev. John Franklin Spalding, D.D., the second Missionary Bishop of Colorado and first Bishop of the diocese of Colorado, was born in Belgrade, Maine, August 25, 1828. He graduated from Bowdoin, 1853; the General Theological Seminary, 1857. He was ordered deacon at St. Stephen's, Portland, Maine, July 8, 1857, by Bishop Burgess, by whom, also, he was advanced to the priesthood July 14, 1858, in Christ church, Gardiner, Maine. He was missionary at St. James' church, Old Town, Maine, for

HISTORY OF ERIE COUNTY. 393

two years, afterwards successively rector of St. George's church, Lee, Mass., assistant minister Grace church, Providence, R. I., and rector of St. Paul's church, Erie, Pa., until his elevation to the Episcopate. He was consecrated in that church, December 31, 1873, by Bishop McCoskry, assisted by Bishops Bedell, Talbot, Coxe and Kerfoot. Upon the erection of the jurisdiction into a diocese he became its diocesan. His bishopric included Colorado, Wyoming, and New Mexico. In 1874 he seconded the letting off of New Mexico, in 1886 of Wyoming, in 1892 of Western Colorado. In 1880 the Cathedral in Denver was built—in 1886 Mathews Hall—in 1888 Jarvis Hall and Wolf Hall. These are the Divinity School, the schools for boys and for girls. The two former were at first located in Golden, but in 1878 were destroyed by fire. St. Luke's Hospital was founded in 1881 and its present fine buildings were erected in 1891. The growth of his work has fairly kept pace with that of the country. The diocese of Colorado was formed in 1887 and admitted into union with the General Convention in 1889 and is one of the leading dioceses of the West. Bishop Spalding has published various works, the principal ones are: "The Church and its Apostolic Ministry," "The Best Mode of Working a Parish" and "Jesus Christ the proof of Christianity."

In 1864 he was married in Erie to Lavina D., daughter of J. C. Spencer, Esq. Mrs. Spaulding's services for the church, in the Bible class and mother's meetings are well known, and by reason of her persevering efforts she will ever be indentified with St. Luke's Hospital in Denver.—*Partly from The Church Standard, June 10, 1893.*

John H. W. Stuckenberg, D.D., member of the Philosophical Society of Berlin, etc., was born in Bramsche, Germany, January 6, 1835; came to the United States at the age of four; graduated in the classical and theological departments of Wittenberg College, and studied in the University of Halle, Germany, from the autumn of 1859 till the spring of 1861, devoting his attention chiefly to theology and philosophy. Returning to the United States, he became the first pastor of the English Lutheran church of Erie in 1861. When the One Hundred and Forty-fifth Regiment of Pennsylvania Volunteers was formed he was appointed chaplain, joining the regiment in September, 1862, on the battlefield of Antietam, where some days were spent in the burial of the dead. He was with the regiment in the battles of Fredericksburg, Chancellorsville and Gettysburg. The church in Erie being in urgent need of his services, he resigned his position as chaplain after being thirteen months in the army. At that time but few of the original members of the brave regiment were at the front, having suffered terribly in the battles mentioned, particularly during the heroic charges at Fredericksburg and Gettysburg. After returning to Erie in the autumn of 1863 he took an active interest in the religious and public affairs of Erie. He resigned his pastorate in 1865 and returned to Germany to study in the universities of Göttingen, Berlin, and Tübingen, remaining abroad eighteen months. After supplying a pulpit in Indianapolis he organized the Messiah Lutheran church in Pittsburg, and was called to Wittenberg College in 1873 as professor of sacred philology. Being anxious to devote himself more fully to a specialty than was possible in this position, he resigned in 1880 and returned to Berlin for the purpose of using the royal library. Soon after his arrrival the management of the American Chapel was committed to him, and in 1887 he organized the American Church of Berlin, of which he is still pastor. This church is a union of different denominations, and is attended largely by American students in Berlin. Besides his work in behalf of this church he has kept up his studies and has been engaged in literary pursuits. Among the works published by him are the following: "History of the Augsburg Confession," "Christian Sociology," "Life of Immanuel Kant," "The Final Science," "Introduction to the Study of Philosophy," "The Age and the Church." In German he wrote: "Grundprobleme in Hume." For a number of years he conducted the European department of the *Homiletic Review*. He has also been an extensive contributor to the *Andover Review*, *Our Day*, and numerous other journals in America and England. He has retained his deep interest in Erie, and numbers many of its citizens as his warm friends. In his various labors he has been efficiently aided by his cultivated wife, a daughter of Henry Gingrich, of Erie.

Yours truly,
Artemas Martin.

HISTORY OF ERIE COUNTY. 395

Artemas Martin, M.A., Ph.D., LL.D., the subject of this sketch, was born August 3, 1835, in Steuben County, New York. He is the only son of James Madison Martin and Orenda Knight (Bradley) Martin.

In 1837 his parents removed to Pennsylvania, and for many years resided near Franklin, Venango County.

He had no schooling in his early boyhood except a little primary instruction while very young, and from that time until in his fourteenth year he was never in a schoolroom as a pupil, but had learned reading, writing, and geography at home, but knew nothing of arithmetic. In his fifteenth year he commenced the study of arithmetic in Dr. Daniel Adams' Scholar's Arithmetic, but did not master the four rules of addition, subtraction, multiplication, and division the first winter. He attended district schools three winters, commencing the study of algebra the last winter. When seventeen years of age he attended a select school in Franklin for six months, studying algebra, geometry, natural philosophy, and chemistry, walking two and one half miles night and morning. Three years afterwards he attended the Franklin Academy about two months and a half, studying algebra and trigonometry. This, at the age of twenty, finished his schooling. He taught district schools four winters in Venango County. In summer he usually worked at farming, and studied mathematics during his spare moments—evenings and rainy days. He also worked in the oil regions at drilling oil wells—mostly in the winter.

Early in 1869 Mr. Martin removed with his parents to Erie County, Pennsylvania, and resided near Erie and in that city until he went to Washington, D. C., in October, 1885.

He began his mathematical career when in his eighteenth year by contributing solutions of problems to the *Pittsburg Almanac*, and soon afterward contributed problems to the "Riddler Column" of the *Philadelphia Saturday Evening Post*, and was one of its principal contributors for about twenty years. In the summer of 1864 he commenced contributing problems and solutions to *Clark's School Visitor*, afterwards *Our Schoolday Visitor*, published in Philadelphia. In June, 1870, he took charge of the "Stairway Department" as editor, the mathematical part of which he had in fact conducted for some years before. He continued in charge as mathematical editor till the magazine was sold to Scribner & Co. in the spring of 1875 and merged into *St. Nicholas*.

In September, 1875, Mr. Martin was chosen editor of a department of higher mathematics in the *Normal Monthly*, published at Millersville, Pennsylvania, by Prof. Edward Brooks, and held the position until the *Monthly* was discontinued in August, 1876. He published in the *Normal Monthly* a series of sixteen articles on the Diophantine Analysis, the most extensive that had been published in this country.

In the spring of 1877 he issued the first number of his *Mathematical Visitor*, which he still publishes at irregular intervals. In January, 1882, he issued the first number of his *Mathematical Magazine*, which he continues to publish.

Although he had never served an hour as apprentice in a printing office to learn the "art preservative," he has done all the type-setting for his publications except for the first three numbers of the *Visitor* and part of the last page of Vol. I., No. 2, of the *Magazine*, and has printed several numbers of the *Visitor* and one of the *Magazine* on a self-inking lever press, only $6\frac{1}{2}$ by 10 inches inside of chase. The numbers he has printed are considered by competent judges to rank among the finest specimens of mathematical printing ever executed.

In June, 1881, he was elected professor of mathematics in the Normal School at Warrensburg, Missouri, but did not accept the position.

His ability and achievements in the science of mathematics have been recognized by three colleges which have conferred on him honorary degrees; Yale College giving him the degree of M.A. in 1877; Rutgers College, Ph.D., in 1882; and Hillsdale College, LL.D., in 1885.

In 1878 he was chosen a member of the London Mathematical Society; in 1884, member of the Société Mathematique de France; in 1885, member of the Edinburgh Mathematical Society; in 1886, member of the Philosophical Society of Washington; in 1889, member, and in 1890, fellow of the American Association for the Advancement of Science; and in 1891, member of the New York Mathematical Society.

In November, 1885, through the influence of Hon. William L. Scott, Dr. Martin was appointed to a position in the office of the United States Coast and Geodetic Survey, and has since resided in Washington, D. C.

Dr. Martin has contributed mathematical problems, solutions, and papers, to the *Analyst*, published at Des Moines, Iowa; to the *Annals of Mathematics* (successor to the *Analyist*); to the *Illinois Teacher* (1865-1867); to the *Iowa Instructor* (1865-1867); to the *National Educator;* to the *Yates County Chronicle;* to *Barnes' Educational Monthly;* to *Educational Notes and Queries;* to the *Wittenberger* (1876-1880); to the *Maine Farmers' Almanac;* and to the *Mathematical Monthly*, published over thirty years ago. He contributed to the *Wittenberger* (1877-1879) a series of thirteen articles on "Average," believed to be the first articles on that subject published in this country.

Dr. Martin has also contributed to the following English mathematical periodicals: The *Lady's and Gentleman's Diary* (1868-1871); the *Messenger of Mathematics;* the *Educational Times* and its *Reprints* (1868-); and the *Quarterly Journal of Pure and Applied Mathematics*. The *Reprint* contains a large number of his solutions of difficult "average" and "probability" problems.

Outside of the time devoted to editing and printing his magazines, Dr. Martin devoted himself for some years to cultivating vegetables and conducting a market-garden near Erie, Pa., and was a regular attendant at the Erie market. He was careful to plant only the best varieties, and prized his skill and reputation as a gardener as highly as he did his fame as a mathematician.

Dr. Martin is not a graduate of any institution of learning, and is almost wholly self-taught. He has a large and valuable mathematical library containing rare and interesting works. His collection of American arithmetics and algebras is one of the largest private collections in the country.

He has also a large miscellaneous library, including many early and scarce school books, among which is a large collection of English grammars.

Rev. G. W. Chamberlain, D.D., was born in Waterford, Pa.,

in 1839. He was educated at Delaware College, and afterwards at Princeton, but was obliged to give up study on account of a difficulty with his eyes. He went to Brazil in 1862, not intending to enter missionary work, but the condition of the ignorant people so appealed to him, he has remained, and was licensed by the Presbytery of Rio. He is a missionary of the Presbyterian Board, and has organized many schools and churches at Sao Paulo, Bahia and Rio Janeiro, and has been remarkably successful in his field of labor. He is also an able and interesting contributor to our missionary magazines. A sister also went with him in 1876, purposing to teach, but her health failed after two or three years and she returned. His oldest daughter has lately joined the mission under appointment of the Board. The Rev. Pierce Chamberlain, long pastor of the Presbyterian Church of Waterford, was his father.

The author of "One Little Injun," *Miss Margaret Emma Ditto*, of Wellesley, Massachusetts, was born in Nunda, Livingston County, N. Y., about the time the Genesee Valley Canal had its inception. Her father had the contract for building that canal, and moved his family from New York City into the then far west of the State, where they resided some years. In 1861 Miss Ditto graduated at Mt. Holyoke Seminary (now college), and came to teach in Erie Academy about 1866, where she remained nine years. In her own words, "Hundreds of Erie boys and girls passed through my hands, and I hope are none the worse for it. I remember them all." We can say we do not doubt but they all remember her with the greatest affection. Since that time her chief interest has been in writing for the press, and she is best known as a writer of short stories for boys. These have appeared in the *Youth's Companion, The Independent*, and *The Congregationalist*. At one time she wrote quite regularly for *Harper's Young People*; and some for the *Bazaar* and the *Weekly*. She says: "I have also done some humerous writing, besides my Indian tracts and Bible studies. I prefer the Bible studies, and I feel that to make known the facts and principles of the Bible is the only permanent use to which literary talent can be put. Life seems a very deep reality to me, and those things which do not make for eternal life do not seem to me worth living for. I have studied the Bible a good deal, and I find that it is a scheme of truth in which if we abide the world and all its doings become belittled almost to extinction. I have a deep conviction that the end of the age is near at hand when our Lord will return in glory to reign, and this truth drives out others, and I cannot write on common themes with zest." Of her humerous writings she says: "They were like foam on the water—a sparkle and gone. They were in the papers under a good many different signatures; as during some years I wrote not under my own name. But Harper used to advertise or notice them as humerous, and I believe had the idea to bring me out in that line. But I hardly think I shall write any more such."

Mr. William C. Kelso, deceased in April, 1892. As a lifelong resident of Erie, the senior member of the bar and the oldest communicant of St. Paul's Episcopal church, his form was well known and his name a household word. As the youngest and sole surviving member of the historic family of Gen. Kelso, whose coming to Erie County was almost identical with its settlement, there was an added interest, especially as his own life had almost bridged the century and his career had been cotemporary with three generations. He was the youngest of seven children of Gen. John and Sarah (Carson) Kelso, and born in Erie about seventy-nine years ago. Gen. Kelso came with his family from Cumberland County in 1798, and to the town of Erie in 1806. He made his home in the square west of State and north of Second Street, where his house and grounds were long a conspicuous landmark, especially as they were adorned by choice vines and shrubs for the first time introduced by them when the family came to Erie. Gen. Kelso was a large landowner and conspicuous, patriotic citizen. He was Associate Judge, Prothonotary, Recorder, and Commissioner of Sales. In the War of 1812 he was brigadier general in active command in charge of the place in repelling invasion and guarding the frontier, especially during the construction of Perry's fleet. He died in 1819, and his widow in 1842. On the 10th of May, 1839, W. C. Kelso was admitted to the bar, after studying with his brother-in-law, Mr. Babbitt. Subsequently he formed a partnership with that renowned lawyer, by which firm a large practice was successfully conducted. In 1862 he was appointed an assistant United States Assessor of the nineteenth collection district of Pennsylvania, and rendered efficient and conscientious service in that important office. After the close of his official duties he never resumed active practice to much extent. He was for probably half a century assiduous and untiring in the discharge of his church duties. These were his life work. As warden, vestryman, and secretary of St. Paul's Episcopal church he was conspicuous. The two latter positions he occupied till his death. Not only was he the oldest member of the church, but as regular in attendance on Sunday and at the week-day services as the rector himself.

Ernest Ingersoll, the naturalist and author, is the son of Dr. Timothy Dwight Ingersoll, of Erie, but was born at Monroe, Mich., March 13, 1852. His taste for natural history was apparent when a lad, and caused him to pursue the study, in spite of obstacles. After a desultory course at Oberlin, he became by his own exertions a student in the Musuem of Comparative Zoölogy at Harvard, where he made a special study of birds, and supplemented this with a season's work at Prof. Agassiz's seaside school on Penikese Island. After Prof. Agassiz's death in 1874, Mr. Ingersoll was appointed to a position on the United States Geological Survey as naturalist and collector, exploring the remotest parts of the southern Rocky Mountains. This appointment was received through the influence of his friend, Prof. S. T. Baird, secretary of the Smithsonian Institute. His work in popular science is, perhaps, best known through his collected essays, "Friends Worth Knowing," and "Country Cousins," and the two volumes, "Old Ocean," and "Birds Nesting." "The Ice Queen" and "Silver Caves" are bright examples of success in the difficult rôle of story telling for young people. He has written also a number of excellent guidebooks; one on the Canadian West is worthy of a more dignified classification, as it embodies large study and experience which he acquired while in charge of the advertising business of the Canadian Pacific Railway in 1887 and 1888. He has delivered many lectures, been for many years correspondent of the *London Field*, and has done a large amount of unsigned work. Mr. Ingersoll lives in New York City, and is at present one of the editors of the "Standard Dictionary," attending to the department of Zoölogy, and having charge of the illustration of that great work. He is assisted by his daughter Helen, who excels as a botanist and an artist.

Dr. Timothy Dwight Ingersoll was born in Lee, Mass., July 4, 1817, but removed with his parents to northern Ohio. His father, Theo. Ingersoll, was a leading citizen and abolitionist, and one of the founders of Oberlin College. His mother, Lydia B. Ingersoll, died at her home in Berea, O., July 25, 1893, at the advanced age of one hundred years and nine months. Dr. Ingersoll is a direct descendant (being in the fifth generation) of the celebrated divine and metaphysician, Dr. Johathan Edwards, who was born in Windsor County, Connecticut, in 1703. He entered the dental profession in 1850, married Miss Eliza Parkinson, and returned to Erie in 1876. Dr. and Mrs. Ingersoll, Prof. G. F. Guttenberg, and Mr. J. Miller founded the Erie "Natural History Society," which has been a nucleus of thought and inspiration here for several years. Dr. T. D. Ingersoll's essays and frequent newspaper articles on scientific subjects and descriptions of scenery in our locality, some of which are found in this work, have awakened much interest. His skill as a dentist has not only been recognized at home, but has a wider reputation through his articles in the dental journals.

The *Rev. William M. Blackburn, D.D.*, author of several interesting works, now President of Pierre College, Dakota, was the first settled pastor of Park church.

Rev. Kemper Fullerton has been appointed provisional instructor in Hebrew and Greek in Lane Theological Seminary at Cincinnati, O., and becomes the successor of Prof. Henry Preserved Smith, D.D. He is the second Erie boy to attain such a position among the instructors of the Presbyterian church, *Rev. Augustus S. Carrier* having for two or three years filled the like professorship of Hebrew in McCormick Theological Seminary at Chicago, after a like high grade of scholarship at Union Seminary, and a like post-graduate period of study in Europe. Erie may justly be proud of two who have attained such honorable positions. Both are sons of former well beloved Erie pastors, Rev. A. H. Carrier, D.D., having been pastor of the First Presbyterian church, and Rev. Thomas Fullerton, D.D., of the Park church.

"ERIE, Pa, May 11, 1893.
"*To the Editor of the Dispatch.*

"I find in the May number of the *Literary Northwest*, published simultaneously at St. Paul, Minneapolis and New York, several poetic contributions from W. R. Perkins, son of R. L. Perkins of this city. They are entitled 'Song of the Lily,' 'Song of the Rose,' and 'Song,' each beautiful in thought and tender and smooth in expression. Indeed, they evince true poetic feeling, serving to show on the part of Mr. Perkins rich gifts in this direction.

"Mrs. Mary J. Reid gives in the same number of the *Literary Northwest* a finely rendered criticism upon Mr. Perkins as a poet of true genius and growing reputation. 'Eleusis and Lesser Herns' of Mr. Perkins, issued in the form of a modern volume, are critically and eulogistically reviewed, and the author awarded distinction, not as a magazine writer of verses to catch the multitudes with rhymes that touch simply upon passing events, but a poet who has for years studied his art with a high and lofty aim.

"It may be added that William L. Perkins was born in Erie in 1847; was graduated in 1868 at Western Reserve College, Ohio, teaching thereafter in his alma mater, and devoting his spare hours to the study of law. In 1879 he was appointed assistant professor at Cornell University, N. Y., where he remained six years. At the expiration of that period he went to Europe, where he attended the Universities of Berlin and Bonn. Upon his return, he was called to the chair of history in the State University of Iowa, Iowa City, a position he still holds. In 1888 he was elected delegate of the Eighth Centenary of the University of Bologna, Italy, thus visiting Europe a second time."

"The several narratives of the resurrection of Christ as confined to the day on which he rose from the dead, in which some have supposed discrepancies to exist, and used them to discredit the truthfulness of the testimony, and to bring in question the inerrant inspiration of the gospels, have been clearly harmonized by a little work, the mechanical execution of which is equal to the beauty of the literary style, written by Rufus Lord Perkins, an elder in the Park church at Erie, Pa. The closing pages of this book contain some forcible thoughts specially adapted to the present, when the plenary inspiration of the Scripture is denied by some within the pale of the Christian church, and the authority of the Bible is put on a level with fallible reason and a fallible church, leaving no solid footing for a soul that turns an anxious gaze toward the solemn future."—*New York Correspondence.*

Samuel Gustine Thompson, appointed by Gov. Pattison to fill the vacancy on the Pennsylvania Supreme Court bench caused by the resignation of Chief Justice Paxson, has been a prominent member of the Philadelphia bar for thirty years, being a superior corporative lawyer. He was born in Franklin, in 1837, his father being judge of the Court of Common Pleas in Venango County. Judge James Thompson was elected to the Supreme bench in 1858 where he officiated for fifteen years, the last six as Chief Justice. The family removed to Philadelphia upon the election of the father to the Supreme Court, and there the son, who had graduated at the Erie Academy, and made himself proficient in several modern languages, took a partial course at the University of Pennsylvania, studied law and was admitted to practice in 1861. He is a director of the Philadelphia & Erie Railway Company. Judge James Thompson died suddenly in 1874, while making an argument before the Supreme Court.—*Condensed from American Press Association.*

A *Dispatch* reporter was told recently by a resident of Erie that in the summer of 1845 he met Rev. Nathaniel and Mrs. Snowden, grandparents of Col. J. Ross Thompson. Mr. Snowden then stated that he heard the old bell ring on the 4th of July, 1776, as independence was proclaimed from Independence Hall, Philadelphia. At the same interview he learned that Mrs. Snowden was among those who escaped— as a child in her mother's arms—at the Wyoming massacre a little later.

Mr. and Mrs. Snowden were then visiting the family of their daughter, Mrs. Judge Thompson, at the corner of Ninth and State streets. The aged minister and the genial old lady were clear in their recollection and positive and entertaining in their statements of the thrilling events each had witnessed. Their memories bridged a longer period than the nation's life. Each survived for some years and witnessed not only the marvelous advance of the State but the leading positions taken by various members of their family in both judicial and legislative, in the federal and State service. Judge Samuel G. Thompson, of the Supreme Court, and A. Loudon Snowden, minister to Greece, are also grandsons of the same persons. Judge Thompson was Chief Justice of Pennsylvania and J. Ross Snowden Treasurer and Director of the United States mint.

Erie has been visited by nine Presidents of the United States, viz: William H. Harrison in 1813, as General of the Western Army, in company with Com. Perry, immediately after the battle of Lake Erie; James Buchanan in 1840, to speak at a political convention; Ex-President John Q. Adams being on a steamer, tarried from 7 o'clock to 9, and was welcomed by Hon. T. H. Sill in the name of the citizens; President Zachary Taylor making a journey for recreation on the lakes, became too ill to proceed farther, and remained ten days at the residence of Dr. W. M. Wood, of the U. S. Navy; Vice-President Fillmore, whose home was in Buffalo, came up to meet him and remained for a day; Gov. Johnson, of Pennsylvania, Surgeon Ward, and Col. Bliss of the army accompanied him in his travels, which he was obliged to abandon and return to Washington, where he died in less than a year. Stephen A. Douglass visited Erie when he was a candidate and made a speech in the West Park. President Lincoln passed through Erie on his way to Washington and made a few remarks from the balcony of the depot just before his inauguration. His remains passed over the Lake Shore road in 1865. Erie was favored by a speech from President Johnson, who was accompanied by Gen. Grant and W. H. Seward; the latter also spoke. Horace Greeley during the campaign of 1872 made a lengthy address to his former townsmen from a window of the

depot. Gen. Garfield made frequent visits to Erie, and during the canvass of 1878 made an address at the courthouse, and in 1880 was a few minutes at the depot, and Benjamin Harrison accompanied him. Father Mathew, the apostle of temperance discoursed in the Pro-Cathedral of St. Patrick's on East Fourth Street.

Hon. William L. Scott was born in Virginia, July 2, 1828, being the son of Maj. R. L. Scott, U. S. A. In 1848 he came to Erie through the influence of Gen. C. M. Reed, and afterwards was in partnership with Messrs. M. B. Lowry and John Hearn in the coal and shipping trade. He contracted to build the Pittsburg & Erie Railroad, was the principal owner and the president during his life. He also built the coal docks and established the coal depot at the mouth of Cascade Run. During the war Mr. Scott gave liberally to the Union cause, and aided in the enlistment of troops, and was widely known as a wealthy and energetic citizen. He made also liberal donations to orphan asylums and churches. In 1866 and 1871 he was elected Mayor, and in 1866 and 1876 was member of Congress. In 1876 and 1880 he was a delegate to the National Democratic Conventions. Mr. Scott married Mary Matilda, daughter of J. A. Tracy, Esq., and granddaughter of Capt. Daniel Dobbins. He died at Newport, September 19, 1891. Prominent as a politician and a citizen of great wealth, his funeral obsequies were fitting and more notable than those of any that had preceded him. We copy from the newspapers of the day in another part of this work. Rev. James Scott, of the Church of England (but being of Scotch descent), was his great-grandfather who graduated at Aberdeen University, was ordained and licensed to preach in Virginia by the Lord Bishop of London in 1735. His grandfather, Gustavus Scott, was educated at Kings College, Aberdeen, and studied law in London, at No. 4 Essex Court, Temple Bar, having entered in 1767 and completed his studies in 1771. Returning to America he settled in Maryland residing in Annapolis and Baltimore. He was a member of the Continental Congress and held many offices of distinction in Maryland. In 1794 he went to Washington as president of the commissioners for laying out the city of Washington. He built and occupied the fine residence

"Kalorama," and died there. The father of Hon. W. L. Scott was also born there. This elegant residence in President Madison's day is now within the city limits and being rapidly built up.

Hon. J. H. *Forster*, of Houghton, Michigan, having been called to Erie by the death of his sister, recalled some matters of interest concerning his grandfathers, Col. Thomas Forster, and Associate Judge William Bell. Mr. Forster is a cousin of W. B. and J. W. Hayes and William E. Bell, of this city. His father, Thomas Forster, resided on the northeast corner of State and Fourth streets; his grandfather, Col. Thomas Forster, at southeast corner of French and Fifth; his grandfather, Judge Bell, corner of French and Sixth. Col. Forster was appointed collector of the port by President Adams, and held the office thirty-six years, until his death. His grandfather Bell was a judge of the Erie courts. Leaving Erie when a boy, Mr. Forster has been much in the public service. He assisted in running the boundary line between the United States and Mexico under the treaty of peace of 1848—the famous Guadalupe-Hidalgo. He himself fixed the initial point for placing the monument at the north of the Gila on the Pacific Coast, under Commissioner Weller. His uncles, Gen. Sumner and Gen. Wright, of the army, are well known. The latter and his wife were drowned en route to California.

Many prominent Erie citizens have passed away since 1861, of which our limited space will allow mention only. Of these are C. M. Reed, Milton Courtright, J. H. Walker, M. B. Lowry, J. C. Spencer, G. A. Elliott, Drs. Stewart and Wallace, M. Sanford, E. Babbitt, A. Scott, P. Metcalf, J. A. Tracy, Rev. Dr. Lyon, B. B. Vincent, Messrs. Tibbals, Grant, Hearn, Follansbee, Gunnison, Cleveland, Selden, Wallace, Mans, Faulkner, Ryan, Neil, and many others.

SECTION V.

Churches—Revivals—Missionary Annual Meeting—Public Schools —Academy—Villa Maria—Lake Shore Seminary—St. Benedict —Clark's Business College—W. C. T. U.—Y. M. C. A.—Hamot and St. Vincent Hospitals—Home of the Friendless—Three New Charities—Bequests of John Weis and R. Wilcox—Sisters of St. Joseph.

THE *Central Presbyterian* church was organized February 23, 1871. David Shirk and J. A. French were chosen elders by a membership of fifty-four persons. Rev. C. C. Kimball was the first pastor. Rev. Solon Cobb, the present incumbent, was ordained December 27, 1878, Mr. Kimball having accepted a call to Kansas City, Mo. The church has been unusually prosperous and fruitful. During the first twelve years of its existence its expenses and charities amounted to about $95,000. Mr. C. C. Shirk has been the superintendent of the Sunday school since its commencement. It has 565 names enrolled. The church built in 1872 was destroyed by fire, but it was replaced in 1890 by a beautiful and commodious structure.

The *Chestnut Street Presbyterian* church originated in 1870 from a Sunday school held in the dwelling of Mr. C. W. Brown, through the efforts of three lay members of the First and Park Presbyterian churches. It was under the Y. M. C. A. until December 1, when Park church had full charge. In order to put in some practical and useful form their quota of the $5,000,000 memorial fund which the Presbyterian church in the United States had resolved to raise as a thank offering to God for the cordial reunion of its dissevered branches, this new church, then Sunday school, was erected and dedicated August 2, 1871. Rev. J. R. Wilson was the first pastor, the church having been organized January 1873. In 1879 he resigned to accept of the chair of Greek Professor in Parsons College, Iowa. Revs. A. C. Wilson, J. D. Kerr, W. J. Haslett and Rev. R. S. VanCleve have succeeded as pastors. In 1890 a beautiful new brick church and chapel were erected.

The *United Presbyterian* church erected a handsome parsonage about 1875. Revs. Robert Reid, Joseph Pressley, and Rev. Dr. J. C. Wilson, for more than eighty years were the only ordained pastors. The First Presbyterian church, in 1891 added to its fine property the Selden Memorial chapel, being largely a donation from Mr. George Selden.

About 1878 Park Presbyterian church built a commodious and beautiful chapel. In 1892 the church was repaired and reseated. This church also organized a Sunday school, and erected a suitable building in East Eighteenth Street, in 1887, in which church services are now being held.

The several Lutheran churches are *St. John's German Evangelical Lutheran and Reformed* church on Twenty-third and Peach streets, Rev. A. L. Benze, pastor, dates from 1815. A new impulse was given about 1834, when Mr. Conrad Brown donated the whole square between Peach, Sassafras, Twenty-third and Twenty-fourth streets, and the church was erected on the same site now occupied. The *German Evangelical* church (Salem) was built in 1843 and rebuilt in 1873. It it is on the corner of Peach and Twelfth streets, Rev. Ernest Koehne is pastor. The *Luther Memorial* church, Eleventh Street and Peach, the Rev. J. O. Baker, pastor, was organized in 1862, and has a mission on the corner of Twentieth and Poplar streets. The *German Evangelical Lutheran Trinity* church, on Eleventh Street near Chestnut, was organized in 1881, and has a parsonage and day-school. Rev. C. C. Morhart was for many years pastor, before his call to Washington City, where he now resides. The *English Evangelical* church is on Twenty-first Street and German, and there is an *English Lutheran* church on Nineteenth and Poplar streets. *St. Paul's German Evangelical* was organized in 1851 and is on Peach Street, between Tenth and Eleventh. It has a parsonage ; Rev. Val. Kern is pastor.

St. Paul's Protestant Episcopal church erected its rich stone structure in 1860. In 1868 *St. John's Protestant Episcopal* church was built in South Erie, and about 1870 *Cross and Crown* and two other *Protestant Episcopal* churches or missions, *Trinity* and *Grace.*

Tenth Street Methodist Episcopal church was built in 1873 ; *Wayne Street Methodist Episcopal* in 1891, and *Simpson Metho-*

dist Episcopal, in South Erie, in 1893. *Evangelical Mission* is on Twenty-first and German streets.

A *Methodist Episcopal* church has lately been built on Brown Avenue, near Cascade Street.

The *African Methodist Episcopal* church on Seventh Street, between Holland and German, suffered from the flood, but has been thoroughly repaired.

Several *Baptist* churches have been erected within the last fifteen years. Rev. Cyrus Thoms, pastor of the *First Baptist* church was noted for his zeal and activity. The *North Star Mission* on East Sixth Street, was commenced as a union work thirty years ago. *Wallace Chapel*, on West Eighteenth Street was so called from the land having been donated by Irvin M. Wallace, Esq., and a *Baptist* church on Seventh and Cascade streets was organized about the same time. On Ash Lane and Twenty-third streets is also a *Baptist* church and Sunday school, and a German *Baptist* church on Seventeenth Street. The *First Baptist* commenced April 1831, with a meeting of ten persons. To-day, sixty years later, they have a fine church and chapel, with five missions, and have admitted as members twenty-five hundred persons.

Christian Science service and Sunday school is held on the corner of Sixth and Holland streets; also the *Bethel* on Front and French streets has preaching, and at 2:30 the Himrod Sunday school meets.

The *United Brethren* have a church on the corner of Cherry and Tenth streets.

A *Swedish* church (Protestant) was erected about 1886 on East Tenth Street. Rev. H. Hagstrom is pastor.

A *Christian* church on the corner of Seventh and Chestnut streets was erected about 1889.

The *Church of Christ* was organized in 1889, and meets in the Tabernacle on Peach Street, between Ninth and Tenth streets. Rev. B. Hayden pastor.

Hebrew—Anvchai Chesed Reform Congregation Synagogue on West Eighth Street, near Sassafras Street. Rabbi, Rev. Nathan Rosenan. Services every Friday evening at 7:30, and Saturday at 10 A. M. Sabbath school Sunday from 10 to 12; Wednesday from 3 to 6.

Many church improvements have been made in the county the last few years. *St. Paul's Protestant Episcopal* in Erie has added, through the liberality of Hon. C. M. Reed, a fine rectory; the *First Presbyterian* church, largely by the gift of Mr. George Selden, a fine convenient chapel. *Park Presbyterian* church has been improved and remodelled, and has erected a mission chapel on Eighteenth Street. At Girard a beautiful new *Presbyterian* church has just been dedicated.

St. Joseph's Roman Catholic (German) is on Twenty-fourth Street, near Peach; *St. John's German Roman Catholic* is on East Twenty-sixth; *St. Andrew's Roman Catholic* is on West Sixth and Raspberry. *St. Peter's Cathedral*, on Tenth and Sassafras, was commenced in 1874, and consecrated August 2, 1893, with great ceremonies. This was also the fiftieth anniversary of Bishop Mullen's ordination to the priesthood. It is 220x130 feet, and its cost is estimated at $250,000. Cardinal Gibbons and Archbishop Ryan were present, and the largest religious procession ever seen in Erie promenaded the streets, with torches and fireworks during the evening. The churches and its appointments are scarcely equalled in Western Pennsylvania.

St. Michael's Roman Catholic church, on Cherry and Seventeenth streets; *St. Stanislaus Roman Catholic* (Polish) Wallace and Thirteenth streets; an *Italian Roman Catholic* church, Seventeenth and Walnut streets, with one on Twenty-sixth and the other on E. Avenue and Tenth streets, make a total of eleven *Roman Catholic* churches in Erie recently built. Regular services are held in five languages, owing largely to our foreign population in the shops and factories.

Hoffman's Roman Catholic Church Directory for 1893 states that Erie diocese has as follows: Bishops, 1; clergy, secular 57; regular, 17; total 74; churches, 105; stations, 35; chapels, 11; secular students, 14; colleges, 1; academies, 5; parochial schools, 58; children attending parochial schools, 5,687; orphan asylums, 1; orphans, 155; charitable institutions, 3; Catholic population, 60,000.

During the pastorate of Rev. George F. Cain in Park church, which terminated in 1870, there was great religious interest, The Rev. E. P. Hammond, Maj. Whittle, and Mr. Rine, the latter about 1876, held series of meetings that were greatly blessed. For many days one of our largest churches was filled, and many business men during business hours held open Bibles and studied under Maj. Whittle. We find in *The Presbyterian*, Philadelphia, the following concerning the revival work of Rev. Dr. Wilbur Chapman in Erie.

"A blessed series of meetings, under the leadership of Rev. J. Wilbur Chapman, D.D., have just been concluded in Erie, Pa. Several churches were united in the movement. Dr. Chapman came to take charge of the work on the 21st of Nov. 1892. He began his work with the Christians: Discouraging impressions had been abroad concerning the religious character of the Erie churches. Erie was pronounced a hard place to move. Early in the course of the meetings it became apparent that such judgment would not stand. The Christians showed interest and willingness to work. A very gratifying spirit of unity was manifest from the beginning to the end of the associated movement.

"As a result, Christians are warmed and stimulated. There is now a more general interest in the cause of the Master. Where there was an appearance of being ashamed of the Master, there is little of that appearance now.

"The Bible has become a book of greater interest. The Evangelist was blessed in making that Book of Books appear full of sweetness and preciousness. He called out the Christians to witness for God's promises in that Book. It was glorifying to God to hear how many there were who could testify to the fact that promises had been tried and proved.

"To many there is a greater reality in prayer. Christians have united in prayer, which was made specific, and prayers have been answered, greatly to the strengthening of the faith of all in the presence of such evidence.

"So great did the interest become that the largest building in the city could not hold all the men who turned out to hear the gospel preached. At one service there were about twenty-five hundred men—possibly more—all that could be packed in the Opera House, and then many were turned away. Men of all creeds and no creed were there—Jews and Romanists, believers and unbelievers. On Tuesday, December 4, the business houses of the city closed at 3:30, and there was a crowded Opera House service at 4 P. M. No one building could accommodate the throngs of people that rushed for entrance.

"There were many inquirers. Nearly a thousand inquirers' cards were signed. Many have become greatly interested who did not sign a card. It is to be regretted that the meetings did not continue somewhat longer, for the power was reaching out beyond the general extent of church influence, and, doubtless, would have reached out more and more.

"The results of the work have exceeded the most sanguine expectation. There are reasons, which are plain, for the great success. The perfect union and sweet Christian fellowship between the churches could not but result in great good.

"The Evangelist proved himself a very wise man, full of power and the Holy Ghost, and just suited to the work in this field. He was free from sensationalism, and preached the gospel in love and earnest simplicity. He drew the ministers to him and builded on their support.

"Dr. Chapman has not only gone away with the love of all the people, but with the approbation and esteem of all the ministers, without exception. He has left behind him a greater love for Christ, for Christ's ministers, for the Bible and the Church, and stronger faith in the word of promise, and in prayer. "Ex. Com."

A REMARKABLE ACHIEVEMENT.

Morning Dispatch, Nov. 15, 1892.

"With the meetings of this day and evening the Evangellist, Rev. Wilbur F. Chapman, closes his labors in Erie. If any one had predicted three weeks ago that prayer meetings at 8:30 o'clock in the morning would be held and be largely attended in all sections of this city; that preaching in the morning and afternoon would draw out audiences completely filling the largest Protestant churches; that the Opera House would not hold the people who assembled at a given hour to hear the gospel story, and two overflow services had to be arranged; that 200 business places in Erie would shut up their stores after 3 P. M. on a week day so near the holidays, in order that a religious service might have uninterrupted right of way; that the Opera House would be filled with men only, interested to hear the words of a preacher and the singing of hymns; that in less than twenty days, more than 1,000 persons in the city of Erie would signify their desire and determination to lead a Christian life—that prophet might have been ridiculed.

"But that and more than that has been done in this city of Erie, and it has been a pleasure to the *Dispatch* to detail as completely as possible the progress of the great movement which has proved of so much interest to many people in this city and whose influence of good for the community cannot be questioned. Systematic method, thorough organization, and the co-operation of church forces under experienced leadership of exceptional ability have accomplished what doubtful means or sensation-dealing could never have done. It is to this superior, active organization, in our view, that is due much of the phenomenal success achieved."

Rev. B. Fay Mills says of Rev. J. Wilbur Chapman, who resigned the pastorate of Bethany church, Philadelphia (best known in the country as John Wanamaker's), with the pressing demand for evangelists of the best sort. "Dr. Chapman's general methods are beyond criticism. His temperament is one of exceeding gentleness, and in his private life he is very attractive and winsome." He was persuaded to visit Erie in this capacity in the winter of '92 and '93 and by so doing brought blessings to hundreds of our citizens. He was the immediate successor of Dr. A. T. Pierson, and entered upon his duties in 1890. Was born in Indiana in 1859; studied at Oberlin and Lake Forest University, and his theological course at Lane Seminary, Cincinnati, where he graduated in 1882, and there manifested his zeal and earnestness with a large measure of God's blessing.

The Twenty-third annual Assembly of the Woman's Foreign Missionary Society of the Presbyterian church met in Erie at the First Presbyterian church, April 1893. Mrs. Charles P. Turner, of Philadelphia, the president, reviewed briefly the work of the society. Hundreds of ladies from the States of Pennsylvania, New Jersey, Delaware, Maryland, Ohio, West Virginia, Tennessee and the District of Columbia were present. Rev. Dr. John Gillespie, of New York, and at least eight returned missionaries from the foreign field, made the meetings, which continued for three days, remarkably interesting.

Erie School Statistics for 1892-93.—The population of the city according to the census of 1893, by William P. Atkinson, Esq., is 47,500. The whole number enrolled in public and parochial schools, 9,335 ; this includes 416 in night school and 40 in mechanical drawing school ; the whole number of regular teachers is 187, with salaries varying from $300 to $1,560 and assistants $250 ; library $1,000 ; total value of public school property is $592,900 ; increase of attendance over previous year is 249. Speaking of the night schools of this year and the last, thirty per cent of the enrollment for both years were foreigners, who could neither read, nor speak English at all, or beyond a few words. These were Germans, Swedes, Italians, Poles, Danes, Finns, Norwegians, Russians, and French. Thirty per cent also were boys from the shops, who had but little or no knowledge of arithmetic beyond the fundamental rules. As usual with night school pupils the average attendance per night was about forty per cent of the whole enrollment. Many could not come every night, and to some, who came under compulsion, a minstrel show, a "dance," or the dime museum was oftentimes more attractive than the school. The ages ran from eleven to thirty-nine years ; and the occupations of all represented every trade and calling in life.

The high school moved into its new quarters in the central school building in September, 1891.

The public schools were closed by the School Board as follows : One in the fall of 1891 for two weeks, without suggestion from the health officer because of the presence of ten cases of diphtheria in that school district ; one in April without suggestion of the health officer, for three weeks *immediately after the spring vacation, because during the vacation fourteen cases of diphtheria appeared in that district;* one for three weeks in May, because of the appearance in the district of twelve cases. All the schools of the city were closed by order of the Board on May 27, 1892, though at that time five schools had already been closed, leaving eleven districts free from diphtheria so far as public school children were concerned.

Columbus Day, Oct. 21, 1891, in honor of the four hundreth

HISTORY OF ERIE COUNTY. 415

anniversary of the discovery of America by Columbus, was celebrated as in other cities, and was a day never to be forgotten, 7,944 children being in line. Erie never witnessed such a display. Oct. 1, D. J. Waller, Jr., State Superintendent of Public Instruction called upon all school principals to see that trees were planted on Columbus Day.

The officers of the School Board for 1893-94 are: H. W. De Witt, President; R. G. Newbegin, Secretary; George P. Colt, Treasurer; John S. Rilling Solicitor; H. C. Missimer, Superintendent; W. G. Arbuckle, Superintendent of Buildings.

The Teachers' Institute of November 1893, held in Erie, was largely attended, and many fine lecturers from a distance assisted. Among the number was Mrs. Mary Hunt, who has introduced temperance teachings in the public school course.

The magnificent central school building finished the last year is worthy of a full description did our space allow.

Report of Public Schools of Erie County.—See page 151 for State Superintendent of Schools' report for 1860. We submit the following statistics for 1892:

```
Whole number of schools..................................... 520
Average number of months taught......................... 834
Number of male teachers..................................... 107
Number of female teachers.................................. 532
Average attendance of scholars...........................10,492
Cost of teaching each scholar per month..........$     1.34
Taxes levied for school purposes.................. 197,817.33
State appropriation...........................................  32,060.67
Total receipts for school purposes............... 329,197.53
Cost of instruction........................................... 143,408.58
Fuel and contingencies......................................  62,517.72
Cost of schoolhouses....................................... 114,899.89
```

This table shows that while the attendance has increased 128 per cent over that of 1860, the combined outlay for instruction, buildings, fuel and contingencies has been increased to 588 per cent.

The proportion of female teachers to the whole number in 1860 was 60 per cent; in 1892 it was 89 per cent. The increase in the proportion of female teachers was first caused by the necessities of the case at the beginning of the late war, from the absence of so many of our best male teachers in the army. But what was begun from necessity has been continued from choice, the ladies having proven quite as satisfactory as teachers as the men, if not more so, and having in this matter secured to themselves the greatest advance in the scope of their influence, usefulness and their opportunities for wage-earning.

The Erie Academy is under the care of Prof. J. A. Wiley, M.A., with Miss S. King and Mrs. Pratt as assistants. It has a kindergarten and is in a prosperous condition.

St. Benedict's Academy has Sister M. Clara, Directress.

The *Villa Maria* Academy, being a large ladies' school occupying a whole square on Plum and Eighth streets, was completed and dedicated the 30th of May, 1892. It is in charge of the Sisters of St Joseph. Also there is a parochial school on Fourth between Holland and German streets.

Lake Shore Seminary, established in Northeast in 1870, though undenominational, was to a certain extent, under the control of the Methodists, having a fine four story brick building in the best vicinity. It did not prosper financially, and was sold at public sale first to the People's Savings Institution, and afterwards, on February 1, 1881, to the Redemptorist Fathers of Annapolis, Md. The price paid was $10,000, and it is used as a preparatory school for young men about to enter the Roman Catholic priesthood, having been dedicated as St. Mary's College.

Clark's Business College.—This organization was established in 1883 and incorporated in 1890. Prof. H. C. Clark, President; Prof. S. M. Sweet, Secretary and Treasurer. Board of managers: H. C. Clark, Hon. Joseph McCarter, Hon. J. F. Downing, J. Foster Hill, Hon. S. M. Brainard, D. C. Weller, S. M. Sweet. This is an exceedingly popular and well patronized institution. It has just presented to the public its tenth annual illustrated catalogue, and has removed to new quarters in the Downing Block, occupying the entire sixth flour of that elegant structure.

M. G. Benedict, A.M., Ph.D., is principal of the State Normal School at Edinboro. It has fine buildings, but has suffered much loss in consequence of dissensions with regard to Prof. Cooper, who was at the head of the institution for nearly thirty years. Many lawsuits and much bitter feeling prevailed which now happily is in the past.

Dr. N. C. Schaeffer, the State Superintendent of Public Instruction, writes editorially in the current number of the *Pennsylvania School Journal* (1893) :

"A visit to the State Normal School at Edinboro revealed an attendance of over 160 students. Of these 110 are prepared to teach and the rest are in the model school. The students are earnest and exceedingly well behaved. The professors are enthusiastic and harmonious. Among them is Miss Anna Buckbee, whose fame as a teacher has reached all parts of the Commonwealth. The superintendent of the model school reports that pupils from the town schools are seeking admission into his department. Edinboro is a beautiful town, free from the temptations of large cities, and well adapted to be the seat of a flourishing school. The buildings and the discipline have been much improved in recent years."

AN APPEAL FROM NINETY-NINE LADIES OF THE BEST CLASS.

Taken from Erie Gazette, September 8, 1853.

An appeal to the voters of Erie County :

We, the undersigned mothers, wives, sisters, and daughters, present this petition to those who hold in their hands the power to drive the demon of intemperance from among us, by procuring the passage of a prohibitory liquor law. We are not *politicians*, nor do we ask for the *right to vote*, but we appeal to you as our protectors and the protectors of our sons and brothers, who are not yet old enough to have a voice themselves, to nominate temperance candidates for the ensuing election. We want men without reference to party politics, who are known to feel deeply and decidedly on this most important subject, who are not actuated by selfish interests to call themselves temperance men, as a last resort of getting the nomination. We want men nominated who have worked for the cause, and are themselves examples of sobriety. We, who are the greatest sufferers, because the weakest party, appeal to you whom both God and our country have appointed our protectors. *Shall we not be heard ?*

Mrs. L. Sanford.	Miss M. McCracken.	Mrs. William Hays.
" G. A. Lyon.	Mrs. Gilson.	" P. Faulkner.
" W. Davenport.	" C. M. Reed.	" R. Faulkner.
" L. M. Richards.	" Carsen Graham.	" Ingersoll.
" Eliza Clark.	" Emily Ottinger.	" M. A. Adkins.

Mrs. T. B. Vincent.
" L. M. Smith.
" H. C. Hoppen.
" David B. Derby.
" H. J. Skinner.
" M. H. Parsons.
" S. L. Gillen.
" J. Constable.
" R. Todd.
" E. Babbitt.
" M. C. Foster.
Miss S. M. Foster.
" Eliza Dunn.
" Letitia Dunn.
Mrs. C. Otis.
" Marg. Graham.
" Jane McCracken.
" H. J. Lowry.
Miss C. M. Zimmerman.
Mrs. E. A. G. Lane.
" E. W. Marshall.
" F. Weatherby.
Miss M. W. Marshall.
" Hamot.
Mrs. W. Himrod.
" Elizabeth Hamot.
" Capt. Dobbins.
" J. F. Hampson.

Miss Virginia Ottinger.
" R. Watkinson.
Mrs. Sophia Camp.
" F. D. Galbraith.
Miss Sarah Davenport.
Mrs. Harriet Vincent.
" A. Tomlinson.
" S. Jackson.
Miss M. Jackson.
Mrs. A. A. Galbraith.
Miss S. M. Wright.
" E. G. Wright.
Mrs. A. M. Low.
" John L. Brown.
" James C. Reed.
Miss Calista Ingersoll.
" Anna E. Casca.
Mrs. J. E. Riblet.
" H. Towner.
Miss Ellen Towner.
" Susan Eddy.
Mrs. E. H. Smith.
Miss Lizzie Martin.
Mrs. O. H. Irish.
Miss E. Hannah.
" Nella Mc. Wade.
" Mary Carter.
Mrs. Wm. Truesdall.

Mrs. J. S. Carter.
" Anna McCann.
" Dr. Vosburg.
" Pierce.
" J. Sill.
" J. Kellogg.
" T. G. Colt.
Miss E. Lyman.
Mrs. S. M. Brewster.
Miss Mary Brewster.
Mrs. Harriet Hulbert.
" Kennedy.
Miss Mariah Kennedy.
Mrs. B. Hubley.
" H. B. Haverstick.
Miss F. Diffenbaugh.
" Diantha Brown.
Mrs. Lucinda E. Irish.
" Nancy Carter.
" L. Moore.
" Mary Metcalf.
" Mary Willing.
" Eleanor Davis.
" Elisa Vanhausen.
" S. M. Kellogg.
" C. E. Gunnison.
" C. H. Seymour.

"An appeal to the voters of Erie County," signed by one hundred ladies, given in a subsequent column, will be found worthy of attention. It is a settled truth that any cause embracing the moral and social well-being of society the ladies take hold of in good earnest, always, sooner or later, succeeds. The passage, therefore, of a prohibitory liquor law, in Pennsylvania, may be classed with the "certainties" of the future. The ladies of Wattsburg, it will be perceived, make a similar appeal.

The Temperance Sentiment (1853).—We observe in the last number of *The Herald*, a monthly temperance periodical published in this city, a resolution signed by a goodly number of well-known Whigs and Democrats pledging themselves to support no man for the Legislature who is not "in favor of the enactment of a prohibitory liquor law similar to the Maine law, and who will not, if elected, use all his influence to secure its passage." It cannot be disguised that there is abroad a deep-seated, determined feeling upon this subject. We have scarce a doubt, from the spirit exhibited in the several counties of the State, that a majority will be chosen to the Lower House favorable to the passage of a prohibitory law. We are opposed to the introduction of temperance into systematic political action, but we are free to say we are perfectly willing that the proposed measure should have a trial. If it can remove the monstrous evils which the sale of intoxicating drinks have entailed upon society, why, in the name of all that's just and good, *let us have it.* We repeat, if it can effect the all-important object contemplated, LET US HAVE IT. We stand ready to accept any panacea for a scourge so dreadful, so desolating, so blasting to human happiness, so detrimental to public and private morals.

The Women's Christian Temperance Union was organized in 1874. Miss Belle Sterrett (afterwards Mrs. Hall) and Miss Stewart took the first active measures. At a meeting September 24, 1874, in the First Methodist Episcopal church Mrs. Longstreet was chosen President, Miss Belle Sterrett, Vice-President; Mrs. J. J. Sterrett, Treasurer, and Miss Abbie Low, Secretary. Mrs. Carrier and Mrs. Ramsey, together with Miss Sanford, were a committee to draft a constitution and report at the next meeting. Miss B. Sterrett was President of the meeting, and Miss L. G. Sanford elected first President. A mass meeting was appointed for November 1874. Mother Stewart lectured in 1875, April 12. Mrs. Judge Marvin, Mrs. C. M. Briggs, Mrs. Wallace Sherman, Misses Burwell and Wittich, Dr. M. A. B. Woods and many other of our ladies have served as officers the last twenty years. Much good has resulted from its efforts, though never as much as desired. The best lecturers have been secured, literature distributed, petitions and remonstrances signed, unfermented wine for communion recommended, pledges given, fountains erected, etc. Several attempts have been made to establish a coffee house, but without much success. Throughout the county many societies exist, as Wattsburg, Girard, Northeast, Waterford, Miles Grove, Harborcreek and Edinboro. A small newspaper, *The Crisis,* edited by Mrs. Dr. Taylor, of Edinboro, has done a good work. The report of Mrs. H. S. Jones of the jail committee is as follows :

During the year ending April 1, 1889, 694 prisoners have been confined in the Erie County jail, of whom thirty-seven were women, and 104 were boys from nine to twenty years of age.

Religious services have been held every Sunday at 3 o'clock P. M., until January, when the time was changed to 9:45 A. M. by request of Sheriff Mehl. By this new arrangement we have been deprived of the valuable services of our assistants who are engaged in Sunday school work at that hour and cannot meet with us. We seldom apply to ministers of the city, as their time is fully occupied with their regular church work on that day. During each week a large package of literature, mostly on temperance, is distributed among the prisoners, which appears to be well received and read with some degree of interest.

During the year scores of prisoners have pledged themselves to abstain from strong drink—men who voluntarily asked for pledges and expressed a desire to lead a better life.

Many affecting as well as heartrending stories of temptation and struggles to be free from the bondage of appetite have been told me. Many who have been incarcerated within the walls of Erie jail have struggled heroically to free themselves from the effects of the blighting curse of drink, while they are assailed on every hand by the almost irresistible fascination of open saloons. To-day I recall the despairing cry of one who said "O, madame, I sometimes think I must do something desperate, that I may again be placed behind the bars out of the reach of the demon that is pursuing me at every turn." A boy only sixteen years of age sent to the Morganza prison reform school for stabbing another with a knife, while frenzied with drink, came to me after his release last month, saying : "What shall I do ? they met me at the depot and wanted me to drink." I kept him at my own home until a place was found for him to work out of town. He writes me that he is doing well and trying to lead a better life. These unfortunates are not all from the lower walks of life. No ! no ! This scourge of despair and death has crossed and is daily crossing the portals of homes of wealth and refinement, striking down and bearing away many of the noblest and best. This skeleton dances behind the tapestry and upon the velvet-covered floors of some of the most beautiful homes in Erie. We have nothing but words of commendation for our jail officials. Sheriff Mehl and Warden Perry Sedgwick, as well as ex-Sheriff Gifford, have done and are doing all they can for our convenience in advancing the work.

The W. C. T. U. donated the city the substantial drinking fountain on the corner of State and Tenth streets. Mr. George D. Selden also presented the large and costly marble fountain in the West Park, to the city in 1883. The two beautiful jets, in the East and West Parks and the Soldiers' monument are evidence of the taste and public spirit of our citizens.

The Union Ice Company, Messrs. Briggs & Kelsey proprietors, generously placed for the season, a tank of ice water, with a faucet and cup (which served also as a sign) in front of their office, 620 State Street, with the legend "Help yourself" —and many hundreds have had reason to thank them.

W C. T. U. officers for 1893 : President, Mrs. Mary Hubble ; Vice-President, Mrs. M. A. B. Woods ; Secretary, Mrs. G. L. Young, Cedar between Seventh and Eighth streets ; Treasurer, Mrs. Titus Berst.

Call for a County Constitutional Temperance Amendment Convention at Erie, March 1, 1889, at Riblet's Hall, corner of Twelfth and Peach streets.

The Legislature having submitted the long sought Temperance Amendment to our Constitution to be adopted, as we hope, the 13th day of June next, it now remains for the good people of every class to unite forces and means to secure success at the polls. Our first work is to complete a county organization, and we, the undersigned, do appoint and call a county convention to assemble at 10 o'clock A. M., March 1, in the city of Erie, in Riblet's Hall, corner of Twelfth and Peach streets.

We cordially invite to meet with us all temperance people, irrespective of sex or party, on a thoroughly non-partisan basis.

ERIE.	UNION.	NORTHEAST.	M'KEAN.
S. T. Pollock.	E. W. Hatch.	D. D. Loop, M. D.	David Stanclift.
Jas. G. Patterson.	H. G. Smith.	J. Higgins.	J. G. Grimler.
Geo. D. Selden.	W. T. Everson.	Z. Rogers.	L. B. Clark.
D. S. Clark.	J. H. Laubender.	Carl Pierce.	D. Hayford.
Solon Cobb.	F. W. Burnham.	Geo. W. Moore.	N. N. Bayle.
W. E. Magill.	W. W. Shrew.	Thos. Porter M.D.	W. J. Stafford.
Robert Williams.	J. E. Thompson.	E. J. Hunter M.D.	
N. Luccock.	T. A. Edwards.	W. O. Wing.	GIRARD.
C. A. Gaither.	Edwin P. Clark.	Wm. E. Marvin,	
M. A. Dunning.	Oscar Glezen.	C. A. Pease.	Rev.C.L.Shipman
Owen Wiard.	L. D. Rockwell.	N. H. Clark.	C. F. Rockwell.

G. E. Barger.
I. B. Gara.
J. C. Thoms.
H. G. Schabacker.
M. G. Sterrett.
F. H. Ellsworth.
J. C. Wilson,
S. S. Caughey.
J. C. Sims.
E. L. Pelton.
J. Boyd Espy.
E. L. Frazier.
Wm. Hardwick.
J. W. Wakefield.
P. B. Sheldon.
J. L. Stratton.

ALBION.

P. D. Flower, M.D.
S. A. Saunders.
L. H. Salisbury.
J. Pelton.
D. G. Spaulding.
G. Runyon.
R. A. Barnes.
Wm. Thornton.
G. V. B. Thomas.
J. Wells.
D. E. Perry.
E. Davenport.
D. E. Flower,
W. Alderman,
E. C. Palmer.
F. C. Callaghan.
D. Sanford.

D. G. Smiley.
C. W. Dabney.
J. W. Sproul.
C. N. McLean.

FAIRVIEW.

Dr. W. J. Weeks.
J. C. Miner.
T. M. Ryan.
Geo. S. Stone.
Rev. H. Webster.
A. J. McCreary.
Chas. Galliard.
B. A. Landis.
J. G. Ziegler.
Allen Sturgeon.
J. A. Daggett.
Elias Bayle.
C. M. French.
Wm. Caughey.

MILL VILLAGE.

S. M. Clark.
F. N. Runnels.
J. S. Ross.
J. N. Reane.
J. R. Hunter.
P. T. Manross.
Wm. McCray.
E. K. Range.
C. S. Edmunds.
S. Beardsley.
Chas. Mitchell.
W. H. Frisbee.
L. M. McKinley.

M. L. Seikregg.
C. C. Hall, M. D.

EAST MILLCREEK.

C. N. Stark.
W. W. Conrad.
H. H. Miller.
G. J. Russell.
F. Fuhrmann, Jr.
G. B. Russell.
J. C. Wood.
Rev. J. P. Irwin.
H. Drown.
Chas. Miller.
R. D. Beardsley,
S. S. Conrad.

WEST MILLCREEK.

C. B. Evans.
J. M. Dunn.
E. Warner.
George Booth.
George Reed.
G. W. Haybarger.
J. G. Reed.
J. C. Munn.

W. SPRINGFIELD.

S. D. Ware.
E. F. Mallory.
N. W. Jones.
C. M. Reed.
F. P. Jones.
S. M. Nickle.
O. W. Anderson.
W. I. Potter.

Dr. O. Logan.
J. M. Ealy.
J. E. Pratt.

EDINBORO.

Joseph Taylor.
I. N. Taylor.
John Proudfit.
F. A. Temple.
H. Lewis.

WAYNE.

J. G. Kincaide.

ELGIN.

Wm. R. Wade.

HARBORCREEK.

G. W. Cleaveland.
Wm. Henton.
T. M. Dodge.

CORRY.

Isaac Colgrove.
Rev. R.M.Warren
Dr. J. A. Marsh.
J. C. Wales.

E. SPRINGFIELD.

John Hughes,
W. T. Manus.
W. M. McMullen.

MILES GROVE.

Chas. Pettibone.

The contest is upon us. Let no friend of temperance fail in the crisis. Only by early, thorough and constant work can we hope for success. The campaign must be planned wisely and prosecuted boldly. The aim of this convention is to inaugurate the movement. We, therefore, appeal to everyone in Erie County who loves his country and his fellow-man to respond to this call in person and to co-operate in this work. "Pennsylvania expects every man to do his duty."

The returns June 30, 1889, showed a majority of about 193,360 votes against the amendment; Erie County's majority, 3,815.

The number of licenses granted for the sale of intoxicating drinks in 1893 in the county of Erie, 163; in the city, 121. Applications denied or refusals to grant, 48.

Woman's Work.—(March 10, 1893.)—In response to the call of the chairman, the members of the Erie County Committee, Board of World's Fair Managers, met at her residence this morning.

The main object of the society, organized a little over a year ago, having been accomplished, and Erie County complimented upon the display to be made, the subject of joining "The Pennsylvania Association for Women's Work" was discussed, and the idea warmly advocated by the ladies present.

At a meeting of delegates from the Congressional districts of Pennsylvania, convened at Philadelphia for the purpose of considering the representation of work of Pennsylvania women at Chicago, it was suggested that the present county auxiliary committees form the nucleus of the permanent organization, which shall be known as the Pennsylvania Association for Women's Work, having for its object the uniting of women of this State for philanthropic and patriotic endeavors and the fostering of all interests of women throughout the Commonwealth. In addition to regular work, it is a part of the liberal plan that in case of any calamity or emergency this association can be relied upon for immediate assistance.

The whole idea is based upon a broad foundation, quite in proportion to the great State it represents. Any woman in the State interested in woman's work, can become a member on the presentation of her name by other members, conditions being the same that secured appointments on the auxiliary committee, i. e., good social standing and the proven capacity to excel in some one line of usefulness.

The membership fee is placed at one dollar per annum. Meetings are to be held yearly, convening by turns in the larger towns. Each county will hold, at its discretion, monthly or quarterly meetings.

The Secretary was requested to notify the State Secretary of the decision of the Erie County Committee, and would request the members absent from to-day's meeting, to kindly send their names and initiation fee ($1) to 138 East Twelfth Street, should they feel disposed to join also.

In regard to ordering the medallions, it was decided to defer the matter until the chairman could send for one for inspection. They are of beautiful workmanship and unique design.

The meeting adjourned subject to the call of the president.

EMMA BREVILLIER, Secretary.

Humane Society.—At a preliminary meeting a vote of thanks was extended to Dr. George A. Bell, the humane agent of the Western Pennsylvania Society, for his work and able report. He was appointed on the 10th day of January, 1891. During the year complaints and investigations made were 448 in number: Domestic animals, 320; children, 110; aged persons, 18. For the year 1892 the total was 372: Domestic animals, 280; children, 84; aged persons, 8.

From the result of investigations there were thirty arrests made and brought before aldermen of this city. They were all fined from ten to twenty dollars each and costs. A few were let off, being very poor, by paying the costs and promising to do better in the future. There were no appeals to a higher court, which can be done when the fines exceed ten dollars.

February, 1893.—Those interested in the organization of a local branch of the Northwestern Pennsylvania Humane Society met at Y. M. C. A. Hall. The attendance was good, many ladies being present. A permanent organization was formed and the following officers and board of managers elected for the ensuing year:

President—F. F. Adams; Vice-Presidents—L. M. Little, J. F. Downing, and Robert J. Saltsman; Managers—Mrs. Willis Churchill, Mrs. J. F. Downing, Mrs. Thomas Baird, Mrs. Myron Sanford, Mrs. W. T. Black, Mrs. J. M. Glazier, Mrs. C. V. Gridley, Mrs. T. D. Ingersoll, Mrs. W. L. Erwin, Mrs. Frank Keplar, Mrs. A. K. McMullen, Mrs. John Walker, Thomas Pickering, James McBrier, Rev. B. H. Hayden, Thomas Brown, Capt. J. S. Richards, W. N. Wilson; Secretary—Mrs. George Talcott; Acting Treasurer—F. A. Bliley.

Dr. Bell was chosen agent for Erie City; F. A. Bliley, solicitor. The adoption of a constitution and code of by-laws followed the election of officers. The annual election of officers will be held on the third Monday of February of each year. Regular meetings will be held on the first Monday of each month. The membership fee was placed at $1 for ladies and $3 for gentlemen.

The Erie Humane Society met in the Y. M. C. A. Hall in monthly session, with Hon. F. F. Adams presiding.

Dr. Bell, the humane agent, made a report of the work of the society during the month of October as follows: Abuse of horses and animals investigated, sixty; children reported to have been neglected, sixty-eight; old ladies neglected or abused, three; and one young man reported to have been badly treated. Two of the old ladies were sent to the almshouse, and the young man was sent to the almshouse infirmary.

The report for the month of November shows that ninety-seven reported cases of abuse to animals were investigated and a number of prosecutions were brought. Seventy children were looked after and their condition improved. Four old ladies were placed amid better surroundings.

Dr. T. D. Ingersoll read a paper on the intelligence of the horse, and the paper was a very philosophical dissertation.

Dr. Bell, in this connection, stated that in the matter of the senses of seeing, hearing, and smelling they were a great deal more acute than those in the human race. The meeting was one of the most interesting held since the organization of the society in this city.

Dr. Bell, who will in all probability be continued as agent of the Erie branch of the Humane Society, concluded his remarks with the following words:

"In conclusion, I must thank the press, police, and citizens in general for the valuable assistance they have given me the past two years. Let every lady and gentleman do all they can to put down cruelty of every nature. There is enough for all of us to do. It is impossible for the agent to be all over the city at one time. Every good citizen has a right to stop any form of cruelty, and then he can report to the agent either by telephone, mail, or in person. All informations are strictly confidential in every respect."

At next Monday's meeting officers will be elected and a constitution and by-laws adopted. Let the good work go on, and the meeting be largely attended, for there is a large and fruitful field in the midst of us for just such a society as the one about to be organized.

A day nursery or *crêche* was incorporated in 1892. The large frame house at No. 235 East Sixth Street was opened December 1st, and a matron installed. The officers were: Mrs. T. C. Gridley, President; Mrs. Wm. T. Black and Mrs. Jno. T. Boyd, Vice-Presidents; Mrs. Chas. Davenport, Treasurer; and Mrs. Wm. Brewster, Secretary. Together with the Humane Society and Bureau of Charities, Erie is much better provided than formerly to help those in want, and it is fortunate that they are popular and funds are amply provided. The flood of May, 1892, made large demands, which were greatly increased by the financial depression a few months later.

The Young Men's Christian Association was organized in Erie August 20, 1860, by a meeting held in Park Hall (609 French Street Park), with Mr. E. L. Pelton as chairman. At the meeting of August 27th, Mr. A. McD. Lyon was elected President. After holding their meetings in the lecture rooms of the different Protestant churches for one year, rooms were fitted up for them in the Beatty Block, West Park. Mr. A. H. Caughey was elected President, and $175 was expended for books and a few periodicals for a reading room. The remains of the Irving Institute Library, consisting of 700 volumes, were entrusted to their keeping. In 1862, Mr. G. S. Berry having an official position in Harrisburg was empowered to apply for a charter, which was granted the ensuing year; also a course of lectures was maintained. The association consists of four departments: First, the general department, providing for the intellectual, social, physical, and spiritual wants of young men, as literary societies, lectures, Bible classes, devotional services, companionship for strangers, gymnastic privileges, etc.; second, the railroad branch, which offers railroad people gospel services, religious literature, with attention to the sick and injured; third, the German branch, providing the German-speaking with meetings in their own language; fourth, the boy's branch, which is conducted with special reference to the wants of that age—practical talks on religious and secular topics, also mechanical, scientific, and other interesting subjects.

The association purchased about 1878, a fine three-story brick building on the corner of Tenth and Peach streets, and in 1889 made a large addition for a lecture room and gymna-

sium. The library now contains about 6,000 volumes, with seventy-five newspapers and periodicals in the free reading room. The number of members is about 500, being of two classes, active and associate. The former hold office or vote in the management, being connected with some church. For a small fee yearly, all the privileges of the institution can be enjoyed—the library, baths, gymnasium, etc. There is also a ladies' auxiliary, which is very useful, with Mrs. F. A. Mizener, President, which has for its work a supervision of the building, refitting, and decorating.

The chairman of the library committee, Mr. (now Rey.) A. H. Caughey, in the *Erie Dispatch*, 1887, recounts one of their past trials, as follows : " It was not until the early part of the year 1867 that the work of soliciting was undertaken with real zeal, and pushed to completion. . . . . Two or three thousand dollars had thus been subscribed, when the late Myron Sanford set down his name for one thousand dollars, with this limitation, namely : ' Provided ten thousand dollars is subscribed and paid in to the treasurer on or before May 25, 1867.' The soliciting committees were delighted, astonished, and—discouraged. . . . . We were in sight of the goal, but it was not reached, and the 25th of May had come. Mr. Sanford kindly extended the time. We worked for a month longer, but were still several hundred dollars short of the full sum ; when our generous helper handed us his check for $1,000, and bade us rest from our labors."

Prof. H. S. Jones, Mr. A. L. Littel, and Rev. A. H. Caughey have been effective and untiring in their efforts for the library. The names of W. R. Davenport, C. C. Shirk, N. J. Clark, George D. Selden, James Metcalf, H. L. Sanford, and of Secretaries Simms, Gordon, and Hatch are recognized as among its active friends. The President (1893) is Mr. L. M. Little, the General Secretary, Mr. W. D. Fellows, and there are twenty-four managers from the different churches. A gospel wagon has the past year been added to the facilities for preaching the Word in points distant from churches. Messrs. Eddy, DeWitt, and I. M. Wallace have aided by their efforts and means.

Hamot Hospital had its origin in a remark made by Rev.

James T. Franklin, and was formally opened July 1, 1881. The property at the foot of State Street, valued at $12,000, was presented to a corporation by the heirs of P. S. V. Hamot for the sole use of a general hospital, being one of the most valuable gifts as yet made for a public purpose. A house physician and a medical board from our first physicians, with a superintendent, a graduate from a New York school for trained nurses, officiated. A ladies auxiliary, representing every Protestant church in the city, is in aid of the regular board of managers. An enlargement of the building was demanded in a few years, and it is now amply equipped and provided. The expense was met by subscription and a small State appropriation. It can now accommodate forty to fifty patients, and is supported by fees from able patients, voluntary donations from business houses, societies, and individuals. It has one yearly income of $500 from a generous citizen; also one perpetual free bed by a donation of $5,000, being the Myron Sanford memorial. Mr. George Selden has bequeathed to the hospital $20,000 provided it ceases to be sectarian. By its constitution the Rector of St. Paul's Protestant Episcopal church is its president and a majority of the managers must be from the same church.

The report of the training school for 1893, which was established in 1889, principally by the efforts of Mrs. Charles H. Strong, is as follows: Eight nurses were sent out, and many calls were refused, as nurses could not be spared from the hospital. There are now three graduates doing private nursing in the town, and one is acting as office nurse to a physician. Four have graduated the past year.

The St. Vincent Hospital was erected in 1875-76; a handsome four story brick structure well fitted for hospital purposes. It is under the care of the Sisters of St. Joseph, being presided over by Sister Ambrosia with a large corps of well-trained nurses. It is one of the most popular institutions of its kind in this region and is on the corner of Twenty-sixth and Sassafras streets.

Home of the Friendless.—This popular and well-established institution, first occupied (Nov. 2, 1871) the "Reed homestead," which was on the southeast corner of State Street and

South Park Row, having been tendered its use by Gen. C. M. Reed. The next year it was removed to the Marine Hospital, now the Soldiers' Home. The managers authorized them to occupy it until the State authorities should direct its use for other purposes. In November, 1875, the Home was removed to its permanent quarters, the Hon. M. B. Lowry having donated the fine property on the corner of Twenty-Second and Sassafras streets. In 1875 the new brick building was completed through much effort to collect funds on the part of its friends. Hon. W. L. Scott made a donation to the institution on Christmas, 1880, of $5,000. Mr. P. Metcalf presented a lot of fifty feet added to the south side. Ten years from its commencement it had a convenient building large enough to accommodate eighty persons, and a property worth $18,000. In 1884 Mr. Dunning's property adjoining on Twenty-Third Street was purchased for $5,000 for an old people's home, an improvement which had been contemplated from the first. A large addition was made on Twenty-Third Street. Thousands of children have been sheltered and cared for, and the ladies of the Protestant churches feel richly rewarded in their labor of love. Mrs. I. B. Gara, Miss Kate Mason, and Miss Sarah Reed have successively held the office of President.

The Old Ladies' Home, under the Home of the Friendless board of managers, commenced in 1886 by the purchase of the "Dunning" place, has proved a very acceptable institution, and will probably soon be enlarged.

St. Joseph's Orphan Asylum is in charge of the Sisters of St. Joseph. Also in charge of the same Sisters is the *Old Folks' Home* corner of Twenty-sixth and Ash streets.

A Charity Society was organized in 1881, mainly through the efforts of Mr. W. L. Scott. J. F. Downing, President; W. S. Brown, Secretary and Treasurer. Objects: To bring into harmonious coöperation with one another and with the overseers of the poor, the various churches, charitable agencies, and individuals in the city, and thus, among other things, to check the evils of the overlapping of relief; to obtain from the people charities, suitable relief for deserving cases; to provide visitors, who shall personally attend cases needing counsel and help, and to procure work for poor persons who are capable of being wholly or partly self-supporting ; to assist from its own funds, as far as possible, all suitable cases for which assistance cannot be obtained from other sources ; to repress mendacity by the above means and by the prosecution of imposters ; to promote the general welfare of the poor by social and sanitary reforms, and by the inculcation of habits of providence and self-dependence. This society was very useful, particularly in 1891-92 when the diphtheria prevailed, but has been superseded by the *Bureau of Charities*, which was incorporated in 1892. The applicants were Harriet V. Gridley, Ella R. Griffith, Filinda W. Walker, Katharine Clark, Minnie Dunning, Emma J. Carroll, Charlotte M. Brevillier. The names of those chosen to act as an advisory board were as follow : Hon. Matthew Griswold, Hon. J. F. Downing, Hon. William A. Galbraith, Rev. John Huske, Rev. Solon Cobb, Rev. H. C. Hall, Hon. Walter Scott, and Messrs. Frederick Brevillier, Charles Jarecki, J. H. Davie, William S. Brown, F. A. Bliley, C. P. Cody, Dr. John Doll and Veterinary Surgeon George W. Bell.

The membership fee was placed at $1 for both ladies and gentlemen.

Commissioner Riblet stated that the board had much to be thankful for on account of the Bureau of Charities, a new organization, which is working in unison with the Commissioners and furnishes the board regularly with a list of persons who have received aid from it. The Commissioners in return furnish the bureau with a similar list.

The total amount expended by the Commissioners during October for groceries and fuel was $299.70 against $243.60 for the same period last year. At present the board is aiding 107 families, an increase of 26. In September of this year, $285.64 was the amount expended in their relief. Every precaution is taken that only worthy persons receive assistance.

The total poor expense last year amounted to $37,151.34, and out of the appropriation $5,450 remained in the treasury at the beginning of the present year. The custom has been to carry over about this amount from year to year, but if 1893 keeps pace with former years with a natural increase in the expense account of $2,000, which it bids fair to do, there will not be much of the $34,000 appropriation made for this year left in the treasury next spring. The amount remaining in the treasury at the present time is $15,000.

Mr. Robertson Wilcox, of Girard, bequeathed $5,000 to a public library in that borough. The amount is to be kept as a reserve fund, and used for the purchase of books and periodicals from year to year. The citizens are erecting the library building, and will meet the running expenses. It will be of brick and two stories high. Nearly $2,000 has already been subscribed. The following persons were selected as incorporators, whose names will appear upon the charter: Mrs. C. F. Rockwell, W. C. Culbertson, A. M. Clark, Mrs. R. S. Battles, A. R. Smith, S. S. Ely, Mrs. U. P. Rossiter, and J. C. Murphy. Five directors to serve for the ensuing year were elected, viz.: Frank May, C. F. Rockwell, R. S. Battles, Geo. W. Kibler, and O. D. Van Camp. The directors will select a building committee, president, secretary, etc., and have general supervision of the affairs of the association.

The cornerstone of the Wilcox Library was laid the 17th of October. After the singing of "America" by the public school children, prayer was offered by Rev. C. D. Shipman, and appropriate remarks were made by Dr. O. Logan. Mrs. C. F. Rockwell read a list of the contents of the box to be deposited under the stone. A contractor of Greenville has charge and good progress may be expected.

Mr. Wilcox contributed largely to the M. E. church of Girard, in which he was a trustee. He had a good common school education and much business capacity, and largely invested in real estate in Erie and Chicago. The Wilcox House in Erie was owned by him. He was born in New London, Conn., in 1811, but came to Girard about 1834, and did a large business working at his trade, which was coopering.

Mr. Wilcox also donated $10,000 for an annex to Allegheny College. The foundation is nearly complete, and, if the work goes on without interruption, the building may be ready for occupancy by the opening of the winter term.

The funds for the building were obtained partly by bequest and partly by subscription. Mr. Robertson Wilcox, formerly of Girard, Pa., left the sum of $5,000 to the college for this purpose, and in honor of him the building will be known as the Wilcox Hall of Science. It is to be devoted entirely to the departments of physics and chemistry, and is being built on a plan especially chosen for the purpose. It will be 40x61 feet on the ground floor, and two to four stories in height. The basement will contain shops ; on the other floors are laboratories, recitation rooms, and a lecture room, seated like a medical lecture room, so that every student can look down upon the experiment table. This will seat about one hundred students. In all there are to be twelve rooms above the basement, and the cost will be between $10,000 and $12,000.

Would that many wealthy citizens would imitate his noble example !

John Weis, a highly respected citizen of West Millcreek, died in 1892, leaving an estate estimated at from $50,000 to $75,000. By his will he provides that a library be built and furnished within the boundaries of Fairview township, or McKean or in West Millcreek. The ground is to be purchased and library opened as soon as possible. The best of books must be provided. Like many of his generation, he felt the absence of an early education, and it was his aim to do all in his power for the education of the young. After the expenses connected with the library are met, the trustees were directed to use the income to assist young people in literary and scientific pursuits. No sum to be paid greater than $100 per year for each person. His father, Jacob Weis, was a typical representative of the Pennsylvania German, and came to Erie from Lancaster about 1797, with the first settlers. First he resided at West Millcreek, but afterwards purchased the Moses Barnet farm, in Fairview township. The site thought the most desirable for the Weis library is in the southern corner of Millcreek, a very healthful as well as beautiful locality. It was undoubtedly the intention of the testator to locate it there. Attorney Henry Riblet was his counsel and near friend. His mother was Elizabeth (Ebersole) Weis, and his sister, Mrs. Hershey, alone survives. John Weis was born January 7, 1819.

In 1888 the *Erie Herald* Publishing Company issued an illustrated, choice paper, " City of Erie, Pennsylvania," and among other items said Erie never had a hurricane, a cyclone, an earthquake or a flood. We trust the first two calamities never may visit us.

The Flood of May 15-18, 1893.—Mill Creek was swollen and raging from the constant and heavy rains of the previous few days. A boy thirteen years of age, Jacob Heberla, was drowned on the 16th, near Twenty-fourth and State streets while attempting to grapple some floating wood. The force of the powerful current drew him into the stream before he realized his danger or could release his hold. A rope was thrown him, but he disappeared at Twenty-third Street culvert, and his body was not found for some days. His recently widowed mother had also lately lost a child by diphtheria, making a grievous affliction. At midnight many women, children, and some invalids were removed to places of safety in a pouring rain. Buildings were picked up, swung around, and carried down stream, often blocking the way. In Erie, French and Holland streets were receptacles for overflow waters. Lakes, pools, and canals were found in unheard of places, and numerous wet cellars and ruined foundations were the result. Sewers at Eighth and Poplar, Eighteenth and Cherry, Tenth and State, Eighteenth and Poplar, were greatly damaged. The Hook and Ladder Company was at E. Eighteenth Street and at Twenty-sixth succeeded in breaking up a jam after midnight. A skating rink on Tenth Street, being an immense structure, was turned about and twisted in an extraordinary manner. Watson's Paper Mill, City Iron Works, Jarecki's and Stearns' were closed for repairs for some days, or isolated by the water and unapproachable, though boats and rafts were useful and in demand. Some rowed over their hitherto beautiful gardens, and many used for entrance and exit second-story windows. Much soil was plowed, and carried down by the rush of waters. Railroad travel was interrupted for days, and the electric car tracks impeded. Bridges and abutments in Glenwood Park disappeared at a great loss. Garrison, Trout, and Brandy Runs, and Elk Creek, Gingrich, and Culbertson dams were partly carried away. Through the county the loss was great at Northeast, Waterford, Wellsburg, Albion, Girard, Lockport, and Fairview. Fortunately there was no loss of life to record, excepting in one case. Many animals, however, perished. The loss of property to the county and city taxpayers, to individuals, for foundations, cave-ins, interruptions in business, railroad companies, etc., was unparalleled.

About 1878 Mr. Jas. Dodsworth and a daughter fifteen years of age, living in a cottage on Eighth Street, were with the house carried down Mill Creek during the night, and the bodies not found until some days after. The storm and overflow were of very short duration, and the catastrophe scarcely had witnesses. Union City, June 5, 1892, suffered by the flood which was so disastrous to Oil City and Titusville. The citizens of Erie made a collection of $6,229.77, $3,736.87 being donated to Titusville and $2,492.90 to Oil City. At Oil City 105 houses were destroyed and many damaged. Titusville and Oil City, according to figures, lost 129 persons in the fiery deluge. It is said the loss to Erie was equal excepting the loss by fire.

The greatest rainfall recorded in the history of Erie commenced on the night of the 15th of May 1893, and ended at about 6 a. m. on the 18th, 6.33 inches of rain having fallen during that period—about fifty-five hours. During the flood, 4.71 inches of rain fell in twenty-four hours. However, two inches of rain fell in Erie in two hours, viz.: from 7:40 to 9:40 a. m., August 25, 1873.

SECTION VI.

Water Commissioners—Hon. W. L. Scott—Palatial Residences— The Wadena—Ore Docks—Trestle—Metric Metal Co.—Railroads— County Roads — Freight Report — Banks --- Disasters — Storage — Homeopathic Hospital—A Synopsis—World's Fair Awards.

THE Board of Water Commissioners realize the importance of bettering the supply of drinking water which is used by the citizens of Erie, and, as true servants of the public, are doing the best they can to obtain it. An intercepting sewer from the vicinity of the Villa Maria Academy to the water front and thence east to the neighborhood of the Soldiers'

Home property at a cost of less than $100,000, was proposed as a measure of immediate relief. A vote for increase of debt for defraying the expense of constructing such a sewer resulted as follows: 1,833 in its favor, and 2,194 against; majority opposed, 361. Judging from this vote (and it was the second upon the subject) the people are not thoroughly aroused to its importance. Notwithstanding the health officer and physicians have recommended to boil the city water used for drinking purposes. Several citizens have written ably upon the subject, and we do not doubt but that a plan will be devised ere long by which the difficulty will be corrected. May it shortly prove an exception to the poet's lines,

"'Twixt truth and error, there is this difference known,
Error is fruitful, truth is only one."

FUNERAL OF WILLIAM L. SCOTT.

From the Evening Herald.

Mayor C. S. Clarke issued the following proclamation:

"The death of Hon. William L. Scott, a former mayor of this city, has occasioned universal sorrow in the community, and in view of his eminent services as an official, citizen, and business man, it is fitting that all due honor should be paid to his memory.

"Therefore I, Charles S. Clarke, mayor, request that all unnecessary business be suspended in this city from three to six o'clock on Thursday, September 24, the day of the funeral, in order that all may have an opportunity to participate in the burial services.

"Given under my hand and the seal of the city of Erie this twenty-third day of September, A. D. 1891.

"CHARLES S. CLARKE, Mayor."

The Rev. John Huske and Rev. William Price conducted the funeral services of the Episcopal church. A quartet composed of Mrs. F. W. Britton, of Cleveland, Mrs. Eggleston, Messrs. Little and Barnhurst, sang "Nearer My God to Thee."

The honorary pall-bearers were ex-President Grover Cleveland, Gov. Robert E. Pattison, Mr. George B. Roberts, Mr. Marvin Hughlett, Mr. E. S. Chapin, Mr. John W. Sterling, Col. Daniel Lamont, Gen. McClelland, Mr. James McCrea,

Mr. Robert Neilson, Capt. John P. Green, Mr. Joseph Wood, Mr. Charles Watts, Mr. J. Twing Brooks, Mr. J. M. Kimball, Capt. Orris A. Browne, Mr. John B. Larkin, Mr. F. F. Marshall, Hon. G. A. Allen, Maj. J. W. Reynolds, Hon. F. F. Adams, Mr. A. R. Lee, Mr. John W. Little, Mr. John Clemens, Hon. E. Camphausen, Hon. C. M. Reed, Col. J. Ross Thompson, Maj. John W. Walker, Hon. F. A. Mizener, Mr. John R. Saltsman, Mr. C. F. Allis, and Mr. Robert J. Saltsman.

The active pall-bearers were Capt. J. S. Richards, Mr. Henry Shannon, Mr. W. S. Brown, Mr. L. M. Little, Mr. M. H. Taylor, Hon. Joseph McCarter, Mr. W. Brewster, and Mr. F. B. Whipple.

Col. J. Ross Thompson addressed the city councils after resolutions of respect had been passed for the loss of "Erie's foremost citizen."

The floral tributes were the finest ever seen in this section of the country and were mostly furnished by Thorley, of New York, who sent his representatives here to look after the flowers.

The emblems which came from Thorley's are as follows:

A four-foot floral mat composed of lilies of the valley, pink roses, white roses, maiden hair ferns with a large white ribbon bow, bearing the card, "From the surviving members of the firm." The casket cross of orchids and lilies of the valley with a lavender knot bearing the name of Mr. John S. Richards. Flat bunch of American beauties with a bow knot of white ribbon from Mr. John E. Payne. A large crescent and wreath of lilies of the valley, la France roses and Scotch heather, tied with lavender ribbon from the Second National Bank.

Five Sago palms and violets tied with lavender ribbon from Hon. Joseph McCarter. A cross from Mr. and Mrs. Geylan, of Philadelphia. Large wreath of white roses from Maj. J. W. Walker. Twelve loose bunches of flowers from Messrs. E. S. Chapin, J. W. Sterling and others of New York.

Those from the Erie florists were a large sheaf of wheat with a ribbon bearing in gilt letters the legend: "Erie Democratic Society, We have lost the leader of Our County." A pillow from W. F. and F. M. Hayes, a crescent of white pinks and Marechal Niel roses from Mr. F. F. Marshall, a pair of palm leaves and bunch of white roses from Dr. and Mrs. C. U. Gravatt, U. S. N., a wreath from Mr. H. C. Shannon, an anchor from the trestle employees, a lyre from the Erie Maennerchor, a harp from the Erie Liedertafel, a wreath from the Mueller Battery, afterwards known as Battery B.

The Philadelphia & Erie Express brought the casket in which Hon. William L. Scott's remains will repose. The coffin, which is from an original design, required the united efforts of the entire force of workmen of the undertaker to complete it in twelve hours. In the construction of it seventy-six pounds of solid silver were used, forty yards of broadcloth, about thirty pounds of silk, and ten pounds of eiderdown. The casket, which is made of Florida red cedar, has straight sides, and heavy fluted columns at the corners. The entire casket, columns, molding, and all, is covered with the heaviest grade of fine black broadcloth, tightly stretched. Along the entire length of each side extend heavy bars of solid oxydized silver. Each one of these bars contains 28½ pounds of pure coin silver. At each end are shorter bars of the same material and design, each one weighing 9½ pounds. The plate on top, which is also of solid silver, is handsomely engraved with the inscription:

> Born July 2, 1828.
> WILLIAM L. SCOTT.
> Died September 19, 1891.

The casket is lined throughout with Bengaline silk. This material is draped with what is known to the professional undertaker as "artistic carelessness." The filling in and all the upholstering is eiderdown.

Thousands of people who followed the remains of Erie's distinguished citizen to their last resting place looked for the first time with wonder upon the imposing edifice he had built for himself and family for their last sleep. The mausoleum, covering 1,000 square feet, rises majestically and stands fifty feet high. The beautiful Gothic structure has the form of a Greek cross and was entered from the east. The granite approaches from the east terminate in a portico which is supported by polished pillars. The ashlar faced Hallowell granite walls, supported by massive buttresses at the corners, rise to the height of seventeen feet. The wings are finished in Gallic panels. The exterior above the buttresses shows a rise of receding granite slabs, one above another till they reach the dome of the mausoleum. This dome is of most exquisite design and on each side has two Gothic niches or windows with polished columns. The dome is in pyramidal shape, terminating in a purely-executed cross-shaped finial. The beautiful polished columns, 22 in number, about the base and at the top of the structure, with their composite capitals in darker granite than the main structure, give the edifice a grandeur that is striking. At the entrance of the rotunda are two standard solid bronze doors. The rotunda, which is eleven feet square, has arranged on the right and left the catacombs, 24 in number. At the west side over the altar there is an apsis of colored designs, and through these a soft light streams down upon the rotunda. Light also admitted from the dome or ventilator shows with fine effect the geometrical patterned marble floor. The walls and wainscot in Florentine, French, African, and native marble are strangely beautiful and artistic.

Erie has palatial residences which merit particular description, as those of Mrs. C. H. Strong, H. F. Watson, M. H. Taylor, H. Shenk, and more than twenty others. Its many business houses and societies must also be passed by for want of space.

The pleasure yacht *Wadena* of Cleveland called for a day at Erie, having crossed from Port Colborne on account of thick and heavy weather. The *Welland* was passed on November 21, 1892. During an absence of over a year the *Wadena* made a voyage of over 25,000 miles. After a winter spent in the Mediterranean, the *Wadena* left for the North Sea. While lying outside of Hammerfest harbor the party, at midnight on July 24, saw the setting sun skirt the horizon and begin to rise again. North Cape, the farthest point to the north, was reached on the following day, and after a visit to the Holland fiord, with its famous black ice, 180 years old, Mr. Wade and his guests turned southward again, skirting Europe, and reaching Gibraltar on September 6. Returning across the Atlantic, Charleston, S. C., was the first United States port touched. This was on October 12, and on the 18th the yacht arrived at Brooklyn. A week later she left for Cleveland. The trip was leisurely taken, stops being made at Halifax, Port Mulgrave, and Quebec—the latter port being reached on October 30. Other stops, generally over night, were made at Charlotte, Valley Field, Cornwall, Lachine, Farran's Point, Morrisburg, and Odgensburg, the yacht being pontooned through the St. Lawrence canals. At Oswego, Fairhaven, and St Catherines, calls were made. The *Wadena*, the property of Com. Wade, of the Cleveland Yachting Club, is about the size of the pleasure yacht *Mystic* of this port.

The Pittsburg Docks in Erie Harbor.—No. 1, the middle dock of the group, so called because first built, is 1,050 feet long, 190 feet wide, and was built in 1864; much of it has since been rebuilt, and the channel on each side deepened and widened.

No. 2 is the west dock, and second built (1868), with trestle and shutes to load soft coal. This practice was abandoned in 1878, trestle and shute taken away, dock widened and extended 500 feet, making its length 1,500 feet, and the width 150 feet. This was in 1882.

No. 3 is the shore dock, running between Nos. 1 and 4, and is 550 feet long by 250 wide, and was built in 1870. This has also been rebuilt, and the channel and basin dredged and deepened.

No. 4, or what is called the Carnegie dock, was built in 1870 and 1871; it is 1,100 feet long, and 350 feet wide. This, however, is but one half the size which the Pennsylvania Company intend to make this dock, as the original plan called for 1,100 feet by 741 feet, and when there is a demand for the other half it probably will be built.

Heavy Ore Shipments.—(1892)—" The work of shipping ore from the Carnegie docks in this city, which was almost suspended during the long strikes of the summer at the Carnegie mills, has been resumed. The daily shipments are about 100 cars. Sometimes it is out of the question to get cars, and the shipments are then retarded. The force of men at work on the Carnegie docks is about eighty, and they will have work all winter, something rather unusual at the ore docks. The shipments from the Erie & Pittsburg docks are slow, and do not run over eight or ten cars a day. There are almost a million tons of ore on both docks at the present time, but it is the intention of the Carnegies to get their ore all off the docks before the opening of navigation. The new donkey hoists on the docks are a great assistance in the handling of ore, and make the work comparatively light.

"The season of navigation, now about closed, has been one of the most notable in the history of this port. During the season the officials of the Pennsylvania Railroad announced their intention of expending $2,000,000 in this city in betterment of their tracks, yards, and dock facilities. An elevator for the receipt and shipment of grain was also promised. The company did expend $200,000 on the extension of the ore docks, and another $60,000 on the ore docks at the Philadelphia & Erie terminus. The fact that the company has, or is about to put up, double-track iron bridges over the western division of the Philadelphia & Erie, and is opening up and extending all its sidings, confirms the report that ere the close of another season the Philadelphia and Erie will have a complete double track. The yards at the lake front are being extended, and everything indicates good faith on the part of the Pennsylvania, and the fulfillment of the predictions of its officials.

"The receipts of freight here during the season were 37,491 tons, mostly from Chicago and Milwaukee. The receipts of corn were 5,595,740 bushels, 112 per cent more than last year. The receipts of wheat were 7,930,788 bushels—a slight falling off from last year, but with that exception the largest ever received in Erie. The receipts of barley were 80,000 bushels, an increase of 60 per cent. The receipts of rye were 414,779 bushels. The flour receipts reached the unprecedented total of 2,000,000 barrels, being more than double last year's, and largely from Duluth. Of flaxseed there were 314,640 bushels, and pig iron 3,940 tons, a slight falling off.

"The advent here of the Carnegies, who occupy the new dock built by the Pennsylvania Company at the Erie & Pittsburg docks, boomed ore receipts largely, and they reached 6,404,434 tons, as against 394,347 tons last year. The receipts of lumber were 12,918,000 feet, 33½ per cent heavier than last season. House-furnishing establishments received 4,850 tons, and building stone from Kelly's Island amounted to 1,023 tons. The copper receipts fell off to 7,704 tons, and plaster from Lake Superior to 1,784 tons.

"Shipments were correspondingly heavy, as follows: Freight, mostly machinery, to Chicago, 110,592 tons; hard coal, 378,067; soft coal, 103,693; brick, 220, and railway iron, 400. There was an increase in foreign shipments from Canada this year in the matter of lumber, and it was for fine house-finishing woods. The imports of white pine were 1,395,087 feet; maple for veneering pianos and for house trimmings, 9,405 feet; lath, 1,047,550; stave bolts for tobacco pails, 345 cords."

The Big Trestle of the Scott Coal Company.—The area covered is 220x400 feet, all under one roof, being the most complete concern of the kind in the country. The machinery is of new design and to be operated by electricity. Coal will be transferred at a cost below any price heretofore, and will not exceed 1¼ cents per ton. The Nickel Plate and Lake Shore cars run into the yards, where thousands of tons of coal will be stored at all times, and the trestle is one of the largest in the United States.

Erie's Coal Shipments (Dec., 1893).—"The last cargo of coal by lake has left this port for this season, being taken by the Schuylkill a few days ago.

"The shipments of hard coal from this port this season were about 440,000 tons, and about 100,000 tons of soft coal, mostly for fuel in the early part of the season, and latterly for the Chicago markets.

"The shipments of coal this season exceed those of last season, especially of soft coal, there being fully 50,000 tons shipped more than last year.

"The new coal trestles at the junction of the Philadelphia & Erie and Lake Shore roads are now in very active use, and the hard coal is being run in on the Philadelphia & Erie Railroad and transferred from the cars into the pockets, or into the general storage in the centre of the building. The pockets are so arranged that cars can be loaded directly from the pocket into the car, saving a great deal of handling by the automatic arrangement.

"The rates for carrying coal this year have been very low. The running rates from this port were 60 cents on hard coal and from 35 to 40 cents on soft coal—that is to Chicago. The rates to Lake Superior have not been so high. Some coal has been carried to Duluth this season for 25 cents a ton, but that was mostly when the coal was wanted for ballast."

Industrial.—November of 1891 the Metric Metal shops were opened, making a great addition to Erie's industries. Many car loads of machinery were transferred from the old plant at Beaver Falls, besides the new machinery from the E. W. Bliss Company, of New York. Twenty acres of ground had been purchased from Hon. C. M. Reed just outside of the eastern limits of the city. The factory is three stories high, in the shape of the letter L, being 201 feet along Ninth Street and 210 feet along the eastern city limit. A switch from the Philadelphia & Erie will be run in along East Tenth Street until it clears the west part of the works, and thence northwest to near Ninth Street, where it will end.

The company is putting in a sewer seven eighths of a mile in length on Payne Avenue from the shops lakeward, and laying pipes to a gas well about a mile distant which they purchased from Mr. Fleming to supply heat for soldering furnaces and light throughout the establishment.

A new residence for the superintendent is under roof north of the buildings. The company opens up Ninth, Tenth, and Twelfth streets, with spills, or drainage, and Hess Avenue, parallel to Payne, is being worked into shape, as is Gilson Avenue still farther east, and real estate has greatly increased in value in the eastern part of the city.

The company will manufacture meters for natural and illuminating gas, iron for natural, and tin for illuminating. The shops will have a capacity of 250 meters a day. That will mean 250 workmen, for by calculation it takes a man to each meter. When running 135 men at Beaver Falls the average output was 135 meters a day. President, C. N. Payne; Superintendent, J. B. Wallace; Secretary and Treasurer, F. H. Payne. Jan. 30, 1893, a great surprise greeted Erie people, the failure of the Car Works, throwing 300 men out of employment. After seven months the whistle was again heard—the Lake Shore road having leased the property for twenty years, with the prospect of purchasing them at that time.

Erie City's five railroads are: Pittsburg, Shenango & Lake Erie; Lake Shore & Michigan Southern; New York, Chicago & St. Louis (commonly called the Nickel Plate); Philadelphia & Erie, and Erie & Pittsburg. At Union City we find the Philadelphia & Erie; New York, Pennsylvania & Ohio, and Western New York & Pennsylvania. At Corry is the Western New York & Pennsylvania, formerly called the Oil Creek road; the New York, Pennsylvania & Ohio, and the Philadelphia and Erie.

Bituminous coal reaches the city at a low charge by way of the New York, Pennsylvania & Ohio road from Mercer and Butler counties, and the Philadelphia & Erie gives it the benefit of competition in securing anthracite from the Eastern Pennsylvania fields.

The Philadelphia & Erie and New York, Pennsylvania & Ohio Railroads both cross the township from Le Bœuf to Concord. A third railroad, the Union & Titusville, comes in from Crawford County and connects with the Philadelphia & Erie at Union City.

It is confidently expected that motor cars will connect Edinboro with Erie in the course of a few months. Maj. Hoyt and Mr. G. E. Ryckman, of Brocton, N. Y., are said to have it in charge.

(Season of 1893). The dockets at the Custom House show the following receipts from the coastwise trade:

Wheat, bu...............	3,659,858	Lath...............	405,000
Corn, bu...............	6,630,347	Limestone, cords...............	2,362
Rye, bu...............	191,100	Package freight, tons...............	20,948
Oats, bu...............	221,887	Copper, tons...............	1,169
Barley, bu...............	156,656	SHIPMENTS.	
Flour, tons...............	105,571		
Flaxseed, bu...............	287,427	Hard coal, tons...............	353,612
Iron ore, tons...............	499,278	Soft coal, tons...............	71,261
Lumber, ft...............	8,562,000	Package freight, tons...............	45,918

There was a very heavy falling off in the receipts of package freight, which were 17,000 tons less than last season.

The receipts of corn were 1,100,000 bushels more than last season. Wheat fell off 4,000,000 bushels; barley receipts showed an increase of 700,000 bushels, or about fifty per cent. This was due to the excellent products of the Northern Minnesota and Dakota farms, which are just now springing into popularity on account of their choice barley. The rye receipts fell off about 300,000 bushels. There were at least a million barrels less of flour received this fall, and the flaxseed fell off 30,000 bushels.

The ore receipts were 150,000 tons less than in 1892, lumber fell off 4,000,000 feet. The receipts of stone were double those of last season, owing to the extension of the north pier. The copper shipments came this way in smaller shipments by 400 tons than in 1892.

Despite the heavy shipments to Chicago early in the spring, the package freight forwarded fell off 60,000 tons. The hard coal shipments fell off 30,000 tons, and the soft coal shipments increased 50,000 tons.

It was observed in this connection, however, that the falling off in the lake traffic was not as great as it was in other lines of business this year.

A local paper has the following of country roads in the spring of 1893 : "If there is such a thing possible as the enactment of any law that will improve our main thoroughfares, it is to be hoped the next Legislature will do so, for the Buffalo road is almost impassible. This should not be so with this road in particular, as it is one of the very oldest in this end of the State, and one of the most traveled. It should have been macadamized long ago. Mr. Carl Walbridge, our efficient road commissioner, is doing all that the road funds on hand will permit, but we must have a law that furnishes more money and a different system of working the roads."

"Good Roads, a matter of Finance" was decided by the bankers at the convention at Chicago. Conservative and reliable statisticians estimate the cost of bad roads in this county at more than $250,000,000.

The First National Bank was organized in February, 1863,

with a capital of $150,000. J. C. Spencer, President; M. Sanford, Cashier; J. L. Sternberg, Teller. In February, 1883, the bank was reorganized for twenty years. Surplus fund $155,000. Present officers are: President, William Spencer; Vice-President, Hon. Charles M. Reed; Cashier, J. L. Sternberg; Directors, William Spencer, Charles M. Reed, M. Griswold, William E. Marvin, and J. L. Sternberg.

The Second National Bank was established in 1864. Capital stock, $300,000; surplus, $200,000; undivided profits, $94,456. President, Joseph McCarter; Cashier, C. F. Allis; Assistant Cashier, W. M. Wallace; Directors, Joseph McCarter, M. H. Taylor, D. D. Tracy, John W. Walker, J. S. Richards, W. S. Brown, Charles H. Strong. The first officers of this bank were: President, William L. Scott; Vice-President, Joseph McCarter; Cashier, W. C. Curry.

The Keystone National Bank. Capital, $250,000. President, Matthew Griswold; Vice-President, J. F. Downing; Cashier, F. V. Kepler; Assistant Cashier, F. M. Lamb; Directors, J. F. Downing, Matthew Griswold, William E. Marvin, George T. Churchill, J. I. Town, F. V. Kepler, F. M. Lamb.

The Marine National Bank. Capital, $150,000. President, F. F. Marshall; Cashier, C. E. Gunnison; Assistant Cashier, Harry Gunnison; Directors, F. F. Marshall, H. Beckman, C. E. Gunnison, Harry Gunnison, John Clemens.

The Erie Dime Savings and Loan Company. Cash capital paid in $150,000; surplus, $50,000; authorized capital $500,000. President, William A. Galbraith; Vice-President, Hon. J. F. Downing; Treasurer, F. F. Curtze; Teller, F. H. Schutte; Directors, Hon. William A. Galbraith, Hon. J. F. Downing, Hon. G. W. Starr, Benjamin Whitman, C. C. Shirk, Davis Rees, John W. Galbraith, Frank Fairbairn.

According to statistics compiled by the *C* *ago Herald*, the season just closed on the great lakes has been uncommonly disastrous. One hundred and twenty-three lives were lost, and fifty-three vessels, with an aggregate tonnage of 24,257, and valued at $1,040,400, passed out of existence, while partial losses by stranding, collision, and fire bring the total of losses up to $2,112,588. The greatest loss of life was on Lake Erie.

Increased storage is required in Erie for grain and fruits of the Northwest. Buffalo is amply provided and millions of bushels are sold in the West for delivery at that point. It is of the greatest importance that Philadelphia should have the benefit of the business done at Erie. The Reading system will soon put Philadelphia in possession of the completest facilities for dividing with the Erie Canal and the New York railways the immense business in Buffalo, and bringing hither a part of the grain, ore, and lumber. There should be a share of Philadelphia business done through the splendid port of Erie, but there is not one tenth of the needed storage.

December, 1893, application was made to the Court of Common Pleas for the incorporation of a hospital, dispensary, and training school for nurses. The name of the corporation is to be "The Homeopathic Hospital and Dispensary Association of Erie," and its purposes are for the establishing and maintaining of a hospital, dispensary, and training school for nurses. The corporators are Drs. W. K. Cleveland, Edward Cranch, Herman C. Galster, J. Louis Ireland, John F. Flint, Joseph R. Phillips, M. A. Wilson, J. C. M. Drake, H. E. Flint, and R. T. Marks, of Erie; and H. L. Stem, of Union City, and W. S. Hubbard, of Albion. The corporation is to be managed by a board of directors consisting of twelve members. The charter and certificate of incorporation were approved by the court, and the Homeopathic Hospital and Dispensary Association is now a matter of fact in organization, and will soon be in operation.

Synopsis.—Some facts concerning Erie have been concisely stated as follows: Erie is built on a bluff overlooking the finest harbor and bay on the chain of lakes. It is one of the healthiest cities on the continent. Altitude, 800 feet. Climate unsurpassed. Has 30 churches, 20 public schools, State Soldiers and Sailors' Home, 40 hotels, 6 banks, 5 daily papers, 5 railroads, natural gas, electric light and power, 15 miles of paved streets, 27 miles of electric street railroad, water sys-system with 77 miles of mains. Home city in every sense of the word. Has most picturesque surroundings. Is a beautiful summer resort. Has pretty parks. Land-locked bay, $4\frac{1}{2}$x$1\frac{1}{2}$ miles in extent. Is in the midst of the great lake shore grape district, and profits by an immense lake trade in lumber, ore, coal, grain, etc.

HISTORY OF ERIE COUNTY. 447

Erie is a manufacturing city with 50,000 population. There are 200 manufactories, employing 8,000 men, with annual output of $18,000,000. Erie enjoys the proud reputation of making more boilers and engines than any city in the world ; has two large piano factories, immense paper mills, 47 iron and brass manufactories, brass works employing 1,000 men, 9 lumber yards and planing mills, 5 large flouring mills, freight car works, lake fishery with 26 steam and 16 sail boats. A State fish hatchery is located in Erie. Bicycles, brick, beer, brooms, barrels, baskets, brushes, car heaters, cements, chemicals, confectionery, electric motors, malt, pails, hollow ware, sleeve pulleys, rubber goods, pearl buttons, stoves, soap, spring beds, novelty show cases, meters and appliances, wringers, mouse traps, and matches, are manufactured and the industries are all prospering.

The following Erie manufacturers received awards at the World's Fair on Thursday, October 12 : Ball Engine Company, high speed, compound condensing engine ; Jarecki Manufacturing Company, Limited, exhibit of brass goods and iron fittings ; Stearns Manufacturing Company, automatic, high speed engine, Gill water tube boiler ; N. A. Watson, Excelsior boiler feeder. The newspaper of the day describes the first named as follows : " The Ball Engine Company has completed the giant 700-horse-power engine for the World's Fair. The engine will be one of eight, from different parts of the United States, which will furnish the motive power in machinery hall at the great Fair. All of these engines will be painted a pure white. The engine will attract considerable attention at the Fair."

The Metric Metal Company has received an award at the World's Fair for spring scales.

The highest honors were awarded the Colby Pianos, at the World's Columbian Exposition.

Why he took the Confederate Flag.—October 20, 1893. Maj. I. B. Brown, who took down the Confederate flag from the Southern locomotive " General," in the Transportation building at the World's Fair says :

" I have no particular hostility to the men who carried the flag during the war, but why any one, twenty-eight years after the war, should deliberately display a flag in the loyal State of Illinois, or, indeed, anywhere else, which never did and never can mean anything but treason, rebellion, and human slavery, I could not understand. I have learned since that it is claimed that the flag was simply hoisted as a relic. The story is hard to believe; but even if there is any truth in it, we can get along without any exhibitions of such relics. There are enough Union soldiers with empty sleeves, wooden legs, crutches and broken constitutions to answer any reasonable demand for relics. I believe the flag was placed in position in defiance of the patriotic sentiment that ought to find a place in the heart of every loyal citizen, and such belief compelled me to take it down."

----, Peter H 291 Wayne 81
ABELL, John 139
ABERCROMBIE, Rev 176
ACADEMIES, 153 160 210
ACTUAL Settlers, 275
ADAIR, W A 172
ADAMS, Daniel 395 F F 106 356
    374 424 436 J Q 289 John Q
    404 Mr 55 Pres 406 Roswell B
    96
ADDISON, Judge 97
ADELPHIC Society, 145
ADKINS, Mrs M A 417
ADLUM, John 62
AGASSIZ, Prof 400
AGRICULTURAL Societies, 137
    138
ALBION Lodge, 139
ALBURT, 197
ALDEN, Roger 99 Timothy 173

ALDERMAN, W 422
ALFRED, Oliver 141
ALGONQUIN, 15
ALLEN, Charles 352 Eleanor 387
    388 Ethan 387 388 G A 436 S K
    387
ALLIS, C F 436 445
ALTHOF, 265
ALVORD, D 207 E 207
AMENDMENT, 421
AMITY Township, 77
ANDERSON, Mr 152 O W 422
ANDREWS, L F 148 R 266
ANGEVINE, Jackson 304
ANGUS, Lt 221
ANTI-ABOLITION, 142
APPALACHIAN, 259
ARBUCKLE, Adam 134 Joseph 175
    P 122 W G 415 William M 122
    Wm 166

ARGILLACEOUS Schist, 206
ARION Musical, 146
ARMOUR, Phillip D 359
ARMSTRONG, Capt 114 William H 151
ARNOLD, Mr 377
ARTERS, John M 368
ARTUS, James 293
ASHLEY, Mr 161 Mrs 161
ASIATIC Cholera, 283
ASSOCIATE Judges, 98
ATCHISON, 104 Adam 106
ATHOF, Mr 265
ATTWANDARONK, 15
ATKINSON, William P 414
AULL, W F 340
AUSTIN, J A 153 John A 157 Richard L 385 T M 136
AVERAGE Articles, 397
AVERY, Janitor 369
AVICULA Speciosa, 261
AYERS, J W 174
AYRES, Amy 212 Robert 212 William 212
BABBITT, E 100 140 146 406 Elijah 98 99 142 304 Henry W 304 Mr 399 Mrs E 418 Per H 306
BABEER, M 36 Mons 333
BACKBONE, 268
BACON, Frank W 325 Wm 141

BADGER, 188 Giles 290 Rev 165 Willard 187
BAGGS, James 82 195
BAHIA, 398
BAILEY, 301
BAIRD, 83 James 105 144 152 Mrs Thomas 424 S T 400
BAKER, Ensign 194 J O 408
BALDWIN, Henry 108 L B 343 L D 344 Mark 100 Mrs 172 W A 352
BALES, 68
BALL, G J 100 133 134 H 138 S 137
BALMORAL, 359
BALTIMORE, Lord 56 57.
BANCROFT, 24 50 George 136 137 378 381
BANKS, 445 John 98
BARATONI, C A 353
BARBIE, Wm P 96
BARCLAY, Commodore 125 232 230 244 Robert Herriot 237
BARGER, 422 G E 422
BARKER, Hezekiah 140 Philo 140 Samuel 140
BARLOW, Stephen 98
BARNES, Isaac 247 R A 422
BARNET, Miles 153 Moses 137 432
BARNETT, 137 Mrs 359 Rev 359

451

BARNETT (continued)
    Richard 281
BARNHURST, Mr 435
BARNUM, T B 148
BARR, 104 James 173 M R 143
BARRETT, D C 174
BARRY, Margaret 205 Mr 194 205
BARTON, 124
BATES, H 101
BATTLES, Asa 336 Mrs R S 431 R
    S 431
BAYLE, Elias 422 N N 421
BEACH, Jesse 81
BEARDSLEY, R D 422 S 422
BEATH, R B 340
BEAVER, 99 J A 340
BECKER, P 106 P A 356 366
BECKMAN, H 445 T 136
BEDELL, Bishop 393
BEDIENT, Mr 194
BEEBE, A 145 Eliphalet 123 124
    374 H 148 J C 133 Taber 174
    Tabor 105
BEEDY, Samuel 143
BELL, 95 Dr 425 George A 424
    George W 430 John 98 134 Wm
    406 Wm E 406 Wm 99 105
BELLE Riviere, 30
BENEDICT, M G 416
BENNET, G A 134 139
BENNETT, E P 139

BENSON, 163 301 Carl 149 Peter
    132 Wm 153 184 Wm Jr 153
BENZE, A L 408
BEREA, 327
BERNARD, 246 Gen 251
BERRY, Capt 346 347 G S 426 R M
    344
BERST, Mrs Titus 421
BEVERLY, William 31
BIDDLE, Clement 65
BIGLER, Gov 121
BIGLOW, 343
BILLY, Seneca 89
BIRD, 246 248 249 Mr 111 288
BISSEL, Mr 370 Russel 276 W C
    156
BISSELL, Russel 90
BITE, Mons 34
BLACK, 164 306 J H 156 Joe 81
    Mrs W T 424 Mrs Wm T 426
    Rock 219 221 S A 352 Wm K
    142
BLACKALL, S E 143
BLACKBURN, W M 175 William
    M 401 William A 131
BLACKMAN, Mr 197
BLACKS, 306
BLAINE, A W 100 133 140 356 E
    M W 101 Ephraim 309 G W
    356 J G 309
BLAIR, Dr 162 J W 138 James 290

BLAIR (continued)
  Mr 189 268 319 William 293
BLAKE, Capt 126
BLICKENSDEFER, Mr 298
BLILEY, F A 424 430
BLISS, 312 Col 404 E W 442 John
  H 382
BLOODGOOD, William A 131
BLOSSOM, Mr 152
BOLIVAR, 283
BOLOGNA, 402
BONE, Ensign 336
BOOTH, George 422 Prof 266
BOOTZ, Jacob 367
BOQUET, 48 Col 55 308 309
BORTHWICK, J L D 344
BOTY, Jacob 139
BOWMAN, C 138 John 176 Rev
  176
BOYD, C C 153 Charles C 184
  David 153 184 815 John 141
  152 184 Mrs Jno T 426 Rev 164
BOYDEN, William 153
BOYER, Col 208
BOYER'S Bluff, 208
BRABOEUF, 20 Father 19
BRACKEN, William 184
BRADDOCK, Gen 28
BRADFORD, 293 Att-Gen 66
  Thomas H 293

BRADLEY, 164 Lewis 156 M B
  184 Orenda Knight 395
BRADSTREET, Col 54
BRADY, 353 J C 106 356
BRAINARD, S M 416
BRAN, Richard 187
BRANDES, Charles 133 334
BRANDT, 71 Capt 75 Joseph 72 Mr
  70
BRANDYWINE, 271
BRANT, Capt 199
BRAWLEY, John 98 106 133 137
  140 142
BRAWLY, John 122 Rebecca 96
BRECHT, Elias 96
BRECKENRIDGE, Judge 97
BREEVOORT, Capt 125
BREVELLIER, F 374
BREVILLIER, Charlotte M 430
  Emma 423 Frederick 430
BREVOORT, Capt 224 226 237
BREWER, 370
BREWSTER, A W 100 106 119 122
  140 156 157 Mary 418 Mr 140
  155 Mrs S M 418 Mrs Wm 426
  W 436
BREYSON, A 343
BRIDGMAN, W R 328
BRIGGS, Mr 421 Mrs C M 419
BRINDLE, 164 Mathias 137 P 157

453

BRISTOL, Mr 189 Philip 141
BRITTON, Mrs F W 435
BROAS, Richard M 336
BROBOA, 19
BROOKS, 246 396 Edward 396 J Twing 436 John 246 Lt 205 225 243 249 Maj Gen 336 343
BROTHERTON, James 108
BROWN, 140 309 B H 379 Benjamin H 379 C W 407 Conrad 408 Conrad Jr 133 David 99 Diantha 418 George 343 H L 339 I B 340 447 Isaac B 339 John L 418 Matthew 309 Mr 222 231 Noah 126 222 R 173 Rasselas 97 Robert 134 135 154 155 284 Roswell H 96 S M 134 Samuel 132 Thomas 424 University 200 W A 133 W S 429 436 445 William H 295 296 William S 430 Wm A 140
BROWNE, Orris A 436
BROWNELL, Capt 377 Thomas 292
BUCHANAN, 404 Alexander 99 James 148
BUCKBEE, 416
BUCKINGHAM, 324
BUDD, Capt 282 George 250
BUEHLER, George 92 105 124 135 Henry 391 Margaretta 391 Mary Wolf 391

BULL, 48 Thomas 45 46
BULLUS, Oscar 343
BURCHFIELD, James 99
BURGES, Tristam 376
BURGESS, 376 Amos 176 Bishop 392
BURINOL, 45
BURLINGHAME, P 158
BURNETT, Jacob 210
BURNHAM, F W 421
BUROTN, D 101
BURR, Aaron 63
BURTON, John 174 P E 134 Peter E 101 133
BURWELL, Miss 419
BUSHNELL, Charles Elmer 385
BUTLER, Gen 73 J W 367 Richard 75 300
BUTTERFIELD, Gen 337
CADWELL, Henry 119
CAIN, George F 410
CALBRAITH, Mathew 380
CALDWELL, Henry 175 J K 101
CALHOUN, David 204 Elizabeth 204
CALLAGHAN, F C 422
CAMERON, Brua 133
CAMP, 163 Irvin 142 153 Rev 169 Sophia 418
CAMPBELL, 162 H S 335 J W 158 James 100 Thomas B 115

CAMPHAUSEN, E 426
CANADOHTA, 375
CANAL, 114
CANFIELD, Jonathan 357
CANNON, Eliza 390
CARMACK, Jacob 100 134
CARMARTHAN, Lord 55
CARNEGIE, 440
CARPENTER, 164 Frank G 204 S
   D 148 S M 106 W B 156
CARR, Mrs 159 Purser 275
CARRIER, A H 167 Augustus S 401
   Mrs 419 Rev 186
CARROLL, Emma J 430
CARSON, 399 Allen W 304 William 184
CARSTENSEN, G A 382
CARTER, A H 402 Comm 342 Capt 341 342 E D 325 J C 332 John C 343 Maj 124 Mary 418 Mrs J S 418 Nancy 418 Thomas 389
CASCA, Anna E 418
CASCADE, 224
CASENOVE, Theophilus 63
CASEY, 306
CASS, Gen 24 235
CASSAWAGO, 70
CASSEY, J 121
CATLIN, H 146 149 Henry 149
CATTARAUGUS, 219

CAUGHEY, 163 A H 114 139 143 149 153 295 389 426 427 Andrew 166 Jane 166 M W 101 122 332 S S 422 Wm 422
CAVALIER, Robert 24
CELERON, 30 31 37 29
CHADAKOIN, 33
CHAMBERLAIN, 81 G W 397 Hinds 81 Pierce 398
CHAMBERS, Col 208 Island 208
CHAMPLAIN, 15
CHAMPLIN, 219 234 237 Capt 377 Mr 229 240 241 S 233 285 Stephen 343
CHANDLER, 210
CHAPIN, E S 435 436 Gen 70 71 73-75 78 Israel 198 199 L 199 L S 188
CHAPMAN, Dr 412 J H 343 J Wilbur 410 413 James H 344 Wilbur 411 Wilbur F 412
CHARLEROIX, 15
CHARLES II, King 56 57
CHASE, Amos 210 Joanna B 210 Joseph 160 Salmon P 377 V O 343 344
CHAUMOUNT, Father 19
CHAUNCEY, 210 343 Comm 218-222 224 226-229 237 246
CHAUVIGNERIE, M 44 M Jr 44

CHESTER, Rev Dr 174
CHICAGO, 211
CHILLIS, Titus D 96
CHIPPEWAY, 225
CHRISTIE, 51 52 P 131 Peter 128
CHURCH, Gaylord 97
CHURCHILL, George T 445 Mrs
    Willis 424
CHUTE, 158
CISSON, Samuel 96
CISTERNS Broken, 206
CITY Hall, 366
CLARA, M Sister 416
CLARK, 243 246 301 343 358 393
    416 A M 431 D S 133 143 421
    Edwin P 421 Eliza 417 G R 343
    H C 416 J D 133 John 246
    Katharine 430 L B 421 Mr 293
    N H 421 N J 427 Rev 178 S M
    422 William 329
CLARKE, C S 356 435 Charles S
    106 435
CLAXTON, Thomas Jr 246
CLAY, H 230
CLEAVELAND, G W 422
CLEMENS, John 436 445
CLEVELAND, Grover 435 Mr 406
    W K 446
CLIFFORD, John 176
CLINTON, Gen 30 Gov 31 33 198
    James 59

CLOUGH, Rufus 134
CLUTE, Mr 150 N 158
COBB, Solon 407 421 430
COBHAM, Col 338
COCHRAN, J P 148 James 99 John
    98 Robert 106 137 Thomas 385
COCHRANE, Rev 172
CODDINGTON, 211
CODY, C P 430
COEUR, Jean 31 35 39 40 42
COFFIN, Stephen 32
COLE, 341 Mr 342
COLSGROVE, Isaac 422
COLSON, Charles 173
COLT, 76 165 Elizabeth 199 George
    P 415 Henry 96 152 Jabez 107
    James H 157 Judah 165 173 190
    196 200 275 282 291 Judah 84
    86 105 108 137 141 143 144
    155 162 Mr 22 85 87 107 108
    123 197-200 274 276 277 369
    Mrs 123 159 163 200 Mrs J 142
    159 Mrs T G 418 S 199 T G
    106 113 Thomas G 106 326
COLT'S Station, 274
COLTRIN, Asa 207 Elizabeth 207
COLTRON, 107
COLTS, 88
CONASTAGUES, 16
CONE-IN-CONE, 260
CONFEDERATE Flag, 447

CONGRESS, 246
CONKLIN, Lt 237
CONNEAUT, 265
CONNELLY, William 99 195
CONNELY, William 314
CONRAD, J M 187 W W 422
CONSTABLE, John Jr 134 Mrs J 418
CONVERSE, Charles Crozat 388 389 Ellen 388 Jacob 388 Lida 389 Manning 388
COOK, 312 J L 153 185 John 143 M B 143 Mrs 190 William 190 Wm 311
COOPER, J Fenimore 215 377 James 116 Prof 416
COPELAND, Charles M 131
CORNPLANTER, 61
CORRY, 358 Hiram 357
CORY, Hiram 357
COURTHOUSE, Bell 290 354
COURTRIGHT, M 119 122 Milton 122 406 Mr 119
COURTRRIGHT, M 295
COUSE, Mr 157
COWAN, Capt 124
COWLES, Timothy S 96
COX, 342
COXE, 342 Bishop 393
CRAIG, A A 106 174 Mary E 387 William 387

CRANCH, Edward 446 Judge 113
CRANE, Elihu Sr 192
CRANE'S Mills, 262
CRAWFORD, 306 James 275 Thomas 254 Wm H 230
CRAWFORDS, 306
CREVECOEUR, 26
CROGHAN, Col 200 311 378 George 30 31 Lt 233 Maj 235
CROSBY, Ebenezer 221
CROSMAN, Alexander 387 Freder 387
CROSS, Wm 138
CROSSMAN, 387
CROUCH, 104
CULBERTSON, Mr 185 W C 305 431 William 83 357
CUMMINGS, Capt 124
CUNNINGHAM, Thomas 99
CURRAN, William 135
CURRY, W C 301 445 William C 122 132 Wm C 175
CURTIN, Andrew G 95 Gov 333 334
CURTIS, C B 98 E 197 Mr 147 R J 147
CURTZE, F F 445
CUSHMAN, Charles 343
CUSIC, 20 David 17
CUTLER, G H 157 George H 189 331

CUTTS, Hannah 387 Lt 387 Mary E 387
D'ALLYON, Father 19
DABNEY, C W 422
DAGGET, 140
DAGGETT, J A 422
DALLAS, A J 65
DANFORTH, Maj 197
DANIEL Book Of, 205
DARWIN, Charles 382 George H 382 Maud 382 Mrs 383
DASH, John 325
DAVENPORT, E 422 Mrs W 417 Sarah 418 W R 427
DAVENPOT, Mrs Chas 426
DAVIDSON, A 153 William 277
DAVIE, J H 430 Ozias J 294
DAVIS, 128 246 248 Eleanor 418 H G 142 Harvey 96
DAVISON, 163 John 37
DAY, 165 J 157 Nursery 425
DEACON, Capt 275 David 250
DEAN, D K 366
DEARBORN, Fort 372 Gen 224 226
DEB, Capt 275
DEBIENVILLE, Celeron 29
DECAMP, G W 332 George W 331
DECHAMPLAIN, Sieur 29
DELANCY, Lt Gov 28
DELAROCHE, Joseph 19
DELASALLE, Sieur 24 29

DEMAN, Capt 35
DEMING, Mr 111
DENIS, Mr 191
DENNY, Capt 64-66 68 69 70 72 73 Ebenezer 199 Maj 78 180
DEPUY, Maud 382
DEQUESNE, Marquis 42
DERBY, Mrs David B 418
DERPONTENCY, Capt 34
DERRICKSON, David 97 Joseph 96
DERUOY, Lt 32
DESTPIERRE, Chevalier 42 Legardeur 40
DEVEREUX, 165 S 157
DEVERGE, Monsieur 44
DEVOTION, Christian 205
DEWIT, Simeon 59
DEWITT, 59 Calvin 387 H W 415 John 387 Julia A W 387 Mary Eleanor 386 Mr 427 W R 386 William R 391
DEXTER, Daniel S 250 387 Hannah 387
DICK, John 98 Mungo 204
DICKEY, 184 James 185
DICKINSON, Mahlon 380
DICKSON, Christina 386 Cyrus 385 390 Delia 386 Dr 386 Mr 282 Wm 385
DIFFENBACH, H L 158
DIFFENBAUGH, F 418

DILL, Robert 363
DILLON, T 101 Thomas 101 106
DINWIDDIE, Gov 37 40 42 43
DINWIDDLE, Gov 38
DITTO, Margaret Emma 398
DIX, Gen 342
DIXON, 59 Jeremiah 58 John 324
DOBBINS, 208 236 328 Capt 113 125 126 207 231 378 D 53 276 D P 328 Daniel 128 152 207 219-222 284 291 327 347 405 Leander 380 Mr 222 282 Mrs Capt 418 William W 285 379
DOCKS, 439
DODGE, John 133 134 T M 422
DODSWORTH, Jas 434
DOLL, C 143 Casper 369 John 430
DOOLITTLE, Giles 171 Miles 172
DORCHESTER, Lord 66
DOUGLAS, 53 95 53 382 404 J W 133
DOUGLASS, David Bates 382 Maj 113 Mr 53 Stephen A 404
DOWNER, Samuel 358

DOWNING, J F 374 416 424 430 445 J L 429 Mrs J F 424
DRAKE, E L 370 J C M 446
DREER, Ferdinand J 385
DROWN, H 422
DRUM, Capt 114

DUDLEY, Richard 134
DUGGEN, J W 143
DULUTH, 322
DUMARS, James 204
DUNCAN, 92 272 James 142 Jonas 134 William 134
DUNDASS, William 162 163
DUNLAP, J D 100 106 137 142 143 145 256 James D 99 John 380
DUNN, 422 Eliza 418 Lettia 418 S 101 Simeon 134 Thomas 290
DUNNING, M A 421 Minnie 430 Mr 429
DUPUY, Charles M 383
DUQUESNE, 28 Gov 32
DURHAM, 59
DURLIN, 164 Fayette 156 Mr 148
DUTCH, 22
DUTLINGER, Capt 135
DWINNEL, Ebenezer 134
EAGLE Hotel, 288
EAGLEY, 165 J 157
EAKENS, John 134
EALY, J M 422
EASTMAN, Nathaniel 152
EATON, 367 Clara J 389 390 Dr 391 Elizabeth 166 J 166 Johnson 281 Johnston 141 166 173 389 Mills 371 Mr 166 167 Rev 168 Samuel John Mills 389 W W 138

EBERSOLE, Elizabeth 432 Jacob
  281 Mr 138
ECKFORD, Henry 222 246 Mr 223
  224
EDDY, D 27 David 20 Mr 427
  Susan 418
EDGERTON, Richard 211
EDMUNDS, C S 422
EDWARDS, Eliza 401 Johathan 401
  T A 421
EGGLESTON, Mrs 435
EILLOT, G A 174
ELDRED, N B 97
ELEUSIS, 402
ELLICOT, 62 78 381 Andrew 59 60
  69 71 77 86 178 179 276 Gen
  83 Mr 64 68 72 73 75
ELLICOTT, Andrew 381 382
ELLIOT, Comm 279 Capt 125 237
  245-248 G A 132 140 141 159
  Geo A 105 J 105 J D 220 221
  Jesse D 250 Lt 224 233
ELLIOTT, 377 G A 406 Jesse 376
  John 374
ELLIS, 165 G 157
ELLSWORTH, F H 422
ELY, 171 Mr 171 S S 431
ENGELBRECHT, F Celestine 175
ENGLEHARD, C 144
ENSIGN, Harmon 172
ERHART, Capt 135
ERIE, & Northeast 119 Bank 207
  Canal 285
ERIES, 270
ERWIN, Mrs W L 424
ESPY, J Boyd 422
EVANS, 26 C B 422 J 173 Robert
  374
EVELETH, Mr 370
EVERSON, 422 W T 421
EWATT, Samuel 99
FAIRBAIRN, Frank 445
FAIRBANKS, Joshua 85 123 Mrs J
  196
FAIRBURN, John 139
FAIRPLAINS, 265
FARRAR, F F 106 355
FARRELLY, J W 98 99 P 98 Patrick 99 210
FAULKNER, 406 Mrs P 417 Mrs R
  417
FAY, Mr 364
FELLOWS, W D 427
FENGER, A A 347
FERGUSON, 165
FETID Bay Of, 26
FIELD, E D 157 John 63
FIESLER, A T 139 F 139
FILLMORE, President 211 Vice-
  President 404
FINCH, William S 148
FINDLEY, 191 312

FINNEY, Darwin A 99
FINNIS, Capt 125 225 237 243
FISH, Capt 127 128 Job 126
FITCH, D W 175
FLEEHARTY, 324 Col 324 Capt 347 John 3223 346
FLEMING, Ben 323 324 Benjamin 292 Mr 442 William 100 101 132
FLINT, H E 446 John F 446
FLOWER, D E 422 P D 422
FLOWERS, 422 James 141
FOLL, Mr 363
FOLLANSBEE, Mr 406
FOLLENSBEE, Joshua 295
FOLWELL, 276
FOLWELLS, 276
FOOT, Capt 279 Warren 174
FORCE, J M 383
FOREST, Lt 240
FORREST, A 386 Rachel 386
FORSTER, Col 159 275 Capt 135 J H 406 S L 101 Thomas 105 106 108 112 134 144 154 155 174 222 251 284 379 406 Thomas Jr 135 Thos Jr 174
FORT, George 225 248
FORWARD, 210
FOSTER, 162 164 A E 156 Alexander W 147 Galen 146

FOSTER (continued)
Hannah 387 Henry D 95 Jane Heron 387 Mr 372 Mrs M C 418 S M 418
FOWZIER, David 324
FRAISER, John 39
FRAIZER, Mr 216
FRANCES, A 138
FRANCISCO, Henry 100
FRANKLIN, 22 313 384 James T 428
FRANZIER, 215
FRASIER, Mr 42
FRAZIER, E L 422 Mr 215-218
FREMONT, Col 290
FRENCH, C M 422 J A 407
FREY, Henry 142
FRISBEE, Robert H 96 W H 422
FRONCE, C 265
FRONTENAC, Count 17 24
FROST, Abijah 174
FRUIT, William 114
FUHRMANN, F Jr 422
FULLER, Adonijah 174 Almond 96 Augustus 289 Mr 364 Wm 145 157
FULLERTON, J H 133 Kemper 401 Thomas 402
GAGGIN, R 101
GAILEY, 164 Richard 156

GAINES, Col 235 244
GAITHER, C A 421
GALBRAITH, 355 A 331 Amy 212
　J 140 John 97 98 120 122 142
　212 John W 445 Judge 120 213
　Mr 213 Mrs A A 418 Mrs F D
　418 W A 97 332 William A 295
　356 366 374 375 430 445 Wm
　A 139 142
GALE, 164 E W 156
GALLAGHER, William M 106 Wm
　M 106
GALLATIN, Mr 64
GALLIARD, Chas 422
GALLOWAY, Rev 204
GALSTER, Herman C 446
GARA, I B 148 334 422 Mrs I B
　429
GARFIELD, Gen 405
GARLAND, Lt 243
GARRISON Hill, 246
GEARY, E R 153
GENESEE River, 260
GENSHEIMER, John 144
GEODETIC, Survey 397
GERGUSON, G 157
GERRISH, E W 158
GERRY, Elbridge 98
GEST, John B 385
GEUTNER, C R 340
GEYLAN, Mr 436 Mrs 436

GIBBONS, Cardinal 410
GIBSON, Gen 73 John 67 300 301
　W P 334
GIFFORD, Ex-sheriff 421 Henry
　175
GILBERT, 24 J 254
GILKERSON, B F 306
GILLEN, Mrs S L 418
GILLESPIE, D 132 John 413
GILLIS, James 343
GILSON, 300 Lloyd 288 Mrs 417
GINGRICH, H 105 Henry 133 134
　394
GIRARD, 421 Stephen 93 187
GIST, Christopher 37 Mr 42
GIWARD, G I 314
GLASS, 186 Philetus 187
GLAZIER, J 134 Mr 348 Mrs J M
　424 P P 266
GLENWOOD, Park 374
GLOVER, Bennet 174 184
GOBIN, 340
GOODRICH, E 174 E C 149
GOODWIN, Daniel 96 Myron 105
GORDON, 54 427
GORHAM, 60 75 84 N 198 Nathan-
　iel 197
GOULD, 163 165 Amos 167 D A
　100 David A 100 J P 153 Mr 23
　N 157 William 141
GRAHAM, Carson 146 Col 58

GRAHAM (continued)
 J 332 John 135 139 Marg 418 Mrs
  Carsen 417
GRANT, B 133 Capt 124 Gen 404
 Mr 406
GRAPES, 359
GRAVATT, C U 437 Mrs C U 437
GRAVES, Amos Jr 96 Chauncey
 143
GRAWOSZ, Peter 134
GRAY, John 101 106 William 142
 143
GREELEY, Horace 160 404
GREEN, I 372 John P 436
GREENVILLE, Lord 89
GREENWOOD, John 152
GREER, John 140 187
GREGG, Capt 332
GREGORY, D D 172 Rev 389
GREYS, Wayne 114 289
GRIDLEY, Harriet V 430 Mrs C V
 424 Mrs T C 426
GRIER, John 98
GRIFFIN, Ella R 430
GRIFFITH, William 140
GRIFFON, 26 27
GRIMLER, J G 421
GRISWOLD, Matthew 430 445
GROSMAN, Gen 387 Hannah 387
GRUBB, 107 Capt 276 John 83 98
 276

GUENTHER, Andrew 367
GUILD, A M 139 A W 133
GUNNISON, 164 C E 143 445 E D
 100 132 134 141 156 174
 Ebenezer 152 Frank 97 356 G
 W 156 Harry 445 J 100 Mr 406
 Mrs C E 418
GUTTENBERG, G F 401
HACKNEY, J 99 Joseph 108
HAGSTROM, H 409
HALDERMAN, John W 336
HALL, C C 422 F A 153 H C 430
 James 259 260 Maj Gen 247
 Mrs 172 419 W S 187
HAMBLETON, 233 243 Mr 240
HAMBURG, 20
HAMILTON, 185 222 312 Gov 36
HAMILTONS, 88
HAMMOND, E P 410 J W 106 356
HAMOT, Adeline 207 Elizabeth
 207 418 Miss 418 Mr 174 207 P
 S V 324 428 P S V 115 128 132
 140 141 173 174 206 284 285 P
 V S
HAMPSON, Mrs J F 418
HAMTRAMCK, Col 276
HANCOCK, Gen 338
HANLEY, 346 347
HANNAH, E 418
HANSON, J 174
HARDWICK, Wm 422

HARRINGTON, Ira 96 Mark W 323
HARRIS, Luman 176
HARRISON, 225 293 404 Benjamin
   405 Gen 290 292 310 380 Gen
   215 226 228 229 232 233 235
   244 245 William H 404
HART, 189 & Bird 287 Edson 143
   H 138 Homer 157 I W 175 J W
   122 L 100 157 Lefferet 189 Mr
   287 Samuel T 131
HARTMAN, Rev 174
HARTSTOWN, 268
HARVEY, H L 52 148
HASLETT, W J 407
HASTINGS, 164 J A 156
HATCH, 427 E W 421 Frank P 357
HATTON, R C 141
HAVERSTICK, Mrs H B 418
HAWKINS, B J 157 Ivory 96
HAWLEY, Gideon 161
HAY, John 106 134
HAYBARGER, G W 422
HAYDEN, B 409 B H 424
HAYES, F M 437 J W 406 S M 357
   W B 406 W F 437
HAYFORD, D 421
HAYS, Mrs William 417 Robert 105
   S 99 173 Samuel 105 132 134
   152 284
HAYWARD, G W 343
HAZELTON, Stephen 140

HEARN, J 114 John 405 Mr 406
HEATH, E C 186 Reuben 81 Robert
   B 340
HEATON, James 140
HEBERLA, Jacob 433
HELLER, W H 157
HELM, 343 J M 344
HENDERSON, William 134
HENNEPIN, 25
HENRY, 104 Mr 49 Robert 134
HERON, Jane 387
HERON, Hannah 387 Hannah
   Foster 387 Hannah Irvine 387
   James 201 James Gordon 387
   Margaret 201 387 Mary Ann
   387 Nancy 387
HERRINGTON, J 99 Jacob 99
   James 99 112
HERRON, 387 Francis 309 James
   135 James E 100 105 108 135
HERSHEY, Mrs 432
HIBBARD, Andrew 131
HIGGINS, J 421
HILL, H A 100 Henry 96 J Foster
   416 Mr 357
HIMROD, 140 A 183 Aaron 152
   Mrs W 418 William 140
HITCHCOCK, J W 133
HOGE, William 98
HOLBURT, Nathan 293
HOLDUP, 250 Lt 230 237 241

HOLLAND, Lt 33 Purchase 84
   Samuel 59
HOLLIDAY, 164 William 157 Wm
   138
HOLMES, 228 Abiel 201 Gen 228
   Mary Jackson 201 Oliver
   Wendell 201
HOMANS, Capt 289
HOME Of The Friendless, 428
HOMEOPATHIC Hospital, 446
HONEOYE, 271
HOOKER, Gen 338
HOPKINS, Andrew 148
HOPPEN, Mrs H C 418
HOPSON, Lt 387 Nancy 387
HORTON, 324
HOSKINSON, James 106 133 324
HOWARD, 326 G W 328 Mr 315
HOWE, Clara J 390 Mr 147
HOWELL, C G 135
HOYT, Maj 443
HUBBARD, W S 446
HUBBLE, Mary 421
HUBLEY, Mrs B 418
HUDSON'S Bay, 29
HUGHES, James 96 106 John 422
   Thomas 134 173 204
HUGHLETT, Marvin 435
HUIDEKOPER, H J 132
HULBERT, E D 134 Harriet 418 R
   O 141 143

HULL, 312 Gen 125 126 215 279
HUMANE Society, 424
HUMPHREY, W J 357
HUNT, Harmon D 146 Mary 415
HUNTER, 225 283 E J 421 John W
   147 Mr 342 Mrs 283
HUNTINGTON, 164 G R 156
HUNTSBURGER, 324
HURD, 165 191 G 157 Gilbert 96
HURST, Henry 99
HUSKE, John 430 435
HUSTON, R 175
HUTCHINS, 163 184 B 174 C J 153
   174 Samuel 98 100 184 Tho
   299
HUTCHINSON, D W 136 Monroe
   96 Myron 98
INDIAN, Blackhoof 235 Broken
   Twig 67 Crane 235 Guyasutha
   55 Gyantwachia 301 Mound 22
   Pallas 161 Pontiac 48-50 54
   Red Jacket 198 Tecumseh 291
   Tiawoncas 67 Tommy Capt 235
INDIANS, Crane 235
INGERSOLL, 424 Calista 418 Dr
   318 401 Helen 401 Mr 26 Mrs
   401 417 Mrs T D 424 T D 401
   425 Theo 401 Timothy Dwight
   400 401
INMAN, William 343
INMANN, William 131

IRELAND, J Louis 446
IRISH, Lucinda E 418 Mrs O H 418
IROQUOIS, 15 271
IRVINE, Callender 100 276 Gen 60
   85 Mary Ann Heron 387 Mr 64
   William 86 276
IRVING, Washington 130
IRWIN, Agnes 196 J P 422 Robert
   105 134
ISHERWOOD, B F 131 Mr 131
JACKSOM, M 418
JACKSON, Gen 208 Mrs S 418 S
   146 Smith 106 119 122 133 142
   326
JAMES II, 2 31 52 King of England
   57 John W 174
JARECKI, Charles 430 Gustavus
   136
JAY, Mr 87 89
JAYNES, Heman 174
JEAN, Coeur 31
JEBB, Prof 383 Richard Claver-
   house 382
JEFFERS, Capt 67 William H 391
JEFFERSON, 19 382 J P 368
JESKAKAKE, 38
JOHNS, William 145 Wm 105
JOHNSON, 104 186 Col 32 33 43
   73 161 George 21 Gov 404 J B
   99 100 146 149 J S 187 Mr 70
   320 Mr 70 Pres 404 S P 97

JOHNSON (continued)
   William 27 47 54
JOHNSON'S Island, 342
JOHNSTONE, 85
JOLIET, 21 Mons 29
JOLLS, Leander 288
JONCAIRE, 32
JONES, 234 Clark 324 Capt 325 D I
   106 356 F P 422 H S 427 Hora-
   tio 199 L S 157 189 Levi 187
   Mr 219 Mrs H S 419 N W 422
   T 293 William 245
JOUETT, James E 343
JUDD, Rev 275
JUDSON, 88 A M 181 Amos 141
   149 153 180 183 184 Col 310
   Mr 153 P E 309 Timothy 184
   William 153 184
JUNKIN, Mr 204
K, Mr 88 89
KANSWANS, 271
KAUTZ, Albert 343
KEEFER, Elizabeth 207 George 207
   S W 106 Samuel 101
KELLEY, George 134 John 155 156
   William 100 104-106 113 119
   122 133 140 157 174 284
KELLOGG, George 157 J 173
   Josiah 106 128 132 141 Mason
   189 Mrs J 418 Mrs S M 418
KELLY, 284 Alfred 120

KELLY (continued)
  Wm 100 132 174
KELSEY, Mr 421 S H 175
KELSO, C W 100 146 Charles W
  106 E J 100 375 Edwin J 106
  Gen 269 277 279 John 98 100
  399 Sarah 399 W C 399 William C 145 399
KENNEDY, Dr 84 Mariah 418 Mrs
  418 Thomas R 313
KEPLAR, Mrs Frank 424
KEPLER, F V 445
KERFOOT, Bishop 393
KERN, Val 408
KERR, David 204 J D 407
KEUSTER, J M 148
KEWENAW, 322
KIBLER, Geo W 431
KIDDER, Perry 191
KILLPATRICK, J 101
KIMBALL, C C 407 J M 436
KINCAID, Robert 184
KINCAIDE, J G 422
KING, A 106 145 332 Alfred 100 B
  359 G F 133 Josiah 288 S 416
  Thomas 182 Wilson 100 106
  184
KINGS, 88
KIRTLAND, Mr 108
KITELINGER, Jacob 182

KNAPP, Abram 278 G 174 Gilbert
  327 347
KNOBLOCK, E 325
KNOLL, M 139
KNOWLTON, W H 142
KNOX, 97 Gen 70 Mr 266 Robert
  106
KOCH, Dr 202 Elizabeth 202
  Michael 139
KOEHNE, Ernest 408
KOHLER, 345
LA, Force 40 Vasseur 282
LACOCK, Abner 98
LADIES' Appeal, 418
LADY, Prevost 225
LAFAYETTE, G W 282 283
LAFORCE, 40
LAIRD, 323 T 173 Thomas 100 134
  148 375 W 100 106
LAKE, Pleasant 317
LAMB, F M 445
LAMONT, Daniel 435
LANDIS, B A 422
LANDON, A C 106 D G 106 E B S
  134
LANE, Mrs E A G 418 W S 332
  Wm S 120
LANMAN, James 293 Joseph 131
  343
LAPSLEY, John 134

LARKIN, John B 436
LASALLE, 24 26 27 39 303
LATTIMORE, William 135
LAUB, 243 Henry 246
LAUBENDER, 421 J H 421
LAUGHEAD, J B 105
LAUGHLIN, 188 James 187
LAVASSEUR, M 282
LAWRENCE, 231 233 Capt 239
LAWSON, Mr 293
LEACH, John 99
LECAIN, Gov 35
LEE, A R 436 Gen 336 Oliver 115
    Thomas 31 Wm 85 86 123 124
LEE'S Run, 223
LEECH, A Q D 379
LEET, C 138 Calvin 134 Charles
    363 Simeon 137
LEMOYNE, 16 17
LEMOYNEE, 16 17
LENNON, 334 Capt 333
LESAMBROW, 46
LESLEY, Peter 375
LESTER, W C 146
LEUSCHEN, 334 N 346
LEUTJE, W F 332
LEWIS, 97 H 422 Lida 389 Mr 149
LICK, Henry 150
LIDDEL, William 356
LIDDELL, 104 117 229 W F 143
    Walter F J 294

LIMBER, 164 John 156
LINCOLN, 95 Pres 335 336 404
LIND, Elizabeth 204 Matthew 204
LINDSAY, 359 Capt 32 John 167
LINDSEY, Mrs R G 359
LINTS, J L 146
LISZT, 388
LITTEL, A L 427
LITTLE, L M 424 John W 436 L M
    427 436 Mr 435
LIVINGSTON, 163 John 153
LIVSEY, William 340
LLOYD, D J 174
LOCKWOOD, 164 R S 156
LOGAN, 306 O 422 431
LOGSTOWN, 32
LONG, John 281 Point 228 232
    Robert H 131
LONGSTREET, Mrs 419
LOOMIS, Dyer 140 Henry 140 R L
    142 Rufus 187 Seth 165
LOOP, D D 421
LOSSING, 381
LOUIS, 37 XIV 24 XV King Of
    France 30
LOW, Abbie 419 Mrs A M 418
    Samuel 133
LOWRIE, 97
LOWRY, 97 162 M B 113 120 332
    405 406 429 Mr 335 Mrs H J
    418

LUCCOCK, N 421
LUCE, N R 357
LULL, 340
LYMAN, Cornelius 276 E 418
LYNN, C R H 149
LYON, A Mcd 143 426 G A 141
    157 George A 173 Mrs G A 417
    Rev Dr 406
LYTLE, James 106 139 174 John
    152 184 John Jr 99
MACHAULT, Ft 44
MACKENZIE, Alexander Slide LL
    376
MACKLIN, John 335
MACLAY, Eleanor 386 William
    299 300
MADISON, 234 238 James 214
    President 245
MAGILL, W E 421
MAGRATH, Purser 233
MAHER, John 326
MALDEN, 236
MALICK, S 186
MALLARY, William 139
MALLORY, E F 422
MANNING, Hannah 196
MANROSS, P T 422
MANS, 406
MANSION House, 287
MANUS, W T 422
MARION, O 290

MARKS, R T 446 William Jr 112
MARLIN, R 99 Ralph 99 108
MARQUETTE, Father 29
MARSH, 104 117 163 J A 422 Run
    265 W R 153
MARSHALL, 374 F F 436 437 445
    J C 114 332 James C 100 122
    142 375 M W 418 Mrs E W 418
    Orsamus H 303
MARTEN, Lt 180
MARTIN, Artemas 395 Charles 152
    Dr 397 James Madison 395
    Lizzie 418 Mr 396 Orenda
    Knight 395
MARTINS, 306
MARVIN, Elisha 137 Elizabeth 199
    Enoch 87 140 155 Mr 335 Mrs
    Judge 419 Selden 106 356
    William E 445 Wm E 421
MASON, 58 59 218 & Dixon 58
    Charles 58 Elizabeth Champlin
    218 John 203 Kate 429
MATCALF, Prescott 355
MATHEW, Father 405
MATHEWS, John 141 184
MATLACK, 61 Timothy 62
MATTHEWS, Mr 182
MAURICE, Capt 282
MAVADA, 306
MAY, Frank 431
MCALLASTER, D 100

MCALLISTER, D 114 David 122
MCARTHUR, Gen 235 William 99
MCBLAIR, 343
MCBRIER, James 424
MCCALL, Capt 276
MCCANN, Anna 418
MCCARTER, I J 106 Joseph 356
    416 436 445
MCCASKEY, 141 J R 153
MCCLASKEY, Alexander 293
MCCLAY, 61 299 Samuel 62
MCCLELLAN, Gen 337
MCCLELLAND, 114 Gen 435 R
    143 173 Robert 141
MCCLINTOCK, J R 158
MCCLOCHLAN, James 41
MCCLURE, J 122 138 John Jr 189
MCCONKEY, James 92
MCCONNEL, Henry 157 N J 157
MCCONNELL, 186 Delia 386 H
    189 James 204
MCCORD, Ann 306 John 101 137
    141 165 172 306 Mary 391 Mr
    164 William 391
MCCOSKRY, Bishop 393
MCCRACKEN, Jane 418 M 417
MCCRAY, Dr 68 Wm 422
MCCREA, 191 312 315 James 435
    Robert 96
MCCREARY, A 142 A J 422 Agnes
    166 D B 175 D P 339

MCCREARY (continued)
    Jackson 145 Mr 335
MCCULLOUGH, John 78
MCCURDY, Elisha 167 Rev 163
    164
MCDONALD, 247 A 233
MCDONNEL, Robert 134
MCDONOUGH, Commodore 201
MCDOUGAL, James 131
MCGILL, 111 Owen 185
MCINTOSH, Alex 125
MCKAY, J L 185
MCKEAN, Warren 98
MCKEE, Thomas 134
MCKENZIE, 217 238
MCKINLEY, L M 422
MCKINNEY, 323 D 141 David 173
    Rev Dr 372
MCKINSTRY, James 131
MCLANE, 334 Col 332 333 337
    Capt 136 John 137 John W 101
    134 135 331
MCLEAN, C N 422
MCMASTER, Bach 385 John Bach
    384
MCMILLAN, John 167
MCMULLEN, M H 374 Mrs A K
    424 W M 422
MCNAIR, David 101 Dunning 107
    193 William E 101
MCNEIL, 364

MCPHERRIN, Rev 168
MCSPARREN, Archibald 134 173 204 C 104 122 146 265 Clark 106
MCWADE, Nella 418
MEAD, David 205 219 Gen 223 230 247 248 Maj Gen 228
MEADE, George G 254
MEHAFFY, Thomas 100
MEHL, 331 Sheriff 420
MEIGS Ft, 228
MERCIE, Mons 33
MEREDITH, 210 Mr 133
MERRIMAN, 163 J R 153
MERSHOM, 165 D 157
MESSICK, Wm 176
METCALF, 297 Charles 133 James 143 427 Joseph 374 Mary 418 P 106 114 122 133 295 406 429 Prescott 122
METZENBURG, Daniel 293
MIDDAUGH, 85
MIDDLETON, 262
MIFFLIN, 312 Gov 62 64-66 69 190 Thos 300
MILES, 334 Capt 333 George 174 249 379 380 James 98 138 157 297 Mr 191 312 Mrs 190 312 William 61 83 96 180 187 190 297 317 Wm 108 137 311 312
MILESES, 88

MILLER, 163 194 422 Chas 422 Edward 116 F M 145 H H 422 J 401 J K 100 J W 153
MILLS, Adelphic 194 B Fay 413
MILROY, John 101
MINER, J C 422
MISSIMER, H C 415
MISSISSAQUES, 17
MITCHELL, 283 422 Chas 422 Samuel L 260
MIZENER, F A 106 356 436 Mrs F A 427
MOESER, C 149
MOHAWK, 16
MOHAWKS, 270
MOLTON, A N 145
MOMEYER, L L 106
MONTGOMERY, J B 233 292 Samuel 172 William 299
MONTOUR, Andrew 36
MOORE, Geo W 421 George 99 100 105 174 251 284 J 175 Jesse 92 97 Mrs L 418 Robert 98 William 135
MOORHEAD, Catherne 386 Christina 386 J T 96 J Y 134 James 142 159 281 386 Mrs 168 T Jr 144 Thomas Jr 132 Thos Jr 100
MORANG, 36 M 35 Mr 33 34
MORAVIAN, Quarry 262
MORGAN, 163 L S 153

MORGANG, 34
MORHART, C C 408
MORRIS, John 101 105 135 147
MORRISON, 340
MORSE, C H 364 Mr 363
MORTON, Rev 159
MOTTIER, Charles H 363
MUELLER, C F 332 Capt 335
MUHLENBERG, P 300
MULLEN, Bishop 410
MULLET, James 115
MUMFORD, George 379
MUNN, J C 422
MURPHY, J C 431 N 174
MURRAY, J 293 William 134
MUZZY, Moses 324
NAGLE, C F 343
NAVY Yard, 223
NAYLOR, James 206 Mary 206
NCNAIR, 312
NEEWMAN, Wm 174
NEGRO, Mckinney 323
NEIL, 406
NEILER, S E 133
NEILSON, R 352 Robert 436
NELSON, 245 Hannah 387 James 142 143 Lord 238 Maj 387
NESBITT, 340
NEUTRAL, 15
NEWBEGIN, R G 415
NEWMAN, Wm H 174

NIAGARA, 231 Falls 249
NICHOLAS, 343
NICHOLS, 163 R R 153
NICHOLSON, 64 343 A 138 J W 64 John 63 65 104 William 82 374
NICKLE, S M 422
NILES, J B 340
NOBLE, O 106 Orange 355
NORMAL School, 185
NORRIS, Col 356 John 293
NORTH, Mr 191
NORTON, 194
NOUE, Father 19
O'BEIL, 69 73 Capt 75
O'BRIEN, 340 J J 346 Mr 347 Richard 374
O'HARA, James 109 110
O'NEIL, R 124
OAK, Hill 369
OAKS, Dolly 196 Jonathan 196
OHIO, 233
OLDS, L W 105
OLIN, Edgar 139
OLIVER, Capt 288 Stephen 290 312
OLMSTEAD, 164 L G 145 156 269 272
ONEIDAS, 270
ONONGAGOS, 270
ORE, 439
ORMSBY, Oliver 206
ORR, 163 R W 153

ORTON, Edmund 172 Rev 178
  Samuel G 172
OSBORN, P 157 354
OSBORNE, 354 P 138
OSGOOD, 290 Mr 291
OTIS, Mrs C 418
OTTINGER, Capt 132 Douglass
  294 295 327 347 Emily 417
  Virginia 418
OWEN, William F 139
P, Mrs 278
PACKER, Gov 97 Wm F 121
PACKET, Lt 237 240
PACKETT, J 233
PADDOCK, Rev 184
PAGE, E 193 Hugh N 292 Mr 193
PAINE, Gen 107 108 Rev 172
PALMER, E C 422
PAMPHLET, Laws 230
PARK, 163 164 James 153 156
PARKER, James 199 O 178 Rowland S 293
PARKINSON, Eliza 401
PARKMAN, 26 50
PARSON, Dr 200
PARSONS, 377 C W 201 Dr 202
  229 238 240 243 376-378 Mary
  Jackson 201 Mr 191 Mrs 201
  Mrs M H 418 Usher 200 201
  236 292 379 381
PARTRIDGE, A 186 H 186

PATRIOT War, 289
PATTERSON, 164 A S 156 Jas G
  421 Mr 165 Rev 166 Robert
  165 168
PATTISON, Gov 340 403 Robert E
  340 435
PAXSON, Chief Justice 403
PAYNE, C N 368 443 F H 443 John
  E 436
PEARCE, George 250
PEASE, 421
PEIFFER, F 144
PELTON, E L 422 426 H 138 J 422
PENIKESE, 400
PENN, 58 59 John 57 Richard 57
  Thomas 57 William 56
PENNYPACKER, S W 385
PENROD, H J 321
PEON, M 35
PEPPER, William 385
PEPPERELL, William 201
PERKINS, J C 194 Mr 402 R L 166
  194 402 Rufus Lord 403 W R
  402 William L 402
PERLEY, James 149 Mr 148 S 148
  Samuel 100
PERRY, 92 226 241-243 378
  Alexander 218 219 Christopher
  Raymond 380 Comm 125 134
  136 200 208 223 236 237 245
  251 252 283-285 291 404

PERRY (continued)
  Capt 217 218 222-228 232 233 235
    236 238-240 244-246 D E 422
  Elizabeth Champlin 218 Mr 293
  Mrs 216 217 240 O H 245 250
    293 294 Oliver 216 217 Oliver
  H 376 Oliver Hazard 215 380
    Square 284
PETER, 290
PETERS, James W 26
PETROLEUM, 265 389
PETTIBONE, Chas 422
PETTIGRU, Lt 219
PETUNS, 15
PHELPS, 60 75 84 & Gorham 60 Ira
    143 O 198 199 Oliver 199
PHILIPPE, Louis 83
PHILLIPPE, Louis 76
PHILLIPS, 359 J H 359 James 96
    James H 363 John 99 141
    Joseph R 446
PICKEN'S Fort, 383
PICKERING, Thomas 424 Timothy
    75 199
PIERCE, Carl 421 Franklin 135 Mrs
    418 Peter 133 145 146
PIERSON, A T 413
PILLSBURY, Mr 157
PIONEERS, 290
PLUMER, A 98
POLHEMUS, Lt 68 72 Mr 69

POLK, President 208
POLLOCK, Capt 180 Elizabeth 202
    James 184 290 Otis W 387 R A
    202 S T 421
PONTIAC, 50
PORT, Dover 232
PORTER, 124 164 Augustus 84 199
    C L 156 George 157 Mr 189
    Robert 141 Thos 421
POTTER, Samuel L 96 W I 422
POTTS, Joseph D 352 385
POWELL, Jerome 335
POWER, 72 James M 113
POWERS, Alexander 107
PRATT, J E 422 Mrs 416
PRENTICE, Thomas 140
PRESSLEY, Joseph 143 408
PRESSLY, Joseph 173
PRICE, William 435
PRIDEAUX, Gen 47
PRINCE, 367
PRIZES, 238
PROCTOR, Gen 244
PROUDFIT, John 422
PROVINCIAL, Marine 225
PUT-IN-BAY, 236 238
PUTNAM, Clark 142
PYMATUNING, 264
RAGNATHA, 18
RAMSEY, Mayor 32 Mrs 419
RANDALL, S W 148

RANGE, E K 422
RANKIN, 248
RANSOM, 68 D 67 Daniel 67
RAWLE, 329 H 106 330 Henry 355 356
REA, S Jr 157 Samuel 100 Samuel Jr 100
REANE, J N 422
REDWAY, George 306
REED, 163 329 422 Adam 187 312 Agnes 196 C M 289 326 405 406 410 422 429 436 442 C M 98 106 113-115 122 132 140 144 157 174 196 286 Charles J 137 Charles M 100 295 355 445 Chas M 98 Col 82 195 196 Dolly 196 G W 183 George 166 195 422 George W 141 Hannah 196 J G 422 J H 153 James C 153 John C 274 John Charles 195 Manning 195 Mr 275 372 Mrs 159 190 Mrs C M 417 Mrs James C 418 Mrs R S 104 159 R S 102 113 114 124 125 128 132 134 137 138 159 200 207 211 221 284 Rufus S 85 101 105 155 156 196 284 Rufus Seth 195 196 S 123 274 Sarah 429 Seth 82 83 85 195 196 324 W W 330 William 207 William W 114 274 Wm W 125

REEDER, 185 312 C 158
REEDS, 88
REES, 107 207 C P 344 Davis 445 Esquire 84 Mr 85 Mrs T 196 T 107 138 Thomas 77 80 83 134 195 Thomas Jr 92
REESE, Lt 347
REID, 164 Elizabeth 202 204 Elizabeth Craig 202 Isaac 202 203 J C 100 James 202 James C 156 202 Mary J 402 Neville Craig 203 R 141 Robert 141 155-157 173 184 202-204 408
REIGERT, 210
REPARTI, Capt 40 41 Mons 40
RESTONE, 163
REY, Mr 427
REYNOLDS, 385 J W 339 352 383 436 Mr 194 William 38
RIBLET, Comm 430 G W 148 Henry 432 Mrs J E 418
RICE, 327 Dan 332 Mr 369
RICHARDS, J S 424 436 445 John 327 347 John S 436 Mrs L M 417
RICHARDSON, 198
RICHMOND, Dean 122
RIDDEL, John 100 134
RIDDLE, D H 309
RILLING, John S 415
RINDERNICHT, W F 133

475

RINE, Mr 410
RIORDY, 356
RITNER, Joseph 158
RITTENHOUSE, 59
ROBERTS, 334 Capt 333 George B
   435 W Milnor 114
ROBERTSON, 67 J 138 Thomas
   165
ROBINSON, Alexander 173 204
   David 204 391 Dr 391 Ellen
   388 John F 391 L 100 Lyman
   188 Mary 391 Mary Wolf 391
   Mrs 172 Philip 306 Samuel 306
   Secretary 28 Thomas 172 391
   Thomas H 309 Thomas Hastings 391 William 391
ROBINSONS, 306
ROCHENWALD, P 139
ROCKWELL, 163 A O 153 C F 421
   431 L D 357 421 Mrs C F 431
RODGERS, Comm 218 Jedediah
   128 Maj 48
ROE, Frances A 343
ROGERS, 264 H D 255 256 Prof
   257 Z 421
ROSENAN, Nathan 409
ROSENGARTEN, 59 Joseph G 385
ROSS, J S 422 James 95 147
ROSSITER, Mrs U P 431
ROUGH, James 124
RUMFORD, Count 389

RUNNELS, F N 422
RUNYON, G 422
RUSH, 253
RUSSEL, George 134 H 109
   Hamlin 277-279
RUSSELL, B 173 Benjamin 101
   137 G B 422 G J 422 H H 357
   W H 357
RUTLEDGE, 76 84 314
RYAN, 406 Archbishop 410 T M
   422
RYCKMAN, G E 443 Mr 364
RYMAN, T 100
SACKETT'S Harbor, 219 223 228
SAGE, O N 174
SALEY, M 186 Marcus 96
SALINA, 207
SALISBURY, L H 422
SALL, Sieur De La 24
SALTSMAN, Jesse 134 John R 436
   Robert J 424 436
SANBORN, William 100 Wm 174
SANDS, W J 374
SANDUSKY, 20
SANFORD, 271 D 422 G 119 137
   138 141 143 145 173 175 251
   273 Giles 155 211 284 H L 427
   John 211 L G 419 M 301 406
   445 Miss 419 Mr 212 Mrs G
   142 Mrs L 417 Mrs Myron 424
   Myron 427 428

SANTA, Anna 388
SARACENIA, 269
SARGEANT, Hosea 292
SATANAS, 235
SATTERFIELD, Rev 164
SAUNDERS, S A 422
SAVAGE, 165 L W 157
SAWDY, David 96 100
SAXTON, Frederick 60
SAYARD, 20 Father 19
SCHABACKER, H C 422
SCHAEFFER, 416 N 417
SCHANTZ, George 105
SCHENCK, Martin 304
SCHEUFFLEN, Mr 149
SCHLAUDECKER, Col 338 F 144
    M 333
SCHMIDT, Mr 367
SCHOOLCRAFT, 21
SCHOTTEN, P 139
SCHOULLER, John 140
SCHULTZ, Frank V 374
SCHUTTE, F H 445
SCORPION, 233
SCOTT, 140 187 A 100 114 295
    406 Andrew 106 Francis 135
    Gen 129 James 405 Mary
    Matilda 405 R L 405 W L 106
    306 330 355 406 429 Walter
    106 356 430 William L 374 397
    405 435 437 445 Wm 140

SCOULER, 23 140 363
SCOULLER, John B 363
SEABURY, Bishop 217
SEARS, S S 153
SEATTLE, 361
SEDGWICH, Perry 420
SEIGEL, C 133
SEKREGG, M L 422
SELDEN, 330 329 G 141 143 157
    173 Geo D 421 George 160 374
    408 410 428 George D 421 427
    Joseph 141 Mr 406 Samuel 96
SELDON, J C 141
SELKREGG, Harley 187
SENAT, 247 G 233
SENECAS, 24
SERGEANT, 210
SEVIN, F 106
SEWALL, Robert 134
SEWARD, W H 404
SEYMOUR, Mrs C H 418
SHADACH, 140
SHADACK, Joseph 140
SHANER, John 148
SHANK, Robert T 134
SHANNON, H C 437 Henry 374
    436 Joseph 99 Mark 367
SHAONONS, 15
SHEFFIELD, 165 C C 157
SHELDEN, Thomas 197
SHELDON, P B 422

SHENK, H 438 Henry 367
SHERMAN, 338 Mrs Wallace 419
    Wallace 96
SHERWIN, 329 330 Ira 133 J P 133
SHINGOWANK, 21
SHIP, Amelia 224 Caledonia 233
    249 Crevecoeur 26 Detroit 233
    Elmer Ruth 206 Exposition
    Flyer 352 Good Luck 291 Jones
    234 Kalorama 406 Little Belt
    225 London Field 401 May
    Flower 282 Philo Parsons 342
    Porcupine 233 247 249 Tigress
    233 Trippe 233 Wocoken 323
SHIPMAN, C D 431
SHIPPEN, Henry 97
SHIRK, C C 407 427 445 David 407
SHIRLEY, Gov 28
SHREW, W W 421
SHUNPIKE, 107
SIBLEY, R J 100
SIEUR-DE-LA, Salle 24
SILL, 124 James 208 James H 208
    Joanna B 210 Mr 209 211 335
    Mrs J 418 Richard 146 Richard
    L 209 T H 98 99 106 115 132
    157 159 289 404 Thomas H 105
    155 284 Thomas Hale 208 Thos
    H 105
SILLIMAN, 186 Prof 370
SILVERTHORN, James 188

SILVERTHORN (continued)
    J W 278
SIMCOE, Gov 87
SIMMERLY, John 106
SIMMS, 427 Alex 141
SIMS, J C 422
SINCLAIR, 206 Arthur 250 Comm
    223 290
SINGER, J 139
SINGLETON, Arthur 206
SISSION, A E 383
SISSON, 383 Giles 82 195
SKINNER, James 99 100 106 122
    Mrs H J 418 S 100 Stephen 100
    133
SLEMMER, Gen 383 Ltc 383
SLOAN, 329 330 B F 96 106 133
    John 134
SLOUGH, George 134
SMEDLEY, E 142 J 145 James 140
    143 172 Jas 96
SMILE, John 300
SMILEY, D G 422
SMITH, 237 262 A R 431 Abraham
    101 Charles 174 G Gary 357 H
    C 421 Henry Preseved 401
    Joseph 96 Judge 182 Mrs E H
    418 Mrs L M 418 S 106 Samuel
    96 98 Sherburn 355 W 99 W H
    L 357 Walter 128 Wm 184 Wm
    C 185 Wilson 98-100

SNOWDEN, A Loudon 404 J Ross 404 Mrs 403 404 Nathaniel 403
SNOWDON, 403
SNYDER, Simon 95
SOBEL, I 374
SOCIETIES, 429 430
SOCIETY Natural History, 212
SOSNOWSKI, Madame 157
SPAFFORD, Calvin 140 O D 106 Oliver 142
SPALDING, Bishop 393 John Franklin 392 Lavina D 392 393
SPANG, Jacob 100
SPAULDING, D G 422
SPENCER, H A 368 J C 122 137 140 145 175 352 393 406 445 Lavina D 393 Mr 383 Mrs William 382 383 S S 141 William 374 445
SPOHR, 388
SPRAGUE, Dr 167
SPROUL, J W 422
STACKHOUSE, Mr 131
STAFFORD, C H 343 W J 421
STAMFORD, Samuel C 185
STANDARD Dictionary, 401
STANDISH, Miles 383 388 Rose 383
STANFCLIFT, David 421
STARK, C N 422

STARR, 163 330 G W 445 George W 330 R W 153
STEM, H L 446
STEPHENS, Thomas W 294
STERLING, J W 436 John W 435
STERNBERG, J L 445
STERRET, J S 174
STERRETT, 22 B 419 Belle 419 J M 98 99 105 Joseph M 106 148 Judge 23 M G 422 Mrs J J 419
STETSON, John A 363
STEVENS, 237 Lt 131 T H 131 332
STEWART, 163 281 304 Dr 406 Gilbert 126 J B 126 John 281 Miss 419 Mother 419 P H 157 186 R T 153 Reid T 156 T I 340 Thomas 105 134 146 152 Thomas J 304 340
STIMER, Alban C 131
STIMSON, Clarilla 96
STOCKMAN, W B 320
STOCKTON, Rev 165
STOKES, Lt 243
STONE, Geo S 422 George 156 Jonas 292 Rev 178
STONY Point, 271
STORAGE, 445
STRANAHAN, P G 265 Pery G 96
STRATTON, J L 422
STRAUB, Mr 367

STRONG, 76 258 Charles H 375
    445 Capt 84 F 135 M 113
    Martin 82 137 141 180 184 262
    280 309 Mrs C H 438 Mrs
    Charles H 428
STRONGS, 88
STRUEBER, Louis 325
STUCKENBERG, J H W 339 John
    H W 393
STUMPTOWN, 248
STURGEON, 193 Allen 422 Jane
    166 William 166 Wm 193
STURZNECKLE, Ernst 149
STVINCENT, 428
SULLIVAN, Josiah 96
SUMNER, Gen 406
SUNBRY, 116
SUPERIOR, 322
SUTTER, John 324
SWATARA, 306
SWEENEY, John 139
SWEET, S M 416
SYMONDS, F M 343
SYNOPSIS, 446
TAGGART, Miles 187
TALBOT, Bishop 393
TALBUT, 197
TALCOTT, Mrs George 424
TALIAFERRO, W T 292
TALLLMADGE, James 290
TALMAGE, 83

TALMON, Benjamin 292
TANACHARISON, 38
TANNEHILL, Adamson 135
TARBELL, A M 139
TATE, Rev 165 168
TAYLOR, 219 I N 422 John 96
    Joseph 422 M H 374 436 438
    445 Mr 238 239 Mrs Dr 419
    Pres 211 W V 223 Zachary 404
TEDEUM, 25
TELLER, 165 H 100 J 157
TEMPLE, F A 422
TERRY, William 325
THAYER, A 100 145
THOMAS, 165 A T 139 Theodore
    388 Z 157
THOMPSON, 124 383 J E 421 J
    Ross 436 436 James 97 98 100
    116 212 403 Mrs Judge 404
    Prof 159 Ross 403 Samuel G
    404 Samuel Gustine 403
THOMS, Cyrus 409 J C 422
THORLEY, 436
THORNTON, Wm 422
THORPE, Francis 370 Francis
    Newton 385 Mr 383-385
TIBBALS, C M 133 Charles M 106
    Mr 406
TIN-TON-HA, 25
TINKER, E L 128
TITUS, 288

TODD, Mrs R 418
TOLEDO, 253
TOMLINSON, Mr 131 Mrs A 418
TOR-A-DA-KOIN, 30
TOTTEN, 246 James G 230
TOTTON, Maj 251
TOUCEY, 131
TOURGEE, Albion Winegar 391
TOWN, J I 445
TOWNER, Ellen 418 Mrs H 418
TOWNLEY, J H 175
TOWNSEND, Charles 128
TRACY, 312 Burrell 291 Capt 182
    D D 445 J A 113 114 122 132
    174 405 406 John 184 John A
    122 133 295 Mary Matilda 405
    Mr 187
TRADE Board Of, 212
TRESTLE, 441
TRIAGLE, 91 274
TRIMBLE, William P 100
TROTTER, John 41
TRUESDALL, Mrs Wm 418
TU-SHU-WAY, 270 272
TUCKER, John 292
TURNER, D 233 Lt 237 240 Mrs
    Charles P 413
TURNEY, J 158
TUSCARORA, 17
TUTTLE, Annie-Robinson 391
    Timothy 165 Truman 142

TYLER, A L 352
TYSON, William Webster 340
VANBRAEM, 37 Mr 42
VANCAMP, O D 431
VANCE, 281 Joseph 96 Thomas
    135
VANCLEVE, R S 407
VANDERSLICE, J M 340
VANHAUSEN, Elisa 418
VANHORN, 68
VANNATTA, Capt 130
VAN RENSSALAER, Gen 215
VAN SICKLE, Jas 72
VAN TICKLER, 72
VIERS, Thomas J 380
VINCENT, 108 B B 106 113 122
    133 146 184 334 406 Daniel
    184 Harriet 418 J 183 J P 97
    John 98 102 108 137 152 180
    184 John P 384 Judge 180 182
    Mrs T B 418 Strong 332 337
    Thomas 101
VINCENTS, 88
VORSE, Lewis 158
VOSBURG, Jacob 145 Mrs Dr 418
VUNK, F C 158
W, C T U 419 421 Dr 202
WADE, Mr 439 Wm R 422
WADENA, 438
WAGNER, F M 139 Louis 340
WAGONER, G H 134

WAKEFIELD, J W 422
WALBRIDGE, Carl 444
WALES, J C 422
WALKER, 27 304 A 129 Filinda W
  430 J C 362 J H 99 100 113 122
  142 406 J W 436 John H 122
  284 331 John W 304 436 445
  Mr 335 Mrs John 424 Thomas
  369
WALLACE, 72 B 282 Benjamin
  387 388 Col 202 David 100 101
  Dr 202 272 273 406 Eleanor
  386 388 I M 427 Irvin M 409
  Irwin M 386 J B 443 J C 90 138
  273 280 282 386-388 J M 388
  Jane 387 John C 100 101 105
  108 144 155 387 John Culbertson 201 Margaret 201 Margaret
  Heron 387 Mary Eleanor 386
  Rachel 386 Wm 144 147 386
  387 Wm M 386 Wm 105
WALLER, D J Jr 415
WALLING, Mr 383
WALLLACE, W M 445
WALSHE, A C 157
WALTER, Thomas H 102
WANEVER, Israel 140
WARE, S D 422
WARFEL, Martin 134
WARNER, 319 348 165 E 422 N W
  357 W 100 W W 96 Wm 157

WARREN, 358 Porter 175 R M 422
WASHBURN, S 138
WASHINGTON, 42 181 Augustus
  37 Gen 39 75 290 381 George
  37 283 Maj 38 40 41 Mr 43
WASHINGTON'S Visit, 29
WATERFORD, 22
WATERS, H E 176
WATKINSON, R 418
WATSON, 370 Archibald 141 184
  H F 374 375 438 N A 447
WATT, Dr 205
WATTS, 186 Charles 436 David
  187 190 312 Wm M 100 113
WAUGH, J Hoge 148
WAY, John 141
WAYNE, 113 186 271 Anthony 89
  90 Col 273 125 201 276 387
  Isaac 90 272
WEATHER, 373
WEATHERBY, Mrs F 418
WEBBER, Daniel E 142 David G
  133
WEBSTER, H 422 James 133 157
  Joseph 140 Thomas 157
WEEKS, Seth 358 W J 422
WEIDLER, Daniel 96
WEIS, 431 Elizabeth 432 Jacob 432
  John 432
WEISER, Conrad 31
WELLER, 406 D C 416

WELLS, 188 J 422 Joseph 96 187
WEST, 297 Branch 317 Holly 13
    Nathaniel 172
WESTON, James 99 100
WETMORE, J W 146 294 295 L D
    97
WHALLON, M 100 106 Murray
    106
WHEELER, Jane 387 Otis 387 T C
    148
WHIPPLE, F B 436
WHITE, David 96 Isaac M 184 J C
    375 J M 153 185 James L 105 R
    L 149 Thunder 38 42
WHITLEY, Benjamin 143
WHITMAN, 329 342 B 330 Benj
    343 346 347 362 445
WHITTAKER, Capt 327 347
WHITTLE, Maj 410 411
WIARD, Owen 421
WICK, Capt 325 Rev 164
WIER, Samuel 203
WIGHT, E 142 Jabez 133 John F
    128
WILBUR, Rev Dr 41
WILCOX, Levi 96 Roberton 431
WILEY, J A 416
WILKINS, Gen 65 66 69 Mr 68
    Thomas 134 174
WILKINSON, 280 Gen 201 James
    299

WILLIAM, Of Orange 202
WILLIAMS, J G 132 J H 122 James
    119 122 133 157 Robert 421 W
    B 96
WILLING, Mary 418 Wm 105
WILLIS, T 174 Zeba 147
WILLSON, Wm 175
WILSON, 191 312 A C 407 Hugh
    143 J C 408 422 J R 407 Jane L
    206 John 205 M A 446 Margaret 205 Mary 205 206 Mr 206
    Mrs 205 Thomas 98-100 105
    124 155 205 W N 424
WING, W O 421
WINGATE, Geo E 343
WINNIE, 81 82 85
WINTERGREEN, Gulch 317
WINTHROP, 388
WISE, Jacob 281
WITTER, George 324
ITTICH, Mrs 419
WOLF, Anna Margaretta 391 Gov
    391
WOMAN'S Work, 422
WOOD, Daniel M 96 J C 422 John
    153 156 297 Joseph 436 Rev
    162 W M 404
WOODBRIDGE, Deacon 161
WOODRUFF, Adeline 207 Charles
    153 Elijah J 96
WOODS, Frank E 368 M A B 419

WOODS (continued)
　Mrs M A B 421
WOODSIDE, John 134
WOODWARD, 97
WOODWORTH, Henry 141 J P 96
WOOLLEY, A K 223
WOOLVERTON, Stephen 99 100 135
WORLD'S Fair, 447
WRIGHT, 343 C B 133 D C 174 E G 418 Eugene 357 Gewn 406 Peter 153 S M 418
WYANDOTS, 15 17 21
WYETH, George 147
WYLLYS, Orrin 96
WYOMING, 403
YAGOWANEA, 18 Queen Of ? 17
YALE, A 174 A E 134
YARNALL, 290 Lt 291
YATES, Jasper 97
YOUNG, Capt 224 J 175 Joseph S M 150 Joshua 175 Mrs G L 421
ZEISBERGER, David 161
ZELLER, Theo 131
ZENOBIA, 17
ZIEGLER, J G 422
ZIMMERMAN, C M 418 Frederick 23

www.ingramcontent.com/pod-product-compliance
Lightning Source LLC
Chambersburg PA
CBHW051333230426
43668CB00010B/1253